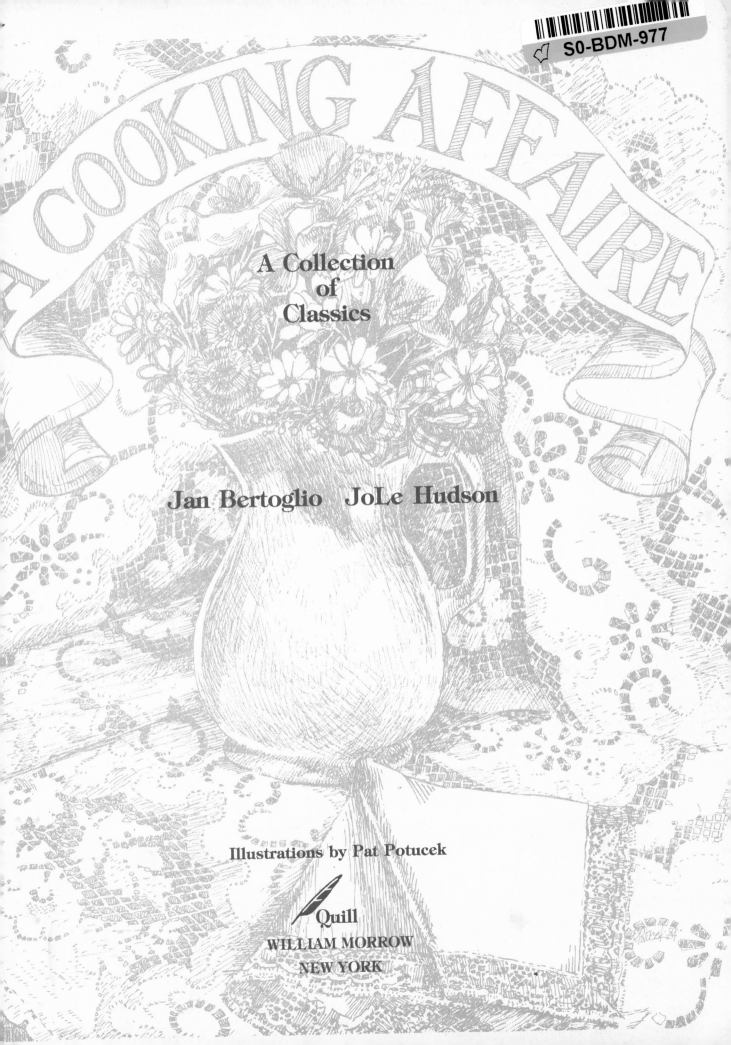

A COOKING AFFAIRE

A Collection
of
Classics

Jan Bertoglio   JoLe Hudson

Illustrations by Pat Potucek

Quill
WILLIAM MORROW
NEW YORK

Library of Congress Catalog Card Number: 86-63042

ISBN: 0-688-07000-0

Printed in the United States of America

First Quill Edition

1 2 3 4 5 6 7 8 9 10

A COOKING AFFAIRE

To our mothers, Vera E. Potucek and Ruby O. Brosius. Their influence has always been with us from our mud-pie days in the backyard to the culmination of *A Cooking Affaire*.

Our thanks to family members and friends who have shared and enjoyed so many of the recipes in *A Cooking Affaire*. Our dreams have been fulfilled.

About the Illustrator

A Kansas artist, Pat Potucek's mastery of pen and ink illustrations appears in this book, reflecting her lifelong interest in Americana art. She was born and raised on a farm in Cowley County. Her love of the country and of Kansas reflect in her still lifes, landscapes, and farm homes. She is the mother of six children and grandmother of thirteen.

Pat is accomplished in several media; her murals, portraits, landscape paintings, and crafts can be viewed in numerous dwellings and establishments across the country. Pat maintains a studio in Hutchinson, Kansas.

Looking back through the years of her work as a painter she says, "I think we create what we most admire."

About the Authors

For me, there was never a moment's doubt that this book would be completed; at least not once my wife, JoLe, and our good friend Jan Bertoglio announced they were actually going to start it.

At the outset it was obvious they were determined to fulfill a longstanding dream that had endured nearly two decades of collecting favorite recipes of family and friends.

To appreciate just how much personal sacrifice and self-discipline is demanded to complete such an enormous project as *A Cooking Affaire* requires one to have been at least in the rooting section on the sidelines, as were cheerleaders Jim Bertoglio and I.

Weeks of kitchen-table brain sessions sorting and culling recipes (the latter a very painful process); hundreds of miles driven between the authors' hometowns for coordination and business confabs; months upon months of typewriter pounding and proofreading copy—sometimes into the wee hours and falling asleep in the middle of describing a sauce velouté or broccoli casserole.

Then all the frustrations of printer deadlines and myriad details too numerous to even attempt to recall.

Three years! That's what was required from day one until the first copies came off the press.

But at no time was there concern that the Dynamic Duo (a moniker proffered by a printer) might be entertaining the slightest notion of giving it up as a lost cause.

And it was more than tenacity that kept the project advancing.

Describe it, instead, as dedication to a host of good cooks among friends and beloved family members of today and to the warm memories of others.

It's their pass-along recipes that contribute so much to the taste-bud pleasures found in these pages.

Although these past months have found more writing and editing paraphernalia on the dining-room table than home-cooked meals, it's been worth the sacrifice. Now it's hubby's retribution time.

"OK, Hon, tonight I'll have the Steak Diane, Greek Salata . . ."

—Jim Hudson

Contents

Overtures · Beverages 1

Appeteasers · Appetizers 9

Great Beginnings · Brunch 27

Love Those Buns · Breads 41

The Warm Up · Soups 71

The Main Event · Entrees 83

Down To Earth · Vegetables 117

Great Toss Ups · Salads 135

Sweet and Saucy · Sauces 151

Sassy and Tart · Pickles, Jellies, Preserves 159

Nine To Five · Quick Meals 165

Melting Moments · Desserts 185

Heirlooms · Recipes from the Past 247

Sugar and Spice · Cooking with Children 261

Under the Mistletoe · Recipes for Christmas 275

R.S.V.P. · Entertaining 309

Fun Do · Fondue Parties 321

La Dolce Vita · Italian Favorites 327

La Fiesta Grande · Mexican Menus 359

Girl Talk · Helpful Hints 375

Finesse · Finishing Touches 381

Index 386

Overtures · Beverages

This beverage section truly offers an array of drinks; whether your taste runs to an ice cream punch or a "heavy duty" cocktail, it is all here—a Peach Daiquiri for two, punch for fifty, beverages for brunches, wedding receptions, and special "you and me" times. Definitely try the Sangria, the Remos Fizz from New Orleans, and Mom's Favorite Kahluà.

Overtures

APPLE JACK CIDER

1 fifth Apple Jack brandy
1 fifth apple cider
6 cinnamon sticks
20 whole cloves

Bring apple cider to a low boil with the cloves and cinnamon sticks. Add brandy and bring to a boil. Strain cloves and sticks. Serve hot in mugs. If filling thermos bottle, add 1 fresh cinnamon stick per 1-quart thermos. Serves 6-8.

GERTRUDE'S ART GALLERY PUNCH

6 cups water
2 large No. 3 cans pineapple juice
Juice of 5 oranges
Juice of 2 lemons
5 ripe bananas, sliced thin
4 cups sugar
Ginger ale

Boil water and sugar together for 3 minutes. Then add all juices and bananas. You may add ginger ale to your liking. This recipe makes 6 quarts without the ginger ale. Freeze like a slush.

Makes 6-8 quarts.

BANANA MILK SHAKE

1 cup milk
1/2 large ripe banana
1/2 pint vanilla ice cream

Combine milk and banana, blend at high speed 1 minute. Add ice cream, blend 1 more minute. Serves 2.

BEAUTIFUL HAIR COCKTAIL

8 ounces whole milk
1 raw egg
1 tablespoon raw wheat germ oil
2 tablespoons raw wheat germ
  Do not use the toasted variety.

Combine all ingredients in blender and mix well. To improve the flavor, add a piece of fruit in season, or add 1 to 2 tablespoons sunflower seeds or sunflower seed meal. They will give the cocktail a fine nutty tang.

Blend at low speed 30 to 60 seconds. Drink the mixture immediately.

This drink should serve as your complete breakfast. Do not eat or drink anything else for two hours after drinking this mixture.

The wheat germ oil, milk and eggs used in this drink should be kept under refrigeration at all times.

Note: Do not supplement the wheat germ oil you use in this drink with wheat germ oil capsules during the day. Serves 1.

BLOODY BULL

1 jigger vodka
1 jigger tomato juice
1 jigger beef bouillon
Dash Worcestershire sauce
Dash Tabasco sauce
Dash black pepper
1 wedge lemon, squeezed

Mix all ingredients, pour into glass over ice. Garnish with dash of seasoning salt and a leafy celery stalk. Serves 1.

Overtures

BRANDY MILK PUNCH FOR 30

4 quarts milk
1 cup brandy
2 1/2 cups rum
1 fifth bourbon
1/2 cup powdered sugar, or to taste
5 teaspoons vanilla
1 quart vanilla ice cream
Nutmeg or cinnamon

Combine milk, brandy, rum and bourbon. Stir well. Add powdered sugar and vanilla, stirring constantly until well dissolved. Cover and refrigerate until well chilled, preferably overnight. Before serving, add ice cream, mixing well until it is dissolved. Return to refrigerator until ready to serve. Sprinkle nutmeg or cinnamon on individual servings. Serves 30.

Jo says, "Careful about that tasting while adding the sugar—you might miss the party! Also remember you will be adding sweet ice cream!"

BRANDY MILK PUNCH FOR 2

2 cups milk
2 cups ice
2 tablespoons sugar
4 teaspoons vanilla
4 to 6 ounces brandy
Nutmeg or cinnamon

Combine all ingredients in blender. Blend on high speed for 10 seconds. Serve in chilled glasses. Sprinkle with nutmeg or cinnamon.

CHAMPAGNE COCKTAIL

2 tablespoons cognac
2 tablespoons Triple Sec
1 sugar cube rubbed with orange
Dash angostura bitters
2 slices orange
8 ounces chilled champagne (1 cup)

Mix together all ingredients except the champagne. Divide between 2 wine goblets. Add 4 ounces champagne to each glass just before serving. This recipe serves two but may be doubled, tripled, etc.

JO'S CHAMPAGNE WEDDING PUNCH

Juice of 6 lemons
4 half pints Orange Curacao
4 half pints Christian Brothers brandy
6 tablespoons sugar
3 fifths dry champagne
1 quart ginger ale

Combine all ingredients, adding champagne and ginger ale at the last minute. Serves 12-14.

FRENCH CHOCOLATE

2 1/2 quarts milk
1 cup heavy cream
1/2 cup Hershey's syrup
1/3 cup sugar

Warm milk. Whip cream, chocolate syrup and sugar until stiff. This can be refrigerated up to 2 hours.

For serving, place whipped chocolate mound in a chilled crystal or silver bowl. Put heated milk in coffee urn. Place bowl of chocolate and urn on serving tray on the table and fill each guests'cup 3/4 full of chocolate. Add enough milk to dissolve chocolate. Stir. Serves 8-10.

BULLSHOT

8 to 10-ounce glass filled with ice
2 drops Tabasco sauce
8 drops Worcestershire sauce
Juice of 1/2 lemon
1 ounce vodka

Place all ingredients in glass, fill remainder with **beef bouillon** and sprinkle with **celery salt** and **freshly ground pepper**. Garnish with **celery stick** or **cucumber spear**. Serves 1.

BUENA VISTA IRISH COFFEE

1 cup piping-hot coffee
3 cocktail sugar cubes
1 jigger Irish whiskey
Whipped cream

Fill glass or mug with very hot water to pre-heat then empty. Pour hot coffee into mug until it is about 3/4 full. Drop in cocktail sugar cubes. Stir until the sugar is thoroughly dissolved. Add full jigger of Irish whiskey. Top with a collar of lightly whipped cream. Serve piping hot. Serves 1.

ICED COFFEE PUNCH FOR BRUNCH

1 gallon strong coffee
1/4 cup Jamaican rum
1/2 gallon half-and-half cream
1 cup sugar
1 quart chocolate ripple ice cream

Prepare coffee, add sugar and refrigerate. At serving time, add half-and-half and rum. Pour over ice cream. Serves 20.

RUM COFFEE COOLER

3 cups brewed coffee
1 pint vanilla ice cream
1 cup heavy cream, whipped
3 tablespoons honey
1/2 cup rum
1 cup crushed ice

Pour hot coffee over ice cream. Add honey to whipped cream. Fold whipped cream mixture into the coffee—ice cream mixture. Add rum and ice.
Makes 2 quarts.

DAIQUIRI

1 can limeade or pink lemonade
1 can Squirt or 7-Up
1 cup white rum
1 cup water
8 to 10 ice cubes

Mix and put into freezer. To serve: Let stand a few minutes until slightly slush.
Jan says, "The daiquiris stay indefinitely in your freezer, but they are so good there won't be any left to refrigerate." Serves 6-8.

PEACH DAIQUIRI

1 can limeade
Small package frozen peaches or 1 cup fresh, mashed
1 cup light rum
5 to 6 ice cubes

Put all ingredients into blender and blend until mushy. You may double or triple this recipe. They keep well in the deep freeze in a tightly covered container. Serves 2.

Overtures

FRESH PEACH DAIQUIRI

1 large peeled fresh peach
1 1/2 ounces white rum
Juice of 1/2 lime
2 teaspoons sugar
1 cup crushed ice

Combine all ingredients in blender. Cover; process at high speed for 10 seconds. Garnish with thick slice of peach. Serves 2.

EGGNOG

6 fresh eggs, separated
1/2 pound granulated sugar
1 1/2 ounces rum
1 pint bourbon or brandy
1 pint heavy cream
1 pint milk
Nutmeg

Beat yolks of 6 eggs. Beat whites separately adding 1/2 pound sugar gradually while beating. Add well-beaten yolks to whites, blend thoroughly. Stir in rum. Add bourbon or brandy, heavy cream and milk. Stir well. Serve chilled. Sprinkle grated nutmeg over top. Serves 10.

IRISH CREAM LIQUEUR

1 can (14-ounce) sweetened condensed milk
3 eggs
1/4 teaspoon coconut extract
1 tablespoon chocolate syrup
1 cup Irish whiskey
1 1/4 cups heavy sweet cream

Blend all ingredients in a blender or food processor. Makes 1 quart.

MOM'S FAVORITE KAHLUA

3/4 of 2-ounce jar Folger's freeze-dried coffee
　crystals
1 pint boiling water
6 cups sugar
1 quart plus 1 1/4 cups water
1 quart 190-proof alcohol
2 tablespoons vanilla

Pour boiling water over coffee crystals. Cover, and allow to cool. Boil sugar and water together 7 minutes. Cool. Add alcohol and vanilla. Mix steeped, cooled coffee with sugar, water, alcohol, vanilla mixture. Cool and bottle. Makes 1 gallon.

KIR

5 parts dry white wine to 1 part Creme de
　Cassis syrup

Serve with ice or thoroughly chilled wine.

LIME RICKEY

1/3 cup lime juice (4 limes)
1 cup crushed raspberries with syrup
1 1/2 quarts water or club soda

Combine lime juice, raspberries and syrup. Add to 2-quart pitcher with water or club soda. Add ice cubes. Serves 8.

Overtures

ORANGE MILK SHAKE

2 cups milk
1/2 pint vanilla ice cream
1/3 cup frozen orange juice, undiluted

Combine all ingredients in blender and blend at high speed several seconds. Serves 4.

JAN'S PUNCH

4 cups orange juice
4 cups lemon juice
2 bottles ginger ale
Sugar to taste
4 cups bourbon

Add ginger ale before serving. Let bourbon, juices and sugar set to blend flavors. Serves 30.

LIME WINE PUNCH

1 cup fresh lime juice
1 cup pineapple juice
1/2 cup sugar
2 bottles white wine
2 fresh limes, thinly sliced
1 orange, thinly sliced
2 cups club soda
Fresh mint

Combine lime juice, pineapple juice and sugar. Stir to dissolve. Add wine and fruits. Chill 1 to 2 hours. Add club soda just before serving. Fresh mint is good and pretty to add. Serves 12.

PARTY PUNCH

6 ounces orange juice
6 ounces lemonade
6 ounces lemon juice
3 quarts 7-Up
Fifth Southern Comfort

Mix all together and serve with chipped ice. Serves 14-16.

PUNCH FOR FIFTY

1 large can pineapple juice
1 large can apricot juice
1 large can grapefruit juice
2 (12-ounce) cans frozen orange juice
4-6 ounces frozen lemon juice
1 large bottle ginger ale
1 pint simple syrup

Mix chilled juices; sweeten with syrup. Pour over crushed ice in punch bowl and add chilled ginger ale.

SYRUP:
2 1/2 cups water
2 cups sugar

Boil mixture 10 minutes.

Overtures

THE HOMEMADE BOMB

1 can lemonade concentrate
1 lemonade can of bourbon
1 can beer

Empty lemonade into blender. Add lemonade can full of bourbon, then add a full can of beer. Add ice and blend well. What a blast! Serves 4.

SHERBET PUNCH

1/2 gallon sherbet
2 liter bottles 7-Up or ginger ale

Place sherbet (you may use any sherbet you desire according to what your color scheme will be) in punch bowl. Allow sherbet to soften slightly. Pour 2 liters of 7-Up over the sherbet and stir gently. As you use the punch you may add the sherbet and 7-Up to the bowl and it may serve any number you desire.

Jan says, "This is one of the best and easiest punches I have ever tasted or used. If you have a doubt as to what kind of sherbet to use, lime sherbet is delicious."

SPECIAL REMOS FIZZ

1 small can frozen lemonade
1 lemonade can of gin
1/2 lemonade can heavy cream
Whites of 2 eggs
1/4 teaspoon vanilla
Orange flower water—just a dash (This is optional, but in New Orleans it's included)

In a blender, combine all ingredients. Add 1 cup crushed ice. Cover and blend 10 seconds on high speed. Serve immediately in chilled glasses. Serves 4-6.

SANGRIA

1 can (6-ounce) lemonade
8 ice cubes
1 fifth burgundy wine
1/4 cup light corn syrup
1 bottle (28-ounce) club soda
Orange and lemon slices
Fresh strawberries, bananas, peaches, cut up

Combine lemonade, corn syrup, wine and fruit. Let chill several hours. At serving time, add ice cubes and club soda. Serve over ice in tall glasses. Makes 2 quarts.

STRAWBERRY-ORANGE COOLER

2 packages (10-ounce size) strawberries (mostly thawed)
1 cup orange juice
1/4 cup lemon juice
Sugar to taste
Ginger ale

Put all ingredients into blender. Blend well. Put ice in punch cups, fill half with mixture and fill remaining with ginger ale.
VARIATION: Pour blended ingredients into punch bowl filled with ice cubes. Pour in 1 quart ginger ale. Serves 8-10.

Overtures

MIMOSA COCKTAIL

1 part champagne
1 part orange juice

Combine and fill champagne glasses. Garnish with a fresh strawberry. Serves 1.

SUNSHINE SLUSH

1 cup sugar
3 cups water
1 can (6-ounce) thawed frozen orange juice
1 can (6-ounce) thawed frozen lemonade
2 medium bananas
2 tablespoons Realemon juice
3 cups pineapple juice
Rum or vodka
Club soda, ginger ale or 7-Up

Boil and cool sugar and water. Combine in blender orange juice, lemonade, bananas, lemon juice and pineapple juice.

Pour water and sugar mixture into the above mixture. Add 1 1/2 cups rum or vodka. Mix well and freeze in a large container with a seal. For best results, freeze overnight. Will keep up to 6 months.

To serve: Scoop slush into glasses about 1/2 full and add any one of the following liquids, until full: club soda, ginger ale, or 7-Up. Garnish with orange slices, cherries or pineapple. Serves 12-14.

HOT SPICED PUNCH

2 1/4 cups pineapple juice
1 3/4 cups water
2 cups apple juice or cider
1 tablespoon whole cloves
1/2 tablespoon whole allspice
2 sticks cinnamon, broken
1/4 teaspoon salt
1/2 cup brown sugar, lightly packed

Using a percolater-type coffee maker, put the spices and sugar in basket and the juices and water in the pot and perk for 10 minutes. Serves 8.

TAOS LIGHTNING

1 jigger Everclear
1 jigger gin
1 jigger white rum
1 jigger tequila
1 jigger vodka
1 splash Peppermint Schnapps, around top of drink
7-Up
2 cocktail onions
1/4 lime, squeezed (at least)
Shaved ice
Fresh mint

Combine all liquors in a tin cup. Add 7-Up and fill with shaved ice. Add lime, onions and mint. Ring top of drink with Schnapps, serve with 2 to 4 straws. Serves 2-4.

Io and Jan both say, "This is lethal, handle with care."

VERA'S SPICED TEA

Juice of 3 lemons
Juice of 3 oranges
3 cups sugar
1 teaspoon each:
   cloves, nutmeg, cinnamon
1/2 cup tea leaves
5 quarts water

Combine juices, sugar, spices and 1 quart of the water. Bring to a boil and pour over tea leaves. Cover and let stand 3 hours. Strain and add 4 quarts of boiling water.
Serves 30.

Overtures

MARGARITAS

1 1/4 cups tequila
1/3 cup Cointreau
1/4 cup superfine sugar
1/2 cup lemon or lime juice
Coarse salt

Mix tequila, Cointreau and sugar in blender. Dip rim of glass in lemon juice, then into coarse salt. Fill glass with ice and pour in mixture. Serves 2.

TOM & JERRY BATTER

12 eggs, separated
2 cups granulated sugar
1 pound powdered sugar
1 can Eagle Brand sweetened condensed milk
Rum and bourbon
Nutmeg

Beat egg whites, gradually adding granulated sugar. Slowly add 1/2 pound of powdered sugar. Add other 1/2 pound of powdered sugar to un-beaten egg yolks. Add Eagle Brand milk. Beat well on electric mixer. Fold yolk mixture into whites. Refrigerate. This will keep for several days; excellent for holidays.

When ready to serve, place 1 tablespoon of bat-ter in a cup, add 1 1/2 ounces rum and bourbon (Mix together in equal proportions ahead of time and keep in a decanter to make it easier at serving time). Stir batter and liquor. Cover with boiling water. Stir well and sprinkle with nutmeg. Makes 2 quarts.

TUMBLEWEEDS — A KANSAS "HAPPENING"

1/4 cup cream
3/4 cup Kahlúa liqueur
1 quart French vanilla ice cream

Combine all ingredients in blender. Blend until proper consistency for pouring into stemmed wine glasses. Serves 6.

VELVET HAMMER

1 quart vanilla ice cream
4 jiggers brandy
2 jiggers Cointreau
2 jiggers creme de cacao

Place all ingredients in blender and mix well. Serve at once in chilled brandy snifters. Serve either as dessert or after-dinner drink. Serves 4.

LEMON VODKA

1 quart vodka
2 tablespoons superfine sugar
12 whole peppercorns
Rind of 1 lemon

Lemon vodka must be made about 10 days be-fore serving; however it will keep refrigerated for months.

Pour off a jigger glass to make room in the bot-tle for the ingredients. Add sugar, peppercorns and lemon peel cut from the lemon in long strips. Cut in 1/4-inch-wide strips.

Cap bottle, invert several times to dissolve sugar and refrigerate for time suggested.

Serve directly from bottle or crystal decanter into small glasses or over ice, which will take some of the "punch" out of it. It is wonderful served with caviar and cream cheese on rye rounds.

Appeteasers · Appetizers

When choosing appetizers consider how you will be serving them. The chafing-dish suggestions are: Beer Balls, Sweet and Sour Chicken Wings, Open Sesame Meat-balls, Oriental Meatballs, Rumaki, Hot Shrimp Balls in Pineapple-Mustard Sauce. Foods that can be passed on trays are: Olive Cheese Shells, Cheddar Cheese Appetizers, Cheese Sticks, Sesame Chicken Bites, Cucumber Canapés, New Potato Appetizers, and Carol's Spinach Balls. Dishes that require the guests to dip or spread with a knife should be placed on level flat surfaces, but don't limit yourself to a buffet table. Included in this category are Red Caviar Mousse, Cheese and Broccoli Dip, Braunschweiger Pâté, and Chutney Cheese Pâté.

Many of these appetizers can be made in advance, even frozen, to allow you more time for other preparations.

Above all, when entertaining, schedule your time so that you have some relaxed, quiet minutes to yourself before the guests arrive. And remember, if you have a good time at your party, everyone else will too.

Appeteasers

ARTICHOKE BOTTOMS WITH CREAM CHEESE AND CAVIAR

1 package Good Seasons old-fashioned French
  dressing mix
1 large can artichoke bottoms
1 package (3-ounce) cream cheese
1 teaspoon grated onion
Lemon juice to taste
Dash Tabasco
Caviar

Make salad dressing according to package directions, cutting oil in half. Drain artichokes and marinate in dressing at least 4 hours.

Mix cream cheese with onion, lemon juice and Tabasco. Add to the cheese some of the marinade. Drain bottoms and fill with cheese mixture. Cut into quarters, top each with caviar and spear with toothpicks.

Serves 12.

HOT ARTICHOKE-CHEESE SQUARES

2 tablespoons oil
1/3 cup finely chopped onion
1 clove garlic, mashed
4 eggs
1 can (14-ounce) artichoke hearts, drained
1/4 cup dry bread crumbs
1/2 pound Swiss cheese or sharp cheddar cheese,
  shredded
2 tablespoons minced parsley
1/2 teaspoon salt, pepper to taste
1/4 teaspoon oregano
1/8 teaspoon Tabasco sauce

Grease a baking dish approximately 7" x 11". Preheat oven to 325 degrees.

In skillet, heat oil and saute onion and garlic until limp but not brown. Beat eggs to froth in mixing bowl, chop artichokes in small pieces and add to bowl. Stir in onion, crumbs, cheese, parsley and seasonings. Turn mixture into baking pan and bake for 25 to 30 minutes until set when lightly touched.

Let cool a bit, cut into 1½-inch squares. If you make ahead, refrigerate, reheat in a 325-degree oven for 10 minutes.

Makes 36 squares.

BEER BALLS

1 pound ground beef
1 small finely chopped onion
1 egg
1/2 cup crushed crackers or bread crumbs
Salt and freshly ground pepper

Combine ingredients. Shape into miniature meatballs and brown in a small amount of shortening. Drain on paper towels.

SAUCE:
1 cup beer
1 cup catsup
3 tablespoons vinegar
3 tablespoons sugar
3 tablespoons Worcestershire sauce
Salt and pepper

Boil sauce ingredients for 10 minutes. Pour over meatballs and simmer 3 hours. Serve hot.

Jo says, "Make up a multiple batch. Freeze meatballs and sauce in separate containers. Take out only what you might need, combine and simmer at that time." Makes 30 small balls.

Appeteasers

BRAUNSCHWEIGER PATE

1 pound Braunschweiger, broken into pieces
Half of 8-ounce package cream cheese, softened
1 tablespoon milk
1 tablespoon grated onion
1 teaspoon sugar
1 teaspoon chili powder

Combine ingredients, beat until smooth. Form into an igloo, place on plate, cover and chill. . . . Whip remaining half-package **cream cheese**, 1 tablespoon **milk**, 1/8 teaspoon **Tabasco sauce**, 1/4 cup chopped **green onion**.

Spread evenly over the chilled mold. Chill until serving time. Garnish with **parsley**, serve with crackers and/or rye rounds. Makes 3 cups.

VARIATION
Spread frosted mound with caviar, sprinkle top with grated hard–boiled egg, or place bowls of caviar, chopped onion and grated egg beside pate and let caviar lovers serve themselves.

CHEESE AND BROCCOLI DIP

1 box frozen broccoli, chopped, cooked and well drained
1 cup celery, chopped
1 cup onion, chopped
1 cup minute rice, cooked
1 can cream of mushroom soup
1 jar (16-ounce) Cheez Whiz

Combine broccoli, celery, onion and rice. Add mushroom soup and cheese. Mix well. Can be made ahead and refrigerated or frozen. Serve hot in chafing dish with corn dippers. Makes 8 cups.

Jo says, "Any leftover can be thinned down if necessary with a little milk and used over chicken breasts. It makes a delicious mock chicken divan. Serve with a spiced peach."

MARINATED BRUSSELS SPROUTS

1 package (10-ounce) frozen Brussels sprouts, cooked and drained
Mix:
1/2 cup Wish-Bone Italian dressing
1/2 teaspoon dill seed
1 tablespoon sliced green onion

Pour over Brussels sprouts and chill several hours or overnight. Serve on toothpicks as appetizer.
Serves 6-8.

CAMEMBERT AMANDINE

1 round (8-ounce) Camembert cheese
Dry white wine
1/2 cup softened butter
1/2 cup chopped toasted almonds
1/2 to 1 tablespoon cognac (adjust to taste)

Score rind of cheese on both sides, place cheese in a dish and cover with wine. Store cheese in refrigerator overnight.

Remove cheese from wine and gently scrape off rind. Blend cheese with butter, beating well with wooden spoon. Beat in cognac, chill mixture.

Shape mixture into original form of the cheese and sprinkle entire outside of round with toasted almonds. Keep refrigerated.

This is delicious served with lavash (cracker bread). Serves 8.

DEEP FRIED CAMEMBERT

6 sections (1 1/3 ounces each) Camembert,
   with rind removed
1 egg
1 cup fine, dry bread crumbs
Vegetable oil for deep frying

Beat egg in small bowl, spread crumbs on shallow dish. Dip Camembert sections in beaten egg and dredge in bread crumbs. Dip in egg again and sprinkle with crumbs on all sides.

Heat oil (2 inches deep) in large deep heavy saucepan until it registers 375 degrees on a deep-fry thermometer. Drop cheese sections in oil and fry 1 to 2 minutes until a golden crust has formed around the cheese. Remove to paper toweling to drain briefly.

Serve fried cheese immediately with fresh fruit wedges. Serves 6.

RED CAVIAR MOUSSE

3 jars (2-ounce size) red salmon or lumpfish caviar
1/4 cup chopped parsley
1 tablespoon grated onion
1 teaspoon grated lemon peel
3 green onions, chopped
3 tablespoons peeled, seeded, diced cucumber
2 cups sour cream
2 envelopes unflavored gelatin
1/4 cup water
1 cup whipping cream
Pumpernickle bread slices

Place first 6 ingredients in large bowl and gently fold in sour cream. In small saucepan gently sprinkle gelatin over cold water and cook over low heat until dissolved. Cool.

Beat cream until stiff, fold dissolved gelatin and whipped cream into sour cream–caviar mixture. Pour into greased 6-cup flat mold. Cover and refrigerate until set. Unmold and serve.

This is very pretty set in a fish mold, or for the holidays use a star mold. Makes 6 cups.

OLIVE CHEESE SHELLS

1 1/2 cups shredded cheddar cheese
1/2 cup mayonnaise
1 cup sliced ripe olives
1/2 cup sliced green onions
1/2 teaspoon curry powder

Mix and put into pastry shells. Broil until golden. Makes 16.

CHEESE BALL

2 packages (8-ounce size) cream cheese
1 jar Kraft Roka-Blue cheese
1 jar Kraft Old English cheese
1 medium onion, grated
Several dashes Worcestershire sauce
1 cup pecans, chopped
1 cup parsley, chopped

Mix cheeses together. Add seasonings and blend thoroughly. Chill for several hours, form into 1 large or 2 small balls. Roll in parsley flakes and chopped pecans. This freezes nicely.

Makes 4 cups.

12

Appeteasers

BROILER CHEESE

1 small package round of Brie or Camembert cheese
1/2 cup melted butter
1 cup sliced almonds

Place cheese on baking dish. Cover with melted butter and sliced almonds. Place under broiler until cheese becomes very soft and almonds are toasted. Cheese must be watched carefully so it does not get too brown. Serve immediately with your favorite crackers. It's marvelous served with apple, pear slices and grapes. Serves 8.

FRUIT CHEESE BALL

2 ripe mangoes or fresh peaches (4 to 6) peeled and chopped
2 tablespoons lime juice
1 pound cream cheese, softened
1 cup coconut, flaked
1 cup nuts, chopped (pecans or macadamia)

Combine mangoes or peaches and lime juice in mixer. Add softened cheese and blend until thoroughly mixed. Add coconut and chopped nuts. Form into ball and refrigerate until serving time. Delicious with wheat crackers. Serves 12.

CHUTNEY CHEESE PATE

1 package (8-ounce) cream cheese
4 ounces cheddar cheese, grated
1/2 to 1 teaspoon curry powder
1/4 cup dry sherry
1 bottle chutney
1 bunch green onions, minced

Cream cheeses. Add curry powder and sherry and thoroughly blend. Form into oval on serving platter, about 1/2 inch thick. Cover and refrigerate.

At serving time, pour chutney over cheese and sprinkle onions generously over chutney.

Serve with Triscuits or wheat crackers.
Serves 10-12.

CHEDDAR CHEESE APPETIZERS

1 block sharp cheddar or coon cheese
1/2 stick butter
1 package almonds, slivered or sliced
1 small package English muffins

Melt cheese and butter. Add almonds and spread on sliced muffins. Cut each slice into four pieces, and place under broiler until bubbly. These can be frozen ahead and broiled before serving.
Serves 12-16.

COCKTAIL CHEESE BALLS

1 stick margarine
1 cup Rice Krispies
1 cup flour
1 cup sharp cheese
Dash cayenne pepper

Mix together. Forms balls about the size of a walnut. Press down with fork. Bake at 350 degrees for 8 to 10 minutes. Makes 36.

Appeteasers

HOT OLIVE CHEESE PUFFS

1 cup grated sharp cheddar cheese
3 tablespoons soft butter
1/2 cup sifted flour
1/4 teaspoon salt
1/2 teaspoon paprika
20 to 24 stuffed green olives

Combine cheese and butter. Stir in flour, add salt and paprika. Mix. Roll about 1 tablespoon of mixture around a well-drained stuffed olive. Bake on ungreased cookie sheet at 400 degrees for 10 to 12 minutes.

These freeze very well. Makes 20-24.

CREAM CHEESE PASTRY

PASTRY:
1 cup butter
1 package (8-ounce) cream cheese
1/2 teaspoon salt
2 cups flour

Mix using fingers. Wrap in foil and chill several hours. Roll out half at a time on slightly-floured board and form into pastry shells.

Bake at 350 degrees for 15 minutes.

FILLINGS FOR SHELLS:
HOT CHEESE AND SHRIMP CANAPES
1 cup mayonnaise
1/2 cup grated cheese
1 or 2 green onions chopped fine
1 can shrimp
1 teaspoon curry powder

Combine ingredients. Fill pastry shells. Place on tray under broiler until bubbly. Makes 24.

CRAB AND/OR SHRIMP MOUSSE

1 1/2 cups shrimp (about 1 pound) chopped
   (crab or lobster may be used)
1 cup chopped celery
1/2 cup chopped bell pepper
2 tablespoons grated onion
1 teaspoon salt
3 tablespoons lemon juice
1 cup mayonnaise
1 tablespoon Worcestershire sauce
1/2 teaspoon Tabasco sauce
1 can tomato soup
3 packages (3 ounces each) cream cheese
3 envelopes plain gelatin
1 cup cold water
1 cup mayonnaise

Combine shrimp, celery, bell pepper, onion, salt, lemon juice, Worcestershire and Tabasco. Mix well and let stand to blend flavors. Combine soup and cream cheese in double boiler. Heat and stir until cheese melts.

Soften gelatin in water for 5 minutes. Add to soup mixture. Remove from heat and cool. When mixture begins to thicken, blend in mayonnaise. Stir in shrimp mixture. Turn into mold and chill. Serve with crackers or may be used as a salad.

To Serve: This is very pretty made in a fish mold, garnished with lemon slices dipped in paprika and sprigs of parsley or watercress. Also makes a lovely salad. Makes 8 cups.

Appeteasers

COTTAGE CHEESE DIP

1/2 cup sour cream
1/2 cup mayonnaise
2 teaspoons parsley
1 package onion soup mix
1 pint cottage cheese

Mix all together and chill. Makes 3 cups.

CRAB SUPREME

1 package (8-ounce) cream cheese
1/2 cup Hellmann's mayonnaise
1/3 cup cream sherry
Juice of 1 lemon
Salt
Couple shakes of Accent
1 teaspoon Worcestershire sauce
1 pound fresh backfin crabmeat. If fresh is not available may use frozen or canned.

Blend and beat all ingredients, adding crab meat at the last. Bake for 20 minutes in preheated 400 degree oven or until brown and bubbly.

If serving as hors d'oeuvres, serve in chafing dish. As a luncheon entree, serve in Pepperidge Farm pastry shells. Garnish with shaved almonds and a dash of red pepper.

Note: Combine all ingredients a day ahead of serving. Bake just before serving. Serves 8.

CHEESE STICKS

2 cups flour
1/2 teaspoon salt
2 teaspoons chili powder
1 1/2 sticks (6 ounce) butter or margarine
1 cup grated cheddar cheese
1/3 cup beer
4 tablespoons heavy cream
1/4 cup ground nuts

Sift together flour, salt and chili powder. Cut in butter and cheese with pastry blender. Stir in just enough beer to make particles adhere, form into bowl and chill 2 hours.

Roll out dough 1/8-inch thick on lightly floured surface. Cut into strips 1/2 by 4 inches long. Arrange on baking pan, brush with cream and sprinkle with nuts. Bake in preheated 425 degree oven 10 minutes, or until browned. Cool on a cake rack. Sticks keep indefinitely in an airtight container. Makes 6 dozen.

SESAME CHICKEN BITES

1/3 cup sesame seeds
2 chicken breasts, skinned and boned
1/2 cup dry white wine
1/2 cup soy sauce
1/2 cup vegetable oil
1 clove garlic, minced
1 tablespoon very finely cut crystallized ginger

Heat oven to 350 degrees. Place sesame seeds in shallow pan. Heat in oven about 20 minutes or until lightly browned, stirring 2 or 3 times.

Cut chicken in 1-inch pieces. Combine wine, soy sauce, oil, garlic and ginger in medium-sized bowl. Add chicken pieces and stir to coat with the mixture. Let stand 20 to 30 minutes.

Coat skillet with shortening, saute chicken bites until done, stirring often. Roll in sesame seeds immediately. Makes 24 appetizers.

Appeteasers

SWEET AND SOUR CHICKEN WINGS

75 to 80 wings

SAUCE:
1 can (15-ounce) Hunt's tomato sauce with tomato bits
4 cups ketchup
2 cups apple cider vinegar
1/2 teaspoon soy sauce
Dash of Worcestershire sauce
2 teaspoons grated onion
2 teaspoons ginger
2 teaspoons dry mustard
2 cups brown sugar
2 cups white sugar

Cut off tip of wing and discard. Cut joints of wings in two and put in baking dish in single layer. Pour sauce over wings. Bake uncovered in 325-degree oven until sauce cooks down and wings are well coated.

Jan says, "When I make this sauce, I make an extra batch so I can use it over chicken or ribs. If I want to make this ahead of time, I partially cook the wings and then freeze until I use them for a dinner or party."

CUCUMBER CANAPES

Bread slices
Butter, softened
2 packages cream cheese (8-ounce size)
1 package Good Season Italian salad dressing mix
1 large cucumber, grated
1/4 cup finely chopped onion
Dash Tabasco sauce
Mayonnaise
Parmesan cheese
Cucumber, sliced paper thin

Cut bread rounds with biscuit cutter, roll out to flatten, lightly butter.

Soften cream cheese and mix with dressing mix. Add cucumber, onion and Tabasco. Mix enough mayonnaise to make spreadable. Spread on bread rounds and top with thin slice of cucumber. Sprinkle lightly with paprika. Serve chilled.

Sandwich loaf yields 50 rounds.

HOT PICKLED EGGS

2 big jars hot, torrid white (banana) peppers
1 quart vinegar
24 to 36 hard-boiled eggs, peeled
1 large onion, cut up
Salt and pepper

Combine all ingredients in large glass container. Cover and let set 24 to 48 hours. Can also add slices of carrots and cauliflower. Refrigerate.

Great for picnics! The marinade will last for months. Just keep adding eggs.

GREEN PEPPER DIP

3 eggs beaten in top of double boiler
3 tablespoons sugar
3 tablespoons vinegar
1 teaspoon butter
1/2 pound (8-ounces) cream cheese
5 drops Tabasco
chopped onions to taste
2 green peppers, chopped

Add sugar, vinegar, butter and cream cheese to egg mixture and stir until thick. Remove from heat after it has become dip consistency. Add Tabasco, onions and green peppers.

Serve warm. Delicious with chips or relishes. Makes 2 cups.

MUSHROOMS STUFFED WITH BACON AND CHIVE CREAM CHEESE

16 medium to large mushrooms
4 tablespoons melted butter
2 containers (4-ounce size) whipped cream cheese with chives
8 slices crisp fried bacon, crumbled

Pull stems off mushrooms and save for another use. With damp sponge or cloth, clean mushroom caps. Brush outside of caps with melted butter.

In bowl, mix cream cheese and bacon bits and spoon into mushrooms, mounding slightly. Place on baking sheet, broil about 6 inches below heat for 3 to 5 minutes until bubbling and brown.

OPEN SESAME MEATBALLS

1 pound lean ground beef
2/3 cup minced onion
1 egg
1/4 cup bread crumbs
1/4 cup milk
1/2 teaspoon salt
1 teaspoon MSG
1/8 teaspoon pepper
1 tablespoon plus 1 teaspoon Worchestershire sauce
1 cup beef broth, bouillon or consomme

Combine all ingredients except broth. Form into miniature balls. Fry in hot oil, at least 3/4 inch deep. Simmer meatballs in broth about 10 minutes or until cooked through. Reserve broth for use in sauce. Makes 60.

SAUCE FOR OPEN SESAME MEATBALLS

2 tablespoons butter
2 tablespoons flour
1/4 teaspoon salt
Dash cayenne pepper
1/2 cup beef broth
1 teaspoon soy sauce
1 teaspoon Worcestershire sauce
2 tablespoons toasted sesame seeds
1 cup sour cream

Melt butter on medium heat. Blend in flour, salt and cayenne. Heat, stirring constantly until bubbly. Add broth all at once and cook, stirring until sauce thickens. Stir in soy sauce, Worcestershire sauce and sesame seeds

Empty sour cream into a medium bowl. Gradually add hot sauce, stirring constantly. Return sauce to pan, fold in meatballs and heat gently to serving temperature. Serve from chafing dish.

Jo says, "If you have any left after your party, it is wonderful served over wild rice or noodles for an entree. Just thin the sauce down with a little milk, or a splash of white wine."

Note: To toast sesame seeds, sprinkle on cookie sheet and bake at 325 degrees about 5 minutes.

VARIATION ON SAUCE

CURRY BALLS

Omit soy sauce, Worcestershire sauce and sesame seeds. Cook 1 teaspoon curry powder in butter for 1 minute. Proceed according to recipe directions. Before adding sour cream, fold in 1 tablespoon lemon juice and contents of 1 can (8½-ounce) of crushed pineapple, well drained.

Appeteasers

HERB MAYONNAISE DRESSING

1 cup mayonnaise
1/2 tablespoon lemon juice
1/4 teaspoon salt
1/4 teaspoon paprika
1/4 cup finely chopped parsley
1 tablespoon grated onion
1 tablespoon chopped chives
1/8 teaspoon curry powder
1/2 teaspoon Worcestershire sauce
1 minced clove garlic
1 tablespoon capers (optional)
1/2 cup sour cream

Combine all ingredients. Chill. This can be made a few days ahead. Serve with a raw vegetable platter or chilled seafood. Delicious!!
Makes 1½ cups.

ORIENTAL MEATBALLS

1 1/2 pounds ground beef chuck
3/4 cup finely chopped water chestnuts
2 tablespoons grated onion
1/4 cup dry bread crumbs
1 egg
Salt and pepper

SAUCE:
1/4 cup soy sauce
1/2 cup pineapple juice
1/2 cup dry sherry
2 tablespoons brown sugar
1/4 teaspoon ground ginger
1 tablespoon cornstarch
1/3 cup chicken broth

Preheat oven to 450 degrees. In a bowl mix together beef, water chestnuts, onion, crumbs, egg. Salt and pepper to taste. Form into balls about 1" in diameter. Place slightly apart on greased, rimmed cookie sheet and bake, uncovered, for 8 to 10 minutes until lightly browned. (If made ahead, cover and chill.)

In large saucepan, stir together soy sauce, pineapple juice, sherry, sugar, and ginger. Add meatballs and simmer 15 minutes. In a cup, stir cornstarch in chicken broth to dissolve. Stir into meatball mixture and simmer until slightly thickened.

Keep meatballs warm in chafing dish. Makes about 55.

CHEESE-STUFFED MUSHROOMS

1/4 pound Roquefort or blue cheese
1 package (3-ounce) cream cheese, softened
2 tablespoons butter or margarine, softened
1 teaspoon grated onion
1/2 teaspoon Worcestershire sauce
36 medium-size mushrooms

Cream cheese and butter until smooth. Stir in onion and Worcestershire. Wash, stem and dry mushrooms. Pipe cheese mixture into caps with pastry bag or spoon and mound it. Garnish with chopped parsley.

Note: Mushrooms may be left raw or poached. To poach, place mushrooms in boiling lemon water for 5 minutes. Drain immediately, chill.

VARIATION

Wash fresh mushrooms, pat dry, remove stems and stuff with Boursin cheese. Bake at 350 degrees until warm.

Boursin is available at cheese shops or delicatessens.

GREEN PEPPER BRICK

Brick of cream cheese
Small jar of green pepper jelly

Pour jelly over cream cheese. Serve with Triscuits or cocktail crackers.

MUSHROOMS A LA GREQUE

MARINADE:
3 cups canned chicken stock
1 cup dry white wine
1 cup olive oil
1/2 cup lemon juice
6 parsley sprigs
2 large garlic cloves, cut up
1/2 teaspoon dried thyme
10 peppercorns
1 teaspoon salt
1 pound fresh mushrooms
GARNISH:
Parsley
Lemon slices

Mix ingredients in 4-quart saucepan. Bring to boil, partially cover pan and simmer slowly for 45 minutes. Using fine sieve, strain marinade into large bowl, pressing down on ingredients with back of spoon to squeeze out juices. Return marinade to saucepan and taste it. To be effective, marinade should be somewhat overseasoned.

Bring marinade to simmer over moderate heat. Drop in 1 pound of fresh mushrooms, whole if small, quartered or sliced if large. Cover pan and simmer for 10 minutes. With slotted spoon, transfer mushrooms to stainless or shallow glass baking dish.

Pour marinade over mushrooms and place in refrigerator to cool mushrooms as quickly as possible. When chilled, cover dish tightly with aluminum foil and refrigerate at least 4 hours before serving.

To serve: Pour off marinade, sprinkle with parsley and garnish with lemon slices.

Note: This marinade is delicious for squash, especially zucchini, or fresh green beans, onions and green peppers. Serves 10.

PECAN SPREAD

1 package (8-ounce) cream cheese
2 tablespoons milk
1/2 cup sour cream
1/4 cup finely chopped green pepper
1 tablespoon minced instant onion
1/2 teaspoon garlic salt
1 jar (2½-ounce) dried beef, chopped
1/2 cup coarsely chopped pecans
2 teaspoons butter
1/2 teaspoon salt

Blend softened cheese, milk and sour cream. Add green pepper, onion and garlic salt. Fold in dried beef. Put into 8-inch pie pan. In small pan, melt butter, add salt and pecans. Heat. Sprinkle pecans over above mixture. Bake in preheated oven 350 degrees for 20 minutes. Serve hot with crackers. Serves 10-12.

VARIATION:
1 package (8-ounce) cream cheese
1/2 cup sour cream
2 tablespoons dry onion soup mix
2 tablespoons milk
1 jar or package chipped beef, chopped
1 can deviled ham

Prepare as in recipe for Pecan Spread. Top with pecan butter mixture.

Appeteasers

PIMENTO CHEESE SPREAD

Place in double boiler:
1 tablespoon sugar
3 tablespoons vinegar
1/2 cup sweet cream
1 tablespoon flour
1 beaten egg
1 tablespoon butter
1/2 teaspoon salt

Mix all ingredients and cook until mixture thickens. While mixture is still hot, add:
2 hard-boiled eggs (chopped)
1 package cream cheese, or 1/2 pound American cheese (cubed)
1 tablespoon grated onion
1 small can finely chopped pimentos

Blend well and put in jars or other containers, cover and store in refrigerator. Makes 3 cups.

NEW POTATO APPETIZERS

Tiny new potatoes, as many as desired, skins left on
Butter
Sour cream with chives
Seasoned salt
Garlic salt
Parsley, minced
Parmesan cheese

Boil potatoes, drain, cool and cut in half. Using melon ball spoon make a hole in each potato half. Roll in melted butter and set on baking sheet. Prepare filling of sour cream, garlic and seasoned salts and minced parsley flakes. Fill cavity in potatoes with mixture, sprinkle Parmesan cheese over tops. Slide baking sheet under broiler for a few minutes until mixture is hot and bubbly. Serve while warm.

BAKED PUMPKIN SEEDS

2 cups pumpkin seeds, unwashed, shells left on, fibers rubbed off
1/2 teaspoon Worcestershire sauce
1 1/2 tablespoons melted butter
1 1/2 teaspoons salt

Combine ingredients. Bake in shallow pan, stirring frequently at 250 degrees for 2½ to 3 hours or until dry. Cool, then store in tightly covered container. Makes 2 cups.

MUSHROOM SHELLS

1/2 pound fresh mushrooms, cut very small
2 tablespoons butter
1/2 teaspoon salt
1/2 cup chopped onion
1 teaspoon lemon juice
1/2 cup sour cream
1 teaspoon dried dill
Pepper
Dash nutmeg

Brown mushrooms and onions in butter. Add remainder of ingredients. Place in pastry shells. Freeze and bake as needed. Fills 16 shells.

❖❖

PARTY SNACK

2 cups Rice Chex
2 cups Wheat Chex
2 cups Cheerios
2 cups pretzel sticks or Pepperidge Farm
   fish pretzels
2 cups Pepperidge Farm fish crackers, plain or
   cheese
1/2 pound mixed nuts
1 1/2 sticks butter, or margarine

Melt butter and add the following:
1/2 tablespoon onion salt
1/2 tablespoon garlic powder
1 tablespoon celery seed
1 tablespoon poppy seed
2 teaspoons Tabasco sauce
2 tablespoons Worcestershire sauce
1/4 teaspoon savor salt
Dash of red pepper

Pour sauce over dry ingredients, stir well and bake in a slow oven (250 degrees) for an hour or so, stirring every 15 minutes. Store in covered containers. Warning: May be habit forming.

Jo says, "You can adjust this as you desire. I adore cashews and hazel nuts, so add some of these along with the other mixed nuts. Also, I have had better luck with the regular canned nuts instead of the dry roasted. Just personal preference." Makes 12 cups.

RADISH, CREAM CHEESE SPREAD

1 package (8-ounce) cream cheese, softened
1/4 cup butter, softened
1/2 teaspoon celery salt
Dash paprika
1/2 teaspoon Worcestershire sauce
1 cup finely chopped radishes
1/4 cup finely chopped green onion

Mix all ingredients. Chill. Makes 1½ cups.

REUBEN ROLL-UPS

1 package refrigerated crescent rolls
1 can (8-ounce) sauerkraut, well drained
8 tablespoons Thousand Island salad dressing
8 thin slices corned beef
2 slices Swiss cheese cut in 1/2 inch strips

Unroll crescent roll dough. Separate dough into triangles. Brush dough with salad dressing. Place one slice corned beef across wide end of each triangle. Spread 2 tablespoons sauerkraut on corned beef across wide end of triangle. Spread 1 tablespoon sauce on each corned beef. Top each with 2 strips of cheese. Roll up, beginning at wide end of triangle. Bake on ungreased sheet at 375 degrees for 10 to 15 minutes. Serves 8.

REUBEN SANDWICHES

1 loaf party rye bread
1 pint jar sauerkraut
1 small jar Thousand Island dressing
1 package sliced Swiss or Mozzarella cheese
1/4 cup shredded ham

Spread Thousand Island dressing on every slice of bread, then shredded ham, cheese, sauerkraut. Top with another slice of bread. Butter outsides and grill both sides in a hot buttered skillet. Serve warm. Makes 12–15 sandwiches.

Appeteasers

RUMAKI

1 can (7½-ounce) water chestnuts
2 bottles (5-ounce size) teriyaki sauce
1 package (2-pound) thick sliced bacon
1 box of brown sugar

Marinate chestnuts in sauce overnight. Drain well. Cut bacon strips in half and roll both chestnuts and bacon in brown sugar. Roll bacon around nut and secure with toothpick. Bake at 400 degrees for 20 to 30 minutes, turning once.

Jo says, "These are wonderful if you will stuff the water chestnut in a pitted prune, and wrap the bacon as in the recipe above. If I'm doing a large party, I bake the rumaki just half the required time, freeze it till the day of the party and finish baking that day. By doing it this way, the rumaki will not get too browned." Makes 40-50.

SALMON BALL

1/4 cup minced onion
1 can (16-ounce) red salmon, drained. Remove skin and bones.
1 package (8-ounce) cream cheese, softened
3 tablespoons lemon juice
1 tablespoon horseradish
2 teaspoons dill
1/4 teaspoon liquid smoke
Dash of Tabasco
1 teaspoon Worcestershire sauce
Salt and freshly ground pepper
1/2 cup parsley leaves
1/2 cup chopped pecans

Mix all ingredients except parsley and nuts until well blended. Adjust seasonings if desired. Refrigerate overnight. Serve as a spread with rye or pumpernickle slices or shape into a mound, garnished with parsley and/or nuts. It is delicious with raw vegetables. Makes 2 cups.

SALMON MOUSSE

1 envelope unflavored gelatin
1/2 cup cold water
1-pound can red salmon
1/2 cup mayonnaise
3/4 cup sour cream
1/2 teaspoon salt
1 tablespoon lemon juice
1 1/4 cups celery, finely chopped
1 tablespoon capers

Sprinkle gelatin over 1/4 cup cold water to soften. Dissolve in 1/4 cup boiling water. Let cool. Put all ingredients except capers and celery in blender, whip until smooth. Add capers and celery. Pour into buttered mold. Chill. Serve with plain cracker bread. Makes 4 cups.

❖❖❖

SALAMI

5 pounds ground beef
2 1/2 teaspoons mustard seed
2 1/2 teaspoons garlic salt
1 teaspoon hickory smoked salt
   (charcoal smoke salt)
5 rounded teaspoons Morton Tender Quick salt
2 teaspoons peppercorns
1 teaspoon black pepper
2 teaspoons liquid garlic
Liquid smoke

Combine ingredients. Keep in cool place 3 days. Knead once each day like bread. Add 10 drops of liquid smoke 1st and 2nd day. Make into rolls and put cheese cloth around, tying both ends. Bake uncovered on sheet on rack 6 hours at 150 degrees. Turn to 200 degrees for 2 more hours.

Jan says, "You may buy Tender Quick salt at: Morton Salt Co. 110 No. Wacker Dr. Chicago, Ill. 60606." Makes 5-6 rolls.

SHRIMP BALLS

1 pound cooked shrimp, ground
1 tablespoon chili sauce
1/4 cup finely minced celery
2 tablespoons finely minced water chestnuts
2 tablespoons grated onion
1 hard-boiled egg, sieved
1 package (8-ounce) cream cheese, softened
1/2 teaspoon white pepper
Dash cayenne pepper
1 teaspoon lemon juice
Minced parsley

Combine all ingredients except parsley. Season to taste. Chill. Form into 1-inch balls, roll in parsley. Makes 25-30.

HOT SHRIMP BALLS IN PINEAPPLE-MUSTARD SAUCE

SHRIMP BALLS
1/3 cup cornstarch
1/4 cup dry sherry
2 tablespoons lemon juice
4 eggs, beaten
1 tablespoon salt
1/2 teaspoon onion powder
6 pounds shrimp, peeled, deveined and cooked
2 cans (8¼-ounce-size) water chestnuts
1 1/2 quarts vegetable oil

PINEAPPLE MUSTARD SAUCE
1/3 cup cornstarch
1 cup water
2 cups pineapple juice
2/3 cups honey
1 tablespoon dry mustard
2 teaspoons ground ginger
1/4 teaspoon salt
2 tablespoons grated orange rind

Dissolve cornstarch in sherry and lemon juice in a large mixing bowl. Add eggs, salt and onion powder.

Chop shrimp very fine or put into blender. Add to cornstarch mixture. Add water chestnuts. Mix until well combined. Cover and refrigerate overnight.

Shape shrimp mixture into small balls. Heat oil to 365 degrees and fry shrimp balls for 2 minutes or until golden brown. Drain on paper towels. If you are doing this in advance, cool to room temperature, wrap and freeze. To reheat, place frozen balls on a cookie sheet in a 325 degree oven for 15 to 20 minutes or until hot.

SAUCE: Slowly add water to cornstarch, add pineapple juice. Cook slowly till sauce thickens. Add honey and rest of ingredients. Keep warm and add to shrimp. Makes 150.

To Serve: Add shrimp balls to hot pineapple mustard sauce in a chafing dish.

SHRIMP IN BEER BATTER

1 pound large, shelled, raw shrimp
1 cup beer
1 cup flour
1/2 teaspoon garlic powder
1/2 tablespoon paprika
1/2 teaspoon Italian seasoning
1 teaspoon salt
1/2 teaspoon white pepper
3 cups vegetable oil

In bowl, beat together beer, flour, garlic powder, paprika, Italian seasoning, salt and pepper.

Heat oil in a large skillet until it just starts to boil. Dip shrimp into batter and fry on both sides until golden brown. Drain on paper towels. Keep warm. Serve with Apricot Dip. Serves 4.

APRICOT DIP

1 cup apricot preserves
2 tablespoons wine vinegar
1/4 cup minced pimentos
2 tablespoons brandy
1 cup scallions

In small saucepan, heat preserves, add vinegar and pimentos. Simmer for 3 minutes. Add brandy and scallions. Cool before serving. Makes 3 cups.

SHRIMP BUTTER

2 cans shrimp or 12 to 14 ounces fresh shrimp, cooked, cleaned and chopped
1 1/2 sticks butter
8 ounces cream cheese
4 tablespoons mayonnaise
Juice of 1/2 lemon
2 tablespoons parsley, finely chopped
2 tablespoons grated onion
1 clove garlic, minced
Salt, pepper to taste

Cream butter and cheese. Combine rest of ingredients in blender. Fold blended mixture into the cheese-butter mixture. Spoon into crock, cover and refrigerate several hours. Allow to soften slightly before serving. Serve with crackers.

Keep covered in refrigerator for 1 week only. Makes 3 cups.

SHRIMP, CRAB AND WATER CHESTNUT DIP

1 can cocktail-size shrimp
1 box (6-ounce) frozen Alaskan king crab. This is optional, some like using just the shrimp.
1 can water chestnuts, chopped fine
1/2 cup mayonnaise
1 teaspoon prepared mustard
Chopped parsley
1 tablespoon chopped green onion
1 teaspoon Worcestershire sauce
2 dashes Tabasco
1 teaspoon dill weed

Mix and chill ingredients. If using crab, be sure to squeeze out excess liquid and cut into small pieces. Makes 2 cups.

Appeteasers

SHRIMP DIP

1 can (4½-ounce) shrimp
1 hard-cooked egg, chopped
1 cup sour cream
1/4 cup mayonnaise
3 tablespoons thinly chopped green onion
1 tablespoon lemon juice
1 teaspoon horseradish
1 teaspoon Worcestershire sauce
1/2 teaspoon dillweed

Combine all ingredients, chill before serving. Serve with Triscuits. Makes 2 cups.

SHRIMP REMOULADE

10 pounds cooked small shrimp
1 1/4 cups salad oil
1/2 cup prepared mustard
1/3 cup white wine vinegar or dry white wine
2 teaspoons salt
2 teaspoons paprika
2 teaspoons Tabasco sauce
2 hard-boiled eggs, chopped
1 apple, cut into small pieces
1 cup finely chopped celery
1/4 cup minced parsley
2 tablespoons chopped scallion
1 tablespoon finely chopped green pepper

Shell and devein cooked shrimp. Combine salad oil with mustard, white wine vinegar or white wine, salt, paprika and Tabasco sauce. Beat until well blended and then add chopped hard-boiled eggs, apple, celery, parsley, scallion and green pepper. Add shrimp and toss well.

Cover and place in refrigerator for at least 12 hours. Stir once after 4 hours and again 1 hour before serving. Drain off excess marinade. Serve on bed of greens with cocktail picks close by.

Jo says, "I've used this recipe as a first course. Place an artichoke bottom on a bed of lettuce, mound drained shrimp on artichoke. Expect raves!" Serves 50.

CAROL'S SPINACH BALLS

1/2 cup sesame seeds
2 packages (10-ounces each) frozen chopped spinach
1/2 cup chopped onions
2 cups garlic or herb-seasoned croutons
1 cup freshly grated Parmesan cheese
4 eggs lightly beaten
3/4 cup unsalted butter, room temperature
1/2 teaspoon freshly ground white pepper
1/4 teaspoon freshly grated nutmeg

Heat a heavy skillet over medium heat; add sesame seeds. Cook, stirring constantly, until seeds are golden, 2-3 minutes.

Cook spinach according to package directions. Drain in sieve, pressing with back of spoon to remove as much moisture as possible.

Grind croutons into fine crumbs in blender or food processor. Mix spinach, crumbs, cheese, eggs butter, pepper and nutmeg thoroughly in medium bowl. Shape mixture into small balls, about 1 rounded teaspoon. Roll in sesame seeds to coat lightly.

Freeze in single layers on waxed-paper-lined baking sheets. Transfer to airtight container. Can freeze 4-6 weeks.

To serve, heat oven to 350 degrees. Place spinach balls on a greased baking sheet. Bake until firm, 10 - 15 minutes. Makes 50 balls.

SPINACH DIP

1 package (10-ounce) frozen chopped spinach, squeezed dry when thawed
1/2 bunch green onions, chopped
1 teaspoon garlic powder
1/2 teaspoon lemon juice
1/2 teaspoon Worcestershire sauce
2 cups Hellmann's mayonnaise
1/4 teaspoon salt

Combine all ingredients and serve at room temperature. Makes 2–3 cups.

SUMMER SAUSAGE

2 pounds extra lean ground beef
2 tablespoons Morton Tender Quick salt
1 1/2 teaspoons liquid smoke
1/2 teaspoon onion powder
1/8 teaspoon garlic powder
1 cup water

Mix and form into 2 or 3 loaves. Wrap in plastic wrap and leave in refrigerator 24 hours. Unwrap and place on rack and bake at 300 degrees for 45 minutes to 1 hour. Slice.
Jan says, "Please do not use tenderizer."

STEAK TARTARE

5 pounds sirloin, fat removed, ground three (3) times
5 tablespoons Worcestershire sauce
1/2 teaspoon sea salt
3/4 tablespoon fresh ground pepper
1 tablespoon mustard
1/2 tablespoon ground nutmeg
1/4 teaspoon anise
1/4 teaspoon cloves
3 garlic cloves, pressed
1/2 cup onion, minced
2 tablespoons capers
4 drops Tabasco
Juice of one lemon
4 tablespoons cognac
2 slightly beaten eggs
1 teaspoon Escoffier Sauce Diable

Mix ingredients together. Firmly press into glass bowl. Cover and refrigerate a few hours before serving. Unmold on platter of red lettuce garnished with parsley and cherry tomatoes. Serve with slices of rye bread sliced silver-dollar thin, or Melba toast.

❖❖❖

TEMPURA BATTER

1 egg, separated
1/2 teaspoon salt
1/2 cup sifted flour
1/2 cup milk
2 tablespoons butter, melted

Beat egg yolk and salt in small bowl. Add milk, then slowly mix in flour. Mix in melted butter. Beat egg white until stiff. Fold into batter.

Use as a batter for frying fish or fresh vegetables, such as mushrooms, zucchini, cauliflower, and eggplant. Makes 1 cup.

TOMATO ASPIC

2 packages lemon-flavored gelatin
2 1/2 cups hot water
1 can (8-ounce) seasoned tomato sauce
1 cup Beefamato juice
2 tablespoons vinegar
1/2 teaspoon salt
1/2 teaspoon seasoned salt
1 tablespoon horseradish

Combine ingredients. Spray mold with Pam. Pour ingredients into mold, chill until firm. Serves 8.

TOASTED PECANS

4 cups raw, shelled pecans
2 tablespoons vegetable oil
3 teaspoons chili powder
1/2 teaspoon garlic powder
2 teaspoons salt
2 teaspoons Worcestershire sauce
1/4 teaspoon Tabasco sauce

Whisk oil and seasonings together in small dish; sprinkle over pecans to coat. Spread evenly on cookie sheet and bake at 300 degrees for 20 minutes or until toasted. Cool and store in airtight container.
Makes 4 cups.

JEANNE'S TIROPETES
(CHEESE TRIANGLES)

1 pound Filo dough
1 cup butter, melted (may need more)
1 pound Feta cheese, crumbled
3 egg yolks
1 cup grated Parmesan cheese (fresh if possible)
2 tablespoons chopped fresh parsley
1 cup milk (hot)
1 1/2 tablespoons flour
2 tablespoons butter
Salt and white pepper to taste

Note: These can be frozen before baking. Spread out on baking sheets in freezer until frozen, then store in bags.

Combine Feta cheese, egg yolks, Parmesan cheese, 3 tablespoons melted butter and parsley. Prepare a white sauce of milk, flour, 2 tablespoons butter, salt and pepper. Let cool. Add to egg, cheese mixture. Stir well.

Cut each of the sheets of Filo dough lengthwise into 3-inch strips. Take one strip at a time (keep others covered to prevent drying), and holding the strip horizontally, brush it with melted butter. Put 1 teaspoon of filling into the lower left corner. Then fold the corner over to make a triangle along the strip. Fold the upper left corner over to close the triangle. Continue to fold dough over and over until strip has become a small triangle of pastry.

Brush the top with butter. Place triangles on a baking sheet and bake in preheated 375-degree oven for 15-20 minutes. Serve hot. Makes 100 or more.

Great Beginnings · Brunch

Whether your brunch is a "before-the-game" affair or a traditional Sunday morning repast, what matters most is simply being with people you enjoy. There is something very special about an out-of-doors brunch where Mother Nature acts as co-hostess and serves up mild temperatures, clear skies, and a whisper of a breeze.

The recipes we present in this section are those we particularly enjoy serving for brunch. The Brunch Eggs Elegante is superb, Sherried Chicken Livers is a delight, many egg dishes will be a hit, as will the Fresh Fruit Tart. In addition, you will find wonderful breads, coffee cakes, and muffins in the bread chapter (Love Those Buns) and more brunch ideas in the party chapter, called R.S.V.P.

Great Beginnings

APPETIZER "ROLL-UPS"

1 package (8-ounce) refrigerated crescent rolls
1/2 cup sour cream
1/2 teaspoon onion salt
1/4 teaspoon mixed herbs
1/2 pound bacon, cooked crisp, drained and crumbled
Parmesan cheese

Unroll the crescent rolls. Cut each roll into three equal wedges, lengthwise. Spread with sour cream mixed with onion salt and mixed herbs. Top with bacon and sprinkle with Parmesan cheese. Roll up each wedge, starting at the point of the wedge. Place "roll-ups" on greased baking sheet and bake at 375 degrees for 12 to 15 minutes or until golden brown. Watch carefully or bottoms will get too dark. Serve warm. Makes 24.

MOCK BLINIS

2 loaves Pepperidge Farm bread. Cut off crusts and roll each slice flat.
2 egg yolks
2 packages (8-ounce size) cream cheese
1/2 cup sugar
Brown sugar and cinnamon mixture — as much as needed
2 sticks butter or margarine

Combine egg yolks, cream cheese and sugar and spread on bread slices. Melt 2 sticks butter or margarine. Roll up each slice of bread. Then roll in butter or margarine mixture, then in mixture of brown sugar and cinnamon. Place on cookie sheet. Freeze.

When ready to serve, cut in thirds. Bake at 350 degrees for 20 minutes. To serve, pass on trays or place on buffet table with a bowl of sour cream so guests can dip. Jo says, "Be ready to replenish because they do not last long." Makes 50.

BROCCOLI CUSTARD MOLD

2 packages (10-ounce size) frozen broccoli
1/4 cup chicken broth
3 tablespoons butter
1/4 cup green onions, chopped
3 tablespoons flour
1 cup sour cream
3 extra large eggs
1/2 cup Swiss cheese, grated
1/2 teaspoon salt
1/4 teaspoon white pepper
1/4 teaspoon dry mustard
1/2 teaspoon nutmeg

Grease a 6-cup ring mold or individual molds. In a medium saucepan, cook broccoli in salted water. Drain and chop. Place broccoli in small mixing bowl, add broth. Preheat oven. In a large skillet, melt butter and saute onions for 1 minute, then blend in flour. Remove from heat and add sour cream. Beat eggs until frothy and add to mixture. Add broccoli and remaining ingredients. Turn into prepared mold. Bake at 350 degrees for 45 minutes. When cool, run a knife around side of mold to loosen. Invert on serving plate. Serves 10-12.

CRAB ON TOAST

1 stick butter or margarine, melted
1 package (8-ounce) cream cheese with chives
1 can crab, drained
English muffins
   or
Toast points

Melt butter, add cream cheese, stir until blended, add crab. Heat thoroughly. Serve on toasted English muffins or toast points. Serves 4.

Great Beginnings

SHERRIED CHICKEN LIVERS

6 slices bacon
1/4 cup butter
2 cups thinly sliced Bermuda onion
4 cups thinly sliced mushrooms
1 tablespoon chopped chives
1 teaspoon salt
1/8 teaspoon pepper
1/8 teaspoon cinnamon
1/2 teaspoon powdered rosemary
1/4 teaspoon powdered savory
1/8 teaspoon chervil
1 pound chicken livers
1/2 cup beef consomme
1/2 cup sherry
2 teaspoons flour mixed with 1/4 cup cold water
2 tablespoons chopped parsley
Freshly made toast points

Cut bacon slices into 1-inch lengths. Pan-broil until crisp and drain on paper toweling. Pour off drippings. In same skillet melt butter, add onion and saute just until tender, adding mushrooms toward the last. Add all seasonings and chicken livers and saute slowly for about 10 minutes. (Prick the livers with a fork to keep them from popping).

Add consomme and sherry and simmer slowly for 10 to 15 minutes more. Blend in flour-water paste and heat, stirring until thickened. Add chopped parsley and crisp bacon and serve immediately over hot buttered toast. Serves 6.

COLUMBIA SPECIALS

Slices of buttered toast
Crisp slices of bacon
Sliced tomatoes
Sliced hard-boiled eggs
Slices of onion (optional), slightly sauteed
Sliced fresh mushrooms, slightly sauteed
1 recipe of Cheese Sauce, doubled if necessary (see index)

Build Specials by stacking bacon on toast, then tomatoes, onion if desired, eggs, mushrooms and topping it off with cheese sauce.

Note: Use as much of the ingredients as you need for the number of people you are serving. We mound them high.

CREAM PUFF BOWL

1 cup water
1/2 cup butter
1/4 teaspoon salt
1 cup sifted flour
4 eggs

Heat water, butter and salt until boiling. Add flour all at once. Stir until mixture forms a smooth ball and leaves sides of pan clean. Remove from heat. Add eggs, one at a time. Beat after each addition. Spread over bottom and up sides of a greased 9-inch pie plate. Bake at 450 degrees for 15 minutes, reduce to 350 degrees for 20 to 25 minutes.
Jan says, "This puff bowl is not only pretty to hold salads or vegetables at your brunch, but very tasty. Do serve at once so bowl won't get soggy."

CREPES BENEDICT

12 cooked crepes, 6 to 6 1/2 inches in diameter
12 slices ham
12 eggs, poached for 6 minutes. (These may be prepared ahead and refrigerated.)
Recipe of Hollandaise Sauce (See index)

On each crepe, center a slice of ham and lay a poached egg on top. Fold over two edges of crepe, then spoon some Hollandise Sauce over the opening. In an oven-to-table dish, broil crepes 6 inches away from the heat for 2 or 3 minutes. Sprinkle with parsley. Serves 6.

Great Beginnings

BASIC CREPES I

1 cup flour
3 eggs
1 1/2 cups milk
Dash of salt
Vegetable oil

Prepare batter an hour or two before baking the crepes. (I like to have the batter sit in the refrigerator all night.) Combine all ingredients except oil in blender. Whirl until smooth. The batter should be the consistency of heavy cream.

Before making each crepe, brush a 6-inch or 6 1/2-inch skillet with oil, covering the bottom and sides. Heat skillet until very hot, but not smoking. Pour in 2 tablespoons of batter, tilt pan to coat bottom, cook about 1 minute or until brown on bottom. Turn, cook thirty seconds more. Repeat until batter is used up. Crepes may be stacked for immediate use or refrigerated and reheated at serving time. Makes 12-14 crepes.

BASIC CREPES II

1 1/4 cups flour
1 1/2 cups milk
Pinch of salt
2 tablespoons melted butter or margarine

Place all ingredients in blender or mixer and beat well. Let batter stand overnight for more perfect crepes. Prepare crepes as instructed in Basic Crepes I. Fill with your desired filling.
Serves 8-10.

EGGS BENEDICT

4 halves of English muffins
4 slices of shredded ham
4 poached eggs
Hollandaise Sauce (see index)

Warm buttered halves of English muffins. Layer ham, poached eggs and pour Hollandaise Sauce over top. Sprinkle paprika over the sauce. Serve hot and immediately. Serves 4.

BRUNCH EGGS ELEGANTE

SAUCE ELEGANTE:
1/4 cup soft butter
1 teaspoon salt
4 tablespoons flour
1/4 teaspoon white pepper
1/4 teaspoon dry mustard
2 cups hot milk
4 tablespoons diced Swiss cheese
4 tablespoons Parmesan cheese

EGGS:
8 hard boiled eggs
Fresh mushrooms, sauteed in butter, drained
   and finely chopped
4 tablespoons soft butter
4 tablespoons Elegante sauce
Grated Parmesan cheese

Place all sauce ingredients into blender, cover and blend at low speed until ingredients are thoroughly mixed. Turn to high speed for 30 seconds. Pour into top of double boiler and cook over simmering water for 15 minutes, stirring occasionally.

Meanwhile, halve eggs lengthwise. Remove yolks and reserve whites. Mix yolks with an equal amount of cooked and chopped mushrooms, butter and sauce. Fill egg whites with mixture, mounding it high.

Spread a layer of sauce in a shallow baking dish, place eggs in sauce and cover with more sauce. Sprinkle with Parmesan cheese and brown under broiler. Can be made a day or two ahead of time, covered and refrigerated.

If refrigerated, set out at least 1 hour before heating. Place in a 325-degree oven for 30 minutes or until sauce is bubbly in center of baking dish. Serves 8-10.

Great Beginnings

POACHED EGGS HARLEQUIN

4 tablespoons butter
1 cup finely chopped mushrooms
1 tablespoon finely chopped shallots
3 tablespoons flour
1 1/4 cup cream
1 cup chicken, cooked and finely chopped
1 1/4 cups sherry
Salt and pepper
4 English muffins
Eggs
Asparagus spears
Pimento and black olives for garnish

Saute mushrooms in melted butter about 3 minutes or until nearly done. Add shallots and cook a few minutes longer. Blend in flour, then add cream and cook stirring constantly until smooth and thick, about 5 minutes. Add chicken and sherry. Season with salt and pepper. Remove from heat and cover.

Toast rounds of English muffins. Place a poached egg on each round. Cover with hot chicken sauce. Garnish each serving with 4 cooked asparagus spears. Place 1 strip of pimento and 1/2 pitted black olive on top of each serving. Serves 4.

RUTHIE'S SCRAMBLED EGG MEDLEY

2 dozen eggs, whipped slightly
1 tablespoon parsley, snipped
14 tablespoons milk
Salt and pepper
1 can cream of mushroom soup
1 carton (10-ounce) sour cream
16 slices of bacon, fried and crumbled
4 ounces extra sharp cheese
4 ounces Jalapeno cheese
Fresh mushrooms, sliced
Butter

Scramble eggs with parsley, milk, salt and pepper. Pour in lightly greased 9 x 13-inch casserole. Mix mushroom soup and sour cream. Spread over eggs. Fry 16 slices bacon, crisp, and crumble. Sprinkle over soup and cream mixture. Mix extra sharp cheese, grated, with Jalapeno cheese. Sprinkle over the bacon. Saute fresh mushrooms in butter. Put on top of bacon and cheese. Bake at 325 degrees for 30 to 40 minutes. Can make the day before or even a week before. Set out at room temperature for 30 minutes before baking.

Jan says, "Before you put this casserole in the oven you may place thinly sliced tomatoes over all." Serves 12.

SAUSAGE STUFFED EGGS

12 eggs
1 pound sausage (mild or hot, as desired)
2 teaspoons lemon juice
4 tablespoons butter
4 tablespoons flour
2 cups milk
Salt and pepper
1 small onion, grated
2 tablespoons dry sherry
Buttered bread crumbs

Hard cook eggs and cut in half, lengthwise. Remove yolks carefully and mash with a fork. Brown sausage, sprinkle with lemon juice, and mix with egg yolks. Stuff eggs with sausage and egg yolk mixture, using drippings if mixture is too dry. Set eggs in greased baking dish and cover with sauce made from butter, flour, milk, salt and pepper.

If there is any sausage-egg mixture left, add it to white sauce. Add onion and sherry to sauce. Spoon sauce over eggs. Top with buttered bread crumbs. Bake at 300 degrees for 45 minutes. Serves 6-8.

Great Beginnings

HOMEMADE SEASONED SAUSAGE PATTIES

2 pounds boneless pork shoulder
4 ounces salt pork
2/3 cup water
1/3 cup finely chopped onion
2 tablespoons snipped parsley
4 teaspoons rubbed sage
1 teaspoon salt
1 teaspoon dried sweet pepper flakes
1 teaspoon chili powder
1/2 teaspoon dried thyme, crushed
1/2 teaspoon dried marjoram, crushed
1/2 teaspoon dried basil, crushed
2 cloves garlic, minced

Using coarse blade on food grinder, grind pork shoulder and salt pork together. Combine rest of ingredients, mix well and grind again. Divide mixture in half. On waxed paper, shape each half into a roll 6 inches long and 2 inches in diameter. Wrap in waxed paper or foil. Chill at least 2 hours.

Just before cooking, slice into rounds 1/2-inch thick. Place a few sausage rounds in a cold skillet. Cover and cook slowly for 10 to 12 minutes, turning once. Drain on paper towels. Makes 24 patties.

PREPARED AHEAD SAUSAGE SOUFFLE

8 slices of bread with crusts, diced
2 cups Cheddar cheese, grated
1 1/2 pound sausage links cooked, cut into thirds, or 1 1/2 pounds of uncooked bulk sausage
4 eggs
2 3/4 cups milk
1 can mushroom soup
3/4 teaspoon dry mustard

Spread bread in bottom of greased 8 x 11-inch baking dish. Sprinkle cheese over top. Arrange sausage on top of cheese. Beat eggs with 2 1/4 cups milk; pour over bread. Mix together soup, milk (remaining 1/2 cup) and mustard; spoon on top of casserole. Cover tightly with foil. Refrigerate overnight.

Place in cold oven. Set oven to 300 degrees and bake about 1 1/2 hours or until puffy and brown. Serve immediately. Serves 8-10.

FRESH FRUIT TART

3/4 package refrigerator sugar cookie dough
1 package (8-ounce) cream cheese, softened
1/3 cup sugar
1 tablespoon milk
2 tablespoons fresh orange rind
Assorted fruits in season--peaches, strawberries, blueberries, kiwi, grapes, pears, etc...

GLAZE:
1 cup sugar
3 tablespoons cornstarch
Salt
3/4 cup water
1 cup orange juice
1/4 teaspoon lemon juice
1 teaspoon orange rind
1 teaspoon lemon rind

Make crust by rolling cookie dough in a thin layer on a pizza pan or 9 x 13-inch baking pan. Prick dough with fork and bake according to package directions. Let cool.

Make cream filling by whipping cheese, sugar, orange rind and milk together. Spread evenly over top of crust. Cover and chill. Decorate with fresh fruit and top with glaze.

Combine sugar, cornstarch and salt. Add liquids and bring to a boil. Cook one minute, then add rinds. Let glaze cool. Carefully pour it over fruit and toss to coat well. Chill thoroughly.

Jo says, "If you are serving he-man eaters, count on serving only 4. There have been a few times I can remember, when the mamas only got to lick the pan. So good." Serves 8-10.

Great Beginnings

BAKED FRUIT

2 cans (No. 303 size) chunked pineapple
2 cans (No. 303 size) fruits for salad
3/4 cup sugar
1/2 cup flour
Juice of 2 lemons
1 jar Old English Sharp cheese (Kraft)

Drain and save juice from pineapple and salad fruits. Place drained fruit in shallow baking dish. Make juice from pineapple juice and enough of the other to make 2 cups.

Mix flour and sugar and combine with pineapple juice mixture and juice of lemons. Cook until thick. Remove from heat and blend in Old English cheese.

Pour over fruit and bake uncovered at 350 degrees for 45 minutes. Serves 6.

HOT CURRIED FRUIT

Pear halves
Apricot or peach halves
3 cups pineapple tidbits
1 small bottle maraschino cherries
1/3 cup melted butter
2/3 cup brown sugar
2 1/2 teaspoons curry powder
3 tablespoons cornstarch
1/4 cup toasted slivered almonds (optional)
8 to 10 coconut or almond macaroons (optional)

Drain fruit thoroughly and place hollow side up in a shallow 2-quart casserole. Melt butter, add sugar, curry powder and cornstarch. Pour over fruit.

If desired, crumble macaroons and mix carefully through the fruit mixture. Top with toasted almonds. Bake at 325 degrees for 1 hour. This is best made a day or two in advance and reheated at 350 degrees for 1/2 hour. Serves 8.

FRUIT SLUSH

1 can (6-ounce) frozen lemonade, slightly thawed
1 can (6-ounce) frozen orange juice, slightly thawed
1 cup sugar
1 (No. 2) can crushed pineapple
1 16-ounce bottle 7-Up
2 large bananas, sliced
2 small boxes frozen strawberries, barely thawed

Mix sugar with juice. Add 7-Up and fruit. Freeze 24 hours. Thaw to slightly slush. Serve as a dessert, salad or for brunch. Serves 18-20.

TIPSY FRUIT

1 medium watermelon
1 medium honeydew
2 medium cantaloupe
1 pineapple cut into chunks
Green grapes
2 cans (6-ounce size) limeade, thawed
4 juice cans water
1/2 cup white creme de menthe
Sprigs of fresh mint

Prepare melon balls and pineapple chunks. Place with green grapes in scalloped, decorated watermelon. Mix limeade, water, creme de menthe. Pour over fruit and garnish with fresh mint. Serve in champagne glasses or let guests serve themselves with toothpicks.

Great Beginnings

SUNDAY EGGS

1/2 stick margarine
3 tablespoons flour
3 tablespoons minced onion
1 cup milk
1 can cream of celery soup, undiluted
1 can mushroom soup, undiluted
3/4 cup processed American cheese, cut up
10 hard-boiled eggs, quartered
1 small can sliced mushrooms, drained
Toast or buns or chinese noodles

Make paste by melting margarine and stirring in flour until smooth. Add minced onion and stir. Add milk, continue stirring and when mixture begins to thicken, add both soups, mushroom and cheese. When mixture is thoroughly heated and thickened, add eggs. Serve over whatever you prefer. This is a basic mixture. Good with crabmeat, ham, lobster or chicken. Add a dash of curry to the above mixture. Serves 16.

THE BEST FRENCH TOAST

8 slices french bread
4 eggs
1 cup cream
Pinch of salt
1/4 teaspoon nutmeg
1/4 teaspoon cinnamon
Optional: 1-ounce Grand Marnier in the egg-
cream mixture

Cut bread on the diagonal, 3/4-inch thick. Beat eggs until frothy and light. Add cream, salt, nutmeg and cinnamon. Soak bread a few pieces at a time so that they absorb egg-cream mixture thoroughly. Preheat oven to 400 degrees.

In a skillet heat 1/2 cup cooking oil. Fry bread on both sides to a golden color or as desired for crispness.

Remove bread from skillet and drain on paper towels to absorb excess grease. Place on baking sheet and allow to bake in oven for 3 to 5 minutes or until puffed.

To serve: Let guests have their choice of warm syrup, powdered sugar and cinnamon or preserves.

Note: Texas toast makes delicious French toast. Serves 4.

CONCH FRITTERS

6 large conch: cleaned, blanched and finely
    chopped (about 2 cups)
1 large green bell pepper, seeded and finely
    chopped
2 medium yellow onions, finely chopped
1 1/2 cups all-purpose flour
1 cup milk
1 1/2 teaspoons baking powder
1 egg
1 teaspoon dried thyme, crushed
1/2 teaspoon oregano, crushed
1/2 to 1 teaspoon minced fresh parsley
Pinch of paprika
Pinch of dried red pepper flakes, or large dash
    of Tabasco sauce
Salt and freshly ground pepper
Bacon fat and corn oil
Chopped parsley for garnish
Cocktail Sauce (See index)

Combine conch and rest of ingredients except bacon fat and corn oil in large bowl and blend well. Let stand for at least 30 minutes. Add equal parts bacon fat and corn oil to depth of 2 inches in heavy skillet and heat to medium-high, or use deep fryer.

Drop conch mixture into skillet in batches by teaspoon and fry until dark brown.

Remove fritters using slotted spoon and drain on paper towels. Transfer fritters to baking sheet and keep warm in low oven while frying the remainder. Arrange fritters on serving platter. Set a bowl of cocktail sauce in center of platter. Sprinkle fritters with chopped parsley. Serve warm.

Great Beginnings

GARLIC CHEESE GRITS

1 cup quick-cooking grits
1 roll garlic cheese
1 stick butter
2 beaten eggs
3/4 cup milk

Cook grits according to package directions. Add cheese and butter. Cool. Combine eggs and milk. Put grits into 2-quart buttered casserole and pour egg-milk mixture over grits. Bake uncovered for 1 hour in 375-degree oven. Can be made ahead.

Note: Egg-milk mixture can be stirred into the cooled grits, if desired, and top dusted with paprika. Serves 8.

BAKED GRITS LEONARDO

2 cups grits, cooked according to package
  directions
1/2 pound butter
1/2 pound sharp cheese
2 tablespoons cooking sherry
2 tablespoons Worcestershire sauce
1 tablespoon Tabasco sauce
2 well-beaten eggs

Cook grits in boiling, salted water until dry. Add butter while grits are still hot. Stir in Worcestershire and Tabasco sauces and eggs. Place in buttered casserole. Soften cheese in sherry and spread over grits in casserole. Cook at 250 degrees for 1 hour--or longer if refrigerated--until bubbly and hot in center. Do not freeze. Serves 12.

HAM AND CHEESE BRUNCH

12 slices white sandwich bread (cut off crusts)
3 cups diced meat (turkey, chicken, ham or
  beef)
3/4 cup of each, diced celery, onion, and green
  pepper
2 tablespoons parsley

Arrange 6 of the bread slices in a 13 x 9 x 2-inch baking dish. Top with meat, celery, onion, green pepper and parsley. Top with remaining slices of bread. Combine and pour over the top:

3 cups milk
3 beaten eggs
1 teaspoon dry mustard
1/2 teaspoon salt
1/4 teaspoon seasoned salt
2 cups grated Cheddar cheese

Refrigerate overnight. Before baking, sprinkle heavily with grated cheddar cheese. Bake at 350 degrees for 30 to 40 minutes or until set. Serve with a sauce of last 3 ingredients.

1 can cream of mushroom soup
1 small jar or can of butter mushrooms, drained
1/3 cup milk

Combine soup, mushrooms and milk. Heat thoroughly and serve as a side dish. Serves 12.

HAM AND EGG CASSEROLE

1 or 2 medium potatoes, cooked, peeled and
  thinly sliced
4 hard-cooked eggs, peeled and sliced
1 cup diced cooked ham
Salt and pepper
1 egg
1 cup sour cream
1/4 cup buttered bread crumbs

Layer potatoes, eggs and ham in buttered 1 1/2-quart baking dish. Season with salt and pepper. Bake 10 minutes in 350-degree oven. Beat egg in medium bowl, blend in sour cream. Pour over casserole and sprinkle with crumbs. Return to oven and bake 5 minutes or until heated. Serve immediately.

Note: For a crowd, triple recipe and bake in 13 x 9 x 2-inch casserole and allow extra time to heat. Serves 4.

Great Beginnings

HAM AND RED–EYE GRAVY

Country ham slices 1/2-inch thick or fully cooked ham slices, cut in half. Trim fat from slices, reserve trimmings. Cook trimmings in skillet until crisp. Discard trimmings and brown ham on both sides in hot fat, 5 to 6 minutes per side. Remove ham to a warm plate. Stir 2/3 cup boiling water and 1 teaspoon instant coffee powder into the drippings in skillet. If ham is mild cured, add a few drops of liquid smoke. Cook, scraping pan often for 2 to 3 minutes. Serve with warm ham slices and grits. Serves 6.

PREPARED AHEAD HAM SOUFFLE

12 slices bread, buttered
1 cup American cheese, grated
1 cup diced ham
3 beaten eggs
3 cups milk
1/2 teaspoon salt
1 teaspoon Worcestershire sauce

Place 6 slices of bread, buttered sides up, in greased baking dish. Arrange diced ham and grated cheese on top of bread. Add remaining 6 slices of bread, buttered sides down. Combine eggs, milk, salt and Worcestershire sauce. Pour over bread and let set in refrigerator overnight or minimum of 1 1/2 hours. Bake at 325 degrees for 1 1/2 hours. Serves 12.

HOPPIN' JOHN

1 package (1 pound) black-eyed peas
3 pints cold water
1/2 pound sliced salt pork or bacon
1 teaspoon Tabasco sauce
1/2 teaspoon salt
2 tablespoons bacon fat
2 cloves garlic, crushed
2 medium onions, chopped
1 large green pepper, chopped fine
1 1/2 cups uncooked long grain rice
1 1/2 cups boiling water
1 can (16-ounce) whole tomatoes, undrained

Cover peas with water in large kettle. Soak overnight. Add pork, Tabasco and salt. Cover and cook over low heat about 30 minutes. While peas are cooking, saute onions and green pepper in bacon fat until tender. Add garlic, rice, tomatoes and boiling water. Cook until rice is tender and water is absorbed, about 20 to 25 minutes, stirring occasionally. Combine mixtures.

Jo says, "A must for New Year's Day." Makes 8 cups.

AUNTIE FAY'S BUTTERMILK HOT CAKES

1 2/3 cups sifted flour
1 tablespoon baking powder
1 1/2 teaspoons soda
1 teaspoon salt
2 tablespoons sugar

Sift all dry ingredients together into a bowl.

2 cups buttermilk
3 beaten eggs
3 tablespoons melted butter or oleo

Add to dry ingredients above, mix lightly and cook on hot griddle. Serves 6.

Great Beginnings

THE BASIC OMELET

3 eggs
1 tablespoon water
1/4 teaspoon salt
Dash pepper
1 tablespoon margarine or butter

In small bowl beat together with a fork, eggs, water, salt and pepper until mixture is blended. In an 8-inch flared, non-stick skillet heat margarine over medium heat until it sizzles, but don't get skillet too hot. Lift pan and swirl margarine around to coat skillet.

Pour egg mixture into pan and continue to cook over medium heat. Shake skillet constantly to keep egg mixture moving so omelet remains even. When eggs are set on the bottom, but soft on top, remove skillet from heat. Spoon a filling of your choice across the center, if desired.

Using a spatula, carefully lift one-third of cooked omelet and fold over filling. Tilt skillet and with a spatula gently fold remaining third of omelet over filling. Invert skillet to roll omelet out onto serving plate. Top with sauce or garnish as desired. Makes 2 servings. Jan says, "Do not make more than a three-egg omelet at a time."

BETTY'S BUTTERMILK PANCAKES

1 egg
1 cup buttermilk
2 tablespoons Wesson oil
1 cup flour
1 teaspoon baking powder
1/2 teaspoon baking soda
1 tablespoon sugar

Beat egg, add buttermilk. Mix flour, baking powder, soda and sugar. Add to buttermilk mixture. Add oil. If mixture is too thick, add a little more buttermilk. Cook on hot griddle. This recipe can be doubled or tripled. Serves 3.

ELEGANT PANCAKE

1 cup flour
1 cup milk
4 eggs, lightly beaten
1 teaspoon nutmeg
1/2 teaspoon cinnamon
1 stick butter
2 tablespoons lemon juice
1 package frozen strawberries and juice, thawed
2 tablespoons powdered sugar

Preheat oven to 425 degrees. Combine flour, milk, eggs, nutmeg and cinnamon. Beat lightly and leave a little lumpy. In a 12-inch skillet with oven-proof handle melt the butter in the oven. When butter is very hot and bubbly, pour in the batter. Bake in oven for 15 or 20 minutes until golden brown.

Remove from oven and pour strawberries and lemon juice over pancake. Return to oven briefly. Sprinkle powdered sugar over pancake and serve. Serves 8.

Great Beginnings

GERMAN POTATO PANCAKES

2 quarts potatoes, grated
Juice of 2 lemons
8 eggs
Flour as needed to hold mixture together
1 tablespoon lemon rind, grated
1 teaspoon nutmeg, ground
Salt to taste
Oil, for frying, as needed

Grate potatoes; add lemon juice to prevent discoloration. Add eggs, flour, lemon rind, nutmeg and salt; blend together with whisk. Place large spoonfuls of batter in frying pan with 1/4-inch of hot oil, turning pancakes to brown and crisp on both sides. Serve piping hot. 24 servings.

ORANGE PANCAKES

Grated rind from 1/2 orange
Juice from 2 or 3 oranges or enough to make
    1 cup
1/2 orange, peeled and sectioned
1 cup packaged pancake mix

Peel and section 1/2 orange, being careful to remove all of the bitter white skin and membranes. Dice and put into bowl, should have 1/4 cup. Combine the cup of pancake mix with the cup of orange juice, the grated orange rind and the 1/4-cup diced orange sections. Heat griddle using 1 tablespoon batter for each pancake. Makes 36 2 3/4-inch pancakes.

HOT SPICED PEARS

1 can (No. 10) pear halves, drained
1 cup syrup from pears
3/4 cup brown sugar
1 teaspoon cinnamon, ground
1/2 teaspoon mace, ground

Place pear halves cut-side up in baking pan, pour in syrup. Combine brown sugar and spices, sprinkle evenly over pears. Place in moderate oven 350 degrees to heat through and glaze. Keep warm until served. Serves 6.

BAKED PINEAPPLE

1 1/2 cups sugar
6 tablespoons flour
6 tablespoons liquid from pineapple, reserved
2 cans (20-ounces each) chunky pineapple, drained
1 cup shredded cheese
2 cups Ritz crackers (crushed)
1 stick margarine (melted)

Combine sugar, flour, juice over low heat until some of the sugar melts. Stir in pineapple chunks and cheese. Pour into 1 1/2 quart casserole. Put crushed crackers on top. Pour melted margarine over crackers. Bake 350 degrees for 20 to 25 minutes. Serves 6 to 8.

Jan says, "This is without a doubt one of the best dishes I have ever tasted. Your company will love it. This may be served with a dinner, brunch or a luncheon."

PINEAPPLE WITH GRAPES

Prepare fresh pineapple. Cut in half, remove fruit, saving shells, and cut into bite-size pieces. Add 1/2 the amount of fresh green seedless grapes. Mix with sour cream, sweetened with brown sugar. Pile into pineapple shells or serve from large bowl.

Great Beginnings

QUICHE LORRAINE

PASTRY for 1 9-inch quiche pan
1 1/4 cups flour-sift before measuring
1/2 cup soft butter
1 egg yolk
1 teaspoon salt
1/2 teaspoon dry mustard
1 tablespoon paprika

FILLING: (for 2 9-inch or 1 12-inch quiche pan)
4 slices bacon, chopped
1 bunch green onions, minced
1 tablespoon butter
1 can (4-ounce) sliced mushrooms, drained
4 thin slices shredded ham
1/2 pound Swiss cheese, grated
4 eggs
1 1/2 cups Pet milk
1 garlic clove, pressed
1/2 teaspoon salt
1/2 teaspoon mustard
Dash nutmeg
Dash black pepper

Sift flour and dry ingredients into bowl. Make well in center and add egg yolk and butter. Form a paste and work in the flour. Sprinkle with ice water. Stir with fork to mix, form a ball and chill. Roll to fit pan and prebake 5 to 10 minutes at 450 degrees. Chill in freezer about 1 hour before filling. (Double recipe for 12-inch pan).

Fry bacon, drain. Saute onions in butter. Layer bacon, onions, mushrooms, ham and cheese in two shells. Combine eggs and other ingredients and beat well into a custard. Pour custard over other ingredients in shells and bake in 350-degree oven for 35 minutes or until knife inserted in center comes out clean. Serves 6-8.

QUICHE LORRAINE

1 unbaked pie shell (9-inch) well chilled. Prick bottom and edges with fork to prevent shrinking.
1 tablespoon soft butter
12 slices bacon cut into 1-inch lengths
2/3 cup onions, thinly sliced
1/4 pound natural Swiss cheese, grated
4 eggs, beaten
2 cups heavy cream
2 dashes Tabasco sauce
1/4 teaspoon sugar
1/4 teaspoon ground nutmeg
3/4 teaspoon salt
Pinch of cayenne pepper
1/4 teaspoon white pepper

Preheat oven to 425 degrees. Fry bacon to crisp. Remove and drain on paper towels. Saute onion in 2 tablespoons bacon fat until tender. Drain on paper towels. Cover bottom of pie shell with soft butter, then onions, bacon and cheese. Combine eggs, cream, Tabasco sauce, sugar, salt, nutmeg, cayenne, and pepper. Using hand beater, beat just enough to mix thoroughly. Pour mixture into pie shell.

Bake at 425 degrees for 15 minutes. Reduce heat to 300 degrees and bake 40 minutes or until knife inserted in center comes out clean. Let stand 15 minutes before cutting into wedges.

If freezing, do not defrost, but bake as directed for about 1 or 1 1/2 hours at 300 degrees.

Jo says, "I had extra mixture when I used a 9-inch shell. You might want to try a 10-inch."

Serves 6.

HOT SAUSAGE BALLS

3 cups Bisquick
1 pound hot bulk sausage
12 ounces Coon cheese or sharp Cheddar cheese, grated

Melt cheese in a double boiler. Mix in sausage, broken into small pieces, and the Bisquick. It will make a thick dough. Form into small balls and bake on a cookie sheet at 350 degrees for about 15 minutes or until brown. These freeze beautifully, just reheat before serving. They are a "MUST" for brunches served with Bloody Marys. Makes 6 doz.

Great Beginnings

CRAB MEAT QUICHE

1 can (7 1/2-ounce) crab meat
3 eggs, slightly beaten
1 cup sour cream
1/2 teaspoon Worcestershire sauce
3/4 teaspoon salt
1/4 teaspoon dill weed
1 cup coarsely shredded Swiss cheese
1 can (3 1/2-ounce) French fried onions
1 9-inch baked pastry shell

Drain crab meat, flake fine. Mix eggs, sour cream, Worcestershire, salt, dill. Stir in cheese, crab and onions. Pour into pastry shell. Bake at 300 degrees for 55 to 60 minutes or until custard is set and knife inserted near center comes out clean. Serve hot. Serves 6.

FRENCH TOAST

3 eggs
Pinch of salt
1/2 cup light brown sugar
1 cup cream
4 slices French bread

Whisk eggs until frothy, add rest of ingredients. Soak slices of French bread and fry in 1/2 cup hot oil until browned as desired. Drain on paper towel to absorb excess oil. Serve with powdered sugar and hot syrup. Serves 4.

YUMMY STRAWBERRIES

Strawberries
Sour cream
Brown sugar

Wash and destem strawberries. Dip into sour cream and then into the brown sugar. Serve.
Jan says, "The cook will get a kiss."

LILLIAN'S CHICKEN CASSEROLE

4 pounds chicken pieces
2 cups water
Celery stalks
1 stick butter
Salt and pepper
1 small package Pepperidge Farm herb stuffing
2 packages (10-ounce size) frozen broccoli spears
3 cans cream of chicken soup
1 cup Hellmann's mayonnaise
Paprika

Cook chicken in 2 cups of water, several stalks of celery and 1 stick butter. Season water with salt and pepper. Mix Pepperidge Farm stuffing with chicken broth until consistency of stuffing for turkey. Debone chicken in large chunks. Put 1/2 stuffing mixture in 9 × 13-inch buttered casserole. Next, place spears (up and down) in pan and sideways at ends.
Combine soup and mayonnaise. Pour over broccoli. Place rest of crumb mixture on top. Sprinkle with paprika.
Bake at 325 degrees for 45 minutes.
Jo says, "If you desire, use chopped broccoli and chicken breasts. This is a 'must-do' recipe given to me by a wonderful cook." Serves 12.

Love Those Buns · Breads

Whether you enjoy baking yeast breads—where you can vent frustrations by kneading dough—or prefer to whip up a coffee cake or a batch of mouth-watering muffins, you'll find many choices in this chapter. The quick breads include Apricot Nut, Apple, Banana Nut, Cinnamon, Cranberry, and many, many more. Our coffee cakes, egg rolls, French breads, and English muffins compete with our Dilly Bread and French Breakfast Puffs, not to mention our rye breads and Khachapuri.

Many of these recipes will complement your brunch and dinner menus, and the various muffins are a must to add to your next luncheons.

Love Those Buns

DIABETIC APRICOT NUT BREAD

2 cups Bisquick
1 cup uncooked oatmeal
1/4 teaspoon salt
1 teaspoon baking powder
1/4 cup chopped nuts
1/3 cup dried apricots (chopped)
Sucaryl
1 1/4 cups skim milk
1 egg

Mix together 4 teaspoons Sucaryl, 1 egg beaten and 1 1/4 cups skim milk.

Add these ingredients to the dry ingredients. Bake in bread pan for 1 hour at 350 degrees.

APRICOT NUT BREAD

1/2 cup firmly filled, finely diced apricots
1 beaten egg
1 cup sugar
2 tablespoons melted butter
2 cups sifted flour
3 teaspoons baking powder
1 cup chopped walnuts
1/2 cup orange juice
1/4 teaspoon soda
3/4 teaspoon salt
1/4 cup water
1 package (8-ounce) cream cheese

Cover apricots with hot water, let soak 2 hours. Drain thoroughly. Whip in blender until pureed. Cream together egg, sugar, and butter. Sift flour with baking powder, soda and salt. Add dry ingredients, alternately with orange juice and water, to sugar mixture. Add apricot puree and nuts. Mix well. Bake in greased loaf pan (9 x 5-inch) for 1 1/2 hours at 350 degrees. Spread with softened cream cheese.

APPLE BREAD

3 eggs
2 cups sugar
1 1/4 cup salad oil
2 teaspoons vanilla
3 cups flour
1 1/2 teaspoons soda
1/4 teaspoon salt
1/2 teaspoon cinnamon
3 cups chopped raw apples
1 cup nuts

Beat eggs and sugar together until light. Add salad oil and vanilla. Add flour to soda, salt and cinnamon. Mix well and add apples and nuts. Bake at 350 degrees in two loaf pans or use one 13 x 9-inch pan plus one 8 x 8-inch pan. If using loaf pans, bake for 1 hour. Check cake pans after 30 minutes until a toothpick comes out clean. Serve with the following Vanilla Sauce.

VANILLA SAUCE

1 stick butter or margarine
1 cup light cream
1 cup sugar
1 teaspoon vanilla
1/2 cup nuts

Put butter, sugar and cream in sauce pan. Cook and stir over moderate heat until clear and slightly thickened. Remove from heat and stir in vanilla and nuts. Serve warm.

Love Those Buns

ELIZABETH'S BAGELS

3 cups warm water
2 packages yeast
1/2 cup honey
6 beaten eggs
5-6 cups flour

1 cup oil
1 tablespoon salt
4-5 cups flour

2 egg whites
Poppy seeds

Mix yeast in warm water. Add honey, well beaten eggs and flour. Beat dough well. Let rise 50 minutes.

Add oil, salt, and flour to the first mixture and knead 5 minutes. Let rise 50 minutes. Punch down. Let rise 20 minutes. Make bagels. Cut out with doughnut cutter. Drop in boiling water for 10 seconds. Beat white of 2 eggs until frothy. Brush on bagels and sprinkle with poppy seed. Place on greased cookie sheet. Let rise 20 minutes. Bake at 425 degrees for 20 minutes. Makes 60.

BANANA BREAKFAST BARS

3/4 cup soft butter or margarine
1 cup packed dark brown sugar
1 egg
1/2 teaspoon salt
1/2 teaspoon cinnamon
1 1/2 cups crushed ripe bananas
4 cups uncooked regular or quick oats
1/2 cup dried currants, chopped raisins, prunes or apricots
1/2 cup chopped nuts
1/2 cup sunflower seeds

Preheat oven to 350 degrees. Cream butter and sugar until light and fluffy with electric mixer. Beat in egg, salt, cinnamon and bananas. Stir in remaining ingredients. Pour into greased 13 x 9 x 2-inch pan. Bake 45-50 minutes, or until tester comes out clean. Freezes well in plastic bags. Makes 12 bars.

BANANA-MINCEMEAT NUT BREAD

2 1/2 cups all-purpose flour
1 tablespoon baking soda
1 teaspoon salt
2 cups granulated sugar
1 cup vegetable oil
4 eggs
2 1/2 cups mashed bananas
1 cup mincemeat (not condensed)
1/2 cup coarsely chopped macadamia nuts
2 tablespoons powdered sugar
2 tablespoons chopped macadamia nuts

Heat oven to 350 degrees. Sift flour, soda, salt together. Beat granulated sugar and oil in large mixer bowl until light. Add eggs, one at a time, beating well after each addition. Beat flour mixture a third at a time alternating with bananas into sugar mixture. Fold in mincemeat and 1/2 cup nuts. Spoon batter into 2 floured and greased 9 x 5 x 2 3/4-inch loaf pans. Bake until toothpick inserted in centers of loaves comes out clean, about 1 1/4 hours. Cool on wire racks; remove from pans.

Combine powdered sugar and 2 tablespoons nuts. Sprinkle evenly over loaves. Makes 2 loaves.

Love Those Buns

BANANA NUT BREAD

3/4 cup butter or margarine
1 1/2 cups sugar
1 1/2 cups mashed bananas (3 medium)
2 eggs, well beaten
1 teaspoon vanilla
2 cups flour
1 teaspoon soda
3/4 teaspoon salt
1/2 cup buttermilk
3/4 cup walnuts, chopped

Cream butter and sugar thoroughly. Blend in bananas, eggs and vanilla. Sift flour, baking soda and salt together. Add to banana mixture, alternating with buttermilk, mixing thoroughly after each addition. Add nuts, mix. Pour batter into greased and floured 9 x 5 x 3-inch loaf pan. Bake at 325 degrees for 1 1/4 hours or until done. Yield 1 loaf.

Jan says, "I put this into 3 small foil loaf pans for 3 small loaves. Freezes well."

BANANA SOUR CREAM COFFEE CAKE

1/2 cup butter
1 cup sugar
2 eggs
1 cup mashed bananas
1/2 cup sour cream
1/2 teaspoon vanilla
2 cups sifted flour
1 teaspoon baking powder
1 teaspoon baking soda
1/4 teaspoon salt
1/2 cup finely chopped nuts
1/4 cup sugar
1/2 teaspoon cinnamon

Preheat oven to 350 degrees. Grease a tube pan. In bowl, cream butter until light. Gradually beat in sugar. Beat in eggs, one at a time. Add mashed bananas, vanilla and sour cream. Sift flour, baking powder, baking soda and salt together. Fold into creamed mixture, stirring just to blend.

In another bowl combine finely chopped nuts, sugar and cinnamon. Sprinkle half of this mixture over the bottom of the tube pan. Spoon in half the batter. Sprinkle the remaining nuts over the batter and cover with the remaining batter. Bake for 45 minutes. Serves 12-16.

DIABETIC DATE BREAD LOAF

1 1/4 cups water
1/2 cup shortening
2 cups dates
3 teaspoons Sucaryl

Bring above mixture to a boil and cool.
Add 2 beaten eggs.

Sift together:
2 cups flour
1/2 teaspoon nutmeg
1 teaspoon soda
2 teaspoons baking powder
2 teaspoons cinnamon
1/2 teaspoon salt

Add the dry ingredients to the cooled mixture and stir well. Bake at 350 degrees for 40 minutes. This will make 1 loaf pan or 2 small loaf pans.

Love Those Buns

DOROTHY'S BLINTZ BUBBLE RING

2 packages (3-ounce size) cream cheese
2 packages refrigerator biscuits (20 biscuits)
1/2 cup sugar
1 teaspoon ground cinnamon
3 tablespoons butter, melted
1/3 cup chopped pecans

Cut cream cheese into 20 pieces. Shape each piece into a ball. Roll each refrigerator biscuit to about 3" in diameter. Combine sugar and cinnamon. Place 1 cheese ball and 1 teaspoon cinnamon mixture on each biscuit; bring up edges of dough and pinch to seal. Pour melted butter or margarine into bottom of 5 cup ring mold. Sprinkle half the chopped pecans and half the remaining cinnamon mixture into mold. Place half the filled biscuits atop mixture, seam side up; repeat layers. Bake at 375 degrees until golden, about 20 minutes. Do not overbake. Cool 5 minutes in pan; invert onto plate. Serves 16.

QUICK BREAD STIX

Slice onion buns in half. Slice each half into 1-inch slices; place on baking sheet. Drizzle a good amount of liquid margarine over each stick, sprinkle with Dip-idy-Dill and Parmesan cheese. Brown under broiler just before serving.

Note: If Dip-idy-Dill is not available at your store substitute with a sprinkling of dried onion flakes and dill weed.

NO KNEAD BUTTERHORN ROLLS

1 cup milk, scalded
1/2 cup shortening
1/2 cup sugar
1 teaspoon salt
1 package yeast
3 eggs, well beaten
4 1/2 cups flour

Combine milk, shortening, sugar and salt and cool to lukewarm. Add yeast and stir well. Add eggs, stir; add flour and mix to form a soft dough. Knead slightly on lightly floured board. Place in greased bowl, cover and let rise until double in bulk.

Divide dough in thirds and roll each on lightly floured surface and brush with melted fat. Let each circle be about 9 inches round. Cut the circles into about 14 wedge-shaped pieces. Starting with wide end, roll to a point. Put in greased baking pans and brush with vegetable oil. Cover and let rise until very light and bake at 400 degrees for 15 minutes.

MOM'S BUTTERMILK BISCUITS

2 cups flour
1/2 teaspoon salt
4 teaspoons baking powder
1/2 teaspoon soda
5 tablespoons shortening
1 cup buttermilk

Combine dry ingredients. Blend in shortening using a pastry blender. Slowly add buttermilk, stirring in with a fork. Turn out onto floured surface and knead several times with floured hands. Roll out 1/2-inch thick and cut with biscuit cutter. Place on baking sheet and bake at 450 degrees for 12-15 minutes. Serves 10-12.

Love Those Buns

RUTHIE'S BUTTERMILK BREAD

2 cups buttermilk (warm a little)
1/2 cup warm water
1/4 cup sugar
2 packages yeast, dissolved in 1/2 cup warm water
1 tablespoon salt
1/4 teaspoon soda
4 tablespoons melted margarine
7 1/2 cups flour

Combine buttermilk, water and sugar. Add yeast mixture and salt. Next add soda and margarine. Add 1/2 of flour and let stand 10 minutes. Mix and knead. Add rest of flour and let rise until double (about an hour and a half). Divide into loaves. Put in pans, let rise until double. Bake at 325 degrees 35 to 40 minutes. This will make 2 1-pound loaves or 4 small ones.

BEIGNETS (FRENCH DOUGHNUTS)

2 3/4 to 3 1/4 cups all-purpose flour
1 package dry yeast
1/2 teaspoon ground nutmeg
1 cup milk
1/4 cup sugar
1/4 cup cooking oil
3/4 teaspoon salt
1 egg
Oil for frying
Sifted powdered sugar

In mixing bowl mix 1 1/2 cups flour, yeast and nutmeg. Heat milk, sugar, oil and 3/4 teaspoon salt just until warm (115-120 degrees). Add to dry mixture; add egg. Beat at low speed of electric mixer for 1/2 minute, scraping bowl constantly. Beat 3 minutes at high speed. By hand, stir in enough remaining flour to make a soft dough. Place in a greased bowl; turn once. Cover and chill. Turn dough out on floured surface. Cover; let rest 10 minutes. Roll to 18 x 12-inch rectangle. Cut into 3 x 2-inch rectangles. Cover; let rise for 30 minutes (dough will not be doubled). Fry in deep hot oil (375 degrees) until golden, turning once, about 1 minute. Drain. Sprinkle with powdered sugar. Makes 36.

BOHEMIAN COFFEE CAKE

1 cup butter or margarine
1 cup white sugar
1 cup brown sugar
3 cups sifted flour

Mix first 4 ingredients. Blend until fine as cornmeal. Take out 1 cup of mixture for topping. To the remainder add:

2 eggs, well beaten
1 cup buttermilk
1 teaspoon soda
1/4 teaspoon salt

Mix well and pour into pan. Cover with dates and nuts.

1 cup chopped dates
1 cup chopped nuts

Cover all with the cup of reserved first mixture. Bake at 375 degrees for 20-25 minutes. Makes 1 large or 2 small.

Love Those Buns

CHERRY COFFEE CAKE

1 can sour cherries
4 eggs, separated
2 cups flour
2 cups sugar
1/2 pound butter
1 teaspoon vanilla
Powdered sugar

Drain cherries. Lay on paper towels to absorb extra juice. Whip egg whites in small bowl, set aside. Beat flour, sugar, butter, egg yolks and vanilla on electric mixer. Fold in egg whites on low speed. Spread mixture on greased pan 11 x 15½-inch (jelly roll pan). Press cherries on top. Bake at 350 degrees for 30 minutes. Remove, wait 5 minutes. Shake powdered sugar on top. Cool. Cut in squares. Can be frozen. Makes 20-24.

CINNAMON BREAD

2 packages yeast
1 tablespoon sugar
1 cup warm water
1 cup milk
6 tablespoons shortening
1/2 cup sugar
7 cups flour
1 teaspoon salt
3 eggs
1 stick butter
1/2 cup brown sugar
2 teaspoons cinnamon

Dissolve yeast and 1 tablespoon sugar in water. Scald milk, shortening and 1/2 cup sugar. Cool to lukewarm. Add 2 cups of flour and salt to make batter. Add yeast, beaten eggs and beat well. Add rest of flour to make dough. Knead lightly and place in greased pan. Cover and keep in warm place. Rise to double and punch down. Roll dough thin. Melt butter, brown sugar, cinnamon and spread on dough. Roll up, folding ends. Put in 4 greased loaf pans. Bake at 250 degrees for 45 to 60 minutes.

CRANBERRY BREAD

1 cup sugar
2 cups flour
1 1/2 teaspoons baking powder
1/2 teaspoon salt
2/3 cup pecans
1 teaspoon grated orange rind
1 1/2 cups cranberries
1 egg
Juice of 1 orange
1/3 cup orange juice
1/2 cup boiling water
1/2 teaspoon baking soda

Mix dry ingredients together, except soda. Add nuts and grated orange rind and cranberries (wet cranberries a little). Add beaten egg. Take the juice of an orange and 1/3 cup orange juice along with boiling water to make 3/4 cup-plus of liquid. Add soda to orange juice mixture and add to first mixture. Bake at 325 degrees for 1 hour. Time depends on size of pan. One loaf will take that long. If you make small loaves it will not take an hour.

Jan says, "I never bake just one loaf of this bread. I always double the recipe. At holiday time I have 3 bowls with a double recipe going in each bowl. Makes around 16 small loaves and this does freeze well. I have been asked what makes this cranberry bread different from others- I do not put any shortening in the recipe. Or had you noticed?"

Love Those Buns

CINNAMON ROLLS

1 quart milk
1 cup shortening
1 cup sugar
4 teaspoons salt
4 eggs
4 packages active dry yeast
Flour to feel (approximately 13-14 cups)
3 sticks butter or margarine, melted
Sugar
Cinnamon
Powdered sugar

Put milk, sugar and shortening in a saucepan and heat until milk bubbles form on side of pan. Let cool to lukewarm. Dissolve yeast in 1 cup warm water. Take a large (2 gallon) bowl, pour in milk mixture, yeast and 4 beaten eggs. Add 4 cups flour and 4 teaspoons salt. Mix well. Add the rest of flour, mixing as you go along until you can handle dough (adding too much flour will make your dough tough). Grease the top of dough and set aside to rise, approximately 1 to 2 hours. Turn out on floured surface and knead lightly for just a few minutes. Divide in 3 parts. Set aside and take one part, rolling out in a thin (not too thin) circle. Spread melted butter or margarine over all the surface well, then sprinkle white sugar and cinnamon generously. Roll up and cut 1/4-inch to 1/2-inch slices and put into greased round pans. Do the rest of the dough likewise. Let rise until doubled, approximately 1 hour. Bake at 350 degrees for 15-18 minutes. After removing from oven make a powdered sugar glaze and spread over the rolls generously.

Remove from pans and wrap tightly in foil.

Jan says, "This makes approximately 90 rolls. They freeze very well. I like this recipe for it does make many and you always have some on hand for company or a pan to take to a friend."

COFFEE CAKE

1 package yellow cake mix
1 package vanilla instant pudding
1/4 cup oil
3/4 cup water
4 eggs, added one at a time
1 teaspoon butter extract
1 teaspoon vanilla

CINNAMON MIXTURE:
1/4 cup sugar
2 teaspoons cinnamon

Mix ingredients; beat for 8 minutes at medium speed. Grease bundt pan. Layer cake mixture with cinnamon mixture beginning and ending with cake batter. Bake at 350 degrees for 40 - 45 minutes. Cool 8 minutes. Glaze while warm.

GLAZE:
1 cup powdered sugar
2 tablespoons milk
1/2 teaspoon butter extract
1/2 teaspoon vanilla

Combine ingredients and spread over cake.

Love Those Buns

ALLECE'S COFFEE CAKE

2 cups sugar
1/2 cup shortening
2 eggs
1 cup milk
3 cups flour
4 teaspoons baking powder
1 teaspoon salt
2 teaspoons vanilla
1 cup nuts

Cream shortening and sugar together. Beat in eggs. Add flour, baking powder and salt alternately with milk. Add vanilla and nuts. Mix filling into batter by swirling it with a spoon. Bake at 350 degrees 40 to 45 minutes.

A powdered sugar icing may be drizzled over cake when cooled.

FILLING:
4 tablespoons butter or margarine
1 cup brown sugar
4 tablespoons flour
4 teaspoons cinnamon

Combine ingredients.

COCOA ZUCCHINI BREAD

2 cups sugar
3 eggs
1 cup oil
2 cups grated zucchini
1/2 cup milk
1 teaspoon vanilla
1/2 cup chocolate chips
3 cups flour
1 teaspoon cinnamon
1 teaspoon soda
1 teaspoon baking powder
1 teaspoon salt
1/4 cup cocoa
1/2 cup nuts

Blend sugar, eggs, oil. Stir in zucchini. Add milk, vanilla and dry ingredients. Blend thoroughly. Stir in chips and nuts. Pour into greased and floured loaf pans. 2 large or 4 small. Bake at 350 degrees for 45 minutes to 1 hour.

JALAPENO CORN BREAD

In a bowl stir together:
2 1/2 cups cornmeal
1 cup flour
2 tablespoons sugar
1 teaspoon salt
4 teaspoons baking powder
In another bowl, beat:
3 eggs, slightly beaten
1 1/2 cups milk
1/2 cup oil
1 pound can cream-style corn
6 - 8 Jalapeno (mild) chili peppers
2 cups grated sharp cheese
1 large onion, grated

Add liquid mixture to the cornmeal mixture. Stir in corn, peppers, cheese and onion, grated. Pour batter into 2 well-greased baking pans (9 x 11-inch) and bake in a hot oven (425 degrees) for 25 minutes or until it tests done.

Love Those Buns

CROISSANTS

3 packages active dry yeast
1 tablespoon sugar
1/2 cup scalded milk, cooled to lukewarm
1 cup water
2 tablespoons butter
1 tablespoon sugar
3 cups all-purpose flour
1 teaspoon salt
3/4 cup softened butter
1 egg, beaten
2 tablespoons water

Dissolve yeast and 1 tablespoon sugar in milk; let stand until bubbly; reserve.

Heat next three ingredients until dissolved. Cool to lukewarm; reserve.

Mix flour and salt in large bowl. Stir in yeast mixture, then butter mixture. Mix until soft dough is formed. Place in greased bowl; turn dough so greased side is up. Cover and let rise until doubled, about 1 hour. Punch down dough, then roll it out on lightly floured surface to 12 x 8-inch rectangle. Place on floured baking sheet; cover and refrigerate 1 hour and 15 minutes.

Roll dough on floured surface to 17 x 13-inch rectangle. Spread 3/4 cup butter over 2/3 of dough, leaving 1/2-inch border. Fold unbuttered 1/3 of dough over half of the buttered; then fold remaining 1/3 over the unbuttered portion. Place on tray, cover and refrigerate 20 minutes.

Roll dough into 16 x 14-inch rectangle. Repeat folding in thirds; top 1/3 to center and bottom 1/3 over center. Cut dough in half. Place on tray, cover and refrigerate 1 hour.

Roll 1 dough half into 16 x 9-inch rectangle. Again, repeat folding in thirds process. Repeat with second dough half. Place on tray, cover and refrigerate 1 hour.

Roll 1 half of dough into 16 x 9-inch rectangle; cut in half lengthwise. Cut each strip into 6 triangles. Roll up triangles starting at wide end; shape into crescents. Repeat process with remaining dough. Place crescents on greased baking sheet, cover and let rise 30 minutes.

Beat egg and water. Brush tops of crescents with this mixture. Bake crescents in pre-heated 425-degree oven 12-15 minutes until puffed and golden brown.

Makes 2 dozen.

LAVASH

1 1/4 pounds (about 5 cups) unbleached all-purpose flour
1 envelope dry yeast
2 1/4 teaspoons salt
3/4 teaspoon sugar
1/4 cup butter, melted
1 1/4 to 1 1/2 cups warm water (120-130 degrees)
3/4 to 1 cup sesame seeds

Grease or butter a large bowl; set aside. Combine first 4 ingredients in mixing bowl. Blend butter with 1 cup water and add gradually to dry ingredients, beating continuously. If dough seems dry add more water as needed. Beat or knead until dough is smooth and elastic. Place in greased bowl, turning to coat entire surface. Cover with plastic wrap and hot damp towel and let rise in warm place until doubled in bulk, about 1 to 2 hours.

Remove oven racks from gas oven; with electric oven place bottom rack in lowest position and place baking sheet on rack. Preheat gas oven to 350 degrees, or electric oven to 375 degrees. Divide dough into pieces about the size of tennis balls. Spread sesame seeds on large breadboard or countertop. Working with one piece of dough at a time, keeping remaining dough covered, place on board and roll out as thinly as possible without tearing dough. It is important to roll it thin.

Bake lavash, one at a time, until light golden with darker highlights, about 2 to 3 minutes on floor of gas oven, or about 13 minutes in electric oven. Cool on racks. Makes 12 to 15 crackers.

Love Those Buns

DILLY BREAD

1 package dry yeast, softened in 1/4 cup warm
   water
1 cup cottage cheese, heated to lukewarm
2 tablespoons sugar
1 tablespoon minced dry onion
1 tablespoon butter
2 teaspoons dill seed
1 big teaspoon salt
1/2 teaspoon soda
1 unbeaten egg
2 1/4 cups flour

Add heated cottage cheese to softened yeast. Add egg, butter and dry ingredients except flour. Add flour, 1/4 cup at a time, beating well after each addition. Dough will be stiff. Cover and let rise in a warm place until light and double in size (50 to 60 minutes). Punch down dough and turn into a well-greased 8-inch round casserole (1½ - 2 quart). Let rise until light (30 to 40 minutes). Bake at 350 degrees for 40 to 50 minutes until golden brown. Cover top with foil last 15 minutes if you feel it is getting too brown. Brush top with melted butter and sprinkle with salt.

Note: Can make 1 large round loaf or 3 small round ones. This bread freezes beautifully.

DILL PICNIC BRAID

1 package active dry yeast
1/4 cup warm water (110-150 degrees)
2 3/4 to 3 cups all-purpose flour
1 cup dairy sour cream
1 egg
1 small onion (1/4 cup)
2 tablespoons sugar
1 tablespoon butter, softened
1 tablespoon dill seed
1 tablespoon dill weed
1 teaspoon salt
1 beaten egg yolk

In large bowl dissolve yeast in warm water. Stir in 1 cup of the flour, sour cream, egg, onion, sugar, butter, dill seed, dill weed and salt. Beat by hand until well-blended. Stir in as much of the remaining flour as you can mix in with a spoon.

Turn dough out onto a lightly floured surface; knead in enough of the remaining flour to make a moderately stiff dough. Continue kneading about 5-8 minutes or until smooth and elastic.

Place dough in a greased bowl, turning once to grease surface. Cover; let rise in a warm place 1 1/4 to 1 1/2 hours or until double in size. Punch down, divide into 3 equal pieces. Cover, let rest 10 minutes.

On a lightly-floured surface roll each piece of dough to an 18-inch long rope. Place the 3 ropes side by side on a large baking sheet. Braid ropes loosely from the center to ends. Press rope ends together to seal. Cover; let rise in a warm place about 30 minutes or until nearly double. Combine egg yolk and 2 teaspoons water; brush top of loaf. Bake in a 350 degree oven for 35 to 40 minutes or until golden and loaf sounds hollow when lightly tapped. Makes 1 large braid.

Love Those Buns

CAROL'S EGG ROLLS

2 packages yeast
2 tablespoons lukewarm water
1/2 cup sugar
1 cup scalded milk
1/2 cup shortening (lard is best)
1 teaspoon salt
3 eggs
4 1/2 to 5 cups sifted all purpose flour
Evaporated milk

Soften yeast in water to which 1 tablespoon sugar has been added. Combine rest of sugar, milk, shortening and salt in bowl. Add beaten eggs. Add 2 cups of flour and yeast and beat about 4 minutes. With a spoon add as much flour as can be stirred into the dough without kneading. Place in greased bowl, cover with towel and let rise in a warm place until double in size.

Turn onto a lightly floured board and cut into 2 equal parts. Roll dough about 3/4-inch thick (for cocktail size, 1/2-inch) and cut with a small cutter. Let rise until double in size and brush with evaporated milk. Heat oven to 425 degrees, place rolls in oven and turn down to 375 degrees. Bake for about 15 minutes. Slice, butter and freeze.

ENGLISH MUFFINS

1 cup scalded milk
3 tablespoons solid vegetable shortening
1 1/2 teaspoons salt
3 tablespoons sugar
1 package dry yeast
1/4 cup lukewarm water
1 egg, beaten
4 1/4 cups flour, sifted

Combine scalded milk, shortening, salt and sugar. Cool to lukewarm. Soften yeast in 1/4 cup lukewarm water; stir and combine with cooled milk mixture. Add egg and 2 cups of flour to milk; mix thoroughly.

Turn dough out on well-floured board. Knead in remaining flour. Continue kneading about 12 to 15 minutes, or until firm and elastic.

Place dough in warm, greased bowl. Brush very lightly with melted shortening. Cover and let rise about 1 1/2 hours, or until double in bulk.

Turn dough out on board and roll to 1/4-inch thickness. Cut with large cutter into 3-inch rounds. Cover dough and let rise on board about 30 to 45 minutes or until doubled in bulk.

Bake muffins slowly on ungreased griddle or heavy skillet. Muffins should brown slowly. Allow 7 to 8 minutes for each side. Makes 1 1/2 to 2 dozen.

JEANNE'S FRENCH BREAD

1 package dry yeast, dissolved in 1/4 cup warm water
1/2 cup milk, scalded to just below boiling
1 tablespoon butter
1 tablespoon sugar
1 1/2 teaspoons salt
1 1/4 cups water
5 cups flour

Add butter, sugar and salt to milk. Cool. Add yeast and water. Mix in flour gradually. Knead 10 minutes. Place in greased bowl, turning dough to grease all sides. Cover, let rise until doubled in bulk. Punch down and let rise again until double in bulk. Knead 1 minute. Make 2 long loaves, place on greased baking sheet. Make slashes diagonally across top and cover. Let rise until double. Bake at 375 degrees for 45 minutes.

Love Those Buns

VERA'S FRENCH BREAD

1 1/4 cups lukewarm water
1 package dry yeast
1 tablespoon butter
2 tablespoons sugar
1 teaspoon salt
3 1/4 cups flour

Dissolve yeast in water. Add butter, sugar and salt to yeast water. Stir in 1 1/2 cups of flour and blend. Add another 1 1/4 cup flour and mix well. Add another 1/2 cup and knead well, about 10 minutes, until smooth. Place in a buttered bowl, turning so top is buttered too. Cover with tea towel and place in warm draft-free area.

Let rise until double, about 1 to 1 1/2 hours. Punch down. Roll to a 12 X 15-inch rectangle. Roll up as a jelly roll, seal edge with water. Place at an angle on greased cookie sheet. Cut diagonally every 2 1/2 inches, about 1-inch deep.

Cover and let rise about 45 minutes. Bake at 375 degrees for 45 minutes. Brush top with butter when taken out of oven. Makes 1 loaf.

Note: While you are in the baking mood, why not double the recipe and make two loaves.

Freezes beautifully.

FRENCH BREAKFAST PUFFS

1/3 cup soft shortening
1/2 cup sugar
1 egg, beaten
1 1/2 cups sifted flour
1 1/2 teaspoons baking powder
1/2 teaspoon salt
1/4 teaspoon mace
1/2 cup milk

Cream shortening. Add sugar, egg and dry ingredients with milk. Fill small muffin pan 1/2 full. 1 teaspoon is about right. Bake at 350 degrees for 20 minutes until very lightly brown. While hot, roll in melted butter, then a mixture of **1/4 cup brown sugar, 1/4 cup white sugar and 1 1/2 teaspoons cinnamon.** Freezes nicely. Wrap in foil and reheat in oven. Makes 2 dozen.

APPLE BUTTER PUMPKIN FRITTERS

1 cup unsifted flour
1 1/2 teaspoons baking powder
1/2 teaspoon salt
1 teaspoon cinnamon
1/4 teaspoon each ground cloves, nutmeg and allspice
1/4 cup raisins
1 egg
1/3 cup canned pumpkin
2 tablespoons each milk, liquid shortening, molasses and apple butter

Mix dry ingredients with raisins. Stir in rest of ingredients just until smooth. Drop from a teaspoon into deep hot fat and fry at 350 degrees about 2 minutes, or until crisp and very brown. Drain on paper towels. Serve at once. Makes 18.

Love Those Buns

BANANA FRITTERS

1 cup unsifted flour
2 tablespoons sugar
1 teaspoon baking powder
1/4 teaspoon salt
1/2 teaspoon cinnamon
1 egg
1/4 cup milk
1 tablespoon melted butter
2 tablespoons drained crushed pineapple
1/4 teaspoon vanilla
1 small ripe banana, peeled and diced

Mix dry ingredients. Stir in rest just until smooth. Drop from a teaspoon into deep hot fat and fry at 350 degrees about 2 minutes or until crisp and brown. Drain on paper towels. Serve at once. Makes 18.

FRESH PEACH FRITTERS

1 cup unsifted flour
2 tablespoons sugar
1 1/2 teaspoons baking powder
1/2 teaspoon salt
1/2 teaspoon cinnamon
1/4 teaspoon nutmeg
1 egg
1/4 cup milk
2 tablespoons melted butter
2 tablespoons drained crushed pineapple
1/4 teaspoon vanilla
1/4 cup diced fresh peaches
Powdered sugar

Mix dry ingredients. Stir in rest of ingredients, except peaches and powdered sugar, just until smooth. Fold in peaches. Drop from a teaspoon into deep hot fat and fry at 350 degrees for about 2 minutes or until crisp and brown. Drain on paper towels. Roll in powdered sugar. Serve at once.

Jo says, "If you dip the spoon into the hot fat between spoonfuls, the batter will slip off easily."

JOYCE'S GRAPENUT BREAD

4 cups boiling water
2 cups Grape Nuts
1 cup wheat germ
1/2 box dark brown sugar
1 stick margarine
1 tablespoon salt
3 packages dry yeast
1 1/2 cups warm water
1 teaspoon sugar
12 cups unbleached flour

Pour boiling water over Grape Nuts, wheat germ, brown sugar, margarine and salt. When lukewarm add: 3 packages dry yeast dissolved in 1 1/2 cups warm water. Add: 1 teaspoon sugar.

Knead in approximately 12 cups unbleached flour. Let double in size. Turn out on floured surface. Knead and form into 6 loaves. Place in greased pans. Let double again. Bake at 375 degrees for 1 hour.

Love Those Buns

IRISH SODA BREAD

1 1/2 cups buttermilk
2 tablespoons butter, melted
1 egg, slightly beaten
1 1/2 cups dark seedless raisins
3 cups all-purpose flour
2/3 cup sugar
1 tablespoon baking powder
1 teaspoon soda
1 teaspoon salt

In medium bowl combine buttermilk, butter, egg and raisins. Set aside. In large bowl combine dry ingredients, mixing with a fork. Add buttermilk mixture and mix until combined. Use a greased 9 x 5-inch loaf pan. Bake at 350 degrees for 50 to 55 minutes. Let cool in pan 1 minute or so.

Jan says, "I always use seeded raisins in my cooking. They are much more flavorful than seedless."

HOMEMADE NOODLES

1 beaten egg
2 tablespoons milk
1/2 teaspoon salt
All-purpose flour (about 1 cup)

Mix egg, milk, and salt. Add enough of the flour to make a stiff dough. Roll very thin on floured surface; let rest 20 minutes. Roll up loosely; slice 1/4-inch wide. Unroll. Cut into desired lengths. Spread out; dry 2 hours. Store in covered container until needed.

TO COOK: Drop noodles into boiling liquid; cook uncovered 8 to 10 minutes. Makes 3 cups uncooked.

HOT CROSS BUNS

1 cup milk
1/4 cup butter
1/2 cup sugar
1 teaspoon salt
2 packages active dry yeast
1/2 cup very warm water
1/2 teaspoon cinnamon
2 teaspoons grated orange rind
2 beaten eggs
4 to 5 cups flour
1/2 cup raisins
1 egg, slightly beaten

GLAZE:
3/4 cup confectioner's sugar
1/2 teaspoon vanilla
1 tablespoon milk

Heat milk until bubbles form on edge of pan. Add butter, sugar and salt. Let cool to lukewarm. Dissolve yeast in water. Stir in lukewarm milk mixture. Then add cinnamon, orange rind and eggs. Add 3 cups of the flour, a cup at a time, mixing well. Mix in raisins. Add enough additional flour to make soft dough.

Place dough on a flour board and knead until satiny and elastic, about 8 minutes. Keep dough soft. Place dough on greased bowl. Turn the dough to grease the top. Cover and set aside to rise until doubled. This will take 1 to 2 hours.

Punch dough down and knead lightly. Pat dough to 3/4-inch thick. Cut with 2 1/2-inch round biscuit cutter into 21 to 24 rounds. Place rounds in greased baking pans, about 1/2-inch apart. Let rise until doubled, 45 minutes to one hour, and buns are touching. Just before rising time is up, preheat oven to 350 degrees. Bake buns 12 to 15 minutes until the tops start to brown. Brush quickly with slightly beaten egg and bake another 10 minutes. Let rolls cool and make powdered sugar glaze. Take a toothpick and dip it into the glaze making a cross on each bun.

Love Those Buns

KHACHAPURI

2 packages dry yeast
1/2 teaspoon plus 1 tablespoon sugar
1 cup milk, scalded and cooled to lukewarm
3 1/2 to 4 cups flour
2 teaspoons salt
1/2 cup butter, melted

2 pounds Muenster cheese
1 egg
2 tablespoons butter

Dissolve yeast in 1/2 cup warm water with 1/2 teaspoon sugar. Put milk, 3 cups flour, 1 tablespoon sugar, 2 teaspoons salt and butter in a bowl. Pour over the dissolved yeast mix, turn onto floured surface and knead, adding more flour as necessary for 10 minutes. Cover and let rise until double in size. (Let rise 2 different times). Roll out to 22-inch circle and gently slip a 9-inch round pie pan under dough, leaving excess dough hanging over edge.

FILLING: Put 2 pounds of Muenster cheese through a food grinder (or grate it). Mix 1 egg and 2 tablespoons butter in the cheese (go ahead and use your clean hands). Place this cheese mixture into center of dough and fold up dough, pleating as you go to form a turban twisting the top. Let rise 30 to 45 minutes covered. Bake at 375 degrees for 1 hour. Before baking, brush dough with an egg-water glaze and again halfway through baking time. Serves 4 to 6.

If you want to make this for dinner, start at least 4 hours before you put it into the oven because of all the rising. This isn't good for the working gal, unless you do it on your day off. Try it for your friend. Serve a spinach salad and a bottle of wine. He will come back.

OLD-FASHIONED RYE BREAD

1/2 tablespoon active dry yeast
1 1/2 cups warm water
1/4 cup molasses or honey
3 to 3 1/2 cups whole wheat flour
1 teaspoon salt
2 tablespoons oil
1/2 tablespoon caraway seeds, whole or ground
1 cup rye flour

Dissolve yeast in warm water and add molasses or honey. Let sit for 5 minutes, then add 2 cups whole wheat flour and beat well to form a smooth, thick, elastic batter. Let sit about 1 hour until light and foamy. Mix in salt, oil and caraway. Add the rye flour and some of the remaining whole wheat flour and begin to knead. Knead well, adding more flour a little at a time until dough is smooth and elastic. The exact amount of flour to be used will vary slightly each time. Let rise 45 minutes to 1 hour, then punch down, knead for a few minutes and let rise for 45 minutes to 1 hour longer.

Shape into a loaf and place in a lightly oiled standard-size bread pan. Let rise in the pan for about 45 minutes, until not quite doubled in bulk. Preheat oven to 350 degrees while rising. Bake 1 hour, remove from pan at once and cool before slicing.

Love Those Buns

TIPPY'S SWEDISH BREAD

2 1/2 cups scalded milk
7 cups flour
2/3 cup sugar
1 envelope yeast
1/2 teaspoon salt
1 egg, well beaten
1/2 cup melted butter
1 tablespoon almond extract

Dissolve yeast in the 1/2 cup scalded milk that has cooled. Add 1/2 cup flour, beat well, cover and let rise. When light add remaining milk and 4 1/2 cups flour. Stir well, cover and let rise again. Add remaining ingredients and 1 1/2 cups flour. Knead, cover and let rise again. Divide dough in half. Divide half into three equal parts and roll in uniform size then braid on cookie sheet. Brush top with one egg yolk diluted with 2 or 3 tablespoons cold water. Bake at 375 degrees for 45 to 50 minutes.

SWEDISH RYE BREAD

2 cups boiling water
1/4 cup quick oats
1/3 cup brown sugar
1 tablespoon salt
1/4 cup shortening
1/4 cup dark molasses
2 packages of yeast
2 cups flour
3 cups rye flour
1 1/2 cups flour

Pour water over oats, brown sugar, salt, shortening and molasses. Cool to lukewarm. Sprinkle yeast into mixture. Stir in well. Add 2 cups flour. Beat 2 minutes with wooden spoon or until batter is smooth and bubbly. Add rye flour gradually. Let dough rest about 10 minutes. Then turn on to floured board and knead in as much of the 1 1/2 cups of flour as needed to make a smooth, elastic, soft dough.

Round up and place in a lightly greased bowl. Cover with a damp cloth or plastic cover. Let rise to double, then punch down. Cover and let rise another 30 minutes. Mold into loaves. Place in greased pan. Cover with damp cloth and let rise until double in size. Bake at 375 degrees for 35 to 40 minutes. Brush with butter. Cover with towel until cool. This recipe will make 2 large, 3 medium, or 6 small loaves.

Jan says, "This is without a doubt one of the best recipes for Swedish rye bread that I have ever tried or tasted."

RYE BREAD

2 packages dry yeast
1/2 cup warm water
1 stick margarine, melted
1/2 cup brown sugar
1/2 cup dark molasses
2 cups warm water
2 cups rye flour
1/2 cup wheat germ
1 tablespoon salt
4 cups white flour

Dissolve yeast in 1/2 cup warm water. Mix margarine, brown sugar, molasses, warm water, rye flour, wheat germ and salt. Beat well. Add yeast and the 4 cups of flour (white). If dough is sticky, add more flour. Knead until smooth. Punch down once and put in pans. Let rise again for 1 to 1 1/2 hours. Bake at 350 degrees for 40 minutes.

Jan says, "Don't forget that rye bread is never as light as other breads. It takes longer to rise and never rises as high."

Love Those Buns

MARY'S BREAD

2 cups milk
8 teaspoons salt
6 cups warm water
8 cups whole wheat flour and
12 cups white flour (or 24 cups white flour)
3/4 cup sugar
3/4 cup margarine (1 1/2 sticks)
4 packages active dry yeast

Jan says: "8 cups whole wheat flour is heavy and equivalent to 12 cups white flour."

Scald milk; stir in sugar, salt and margarine. Cool to lukewarm. Measure warm water into large bowl. Sprinkle in active yeast; stir until dissolved. Add lukewarm milk and 12 cups flour, beat until smooth. Add remaining flour to make stiff dough. Turn out on lightly floured board, knead 10 to 12 minutes. Place in greased bowl, turning to grease top. Cover; let rise in warm place until double (1 hour). Punch down. Cover. Rest 15 minutes. Divide into 6 pieces, roll and shape into loaves. Place in greased pans. Cover; let rise until double. Bake at 400 degrees for 30 minutes. Makes 6 loaves.

NOTES ON MUFFINS

If your batter has lumps in it, it is just right.

To make muffins lighter, place greased pans into oven for a few moments before adding batter.

To keep edges of muffins from getting too brown, fill one section with water instead of batter.

If muffins do not want to come out of pan, set hot pan on a wet towel for a few moments. Muffins will come out nicely.

APPLE BRAN MUFFINS

2 large Jonathan, Delicious or Rome apples
   pared, cored and chopped
1/2 cup butter or margarine
1 cup boiling water
3 cups whole bran cereal
2 cups buttermilk
2 eggs slightly beaten
2/3 cup sugar
1 cup finely chopped dates or raisins
2 1/2 cups flour
2 1/2 teaspoons baking soda
2 teaspoons ground cinnamon
1 teaspoon ground nutmeg
1/2 teaspoon ground cloves
1/2 teaspoon salt

Saute apples in butter 10 minutes or until tender. Pour boiling water over bran; add apples, buttermilk, eggs, sugar and raisins. Combine flour, baking soda, spices and salt; stir into bran mixture just until combined. Refrigerate in tightly covered container at least 24 hours. Use within 3 weeks. Fill greased muffin pans 3/4 full and bake at 400 degrees 20 to 25 minutes. Makes 30 to 36 muffins.

Love Those Buns

FRESH APPLE MUFFINS

3/4 cup milk
1 egg, beaten
1/4 cup shortening or margarine
2 cups unsifted flour
1/2 cup sugar
1 tablespoon baking powder
1/2 teaspoon salt
1 teaspoon cinnamon
1 cup finely chopped apples
1/4 cup raisins

Beat egg in small bowl. Add milk to egg. Stir in melted margarine or shortening. Measure and mix dry ingredients. Stir in apples and raisins. Add liquid mixture and stir just until most of the dry ingredients are moistened (do not overmix; the batter should be lumpy). Grease muffin tins or line with paper cups. Fill each cup about 1/2 full. Bake at 375 degrees for 20 to 25 minutes or until golden brown. Makes 12 muffins.

BANANA NUT MUFFINS

1 3/4 cup sifted cake flour
2 teaspoons baking powder
1/4 teaspoon baking soda
1/2 teaspoon salt
1/4 cup sugar
1 large egg
1 cup mashed ripe bananas (3 medium size)
1/3 cup butter, melted
3/4 cup chopped walnuts

Sift together flour, soda, baking powder, salt and sugar. Thoroughly beat together egg, banana, and butter. Add flour mixture and nuts. Stir only until dry ingredients are moistened. Turn into well-buttered muffin tins (2 1/2 x 1-inch), filling each 2/3 full. Bake in preheated 400-degree oven about 20 minutes. Serve hot. Makes 12.

CORNBREAD MUFFINS OR CORN STICKS

1 cup Quaker Yellow Corn Meal
1 cup flour
1/4 cup sugar
4 teaspoons baking powder
1/2 teaspoon salt
1 cup milk
1 egg
1/4 cup liquid shortening

Combine cornmeal, flour, sugar, baking powder and salt. Add milk, egg and shortening. Beat until smooth. Bake in muffin cups or well-greased corn stick pans. Preheat oven to 400 degrees and bake for 15 to 20 minutes. Makes 1 dozen.

CRANBERRY MUFFINS

1 cup white flour
3/4 cup whole-wheat flour
1/4 cup sugar
2 1/2 teaspoons baking powder
3/4 teaspoon salt
1 egg
3/4 cup orange juice
1/3 cup vegetable oil
1 cup fresh or frozen cranberries
2 teaspoons grated orange peel

In large mixing bowl, stir together flours, sugar, baking powder and salt. Stir in cranberries, coating with dry ingredients. Combine egg, juice, oil, grated orange peel. Add to dry ingredients. Stir until moistened. Bake 25 minutes at 400 degrees or until toothpick comes out clean after inserted into middle of muffin. Makes 1 dozen.

Love Those Buns

CREAM CHEESE SPICED MUFFINS

2 packages (3-ounce size) cream cheese
1 egg
1 tablespoon sugar
MUFFIN:
1 3/4 cups flour
3/4 cup toasted chopped almonds
1/2 cup packed brown sugar
1 tablespoon baking powder
2 teaspoons cinnamon
2 teaspoons nutmeg
1 teaspoon cloves
1 teaspoon salt
1 cup canned pumpkin
3/4 cup Pet milk
1/4 cup margarine, melted
2 eggs, well beaten

In small bowl beat cheese, egg and sugar until well blended. Set aside. In mixing bowl combine flour, almonds, brown sugar, baking powder, spices and salt. In third bowl combine pumpkin, milk, margarine and eggs, mixing until blended. Stir pumpkin mixture into dry ingredients, mixing just until moistened. Fill 18 greased muffin cups with half the batter, dividing equally. Spoon cream cheese filling over batter, dividing equally. Top with remaining batter to cover cream cheese layer. Bake in 400 degree oven 20 to 25 minutes. Cool. Remove from pans. Makes 1 1/2 dozen.

FRESH PEACH MUFFINS

1 egg
1 cup milk
1/4 cup melted shortening
2/3 cup sugar
1/2 teaspoon salt
3/4 teaspoon cinnamon
1 teaspoon lemon juice
1/4 teaspoon vanilla
2 cups unsifted flour
3 teaspoons baking powder
1 cup unpeeled, chopped fresh peaches

Beat egg. Stir in milk, shortening, sugar, salt, cinnamon, lemon juice, vanilla. Sift together flour, baking powder. Stir into milk mixture just until blended. Do not overmix. Fold in peaches. Fill greased muffin cups 2/3 full. Bake at 450 degrees about 20 minutes or until golden brown. Makes 12.

PINEAPPLE MUFFINS

2 cups flour
4 teaspoons baking powder
1/2 teaspoon salt
1/4 cup butter
1/2 cup sugar
1 large egg
8 1/2-ounce can crushed pineapple in heavy syrup, undrained

Stir together flour, baking powder and salt. Cream butter and sugar; thoroughly beat in egg. Add flour mixture and pineapple; stir only until ingredients are moistened. Fill buttered muffin cups about 1/2 to 2/3 full. Bake at 375 degrees for 25 minutes. Makes 12 muffins.

Love Those Buns

PUMPKIN MUFFINS

1 cup white flour
3/4 cup whole-wheat flour
1/4 cup sugar
2 1/2 teaspoons baking powder
3/4 teaspoon salt
1 egg, beaten
3/4 cup apple juice
1/3 cup vegetable oil
1 cup canned pumpkin
1 teaspoon cinnamon
1 teaspoon nutmeg

In large mixing bowl stir together flours, sugar, baking powder, salt and spices. Make a well in the center and combine egg, juice, oil and pumpkin. Add egg-pumpkin mixture to flour mixture. Stir until just moistened. Grease muffin cups or line with paper baking cups. Preheat oven to 375 degrees. Fill muffin cups. Bake 25 minutes or until toothpick inserted in middle of muffin comes out clean. Makes 1 1/2 dozen.

RASPBERRY MUFFINS

1 cup raspberries
2 cups sifted all-purpose flour
1/4 cup sugar
4 teaspoons baking powder
1/2 teaspoon salt
1 egg
3/4 cup milk
1/4 cup melted butter or margarine

Preheat oven to 425 degrees. Lightly grease 12 muffin-pan cups. Wash and pick over raspberries and drain well. In medium bowl, sift together flour, sugar, baking powder and salt.

In small bowl, beat egg with milk. Add melted butter or margarine. Make a well in flour mixture; pour egg mixture, all at once, into well; stir just until combined (do not overmix; batter should be lumpy). Gently fold raspberries into batter. Fill muffin-pan cups no more than 3/4 full. Bake 20 to 25 minutes or until golden-brown. Makes 12.

SIX-WEEK BRAN MUFFINS

8—10-ounce box of Bran Buds
2 cups boiling water
5 cups flour
5 teaspoons baking soda
1 teaspoon cinnamon
1 cup chopped walnuts or pecans
1 regular-size box white raisins
3 cups sugar
4 eggs
1 cup cooking oil
1 quart buttermilk

Pour boiling water over 2 cups Bran Buds. Set aside. Mix together dry ingredients, the remaining Bran Buds, flour, soda, sugar, cinnamon, nuts and raisins. Mix together eggs, oil, buttermilk into Bran Buds with water added. Add liquid mixture into dry ingredients. Blend. Store in 4 1-quart covered containers or in a 1 gallon jar. Let sit in refrigerator overnight. Bake in small muffin tins, lightly greased, or in paper muffin cups. Bake at 350 degrees about 25 minutes. Makes 8-10 dozen muffins. Batter keeps 6 weeks in refrigerator.

Love Those Buns

✧✧

ONION HAMBURGER BUNS

8 cups all purpose flour
2 envelopes dry yeast
2 cups warm water (120-130 degrees)
3/4 cup oil
1/2 cup sugar
1 tablespoon salt
4 eggs
Flour
1 tablespoon butter
1 large onion, thinly sliced
1/2 teaspoon milk

Generously grease a large bowl and 2 large baking sheets; set aside.

Combine 4 cups flour with all of yeast in mixing bowl and blend well. Combine water, oil, sugar and salt and add gradually, mixing thoroughly. Add 3 eggs. Using electric mixer, beat at low speed 30 seconds, scraping bowl frequently. Increase speed to high and beat an additional 3 minutes. Blend in remaining 4 cups flour.

BY HAND:

Turn dough out onto lightly floured board and knead until smooth and elastic. Place in greased bowl, turning to coat entire surface. Cover and let rise until doubled, about 1 1/2 hours.

Punch dough down and divide into 3 equal pieces. Cover and let stand 5 minutes. Divide each piece into 8 balls. Gently flatten each ball in your hands, folding edges under to make even circle about 3 1/2 inches in diameter. Place on baking sheets and let rise uncovered in warm place until doubled.

Meanwhile, melt butter in small skillet over medium-low heat. Add onion and cook until soft but not brown. Remove from heat and set aside. Beat remaining egg with milk and set aside.

About 15 minutes before baking, preheat oven to 375 degrees. When ready to bake, brush buns with egg mixture. Gently press small amount of onion over tops. Bake about 10 -12 minutes or until golden. Remove to rack and cool slightly.

Split with serrated knife. Makes 24.

ZUCCHINI WALNUT BREAD

2 cups sugar
1 cup vegetable oil
3 large eggs
1 1/2 tablespoons ground cinnamon
1 teaspoon baking powder
1 teaspoon baking soda
1 teaspoon vanilla
1/2 teaspoon ground ginger
1/2 teaspoon salt
3 1/4 cups sifted all-purpose flour
3 cups shredded, unpeeled zucchini (about 3)
1 cup ground walnuts

Preheat oven to 325 degrees. Grease loaf pans with shortening. Line bottom with waxed paper and grease that also. Combine all ingredients except flour, zucchini and walnuts in large electric mixer bowl. Beat for 2 minutes, until well blended, scraping side of bowl often with spatula. Fold in flour until blended, then fold in zucchini and walnuts.

Divide mixture evenly in pans. Bake on center rack at 325 degrees until toothpick comes out clean, about 1 hour and 15 minutes for large loaves and 1 hour for small. Let cool 5 minutes in pans, then turn out on racks to cool.

For best flavor, serve warm. Heat bread wrapped tightly in foil in 300-degree oven until warm. Makes 2 8 x 4-inch loaves or 6 5 x 3-inch loaves.

Love Those Buns

OUT OF THIS WORLD ROLLS

2 packages active dry yeast
1/4 cup warm water
1/2 cup shortening
1/2 cup sugar
3 eggs, well beaten
1 cup warm water
4 1/2 cups flour
2 teaspoons salt
1 stick softened butter

Soften yeast in the 1/4 cup warm water. In large bowl combine shortening, sugar, beaten eggs, 1 cup warm water and salt. Stir in softened yeast and 2 1/2 cups flour. Beat with hand mixer until smooth and well-blended. Add remaining flour to make a soft dough. Mix well. Cover and allow to rise in a warm place until doubled in bulk, about 1 hour. Punch down and place in refrigerator overnight.

3 hours before serving, roll out by dividing dough in half and rolling each portion on lightly floured surface to a rectangle 1/2-inch thick. Spread with softened butter. Roll jelly-roll style and cut into 1-inch slices.

Place cut side down in greased muffin tins. Cover and allow to rise 3 hours. Bake in 400-degree oven for 15 minutes. Makes 2 dozen large rolls.

PITA BREAD

3 1/2 - 4 cups all-purpose flour
1 package active dry yeast
1 1/4 cups warm water (115 - 120 degrees)
2 tablespoons cooking oil
1 teaspoon salt
1/4 teaspoon sugar

In large mixer bowl combine 1 1/2 cups of flour and yeast. Combine warm water, cooking oil, salt and sugar. Add to yeast mixture; beat on low speed of electric mixer for 1/2 minute, scraping sides of bowl constantly. Beat 3 minutes at high speed. By hand stir in enough of remaining flour to make a moderately stiff dough. Turn dough out on a lightly floured surface; knead dough about 5 minutes or until smooth and elastic. Cover; let rise 45 minutes.

Punch down and divide into 12 equal pieces. Shape into balls; cover and let rest 10 minutes. Roll 2 or 3 of the balls on lightly floured surface to 5-inch round, beginning at center and rolling to edges. (Do not roll back and forth or bread will not puff.)

Place 2 inches apart on ungreased baking sheet. Cover; let rise 20-30 minutes. Bake in 400-degree oven for 10 to 12 minutes or until puffed and brown. Repeat rolling and baking remaining dough. To serve, slice bread partway along one side and stuff with desired filling. Makes 12.

Love Those Buns

JANE'S PECAN ROLLS

1 package active dry yeast
1 cup warm water (105-115 degrees)
1/4 cup granulated sugar
1 teaspoon salt
2 tablespoons margarine, softened
1 egg
3 1/4 to 3 1/2 cups all-purpose flour
1/3 cup margarine, melted
1/2 cup brown sugar, packed
1 tablespoon corn syrup
2/3 cup pecan halves
1/2 cup granulated sugar
2 teaspoons cinnamon
1/2 cup melted margarine

In mixing bowl, dissolve yeast in warm water. Stir in 1/4 cup sugar, salt, 2 tablespoons margarine, egg and 2 cups of flour. Beat until smooth. With spoon or hand, work in enough of remaining flour until dough is easy to handle. Place greased-side up in greased bowl; cover tightly. Refrigerate overnight or up to 4 or 5 days.

Combine melted margarine, brown sugar, corn syrup and pecan halves. Pour into greased oblong pan, (13 x 9 x 2-inch). Combine 1/2 cup sugar and cinnamon. On floured board, roll dough into 15 x 9-inch oblong. Spread with melted margarine and sprinkle with sugar-cinnamon mixture. Roll up tightly, beginning at wide side. Seal edge well. Cut into 1-inch slices and place in prepared pan. Cover; let rise in warm place (85 degrees) until double, about 1 1/2 hours. (If kitchen is cool, place dough on a rack over a bowl of hot water and cover completely with a towel). Heat oven to 375 degrees. Bake 25 to 30 minutes. When through baking, invert baking pan. Makes 15 rolls.

POLENTA

6 cups water
1 1/2 teaspoon salt

1 1/4 cup cornmeal

1/2 pound grated American cheese

1 egg, well beaten

Bring salt and water to rapid boil. Add cornmeal and stir well.

Cook over direct heat 5 minutes then place over boiling water and cook 30 minutes. Add cheese and stir until it melts.
Remove from heat and add egg.

While still hot, drop by tablespoons onto platter and cool. When cold these patties may be fried on slightly greased fry pan or placed in baking dish, dotted with butter and browned in 375-degree oven.
Makes 20 cakes or fills an 8-inch baking dish.

PRALINE ROLLS

1/2 stick margarine, melted (coat pan with this)
1/2 cup brown sugar
1 small jar maraschino cherries (cut up)
1 cup chopped pecans
1 stick melted margarine
1 cup sugar
1 tablespoon cinnamon
1 package (24) frozen yeast rolls

Layer ingredients in bundt pan. Place 1 package (24) frozen yeast rolls on top of ingredients. Cover with dish towel, let stand overnight in refrigerator. Bake at 325 degrees for 30 minutes. Cool 15 minutes in pan. Then invert onto plate.

Love Those Buns

PUMPKIN BREAD

3 1/2 cups all-purpose flour
3 cups sugar
2 teaspoons baking soda
1 1/2 teaspoons salt
2 1/2 teaspoons cinnamon
1 teaspoon nutmeg
1 teaspoon ground cloves
1 cup vegetable oil
4 eggs
2/3 cup water
2 cups canned pumpkin

Sift dry ingredients together. Mix pumpkin, water, oil and eggs together. Pour into dry mixture and mix well. Pour into greased and floured bundt cake pan and small loaf pan or two medium loaf pans. Bake 1 hour and 15 minutes at 350 degrees. Cool 30 minutes before removing from pan. Wrap in foil to store. Freezes beautifully.

PUMPKIN-RAISIN LOAVES

Canned pumpkin
1/3 cup water
1 egg
1 teaspoon pumpkin pie spice
Apple-cinnamon muffin mix
1/2 cup raisins
2 cups powdered sugar

In mixing bowl, combine 3/4 canned pumpkin, 1/3 cup water, 1 egg, and 1 teaspoon pumpkin pie spice. Add one 14-ounce package apple-cinnamon muffin mix and raisins; stir just until moistened. Turn into 3 greased 5 x 3 x 2-inch loaf pans or one 9 x 5 x 3-inch loaf pan. Bake small loaves in 350 degree oven 35 to 40 minutes. Bake large loaf 50 minutes. Turn from pans. Cool. Drizzle loaves with powdered sugar icing: add enough milk to 2 cups sifted powdered sugar to make pouring consistency.

Jan says, "I use boiling water instead of milk. Gives it a smooth consistency."

RASPBERRY COFFEE CAKE

1 package (3-ounce) cream cheese
1/4 cup butter
2 cups packaged biscuit mix
1/3 cup milk
1/2 cup raspberry preserves

In mixing bowl cut cream cheese and butter in biscuit mix until mixture is crumbly; blend in milk. Turn biscuit dough out onto lightly floured surface and knead 8 - 10 strokes. On waxed paper roll dough to form a 12 x 8-inch rectangle. Carefully turn onto greased baking sheet; remove waxed paper. Spread raspberry preserves evenly down center of dough. Make 2 1/3-inch long slits at 1-inch intervals on long sides of rectangle. Fold each strip over raspberry filling. Bake coffee cake at 425 degrees for 12 to 15 minutes. Drizzle warm coffee cake with confectioners' icing.

CONFECTIONERS' ICING:

1 cup sifted confectioners' powdered sugar
1/4 teaspoon vanilla
1 1/2 tablespoons milk (approximately)

Mix all ingredients, adding milk slowly, using just enough to make spreading consistency.

Love Those Buns

REUBEN BREAD

1 package dry yeast
3/4 cup warm water
1/2 cup potato flakes
3 tablespoons brown sugar, packed
1 teaspoon salt
1/2 teaspoon caraway seed
2 tablespoons cooking oil
1 can (8-ounce) or 1 cup chopped drained
   sauerkraut
3 to 3 1/2 cups flour

In large bowl, sprinkle yeast over warm water. Stir until dissolved. Blend in the potato flakes, brown sugar, salt, caraway seed, oil and kraut. Gradually add the flour to make a stiff dough. Knead on floured surface until smooth, about 4 minutes. Cover, let rise until light and doubled in size, about 45 minutes. Punch down the dough and shape into a loaf. Place in a greased 9 x 5-inch loaf pan. Cover, let rise until light and doubled in size, about 45 minutes. Bake at 350 degrees for 50 minutes until bread is a deep golden brown. Remove from pan and cool.

LEMON NUT BREAD

1 cup Crisco
3 cups sugar
6 egg yolks
3 cups flour
1/4 teaspoon salt
1 cup buttermilk
1 ounce lemon extract
6 egg whites, beaten
2 1/2 cups chopped pecans

Cream Crisco, sugar, egg yolks. Add sifted dry ingredients, alternately with buttermilk. Add lemon extract. Fold in beaten egg whites, then pecans. Pour into 3 greased loaf pans (bread size) and bake at 350 degrees for 1 1/2 hours.

SHREDDED WHEAT BREAD

3 to 4 shredded wheat biscuits
1/2 cup vegetable shortening
1/2 cup molasses
2 3/4 cups boiling water
1 teaspoon salt
1 package dry yeast
1/4 cup warm water (110-115 degrees)
2 tablespoons lecithin granules
2 cups sifted whole wheat flour
5 to 6 1/2 cups sifted white flour

Crush 3 shredded wheat biscuits into large bowl. Add shortening and molasses. Measure boiling water in molasses cup and pour over biscuits. Add salt, stir and set aside to cool just until shortening starts to congeal into little "money" spots on top of mixture. Soften yeast in lukewarm water and add to warm (not hot) mixture.

Add lecithin and whole wheat flour and beat mixture a minute or two. Stir in white flour and the 4th biscuit until dough is too stiff to stir. Measure balance of flour onto breadboard and use as a base for kneading. Turn out soft dough and knead 10 minutes (to develop protein). Add a little more flour if necessary.

Place in greased bowl and let rise at 90 degrees or until double. Turn out, punch down and divide into 4 or 5 parts. Let rest 10 minutes. Put into cans and bake 45 minutes to 1 hour at 375 degrees.

Jan says, "I use the 1-pound coffee cans."

Love Those Buns

SHEEPHERDER'S BREAD

3 cups very hot tap water
1/2 cup butter, margarine
1/2 cup sugar
2 1/2 teaspoons salt
2 packages active dry yeast
9 1/2 cups (approximately) all-purpose flour, unsifted
Salad oil
10-inch cast iron covered Dutch oven (5-quart size)

In a bowl, combine hot water, butter, sugar and salt. Stir until butter melts; let cool to warm (110-115 degrees). Stir in yeast, cover and set in a warm place until bubbly, about 15 minutes.

Add 5 cups of flour and beat with a heavy-duty mixer or wooden spoon to form a thick batter. With a spoon, stir in enough of remaining flour (about 3 1/2 cups) to form a stiff dough. Turn dough out onto a floured board and knead until smooth, about 10 minutes, adding flour as needed to prevent sticking. Turn dough over in a greased bowl, cover, and let rise in a warm place until double, about 1 1/2 hours.

Punch down dough and knead on floured board to form a smooth ball. Cut a circle of foil to cover the bottom of Dutch oven. Grease the inside of Dutch oven and underside of lid with salad oil.

Place dough in pot and cover with lid. Let rise in a warm place until dough pushes up the lid by about 1/2-inch, about 1 hour (watch closely).

Bake covered with lid in a 375-degree oven for 12 minutes. Remove lid and bake for another 30 to 35 minutes or until loaf is golden brown and sounds hollow when tapped. Remove from oven and turn loaf out (you will need a helper) onto a rack to cool. Makes 1 very large loaf.

SOURDOUGH STARTER

1 package active dry yeast
2 1/2 cups warm water
2 cups sifted all-purpose flour
1 tablespoon sugar

Dissolve yeast in 1/2 cup of the water; stir in remaining water, flour and sugar. Beat until smooth. Cover with cheesecloth; let stand at room temperature 5 to 10 days, stirring 2 to 3 times a day. (Time required to ferment will depend upon room temperature; if room is warm, let stand a shorter time than if the room is cool.) Cover and refrigerate until ready to use.

TO KEEP STARTER GOING: Add 3/4 cup water, 3/4 cup sifted all-purpose flour and 1 teaspoon sugar to remaining starter after some is used. Let stand at room temperature until bubbly and well fermented, at least 1 day. Cover and refrigerate until used again. If not used within 10 days, add 1 teaspoon sugar. Repeat adding sugar every 10 days. Mark your calendar.

NOTE: Do not use metal containers.

Love Those Buns

SOURDOUGH BISCUITS

1 cup whole wheat flour
1 cup all-purpose flour
1 tablespoon sugar
2 teaspoons baking powder
1/2 teaspoon salt
1/2 cup margarine
2 cups sourdough starter

Measure whole wheat flour into bowl. Sift in all-purpose flour, sugar, baking powder and salt. Cut in margarine until mixture looks like bread crumbs. Stir in sourdough starter. Turn dough onto floured board and knead. Roll out 1/2-inch thick and cut into biscuits. Place on lightly oiled cookie sheet. Let rise 1/2 hour. Bake at 425 degrees for 20 to 25 minutes.

Recipe can be made using all white flour. Reduce starter to 1 2/3 cups. Makes 22 biscuits.

SOURDOUGH BREAD

1 package active dry yeast
1 1/2 cups warm water
1 cup sourdough starter
2 teaspoons salt
2 teaspoons sugar
5 1/2 cups sifted flour
1/2 teaspoon baking soda

In large bowl, soften yeast in warm water. Blend in sourdough starter, salt and sugar. Add 2 1/2 cups of flour. Beat 3 to 4 minutes with electric mixer. Cover and let rise until light and bubbly, about 1 1/2 hours. Combine soda and 2 1/2 cups of flour; stir into dough. Add enough additional flour to make a stiff dough.

Turn out onto lightly floured surface; knead 5 to 7 minutes. Divide dough in half, cover and let rest 10 minutes. Shape into 2 round loaves. Place on lightly greased baking sheets. With sharp knife, make diagonal slashes across top of loaves. Let rise until double, 1 to 1 1/2 hours. Bake at 375 degrees for 30 to 40 minutes. Brush with butter. Makes 2 loaves.

SOURDOUGH JACK BREAD - EXTRA SOUR

1 cup sourdough starter
1 cup warm water
2 cups flour
2 tablespoons sugar
2 teaspoons salt
2 cups flour

Put starter in large bowl. Stir in cup of warm water and 2 cups flour. Mix well. Let stand 14 to 36 hours. Work in sugar, salt and 2 cups flour (more if mixture is sticky). Turn dough onto board and knead until silky smooth. Let rest 10 minutes. Shape into 1 or 2 loaves. Let rise on cookie sheet 30 minutes. Bake at 400 degrees for 40 to 50 minutes.

Love Those Buns

SOURDOUGH PANCAKES

1 cup sourdough starter
2 cups warm water
2 1/4 cups all-purpose flour

2 eggs
2 tablespoons sugar
2 tablespoons corn oil
1/3 cup milk
1 teaspoon soda

Mix first three ingredients, cover bowl and let stand overnight. Beat in rest of ingredients.

Let batter stand 10 minutes. Using hotter griddle than usual, make silver-dollar-size pancakes, using 1 tablespoon batter for each. Makes 4 1/2 cups batter, about 70 pancakes.

SOUR CREAM COFFEE CAKE

2 sticks butter
2 cups sugar
3 eggs, add 1 at a time
2 cups flour
1/4 teaspoon salt
1 teaspoon baking powder
1 cup sour cream
1 teaspoon vanilla

SUGAR MIXTURE:
3 tablespoons sugar
2 teaspoons cinnamon
1/2 cup chopped pecans

Cream butter and sugar, add eggs 1 at a time. Sift together the flour, salt, baking powder. Add this mixture and sour cream alternately to first 3 ingredients. Add vanilla. Mix well and pour 1/2 of batter into a greased bundt pan. Sprinkle 1/2 of the following sugar mixture over the batter, then add other 1/2 of batter. Sprinkle remaining sugar on top.

Bake 65 to 70 minutes at 325 degrees. Cool in pan for about 2 hours.

Jo says, "If you own the baking pan that has 6 individual bundt cakes in it, this is a wonderful idea for a brunch, to serve each guest his own mini coffee cake."

STICKY BUNS

1/2 cup butter
1/2 cup pecans, chopped
1 cup brown sugar
2 tablespoons water, perhaps a bit more
2 packages refrigerator crescent rolls

Melt butter; put 2 to 3 tablespoons in bundt pan and swirl to coat. Sprinkle about 3 tablespoons nuts. Put rest of nuts in remaining butter along with sugar and water. Bring to a boil.

Cut each package of rolls into 8 slices as for cinnamon rolls (16 altogether). Pull rolls apart just slightly.

Put 8 rolls in bottom of pan. Add 1/2 of sauce. Add other 8 rolls and top with remaining sauce. Bake at 350 degrees for 30 minutes. Cool in pan about 3 minutes and turn out.

Jo says, "Takes about 40 minutes from start to finish and so easy."

Love Those Buns

MONKEY BREAD

5 cups flour (approximately)
3 envelopes dry yeast
2 tablespoons sugar
1 teaspoon salt
1 1/2 cups milk
1/3 cup butter or margarine
1 egg
3/4 to 1 cup margarine, melted

In large bowl or mixer stir together 1 1/2 cups flour, yeast, sugar and salt; set aside. Heat milk and the 1/3 cup butter until very warm and pour over flour-yeast mixture. Add egg and beat 3 minutes at medium speed, scraping bowl occasionally. Add 1 cup flour and beat 3 minutes longer. Stir in remaining 2 1/2 cups flour and mix with wooden spoon until thoroughly blended. Grease top of dough. Cover and let rise in warm draft-free place until double in bulk, about 30 minutes.

Turn out on lightly floured surface and knead lightly until smooth. Divide dough in half. Roll out each half in 18 x 12-inch rectangles. Cut in 3/4-inch strips, then crosswise in 3-inch pieces. Dip each piece in melted butter, then toss helter-skelter into a 10-inch angel-cake pan or bundt pan. Cover and let rise in warm draft-free place until double in bulk, about 1 to 1 1/2 hours.

Bake on bottom rack in preheated, 375-degree oven about 25 to 30 minutes or until golden brown and done. Turn out on rack to cool slightly. Serve in basket.

Jan says, "This is a great bread to replace the garlic bread. It does not have to be cut. Just pull it."

VIENNA BREAD

1 tablespoon salt
1 tablespoon sugar
2 tablespoons shortening
1 cup boiling water
3/4 cup cold water
1 package yeast
1/4 cup warm water
5 to 5 1/2 cups flour
1 egg white, beaten

Mix salt, sugar, shortening and boiling water together. To this mixture, add cold water and the 1 package of yeast that has been dissolved in 1/4 cup warm water. Mix well, adding the flour slowly. Knead 5 minutes and put in a greased bowl. Cover and let rise 1 1/2 hours.

After rising, divide dough into 2 portions. Roll each portion into a jelly-roll fashion. Pinch ends together and put side down on a cookie sheet. Brush with beaten egg white and make diagonal slashes across the top of each portion of bread.

Let rise for 1 hour. Put bread in a preheated 425-degree oven for 15 to 30 minutes. Reduce heat to 350 degrees and bake 30 more minutes. Let cool and slice bread through the slashes.

Jan says, "This is one of my favorite hard bread recipes and it is easy."

Love Those Buns

CORNBREAD STUFFING CASSEROLE

2 boxes Jiffy cornbread, baked and crumbled
1 loaf sandwich bread, crumbled
5 ribs of celery, diced
1 big onion, chopped
3/4 stick butter, melted
3 eggs, beaten
2 teaspoons sage
1 teaspoon Accent
Salt and pepper
4 or 5 cans chicken broth
1 teaspoon poultry seasoning

Saute celery and onion in melted butter. Mix beaten eggs with sage, Accent, salt and pepper. Add sauteed ingredients, mix with cornbread and crumbled sandwich loaf. Add cans of chicken broth until the desired consistency. Bake at 350 degrees in greased casserole about 1 1/2 hours.
Serves 16-18.

BEAUTIFUL FINGERNAILS BREAD

3 cups lukewarm water
2 packages dry yeast
2 tablespoons honey
6 cups (approximately) unbleached enriched bread flour
1/2 cup full-fat soy flour
3/4 cup nonfat dry milk solids
3 tablespoons wheat germ
4 teaspoons salt
2 tablespoons sunflower oil
Melted butter, optional

Place water, yeast and honey in large bowl. Stir to mix and let stand in warm place 5 minutes. Sift together flour, soy flour, and dry milk solids. Stir in the wheat germ.

Add salt to yeast mixture and about 1/2 to 3/4 of flour mixture so that batter has a consistency that can be beaten. Beat for 2 minutes in an electric mixer or 75 strokes by hand.

Add oil and work in remainder of flour mixture adding extra flour if needed to form a dough. Turn dough onto floured board and knead 10 minutes or until dough is smooth and elastic.

Place in a greased bowl. Grease top of dough lightly, cover and let rise in a warm place until almost doubled in bulk, about 45 minutes. Punch dough down, fold over the edges and turn upside down in bowl. Cover and let rise 20 minutes longer.

Turn onto a board, divide into 3 parts. Form into balls, cover and let stand 10 minutes.

Roll out one ball into a rectangle twice as big as an 8½ x 4½ x 2½-inch loaf pan. Fold the long sides into the center. Pinch to seal layers and fit into a greased loaf pan. Repeat with the other two balls.

Cover pans and let rise in a warm place until doubled in bulk, about 45 minutes.

Preheat oven to 350 degrees. Bake loaves 50-60 minutes. Cover lightly with foil if tops begin to overbrown. Bread is done when it sounds hollow when tapped. Brush tops with melted butter for a soft crust. Cool on a rack. Makes 3 loaves.

Jo says, "Keep this bread in the refrigerator as it contains no preservatives. It freezes nicely."

The Warm Up · Soups

There is nothing that warms the soul quite like a hot bowl of Vegetable Soup, Chowder, San Juan Black Bean or Loco's Chili. And when cooling soups are wanted on those hot summer days, nothing refreshes quite like Iced Lemon, Cucumber, or the Peach-Blueberry Soup.

As most soups are freezable, we love making multiple batches to have ready upon call whether it be a light lunch, a hearty cold meal, or to fill a thermos for hunters, sledders, or tail-gate picnickers.

The Warm Up

APPLE VICHYSSOISE

3 large Delicious apples
2 quarts chicken stock
1 cup chilled heavy cream
Salt to taste
Sugar to taste
Fresh lemon juice to taste
1/2 apple, cut in very fine strips

Peel and core apples. Cut into small pieces and cook in broth for about 20 minutes, or until tender. Force through sieve or whirl in blender. Cool and chill. Add cream and mix well. Add salt, sugar and lemon juice.

Make the julienne of apple at the last moment so it will not discolor. Sprinkle on top of soup and serve at once. Serves 6.

APRICOT SOUP WITH SOUR CREAM

1 pound dried apricots
1/2 cup dry white wine
Lemon juice to taste
1 cup heavy cream
Sour cream

Soak apricots in warm water to cover for 1 hour. Whirl apricots in blender with water in which they soaked until pureed. Strain and add wine. Add lemon juice to taste and stir in cream. Chill. Serve with garnish of sour cream. This is a tart, delicious soup, excellent as a first course of a game dinner. Serves 6.

ASPARAGUS SOUP

1 can cream of asparagus soup
1 can cheddar cheese soup
1 cup milk
1 cup water
2 tablespoons butter or margarine
Salt, black and red pepper to taste
1 can asparagus, drained and chopped

Heat soups, milk, water, butter and seasonings slowly in heavy pot. Add asparagus. Heat and stir occasionally. Serves 6.

AUTUMN TOMATO BOUILLON

1 can (10-ounce) tomato soup
1 can (10-ounce) beef bouillon
1 can water
2 tablespoons butter
2 tablespoons Worcestershire sauce
1 teaspoon curry powder
1 teaspoon soy sauce
1 tablespoon sherry
1 teaspoon salt
1 tablespoon fresh or dried chives
1 teaspoon parsley
Fresh pepper

Bring all ingredients except sherry to a boil. Reduce heat and simmer 20 minutes. When ready to serve, put one tablespoon of sherry in pan and stir. Makes 1 quart.

The Warm Up

AUTUMN SOUP

1 pound ground beef
1 cup chopped onion
4 cups water
1 cup carrots, cut up
1 cup diced celery
1 cup cubed pared potatoes
2 teaspoons salt
1 teaspoon Kitchen Bouquet
1/4 teaspoon pepper
1 bay leaf
1/8 teaspoon basil leaves
6 fresh tomatoes, chopped

Cook and stir meat; drain off fat. Cook and stir onions with meat until onions are tender, about 5 minutes. Stir in remaining ingredients, except tomatoes. Heat to boiling. Reduce heat, cover and simmer 20 minutes. Add tomatoes; cover and simmer 10 minutes or as long as desired. If fresh tomatoes are not used, use 1 (28-ounce) can tomatoes with juice and reduce water to 3 cups.
Serves 6-8.

BAHAMIAN CONCH CHOWDER

3 bacon strips
1 large onion, chopped
1 large green pepper, chopped
2 stalks celery, chopped
4 cups water
6 diced conch (pound the conch for tenderness)
2 large cans V-8 juice
3 large potatoes, cut in cubes
1 large can tomatoes, quartered
2 bay leaves
2 cloves garlic, crushed
1 teaspoon oregano
Tabasco sauce
Peppercorns
Salt, pepper, seasoning salt

Fry bacon strips, crumble and set aside. Add onions, celery, green pepper to the pan. Saute until tender. Add bacon and remaining ingredients and simmer four hours. This is even better on the second day.
Serves 14-16.

BEEF AND BARLEY VEGETABLE SOUP

2-pound soup bone (have butcher crack it for you)
1 pound stew meat
2 tablespoons oil
2 quarts water
1 1/2 tablespoons salt
1/4 teaspoon pepper
1 bay leaf
2 tablespoons minced parsley
1/4 cup barley
1 cup cubed carrots
1/4 cup chopped onion
1/2 cup chopped celery
1 cup cubed potatoes
1 cup green beans
2 cups cut cabbage
2 cups cooked tomatoes
1 cup frozen corn
1 cup fresh or frozen peas

Remove meat from cracked soup bone, cut into cubes and brown lightly with stew meat in hot oil. Place meat, bone, water and seasonings in soup kettle. Cover tightly and cook slowly 1 hour. Add barley and cook 1 hour longer. Cool and skim off excess fat. Remove soup bone. Add vegetables and cook 45 minutes.

Jo says, "Be creative! I never make this the same way twice. You might desire more of one veggie, less of another. Also, I usually double or triple the recipe and freeze in small enough containers for a family meal." Makes 5 quarts.

The Warm Up

BEET BORSCHT

12 medium-sized beets
2 medium-sized onions, peeled and finely minced
2 carrots, peeled and finely grated
1 tablespoon unsalted butter
6 cups chicken or beef broth
2 teaspoons sugar
3 tablespoons freshly squeezed lemon juice
Salt and pepper, to taste
2 cups sour cream

Wash unpeeled beets, cook in boiling water until fork tender. Cool, peel and grate.

Saute onions and carrots in butter 10 minutes. Add beets, broth and sugar. Simmer 20 to 30 minutes. Remove from heat. Stir in lemon juice. Season. Puree mixture in food processor. Chill well.

Stir sour cream into soup and serve with bowls of garnish, such as cubed boiled potatoes, chopped fresh dill, cubed cucumber, hard-boiled eggs, and extra sour cream.

Delicious served with slices of black bread. Serves 4-6.

BROCCOLI SOUP

1/4 cup salad oil
1 medium onion, diced
1 large potato, diced
2/3 cup celery, diced
1 garlic clove, minced
1/2 teaspoon pepper
3 cups chopped broccoli or 1 package
   (10-ounce) frozen chopped broccoli,
   thawed
5 cups chicken broth
1/4 teaspoon fresh chopped basil or
   1 teaspoon dried basil
Salt and pepper to taste

In large saucepan, heat oil. Add onions, saute until tender, about 10 minutes. Add potato, celery, garlic and pepper. Cook for 10 minutes, stirring occasionally. Stir in broccoli, broth and basil, cover and simmer for 20 minutes.

Into blender, pour half of soup. Blend till smooth. Repeat with remaining soup. Taste for seasonings and add salt if needed. Reheat soup. Serves 4-6.

BOSTON CLAM CHOWDER

1/4 pound salt pork, diced
2 cups sliced onions
4 cups diced potatoes
3 cups milk
1 teaspoon salt
1/2 teaspoon coarse black pepper
3 cans (7-ounce size) shelled clams
2 cups clam liquid
1/4 cup cream

In large saucepan gently heat salt pork until fat is melted and crisp. Stir in onion and saute 2 to 3 minutes. Add potatoes, milk, salt and pepper. Simmer gently covered 10 to 15 minutes or until potatoes are just tender. Add the cans of clams and clam liquid. Simmer until potatoes are completely cooked. Stir in the cream just before serving. Always use good clams. Serves 6-8.

CLAM CHOWDER

1 can (10-ounce) Snow's clam chowder
1 can (6 1/2-ounce) minced clams
3/4 cup Pet milk or cream
2 tablespoons sherry
3 tablespoons parsley
Several flicks of Worcestershire sauce

Pour juice off clams. Add ingredients as stated and simmer until hot. DO NOT BOIL.

Jan says, "Use the above clam chowder recipe, but add one can of tomatoes or 1 can of tomato bisque soup. This makes a good red clam chowder." Serves 2.

The Warm Up

CHEESE SOUP

8 tablespoons butter
6 tablespoons flour
1/4 teaspoon dry mustard
1 quart milk
2 cups grated American cheese
2 cups chicken stock
1/2 cup celery, finely chopped
1/2 cup green pepper, finely chopped
1/2 cup onion, finely chopped
1/2 cup grated carrots
Several drops Tabasco sauce
Salt to taste
1/2 teaspoon paprika

Melt 6 tablespoons butter. Add flour and dry mustard, blending well. Pour milk in gradually, blend well. Bring to boil. Add cheese and remove from heat but keep warm.

Melt remaining butter in another pan. Add celery, green pepper, onion and carrots. Cook until transparent, then put through sieve. Add chicken stock and mix well. Combine two mixtures and season with hot pepper sauce, salt and paprika. Do not boil. Serves 4-6.

CHICKEN GUMBO

1 to 2 cups cooked chicken, cut into bite-size pieces
1 slice ham, cut into small pieces
2 tablespoons bacon or chicken fat
1 medium onion, diced
1/3 cup diced green pepper
2 ribs celery, sliced
4 cups chicken broth
1 can (16-ounce) tomatoes, undrained
2 teaspoons salt
1/8 teaspoon pepper
2 tablespoons chopped parsley
1 bay leaf
1/2 teaspoon thyme
1/2 teaspoon file' powder
Dash of Worcestershire sauce
1/3 cup long-grained rice, uncooked
1 cup canned or frozen cut okra

Saute chicken and ham lightly in fat. Combine rest of ingredients, add to chicken and bring to a boil. Cover and reduce heat; simmer until vegetables and rice are tender, about 20 minutes. Remove bay leaf and serve. Better even on 2nd or 3rd day!!

Note: Do not put file' powder in while cooking if you intend to freeze. Add before serving. Do not boil soup after adding file' powder. Serves 6.

CHICKEN SOUP WITH RICE AND MUSHROOMS

1 stewing hen, 5 pounds
6 quarts water
1 whole onion, stuck with 2 cloves
2 whole stalks celery
2 tablespoons salt
1/2 teaspoon Tabasco sauce
1/4 teaspoon green hot sauce
2 medium onions, chopped
3 to 4 cups celery, chopped
2 large carrots, grated
1 pound fresh mushrooms, sliced
2 cans, stewed seasoned tomatoes
1 cup rice, uncooked
1 teaspoon leaf thyme
Salt and pepper to taste
Fresh chopped parsley to garnish

In pot of salted water add hen, Tabasco sauce, green hot sauce, whole onion and celery stalks. Simmer at least 3 hours. Cool.

Remove hen, discard whole onion and celery stalks. Strain broth, return to pot. To the broth add remaining ingredients except chicken and parsley. Simmer about 15 minutes. Add the skinned, deboned chicken which has been cut into bite-size pieces. Adjust the seasonings to taste.

Freezes well but, if frozen, do not add the parsley until serving time. Makes 1 1/2 to 2 gallons.

The Warm Up

LOCO'S CHILI

1 cup beef suet
2 1/2 pounds coarse lean meat
1 cup minced onion
1 clove crushed garlic
1 large green pepper, minced
1 large bay leaf
1 teaspoon oregano
2 1/2 tablespoons chili powder
1 teaspoon ground cumin
1/4 teaspoon cayenne
1/2 teaspoon fresh ground black pepper
2 chili pods, minced very fine
1/2 tablespoon paprika
Salt as desired
3 tablespoons flour
1 1/2 quarts tomato juice
1 can beef bouillon
3 cans red beans
1/4 cup cracker crumbs

Melt beef suet over low heat. Remove pieces that remain after fat melts. Add lean meat, stirring frequently until it loses red color. Add next 12 ingredients and stir in well. Cover and saute 5 minutes.

Blend in well 3 tablespoons of flour. Add tomato juice and beef stock. Bring to a boil, reduce heat and simmer 1 hour. Add beans with liquid, heat through. Stir in cracker crumbs 10 minutes before serving. Serves 8.

COLONIAL SOUP

1 medium onion, chopped
2 ribs celery, chopped
1/4 cup butter
1 tablespoon flour
2 quarts chicken broth
1 cup smooth peanut butter
2 cups heavy cream
Chopped peanuts

Saute onion and celery in butter until soft. Stir in flour and blend well. Add chicken broth; bring to boil stirring constantly. Remove from heat and rub through a sieve. Add peanut butter and cream, blend well. Garnish with peanuts. May be made a day in advance. Reheat until piping hot.
Serves 8-10.

CREAM OF CORN SOUP

3 tablespoons butter
1 medium onion, chopped
1 tablespoon flour
1 large package frozen corn
8 ounces whipping cream
1 pint half-and-half
Salt and pepper to taste
4 or 5 sprigs of parsley, chopped
1 small bay leaf
Pinch of dried sage
Dash of Tabasco sauce

Melt butter, add flour slowly and chopped onion. Saute about 10 minutes. Add the frozen corn, slowly simmering until corn is very soft. Add cream and half and half, cook until blended. Add parsley, salt, bay leaf, sage, Tabasco and pepper. Blend well. Puree mixture in blender and strain to remove corn husks. Straining makes a difference both in the texture and taste of this soup. Reheat and serve warm. Garnish with paprika.
Serves 4-6.

The Warm Up

CREOLE COURTBOUILLON

4 to 5 pounds fish (cat, red)
1/2 cup cooking oil
2 tablespoons flour
3 cups onion, finely chopped
1 large green pepper, chopped
1 large can tomatoes
1 small can tomato paste
1 cup celery, chopped
3 cloves garlic, pressed
4 cups water
1 teaspoon Worcestershire sauce
Salt and freshly ground pepper to taste
1/3 cup parsley, minced
1 cup white wine
1 lemon, thinly sliced

Heat oil, add flour and cook until medium brown. Add onions and saute until transparent. Add tomatoes, tomato paste, green pepper, celery and garlic. Cook slowly for 25 minutes. Add 1 cup of water and allow to cook down again. Add remainder of water and fish, Worcestershire sauce, salt, pepper and parsley. Simmer 20 to 25 minutes. The last 5 minutes, add wine and sliced lemon. Serve with bowls of cooked rice.
Serves 10-12.

CREOLE GUMBO

3 tablespoons butter
3 tablespoons all purpose flour
1/2 cup chopped onion
1 clove garlic, minced
1 can (16-ounce) tomatoes, cut up and undrained
1/2 cup chopped green pepper
2 bay leaves
1 teaspoon dried oregano, crushed
1 teaspoon dried thyme, crushed
1/4 teaspoon Tabasco sauce
1 1/2 cups water
1/2 teaspoon salt
2 cans (4 1/2-ounce size) shrimp, drained and cut up
1 can (7 1/2-ounce) crab meat, drained and cartilage removed
1 tablespoon file' powder
Hot cooked rice

In large saucepan melt butter; blend in flour. Cook and stir until golden brown, about 7 to 8 minutes. Stir in onion and garlic; cook until onion is tender. Stir in tomatoes, green pepper, bay leaves, oregano, thyme, Tabasco sauce, 1 1/2 cups water and 1/2 teaspoon salt. Bring to a boil, reduce heat and simmer, covered, about 20 minutes. Remove bay leaves. Stir in shrimp and crab; heat through. Remove from heat. Blend moderate amount hot liquid into file' powder. Return to remaining hot mixture in saucepan, stirring until combined. Serve over rice. Serves 4-6.

ICED CUCUMBER SOUP

2 medium cucumbers
3 1/4 cups buttermilk
1 cup sour cream
Dash of Tabasco sauce
Dash of garlic powder
2 tablespoons wine vinegar
Dash of Worcestershire sauce
3/4 teaspoon salt
1/2-inch slice of a medium onion
3 tablespoons chopped parsley
4 or 5 fresh mint leaves or 1/4 to 1/2 teaspoon dry mint leaves
1 1/2 teaspoons dill weed

Peel cucumbers. Remove seeds. Cut into thick slices. Put into blender with 1 cup of buttermilk, onion, seasonings, and vinegar. Blend until cucumbers are grated fine but not liquefied. Combine rest of buttermilk, sour cream. Gradually stir in the cucumber mixture. Blend well and refrigerate at least one hour. Serve cold with garnish of dill weed on top and/or a cucumber slice.
Note: Can be made a day or two ahead.
Serves 4.

DOWN SOUTH SHRIMP GUMBO

6 strips bacon
6 onions, medium sized
4 green peppers
1 bunch of celery
1 bunch of parsley
4 cloves of garlic, minced
1 can (1 quart, 14 ounces) tomato juice
2 cans (28 ounces each) tomatoes
2 cans (6 ounces each) tomato paste
1 pouch of seafood seasoning
1 tablespoon salt
5 tablespoons Worcestershire sauce
6 drops Tabasco or 1 teaspoon red pepper
1 tablespoon pepper
3 pounds cleaned and deveined fresh shrimp
1 sack frozen chopped okra
1 pound regular or lump fresh crab meat

Fry the 6 strips of bacon. Eat the bacon while you chop onions, green peppers, celery, parsley and garlic. Saute in bacon grease until transparent. Add next eight ingredients and cook slowly for 2 hours. Remove seafood seasoning pouch. Add shrimp and cook for 30 minutes. Add okra and cook slowly for another hour. Stir in crab meat and mix thoroughly. Set aside to cool before refrigerating overnight. Reheat next day, adjust seasonings, and, if too thick, add a can of consomme. Serve with rice. Serves 12.

EGG-LEMON SOUP/SOUPA AVGOLEMONO

8 cups chicken broth
1 cup rice
4 eggs, separated
Juice of 2 lemons
Salt
Lemon slices for garnish
Stewed chicken breasts (optional)

Bring chicken broth to a boil, salt to taste, add rice and simmer, covered, for 20 minutes; then remove from heat. In a bowl, beat egg whites until stiff, add yolks and beat well. Slowly add lemon juice to eggs, beating constantly, then add 2 cups of hot chicken broth. Do not stop beating. Constant beating prevents curdling and that's the secret of this soup. When eggs and broth are well mixed, pour this mixture back into remaining broth and rice. Stir well over heat, but do not allow to boil. Serve at once in bowls garnished with thinly sliced lemons. If you desire, cut up some cooked chicken breasts into the soup.
Serves 6.

ICED LEMON SOUP

4 cups chicken stock
2 cups half-and-half
2 tablespoons cornstarch
6 egg yolks
Juice of 6 lemons
1 teaspoon Accent
1/2 teaspoon Bon Appetit
Dash of cayenne
1/2 teaspoon grated lemon peel
Salt to taste
Thin slices lemon
Chopped parsley or mint leaves

In saucepan, combine chicken stock and cream. Heat, stirring constantly. Stir in cornstarch. Cook over low heat until thickened, without letting boil. Beat egg yolks lightly and gradually pour just a bit of the hot soup into them. Stir briskly. Pour yolk mixture into soup and add lemon juice, Accent, cayenne, Bon Appetit and grated lemon peel. Let cool. Chill at least 8 hours. Serve soup well chilled, garnished with thin slices of lemon and chopped parsley or mint leaves. Serves 12.

The Warm Up

OLD-FASHIONED MUSHROOM SOUP

6 tablespoons butter
1 pound mushrooms, thinly sliced
2 medium-sized onions, chopped
2 cloves garlic, finely chopped
2 carrots, finely chopped
3 stalks celery, finely chopped
3 tablespoons flour
8 cups beef broth
2 ripe tomatoes, peeled, seeded and chopped
1 cup tomato puree
2 tablespoons tomato paste
3 tablespoons finely chopped parsley
1 cup sour cream
3 tablespoons sherry
Salt and pepper to taste

Heat 4 tablespoons of butter in large kettle. Saute mushrooms for 3 minutes. Remove and reserve mushrooms. Heat remaining butter and saute remaining vegetables for 5 minutes. Stir in flour and cook for 2 minutes.

Add beef broth, half of the reserved mushrooms, tomatoes, tomato puree and tomato paste. Season with salt and pepper. Bring to boil. Partially cover the kettle, reduce heat and simmer for 30 minutes.

Add the remaining mushrooms, sherry and parsley and simmer for another 5 minutes. Serve the soup in a warm tureen, topped with sour cream. Serves 8.

PEACH-BLUEBERRY SOUP

2 cups buttermilk
1 cup yogurt
1/2 cup cottage cheese
2 tablespoons honey
1 tablespoon minced fresh mint
1/2 teaspoon grated orange peel
2 cups peaches
1 1/2 cups blueberries
Reserve 1 cup blueberries and 1/2 cup peaches

Whip all ingredients for 1 minute at medium speed on blender and 1 minute at high speed. Serve chilled and garnish with reserved peaches and blueberries. Serves 4-6.

PEA POD SOUP

1 cup sliced leeks
3 tablespoons butter
3 tablespoons flour
4 cups chicken broth
1 teaspoon salt
1 package (10-ounce) frozen peas
1 pound fresh snow pea pods, strings and tips removed
1 1/2 cups water
1 scallion, green and white parts chopped
8 large leaves Boston lettuce
1 tablespoon butter
1 cup milk
1/4 to 1/2 cup heavy cream
Salt to taste
White pepper to taste

Saute leeks in butter 10 minutes until tender. Add flour, stirring constantly. Add broth, salt, peas. Simmer 20 minutes. Puree in food processor. Set aside.

Cook together pods, water, scallion, lettuce and butter until pods are tender, about 15 minutes. Remove from heat, puree in food processor. Put through strainer. Add to puree base, thin with milk. Chill well.

To serve, enrich with cream, season with salt, white pepper. Garnish with finely shredded lettuce leaves. Serve this with whole wheat bread. Serves 4-6.

The Warm Up

POTAGE ST. GERMAIN
(CREAM OF PEA SOUP)

1 pound package dry split peas
1 large or 2 medium leeks
2 ribs celery
1 large onion
1 tablespoon butter
1/2 gallon chicken stock
1 small potato
Ham pieces (2 ham hocks or prosciutto bone)
Pinch dried chervil
1/2 teaspoon sugar
1/4 teaspoon thyme
1/2 to 1 cup whipping cream
1 tablespoon butter

Soak peas overnight in water to cover well. Rinse peas before cooking.

Chop leeks, green and white part. Chop celery and onion. Melt butter in large pot; add leeks, celery and onion. Salt and cook covered 8 to 10 minutes. If using prosciutto bone, cut down on salt. Add cut up potato, peas, chicken stock and ham or whatever you are using.

Add chervil, sugar and thyme. Simmer for 1 hour or until done. Skim any fat off top. Put into blender or food processor and puree, a small amount at a time. If using ham or ham hocks, put meat through blender also. If too thick, add more stock. Add whipping cream and tablespoon of butter. Adjust seasonings. Do not let boil again after adding cream. Serves 8-10.

POTATO SOUP

3 cups onions, thinly sliced
3 cups potatoes, peeled and thinly sliced
1 quart chicken broth
1 cup heavy cream
5 tablespoons lightly salted butter
Salt and pepper to taste

Peel and slice potatoes and onions. Put in pot with chicken broth. Bring to boil, salt and pepper to taste. Simmer for 40 minutes or until potatoes are tender. Put mixture into blender and puree. (For the best soup, leave it chunky with bits of potatoes when blending.) Put mixture back into pot, add cream and butter. Cook until warm. Serves 4.

PUMPKIN SOUP

2 tablespoons butter
4 scallions, chopped
1 large onion, sliced
1 can (29-ounce) pumpkin
1 bay leaf
2 carrots, chopped
3 cans (13 3/4-ounce size) chicken broth
1 tablespoon brown sugar
1/4 to 1/2 teaspoon nutmeg
1/4 teaspoon ginger
1/4 teaspoon cinnamon
1 cup light cream
Salt and pepper
Sherry (optional)
Chopped chives or scallions
Lightly salted whipped cream

In a large saucepan, melt butter and saute scallions and onion until limp. Add canned pumpkin, bay leaf, carrots and chicken broth; bring to a boil. Reduce heat, cover and simmer for 15 minutes. Remove bay leaf and puree mixture in electric blender or push through a sieve and return to saucepan. Stir in sugar, nutmeg, ginger and cinnamon to taste.

Here, if you like, cover and refrigerate.

To serve: Bring soup to a boil, reduce heat, stir in cream, salt and pepper to taste. Garnish with a tablespoon of sherry, chopped chives or scallions and a dollop of lightly salted whipped cream.

Jo says, "I've served this as a beginning to festive holiday dinners. It is elegant and delicious."

Serves 12.

The Warm Up

COLD RASPBERRY SOUP

1 1/2 tablespoons unflavored gelatin
1/3 cup cold water
3/4 cup hot water
3 packages (10-ounce size) frozen raspberries, thawed or:
  4 cups fresh raspberries
3 1/2 cups sour cream
1 1/3 cups pineapple juice
1 1/3 cups half and half
1 1/3 cups dry sherry
1/3 cup grenadine
Juice of 1 lemon
Sugar to taste

Soak gelatin in cold water 5 minutes. Stir in hot water and dissolve over low heat. Push raspberries through a sieve to remove seeds, then puree. Combine remaining ingredients and place in a glass container. Cover and refrigerate overnight. Garnish with a few whole raspberries and a mint leaf. Serves 12.

SAN JUAN BLACK BEAN SOUP

2 cups black beans
1/2 pound cubed ham
3 quarts water
2 tablespoons olive oil
2 chopped onions
2 cloves garlic, crushed
1 large carrot, chopped
1/2 cup celery, chopped
1 large green or red pepper, chopped
2 tomatoes, chopped
1 bay leaf
2 teaspoons salt
1/4 to 1/2 teaspoon dried ground chili peppers
1 teaspoon paprika
2 tablespoons butter
2 tablespoons flour
2 tablespoons rum or sherry

Wash the black beans and soak overnight in water to cover. Drain and rinse. Then add cubed ham and 3 quarts of water. Bring this to a boil, simmer over low heat for about 3 hours.

Heat olive oil in a skillet. Add onions, garlic, carrot, celery, and green or red pepper. Saute just until onion is yellow and limp, stirring occasionally.

Add to beans the tomatoes, bay leaf, salt, chili peppers, and paprika. Cover and simmer 1 hour.

Now press all through a sieve or use the blender. Return to kettle and reheat. Just before mealtime, blend together butter and an equal amount of flour. Form into a ball, divide the ball in half and add both to the soup, stirring constantly to the boiling point. That's an easy way of thickening, when necessary. Adjust seasonings, adding whatever you think necessary. At this point add rum or sherry if desired. Ladle soup into bowls and have side garnishes of chopped onion, hard-cooked egg, chopped, and Parmesan cheese. Serves 12-16.

HOT TOMATO BOUILLON

1 can condensed tomato soup
1 can condensed beef broth
1 cup water
1/4 teaspoon horseradish
Dash Tabasco
Sour cream

Combine all ingredients except sour cream. Simmer uncovered for 5 minutes and blend well. Pour into mugs and float a spoonful of sour cream in each. Serves 6.

The Warm Up

CREAM OF SPINACH SOUP

4 cups canned beef or chicken broth
2 packages (10-ounce size) frozen chopped
  spinach
2 cups sour cream
Nutmeg (optional)
Hot sauce (optional)

Combine broth and spinach and bring to boil, breaking spinach apart as quickly as possible. Place in blender or puree through a strainer. Add sour cream and blend. Reheat or chill before serving. Top with nutmeg or hot sauce if desired. It is delicious garnished with grated hard-boiled eggs.
    Serves 4-6.

STEAK SOUP

1 stick butter
1/2 cup flour
4 cans (10-ounce size) beef consomme
1/2 cup diced fresh carrots
1/2 cup diced fresh celery
1/2 cup diced fresh onions
1 can (8-ounce) tomatoes, chopped
1 1/2 teaspoons Kitchen Bouquet
2 beef bouillon cubes
1/2 teaspoon ground black pepper
1 teaspoon Accent
1 package (10-ounce) frozen mixed vegetables
1 pound ground beef steak, browned and drained
1 1/2 pounds sirloin, cut into small pieces,
  browned but not drained

Place butter in soup pot. Allow to melt without browning. Add flour to butter and stir to form a smooth paste. After mixture is smooth, cook over medium heat — without browning — for 3 minutes, stirring constantly. Add consomme to flour-butter mixture and stir until smooth and lightly thickened. Bring to full boil. Add fresh vegetables, seasonings and tomatoes to the boiling soup. Allow soup to regain boil, then reduce heat and simmer 30 minutes. Add frozen vegetables and browned ground steak and sirloin. Simmer 15 minutes. Serves 8.
    Jo says, "Better double or triple the recipe. It will not last long, and it freezes so beautifully."

TOMATO SOUP WITH PESTO

2 tablespoons creme fraiche or sour cream
1 to 2 teaspoons pesto (See index for Pesto)
4 cups tomato soup, chilled
Fresh basil for garnish

Combine cream and pesto. Spoon a dollop onto soup. Garnish with chopped fresh basil. Serves 4.

JACK'S TURKEY CHOWDER

1 can chicken stock (or turkey, if you are
  cooking down the turkey carcass)
3 cups chopped cooked turkey
Salt and pepper
1/2 cup very fine noodles
1 1/2 cans cream-style corn
3 green onions, chopped, using tops
1 rib celery, sliced very thin
1 sprig parsley, chopped
1 teaspoon sugar
1 cup milk
1/4 cup whipping cream

Combine meat and stock, heat but do not boil. Add noodles and corn. Heat. Add green onions, celery and parsley. Add sugar, milk and cream. Heat through. Thin with more milk if needed.
    Serves 4-6.

The Warm Up

VICHYSSOISE

6 to 8 leeks, white parts only (1 1/4 to 1 1/2-inch diameter)
4 tablespoons butter
8 white potatoes, peeled, thinly sliced
1 tablespoon salt
5 cups chicken broth
2 cups half and half
Pinch of nutmeg
White pepper, to taste
1 cup heavy cream

Saute leeks in butter 8 to 10 minutes. Add potatoes, salt and broth. Simmer 30 minutes or until potatoes are very tender. Puree potato mixture in food processor then put through fine strainer to remove any lumps. Add half and half, nutmeg and pepper. Check for seasoning. Chill well. To serve, stir in cream, garnish with chives. Serves 4-6.

WATERCRESS SOUP

1/3 cup minced onion
3 tablespoons melted butter
3 or 4 cups watercress with stems (tightly packed)
1/2 teaspoon salt
3 tablespoons flour
5 1/2 cups chicken broth
1 cup whipping cream
2 egg yolks
2 tablespoons butter

Saute onions in butter 5 to 7 minutes, until tender and transparent. Stir in watercress and salt. Cook slowly until tender, about 5 minutes. Sprinkle flour into watercress mixture. Stir over moderate heat for 3 minutes. Add chicken broth and bring to boiling point. Simmer 5 minutes. Strain watercress mixture. Place strained watercress in blender and puree. Return puree to chicken broth, correct seasonings.

Blend the yolks and cream in mixing bowl. Beat a cupful of hot soup into yolks by drops. Gradually beat in the rest of the soup in a thin stream. Place saucepan over heat for a few minutes; simmer but do not let boil. Turn off heat, stir in the butter a tablespoon at a time. Cool and refrigerate. May be served hot or cold.

Garnish top with unsweetened whipped cream and watercress sprigs, or seasoned croutons. Serves 6.

WHITE BEAN SOUP

2 cups navy beans
2 quarts water
2 big onions
1 carrot, cut in half
Ham bone
2 cups ham, cut into bite-size pieces
Bay leaf
Salt and pepper
1 tablespoon cornstarch
1 cup tomato juice
2 tablespoons butter

Soak beans in water overnight. Measure water again in the morning. Put on to cook with ham bone, pieces of ham, chopped onions and carrot, bay leaf, salt and pepper. Simmer for 3 hours, adding more boiling water if needed. Dissolve cornstarch in cold tomato juice, add to the soup the last 15 minutes. Remove carrot and discard. Add butter to soup just before serving. Serves 8.

The Main Event · Entrees

We urge you to look through this section on main courses to discover the diverse selection of meat, fish, and fowl recipes within. From the down-home Family Request for Pot Roast to the more sophisticated Le Steak au Poivre Vert en Chemise, or from a prideworthy collection of chicken breast recipes to the well-loved Chicken Marengo for Twelve, Chicken Rococo, Chicken in the Sack, and more. If you get tired of chicken, please try Josef's Duck Breast or the Curried Turkey Breast. Your hunters will be proud of their bag when you serve the Baked Pheasant, Quail, or Dove.

The seafood section is full of simple delights such as Fillet of Fish Amandine, Fillet of Fish Coconut Grove, and Fillet of Fish Florentine. Bar-B-Q Lobster Tails, Shrimp Étouffé, and Snapper Normande are favorites of ours and our guests'. If you have had a hectic day or a late invitation for dinner, why don't you fix the Tuna-Almond Bake or the Easy Fixin' Tuna Casserole for the kiddies.

The Main Event

❖❖❖

Meats

FILET OF BEEF WELLINGTON

Parts 1, 2, 3, and 4 are to be completed a day or two before serving. Part 5 can be completed prior to guests' arrival.

Part I: The Filet

Roast 1 whole beef tenderloin (6-7 pounds). Trim fat and membranes off tenderloin, tuck small end under, or cut it off. Reserve fat to cover meat. Preheat oven to 475 degrees. Cover beef with reserved fat. Place in buttered pan and roast for 7 minutes. Remove at once, discard fat, cool, cover and refrigerate.

Part 2: The Pastry

4 cups flour
2 sticks butter, chilled
6 tablespoons chilled solid vegetable shortening
2/3 cup ice water
2 teaspoons salt
2 eggs
1/4 teaspoon sugar

Cut butter and shortening into flour until mixture resembles meal. Mix remaining ingredients and add to flour mixture. Scrape dough into a ball, dust with flour, cover and refrigerate several hours.

Part 3: English Forcemeat

1/2 pound ground lean veal
1/2 pound ground pork
3/4 stick butter
2 tablespoons oil
1 pound fresh mushrooms, chopped
6 green onions, bottom halves, chopped
3/4 cup filbert nuts, chopped
3 tablespoons fresh parsley, chopped
1 teaspoon salt
1/2 teaspoon tarragon
1/2 teaspoon rosemary
1/4 teaspoon cracked fresh pepper
1/4 cup cognac

Saute veal and pork together until just begins to brown. Drain on paper towels. In butter and oil, saute mushrooms and green onions for 10 minutes. Stir in filberts, parsley, salt, tarragon, rosemary and cracked pepper. Add veal, pork and cognac. Cover and simmer over low heat for 15-20 minutes. Correct seasonings. Cover and refrigerate.

Part 4: Perigeux Sauce

2 tablespoons butter
2 tablespoons finely minced shallots
2 cups beef bouillon
1/2 cup Madeira wine
1 tablespoon cornstarch
3 chopped truffles. These are very expensive so some use chopped pitted ripe olives. We won't tell.

Saute shallots in butter. Add beef bouillon and cornstarch dissolved in wine. Stir over low heat until thick. Add chopped truffles and season with salt and pepper. Store in refrigerator but serve hot.

❖❖

Part 5: The Assembly

Warm filet and forcemeat to room temperature. Break an egg into forcemeat and mix well. Roll out pastry on floured surface to 1/4-inch thick to make a 10 x 18-inch rectangle. Place filet 3 inches from one end, pack forcemeat around it and fold pastry over it, creating a closed pastry envelope. Seal edges with fingertips moistened with a slightly beaten egg. Seal ends also. Transfer pastry wrapped meat to baking sheet by using two well-chilled spatulas for lifting.

Decorate top of pastry with bits of remaining pastry cut into flower and leaf designs. Brush top of pastry with beaten egg. Insert meat thermometer through pastry on side so pastry is not marred on top. Bake in preheated 400 degree oven 30 to 45 minutes until pastry is browned and meat thermometer registers rare to medium-rare. Allow to sit 20 minutes before slicing. Serve with warm Periguex sauce. Serves 8.

LE STEAK AU POIVRE VERT EN CHEMISE (GREEN PEPPERCORN STEAK IN A CREPE)

8 boneless top sirloin steaks (6-8 ounces each)
4 teaspoons whole black peppercorns, crushed
1 stick butter (1/2 cup)
4 tablespoons oil
6 tablespoons red wine vinegar
4 cups heavy cream
4 teaspoons green peppercorns, drained
  (purchase at a gourmet shop)

STEAKS:
Press crushed black pepper into steaks. Brush off excess. Bring steaks to room temperature—may need to use two pans for cooking. Melt about 1 1/2 to 2 tablespoons butter and a little oil per steak in the pans. Cook quickly over medium high heat to desired doneness. (Meat is soft on top to the touch when medium rare.) Remove steaks to heated platter when done; slice each steak in half, wrap each half in an herb crepe and place on platter, seam side down. Allow 2 crepes per person.

CREPES:
1 1/4 cup flour
1 cup milk
1/4 teaspoon pepper, coarse grind
3 tablespoons melted cooked butter
2 teaspoons chervil
2 teaspoons dried chives
3 large eggs
1/4 cup water
1/2 teaspoon salt
Pinch nutmeg
1 tablespoon dried parsley (or 2 tablespoons fresh)

Mix all crepe ingredients well. Let batter stand in refrigerator at least 1 hour or overnight. Season crepe pan with oil; heat pan and pour in from ladle about 2 ounces of batter at an angle to evenly coat pan thinly. Cook a minute or so until lightly browned. Turn gently with a spatula or fingertips and cook other side briefly. Slide gently onto a plate with waxed paper in between crepes. These may be made ahead and refrigerated or frozen. Allow 2 crepes per steak.

GREEN PEPPERCORN SAUCE:
Pour off excess fat from pans. Deglaze pans with vinegar; let it evaporate completely. Immediately pour in cream and let it boil down and thicken somewhat. Test for seasoning, adding salt 1/4 teaspoon at a time to correct. Add 4 tablespoons butter and green peppercorns. Spoon sauce over crepes and serve immediately. Pass any extra sauce. Serves 8.

❖❖

JEAN'S SWEET AND SOUR MEATBALLS

1 egg
1 cup bread crumbs
2 tablespoons chopped onion
2 tablespoons milk
3/4 teaspoon salt
1 pound ground beef
2 tablespoons shortening
1 can (8 1/4-ounce) pineapple tidbits
1 can (8-ounce) cranberry sauce
1/2 cup barbeque sauce
1/4 teaspoon salt
1/4 teaspoon pepper
1 tablespoon corn starch
1/4 cup cold water
1/2 cup green pepper, chopped

Combine egg, bread crumbs, onion, milk, salt. Add to ground beef and mix well. Shape into little meatballs and brown in shortening. Remove balls from skillet, drain on paper towels and pour grease from skillet; return balls to skillet. Add water to pineapple juice to make 3/4 cup of syrup. Pour over meatballs with cranberry sauce, barbeque sauce, salt and pepper. Bring to boil, then simmer.

Combine cornstarch and cold water, stir into skillet, cook until thick. Add pineapple tidbits and green peppers. Simmer 1 hour. Serve over hot rice. Serves 8.

ITALIAN MEAT LOAF

1 1/2 pounds lean ground beef
1 egg
3/4 cup cracker crumbs
1/2 cup finely chopped onion
2 cans (8-ounce size) tomato sauce with cheese
1 teaspoon salt
1/2 teaspoon oregano
1/8 teaspoon pepper
2 cups shredded Mozzarella cheese

Combine ground beef, egg, cracker crumbs, onion, 1/3 cup tomato sauce, salt, oregano, and pepper. Mix well and shape into a flat rectangle about 10 x 12-inch on waxed paper. Sprinkle Mozzarella cheese evenly over meat mixture. Roll up like a jelly roll and press ends to seal. Place in shallow baking dish. Bake at 350 degrees for 1 hour. Drain off excess fat. Pour on remaining tomato sauce and bake additional 15 minutes. Serves 4-6.

BEEF TENDERLOIN

1 beef tenderloin (6-pounds)
Garlic powder
Lemon pepper
Paprika

Wipe beef with damp paper towels. Generously coat meat all over with garlic, pepper and paprika. Tuck small ends under and place meat on greased broiler rack. Lay a strip of bacon on top. Bake in preheated 425-degree oven 25 minutes for very rare meat or 30 to 40 minutes at 450 degrees for meat rare in the center.

After removing from oven, let meat set 15 minutes before slicing. Serve with Bearnaise sauce. Serves 12.

Jo says, "Place a large pan with a small amount of water under the broiler pan to catch splatters and prevent smoking." Serves 12.

❖❖

VARIATION: TOURNEDOS

1/2 cup butter
12 (3-inch) white bread rounds
12 slices filet of beef, 1 inch thick (6 pounds)
4 tablespoons melted butter

In butter saute bread rounds until lightly browned all over. Set aside.

Prepare beef slices as in Tenderloin recipe. Brush top with melted butter. Broil 4 inches from heat for 5 minutes. Turn steaks; brush with remaining melted butter, broil 5 minutes longer for medium rare. To serve, arrange meat on bread rounds, garnish with watercress and pass Bernaise sauce (see index). Serves 6.

Jo says, "Place a baking pan with an inch of water on the rack below the broiler pan. This will help take care of some of the grease splatters and smoke.

STEAK DIANE

2 small sirloin steaks
Salt and freshly ground pepper
2 tablespoons butter
1 tablespoon chopped shallots or green onions
1 tablespoon chopped chives
1 tablespoon chopped parsley
1 tablespoon Worcestershire sauce
1 teaspoon A.1. sauce

Pound steaks lightly. Trim off excess fat. Sprinkle salt and pepper over meat. Melt butter in chafing dish. Saute shallots until golden. Quickly brown steaks on both sides. Add remaining ingredients. Spoon sauce over steaks and serve immediately. Serves 2.

Jo says, "I use slices of beef tenderloin."

SAVORY PEPPER STEAK

1 pound round steak, cut in very thin strips
2 tablespoons salad oil
1 1/2 cups sliced fresh mushroom or 4-ounce can (drained)
1 1/2 cups diagonally sliced celery
1 cup green pepper cut in 1-inch squares
1/2 cup green onion diagonally cut in 1-inch pieces
1 can Campbell's beef broth
2 tablespoons soy sauce
2 tablespoons cornstarch
1/2 cup water
Cooked rice

Brown meat in skillet with the oil. Add vegetables, soup and soy sauce. Cover; cook over low heat 20 minutes or until meat is tender. Stir now and then. Blend cornstarch and water; stir into sauce. Cook, stirring until thickened. Serve with rice. Serves 4.

CORNED BEEF AND CABBAGE

5 pounds corned beef
4 whole cloves
1 bay leaf
1 whole onion
2 stalks celery, sliced
1 medium-sized head cabbage

Place corned beef in Dutch oven. Cover with cold water. Add cloves, bay leaf, onion and celery. Bring to a boil over medium-high heat. Reduce heat to low and simmer 5 minutes. With a large metal spoon, skim off fat and meat particles from top of liquid. Cover tightly with lid secured and simmer 3 to 4 hours or until corned beef is tender. Add hot water during cooking, if it is needed. Cut cabbage into wedges, removing part of the center core. Place cabbage on top of meat and cook until cabbage is tender, 10 to 15 minutes. Remove cabbage with a slotted spoon to drain. Remove corned beef and slice. Serves 6.

Jan says, "Boiled potatoes are very good with this dish."

PAPRIKA GOULASH

1/4 cup peanut oil
2 1/2 pounds round of beef, cut into 1-inch cubes
1 1/2 teaspoons salt
1/4 teaspoon pepper
4 cups sliced onions
1 green pepper, chopped
2 cloves garlic, minced
1 bay leaf
1 can (6-ounce) tomato paste
1 1/2 cups beer
1 tablespoon paprika
1 teaspoon lemon juice

Heat oil in heavy kettle and cook meat until well browned on all sides. Sprinkle with salt and pepper. Add onions, green pepper and garlic. Cook, stirring occasionally, 10 minutes longer. Add bay leaf and tomato paste mixed with beer. Add paprika, cover and cook over low heat until meat is tender, about 2–2 1/2 hours. Before serving, stir in lemon juice. Correct seasonings with salt and pepper. Serve with buttered noodles. Serves 6.

BAR-B-QUED STUFFED FLANK STEAK

1 flank steak (2 1/2 pounds)
Instant meat tenderizer
1/2 teaspoon dried rosemary, crushed
1/4 teaspoon dried tarragon leaves
4 whole cloves
1/4 teaspoon thyme
1 tablespoon instant minced onion
1 1/2 cups vegetable oil
1 1/2 cups water
1/2 cup wine vinegar
cornbread stuffing (next page)

Cut steak in half, crosswise. Starting at cut end, make a pocket in each half to within 3/4-inch of edge of steak. If desired, have butcher make pockets. Sprinkle meat tenderizer on all surfaces of meat, allowing about 1/2 teaspoon per pound. Pierce deeply with meat fork at 1 inch intervals. Combine all other ingredients in saucepan. Bring to boil over moderate heat. Simmer 1 minute. Remove from heat and cool. Pour marinade over meat; cover and refrigerate 4 hours or overnight. Turn occasionally. Remove meat from marinade and wipe excess with paper towels. Fill pockets with cornbread stuffing. Close with skewers. Place on grill and cook 10 to 15 minutes on each side or until cooked to degree of doneness desired. Cut in crosswise slices to serve. Serves 6.

FLANK STEAK - CORNBREAD STUFFING

1 package (10-ounce) frozen chopped spinach
1/4 cup butter
1/2 cup finely chopped celery
1/2 cup finely chopped onion
1 package (8-ounce) cornbread stuffing
1/2 cup water

Cook spinach. Drain well and reserve. Melt butter in skillet over moderate low heat. Add celery and onion and cook until onion is tender. Combine spinach, butter mixture, cornbread stuffing and water. Toss with a fork. Mix well.

VERA'S BARBEQUED BRISKET

3 to 4 pound brisket
2 tablespoons liquid smoke
1 teaspoon garlic salt
1 teaspoon onion salt
2 teaspoons celery seed
1 1/2 teaspoons salt
2 teaspoons Worcestershire sauce
2 teaspoons freshly ground pepper
1 cup barbecue sauce

Cover both sides of brisket with liquid smoke, garlic and onion salt, celery seed and Worcestershire sauce.

Place brisket on baking pan and marinate meat in refrigerator overnight. Add salt and pepper, cover with foil and bake in slow oven 300 degrees for 5 hours.

Add barbeque sauce and leave uncovered last hour. Baste occasionally. This may be cooked outdoors on a rotating spit. Serves 6.

COMPANY'S COMING

1 package (8-ounce) noodles
1 clove garlic, minced
1 1/2 pounds lean ground meat
1 tablespoon butter
1 teaspoon oregano
1/4 teaspoon basil
2 cans (8-ounce size) tomato sauce
Salt and pepper
1 tablespoon sugar
1 cup cottage cheese
1/2 cup sour cream or 1 package (8-ounce)
  cream cheese
1/2 cup chopped onion
1/4 cup chopped green pepper
7 cups Cheddar cheese, shredded

Cook noodles. Brown meat and garlic in butter. Add oregano, basil, tomato sauce, salt, pepper and sugar. Blend cottage cheese. Add sour cream or cream cheese, onion and green pepper to cheese. In greased 9 x 13-inch casserole, put 1/2 cup cooked noodles. Layer with cheese, meat mixture, then repeat layers. Put Cheddar cheese on top. Bake at 350 degrees for 30 minutes. Serves 10-12.

STUFFED GRAPE LEAVES

1 pound ground beef
1/2 to 3/4 cup uncooked rice
1 medium onion, chopped fine
Salt and pepper to taste
1/2 teaspoon garlic salt
1/2 teaspoon basil
1/4 teaspoon dill
1 jar (15-ounce) grapevine leaves
1 can tomatoes

Combine all ingredients except tomatoes. Mix well. Place heaping spoonful of mixture in center of each grape leaf and fold over. Place in baking dish and pour tomatoes over top. Cover and cook at 350 degrees for 30 minutes or longer. Serves 4.

BEEF POT ROAST IN WINE

1 beef roast (3 to 4 pounds)
1/3 cup flour
1 teaspoon salt
1 teaspoon garlic powder
1/2 teaspoon pepper
1/2 teaspoon paprika
1/4 cup melted shortening
2 medium onions, sliced
1 bay leaf, crumbled
1/4 teaspoon rosemary
1/4 teaspoon thyme
1 bay leaf, crushed
1/2 cup water
1 1/2 cups red wine or sherry
3 large white potatoes, quartered
6 carrots, quartered lengthwise

Combine flour with salt, garlic powder, pepper and paprika. Completely coat roast with mixture on both sides.

Brown meat in small amount of shortening. Put in Dutch oven. Place onions on top of meat. Sprinkle with rosemary and thyme, and crushed bay leaf. Add wine and 1/2 cup water. Cover meat tightly. Bake in 350-degree oven until tender (about 2 1/2 to 3 hours).

Add potatoes and carrots about 45 minutes to 1 hour before meat is done. Add water if necessary. Serves 8.

THREE-DAY MARINATED ROAST

3 to 5 pound roast
3 cloves garlic
1 teaspoon salt
1/2 teaspoon pepper
1 teaspoon chili powder or cloves
1 teaspoon thyme
1 cup vegetable oil
1/2 cup red wine vinegar

Pierce meat with fork. Put roast in plastic bag. Combine rest of ingredients to make marinade. May be marinated for 3 days. Bake the roast according to your baking preference. Serves 6.

BROWN ROAST

3 pounds rump, pikes peak or sirloin tip roast
1 bottle catsup
1/3 bottle Heinz 57 sauce (10-ounce)
Smoke salt, to taste
Tabasco, to taste

Combine ingredients and pour over roast. Bake in 275-degree oven several hours or overnight until meat shreds easily. Serves 6.

FAMILY REQUEST FOR POT ROAST

1 pot roast (4-5 pounds)
Cooking oil
1 package Lipton onion soup mix
1 can cream of mushroom soup
1/2 soup can of water
Potatoes, cut in half or quartered
Carrots, cut in pieces
Onions, quartered

Brown meat in small amount of oil in a Dutch oven. Combine remaining ingredients and pour over meat. Cover and cook in a 350-degree oven 4 to 5 hours.

Add vegetables last hour.
Note: Do not add salt.
Serves 6.

✦✦✦

BEEF STROGANOFF

1/2 pound fresh mushrooms, sliced
1 large onion, chopped
3 tablespoons butter
2 pounds round steak (1/4 to 1/2-inch thick)
3 tablespoons flour
1 teaspoon salt
1 1/2 teaspoons paprika
1 cup water
3 tablespoons sherry
2 tablespoons tomato paste
1 can bouillon or consomme, diluted to make
   2 cups
1/2 cup sour cream

Saute mushrooms and onion in 2 tablespoons butter and remove from skillet. Cut steak into strips 2 1/2-inches long and 3/4-inch wide, removing fat and bone. Add another tablespoon butter to skillet and brown meat. Sprinkle flour, salt and paprika over meat and add water and tomato paste. Add sherry, bouillon-water mixture and bring to a boil. Simmer until meat is tender, about 1 1/4 hours. Add sour cream and heat, adding sauteed onions and mushrooms. Serve hot with fluffy white or wild rice, or buttered noodles. Serves 6.

AN ALSATIAN DINNER

2 pounds sauerkraut
3 medium onions, chopped
2 tablespoons bacon or pork fat
2 tart apples, peeled, cored and chopped or
   1 16-ounce can applesauce
6 peppercorns
10 juniper berries or 1/4 cup gin
2 1/2 cups white wine (optional)
6 slices cooked ham, 1/4-inch thick
6 smoked pork chops
6 franks, or knockwurst or bratwurst
12 link sausages

Soak sauerkraut in cold water for 15 minutes. Squeeze dry. Saute onions in fat until tender. Add kraut and toss. Cook for 5 minutes, stirring. Add apples or applesauce, peppercorns and juniper berries or gin. Pour in white wine if you use it. Cook slowly 1 hour.

Cook sausage and drain on paper towel. Add meats to kraut. Cook covered 30 minutes. Discard peppercorns and berries.

To serve: Pile Sauerkraut in center of a large warm platter. Arrange meats around kraut. Serve with boiled potatoes and mustard. This can be made ahead and reheated. Serves 6.

GLAZED PORK ROLL

1 whole pork loin roast, boned and tied
   (5 pounds)
3 jars (4 3/4-ounce) baby food strained apricots
1/3 cup honey
1/4 cup lemon juice
1/4 cup soy sauce
1/4 cup finely chopped onion
1 cup ginger ale
1/2 clove garlic, minced
1/8 teaspoon ground ginger
1/8 teaspoon pepper
1 can (1 pound, 13-ounce) apricot halves
1 tablespoon grated lemon peel
2 tablespoons cornstarch
1/4 cup shredded coconut

Place pork roast in a large shallow dish. Combine 2 jars of strained apricots with honey, lemon juice, soy sauce, onion, ginger ale, garlic, ginger and pepper. Pour over pork. Cover and marinate in refrigerator 4-5 hours, turning occasionally. Remove pork from marinade and place on barbecue spit. Reserve marinade. Place over low coals and cook about 3 1/2 hours brushing occasionally with marinade. A meat thermometer will register 185 when pork is cooked. Drain syrup from apricot halves in heatproof pan. Add remaining jar of strained apricots and lemon peel. Set aside apricots. Gradually stir 1/3 cup of cold marinade into cornstarch. Blend into apricot syrup mixture in pan. Cook until smooth and thickened. Stir in apricots. Keep sauce warm on grill. Sprinkle with coconut and serve. Serves 10.

❖❖

ENCORE FOR ROAST PORK WITH FRIED RICE

1/4 teaspoon salt
1 egg
1/4 cup diced leftover roast pork
1/4 cup diced onion
1/4 cup bean sprouts
3 cups cooked, cooled rice
1 teaspoon soy sauce
1/4 teaspoon Accent
Dash of pepper

Grease a skillet well, add salt and heat very hot. Add egg and scramble. Mix in the pork, onion, bean sprouts and rice. Stir and fry for 2-3 minutes. Season with soy sauce, Accent and pepper. Cook and stir 1 more minute. Serves 4.

SHERRY PEARS AND PORK CHOPS

3 fresh Bartlett pears
6 pork chops
1 tablespoon lemon juice
1/2 cup brown sugar
1/2 teaspoon cinnamon
2 tablespoons butter
Salt and pepper
1/4 cup sherry wine

Core and slice pears, leaving skins on them. Brown pork chops on both sides in a little fat trimmed from edges. Arrange half of pear slices in baking dish. Sprinkle with half of lemon juice, brown sugar and cinnamon. Dot with 1 tablespoon butter.

Place browned pork chops over pear slices. Sprinkle with salt and pepper. Layer remaining pears over chops, sprinkle with remaining lemon juice, brown sugar and cinnamon. Dot with 1 tablespoon butter. Pour sherry wine over all. Cover and bake at 350 degrees for 10 minutes. Uncover and continue baking 40-50 minutes or until chops are done. Serves 6.

RUTH'S PORK CHOPS

4 pork chops
1/4 cup margarine
3/4 cup crushed corn flakes
1 teaspoon salt
Dash of pepper
1 egg, well beaten
1/2 cup orange juice
1/4 teaspoon orange rind

Dip the pork chops in well-beaten egg. Put salt and pepper with crumbs and dip the pork chops in that mixture. Brown slowly in melted margarine. Place chops in a 9 x 9-inch casserole and pour the orange juice and rind over them. Cover with foil. Bake at 350 degrees for 30 minutes. Serves 4.

SAUCY PORK CHOPS

4 loin chops, 1-inch thick
Salt
Pepper
3 tablespoons chopped onion
Flour
2 tablespoons chopped green pepper
3/4 cup pineapple juice
1/2 cup catsup
5 drops Tabasco sauce

Season and flour pork chops. Brown in a heavy skillet. Add onions and green pepper. Combine pineapple juice, catsup and Tabasco sauce. Pour over meat. Cover and cook slowly about 1 hour or until chops are thoroughly done. Serves 4.

The Main Event

SWEET AND SOUR PORK CHOPS

4 center cut loin chops
2 tablespoons vegetable oil
3/4 cup finely chopped onion
1 clove garlic
1 1/2 tablespoons cornstarch
1 cup pineapple juice
3 tablespoons tomato juice
2 tablespoons vinegar
1 tablespoon soy sauce
1 tablespoon brown sugar
3/4 teaspoon curry powder
3/4 teaspoon pepper
3 small strips lemon peel
1/3 cup coarsely chopped walnuts

In large skillet brown chops on both sides in vegetable oil. Transfer to a casserole in which they lie flat. Pour off all but 2 tablespoons of fat in skillet and add onions and garlic. Sprinkle cornstarch over onions and stir in rest of ingredients, mixing well. Cook over low heat for 5 minutes, stirring constantly. Pour over pork chops. Cover and bake for 1 hour at 350 degrees. Sprinkle walnuts over top after the first half hour; cover and continue cooking. Serves 4.

SAUSAGE STUFFED PEPPERS

1 pound sausage
4 green peppers
1 teaspoon parsley flakes
1 clove garlic, crushed
1/4 cup celery, chopped
2 tablespoons grated sharp cheese
1 egg

SAUCE:
1 can (16-ounce) tomato sauce
1/2 teaspoon salt
1/2 teaspoon pepper
1/3 cup vinegar
1 tablespoon brown sugar
1/4 teaspoon cinnamon
1 tablespoon chili powder
1/4 cup onion, chopped
1/2 teaspoon cumin
1/4 teaspoon allspice
1/4 cup water

Blanch green peppers for 3-4 minutes, drain on paper towels. Combine sausage, parsley, garlic, celery, cheese and egg. Stuff peppers and place in greased baking dish.

Combine sauce ingredients and cover stuffed peppers. Bake in 325-degree oven for 45 minutes. Serves 4.

HAM

Preheat oven to 350 degrees. Wet ham down liberally with liquid smoke. Then pat dry mustard over it mostly on top. (If 1/2 ham, do not put anything on cut end.) Cook on rack, reduce heat to 325 degrees and put ham in oven. Cook 20 minutes per pound. Take out ham and raise oven to 400 degrees. For whole ham, mix with liquid smoke, then pat on sugar mixture and bake till glazed. Not over 20 minutes. Remove to tray and cover with foil. Serves 10-12.

❖❖❖

HAM BALLS

1 pound ground ham
1 1/2 pounds ground pork
2 cups bread crumbs
2 eggs
1 cup milk

SAUCE:
1 cup brown sugar
1/2 cup water
1/2 cup vinegar
1 teaspoon dry mustard
Simmer into a sauce

Shape this mixture into 30 balls.

Place balls in baking pan or chafing dish. Cover with sauce. Bake or simmer for 2 hours at 300 to 325 degrees.

Jan says, "These ham balls freeze well before you bake them."

UPSIDE DOWN HAM LOAF

1 1/2 pounds ground lean pork
1 1/2 pounds ground cured ham
2 eggs
1/2 cup fine bread crumbs
1 can Campbell's tomato soup
3 tablespoons butter
Brown sugar
8 slices pineapple
Maraschino cherries

In large mixing bowl, beat eggs slightly. Add soup and crumbs. Mix and blend meat in thoroughly. Using a 12-cup ring mold, melt 3 tablespoons of butter in ring. Sprinkle a small amount of brown sugar on butter. Lay 8 slices of drained pineapple in ring. Place maraschino cherries in middle of pineapple. Pack in ham loaf. Bake at 350 degrees approximately 1 1/2 hours. Drain off fat. Place plate on top and turn out. Garnish.

Jan says, "I like to make this a day ahead and refrigerate until ready to bake. This also freezes well wrapped until ready to bake. Time is 2 hours if put in oven frozen. When you buy the meat have your butcher grind the pork and ham together. Serves 8-10.

IMPOSSIBLE PIE

2 cups diced cooked chicken, turkey or ham
14-ounce can sliced mushrooms (drain)
1/4 cup diced onions (green or white)
1 cup shredded cheese
    Spread in bottom of greased pie plate, or 1-quart casserole.
Beat:
3 eggs
3/4 cup milk
3/4 cup Bisquick
1/2 teaspoon salt
Pinch of sage

Pour the egg, milk ingredients over other ingredients. Bake at 400 degrees for 35 minutes.

Jan says, "You can add broccoli or other fresh vegetables or you can make this with only vegetables." Serves 4.

The Main Event

LONNIE'S GREEK ROAST LEG OF LAMB

1 leg of lamb (5 to 6 pounds)
Salt and pepper
3 cloves of garlic, slivered
1 tablespoon oregano
1/2 teaspoon thyme
Juice of 1 lemon
1/2 cup olive oil
1/2 cup white wine
1/2 cup melted butter
1/2 cup white wine

Insert slivered garlic into slits in lamb and season with salt and pepper. Rub oregano and thyme on all sides of lamb; sprinkle with juice of lemon. Pour combined 1/2 cup of wine and olive oil over lamb and turn to coat. Marinate overnight. Roast lamb uncovered at 350 degrees for 2 hours or until correct temperature is reached using a meat thermometer. Baste frequently with 1/2 cup wine and melted butter, adding water to pan juices if needed.

EAST INDIAN LAMB CURRY

8 ounces oil
5 pounds boneless lamb, cut into 3/4-inch cubes
4 onions, chopped fine
4 celery ribs, chopped fine
15 pieces garlic, finely minced
2 green peppers, chopped fine
1 can (8-ounce) tomato puree, more if needed
1 cup chicken broth, more if needed
2 tablespoons paprika
4 tablespoons curry
2 tablespoons cumin
1 tablespoon white pepper
1 teaspoon tumeric
1/2 teaspoon mace
1/2 teaspoon nutmeg

BOUQUET GARNI:
4 bay leaves
3 small cinnamon sticks
10 cloves
1 teaspoon coriander
8 pieces cardamom seeds
Tie these ingredients in a cheesecloth bag.

Heat oil in deep casserole, brown lamb then brown onions, celery, garlic, green peppers. When browned, add tomato puree and chicken broth, then remaining ingredients, including Bouquet Garni.

Cover casserole and cook over low heat for 1 hour or until meat is tender. Serve over rice. Serves 12.

Jo says, "Serve with bowls of garnishes such as chopped peanuts or cashews, chutney, raisins, coconut. This is perfect for that special and different dinner."

BEV'S LAMB SHANK

1 lamb shank
3/4 cup coffee
3/4 cup bourbon
1 package onion soup mix

Put lamb shank into a plastic oven bag. Combine rest of ingredients and pour over lamb. Punch holes in bag, place in oven pan and bake at 250 degrees for 5 hours.

Jan says, "This is delicious and a very easy piece of meat." Serves 4-6.

The Main Event

GOURMET VEAL

4 tablespoons butter
1/2 pound fresh mushrooms, sliced
8 veal scallops 1/4-inch thick or
1 1/2 pounds veal, round or sirloin, cut 1/4 to
    1/2-inch thick
Salt and fresh ground pepper
Flour
3 tablespoons butter
1 tablespoon olive oil
2 tablespoons finely chopped shallots or
    scallions
1 clove garlic, minced
1/2 cup dry white wine
1/2 cup heavy cream
1 teaspoon lemon juice
3 tablespoons minced parsley

In a separate skillet, saute mushrooms in butter. Drain and set aside.

Season scallops with salt and pepper on both sides and dust lightly with flour. Heat butter and olive oil in a large skillet. Brown scallops on each side 5 to 6 minutes until golden. Remove from skillet. Stir in garlic and shallots, saute 1 minute.

Pour in wine and bring to boil over high heat, scraping any browned pieces that may cling to the pan. Boil wine 2 to 3 minutes until it has reduced to 1/4 cup, lower heat, stir in cream and simmer, stirring constantly until mixture thickens. Season with lemon juice, salt and pepper.

Add veal scallops and mushrooms to sauce and simmer to heat well. Remove scallops to a warm platter, pour sauce over them, garnish with parsley and serve while hot. Serves 4.

VARIATION ON VEAL

Prepare veal and mushrooms as in above recipe. Generously butter a large baking dish, arrange mushrooms on butter, cover with browned veal scallops and cover with Bechamel Sauce (see index). Sprinkle grated Parmesan cheese on top of sauce to cover evenly.

Place casserole in 400-degree oven until sauce begins to bubble, then turn on broiler to brown the Parmesan cheese. Serve immediately.

VEAL PARMESAN

3 tablespoons olive oil
1 pound thin veal cutlets
3 cloves garlic, finely minced
1 onion, minced
1 can (16-ounce) tomatoes
Salt and pepper
1 can (16-ounce) tomato sauce
1/4 teaspoon oregano
1/2 teaspoon parsley flakes
1 egg
1/4 cup packaged dried bread crumbs
1/2 cup grated Parmesan cheese
1/2 pound Mozzarella cheese

Cut veal into 8 pieces, about 4 1/2 x 2-inches in size. Heat 3 tablespoons of olive oil in saucepan over medium heat. Add garlic and onion and cook until lightly browned. Add tomatoes, salt, pepper, tomato sauce, oregano, parsley. Do not cover. Simmer about 30 minutes, stirring occasionally to break the tomatoes.

Beat egg lightly with a fork. Combine crumbs and 1/4 cup parmesan cheese onto a piece of wax paper. Dip each piece of veal in the beaten egg, then into the crumbs. Heat 1 tablespoon olive oil in a skillet over medium high heat. Add 3 pieces of the veal and cook until golden brown on both sides. Repeat process, using remaining 2 table-spoons of olive oil and cooking the rest of the veal.

Place browned pieces of veal in a 12 x 8 x 2-inch baking pan. Heat oven to 350 degrees. Cut mozzarella cheese into very thin slices. Pour about two-thirds of tomato sauce over veal in pan. Add mozzarella. Top with remaining tomato sauce. Sprinkle remaining Parmesan cheese over top. Bake uncovered 30 minutes. Serves 4.

RABBIT IN PEPPER SAUCE

1 young rabbit, cut into pieces
1 1/2 teaspoons salt
3 tablespoons butter
1 medium onion
4 cloves
1 1/2 cups port wine
12 peppercorns
1 tablespoon lemon juice
1 herb bouquet (parsley, thyme, bay leaf)
3 cups beef bouillon
2 tablespoons butter, melted
1 tablespoon flour

Rinse rabbit and pat dry. Rub with salt. Saute in 3 tablespoons butter until brown, approximately 20 to 30 minutes. Place in casserole with onion and cloves. Add 3/4 cup wine, peppercorns, lemon, herbs and stock. Cover and bake at 350 degrees for 2 to 2 1/2 hours. 1/2 hour before rabbit is finished, blend melted butter, flour and stir in the hot mixture into the casserole. Add the remaining wine and needed seasonings. Cover and cook the remaining 30 minutes. Place on a hot serving platter and cover with the sauce. Make a day ahead to blend the flavors. Serves 4.

The Main Event

Poultry

CHICKEN A L'ORANGE

3 pounds chicken breasts, split
6 tablespoons chopped shallots or scallions
1 teaspoon paprika
1/2 teaspoon dried crushed rosemary
1 teaspoon dried basil
1/2 teaspoon garlic salt
1/2 teaspoon white pepper
1 1/2 cups fresh orange juice
Fresh carrots, peeled and cut into strips

Wash and dry chicken. Mix scallions, herbs, garlic salt, pepper and paprika. Rub pieces of chicken with mixture to cover well. Place in shallow casserole. Place carrot strips around chicken and bake in 300-degree oven for 1 1/2 hours or until done. Baste frequently with orange juice until chicken is brown. Serves 4.

BREAST OF CHICKEN IN CREAM WITH FRESH APPLES

8 chicken breasts (6-8-ounce size), dusted
  with flour
8 tablespoons butter
4 tablespoons minced onion
8 peeled fresh apple rings, cut 1/2-inch thick
1 1/2 cups apple cider
1/2 cup brandy
2 cups heavy whipping cream
Salt and pepper

Saute chicken breasts in butter with onion over low heat. Poach the apple rings in the cider until soft. Add brandy to chicken and ignite. Add cider left from poaching apples. Cook at low temperature until chicken is tender, about 10 minutes. Add cream and continue cooking until sauce is thickened. Season to taste.

Place chicken on serving platter with a slice of apple on each piece. Pour sauce over all. Run under the broiler to brown. Serves 8.

LEMON HONEY BREAST OF CHICKEN

8 chicken breasts

SAUCE:
1/2 cup honey
Juice of 2 lemons
Grated rind of lemon
1/2 cup sherry
1/2 cup cooking oil
1 teaspoon paprika

Heat ingredients over water so honey mixes with the other ingredients. Marinate 8 breasts of chicken in sauce for several hours or over night. Be sure the chicken is salted. Heat oven to 400 degrees. Bake chicken for about 45 minutes, basting occasionally with sauce. Serve on platter with spiced crab apples and parsley. Serves 6-8.

CHICKEN CASSEROLE

1 chicken (3 1/2 to 4 pounds)
1 can mushroom soup
2 beaten eggs
2 cups chicken broth
4 cups crushed Ritz crackers
1 medium diced onion
1 1/2 cups cubed cheese
Small jar of pimento
1/2 can of ripe olives
Slivered almonds, if desired

Cook chicken until tender; cube (don't use the skin). Add rest of the ingredients. Mix well. Yes, that means the Ritz crackers, too. Put in flat pan and bake at 350 degrees for 40 minutes. Cut into 4-inch squares. This makes a great luncheon casserole. Will freeze well until baked. Serves 10-12.

❖❖❖

SESAME CHICKEN BREASTS

1 egg
1 tablespoon milk
1/2 cup dry bread crumbs
1/4 cup sesame seeds
1 tablespoon finely chopped fresh parsley
1 teaspoon salt
1/2 teaspoon garlic powder
1/8 teaspoon ground pepper
1 1/2 teaspoons mixed herbs
2 whole chicken breasts, skinned, boned and halved
2 tablespoons vegetable oil
2 tablespoons unsalted butter
Lemon wedges

Whisk egg and milk in small bowl. Combine bread crumbs and seasonings in shallow dish. Dip each chicken breast into beaten egg mixture, then in bread crumb mixture, pressing so crumbs will adhere. Place breaded breasts on waxed paper-lined plate, uncovered, and refrigerate for at least 10 minutes.

Heat oil and butter in large skillet over medium-high heat until bubbly. Brown chicken breasts 1 to 2 minutes per side in skillet. Lower heat to medium; continue to cook until tender, turning the breasts once 4 to 5 minutes per side. Remove breasts to warm platter; garnish with lemon wedges. Serve immediately. Serves 4.

CHICKEN CACCIATORE

1 cut up fryer (3-pounds)
Salt, pepper
1/4 cup olive oil
1/2 cup chopped onions
1 cup water
1 can tomato paste
1/2 cup dry white wine
1 teaspoon salt
1/4 teaspoon pepper
1/8 teaspoon thyme
1/4 teaspoon marjoram
1 medium-size bay leaf

Saute chicken pieces that have been salted and peppered in 1/4 cup olive oil. Remove chicken and add 1/2 cup chopped onions. Cook until golden and drain. Add rest of ingredients.

Simmer sauce until flavor goes through. Add chicken pieces and simmer 1 1/2 hours more. Serves 4.

CRUNCHY CHICKEN ROLL-UPS

8 to 10 split chicken breasts
1 stick (10-ounce) mild Cracker Barrel cheese
1 cup melted butter
1 package Good Seasons Italian salad dressing mix
1 package Pepperidge Farm dressing

Cut cheese into 8 to 10 equal sticks. Combine butter and salad dressing mix. Pound each split chicken breast. Dip each in butter mixture and press into dressing to coat well. Roll each piece of chicken around a cheese stick and secure with a toothpick.
Place breasts in well-greased casserole. Cover with foil. Bake 1 hour in 350-degree oven. Uncover and bake 20 minutes more.

VARIATION:

Leave out the cheese sticks. Follow recipe as above, leaving chicken breasts flat, baking skin side up. Be sure to separate in baking dish. Serves 8-10.

The Main Event

CHICKEN GARDEN SKILLET

3 to 4-pound fryer, or breasts, legs and thighs
Seasoned flour
1/4 cup fat
3/4 cup chicken broth
3/4 cup cooking sherry
1 package (10-ounce) frozen artichoke hearts
2 tomatoes, cut in wedges
1 onion, sliced
1/2 green pepper, sliced
Garlic salt and pepper to taste

Preheat electric skillet to 360 degrees. Dredge pieces of ready-to-cook frying chicken in seasoned flour. Brown slowly in fat, turning once. Reduce temperature to 230 degrees, pouring in 3/4 cup chicken broth and cooking sherry. Cover and cook 45 minutes. Push chicken to side, add artichokes, tomatoes, onion, green pepper. Sprinkle vegetables with salt and pepper. Cover and cook just until artichokes are done, about 15 minutes. Serves 4.

CHICKEN LIVERS

1/2 pound chicken livers
Cold water
1 stick butter, melted
1 tablespoon green pepper, minced
1 tablespoon parsley, chopped
1 tablespoon onion, chopped
1 pound mushrooms, washed and sliced
2 tablespoons flour
1/2 cup dry white wine
1/2 cup chicken stock
1 small bay leaf
1 tablespoon catsup
1 tablespoon Worcestershire sauce
Dash of pepper
Dash of nutmeg

Rinse livers in cold water and cut each into 3 pieces. Saute green pepper, parsley, onion and mushrooms in melted butter for 4 minutes. Add livers. Cook another 4 minutes, stirring frequently. Sprinkle flour over all. Add wine and chicken stock. Cook until thickened. Add rest of seasonings. Transfer to chafing dish. Serves 8-10.

BAKED CHICKEN IN MACADAMIA NUT CREAM

3 medium-size boiler chickens, split
Salt and pepper
1/2 cup finely ground macadamia nuts
1/2 cup flour
2 tablespoons butter
1 cup rich cream (or half-and-half)

Split chickens and season them with salt and pepper. Place them in a buttered baking pan. Combine the ground nuts with flour and sprinkle over the broilers. Put a teaspoon of soft butter on each half and cover them with 1 cup rich cream. Let stand in refrigerator overnight.

Preheat oven to 400 degrees. 45 minutes before serving, set the baking pan with the chicken in oven for about 15 minutes or until chickens are well browned. Reduce temperature to 350 degrees. Cover the pan tightly and continue to cook for another half hour. The cream will be absorbed by the chicken while baking. If necessary, add a small amount of cream during the baking period. Serves 6.

◆◆

CHICKEN MARENGO FOR TWELVE

3/4 cup white dry wine
1 cup sour cream
2 cans (10-ounce size) cream of chicken soup

5 cups cooked chicken, diced
1 package (14-ounce) medium noodles
Cook and drain noodles. Set aside.
1 large onion chopped
1/2 cup chopped green pepper
1 large can pitted ripe olives, sliced
1 large can artichoke hearts, each heart cut up
1/2 cup chopped pimento
1 cup Parmesan cheese

Combine ingredients for sauce. Stir well. Set aside.

In a large casserole layer half the noodles, then half of chicken, then half of other ingredients. Repeat a 2nd layer. Pour sauce over all and cover with 1 cup of Parmesan cheese. Bake at 350 degrees for 45 minutes.

PARMESAN CHICKEN

8 chicken breasts, boned
3 eggs
1/3 cup milk
2 cups seasoned bread crumbs
1/4 teaspoon garlic powder
1 teaspoon oregano
1 teaspoon basil
1 teaspoon chopped parsley
1/2 cup olive oil
2 jars (15-ounce size) Spaghetti Sauce or 4
   cups Jan's Tomato Sauce (see index)
8 thin slices Swiss cheese
8 thin slices Mozzarella cheese
Parmesan cheese

Pound chicken breasts flat. Combine bread crumbs, garlic powder, oregano, basil and parsley. Dip chicken breasts in beaten eggs and milk, roll in bread crumb mixture and saute in olive oil. Layer bottom of casserole with sauce, then chicken breasts, then cover each with a slice of Swiss and a slice of Mozzarella. Pour remaining sauce on top and sprinkle with Parmesan cheese and parsley. Bake 30 minutes in a 350-degree oven.
   Jo says, "Substituting veal cutlets for the chicken and following this recipe will give you a delicious Veal Parmesan." Serves 8.

CHICKEN IN THE SACK

1 fryer (3-pounds)

SAUCE:
3 tablespoons catsup
2 tablespoons vinegar
1 tablespoon lemon juice
2 tablespoons Worcestershire Sauce
4 tablespoons water
2 tablespoons melted butter
3 tablespoons brown sugar
1 teaspoon salt
1 teaspoon dry mustard
1 teaspoon chili powder
1 teaspoon paprika
1/2 teaspoon cayenne pepper

Simmer sauce for 20 minutes. Dip chicken pieces in sauce; then take 2 brown sacks that have been greased very well, put chicken in sack, adding the remaining sauce. Tie the ends of the sacks with string securely. Put in broiler pan and bake 15 minutes at 450 degrees and then 1 hour 45 minutes longer at 350 degrees. Serves 4-5.

The Main Event

PARTY CHICKEN FOR EIGHT

8 good size chicken breasts, boned
8 slices bacon
1 package (jar) chipped beef
1 can undiluted mushroom soup
1/2 pint sour cream

Wrap each breast in bacon. Cover bottom of flat dish with chipped beef. Arrange breasts on chipped beef. Mix soup and sour cream and pour over chicken. Bake at 275 to 300 degrees for 3 hours, uncovered.

Jan says, "This is a great company dish. It may be made 1 or 2 days ahead and kept covered in the refrigerator."

CHICKEN ROCOCO

1 stick (10-ounce) Mild Cracker Barrel cheese
4 chicken breasts (skinned and boned)
2 eggs beaten
3/4 cup bread crumbs
Melted margarine
2 chicken bouillon cubes
1 cup boiling water
1/2 cup chopped onions
1/2 cup chopped green pepper
Margarine
2 tablespoons flour
1/2 teaspoon thyme
1/2 teaspoon sage
1 teaspoon salt and pepper
2 cups cooked white rice
1 cup cooked wild rice
1 cup sliced fresh mushrooms

Cut cheese into 8 equal sticks. Cut chicken breasts in 2 pieces. Pound each piece out and roll around cheese stick, secure with a toothpick. Dip in beaten egg, then in bread crumbs and brown in melted margarine.

Cook rice. Dissolve bouillon cubes in water. Saute onions and green pepper in a little margarine until tender. Add flour, seasonings and bouillon. Cook until thick. Add rice and mushrooms and pour into a buttered 10 x 8-inch baking dish, top with chicken and bake at 400 degrees for 20 minutes. Serves 8.

CHICKEN AND STUFFING SCALLOP

1 package (8-ounce) (3 1/2 cups) herb-seasoned stuffing (Pepperidge Farm)
3 cups cubed chicken (you may use canned)
1/2 cup butter or margarine
1/2 cup flour
1/4 teaspoon salt
Pepper
4 cups chicken broth
6 slightly beaten eggs
1 recipe Pimento-Mushroom sauce

Prepare stuffing according to package. Use the directions for dry stuffing. Spread in a 13 x 9 x 2-inch dish. Top with layer of chicken. In a large saucepan melt butter, blend in flour and seasonings. Add cool broth. Cook and stir until mixture thickens. Stir small amount of hot mixture into eggs, return to hot mixture; pour over chicken. Bake in slow oven (325 degrees) for 40 to 45 minutes, or until the knife comes out clean. Let stand 5 minutes to cut. Cut in squares and serve with the Pimento-Mushroom sauce. Serves 10-12.

PIMENTO-MUSHROOM SAUCE

Mix 1 can condensed cream of mushroom soup, 1/4 cup milk, 1 cup dairy sour cream and 1/4 cup chopped pimentos. Heat and stir until hot.

Jan says, "This recipe serves 12 people and it is a great dish for a luncheon or dinner. Freezes well so you may make it ahead."

‹‹

STIR-FRY CHICKEN

2 whole chicken breasts
2 teaspoons cornstarch
3 tablespoons oil
2 tablespoons sherry
6 big mushrooms
1 can water chestnuts, diced
1/2 cup bamboo shoots, diced
1 medium green pepper, diced
3/4 cup celery, diced
6 green onions, chopped
2 to 3 tablespoons Kikkoman Sweet and
   Sour sauce

Skin and bone chicken breasts. Dice chicken and put chicken in sherry and cornstarch. Heat the oil in wok or skillet over high flame. Stir-fry chicken about 3 minutes until meat whitens. Do not brown. Add the remaining vegetables and stir-fry thoroughly. When still crisp, add Sweet and Sour sauce and mix thoroughly. You may garnish with slivered toasted almonds before serving. Serves 4-5.

SWEET AND SOUR CHICKEN

1 3-pound fryer
1 can (3 1/2-ounce) chunk pineapple
1 cup sugar
2 tablespoons cornstarch
3/4 cup cider vinegar
1 tablespoon soy sauce
1/4 teaspoon ginger
1 chicken bouillon cube
2 green peppers, cut into 1/2-inch squares
1/2 cup celery strips

Flour and brown chicken. Meanwhile drain pineapple juice to measure 1 1/4 cups. If not enough juice you may add water. Blend in sugar, cornstarch, vinegar, soy sauce, chicken cube, ginger and boil for 2 minutes.

Place chicken in casserole dish and pour sauce over it and top with pineapple, pepper and celery strips. Bake 30 to 40 minutes in a 350-degree oven. Serves 4.

ANN'S CHICKEN TETRAZZINI

5 pounds boned chicken breasts, stewed
1/2 pound spaghetti
1/2 cup green pepper, chopped
1/2 cup chopped onion
2 cans (4 1/2-ounce) mushrooms, whole
   (or fresh ones)
2 sticks margarine
2/3 cup flour
4 cups milk
1 teaspoon salt
1/2 pound American cheese
1 cup cracker crumbs (Hi Ho)
Melted butter

Cut stewed chicken in large bite-size pieces. Cool broth and remove fat, strain. Keep 1 quart. Cook spaghetti in broth until liquid is almost entirely absorbed. Saute green pepper, onion and mushrooms in margarine. Blend in flour. Gradually add milk and 1 teaspoon salt to sauteed mixture. Stir constantly until thickens. Stir in cheese until melted. Combine chicken, spaghetti and sauteed ingredients in a greased 9 x 13-inch casserole. Top with crushed buttered cracker crumbs. Bake in 350-degree oven for 30 minutes or until it is hot in the center of casserole. Serves 10-12.

GLAZED CORNISH HENS

1 cup celery, chopped
1 cup onion, chopped
1 cup mushrooms, sliced
1/2 cup chopped pecans
1/2 cup butter or margarine
1 cup water
1 package (7-ounce) stuffing mix
1 1/2 cups cranberries
3 tablespoons sugar
1/2 cup chopped parsley
Grated peel of 1 orange
6 cornish hens
Salt and pepper to taste
1/2 cup marmalade mixed with
    1/4 cup soy sauce

In large skillet, saute celery, onions, mushrooms and pecans in butter for 5 minutes. Add water and bring to a boil. Stir in stuffing, cranberries, sugar, parsley and orange peel, stirring to blend. Wash and dry hens; sprinkle with salt and pepper. Stuff hens and skewer openings. Roast at 350 degrees for 45 minutes. Spread with marmalade mixture and roast another 15 minutes, or until legs can be moved up and down easily. Serves 6.

DUCK BREAST

MARINATE - 1 hour to overnight in brandy and pepper
DIP - in flour
GRILL - in hot skillet with Crisco, 4 minutes on each side
FLAME - with Triple Sec or Cointreau
PUT DUCK - in warm oven for 10 minutes to set up
SERVE
Jan says, "Thank you Josef Auerbach for sharing your duck breast recipe."

CURRIED TURKEY BREAST

1 turkey breast (4 to 6 pounds)
1 tablespoon curry powder
1 tablespoon mixed herbs or
    1 teaspoon basil
    1/2 teaspoon thyme
    1 teaspoon oregano
    1/2 teaspoon marjoram
1 tablespoon garlic salt
1 teaspoon paprika
1 cup gin
1 cup water
2 onions, cut in wedges
3 carrots, cut in strips
2 ribs celery, cut in large pieces
1 unpeeled orange, cut in fourths

If turkey breast is frozen, defrost, wash and dry. Mix curry powder, herbs, garlic salt and paprika. Rub mixture inside and outside the turkey. Place in roaster with vegetables and orange. Roast uncovered at 350 degrees for 3 hours or until tender. Baste often with gin and water. Serve sliced thin.
    Serves 4-6.

The Main Event

ROAST TURKEY

Wash bird inside and outside. Dry well and rub the inside with salt. Fill neck cavity with stuffing. Fasten neck skin to back with skewer or pin then lace shut. Tie leg ends to tail. Brush entire bird with butter or margarine. Place bird on rack with breast side up. Cover with cloth dipped in melted butter or margarine. You may use foil instead of cloth. Remove the foil the last 20 minutes so bird will brown. Baste with a baster off and on during cooking.

CHART FOR ROASTING TURKEY

8 to 10 pounds	325 degrees	3 to 3 1/2 hours
10 to 14 pounds	325 degrees	3 1/2 to 4 hours
14 to 18 pounds	300 degrees	4 to 4 1/2 hours
18 to 20 pounds	300 degrees	4 1/2 to 6 hours
Half turkey	325 degrees	25 to 30 minutes per pound

To test the turkey when done, press the fleshy part of drumstick. It is done when the meat feels soft. Move drumstick up and down. If it breaks away it is done.

BAKED PHEASANT, QUAIL OR DOVE

Flour
Butter or margarine
1 can cream of chicken soup
1/2 cup apple cider
1 tablespoon Worcestershire sauce
3/4 teaspoon salt
1/3 cup onions, chopped fine
1 minced garlic clove
1 can mushrooms
Paprika

Roll fowl in flour and brown lightly in a little butter or margarine. Put in casserole depending on how many birds. Blend ingredients and pour over the birds. Bake 2 hours in a 325-degree oven. Baste with sauce occasionally. This recipe may be doubled.

BAKED QUAIL OR PHEASANT WITH WHITE GRAPES

1 pheasant or 6-8 quail
4 tablespoons butter or margarine
Salt, pepper and flour
1 can chicken stock
2 cans golden mushroom soup
1/2 cup dry sherry, white wine or vermouth
1 small onion, chopped fine
1 can mushrooms
Paprika
30 seedless grapes
1/4 cup sherry
1/4 cup chicken stock
Uncle Ben's rice

Season birds with salt, pepper and paprika. Flour lightly and brown in butter. After browning, set birds aside and saute onions in butter. Add chicken stock, mushroom soup, wine. Heat and pour over the birds that have been put in a roasting pan or casserole. Cover and bake 2 to 3 hours in a 300-degree oven.

While the quail or pheasant are roasting, gently heat about 30 Thompson seedless grapes or white seeded grapes in 1/4 cup sherry and 1/4 cup chicken stock. Remove grapes with a slotted spoon. Add with drained mushrooms to quail or pheasant and roast 5 more minutes. Serve with Uncle Ben's rice using extra gravy to pour over rice. Serves 2-4.

The Main Event

SHERRY QUAIL

6 quail
Green seedless grapes for stuffing
3/4 cup butter
1 1/2 cups cream sherry
2 teaspoons butter paste
1/2 pint whipping cream
Salt and pepper
1 teaspoon parsley flakes
1 teaspoon Worcestershire sauce
1 cup chicken stock or soup

Melt 3/4 cup butter. Add the stuffed quail and brown. Add 1 cup sherry. Cover and cook in oven for 20 minutes at 350 degrees. Remove quail and excess butter, add in skillet 1/2 pint cream, 2 teaspoons butter paste. Add salt, pepper, Worcestershire sauce, parsley, chicken soup and 1/2 cup of sherry. Bring to a simmer point and add quail to the sauce with breast down and simmer 5 minutes covered.

BUTTER PASTE:
2 tablespoons flour, 2 tablespoons melted butter. Mix together until blended.
Serves 2-4.

Seafood

FILLET OF FISH AMANDINE

6 fish fillets
Salt and pepper
Flour
1 1/2 cups butter
1 cup almonds, sliced
1 lemon

Wipe fillets with a damp cloth. Sprinkle with salt and pepper and dredge in flour. Saute in 1/2 cup melted butter until done but not too brown. Place fillets in a pan. Mix almonds and 1 cup melted butter. Heat until almonds are light brown. Pour almond mixture over fillets and sprinkle with lemon juice. Place in a 375-degree oven for 3 to 5 minutes or until nicely browned. Serve immediately. Serves 6.

FILLET OF FISH COCONUT GROVE

2 pounds fish fillets — sole, flounder, grouper, yellowtail, skinned and boned
Salt and pepper
1 cup flour
2 ripe bananas
1 cup butter, melted
1/2 cup vermouth
1 cup finely chopped macadamia nuts (optional)

Wash fillets and dry with paper towels. Season with salt and pepper and dredge in flour to coat well. Place in a buttered baking dish. Peel bananas and cut in halves or quarters and place on top of each fillet. Melt butter and add vermouth and pour over fillets. Bake at 450 degrees for 10 to 15 minutes or until fish flakes when tested. Baste frequently. Before serving spoon pan juices over fillets and sprinkle chopped nuts on each fillet if desired. Serves 4.

✦✦✦

FILLET OF FISH FLORENTINE

3 packages frozen chopped spinach
3 tablespoons flour
2 cups sour cream
1/2 cup finely chopped green onions, using tops
2 tablespoons lemon juice
2 teaspoons salt
2 pounds fish fillets, sole, flounder, snapper, grouper
2 tablespoons butter
Paprika
Butter

Cook spinach according to package directions and drain. Blend sour cream, flour, onions, lemon juice and salt. Combine mixture with spinach and spread half over bottom of shallow, greased 9 x 13 x 2-inch baking dish. Arrange fillets on top of spinach mixture. You may overlap them if necessary. Dot with butter. Spread remaining spinach and sour cream mixture over fish.

Bake at 375 degrees for about 25 minutes or until fish is flaky when tested with a fork.

This dish can be refrigerated overnight before cooking. Serves 4-6.

FISH FILLET PARMESAN

2 pounds fish fillets, fresh or frozen
1/4 cup grated Parmesan cheese
1 tablespoon lemon juice
1 tablespoon grated onion
1/2 teaspoon salt
Dash of Tabasco
Paprika
Chopped parsley
1 cup sour cream

Cut fillets into serving-size portions. Place in a single layer in a well-greased baking dish (9 x 12 x 2-inch).

Combine remaining ingredients except paprika. Spread sour cream mixture over fish. Sprinkle with paprika. Bake in a 350-degree oven for 25 to 30 minutes or until fish flakes easily when tested with a fork. Garnish with parsley. Serves 6.

FISH FILLET SUPREME

6 fish fillets
6 tablespoons butter
Salt and pepper to taste
8 tablespoons shallots, minced
7 tomatoes, peeled, seeded and chopped
3 cups white wine
2 cups heavy cream
3 tablespoons parsley, minced

In a baking dish, make a single layer of the fillets. Dot the fish with butter and season with salt and pepper. Sprinkle the shallots and 6 chopped tomatoes over the fillets, then add the wine. Bake at 350 degrees for 15 minutes. Remove fish from oven. Drain off the cooking liquid to a saucepan and over high heat reduce the liquid to 1/2 cup. Lower heat and gradually add the cream, stirring constantly. Heat sauce, but do not boil. Add parsley, and more salt and pepper if necessary. Pour sauce over the fillets and garnish each one with the remaining chopped tomato. Place under the broiler until the sauce is browned. Remove and serve immediately. Serves 6.

FISH FILLET VERONIQUE

2 pounds snapper, sole, flounder or other fish
   fillets, fresh or frozen
1 can (8 3/4-ounces) seedless green grapes
2 tablespoons butter or margarine
1/2 cup chopped onion
1 pound fresh sliced mushrooms, sauteed in
   4 tablespoons butter (optional)
1/4 cup dry white wine
3/4 cup light cream
1 egg yolk
1 tablespoon flour
1/4 teaspoon salt
Dash nutmeg
Paprika

If using frozen fish, let thaw in refrigerator. Sprinkle both sides with salt and pepper. Roll fillets and secure with toothpicks. Drain grapes, reserving liquid. Cook onion until tender in melted butter. Add fish rolls. Pour in wine and reserved grape liquid. Cover and simmer 8 to 10 minutes or until fish flakes when forked.

Remove fish to serving platter, and remove toothpicks. Combine cream, egg yolk, flour, salt, and nutmeg. Gradually add liquid to hot pan and cook and stir until thick. Taste and correct seasonings if necessary. Stir in grapes and mushrooms, and pour over fish. Sprinkle with paprika. Serves 6.

HERB–STUFFED FISH

2 pounds red snapper, or other whole fish,
   dressed with pocket for stuffing
Salt, pepper
1 cup herb-seasoned stuffing mix
2 teaspoons snipped parsley
1/2 teaspoon grated lemon rind
1/2 teaspoon basil leaves
1/8 teaspoon garlic powder
2 tablespoons melted butter
1 tablespoon lemon juice
1 small onion, sliced thin

Place length of Heavy Duty Reynolds Wrap in pan. Salt and pepper fish, cavity and outside. Prepare stuffing mix as package directs, stir in next 4 ingredients. Stuff cavity of fish. Combine butter and lemon juice; pour over fish. Top with onion. Bring 2 sides of foil up over fish, fold down loosely in a series of locked folds. Fold short ends up and over. Cook at 350 degrees for 50 minutes or until fish flakes easily. Serves 2.

BAR-B-Q LOBSTER TAILS

4 medium lobster tails
4 tablespoons melted butter
2 teaspoons lemon juice
1/8 teaspoon chili powder
1/2 cup mayonnaise
1/4 teaspoon dried dill
2 to 3 teaspoons lemon juice

In saucepan, combine mayonnaise and dill, add lemon juice until desired consistency for basting. Place on edge of grill to warm.

Cut through lobster shells to spread tails open butterfly-style to expose meat on top. In a small bowl, combine butter, 2 teaspoons lemon juice, chili powder and brush on lobster meat. Place on grill, meaty side down, broil over hot coals for 5 minutes, turn tails meaty side up. Brush again with sauce, continue broiling 5 to 10 minutes or until meat has lost its transparency. Serve immediately with Dill Mayonnaise. Serves 4.

The Main Event

SALMON CROQUETTES

1 can (8-ounce) salmon
1/2 stick butter or margarine
1/4 cup flour
3/4 cup cooked rice
3/4 cup milk or 3/4 cup of Pet milk
1 teaspoon chopped parsley
Salt, pepper and lemon juice according to
   taste
1 egg
1 tablespoon peanut oil. You may use salad
   oil.
Flour
Bread crumbs

Strain salmon well. Debone, skin and mash the salmon and set aside. Melt butter in a heavy pan and blend in flour. Add milk and salmon juice. Cook stirring constantly until sauce is very thick. Add rice and salmon. Remove from heat and mix well, stirring in parsley, salt, pepper and lemon juice. Put in a bowl, cover and chill.

Make mixture into croquettes. Beat egg with salad oil or peanut oil. Dip croquettes in flour, then egg mixture, and then in the bread crumbs. Coat well. Chill for several hours.

Heat enough grease in small heavy pan or deep skillet to cover the croquettes. They will brown quickly. Drain on paper. Keep warm until they all are cooked. Serve with lemon wedges.

Makes 12-14.

WHOLE POACHED FRESH SALMON

1 8 to 9 pound fresh salmon
1 recipe court bouillon — measure water to
   completely cover salmon. For each gallon
   of water, prepare 1 recipe court bouillon,
   as follows:
1 carrot, chopped fine
2 small onions, cut into pieces
2 tablespoons tarragon vinegar
2 tablespoons salt
4 cloves
1 cup dry white wine
4 sprigs parsley
2 bay leaves
4 peppercorns

Combine all ingredients except salmon and bring to a boil. Simmer for 1/2 hour, strain and cool.

Wash salmon. Wrap it in a triple thickness of cheesecloth, and sew it so that it fits the fish snugly, leaving extra cheesecloth on the ends for handles. Lay fish in a large roaster and cover with court bouillon. Let water boil over fish, then reduce heat. Simmer slowly 10 minutes per pound. Fish is done when it flakes. Cover pan for 1 hour after removing it from heat. Then uncover and let it come to room temperature. When cool, remove cheesecloth by slitting it and removing from the top side of the fish. Remove skin and any dark flesh. Turn fish gently onto platter and do the same on the other side. Chill in refrigerator 24 hours lightly covered with foil. Garnish with cucumbers, cherry tomatoes, lemon wedges and fresh dill springs, or bibb lettuce. Serve with Cucumber Sauce. Serves 12-14.

CUCUMBER SAUCE

6 cucumbers
3 cups heavy cream
1 1/2 tablespoons sugar
1 teaspoon salt
1/4 teaspoon white pepper
1/2 to 3/4 cup white vinegar as desired

Pare, remove seeds, chop, drain cucumbers. Beat cream until stiff, seasoned with sugar, salt and pepper. Add vinegar and cucumber. Pile lightly into a bowl.

The Main Event

JUDY'S SEAFOOD CASSEROLE

1 can (6-ounce) tuna
1 can (6 1/2-ounce) crab
1 can (6 1/2-ounce) shrimp (rinse shrimp
  in cold water, drain)
1 1/2 cups Minute rice
1 cup grated Cheddar cheese
1 can mushroom soup
1/2 cup milk
1/2 green pepper, diced
1/2 small onion, diced
1 small can mushrooms
Potato chips

Mix all ingredients together and put in casserole. Top with crushed potato chips. Bake at 350 degrees for about 40 minutes. (If you want to make ahead of time and freeze, do not add potato chips until ready to bake.) Serves 6.

Splurging on shrimp for the holidays? When buying shrimp, remember that one pound of raw, headless, unpeeled shrimp yields about 1/2 pound cooked, peeled and deveined shrimp. Raw shrimp known as "green shrimp" can be cleaned before or after cooking.

STIR-FRIED SHRIMP WITH ASPARAGUS

1 pound raw shrimp

MARINADE:
1/2 egg white, slightly beaten
2 teaspoons water chestnut powder
1 tablespoon sherry
1 teaspoon salt

3 cups slant-cut asparagus or broccoli, or
  snow peas
6 scallions
2 cloves garlic
2 teaspoons ginger root, minced
1/4 cup almonds

BINDER:
2 teaspoon water chestnut powder
1 to 2 teaspoons hot sauce
1 tablespoon sherry

1 tablespoon peanut oil
1/2 teaspoon salt
2 1/2 tablespoons peanut oil
1/3 cup chicken stock

Shell, devein, split, wash, drain and dry shrimp. Marinate shrimp in egg white, 2 teaspoons water chestnut powder, 1 tablespoon sherry, and 1 teaspoon salt. Refrigerate for at least 1/2 hour, up to 12 hours. Slant-cut asparagus in 1 1/2-inch pieces. Chop scallions. Mince garlic and ginger. Roast almonds. Mix binder.

Place wok over high flame for 30 seconds. Add 1 tablespoon oil and heat for 20 seconds or until oil is very hot but not smoking. Add asparagus and stir-fry for 2 to 3 minutes. Add 1/2 teaspoon salt and mix well. Empty asparagus into a heated serving dish. Heat remaining 2 1/2 tablespoons oil in wok over high flame. Add scallions, garlic and ginger; stir-fry 1/2 minute. Add shrimp to wok and stir-fry for 2 to 3 minutes or until almost pink. Again add asparagus, pour in stock and bring to a boil. Restir binder and add it with one hand while stir-frying with the other until sauce has thickened. Empty contents into heated dish and sprinkle with almonds. Serves 4.

SHRIMP AND ARTICHOKE CASSEROLE

2 pounds frozen shrimp
1 No. 2 can artichoke hearts

2 tablespoons butter
3 tablespoons flour
1 pint half-and-half
1/2 teaspoon paprika
1/4 teaspoon red pepper
1 tablespoon catsup
1 tablespoon lemon juice
1 tablespoon Worcestershire sauce
3 tablespoons sherry
1 cup sharp grated cheese
1 teaspoon hot mustard

Boil, shell, and devein shrimp. Place shrimp in greased baking dish with quartered artichoke hearts. Pour over them the following sauce:

Make sauce of butter, flour, cream, paprika and red pepper. Cook until thick. Then add remaining ingredients. If mixture is too thin, thicken with cornstarch to suit. Pour sauce over shrimp and artichokes and add a little grated cheese on top. Heat in moderate oven. Serves 6.

"BETTER WEAR BIBS" SHRIMP

6 pounds shrimp
8 tablespoons fresh ground pepper
1 pound butter
1 pound margarine
Juice of 4 lemons
1 package Good Seasons Italian
  dressing mix

Place shrimp, with shells on, in a 2-inch-deep baking dish. Cover with the fresh ground pepper, butter and margarine in chunks, Italian dressing mix and lemon juice. Bake uncovered in a 500-degree oven for 10 minutes; pour off the melted butter, margarine, lemon juice mixture and reserve as a dip for the shrimp. Return the shrimp to oven for another 2–3 minutes, until the tails are crisp.
Serves 8.
Jo says, "This is a great patio dish. Be sure to tell your guests to wear clothes that wash, and put newspapers on the table."

SHRIMP ELEGANTE

3 pounds fresh or frozen shrimp in shells or 50
  large shrimp
Boiling water
2 packages (6-ounce size) frozen pea pods
3 chicken bouillon cubes
2 1/2 cups boiling water
1/2 cup sliced green onion with tops
3 tablespoons soy sauce
1 teaspoon salt
1/4 cup cold water
1/4 cup cornstarch
4 medium tomatoes, cut into eighths

Thaw frozen shrimp. Peel and devein shrimp, set aside. Pour a little boiling water over pea pods and carefully break apart with fork; drain immediately and set aside. In large saucepan dissolve bouillon cubes in the 2 1/2 cups boiling water; add shrimp, green onions, soy sauce and salt. Return to boiling; cook for 3 minutes, stirring occasionally. Slowly blend cold water into cornstarch, stir into shrimp mixture. Cook stirring constantly until the mixture is thick and bubbly. Add tomatoes and pea pods. Cook until tomatoes are heated through, about 3 minutes. Serves 12.

The Main Event

DEEP-FRIED BUTTERFLY SHRIMP

1 pound large-size shrimp (15 to 20)
1 teaspoon ginger
1 teaspoon minced garlic
1 tablespoon sherry
1 teaspoon salt
Oil for deep frying
1/2 cup flour
1/3 cup cornstarch
1/2 teaspoon garlic powder
1 teaspoon soy sauce
1/2 to 2/3 cup cold flat beer
1 tablespoon peanut oil
2 teaspoons baking powder
1/2 teaspoon salt

Prepare shrimp by butterflying but leaving the tail intact. (Follow procedure as directed in Scampi Livornese.) Prepare marinade by combining ginger, garlic, sherry and salt. Dip each shrimp into the marinade, one at a time on the split side only. Refrigerate at least 1 hour and up to 12 hours, until ready to fry.

Prepare batter by placing flour, cornstarch, garlic powder and salt in a bowl. Mix and add the soy sauce and oil. Mix again. Gradually add the cold beer. Mix in the baking powder last.

Heat oil in wok or large skillet until it reaches the temperature of 350 degrees.

Take each shrimp by the tail, dip it into the batter and put into hot oil. After 15-30 seconds the shrimp should be brown. It will puff up and float to the surface immediately upon immersion into the hot oil. Turn and fry another 15-30 seconds or a bit longer. Do not fry more than 6 at a time. Repeat procedure until all shrimp have been fried.

Drain well on paper toweling. Serve immediately with sauces. (See Seafood Cocktail Sauce and Ft. Lauderdale Mustard Sauce in index.) Serves 4.

SCAMPI LIVORNESE

12 large raw shrimp
Flour, salt, pepper
1/2 cup butter
1 large clove garlic, chopped fine
1/2 cup sweet sherry
1/2 cup heavy cream
1/8 teaspoon cayenne pepper, scant
1 tablespoon fresh parsley, minced

Peel shrimp and butterfly them. To do this, remove the back vein, then cut the shrimp from the underside almost through to the back, not cutting completely through. Turn shrimp over and make a few vertical cuts. Wash, drain and dry shrimp well. Dredge shrimp in flour, seasoned with salt and pepper.

Cook lightly floured shrimp in hot butter until lightly brown. Remove shrimp to warm platter. Add garlic to butter, then add cream, sherry, cayenne pepper and fresh parsley. Do not boil. Stir and add shrimp to mixture, so they are well covered with sauce. Serve immediately, with lemon wedges and lightly sprinkled with paprika. Garnish with sprig of fresh parsley.

Delicious as an appetizer or entree. Serves 4.

The Main Event

PASTA SCAMPI SAUCE

3 tablespoons butter
2 tablespoons minced garlic
1 1/2 pounds fresh shrimp, shelled and deveined
1/4 cup dry white wine
1/2 cup tomato sauce or Ragu marinara
1 1/4 cups heavy cream
1/2 teaspoon basil
1/2 teaspoon oregano
1/4 teaspoon cayenne pepper
2 egg yolks
Salt and pepper
2 tablespoons finely minced parsley
Thin spaghetti

Melt butter in skillet. Add garlic and cook, stirring constantly, for 1 minute. Add shrimp and cook over medium-high heat, stirring constantly, until shrimp are bright pink on both sides. Add white wine and tomato sauce and cook for 1 minute. Blend in 1 cup heavy cream, basil, oregano, and cayenne. Beat egg yolks with remaining 1/4 cup cream and add to sauce, stirring over medium heat until sauce thickens. Do not boil. Season to taste with salt and white pepper.

Spoon over hot buttered pasta, sprinkle with parsley. Serves 4-6.

SHRIMP ETOUFFE

1 1/2 pounds fresh or frozen shelled shrimp
2 tablespoons all-purpose flour
1/4 cup butter or margarine
1/4 cup finely chopped celery
2 tablespoons sliced green onion with tops
1 clove garlic, minced
1 cup water
2 tablespoons snipped parsley
1 teaspoon salt
Dash cayenne
Hot cooked rice

Thaw frozen shrimp. In saucepan cook flour in butter until golden brown, about 5 minutes; stirring often. Stir in celery, onion and garlic; cook and stir for 3 to 4 minutes. Add water, parsley, salt, cayenne and shrimp. Simmer covered for 15 minutes. Serve over hot cooked rice. Serves 6.

SEAFOOD IN CHEESE SAUCE

1 pound cooked shrimp
1 pound cooked crab meat
1/2 cup butter
1/2 cup flour
4 cups milk
1 teaspoon salt
1 can (6-ounce) sliced mushrooms, drained
1/4 cup celery, chopped fine
1/4 cup green pepper, chopped fine
1 teaspoon Beau Monde
2 teaspoons dried parsley
1/2 teaspoon Worcestershire sauce
1/4 teaspoon prepared mustard
1/3 cup green onions, chopped fine
1/2 cup black olives, chopped
1 1/2 teaspoons chopped pimento
4 cups grated sharp Cheddar cheese

Melt butter, stir in flour; mix well. Remove from heat and add milk, stirring until smooth. Return to heat and cook until thick. Stir in the next 11 ingredients. Mix well. Stir in fish and 3 cups cheese. Cook over very low heat until cheese is melted. Put in a shallow casserole and top with 1 cup cheese. Refrigerate until serving time. Bake in a 350-degree oven for 25 to 30 minutes. Serve with rice.

Jo says, "You may wish to substitute a little sherry for some of the milk in the white sauce. Adjust seasonings to individual taste."

Serves 12-14.

The Main Event

SHRIMP THERMIDOR

3/4 pound cooked shrimp
1/2 cup sliced mushrooms
1/4 cup butter, melted
1/4 cup flour
1 teaspoon salt
1/2 teaspoon dry mustard
Dash cayenne pepper
2 cups milk
Grated Parmesan cheese
Paprika

Cut large shrimp in half. Cook mushrooms in butter for 5 minutes. Blend in flour and seasonings. Add milk gradually and cook until thick, stirring constantly. Stir in shrimp. Place in 6 well-greased individual shells or 6-ounce custard cups. Sprinkle with cheese and paprika. Bake in 400-degree oven for 10 minutes or until cheese browns. Serves 6.

SNAPPER NORMANDE

6 snapper fillets, 6 to 8 ounces each
Salt, pepper and flour
4 tablespoons sweet butter
2 tablespoons shallots, chopped
1/2 cup Calvados or Apple Jack brandy
1 cup creme fraiche (see index)

Salt, pepper, and flour the fish. Saute in 3 tablespoons butter. Transfer to heated plate and hold in a warm oven. Add more butter if necessary. When all fish is cooked, saute the shallots in no more than 1 tablespoon of butter. When cooked, but not brown, pour in the Calvados. Deglaze pan, reducing Calvados by no more than half. Add creme fraiche and reduce slightly. Do not boil too long or it will separate and look curdled. The sauce should be thin. Either brush fish or pass sauce separately. A few springs of watercress and a few lemon wedges make an attractive garnish.
Serves 6.

FILLET OF SOLE GOURMET

1 package (6-ounce) white, brown or wild rice mix
1 package (10-ounce) frozen asparagus or 1 1/2 pounds fresh
1 cup finely chopped celery
3 tablespoons butter
3 tablespoons flour
1 cup milk
1/2 teaspoon salt
1 teaspoon Worcestershire sauce
1 tablespoon fresh lemon juice
1 cup sour cream (room temperature)
6 sole fillets (1 1/2 to 2 pounds)
1/2 fresh lemon
2 tablespoons Parmesan cheese
2 tablespoons sliced almonds, lightly toasted

Cook rice according to package directions. Spoon into baking dish. Cook asparagus according to directions. Drain.

Saute celery in butter. Stir in flour and cook 1 minute, add milk all at once and cook, stirring until thickened. Add salt, Worcestershire and lemon juice. Empty sour cream into medium bowl, gradually add hot sauce, stirring constantly. Sprinkle fillets lightly with juice of half of lemon, salt to taste. Roll each around 2 or 3 asparagus spears. Arrange roll-up on top of rice. Spoon sour cream sauce over fish, sprinkle with cheese and almonds. Bake at 350 degrees for 25 minutes or until fish is flaky.

❖❖

SPICED FILLET OF SEA TROUT WITH BROCCOLI

3/4 pound Sea Trout fillet

MARINADE:
1 egg white
1/2 teaspoon salt
1 tablespoon sherry
2 teaspoons water chestnut powder
3/4 pound Chinese broccoli
4 mushrooms
1/4 cup bamboo shoots, diced
3 scallions (white and green parts)
1 teaspoon ginger root, minced

SEASONING SAUCE:
1 1/2 to 2 teaspoons Tabasco sauce
1/2 teaspoon sugar
1 1/2 teaspoons sherry
2 tablespoons mushroom stock
1 tablespoon dark soy sauce
1 teaspoon water chestnut powder
1 teaspoon sesame-seed oil with chili

BROCCOLI SEASONING:
1 teaspoon sherry
1 teaspoon salt
1/2 teaspoon sugar
2 cups peanut oil (for deep frying)

Have fish market bone and skin sea trout. Cut fillet into 1-inch cubes. Marinate the fish cubes in egg white, salt, sherry and water chestnut powder for at least 1/2 hour (up to 12 hours) in the refrigerator.

Saute broccoli and blanch (cook in boiling water) for 2 minutes. Remove broccoli from boiling water and plunge into a bowl of ice water. Drain broccoli well, then dry well with paper towel. The preparation up to this point can be done up to 24 hours before. Refrigerate all prepared ingredients until ready to stir-fry.

Rinse mushrooms, cover with warm water, and soak for 30 to 60 minutes or until soft. Save mushroom stock. Cut each mushroom into 4 or 6 pieces.

Slice bamboo shoots. Slant-cut scallions in 1-inch pieces. Mince ginger. Mix seasoning-sauce ingredients in a bowl; Tabasco, sugar, sherry, mushroom stock, soy sauce, water chestnut powder, and sesame-seed oil with chili. Put broccoli seasoning (sherry, salt and sugar) in a small cup.

COOKING PROCEDURE

Heat 2 cups peanut oil in wok until it reaches 325 degrees on a deep fat frying thermometer. While the oil is heating, place another wok over high flame for 3 seconds. Add 1 tablespoon oil, and heat for 20 seconds or until oil is very hot but not smoking. Add broccoli and stir-fry 1 minute. Add broccoli seasoning and stir fry for 1 more minute. Remove the broccoli and place on a heated serving dish. Keep the broccoli warm in preheated 200-degree oven.

When the two cups of oil in the first wok registers 325 degrees, gently lower the marinated sea trout cubes into the oil and stir carefully with chopsticks for about 2 minutes. Remove fish from oil with a wire strainer and drain on several layers of paper towels. Pour off the oil into a pot or bowl, leaving about 1 tablespoon oil in the wok. Do not wash wok. Turn the flame to high and add scallions, ginger, mushrooms, and bamboo shoots. Stir-fry for 1 minute. Restir the seasoning sauce. Add fish cubes and seasoning sauce. Mix thoroughly for about 1 more minute. Empty the contents of the wok (the sea trout) over the middle of the broccoli, which had been placed on a heated serving platter a few minutes before. Serve immediately. Serves 6.

TUNA-ALMOND BAKE

2 cups chopped celery
1 cup toasted slivered almonds
2 onions, peeled and minced
2 cans (6 1/2-ounce size) tuna, drained and
   and broken into pieces
1/2 teaspoon Worcestershire sauce
2 cups evaporated milk
2 cans (10 1/2-ounce size) cream of celery soup
1 can (3-ounce) Chinese noodles
Cooked rice (optional)
Soy sauce

Combine celery, almonds, onions, tuna and Worcestershire sauce. Also combine milk and celery soup and fold into the tuna mixture. In the bottom of a 3-quart casserole spread a layer of Chinese noodles, just enough to cover the bottom. Pour in the tuna mixture and top with a layer of the Chinese noodles. Bake in a 375-degree oven for about 45 minutes or until bubbly. Serve with soy sauce and over rice if you desire. Serves 6.

EASY FIXIN' TUNA CASSEROLE

1/4 cup butter
1 cup chopped onion
1/4 cup flour
2 1/2 cups milk
1/3 cup prepared mustard
1 teaspoon salt
1/8 teaspoon pepper
1 1/2 teaspoons dill
3 cups tuna, drained
3 cups cooked well-drained broad noodles
1 package (10-ounce) frozen peas, cooked
   and well drained
1 cup grated American cheese

Melt butter in saucepan. Saute onion in the butter. Remove from heat; stir in flour. Gradually add milk. Cook over low heat, stirring constantly, until sauce thickens and comes to a boil. Add all ingredients except cheese. Pour tuna mixture into a well-greased 2-quart casserole. Bake in a 350-degree oven for 20 minutes. Top with grated cheese and bake 15 minutes longer. Garnish with parsley. Serves 6.

Down To Earth · Vegetables

In this chapter we tried to provide you with recipes for every vegetable from asparagus to zucchini with a mix of recipes to meet every type of need. You'll find picnic dishes such as Baked Beans and Copper Pennies, quick steamed vegetables, and special accompaniments such as Stuffed Zucchini Boats, Jeanne's Tomatoes à la Provençal, and Fried Parsley. Remember to check the Nine to Five section for more quick, easy vegetable dishes.

Down to Earth

ASPARAGUS AU GRATIN

2 pounds fresh or equal amount frozen asparagus

SAUCE:
2 tablespoons butter
2 tablespoons flour
1 cup hot milk (use part asparagus liquid)
1/4 teaspoon salt
1/8 teaspoon pepper
1 teaspoon Worcestershire sauce
2 eggs, hard-boiled

Cook and drain asparagus, reserving liquid to use in making cream sauce. Do not use too much or the sauce will be gray. Place drained asparagus in buttered baking dish.

Melt butter, add flour, salt and pepper. Cook one minute, remove from heat, slowly add milk and asparagus liquid. Return to heat and stir constantly until thickened. Add Worcestershire sauce, and chopped hard-boiled eggs. Pour over asparagus, sprinkle with bread crumbs and dot with butter. Brown in 375-degree oven until heated thoroughly. Serves 6.

BAKED BEANS I

2 cans (1-pound size) pork and beans
1 small chopped onion
2 teaspoons Worcestershire sauce
1/2 cup catsup
1/4 cup brown sugar
2 tablespoons molasses
2 teaspoons prepared mustard
1/2 cup bacon, chopped and browned

Combine all ingredients, adjust seasonings. Bake uncovered in 250-degree oven for at least 2 hours, or until mixture thickens. Serves 6.

BAKED BEANS II

1/2 pound hamburger
5 slices bacon
1 small onion, chopped
1/3 cup brown sugar
1/2 cup catsup
2 tablespoons prepared mustard
1/4 teaspoon pepper
1/3 cup white sugar
1/3 cup barbeque sauce
2 tablespoons molasses
1/2 teaspoon salt
1/2 teaspoon chili powder
1 can (46-ounce) pork and beans. Drain, but save liquid to add some back if necessary.
1 can black-eyed peas, drained
1 can red kidney beans, drained and rinsed

Brown hamburger, bacon and onion, drain well. Combine rest of ingredients, except beans, and add to browned meat mixture. Add beans, mix well and bake at 350 degrees for 1 hour. This can be frozen. Serves 8-10.

BROCCOLI CASSEROLE

4 packages (10 ounce) frozen broccoli
2 sticks margarine, melted
1 envelope dried onion soup
1 cup pecans, chopped
1 cup sliced water chestnuts
Bread crumbs

Mix together last 4 ingredients. Pour over broccoli. Top with bread crumbs. Bake at 300 degrees 1 hour. Serves 8.

Down to Earth

MARINATED BLACK-EYED PEAS

2 cans (1-pound size) black-eyed peas, drained, or use frozen black-eyed peas, of same amount, cooked according to package directions and drained
1/3 cup oil
1/3 cup wine vinegar
1 clove garlic
1 large onion, sliced
1/2 teaspoon salt
Fresh ground pepper as desired

Mix all ingredients and store in refrigerator 24 hours. Remove garlic and keep in refrigerator for 2 days to 2 weeks before eating.

Jo says: "This is a wonderful dish for New Year's buffets. My family did a taste test for me the first time I served it, we served some of it cold and I heated the remainder. I can't remember which disappeared first. —Cornbread is a 'must' with it."

RED CABBAGE

1 head red cabbage
3 slices bacon
2 tablespoons finely chopped onion
2 apples
1/4 teaspoon salt
2 tablespoons flour
1/2 cup diluted vinegar or red wine
1 tablespoon sugar

Shred cabbage and soak in water. Cut bacon into small pieces and place in a saucepan. Saute over low heat. When it is well-fried, remove from fat and saute the chopped onion.

Lift cabbage from cold water with hands, leaving it moist. Place it in saucepan, cover and simmer 10 minutes. Core apples and cut into very thin slices. Add them to the cabbage with salt and 1/8 cup boiling water. Stir. Simmer in covered saucepan 1 hour and 20 minutes. If the water has not been absorbed when the cabbage is done, remove the lid and permit water to be absorbed.

Dissolve flour in vinegar or red wine and add 1 tablespoon sugar. Add these ingredients to cabbage and simmer 10 minutes longer. Serves 4.

SCALLOPED CABBAGE

1 head cabbage (2 1/2 pounds)
Salt and boiling water
5 tablespoons butter
1/2 cup soft bread crumbs
6 tablespoons flour
Dash nutmeg
1 1/2 cups milk

Cut cabbage into eighths. Place in dutch oven, add 1 teaspoon salt and just enough boiling water to cover. Boil gently, covered, 15 minutes. Drain well, reserving 1 1/2 cups cooking liquid.

Preheat oven to 350 degrees. Arrange the cabbage in a 12x8x2" dish. Melt butter. Remove 1 tablespoon and toss with bread crumbs. Set aside.

Combine flour, 3/4 teaspoon salt and nutmeg in saucepan. Gradually stir in milk and reserved cooking liquid. Bring to a boil, stirring constantly. Boil 2 minutes. Pour over cabbage. Sprinkle buttered bread crumbs over top.

Bake 20 minutes or until bread crumbs are golden brown and sauce bubbles around edge. 6-8 servings.

Down to Earth

CABBAGE WITH SOUR CREAM

6-8 slices bacon
Head of cabbage, washed, chopped and
  drained
Bunch of green onions, chopped
8-ounce container sour cream

Fry bacon until crisp. Drain on paper towels and crumble. Fry cabbage in bacon fat to coat well, until just crispy. Season with salt and white pepper. Mix bacon, green onions and sour cream into cabbage. Sprinkle with paprika.
  Serves 4.

HUNGARIAN CARROTS

1 bunch carrots
2 tablespoons butter
1 cup hot water
2 tablespoons flour
1/2 teaspoon salt
4 tablespoons orange or lemon juice
3 tablespoons brown sugar

Cut carrots into sticks. Melt butter and add carrots and season with salt. Cover and cook 5 minutes. Add flour, stirring, add juice and brown sugar and hot water. Cook until tender crisp. Serves 4.

CELERY CASSEROLE

6 cups celery, diced
2 cans cream of chicken soup
1 cup chopped water chestnuts
1 small jar pimentos

Boil celery 4 minutes. Drain and spread in 10 x 13-inch pan. Add soup, water chestnuts and pimentos. Serves 4.

TOPPING:
1/2 cup sliced almonds
3/4 cup butter
1 1/2 cups crushed French onion crackers

Saute almonds and butter for 1 minute. Spread topping on celery mixture. Sprinkle crushed crackers over the top of mixture. Bake at 350 degrees 20 minutes. Serves 6-8.

CAULIFLOWER MIXTURE

1 cup mayonnaise
1 teaspoon vinegar
1 teaspoon minced onion
1 tablespoon sugar
2 tablespoons chopped parsley
4 hard-boiled eggs, chopped
Salt to taste

Put in double boiler. Heat through, but do not boil as it will separate. Pour this mixture over prepared head of cauliflower. Sprinkle paprika over top. Serves 6.

CAROL'S BROCCOLI

4 cups frozen broccoli stems and buds,
  cooked and drained
1/2 can mushroom soup
2 ounces chopped pimento
1 carton (8-ounce) sour cream
1 cup chopped celery
1 tablespoon Worcestershire sauce
Fresh ground pepper
1 tablespoon dry onion flakes
1 teaspoon salt
1/2 cup grated sharp Cheddar cheese
1 cup canned boiled onions

Mix all ingredients except cheese and place in a greased casserole. Top with cheese and bake at 350 degrees for 1 hour. Serves 6-8.

SAUSAGE-STUFFED ONIONS

8 medium-size red onions
1 cup packaged herb stuffing mix
3 tablespoons butter, melted
2 tablespoons chopped parsley
3 precooked sausage links, sliced

Peel onions. Remove 1 or 2 outer layers. With a sharp knife or apple corer, scoop out onions to make a deep cavity in each. Finely chop enough of the removed onion to make 1/4 cup. In a small bowl, toss stuffing mix with 1/4 cup chopped onion, butter, parsley and sliced sausage. Fill each onion cavity with about 2 tablespoons of mixture, packing well. Place onions in a greased baking dish, cover with aluminum foil and seal well. Bake at 350 degrees for 1 to 1 1/2 hours or until onions are crisp tender.

Note: These are delicious done on a broiler. Wrap each onion in a square of foil and seal well. Roast on grill 3 to 4 inches from coals for 50 to 60 minutes turning occasionally. Serves 8.

CARROTS WITH LEMON JUICE

3 tablespoons sugar
1 tablespoon cornstarch
1/2 teaspoon salt
Juice of 1/2 lemon or 1 tablespoon concentrated
  juice
1 tablespoon butter
1 cup carrot juice
Canned or fresh-cooked carrots

Mix sugar, cornstarch and salt together. Add lemon juice, butter and carrot juice. Pour over carrots and cook for 1 or 2 minutes. Serves 4.

COPPER PENNIES

1 sack frozen sliced carrots or 2 packages
  of whole fresh carrots
1 medium onion, chopped
1 medium green pepper, chopped
1 can tomato soup
1/3 cup salad oil
3/4 cup vinegar
1 cup sugar

Cook carrots until tender. Drain. Chop onion, green pepper, and add to tomato soup, oil, vinegar and sugar. Mix with carrots. Marinate overnight in refrigerator. This will keep several days.

Jan says, "The Pennies are delicious served warm." Serves 6-8.

CORN BALLS

1/4 cup butter
1/2 cup onion, chopped
1/2 cup celery, chopped
1 can (13-ounce) cream-style corn
1 cup water
1 teaspoon salt
1/4 teaspoon pepper
1 1/2 teaspoons poultry seasoning
2 cups Pepperidge Farm stuffing
3 egg yolks
1/2 cup butter, melted

Saute onion, celery in butter until tender but not brown. Add corn, water, salt, pepper, poultry seasoning. Bring to a boil. Pour over the 2 cups of stuffing. Stir in egg yolks lightly. Makes 12 or 13 balls. Place in baking dish. Pour butter that has been melted over the balls. Bake at 375 degrees 15 minutes.

Jan says, "This recipe may be made ahead. It is very good with poultry or wild game."

SCALLOPED CORN

1 can (16 1/2-ounce) golden cream-style corn
1 cup milk
1 egg, beaten
1/4 cup green pepper, chopped
1/4 cup onion, chopped
3/4 teaspoon salt
Dash pepper
1 cup coarse cracker crumbs, buttered

Combine corn and milk, heat to lukewarm. Stir in remaining ingredients except crumbs. Pour into greased 10 x 16-inch baking dish. Top with buttered crumbs. Bake at 350 degrees about 35 minutes or until set. Serves 6.

MOM'S GREEN BEANS

3 packages (10-ounce size) frozen French green
  beans
1/2 cup butter
1 can mushrooms, sliced
1 medium onion, chopped
1/4 cup flour
2 cups milk
1 cup light cream
3/4 pound sharp Cheddar cheese
1/8 teaspoon Tabasco
2 teaspoons soy sauce
Salt and pepper
1 can (15-ounce) water chestnuts
Slivered almonds

Cook green beans according to package directions, drain well. Saute mushrooms and onion in 1/2 cup butter. Add flour, milk and light cream. Cook in double boiler, stirring constantly. Add 3/4 pound cheese, Tabasco, soy sauce, salt and pepper to taste. Pour over drained green beans. Sprinkle with sliced water chestnuts and slivered almonds. Bake at 375 degrees until bubbly. Serves 12.

GREEN BEAN CASSEROLE

2 packages frozen french-style green beans
1 can water chestnuts
1 can bean sprouts
1 can mushrooms
1 large onion, chopped
Salt to taste
1/2 pound grated Cheddar cheese
1 can chow mein noodles
2 1/2 cups thick white sauce (see index)

Cook beans and drain. Add the next 6 ingredients to beans. Put in 2-quart casserole the bean mixture alternating with the white sauce. Top with the chow mein noodles. Bake at 300 degrees 30 minutes. Serves 6-8.

HERB GREEN BEANS

1 pound fresh green beans, or 1 large can whole
    green beans, or 2 packages (10-ounce size)
    frozen whole green beans
1/4 cup butter
1/2 cup minced onion
1/4 teaspoon garlic salt
1/4 cup minced parsley
1/4 teaspoon dried rosemary
1/4 teaspoon dried sweet basil
1/2 teaspoon salt

Cook green beans until just tender. If canned or frozen beans are used, cook according to directions. While beans are cooking, melt butter in a small pan. Add minced onion and cook about 5 minutes. Then add garlic salt, parsley, rosemary, basil and salt. Simmer about 10 minutes. When ready to serve, toss beans with herb-flavored butter. Serves 4-6.

GREEN CHILE RICE

2 cups uncooked long-grain white rice
2 cups sour cream
2 small cans Ortega green chiles
3/4 pound Jack cheese, grated
Seasoned salt
1 teaspoon chopped chives

Cook rice. Wash and rinse green chiles, removing seeds, and chop. Grease 9x13-inch pan. Layer ingredients beginning with rice. Spread with sour cream, then a layer of green chiles and a layer of Jack cheese. Sprinkle seasoned salt. Repeat, ending with cheese. Sprinkle with chives. Bake at 300 degrees 45 minutes. Serves 6.

GREEN PEPPER CASSEROLE

6 cups green pepper, cut in chunks
2 cups boiling water
1 onion, chopped
2 eggs
1 cup mayonnaise
1 cup grated Parmesan cheese
1 tablespoon butter
2 tablespoons buttered bread crumbs
Salt and pepper

Cook green peppers in boiling water 3 minutes (no longer). Beat eggs in large bowl. Stir in mayonnaise, onion, cheese, salt and pepper. Add green peppers. Turn into greased casserole. Dot with butter, sprinkle with bread crumbs. Bake 30 minutes at 350 degrees or until bubbly. Serves 4.

Down to Earth

FRIED PARSLEY

Quickly deep-fry washed, thoroughly dried parsley sprigs in equal amounts of light olive and vegetable oils heated to 375 degrees. Serve hot and lightly salted.

AU GRATIN POTATOES

4 to 5 pounds potatoes

SAUCE: (Makes 4 cups approximately)
4 tablespoons butter
3 to 4 tablespoons flour
1/2 teaspoon dry mustard
1/2 teaspoon salt
1/4 teaspoon pepper
1 tablespoon grated onion
1 tablespoon chopped parsley
2 cups milk
1 cup American cheese
Grated Cheddar cheese for topping
Paprika

Wash potatoes. Leave whole or cut in large pieces or slices. Cook covered in 1-inch boiling salted water. While potatoes are cooking, prepare sauce. Allow at least one cup of sauce for 4 medium or 8 small potatoes.

Melt butter over low heat in heavy saucepan. A wooden spoon or whisk is very good to use when making sauces. Blend in flour, seasonings. Cook over low heat, stirring until mixture is smooth and bubbly. Remove from heat. Stir in milk and bring to a boil, stirring constantly. Boil 1 minute. Add cup of cheese and stir until it melts.

Peel and dice potatoes, salt and pepper. Add cheese sauce. Pour mixture into a buttered casserole. Top with grated Cheddar cheese and sprinkle with paprika. Heat in 350-degree oven until hot and bubbly.

Serves 12.

POTATO BASKETS

Potato baskets can be made in two sieves, one slightly smaller than the other, but the special fryer that is available in cookware shops makes the job easier. The fryer should be 4 to 5 inches across, and the inside sieve or basket should be slightly smaller.

To make 12 baskets you will need about 6 medium-size baking potatoes. Grate the peeled potatoes, place them in a sieve under cold running water and then squeeze moisture out with your hands and place grated potatoes in a single layer on paper towels on a tray.

In a deep-fryer or kettle, heat oil (make sure oil is deep enough to completely cover basket) to a temperature of 375 degrees. Dip the basket in oil and place about a 1/2 inch layer of potatoes completely around the inside. Clamp on the insert or press down with the smaller sieve.

Dip the potato nest in hot oil until the vigorous bubbling subsides, then submerge it completely and fry for 3 minutes or until golden brown. Drain off as much oil as possible and allow to cool for 3 minutes. Carefully remove inside basket and then unmold nest by turning upside down and gently releasing it with the tip of a knife. Salt nest lightly and drain on paper towels. Place completed baskets on a baking sheet and cover until ready to reheat.

To warm baskets, place in a 300-degree oven for about 10 minutes.

These are delicious and so colorful filled with sauteed cherry tomatoes, baby carrots and green peas. They make an excellent accompaniment to tenderloin.

Makes 12 baskets.

Down to Earth

POTATO CASSEROLE

2 pounds frozen hashbrown potatoes
1/2 cup melted butter
1 teaspoon salt
1/4 teaspoon pepper
1/4 cup onion, chopped fine
1 can cream of chicken soup
2 cups sour cream
1 cup (I like 1/2 cup) buttered bread crumbs

Defrost potatoes, combine with all remaining ingredients. Pour into buttered 3-quart casserole. Bake covered at 350 degrees for 1 hour.
Jan says, "You may freeze this until used."
Serves 8-10.

COMPANY PEA CASSEROLE

1 package (20-ounce) frozen peas, cook as directed
1/4 cup butter or margarine
1/3 cup onion, chopped
1/3 cup green pepper, chopped
1 small jar pimento, drained
1 can water chestnuts, sliced and drained
1/3 cup celery, chopped
1 can cream of celery soup, undiluted
1/2 cup shredded cheese

In pan saute butter, onion, green pepper, pimento, water chestnuts and celery. When sauteed, add soup. Mix with peas and put in casserole. Top with cheese. Bake at 350 degrees 30-40 minutes. Serves 8.

NASSAU PEAS 'N' RICE

1 small onion, diced
1/2 teaspoon thyme
2 cups white or brown rice
2 1/2 ounces tomato paste
1 No. 2-size can pigeon peas
4 cups water

Cover bottom of heavy pan with grease 1/4-inch deep. (1/2 bacon fat and 1/2 cooking oil is the best mixture.) Fry diced onion until brown, add thyme, tomato paste and cook about 5 minutes. Drain peas and add to tomato mixture with water. Season to taste. When mixture is boiling, add rice and boil about 30 minutes until soft. Stir peas frequently, adding more water if needed. Can reheat and serve later, adding water or tomato juice before reheating. To give it a little zip, substitute V-8 Juice or Snap.E. Tom for the tomato juice. Serves 6-8.

CURRIED POTATOES

4 tablespoons flour
8 potatoes
6 tablespoons butter
1 cup heavy cream
1 cup evaporated milk
4 tablespoons finely chopped onion
2 teaspoons salt
3/4 teaspoon black pepper
1 tablespoon curry powder

Boil potatoes, peel and cube. Brown flour in 4 tablespoons butter. Stir to smooth flour. Slowly add cream and milk, cook until sauce bubbles and thickens, stirring constantly. Add onions, curry, salt and pepper. Taste. Mix well. Combine potatoes and sauce. Pour into 2-quart lightly buttered baking dish. Dot remaining butter on top. Bake at 350 degrees until top is browned, about 45 minutes. Serves 6.

❖❖❖

MICROWAVE PARMESAN POTATOES

2 tablespoons margarine or butter
2 medium potatoes, unpeeled (about 2/3 pound), sliced 1/4-inch thick
1/3 cup chopped onion
1 garlic clove, minced
1/2 cup (1 inch) green pepper chunks
1/4 teaspoon salt
1/8 teaspoon pepper
1/4 cup grated Parmesan cheese
Paprika
Chopped parsley

Melt butter in shallow 9-inch dish in microwave oven. Add potatoes, onion and garlic, toss. Cover loosely with plastic wrap and place in microwave on full power for 5 minutes. Stir in green pepper, salt and pepper. Toss. Cover and microwave on full power 3 minutes. Gently mix in cheese. Toss gently and dust with paprika. Microwave on full power, uncovered, 3 minutes. Let stand 2 minutes. Sprinkle with parsley. Serves 3-4.

MRS. APPLEYARD'S PATRICIAN POTATOES

4 cups freshly cooked mashed potatoes (about 6 medium-size potatoes cooked with 2 teaspoons salt)
3 cups cream-style cottage cheese
3/4 cup commercial sour cream
1 1/2 tablespoons finely grated onion
1 teaspoon salt
1/4 teaspoon white pepper
Melted butter
1/2 cup chopped toasted almonds

Mash potatoes thoroughly, add no milk or butter. Mix cottage cheese with warm mashed potatoes, add sour cream, onion, salt and pepper. Mix well. Spoon into a shallow, buttered 2-quart casserole. Brush surface with melted butter. Bake in moderate oven (350 degrees) for 1/2 hour. Place under broiler for a few minutes to brown the surface. Sprinkle with almonds. Serves 8.

POTATO PUFFS

1 1/2 cups mashed potatoes, unseasoned
2 eggs
1/2 teaspoon salt
1 teaspoon onion, grated
1/2 cup fine dry bread crumbs
1 tablespoon oil
Italian herbs

Combine potatoes with eggs, salt and onion. Roll small balls of the potato mixture in fine dry bread crumbs seasoned with Italian herbs mixed with 1 tablespoon oil. Place on cookie sheet. Bake at 400 degrees for 5 minutes, then broil 5 inches from heat for 1 or 2 minutes, or until golden brown. Makes 6 balls.

REFRIGERATOR MASHED POTATOES

5 pounds potatoes (9 large)
2 packages (3-ounce size) cream cheese
1 cup dairy sour cream
1 teaspoon onion salt
1 teaspoon salt
1/4 teaspoon pepper
2 tablespoons butter or margarine

Cook peeled potatoes in boiling salted water until tender. Drain. Mash until smooth, and no lumps. Add remaining ingredients and beat until light and fluffy. Cool.

Cover and place in refrigerator. May be used anytime within 2 weeks. To use, place desired amount in greased casserole, dot with butter and bake in moderate oven at 350 degrees until heated, about 30 minutes.

Note: If you use the full amount, heat in a 2-quart casserole and dot with 2 tablespoons butter. It is also very good topped with shredded cheddar cheese. Serves 12.

Down to Earth

OVEN–CREAMED POTATOES

1/4 cup butter or margarine
1/4 cup flour
1/8 teaspoon salt
1/8 teaspoon pepper
2 cups milk
3 tablespoons dehydrated horseradish
1/4 pound cheddar cheese
3 1/2 cups diced cold potatoes

Blend first 6 ingredients and cook until done over medium heat. Stir in grated cheese and mix until blended, but do not boil. Pour over diced potatoes in large casserole. Bake at 350 degrees 20 to 25 minutes. Serves 8.

SOUFFLED POTATOES FOR FREEZER

6 large baking potatoes
Butter or margarine
1 cup commercial sour cream
1/4 cup butter
1 egg
1 teaspoon salt
1/8 teaspoon pepper
9 crisp bacon slices, crumbled

Preheat oven to 400 degrees. Wash potatoes, rub skins with butter. Prick with fork and bake directly on oven rack for 45 minutes or until fork-tender. Holding one of the potatoes in pot holder, cut out an oval from one side of the skin. Scoop potato out, repeat process with all the potatoes. Mash potatoes with sour cream, 1/4 cup butter, egg, salt and pepper, stir in bacon. Heap back into potato shells, fluffing up with a fork. Allow to cool, then freezer wrap individually and freeze.

To serve: Preheat oven to 400 degrees. Unwrap frozen potatoes; place right on oven rack, then bake until heated through, about 30 to 45 minutes. Serves 6.

POTATO SKINS

2 medium-size potatoes (about 8 ounces each)
1 tablespoon melted butter
1 teaspoon Parmesan cheese

Rinse and scrub potatoes thoroughly. Pierce once with fork so potatoes will not burst while cooking. Bake at 375 degrees 1 hour, until soft and cooked. Remove from oven and cover with damp paper towel to cool without skins drying out. Cut potatoes in half lengthwise. Scoop out the insides, leaving about 1/4-inch potato next to skin. Brush with melted butter, sprinkle with Parmesan cheese. Bake at 375 degrees about 35 minutes until crisp and brown. Serves 2.

GREEN RICE

1 cup long-grain white rice
1 medium onion, minced
8 ounces sharp Cheddar cheese
1 minced clove garlic
1 package chopped frozen broccoli
2 1/2 cups boiling water
5 beef bouillon cubes

Combine rice, onion, cheese, garlic and broccoli. Dissolve cubes in boiling water and pour over rice. Cover and bake 1 hour 15 minutes at 350 degrees. Serves 4.

Down to Earth

BOHEMIAN SAUERKRAUT

2 tablespoons butter or bacon drippings
1/2 cup sliced onion
1 quart sauerkraut
1 medium-sized potato or tart apple
Boiling chicken or beef stock, or water

Saute sliced onion in bacon drippings or butter until clear. Add sauerkraut and saute for 5 minutes. Peel, grate and add potato or tart apple, cover with boiling stock and cook uncovered 30 minutes. Cover and bake at 325 degrees for 30 minutes.

Kraut may be seasoned with 2 tablespoons brown sugar and 1 teaspoon caraway or celery seed. Serves 6.

SPINACH ON ARTICHOKE

2 packages (10-ounce size) frozen chopped spinach
1/2 pound fresh mushrooms
6 tablespoons butter
1 tablespoon flour
1/2 cup milk
1/2 teaspoon salt
1/8 teaspoon garlic powder
1 can artichoke bottoms (No. 2 size)

Cook spinach according to package directions. Drain. Chop mushroom stems and saute in 2 tablespoons butter. Saute mushroom caps separately in 2 tablespoons butter. Set aside.

Melt 2 tablespoons butter in saucepan. Add flour and cook until bubbly. Add milk, stirring constantly until smooth. Add salt, garlic powder, mushroom stems and spinach. Mix well.

Drain artichoke bottoms and arrange in casserole. Cover with creamed spinach. Pour hollandaise sauce over spinach and top with mushroom caps. Bake uncovered at 375 degrees for 15 minutes. Serves 12.

EASY HOLLANDAISE SAUCE

1/2 cup sour cream
1/2 cup mayonnaise
1/4 cup lemon juice

Combine ingredients and mix well. Heat over hot water, do not boil.

BAKED HERBED SPINACH

1 cup finely chopped onion
2 cloves garlic, minced
1/4 cup butter or margarine
5 packages (10-ounce) frozen chopped spinach, thawed
1 cup heavy cream
1 cup milk
1/2 cup grated Parmesan cheese
1/2 cup packaged bread crumbs
1 teaspoon leaf marjoram, crumbled
1 teaspoon salt
1/4 teaspoon pepper
1/4 cup grated Parmesan cheese

Heat oven to 350 degrees. Saute onion and garlic in butter just until tender. Combine all ingredients, except for 1/4 cup grated cheese. Turn into greased 2-quart baking dish. Sprinkle top with reserved cheese. Bake 30 minutes or until cheese on top is browned. Serves 8.

Down to Earth

SPINACH INTRIGUE

3 packages frozen chopped spinach
1/2 pint sour cream
2 small cans tomato paste
2 teaspoons grated onion (more if desired)
1/2 cup canned mushrooms
Butter
Paprika

Cook spinach. Set aside to drain. Saute mushrooms and onions in butter. Place spinach in casserole, add onions and mushrooms. Mix lightly but thoroughly. Spread tomato paste on top. Cover with sour cream, covering paste completely. Sprinkle with paprika. Bake uncovered, 350 degrees until heated through, about 20 minutes. Serves 6.

SCALLOPED SPINACH

2 packages (10-ounce size) frozen chopped
  spinach, cooked and drained
2 tablespoons onion, chopped
2 eggs, beaten
1 1/2 cups milk
1 1/4 cups cheddar cheese, grated
Salt, pepper
1/2 cup buttered bread crumbs

Combine drained spinach with all other ingredients except bread crumbs. Pour mixture into greased baking dish. Top with bread crumbs. Bake in 350-degree oven for 20 minutes. Serves 4-6.

JEANNE'S SPANATOPITA
(Greek Spinach Pie)

2 pounds fresh spinach
2 bunches green onions
1 bunch parsley
1 pound crumbled Feta cheese
1 dozen eggs
1/2 to 1 pound Filo leaves. (These are tissue
  thin Greek pastry available at specialty
  food stores.)
1 cup Wesson oil
3 sticks butter

Wash spinach, cut off stems, dry completely and chop fine. Chop onions fine and mince parsley. Combine spinach, onions and parsley in large bowl. In another bowl beat eggs well and add Feta cheese. Pour egg mixture over spinach mixture and combine well. Melt butter and oil and keep warm.

Using large pan, about 10 x 15-inch, place a whole Filo leaf on bottom of pan and brush with butter. Repeat with Filo leaves until you have 6-8 leaves on bottom of pan.

Spread 1/3 of spinach mixture on Filo leaves. Place 3 more layers of Filo leaves on spinach mixture and brush each leaf with butter.

Place another 1/3 of spinach mixture and repeat process. Then place remaining mixture and cover with 7 or 8 more Filo leaves, brushing each with butter.

Bake at 350 to 375 degrees for 45 minutes to 1 hour. Cool and cut into squares. Serves 20-24.

SPINACH RING WITH SAUTEED TOMATOES

4 tablespoons butter
1/2 cup chopped onion
2 packages (10-ounce size) frozen chopped spinach
3/4 cup light cream
4 eggs, slightly beaten
3/4 cup milk
1/4 teaspoon garlic salt
1 tablespoon grated Parmesan cheese

Preheat oven to 325 degrees. Generously butter a 5½-cup ring mold. In 4 tablespoons hot butter, saute onion until tender. Add spinach. Cook, covered, breaking up with a fork, about 5 minutes or until thawed, then cook uncovered, and stirring occasionally, until liquid has evaporated.

Stir in cream, simmer 2 minutes. In medium bowl, beat eggs with milk, 1 teaspoon salt and garlic salt just until combined. Stir in spinach mixture and Parmesan cheese. Pour into prepared mold. Place in shallow pan, pour hot water to 1-inch depth around mold. Lay sheet of waxed paper over top of mold. Bake 40 minutes or until knife comes out clean. Make tomatoes. Serves 6.

SAUTEED TOMATOES

2 tablespoons butter
1/2 teaspoon salt
1/8 teaspoon dried oregano
1 pint cherry tomatoes

Heat butter in medium skillet. Stir in salt and oregano. Add tomatoes and cook over medium heat, stirring occasionally until skins start to break (3 to 5 minutes). Keep warm.

Run small spatula around side and center of mold to loosen. Invert onto heated plate. Spoon tomatoes into center. Serves 6.

AUNT FANNY'S BAKED SQUASH

3 pounds yellow summer squash
1/2 cup chopped onions
1/2 cup cracker meal or bread crumbs
1/2 teaspoon black pepper
1/2 teaspoon salt
2 eggs, beaten
1 stick butter
1 tablespoon sugar
Bread crumbs for top

Wash and cut up squash. Boil until tender, drain thoroughly, then mash. Add all ingredients except 1/2 of butter to squash. Melt remaining butter. Pour mixture in 7 1/2 x 11 1/2-inch baking dish, then spread melted butter over top and sprinkle with cracker meal or bread crumbs. Bake in 375-degree oven for 1 hour or until brown on top. Serves 8.

APRICOT SWEET POTATOES

1 can (16-ounce) yams or 6 large sweet potatoes
1 can (17-ounce) apricot halves
3 tablespoons brown sugar
1 tablespoon cornstarch
1/4 teaspoon salt
1/8 teaspoon cinnamon
1/3 cup light raisins
3 tablespoons dry sherry
1/8 teaspoon grated orange peel

Drain yams, or cook sweet potatoes until soft. Arrange in 10 x 6 x 2-inch baking dish. Drain apricots, reserving syrup. Add water as required to equal 1 cup liquid. Set aside. Arrange apricot halves over yams.

In saucepan, combine brown sugar, cornstarch, salt and cinnamon. Stir in apricot syrup and raisins. Cook over high heat, stirring constantly until mixture boils. Stir in sherry and grated orange peel. Pour over mixture of yams and apricots. Bake uncovered 350 degrees for 20 minutes. Serves 4-6.

TROPICAL GLAZED SWEET POTATOES

3 pounds sweet potatoes
3/4 cup brown sugar
1 1/2 tablespoons cornstarch
1/4 teaspoon salt
1/4 teaspoon cinnamon
1 cup apricot nectar
1 cup crushed pineapple, drained, reserving
    1/3 cup syrup
2 teaspoons grated orange peel
2 tablespoons butter
1/2 cup chopped pecans

Cook sweet potatoes in boiling water until tender, peel. Drain and slice in half, place in buttered casserole.

In saucepan, combine sugar, cornstarch, salt and cinnamon. Blend in nectar, pineapple syrup and orange peel. Bring to boil, stirring constantly. Remove from heat. Stir in butter. Cool slightly and stir in pecans and pineapple. Pour sauce over potatoes and bake at 375 degrees for 25 minutes or until sauce is bubbly. Serves 8.

SWEET POTATO SCALLOP

6 medium sweet potatoes (2 3/4 pounds)
2 oranges, peeled and thinly sliced
1/4 cup brown sugar, firmly packed
1 1/2 teaspoons cornstarch
1/4 teaspoon salt
1/4 teaspoon pumpkin-pie spice
1 cup orange juice
2 tablespoons butter

Wash potatoes, place in pan, cook in boiling water for 30 minutes or until tender. Peel. Heat oven to 350 degrees.

Cut potatoes in slices, place in pan alternately with orange slices. Make a sauce of brown sugar, cornstarch, salt and spice. Gradually stir in orange juice and add butter. Bring to a boil, stirring constantly. Boil 2 minutes. Pour over potatoes and orange slices. Bake, uncovered, 45 minutes or until hot and bubbly.

Note: Can also add 1/2 cup mini-marshmallows and 1/2 cup walnuts or pecans to sauce before pouring over potatoes. Serves 6.

RATATOUILLE

1/2 cup olive oil
2 pounds Italian sausage: if not bulk, remove
    from casing and chop
1 cup celery, chopped
1 cup onion, chopped
4 garlic cloves, minced
1 can (28-ounce) Italian tomatoes
4 medium zucchini, sliced in 1/2-inch pieces
1 medium eggplant, cubed but not peeled
2 large green peppers, seeded and sliced in
    1-inch pieces
2 large onions, sliced in 1/2-inch pieces
1/2 cup Burgundy wine
1 tablespoon Italian seasoning
1 tablespoon basil
1 tablespoon oregano
Salt and pepper to taste
Parmesan cheese, grated

In large heavy saucepan, saute sausage in olive oil until lightly browned. Remove sausage and add chopped celery, onion and garlic. Saute until vegetables are limp, about 5 minutes. Return sausage to saucepan, add tomatoes and zucchini and simmer, covered, for 5 minutes. Add rest of sliced vegetables and seasonings. Simmer gently for 1/2 hour or until vegetables are tender. Add wine and adjust seasonings to taste. Pass Parmesan cheese to sprinkle over top. This dish is better prepared a day or so ahead of serving. Flavors will have a chance to blend. Serves 10-12.

RATATOUILLE II

8 tablespoons olive oil
2 large onions, sliced
2 green peppers, diced
1 eggplant, unpeeled
2 to 4 zucchini, unpeeled, cut in 1/2-inch slices
4 to 6 ripe tomatoes
1 can tomato paste
Salt and freshly ground black pepper
2 tablespoons chopped parsley
1 teaspoon marjoram or oregano
1 teaspoon basil
1 large clove garlic, crushed

Slice unpeeled eggplant in circles. Place on paper toweling, sprinkle with salt and allow to stand 30 minutes on each side to draw out moisture. Then cut rounds into eighths or smaller if desired.

Place eggplant and cut zucchini on baking sheet. Place under broiler to brown skins a bit.

Heat olive oil in a large saucepan, add onion slices and saute until they are transparent Add diced green pepper, eggplant, and 5 minutes later, the zucchini, tomatoes, and can of tomato paste. The vegetables should not be fried but stewed in the oil to simmer gently in covered pan for 30 minutes. Add salt and pepper to taste, then parsley, marjoram, basil and crushed garlic. Cook uncovered 10 to 15 minutes.

Serve hot from casserole or cold as a delicious beginning to a summer meal.

Jo says, "You can bake this in the oven uncovered rather than on top of the stove." Serves 6.

JEANNE'S TOMATOES A LA PROVENCAL

6 small tomatoes (1 1/2"-2" in diameter)
   OR
3 large tomatoes (3"- 4" in diameter)
   large preferred
1 cup coarse dry white bread crumbs
2 tablespoons dried basil
1/2 cup chopped fresh parsley
2 tablespoons green onion tops, chopped
1/2 teaspoon salt
1/4 teaspoon pepper
1/3 cup olive oil

Cut tomatoes in halves if using large ones. If using small, cut slice off top. Cut a small slice off bottoms so they will sit flat in pan. Arrange tomatoes cut side up in a lightly oiled baking dish.

Sprinkle each half with a few drops of oil and salt and pepper.

In mixing bowl, stir together the crumbs, parsley, onion tops, basil, salt, pepper, and enough oil to moisten but still leave it crumbly. Top each tomato half with about 2 tablespoons of crumb mixture (for large tomatoes), patting it in and letting it mound up a little in the middle. Sprinkle a few drops of oil over each half. Bake in a preheated oven for 20-30 minutes at 350 degrees. They should get hot and tender but not limp.

Serves 6.

TOMATO PUDDING

1 stick butter
1 cup light brown sugar
2 cups bread cubes
1 can tomato puree (10 1/2-ounce size)
1/4 cup water
1/4 teaspoon salt

Melt butter. Pour over cubes and toss. Heat puree with water, add salt and sugar. Simmer about 5 minutes. Pour mixture over cubes, toss, put in casserole. Bake covered for 45 minutes at 325 degrees. Serves 8.

Down to Earth

MARINATED VEGETABLES

1 cauliflower, cut in florets, cooked and chilled
1 pound mushrooms, lightly sauteed and chilled
1 bunch fresh broccoli, cooked and chilled
2 packages (10-ounce size) frozen artichoke
    hearts, cooked and chilled
2 packages (10-ounce size) frozen regular cut
    green beans, cooked and chilled
2 packages (10-ounce size) frozen asparagus
    spears, cooked and chilled
2 packages (10-ounce size) frozen green lima beans,
    cooked and chilled
1 can (1-pound) sliced beets, chilled

MARINADE:

1/2 cup tarragon vinegar
2 teaspoons Accent
2 teaspoons salt
2 teaspoons sugar
2 tablespoons dried fine herbs
1/4 teaspoon cayenne
1 cup vegetable oil
1/2 cup chopped fresh parsley
Capers, according to taste

Combine vegetables in large bowl. For marinade, measure vinegar into small bowl. Add Accent, salt, sugar, herbs and cayenne, stirring until dissolved. Add oil and parsley. Beat or stir vigorously until blended.

Pour over vegetables, cover and refrigerate several hours or overnight. Drain off excess marinade.

Arrange attractively on large chop-plate or platter. Serves 8-10.

VEGETABLE MEDLEY

2 medium carrots
2 celery stalks
1 medium onion
1 medium bunch broccoli
1/2 pound fresh mushrooms
1/4 cup salad oil
1 garlic clove
1 chicken bouillon cube
1/3 cup water
1 1/2 teaspoons salt
1/2 teaspoon sugar

Cut each carrot crosswise in half, then lengthwise into thin strips. Cut each celery stalk crosswise into 3 pieces, then lengthwise into thin strips. Thinly slice onion. Cut broccoli into 2-inch by 1/2-inch pieces. Cut mushrooms in quarters or cut in half if small.

In a 12-inch skillet over high heat, in hot salad oil and garlic clove, cook carrots, celery, onion, and broccoli, stirring quickly and frequently, about 5 minutes. Add mushrooms, chicken bouillon cube dissolved in the water, salt, and sugar. Cover and cook 5 to 6 minutes longer until vegetables are tender but still crisp, stirring frequently. Makes 8 servings.

STIR-FRIED VEGGIES

2-3 tablespoons oil
1 clove garlic, crushed
1 cup chicken broth

Heat oil, add garlic. Place veggies in skillet and stir to coat with the oil. Add the chicken broth, cover and cook approximately 8-10 minutes or until tender as desired, depending on the vegetable you are using.

Jo says, "You must try brussels sprouts, fresh green beans, carrots, broccoli, zucchini, etc., etc."

❖❖❖

VEGETABLE TRIO WITH ZIPPY SAUCE

1 cup mayonnaise or salad dressing
1 hard boiled egg, chopped
3 tablespoons lemon juice
2 tablespoons minced onion
1 teaspoon Worcestershire sauce
1/4 teaspoon prepared mustard
1/4 teaspoon garlic salt
Dash of Tabasco sauce
1 can (No. 2 - 2 1/2 cups) or 1 package frozen
    French-style green beans
1 can (No. 2) or 1 package frozen peas
1 package frozen baby lima beans

Combine ingredients except vegetables. Heat and stir over low heat just until hot; do not boil. Cook vegetables according to package directions. Drain and mix. Pour sauce over hot vegetables. Serves 10.

Jan says, "You may do this ahead of time, but do not add the sauce to the veggies until you are ready to serve. This is a unique dish to serve anytime or anywhere."

WILD RICE

2 cups wild rice
1 cup butter
3 medium onions, chopped
2 medium green peppers, chopped
2 pimentos, chopped, or 1 small jar
1 teaspoon thyme
1/2 teaspoon sage
Salt and pepper

Cook rice according to directions on package or use 1 quart boiling water and 1 teaspoon salt for 2 cups rice.

Melt butter in skillet. Saute onions, green pepper, and pimentos until tender. Add remaining ingredients to onion-pepper mixture. Add to rice and bake at 300 degrees—will keep in warming oven nicely. Serves 6.

Jo says, "A must with Chicken Roquefort."

STUFFED ZUCCHINI BOATS

2 zucchini (1 1/4 pounds)
4 tablespoons olive oil
1/2 cup chopped onion
1 clove garlic, minced
1/4 pound ground veal
1/4 pound ground pork
1/2 cup plus 1 to 2 tablespoons bread crumbs
Salt and freshly ground pepper
1 egg yolk
3 tablespoons finely chopped dill
2 tablespoons finely chopped parsley
1 to 2 tablespoons grated Parmesan cheese

Preheat oven to 425 degrees. Trim off small portion of stem from each zucchini, and split in half lengthwise. Scoop out center seed portion of each zucchini leaving casing to be stuffed. Chop the scooped-out pulp (should be 1 cup). Heat 2 tablespoons oil in large saucepan. Add onion and garlic, cook until onion is wilted. Add meat and cook, stirring down with a heavy wooden spoon to break up lumps, until meat loses its red color. Add reserved chopped zucchini pulp and cook about 3 minutes, stirring often. Add 1/2 cup bread crumbs and stir to blend. Add salt and pepper to taste. Add egg yolk, parsley and dill. Heat briefly, stirring, until mixture is slightly thickened. Do not overcook or yolk will curdle.

Sprinkle insides of zucchini with salt and pepper. Stuff zucchini halves with equal portions of filling, smoothing over the tops. Blend cheese and remaining bread crumbs and sprinkle over top.

Dribble remaining oil over all and bake 30 minutes. Serve with Jan's Tomato Sauce (see index). Serves 4.

Down to Earth

ZUCCHINI CREPES

2 cups zucchini, grated
1/2 cup onions, grated
1/2 cup Cheddar cheese, grated
1 cup self-rising or pancake flour
2 eggs
1/2 cup milk

Mix all ingredients and fry like a pancake.

ZUCCHINI RICE

1 zucchini squash
1 cup long-grain rice, uncooked (or saffron rice)
1 cup grated sharp Cheddar cheese (I like medium)
6 tablespoons melted butter
3 eggs, beaten
Salt and pepper to taste

Peel and slice squash. Cook rice per package directions. Add squash when rice is about 1/2 cooked. Stir in remaining ingredients. Bake in 1 1/2 quart casserole, uncovered, 30 minutes at 350 degrees or until done in center. (Like a souffle or custard.) Serves 4.

Jo says, "This is marvelous with meat."

GREAT TOSS UPS

Great Toss Ups · Salads

Are you in the same old salad routine? It is definitely time for a change! Must-trys are Mom's Frozen Fruit Salad, the Overnight Green Tossed Salad, and our spinach salads—each and every one will bring raves.

We think some of the loveliest luncheons consist of a perfect salad, roll or muffin, and dessert. Three of our favorite luncheon salads are Apricot Soufflé Ring with Chicken Salad, Auntie K's Favorite Fruit Salad, and Salmon Mousse.

Some of our salads—like the Frozen Fruit Salad—make perfect garnishes—a small portion is all that's needed to brighten up a meal. A good dressing counts too—so don't miss the salad dressings at the end of this chapter.

Great Toss Ups

Jo and Jan say, "Don't abuse and bruise your salad greens. Tear pieces gently into bite-size pieces."

APRICOT SOUFFLE RING WITH CHICKEN SALAD

SOUFFLE RING:
1 cup apricot juice (from can of apricots)
1 cup apricot nectar
6-ounce package lemon Jell-O
2 cups heavy cream, whipped
Fresh mint leaves for garnish
Paprika

Bring apricot juice and apricot nectar to a boil. Add Jell-O and stir until dissolved. Chill until mixture is consistency of honey. (Check after 45 minutes.) Fold into whipped cream and chill in greased 6-cup ring mold.

CHICKEN SALAD:
1 large onion, sliced
4 stalks celery with leaves, sliced
Salt and pepper
4 whole chicken breasts
2 teaspoons minced onion
8 hard-boiled eggs, chopped
1 can (6-ounce) water chestnuts, sliced
3-4 stalks celery, chopped
1/2 cup seedless grapes
1/2 cup chopped nuts (pecan, cashew, macadamia)
3/4 cup mayonnaise

Place onion, celery, salt and pepper in large kettle of water. Bring to a boil and add chicken breasts. Simmer 1 hour, or until tender. Remove breasts and chill. Skin and bone chicken and cut into cubes. Add eggs, minced onion, water chestnuts, celery, grapes and nuts. Add only enough mayonnaise to mix thoroughly.

TO SERVE:
Dip souffle ring very quickly into hot water and unmold on round serving platter. Mound chicken salad in center of ring. Dust with paprika and garnish with fresh mint leaves. Serves 8-10.

MOLDED BEET SALAD

1 1/2 packages lemon Jell-O
1 can shoestring beets (1 pound)
1 cup chopped celery
1/2 cup finely chopped cucumber
4 teaspoons grated onion
1/3 cup sugar
4 tablespoons vinegar
2 tablespoons horseradish
1/8 teaspoon salt

Drain beets. Add enough water to beet juice to make 2 1/3 cups liquid. Heat to boiling, add Jell-O, sugar, salt, vinegar and horseradish. When slightly thickened, add remaining ingredients. Pour into greased individual molds or a ring mold. Chill overnight. Serve on a bed of lettuce with real mayonnaise, to which has been added red wine vinegar to taste. Serves 6.

BLACK CHERRY SALAD

1 large can fruit cocktail, discard liquid
1 medium can pineapple tidbits
1 quart pitted black cherries
1 cup chopped nuts
1/2 cup sugar
4 tablespoons cornstarch
1 package (3-ounce) cherry Jell-O
6 bananas
1 pint heavy cream

Drain juice from pineapples and cherries into pan. Add sugar; thicken with cornstarch. When thick, stir in Jell-O. Pour this thickened juice over fruit while juice is still hot. Let set 3 or 4 hours then add sliced bananas when ready to serve. Spread whipped cream on top and sprinkle with chopped nuts.
Serves 6.

Great Toss Ups

BROCCOLI SALAD

1 tablespoon Dijon mustard
2 tablespoons red or white wine vinegar
Juice of 1 large orange
6 tablespoons Bertolli olive oil
1/2 teaspoon salt
1/2 teaspoon freshly ground pepper
1/4 teaspoon sugar
2 heads of broccoli, cut into florets
1 green pepper, cut into 1/4-inch strips

Mix in small bowl mustard, vinegar, and orange juice until blended well. Slowly beat in the olive oil, then beat in the salt, pepper and sugar. Steam broccoli until just tender. Arrange broccoli in a bowl and pour over the dressing. Toss with the green pepper and serve warm. Makes 6 servings.

BROCCOLI-CAULIFLOWER-RED ONION SALAD

1 head of broccoli
1 head of cauliflower
1 medium-size red onion
Mayonnaise, salt and pepper to taste
Sour cream is optional

Jan says, "This is one of the most delicious salads and the easiest. It will go with any meal including cocktail parties. It's like potato chips-you can't leave it alone." Serves 6-8.

MOM'S CAESAR SALAD

1/2 cup salad oil
1/4 cup lemon juice
1 tablespoon Worcestershire sauce
1 teaspoon salt
1/4 teaspoon pepper
1 egg
1 teaspoon garlic juice or 2 garlic cloves, peeled and crushed

Whip all ingredients with electric mixer. Can be made a day ahead. When ready to serve, tear **two heads of romaine lettuce** into bite-size pieces. Toss with **2 cups toasted croutons, 1/4 cup grated Parmesan cheese,** and **1 wedge Blue cheese,** diced. Pour dressing over salad and toss gently. Season with salt if desired and coarse **freshly ground black pepper.** Serves 8.

CHICKEN SALAD

2 cups chicken or turkey (chopped)
2 cups celery (sliced)
1/2 cup toasted slivered almonds
1/2 teaspoon salt
2 teaspoons onion, grated
2 tablespoons lemon juice
1 cup mayonnaise
1/2 cup cheese, grated
1 cup crushed potato chips

Mix all ingredients together except the cheese and potato chips. Add these last and bake at 450 degrees for 10 minutes. Serves 6.
Jan says, "This is a very good luncheon dish served with a vegetable and hot bread. Also good for a light supper dish."

HOT CHICKEN SALAD

2 cans mushroom soup
1 cup Miracle Whip
1/4 teaspoon curry powder
3 cups chopped chicken breasts
2 cups water chestnuts
1/2 cup walnuts or almonds
Top: 6 teaspoons butter
    1 cup Pepperidge Farm dressing

Combine first 6 ingredients. Put in baking dish. Combine and add the topping. Bake at 350 degrees for 30 to 45 minutes. Serves 6.

Great Toss Ups

CHERRY-PEPSI-COLA SALAD

2 packages cherry Jell-O
1 can pie cherries, drained and water added
   to make 1½ cups liquid
3/4 cups sugar
1 envelope unflavored gelatin, dissolved in 1/4
   cup cold water
1 can (No. 2½) crushed pineapple, juice and all.
1 cup Pepsi-Cola
Nuts may be added, if desired

Put cherry Jell-O in a bowl. Add 1 cup boiling water, stir until well dissolved. Add liquid from drained cherries and the water to make 1 1/2 cups.

Add cherries and sugar. Bring to a boil. Remove from heat. Add gelatin dissolved in water. Add crushed pineapple and nuts. Last, add 1 cup Pepsi-Cola. Chill until firm. This makes a large salad. Serves 12.

CHERRY SALAD

1 can Wilderness cherries
1 can (20-ounce) pineapple tidbits, drained
   desired
2 cups mini marshmallows
2 cups sliced bananas
1 cup or more large pieces of pecans or English
   walnuts

Stir all together. Let set.
Note: If prepared the day before, add bananas just an hour before serving. May add Cool Whip on top. Serves 8.

ERMADENE'S CHERRY TOMATOES

2 baskets cherry tomatoes
Boiling water
1/4 cup red wine vinegar
2 tablespoons instant minced onions
1/2 teaspoon whole sweet basil, crushed
1/4 teaspoon whole oregano, crushed
1 teaspoon garlic salt
1/4 teaspoon pepper
1/2 cup salad oil or olive oil

Put tomatoes a few at a time into collander and dip into pan of boiling water for 15 seconds. Rinse in cold water and peel. Place in refrigerator.

Combine remaining ingredients and add tomatoes. Let marinate overnight in refrigerator before serving. Serves 6-8.

GOURMET CHICKEN SALAD

3 cups cooked chicken (about 3 chicken breasts
   cut up)
1 1/3 cups celery
1 bottle (8-ounce) French dressing
1 1/2 cups green grapes, halved
1/3 cup toasted slivered almonds
1 1/2 cups shredded cheddar cheese
1 1/2 cups sour cream
1 1/2 teaspoons mustard
1/2 teaspoon salt
Potato chips

Marinate chicken and celery in dressing 1 hour. Drain excess dressing, if necessary. Combine grapes, almonds, 1/2 cup cheese, sour cream, mustard and salt. Mix well and add to chicken mixture. Toss. Place in casserole. Top with crushed potato chips and 1 cup shredded cheese. Bake 300 degrees for 30 minutes. Serves 8. This recipe freezes well.

Great Toss Ups

HOT GERMAN SALAD

5 medium potatoes
6 slices of bacon
3/4 cup thinly sliced onions
2 tablespoons flour
1 tablespoon sugar
1 1/2 teaspoons salt
1/2 teaspoon celery seed
Dash of pepper or lemon pepper
1/2 cup vinegar
3/4 cup water

Boil potatoes until not quite done. Peel and slice thin. Fry bacon till crisp. Set bacon aside. Cook onions in 2 tablespoons of bacon grease. Mix in flour, sugar, salt, celery seed and pepper. Gradually stir in vinegar and water. Cook, stirring, until mixture boils. Pour over potatoes. Sprinkle bacon bits and parsley on top of salad. Serves 5-6.

WHOLE CINNAMON APPLES FOR SALAD

6 tart apples
1 cup red cinnamon candies
Miracle Whip salad dressing
1 cup Kraft miniature marshmallows
1/2 cup chopped celery
1 cup seedless raisins
1/3 cup chopped pecans

Pare and core apples. Cook candies in 2 cups water until dissolved. Add apples, simmer until tender. Chill thoroughly in syrup.

Blend 1/2 cup Miracle Whip with remaining ingredients and fill apples. Top with more Miracle Whip. Serves 6.

MOLDED CINNAMON-APPLESAUCE SALAD

1 package (3-ounce) red gelatin
1/2 cup red hot candies (cinnamon)
1 cup boiling water
2 1/2 cups applesauce (No. 2 can)
1 package (8-ounce) cream cheese
1/2 cup chopped celery
1/2 cup chopped pecans
1/4 cup milk
2 tablespoons mayonnaise

Stir red hots in boiling water until completely dissolved. Add gelatin and applesauce. Mix well. Pour half of mixture into 8 x 8 x 2-inch pan. Chill until set. Leave other half at room temperature.

Mix cream cheese, milk, mayonnaise, celery and nuts. Spoon on top of applesauce mixture after it is set. Pour remaining applesauce-gelatin mixture on top and refrigerate.

Jo says, "If desired, you can let the entire gelatin mixture set until firm, then cover with cream cheese mixture to frost." Serves 8.

COLE SLAW DELUXE

1 medium head cabbage, chopped
1 medium onion, chopped
1 green pepper, chopped
12 stuffed olives, sliced
3/4 cups sugar

Sprinkle sugar over top of combined first 4 ingredients. In a saucepan, mix the following and boil together for 3 minutes.

1 cup white vinegar
1 teaspoon salt
1 teaspoon celery seed
1 teaspoon dry mustard
1 pinch of pepper
1/2 cup salad oil

After boiling, pour hot ingredients over cabbage mixture. Mix well. Cover and refrigerate for 24 hours. Serves 8-10.

Great Toss Ups

CORNED BEEF SALAD

2 packages lemon Jell-O
1 3/4 cup boiling water
2 cups corned beef, diced
4 to 6 chopped hard-boiled eggs
2 cups diced celery
2 tablespoons green pepper
2 tablespoons chopped onion
1/4 cup sweet pickle relish
1 1/2 cups salad dressing

Dissolve Jell-O in water. Add salad dressing until dissolved, then add rest of ingredients. Serves 8.
Jan says, "This is a very good salad for a luncheon."

CRANBERRY SALAD

6 cups cranberries
3 cups sugar
2 cups cut grapes
2 cups celery, diced
2 red apples, diced
1 cup nuts, chopped
1 large box raspberry Jell-O

Grind cranberries and add diced apple. Mix with sugar and let stand 2 hours. Dissolve Jell-O in large bowl, using 2 cups hot water. Chill. Add celery, grapes and nuts to cranberry mixture and add to the Jell-O. Chill until firm. Serves 12.

CRANBERRY SAUCE

2 cups sugar
2 cups water
1 package fresh cranberries

Boil sugar and water together until sugar dissolves. Add rinsed berries and cook over medium heat for 15 minutes after the mixture begins to boil. Cool. Makes 4 cups.

FROZEN CRANBERRY SALAD

2 cups cranberry sauce (recipe above)
6 tablespoons lemon juice

Mix and spread in greased mold. Freeze.

COMBINE:
1/4 cup powdered sugar
1/4 cup mayonnaise
1 cup chopped nuts to 1/2 pint of cream, whipped

Pour the cream mixture over frozen cranberry sauce and freeze. Serves 4-6.

MOLDED CRANBERRY SALAD

1 can (9-ounce) crushed pineapple
1 package (9-ounce) cherry Jell-O
1 tablespoon lemon juice
1/2 cup sugar
1 small unpeeled seedless orange ground in a food grinder (use fine blade)
1 cup ground fresh cranberries (using fine blade)
1 cup finely chopped celery
1/2 cup chopped walnuts

Dissolve Jell-O and sugar in 1 cup boiling water. Drain pineapple. Reserve syrup and add enough water to make 1/2 cup. Add syrup and lemon juice to Jell-O. Chill until partially set. Add cranberries, pineapple, orange, celery and nuts. Pour into individual molds and chill overnight. Serves 6.

Great Toss Ups

CRANBERRY WHIP

1 pound cranberries
2 Jonathan apples
2 cups sugar
1 cup finely chopped celery
1/2 cup chopped pecans
1/2 pound marshmallows, cut up
1/2 pint heavy cream, whipped

Put cranberries and apples through food grinder or food processor. Mix rest of ingredients except heavy cream. Stir well. Fold in the whipped cream and chill. Serves 6.

CURRIED CHICKEN SALAD

4 chicken breasts, cooked and diced
1 package wild rice, cooked
1 cup green seedless grapes or raisins
1 cup diced celery
1 cup diced apples, unpeeled
1 cup slivered almonds or cashews
1/2 cup mayonnaise or to taste
3 teaspoons mango chutney
2 tablespoons soy sauce
2 to 3 teaspoons curry powder

Mix chicken, rice, grapes or raisins, celery, apples and nuts. Add mayonnaise and stir thoroughly. Add chutney, soy sauce and curry powder. Blend. Adjust seasonings to taste and chill 2 hours. Serves 10-12.

JANE'S DELAROBIA SALAD

1 can (1lb. 13 oz.) pear halves
1 can (8½ ounce) pineapple slices
1 can (1 pound) peach halves
1 jar (1 lb.) spiced crabapples
1 jar (12 oz.) kumquats
2 packages (3-ounce size) cream cheese
1 large box pitted dates
2 tablespoons chopped walnuts
1 bunch watercress
1 package (10 ounce) pecan halves

Refrigerate all fruit until well chilled. Drain well. Soften cream cheese, add walnuts, mix. Make 4 whole pears stuffed with cheese. Wash watercress, drain, and remove stems. Form wreath with cress around edge.

On cress, alternate pears and pineapple. Top slices with peach, round side up. On outer edge of wreath place 1 crabapple between each pear and pineapple. On inner edge of wreath place 2 kumquats opposite each crabapple. Bunch pecans and dates here and there. Refrigerate. Serve with dressing on the side. Serves 8.

DELAROBIA SALAD DRESSING

1 can (6 ounce) frozen orange juice, thawed
1/3 cup sugar
3 tablespoons lemon juice
1 teaspoon grated lemon peel
3 tablespoons salad oil
1/4 teaspoon salt

Combine orange juice and sugar. Add rest of ingredients. Refrigerate 2 hours. Lovely for holiday dinners.

Great Toss Ups

AUNTIE K'S FAVORITE FRUIT SALAD

4 eggs
Juice of 1 lemon
1/4 teaspoon prepared mustard
1/2 cup warm milk
1 pound marshmallows, cut into eights
1 large can white (Queen Ann) cherries, drained and pitted
1 large can diced pineapple, drained
1/4 pound slivered almonds (can lightly toast, if desired)
2 cups red grapes, halved and seeded (optional)
1 pint heavy cream, whipped

Combine eggs, lemon juice and mustard. Beat well and add warm milk. Cook in top of double boiler until thick. Cool. Add marshmallows, cherries, almonds, grapes and pineapple. Stir until mixed. Fold in whipped cream. Chill overnight. Serve in lettuce cups. Serves 12-16.

Jo says, "Be very sure your fruits are well drained. This salad is one of our all-time favorites, dating back to the 1930's."

FROSTED SALAD

2 small packages lemon Jell-O
2 cups boiling water
2 cups 7-Up (ginger ale may be used)
1 can (20 ounce) crushed pineapple, drained; reserve liquid
1 cup mini-marshmallows
2 large bananas, sliced into rounds

Dissolve Jell-O in boiling water. Stir in beverage and chill until partially set. Drain juice from pineapple and save for topping. Fold in pineapple, marshmallows and bananas. Pour into 9 x 12-inch pan and chill until firm.

TOPPING:
1/2 cup sugar
2 tablespoons cornstarch
1 cup pineapple juice
1 egg, slightly beaten
2 tablespoons butter
1 cup cream, whipped, or Cool Whip
1/4 cup shredded American cheese

Combine sugar, cornstarch and juice. Cook until thickened, add a little to the egg to mix, then gradually add the rest. Add butter, chill.

When chilled, fold in whipped cream and frost top of salad. Sprinkle with grated cheese.

Serves 10-12.

GREEK SALATA

1 head lettuce, shredded (6 cups)
3 tomatoes, peeled and chopped
1 large unpared cucumber, chopped
1 bunch watercress, chopped (1½ cups)
1 medium green pepper, chopped
1/3 cup green onions, finely chopped
1/4 cup sliced Greek olives or ripe olives
3 tablespoons lemon juice
1 teaspoon salt
1/3 cup olive oil
1 teaspoon oregano
1 pound Feta cheese, cut in small pieces

Combine lettuce, tomatoes, cucumber, watercress, green pepper and green onions. Add olives, lemon juice, oregano and salt; toss together. Mound on platter, garnish with tomato wedges, cucumber slices, pieces of Feta cheese and Greek olives. Pour olive oil over the salad and allow to stand 15 minutes to blend flavor. Serves 8-10.

Great Toss Ups

MOM'S FROZEN FRUIT SALAD I

1 can (No. 2 or 2 1/2 cups) pineapple,
   reserve juice
1 can (No. 2½ or 3½ cups) white Queen Ann
   cherries
1 can (No. 2½ or 3½ cups) apricots
1 tablespoon butter
1 tablespoon flour
1 tablespoon sugar
1 tablespoon lemon juice
1 egg
1 cup heavy cream, whipped

Drain fruit well. Cut pineapple and apricots into pieces and pit cherries, if necessary.

Melt butter in top of double boiler. Add flour and stir until blended. Add pineapple juice, sugar, lemon juice and egg. Cook and stir until smooth. Be very careful to not overcook. Cool and fold whipped cream into fruit mixture and freeze. Serve on lettuce cups. Serves 12.

FROZEN FRUIT SALAD II

1 package (3-ounce) softened cream cheese
1/3 cup mayonnaise
1 teaspoon lemon juice
2 egg whites
1/3 cup sugar
1 cup whipping cream
8 marshmallows, cut into eighths
1/4 cup drained mandarin orange slices
1 pound can fruit cocktail, drained
2 tablespoons chopped maraschino cherries
1 tablespoon chopped walnuts

Blend cheese, mayonnaise, lemon juice. Beat egg whites until foamy. Beat in sugar, a tablespoon at a time, until stiff peaks form. Whip cream until stiff. Fold cream into egg whites then fold into cheese mixture. Fold in rest of ingredients. Pour into 8-inch square pan. Freeze. Serves 6-8.

GREENGAGE DESSERT SALAD

1 1/2 tablespoons (1½ envelopes) unflavored
   gelatin
1/4 cup cold water
3/4 cup boiling water
3/4 cup plum juice (from can)
1/4 cup fresh lime juice
1 can (No. 2½) greengage plums

Sprinkle gelatin over cold water and let stand 5 minutes. Dissolve in boiling water. Add plum juice, lime juice and cool. When mixture begins to thicken, stir in plums cut into fairly large pieces, and turn into 1 large or 6 individual molds. Chill. Serve on watercress. Pass cooked fruit salad dressing mixed with whipped cream. See index for Pauline's Salad Dressing. Serves 6.

DOROTHY'S LAYER SALAD

1 bag of spinach
1 purple onion, chopped
1 head iceberg lettuce, chopped
12 eggs, sliced
1 large can peas, drained
2 pounds Swiss cheese, shredded
10 slices bacon
DRESSING:
3/4 quart jar Hellmann's mayonnaise
1/4 quart jar Miracle Whip

Layer ingredients as listed. Blend dressings and spread on salad. Top with Swiss cheese and bacon, cooked crisp and crumbled. Cover tightly and allow to chill several hours.

Jo says, "I don't use this much cheese. It is a matter of individual taste."

This recipe is very pretty if put in a clear glass bowl. Be sure to salt and pepper each layer.
Serves 10.

Great Toss Ups

MYSTERY SALAD

3 small packages raspberry gelatin
1 1/2 cups boiling water
32 ounces canned stewed tomatoes
10 drops hot sauce
1 carton sour cream
1 teaspoon horseradish sauce
Sugar and salt to taste

Dissolve gelatin in boiling water. Add the tomatoes and mix in a blender or an electric mixer; stir in the hot sauce. Refrigerate until firm. Make a topping of sour cream, 1 teaspoon horseradish sauce, sugar and salt to taste. Serves 8.

Jan says, "I like the Reese horseradish sauce."

ORIENTAL SALAD

1/2 pound spinach, washed, dried and torn into bite-size pieces
1/2 head lettuce, washed dried and torn into bite-size pieces
1 can bean sprouts, drained
1 can water chestnuts, drained and slivered
3 hard-boiled eggs
5 strips bacon, fried crisp and crumbled

Layer ingredients. They look very pretty in a glass bowl. Prepare dressing.

DRESSING:
1 cup salad oil
1/3 cup catsup
1 tablespoon Worcestershire sauce
1/2 cup white sugar
1/4 cup brown sugar
1 medium onion, grated

Gradually add salad oil to rest of ingredients. Drizzle dressing over salad. Serves 8-10.

OVERNIGHT GREEN TOSSED SALAD

1 medium head iceberg lettuce
1 package (10 ounce) fresh spinach
1/2 cup sliced green onions
1 pint cherry tomatoes, cut in half
1 package (10 ounce) frozen peas, thawed, not cooked
1 pound bacon diced, cooked and drained
1 1/2 cups mayonnaise
1 cup sour cream
2 teaspoons lemon juice
1/2 teaspoon oregano leaves
1/4 teaspoon basil leaves
1/4 teaspoon salt
1/8 teaspoon pepper

Tear lettuce and spinach into bite-size pieces and place in large bowl. Add onion, tomatoes, peas, bacon. Toss gently. Combine mayonnaise, sour cream lemon juice and seasonings. Mix well. Spread dressing over entire surface. Seal dressing to sides of bowl to make air tight. Do not mix in. Cover salad mix overnight. Toss when ready to serve. Serves 14-16.

Jan says, "This is a wonderful way to have a tossed salad already prepared when company comes. I also don't use a full pound of bacon. And if you can't find spinach, use more lettuce."

Great Toss Ups

HEARTS OF PALM SALAD

1 can hearts of palm, chilled

DRESSING:
1 clove garlic, mashed
1 1/2 teaspoons salt
1 to 1 1/2 tablespoons red wine vinegar
1 teaspoon Dijon mustard
1/8 teaspoon fresh ground pepper
6 to 8 tablespoons olive oil
1 teaspoon chopped fresh parsley
1 egg yolk (optional)

Combine dressing ingredients in blender. Drain can of hearts of palm and cut into crosswise pieces. Marinate in salad dressing for several hours or overnight. Drain and serve on a bed of lettuce. Garnish with strips of pimento. Serves 2-4.

CREAM CHEESE SALAD

2 packages (3-ounce size) cream cheese
1 can spiced white grapes, drained
1 small can crushed pineapple, drained
1/2 cup blanched almonds (more, if desired)
Mayonnaise
Tabasco sauce
Salt

Mix ingredients together, adding a small amount of mayonnaise and a dash of Tabasco sauce and salt. Chill well and serve in lettuce cups. Serves 4.

FROZEN PINEAPPLE-CHERRY SALAD

1 carton (12 ounce) sour cream
2 teaspoons lemon juice
3/4 cup sugar
1 can (9 ounce) crushed pineapple, drained
1/4 cup maraschino cherries, chopped
1/4 cup pecans, chopped

Pour mixture into 8 paper liners in muffin tins or 5-ounce size paper cups. Freeze. Serve on lettuce cups.

THE "BEST" POTATO SALAD

6 medium-sized potatoes, cooked and diced
1 cup Italian salad dressing
1 onion, finely chopped
1 cup mayonnaise
2 teaspoons prepared mustard
3 hard-boiled eggs, chopped
1/2 teaspoon celery seed
1/2 cup celery, chopped
2 tablespoons sweet pickle relish
Seasoned salt to taste
Salt and pepper to taste

Marinate potatoes in Italian dressing in refrigerator for several hours. Combine with other ingredients and chill until serving time. May garnish with hard-cooked eggs, cherry tomatoes, or green pepper rings. Serves 6-8.

Great Toss Ups

RASPBERRY SALAD

1 large package raspberry Jell-O
1 small package (10 ounce) frozen raspberries
1 can (20 ounce) crushed pineapple, drained
1 large banana, mashed, or 2 small bananas
1 package (8 ounce) cream cheese softened
with mayonnaise

Dissolve Jell-O and divide in half. Into first half, dissolve frozen berries, banana and pineapple. Refrigerate until set up. Spread the layer with cream cheese. Put other half of Jell-O on top and let set up.

NOTE: Use a smaller pan than 9 x 13-inch, as the larger pan makes the layers too thin. Serves 8.

SALMON MOUSSE

2 envelopes unflavored gelatin
1/2 cup boiling water
2 tablespoons lemon juice
1 teaspoon salt
1 small onion, diced
1 cup mayonnaise
1 cup sour cream
1 can (1 pound) drained, boned, flaked red
salmon
2 tablespoons Durkee's sandwich spread
1/2 teaspoon paprika
1 to 2 teaspoons dill weed
1/8 teaspoon freshly ground pepper

Stir gelatin into boiling water until dissolved. Put gelatin, lemon juice and onion in blender and blend at high speed for 1 minute. Add dill weed, paprika, salmon, Durkee's spread, salt, pepper, 1/2 cup mayonnaise and 1/2 cup sour cream. Cover and blend well. Add other 1/2 cup mayonnaise and 1/2 cup sour cream. Cover and blend again. Pour into 4-cup fish or shell mold that has been lightly greased with salad oil. Refrigerate until firm.

To Serve: Unmold on platter. Garnish top of mousse by overlapping thin slices of scored cucumbers or radishes to simulate scales. Use strips of pimento to form mouth, and a slice of olive for eyes.

Garnish wedge with watercress, cherry tomatoes and artichoke hearts or wedges of hard-boiled eggs, small whole pickled beets and Belgian endive. Serve with Cucumber Dill Sauce or Avocado Dressing. Serves 6-8.

AVOCADO DRESSING

1 large overripe avocado
1/4 teaspoon garlic salt
Juice of 1 lemon
1/4 teaspoon onion salt
1/4 cup mayonnaise

Put all ingredients into blender at high speed until creamy smooth. Garnish with paprika.
Makes 3/4 cup.

CUCUMBER DILL SAUCE

1 cucumber, peeled and seeded
Salt
1 cup sour cream
1 tablespoon lemon juice or tarragon vinegar
1 teaspoon dill weed
1 teaspoon chopped chives
1/4 teaspoon white pepper

Shred cucumber with coarse grater. Sprinkle with salt; let stand at room temperature for 1 hour. Drain thoroughly. Combine with remaining ingredients. Chill. Makes 1 1/2 cups.

Great Toss Ups

SESAME CHINESE CABBAGE

1 medium head Chinese cabbage
2 tablespoons sesame seeds
2 tablespoons vegetable oil
1/2 cup chopped onion
2 tablespoons butter
1 tablespoon soy sauce

Separate leaves of cabbage. Wash and drain. Cut leaves across 1/2 inch thick. Brown seeds lightly in skillet, stirring often. Remove from pan. Heat oil in skillet. Saute onion 1 minute. Add cabbage. Cook tender but crisp, stirring often. Spoon off liquid. Stir butter, soy sauce, seeds into cabbage. Serves 6.

SPINACH SALAD A LA GREQUE

6 cups (2/3 pound) washed, drained, bite-size pieces of spinach
1 small Bermuda onion, sliced thin
1/4 cup diced celery
4 hard-cooked eggs, sliced
1/2 teaspoon salt
1/8 teaspoon freshly ground black pepper
1 cup sour cream
1 package Good Season's garlic-cheese salad dressing mix
3 tablespoons lemon juice
5 slices crisp, crumbled bacon

Combine spinach, onion, celery, eggs, salt and pepper; toss well. Refrigerate. In separate bowl, combine sour cream, salad dressing mix, lemon juice. Mix well and refrigerate.

When ready to serve, thoroughly toss 1/2 of the sour cream mixture with spinach mixture. Add bacon. Serve immediately. Refrigerate the remaining sour cream mixture for future use. Serves 6.

SPINACH APPLE SALAD

2 Golden Delicious apples
1 1/2 quarts fresh spinach
1/2 cup sunflower seeds

DRESSING:
1/3 cup Bertolli olive oil
1/2 cup orange juice concentrate
2 tablespoons tarragon wine vinegar
1/4 teaspoon salt
1 teaspoon sugar
1/8 teaspoon pepper
1/8 teaspoon dry mustard

Slice and core apples. Combine apples, spinach and sunflower seeds in salad bowl. Combine dressing ingredients in small jar and shake well to blend. Drizzle dressing over salad and toss. Serves 6.

WATERCRESS SALAD

2 large bunches watercress
1 to 2 teaspoons garlic
2 tablespoons Dijon mustard
1 teaspoon salt
1/2 teaspoon freshly ground black pepper
3 tablespoons red wine vinegar
1/2 cup olive oil
2 cups fresh mushrooms, sliced
1/2 cup toasted slivered almonds

Toast almonds in flat pan in oven until lightly browned; set aside. Wash and dry watercress. Reserve.

Chop garlic. Place in small bowl with all ingredients except olive oil, mushrooms, and almonds. Whisking continuously, add olive oil in a thin stream. Toss dressing with salad, nuts and mushrooms at the last moment. Serves 4.

Great Toss Ups

SPINACH-MUSHROOM SALAD

1/2 cup dry white wine
2 tablespoons lemon juice
1/2 cup dried apricots
1 1/2 pounds fresh spinach
1/2 pound fresh mushrooms
6 tablespoons olive oil
1/2 teaspoon dill
Salt and pepper
Sliced almonds, if you like

Combine wine, lemon juice, dried apricots and simmer over low heat about 20 minutes. Cover these ingredients tightly for 1/2 hour. In the meantime, slice mushrooms thin. Then drain apricots (saving liquid) and cut into bite-size pieces. Add liquid, olive oil, salt and pepper and whip. Toss and sprinkle apricots and almonds on top. Serves 6.

SPINACH SALAD FLAMBE

6 bunches of spinach (12 ounces each), washed
   and dried thoroughly
6 hard-boiled eggs, sliced
1/4 teaspoon salt
1/2 teaspoon ground pepper
1 cup chopped green onion
18 bacon strips, chopped and fried crisp
3/4 cup bacon drippings
1/2 cup malt vinegar
1/4 cup lemon juice
4 teaspoons brown sugar
1 teaspoon Worcestershire sauce
1 1/2 ounces 100-proof brandy

Tear spinach into bite-size pieces and place in large salad bowl. Add egg slices, onion, bacon, salt and pepper. Mix remaining ingredients except brandy into small saucepan and heat until very hot. Heat brandy briefly, add to saucepan and ignite. Pour flaming dressing over spinach and toss gently but thoroughly. Serve on warm salad plates. Serves 8-10.

SPINACH SALAD AND DRESSING

1 pound fresh spinach
2 medium oranges, peeled and sliced
1 medium red onion, thinly sliced
1/2 cup bacon, cooked and crumbled

DRESSING:
1/2 cup mayonnaise
1/2 cup olive oil
1/4 cup lemon juice
2 teaspoons dark mustard

Just before serving, combine spinach, orange, onion and bacon. Toss with dressing. Add garnish and serve with sesame crackers.

Blend mayonnaise, olive oil, lemon juice and mustard. Add salt and pepper to taste. Serves 6-8.

THREE BEAN SALAD

2 cans green beans
2 cans wax beans
1 can kidney beans
Green pepper, chopped
Small onion, chopped
1 can water chestnuts, sliced
3/4 cup sugar
2/3 cup vinegar
1/2 cup salad oil
1 teaspoon salt
1/8 teaspoon pepper

Drain all vegetables. Add chopped green pepper, onion. Boil sugar, vinegar, salad oil, salt and pepper together for a few minutes. Pour over drained vegetables and mix well. This will keep a week or 10 days in the refrigerator. Serves 12-14.
Jan says, "The older it gets, the better it is."

Great Toss Ups

TWENTY-FOUR HOUR FRUIT SALAD

4 egg yolks
Juice of 1 lemon
1/4 cup heavy cream
1 pound tokay grapes
1 small bag marshmallows, cut into fourths
Cans of fruit cocktail, peaches, pears, pineapple,
    mandarin oranges
1/2 pint heavy cream

Cook egg yolks, lemon juice, 1/4 cup heavy cream until thick. Put hot salad dressing over drained fruit; add marshmallows. Whip 1/2 pint heavy cream until peaks. Mix gently into the first mixture. Let salad stand 24 hours. Serves 10-12.

Jan says, "You may add any amount of fruit and any kind that you prefer to the amount of dressing you have prepared. A very good salad to serve, especially at holiday time."

JEANNE'S V-8 TOMATO ASPIC

4 cups V-8 juice
2 tablespoons gelatin
1 teaspoon salt
1/2 teaspoon paprika
1/2 teaspoon sugar
2 tablespoons lemon juice
3 tablespoons chopped green onion
4 stalks chopped celery
2 tablespoons chopped green pepper

Place gelatin in 1/2 cup V-8 juice to soften. Heat remaining 3 1/2 cups juice with salt, paprika, sugar, lemon juice. Dissolve gelatin in heated juice. Add onion, celery, and green pepper. Pour into greased ring mold and chill until firm.

VARIATIONS:
When partially congealed, drop marinated artichoke hearts into aspic, all the way around ring.

Fill center of ring with mayonnaise mixed half and half with sour cream, well-laced with horseradish.

Mix mayonnaise and sour cream with curry powder to taste.

The aspic with horseradish goes beautifully with roast beef. The curry-flavored sauce is good when you are serving aspic with shrimp, chicken or lamb. Serves 12.

WALDORF SALAD

2 cups diced tart red apples
1 tablespoon sugar
1 teaspoon lemon juice
Dash of salt
1 cup coarsely diced celery
1/3 cup seedless raisins
1 cup quartered marshmallows
1/2 cup walnut chips
1/4 cup mayonnaise
1/2 cup cream, whipped

Sprinkle diced apples with sugar, lemon juice and salt. Add celery, raisins, marshmallows and nuts. Fold mayonnaise into whipped cream, then fold into apple mixture. Chill. Serve in lettuce cups. Serves 6.

HOT SLAW

2 egg yolks
1 tablespoon butter
1/4 cup cider vinegar
1/4 cup water
4 cups shredded cabbage
Salt to taste

In heavy saucepan mix yolks, butter, vinegar and water. Stir over low heat until thickened. Add cabbage and stir briskly to coat. Serves 6.

Great Toss Ups

FRESH FRUIT SALAD DRESSING

1 cup mayonnaise
2 tablespoons honey
3 tablespoons pineapple juice
4 tablespoons creme de menthe
Dash of salt

Mix well and refrigerate. Makes 1 1/2 cups.

ONION FRUIT SALAD DRESSING

2 tablespoons grated onion
1 teaspoon dry mustard
2 tablespoons vinegar
1 teaspoon salt
1/2 cup sugar
1 cup salad oil
1 teaspoon celery seed
1/4 teaspoon paprika

Combine first five ingredients. Add 1 cup salad oil very slowly, mixing on blender or electric mixer. Add 1 teaspoon celery seed and 1/4 teaspoon paprika. Chill. Keeps well. Makes 2 cups.

RUTHIE'S FRUIT SALAD DRESSING

1 egg, well beaten
1 1/2 cups orange juice
1/4 cup lemon juice
1/2 cup pineapple juice
1 cup sugar
3 rounded tablespoons cornstarch

Blend together. Cook over low heat until thickened. Layer fruit in dish. Add dressing after each layer. You may use any fruit. This dressing will not color fruit. If you use bananas, add them last. Makes 2 cups.

GORGONZOLA DRESSING

1 cup Gorgonzola cheese, grated or chopped
1/2 cup mayonnaise
1/2 cup sour cream
1 tablespoon Dijon mustard
2 cloves garlic, crushed
2 tablespoons red wine vinegar
1 tablespoon celery seeds
1 teaspoon oregano
1/4 cup grated Parmesan cheese
Salt, pepper
Dash of Lea & Perrins sauce
Dash of Maggi seasoning

Blend all ingredients and mix well. Makes 2 cups.

HONEY POPPY SEED DRESSING

3 tablespoons poppy seed
1 tablespoon celery seed
1 cup honey
1/2 cup vinegar
3 tablespoons lemon juice
3 cups salad oil
2 cups sugar
1 teaspoon salt

Combine all ingredients except oil. Slowly add oil, beating constantly until well mixed. Refrigerate overnight to thicken. Pour over fresh fruit. Makes 1 1/2 quarts.

Great Toss Ups

HUBBLE HOUSE DRESSING

1 can tomato soup
2/3 cup Mazola oil
2/3 cup brown sugar
1/2 cup catsup
Juice of 1 lemon
1/4 cup vinegar
1 teaspoon salt
1 teaspoon dry mustard
1 small grated onion
1/2 green pepper, cut fine
1 quart Miracle Whip

Boil first 10 ingredients for 10 minutes; let cool and add 1 quart Miracle Whip salad dressing. Mix well. Makes 2 quarts.

PAULINE'S SALAD DRESSING

2 egg yolks
2 tablespoons sugar
Juice of 2 lemons
1 tablespoon flour
1/2 cup honey or maple syrup
1/2 cup whipped cream

Mix syrup, flour, sugar and cook in double boiler 10 minutes. Add lemon juice and beaten egg yolks slowly and cook 5 minutes, stirring constantly. Remove from fire and cool. Add whipped cream to salad dressing before serving.
Makes 1 1/2 cups.

DRESSING FOR WILTED LETTUCE

1 egg, beaten
1 tablespoon sugar
1/2 teaspoon salt
1/4 cup sour cream
1 tablespoon vinegar
1 1/2 tablespoons butter

Combine beaten egg, sugar, salt, cream and vinegar, then beat. Brown 1 1/2 tablespoons butter in skillet, add creamed mixture and cook, stirring constantly until thick. Makes 1/2 cup.

ORANGE FRUIT SALAD DRESSING

1 cup sugar
2 tablespoons flour, heaped
1 egg
1 cup boiling water
Juice and grated rind of 1 orange
Juice of 1 lemon
1 teaspoon butter
1 cup heavy cream, whipped

Mix dry ingredients. Add egg and mix. Add water then juices, rind and mix. Cook, stirring constantly until thick. Add butter. Cool. To serve, add whipped cream. Measure the cream before whipping. Makes 3 cups.

Sweet and Saucy · Sauces

This chapter offers every type of sauce except for dessert sauces, which are in the dessert chapter called Melting Moments. It's here that you will find cocktail sauces, cheese sauces, crème fraîche, cranberry sauces, barbecue sauces, even a sauce for baked potatoes. If you have an abundance of ripe tomatoes, do try the Ripe Tomato Catsup. The Herb Butter recipe is great on French bread and the Mock Hollandaise is easy, delicious, and not as rich or fattening as the regular Hollandaise.

Sweet & Saucy

BARBECUE SAUCE

2 teaspoons salt
1/2 cup water
1/2 cup chopped onion
1 clove garlic, minced
1 can tomato paste
1 cup catsup
3/4 cup brown sugar
1/2 cup vinegar
2 tablespoons prepared mustard

Combine all ingredients, mix well. Simmer for 30 minutes. Keep warm when serving over meat. Makes 3 cups.

GINA'S BARBECUE SAUCE

2 bottles (14 ounces each) ketchup
1 bottle (12 ounces) chili sauce
1/3 cup prepared mustard
1 tablespoon dry mustard
1 1/2 cups firmly packed brown sugar
2 tablespoons coarse, freshly ground black pepper
1 1/2 cups wine vinegar
1 cup fresh lemon juice
1/2 cup bottled thick steak sauce
Dash Tabasco, or to taste
1/4 cup Worcestershire sauce
1 tablespoon soy sauce
2 tablespoons salad oil
1 can (12-ounce) beer
Minced or crushed garlic, if desired

Combine all ingredients except the garlic and mix well. Pour into pint jars to store. This sauce may be stored for several weeks in the refrigerator. For longer storage, freeze. About an hour before using the sauce, add the garlic if desired. Makes 6 pints.

HELENA'S BARBECUE SAUCE

2 tablespoons oil
1 onion, chopped
1/4 cup vinegar
2 tablespoons sugar
1 cup catsup
1/2 cup water
3 tablespoons Worcestershire sauce
1 teaspoon prepared mustard
1/2 cup finely diced celery
2 teaspoons salt

Combine all ingredients. A delicious sauce for basting chicken, chops and ribs. Makes 2 1/2 cups.

BECHAMEL SAUCE

4 tablespoons butter
4 tablespoons flour
1 cup milk
1 cup heavy cream
1 teaspoon salt
1/8 teaspoon white pepper

Melt butter, stir in flour. Gradually add milk and cream, whisking constantly. Stir until mixture comes to a boil and is smooth. Still stirring, simmer 2-3 minutes more or until sauce coats wires of whisk heavily. Remove from heat and season with salt and pepper. Makes 2 cups.

Sweet & Saucy

BEARNAISE SAUCE

1 tablespoon tarragon wine vinegar
2 tablespoons dry white wine
2 tablespoons shallots, chopped
Dash fresh ground pepper
3 egg yolks
Pinch of salt
3/4 cup butter

Combine vinegar, wine, shallots and pepper in saucepan and cook until almost all liquid is evaporated. Cool slightly. Place egg yolks, salt and tarragon mixture in blender. Melt butter and heat until bubbles, but not brown. Add butter in steady stream into blender mixture on blending speed. Sauce may be prepared early in the day. Do not boil if reheating. Makes 1 cup.

CHATEAUBRIAND SAUCE

1 small onion, finely chopped
1 small carrot, minced
2 tablespoons oil
3/4 cup finely chopped mushrooms
2 tablespoons flour
1/4 cup red wine
1 1/2 cups beef stock or bouillon
1 tablespoon tomato paste
1 small bay leaf
1/2 teaspoon salt
Fresh ground pepper

Cook onion and carrot slowly in oil until golden. Add mushrooms and flour and cook until brown but not scorched. Add remaining ingredients. Bring to a boil and simmer uncovered for 30 minutes. Remove bay leaf. The sauce should be well-flavored and glossy. Taste for seasonings before serving with steak slices. Makes 1 1/2 cups.

CHEESE SAUCE

4 tablespoons butter
3 to 4 tablespoons flour
1/2 teaspoon dry mustard
1/2 teaspoon salt
1/4 teaspoon pepper
1 tablespoon grated onion
1 tablespoon chopped parsley
2 cups milk
1 cup American cheese, shredded

Melt butter over low heat in heavy saucepan. Blend in flour and seasonings. Cook over low heat, stirring until mixture is smooth and bubbly. Remove from heat, stir in milk. Bring to boil, stirring constantly. Boil 1 minute. Add American cheese, stir until cheese is melted. Makes 3 cups.

LOIS' CHILI SAUCE

10 cups tomatoes
4 large mango peppers
5 onions
8 stalks celery
1 teaspoon celery seed
2 cups sugar
1 tablespoon salt
1 tablespoon whole allspice
1 tablespoon cloves
1 to 2 sticks cinnamon
2 bay leaves
3 dried chili peppers
2 cups vinegar

Grind or finely mince peppers, onions and celery. Chop tomatoes.
Combine all ingredients. Boil until vegetables are tender. Seal in sterile jars. Makes 4 quarts.

Sweet & Saucy

CRANBERRY SAUCE

1 pound cranberries
1/2 cup raisins
1/4 cup candied ginger, minced
2 cups sugar
1/2 cup orange juice
3/4 teaspoon curry powder
1/2 teaspoon Tabasco sauce
1 stick cinnamon
1 clove garlic, minced
4 navel oranges

Peel oranges thinly, getting only the brightly colored peel. Grind in meat grinder or cut into tiny slivers. Put into saucepan with rest of ingredients except oranges and bring to a boil over moderate heat. Stir until sugar dissolves, then continue cooking, uncovered, until all the cranberries pop. Meanwhile, cut off all the white membrane from the oranges and cut into slices 1/4-inch thick. Cut the slices into quarters and remove seeds. When cranberries have all popped, remove pan from fire and discard cinnamon stick and garlic. Add orange pieces, folding them in gently but thoroughly.
Makes 2 pints.

CREME FRAICHE

1 pint whipping cream. If possible do not use cream sterilized to have a shelf life of 2 months.
2 tablespoons buttermilk
Sugar or freshly grated nutmeg (optional)

Combine cream and buttermilk in glass jar and whisk until well blended. Cover and let stand at room temperature in draft-free area, whisking several times, until mixture has thickened (about 24 hours).

Chill thoroughly before using. Serve with sugar, nutmeg, or plain. Creme Fraiche will keep covered in refrigerator for 10 days to 2 weeks.

Jo says, "You have not lived until you have tried fresh berries, any kind will do nicely, covered with creme fraiche." Makes 1 pint.

COCKTAIL SAUCE FOR SEAFOOD

1 cup tomato catsup
1/2 cup finely chopped celery
1 tablespoon finely chopped onion
1/4 cup prepared horseradish
1/2 cup lemon juice
1/4 teaspoon Tabasco sauce

Combine ingredients. Chill sauce and seafood before serving. Will keep a long time in refrigerator. Makes 2 cups.

GOURMET MEAT SAUCE

2 shallots, chopped
1 cup wine vinegar
1/2 bottle Sauce Robert
1/2 bottle Sauce Diablo
1 tablespoon Worcestershire sauce
1/2 teaspoon lemon juice
3 tablespoons English mustard
1 quart brown stock or very strong consomme
1 cup heavy cream
Salt, pepper
Dash of Tabasco

Combine first 5 ingredients. Bring to a boil and reduce to 1/3. Add lemon juice, mustard and stock. Simmer 1 hour. Add cream, salt, pepper and Tabasco. Simmer 10 minutes. Strain. Keep warm for serving. This sauce can be left in the refrigerator for a week to 10 days. Makes 2 quarts.

Sweet & Saucy

DEGLAZING SAUCE

1 tablespoon of minced shallots or scallions
3/4 cup of chicken stock or a combination
   of stock and white wine
2 tablespoons butter

Saute the minced shallots or scallions in a teaspoon butter. Cook over moderately high heat stirring constantly. Pour in 3/4 cup chicken stock and wine. Boil rapidly, scraping up coagulated saute juices from bottom of pan, and continue to boil rapidly until liquid is almost syrupy. Remove pan from heat and swirl a tablespoon or two of butter to enrich the sauce. Pour the sauce over chicken. Makes 3/4 cup.

ORANGE FRUIT DRESSING

In saucepan, combine half of a 6-ounce can orange juice concentrate, thawed (1/3 cup), 1/4 cup sugar, 1/4 cup water, and 2 beaten eggs. Cook and stir over low heat until thickened. Cool. Whip 1/2 cup heavy cream. Fold whipped cream and 1/2 cup mayonnaise into cooled mixture. Chill. Makes 2 1/2 cups.

RIPE TOMATO CATSUP

1/2 bushel ripe tomatoes, juiced
2 pounds brown sugar
1 pound salt
1/4 pound black pepper
1/4 teaspoon cayenne pepper
1/4 pound whole cloves
1/4 pound whole allspice
6 whole onions, medium size
1 quart cider vinegar

Add brown sugar, salt, pepper, cayenne and vinegar to tomatoes. Put cloves and allspice in a bag and tie. Put onions in whole. Place all in saucepan and boil 3 hours; heat tomatoes to a boiling point, run through a sieve, strain and bottle. Will keep indefinitely. Makes 6 quarts.

HERB BUTTER

1 pound unsalted butter, room temperature
1 small bunch parsley, chopped
1 small bunch dill, chopped

Add chopped herbs to softened butter and beat until fluffy and herbs are well distributed. This butter is delicious on freshly baked breads. If the herbs are chopped in the food processor, the butter becomes a brighter green. Herb butter may be stored in the refrigerator or frozen indefinitely.
Makes 1 pound.

MUSTARD SAUCE

4 tablespoons butter
1 cup plus 2 tablespoons sugar
2 eggs, well beaten
1/2 can tomato soup
1/2 cup apple cider vinegar
1/2 cup Dijon mustard

Mix all ingredients together and cook in double boiler until thick. Pour into jar and refrigerate. This sauce keeps very well. Makes 3 cups.

Sweet & Saucy

MOCK HOLLANDAISE SAUCE

1 cup Hellmann's mayonnaise
2 eggs
3 tablespoons lemon juice
1/2 teaspoon salt
1/2 teaspoon dry mustard

Stir all ingredients with a wire whisk in small saucepan until all ingredients are smooth. Stir over medium-low heat until thick (do not boil). Serve over vegetables, seafood or eggs. Sprinkle with paprika. Makes 1 2/3 cups.

HOLLANDAISE SAUCE IN LARGE QUANTITY

2 1/2 cups butter
20 egg yolks
2 teaspoons salt
1 1/4 cups lemon juice
1 1/4 cups light cream

Heat butter in double boiler until just melted. Add salt and lemon juice to egg yolks and mix well. Turn down heat so water is just simmering. Stir the egg mixture into butter and beat until thick. Add cream and beat 2 minutes more.

Note: This large quantity of sauce might be helpful for brunches or buffets, when serving eggs or vegetable dishes for a crowd. Makes approximately 6 1/3 cups.

MARINADE FOR STEAKS

9 tablespoons bourbon
6 tablespoons soy sauce
2 tablespoons lemon juice
2 tablespoons salad oil
1/2 teaspoon Accent
2 cloves minced garlic
1/2 teaspoon smoked salt
1/2 teaspoon mixed herbs
1/2 teaspoon ground pepper

Combine all ingredients. Pour over steaks placed in a glass container. Let the steaks marinate for several hours, turning frequently. Prepare the steaks in your favorite fashion. Makes 1 cup.

GREEN MAYONNAISE

1 1/2 cups mayonnaise or cooked salad dressing
1 cup torn raw spinach
1/4 cup parsley sprigs, no stems
1/4 cup watercress, no stems
1 tablespoon chives
2 tablespoons dry white wine

One day before serving, place half of all ingredients in electric blender. Cover, blend at high speed until smooth. Add remaining ingredients and blend well. Refrigerate, covered, overnight. Served with poached salmon. Makes 1 1/3 cups.

CUCUMBER SAUCE

1 medium cucumber, seeds removed
1/2 cup sour cream
3 tablespoons mayonnaise
2 teaspoons vinegar
1 tablespoon parsley
1 teaspoon finely chopped green onion
Salt and pepper to taste

Combine all ingredients in blender. Makes 1 1/2 cups.

Sweet & Saucy

MUSTARD SAUCE

4 ounces mayonnaise, Hellmann's
1/2 teaspoon Dijon mustard
1 tablespoon sour cream
1/4 teaspoon garlic powder
1/4 teaspoon anchovy paste
1/4 teaspoon lemon juice
1/4 teaspoon brandy, optional
Salt and pepper to taste

Mix all ingredients together, refrigerate.
Makes 1 cup.

FT. LAUDERDALE MUSTARD SAUCE

2/3 cup sour cream
1/4 teaspoon parsley flakes
1/4 teaspoon dry mustard
2 tablespoons Dijon mustard
Big pinch of salt
2 teaspoons butter

Heat to blend but do not boil. Serve hot or cold. Makes 1 cup.

SAUCE NOISETTE

Add 1/4 cup grated hazelnuts or filberts to 1 recipe hollandaise sauce and season well. Serve with chicken or asparagus.

NUT GLAZE FOR HAM

3/4 cup brown sugar
1 tablespoon dry mustard
2 tablespoons cooking sherry
1/2 cup chopped walnuts

Combine all ingredients. Last 1/2 hour of baking ham, spread glaze on top. Glazes 5-pound ham.

BAKED POTATO SAUCE

4 tablespoons margarine
1/2 cup sour cream
2 tablespoons chives
1/2 cup bacon bits
1/2 cup sharp process cheese, grated

Whip the above ingredients together. May be made ahead and kept in the refrigerator. Remove to room temperature before serving.
Makes 1 1/2 cups.

HOLLANDAISE SAUCE

3 egg yolks
3 tablespoons cold water
Pinch pepper
1/2 pound butter, melted
1 tablespoon lemon juice
1/8 teaspoon salt

Beat yolks, water, salt and pepper in top of a double boiler until blended. Place over **just-simmering** water, heat and beat until mixture thickens and is custardlike, a minute or two. Turn heat to low and add butter, a tablespoon at a time, beating all the while. When all butter is added, remove sauce from heat and stir in the lemon juice. Serve hot. Makes 1 cup.

Sweet & Saucy

PESTO TIPS

Store in jar with tight-fitting lid. When storing basil pesto in refrigerator or freezer, add a film of olive oil about 1/8-inch thick to the top before sealing. Mix it in when ready to use. Always bring chilled pesto mixtures to room temperature before serving. Before dressing hot pasta with pesto, add 2-3 teaspoons of hot water to pesto for better consistency.

BASIC PESTO SAUCE

2 cups tightly packed fresh basil leaves
1/4 cup fresh grated Parmesan cheese
2 cloves garlic
1 tablespoon toasted pine nuts
2/3 to 1 cup olive oil

Combine all ingredients in blender, adding just enough oil to make a thick sauce. Makes 3 1/2 cups.

PESTO SAUCE

1/2 cup pine nuts
4 cloves garlic, peeled
1 teaspoon salt
1/2 teaspoon freshly ground pepper
3 to 4 cups fresh basil leaves
1/4 pound freshly ground Parmesan cheese
1/4 pound freshly grated Romano cheese
1 1/2 to 2 cups olive oil

Chop nuts, garlic, salt and pepper until very fine. Add basil, chopping until very fine. Put in bowl, adding cheeses and olive oil, drop by drop, mixing well until creamy smooth. If using a food processor, grind all ingredients until smooth with 1/2 cup olive oil. Add remaining oil and process until smooth and creamy. Makes 4 cups.

STIR-FRY SAUCE

3 tablespoons dark brown sugar
1/3 cup cornstarch
2 teaspoons fresh minced ginger root or
     2 teaspoons ground ginger
4 garlic cloves, crushed
1/2 cup soy sauce
1/2 cup dry sherry
1 tablespoon Worcestershire sauce
1/4 teaspoon Tabasco sauce
3 tablespoons red wine
2 1/2 cups chicken broth or beef broth

Combine all ingredients except broth in blender and blend until smooth. Pour into jar; add broth and shake. Store in refrigerator 10 days to 2 weeks. Shake before using. Makes 4 cups. You may freeze this sauce in 1-cup portions and thaw at room temperature.

TERIYAKI SAUCE

2/3 cup soy sauce
1/4 cup salad oil
2 tablespoons molasses
2 teaspoons Accent
2 teaspoons ginger
2 teaspoons dry mustard
3 to 6 garlic cloves, crushed

Combine all ingredients. Marinate steaks or pieces of sirloin for kabobs for several hours, turning frequently. Marinade for 2 pounds of meat.

Sweet & Saucy

SAUCE VELOUTE I

1 tablespoon butter
1/2 cup flour
4 cups strained chicken stock
Salt, white pepper
1 pinch nutmeg, optional
1/2 cup white sliced mushrooms (optional)

Melt butter in a heavy saucepan over low heat, stir in the flour, and cook, stirring constantly, until the roux is smooth but not brown. Add heated chicken stock gradually, stirring constantly until it starts to thicken. Add seasonings to taste, then mushroom slices, and simmer over very low heat, stirring occasionally, for 1 hour.

Strain the sauce and stir until cold. This sauce is improved by the long simmering, but if time is not available, the stock can be reduced to 3 cups and simmering time cut to 20 - 30 minutes. Serve with chicken dishes. Makes 3 cups.

SAUCE VELOUTE II

1 recipe chicken veloute sauce I
1 cup strained chicken stock
1 teaspoon lemon juice
2/3 cup heavy cream
3 egg yolks, beaten
1 teaspoon butter
Salt, white pepper

Combine veloute sauce, stock and lemon juice. Bring to a boil in a heavy saucepan, stirring constantly. Reduce heat and simmer, stirring frequently, until sauce is reduced by about 1/3. Add a small amount to combined cream, egg yolk mixture, then add it back to saucepan, stirring constantly. Simmer 5 minutes longer. Add butter, salt and pepper. Makes 5 1/2 cups.

WHITE SAUCE FORMULAS

White Sauce	Liquid	Thickening Material	Butter
No. 1 – Thin	1 cup milk	1 tablespoon flour	1 tablespoon
No. 2 – Medium	1 cup milk	2 tablespoons flour	1 1/2 tablespoons
No. 3 – Medium	1 cup milk	3 tablespoons flour	2 tablespoons
No. 4 – Thick	1 cup milk	4 tablespoons flour	2 1/2 tablespoons

Melt butter, add flour and stir to blend. Continue stirring over heat for 2 minutes to blend flavors. Add salt, pepper and any other seasonings you desire. Some prefer adding 1/2 teaspoon of paprika or dry mustard. Remove from heat and stir in the milk. When completely blended return to heat and cook until thickened.

Sassy and Tart · Pickles, Jellies, Preserves

So many of these recipes have been handed down through the years. They easily could have been in the Heirlooms section, but we felt they deserved a place of their own.

And so many of them make wonderful gifts that lovingly say "I care." When someone goes to the effort of baking or preserving and giving, those receiving know they are special. Don't miss the Green Pepper Jelly, the Bread and Butter Pickles, Hattie's Piccalilli, or the other variations of pickles.

Sassy & Tart

APPLE BUTTER

6 pounds tart apples
6 cups apple cider or apple juice
3 cups sugar
2 teaspoons ground cinnamon
1/2 teaspoon ground cloves

Core and quarter apples. Cook with cider in large heavy saucepan until soft, about 30 minutes. Press through a food mill. Boil gently 30 minutes, stirring often. Stir in sugar and spices. Cook and stir over low heat until sugar dissolves. Boil gently stirring often, until desired thickness, about 1 hour. Pour into hot 1/2-pint jars, adjust lids. Process in boiling-water bath 10 minutes (start counting time after water returns to a boil). Makes 8 half pints.

PICKLED BABY BEETS

2 quarts vinegar
1 pint water
4 cups sugar
2 teaspoons salt
3/4 teaspoon pepper

Mix and let boil. Fill jars filled with beets to overflowing with boiling mixture. Makes 4 quarts.

MANGO CHUTNEY

4 pounds mangos (8 cups) 4 large, 5 or 6 medium mangos
2 tablespoons white mustard seed
1 tablespoon ground chili pepper (chili powder)
1 pound preserved syrup and ginger
2 pounds sugar, combine brown and white
2 quarts cider vinegar
1 1/2 cups white raisins
1 clove garlic

Peel and cut fruit into 1/4-inch pieces. Add 1 quart of vinegar. Boil for 20 minutes. Combine sugar and 1 quart of vinegar. Boil until it is a thick syrup, about an hour. Pour off most of liquid from the fruit and add to the syrup. Boil this until it is thick. Combine the thick syrup to fruit and remaining ingredients, except the ginger. Cook for 30 minutes. Add chopped ginger and cook for 10 more minutes. Pour into sterilized jars and pour melted paraffin on top. Seal. Will keep indefinitely. Makes 6 quarts.

LOIS' CORN RELISH

2 quarts corn
1 quart chopped cabbage
1 cup green sweet peppers
1 cup red sweet peppers
2 large onions
1 cup sugar
2 teaspoons ground mustard
1 tablespoon mustard seed
1 tablespoon salt
1 tablespoon celery seed
1 quart vinegar and 1 cup water

Boil corn 5 minutes. Cold water dip, cut from cob, measure. Chop and measure cabbage, peppers and onions. Combine all and simmer 20 minutes. Pack into hot sterile jars and seal. Makes 5 quarts.

BEV'S CUCUMBERS

1 cup sugar
1/2 cup salad oil
1/2 cup vinegar
1 teaspoon celery seed
2 cucumbers - peeled and sliced

Shake well and cover. Leave in refrigerator at least overnight. Makes 1 quart.

Sassy & Tart

RED CUCUMBER RINGS

7 pounds cucumbers, peeled, sliced and cored
2 cups hydrated pickle lime
2 gallons water

2 quarts white vinegar
4 1/2 pounds sugar
1 tablespoon celery seed
1 tablespoon mustard seed
2 tablespoons salt
1 tablespoon whole cloves
1 tablespoon mixed pickling spice
8 sticks cinnamon
2 capfuls (according to color) red or green
   food coloring

Mix lime and water and pour over cucumbers and let stand 24 hours. Drain and wash. Soak in cold water for 3 hours. Drain and cover. Mix:

Soak cucumbers overnight. Then boil 35 minutes in the solution or until clear. Seal in sterilized jars. This makes a beautiful Christmas pickle that tastes like apple rings. Makes 10 pints.

GRAPE JELLY

3 cans (6-ounce size) grape juice, frozen
6 1/2 cups sugar
2 1/2 cups water
1 bottle Certo pectin

Put sugar and water in an 8-quart kettle. Place over high heat. Bring to a full rolling boil, stirring constantly. Boil hard 1 minute. Remove from heat and stir in 1 bottle Certo pectin and grape juice. Pour into scalded glasses and seal with paraffin. Makes 12 (6-ounce) glasses.

GREEN PEPPER JELLY

1 cup green pepper, ground
1/4 cup yellow pepper (hot), seeded, ground
2 1/4 teaspoons crushed red pepper
6 1/2 cups sugar
3 1/2 cups cider vinegar
Green food coloring to suit eye
1 bottle (6-ounce) Certo

Combine first 5 ingredients; bring to a boil and allow to boil for 5 minutes, stirring frequently. Cool 10 minutes. Add food coloring and Certo; stir well. Bring to boil and boil 1 minute. Cool 10 minutes. Pour into scalded glasses and seal with paraffin. Makes 10 (6-ounce) glasses.

MOM'S BREAD AND BUTTER PICKLES

6 quarts medium cucumbers, thinly sliced
   (Do not use waxed cucumbers)
6 medium onions, thinly sliced
3/4 cup salt (non-iodized)
1 quart white vinegar
4 cups granulated sugar
2 tablespoons celery seed
2 tablespoons mustard seed
1 cup water

Wash cucumbers thoroughly before slicing. Arrange sliced cucumbers and onions in layers in an earthenware crock bowl. Sprinkle each layer with salt. Cover and let stand 3 hours. While you wait, combine water, vinegar, sugar, celery seed and mustard seed. Bring to a boil, stirring until sugar is dissolved. Boil 3 minutes. Sterilize 8 pint jars and lids. After 3 hours, drain off juice which has accumulated in layers of cucumbers and onions. Add cucumber mixture to vinegar syrup mixture; bring to a boiling point but do not boil. Pack immediately into hot sterilized jars. Seal at once. Boil in water bath. Let rest for 2 weeks or more.
Makes 8 pints.

❖❖❖

PEACH SUN PRESERVES

2 pounds fresh ripe peaches
3 cups sugar
1/4 cup lemon juice

Peel peaches and cut into 1/2-inch-thick slices, discarding pits. Measure 4 cups of the fruit and combine with the sugar and lemon juice in a 4-quart saucepan; stir gently. Cover and let stand for 1 hour.

Bring to a boil over medium heat; stirring constantly. Increase heat and boil vigorously, uncovered, for 4 minutes without stirring. Remove from heat; let cool for 30 minutes. Pour mixture into shallow baking pans or plastic trays (fruit should be 1/2 to 3/4-inch deep). Cover containers with clear plastic wrap, leaving a 1-inch-wider opening at 1 side.

Place in direct sunlight. Once every hour, stir mixture gently, turning fruit over. Let remain in sun from 2 to 10 hours, or until fruit is plump and syrup is the consistency of corn syrup. If necessary, fruit can be brought in at night and returned to sunlight the next day.

Spoon into sterilized jars and cover and store in refrigerator. Will keep 4 weeks.

You can store preserves by freezing. Fill containers to within 1 inch of top; cover with tight lids and freeze. Jan says, "Strawberries are good too!"

Makes 6 pints.

HATTIE'S PICCALILLI

1/2 bushel solid green tomatoes
2 medium-size heads cabbage
1 dozen green peppers
1 dozen red peppers
2 ounces white mustard seed (1 ounce equals
    2 tablespoons)
2 dozen white onions, ground
1 ounce celery seed
1 teaspoon cinnamon
6 cups white sugar
1 gallon vinegar

Grind the tomatoes, cabbage and peppers. Add 1 pint salt and place in cloth bag. Hang to drain overnight. In morning add rest of ingredients.

Cook over low heat approximately 1 hour after coming to boil. Place in hot sterilized glass jars and seal. Use white-coated jar lids, because of acid. Yields 14 to 18 quarts depending on size of vegetables.

MYSTERY JELLY OR RELISH

5 cups green tomatoes, pureed
4 cups sugar
1 package raspberry Jell-O

Puree tomatoes in blender or food processor. Put tomatoes and sugar in heavy pan and bring to a boil and boil for 20 minutes. Remove from heat and add 1 package raspberry Jell-O and stir well. Put in sterilized jars and seal. Makes 1 quart or 4 small jars.

Sassy & Tart

BREAD AND BUTTER PICKLES

1 gallon cucumbers, cut up
8 small onions
2 bell peppers
1/2 cup salt

Soak mixture in 2 quarts crushed ice for 2 hours. Drain and mix in large pan:

4 cups sugar
1 1/2 teaspoons turmeric
2 teaspoons cloves
2 teaspoons mustard
1 teaspoon celery seed
5 cups vinegar

Bring to a rolling boil. Remove from heat and put the pickles in sterilized jars and seal.

MRS. PENNY'S OIL PICKLES

100 small cucumbers (about finger size)
2/3 of 10 cent sack of salt (2 cups)
3 pints small white onions (walnut size)
Alum the size of a walnut (or equivalent granulated)
1 pint cold water
3 ounces white mustard seed
1 ounce celery seed
2 ounces fresh ground pepper berries
1 pint olive oil
White vinegar

Slice cucumbers very thin, mix with salt and let stand 3 hours. Dissolve alum in cold water, peel and slice onions very thin. Mix alum water and onions and let stand while cukes are soaking. At end of 3 hours, drain liquid off cukes, and if too salty, rinse in cool water until they suit taste. Wash alum off onions in cold water. Mix mustard seed, celery seed, ground pepper and put in big jar or crock with cukes and onions and mix all very thoroughly. Pour on olive oil and stir well. Add enough cold vinegar to cover the mixture, mixing all very well. Let stand in jar about a week, or indefinitely until all are used. The pickles may be put in sterilized jars and canned for future use. Can them cold.
Makes about 2 gallons. — This recipe is from the 1920's.

OKRA PICKLES

2 1/2 pounds small okra
1 quart white vinegar
1 quart water
1 cup salt
1 tablespoon fresh dill (or dill seed)
Hot peppers (1 or 2 to a jar)
Garlic buds (1 to a jar)

Sterilize wide-mouth jars. Wash okra; pack in jars. Place garlic buds and peppers in each jar. Divide dill among jars. Bring water, vinegar and salt to a boil. Pour over okra and seal. Let set 4 weeks. Chill before serving. Makes 4 quarts.

Sassy & Tart

OLD SOUTH SWEET LIME PICKLES

7 pounds cucumbers (slice crosswise)
Mix 2 cups of pickling lime to 2 gallons water

SYRUP:
2 quarts vinegar
8 cups sugar
1 tablespoon salt
Few drops green food coloring if desired
1 tablespoon whole cloves or allspice

Soak cukes 24 hours, stirring occasionally, in lime water. Do not use aluminum ware. Remove from lime water and rinse in 3 cool waters. Soak 3 more hours in ice water. Remove carefully to drain. Prepare syrup.

Combine ingredients and stir until dissolved. Pour over cukes, let set 5-6 hours or overnight. Add whole cloves or allspice. Boil mixture for 35 minutes. Fill sterilized jars with cuke slices and pour syrup over, leaving 1/8-inch head space. Seal. If syrup does not cover cukes while boiling, mix partial recipe of syrup and add to mixture.
Makes 4 quarts.

SWEET PICKLES OUT OF DILLS

1 1/2 quart (48-ounce jar) dill pickles
2 cups sugar
1 teaspoon mustard seed
Dark cider vinegar

Quarter the pickles, put back in jar. Pour 1 cup sugar, mustard seed and a little vinegar over sugar. Pour 1 more cup sugar over pickles. Fill the jar with vinegar. Seal and shake every so often. Let stand for 2 weeks. Makes 2 quarts.

LETHA'S PYRACANTHA JELLY

3 cups pyracantha berries, very ripe
6 cups water
Juice of 1 lemon
Juice of 1 medium-size grapefruit
1 package (1 3/4-ounce) powdered pectin
4 1/2 cups sugar

Wash and stem berries. In a pan bring the berries and water to a boil. Reduce heat and simmer 20 minutes. Stir in lemon and grapefruit juice. Strain, but do not squeeze, through a fine cloth or several thicknesses of cheesecloth. You should have 4 1/2 cups of juice.
Return juice to pan and stir in pectin. Place over high heat and stir until mixture comes to full rolling boil. Add sugar, stirring constantly, and bring to a boil for 2 minutes. Remove from heat, skim and pour into hot jars. Makes 4 half-pints.

Sassy & Tart

SAND PLUM JELLY

4 1/2 cups prepared plums
1/2 cup water
7 1/2 cups sugar
1 pouch Certo fruit pectin

Pit and wash berries. In a pan bring the berries and water to a boil. Reduce heat and simmer 5 minutes. Stir sugar into prepared fruit. Bring to a full rolling boil over high heat, stirring constantly. At once stir in Certo fruit pectin. Stir and bring to a full rolling boil (that cannot be stirred down) and boil hard 1 minute, stirring constantly. Remove from heat. Skim off foam. With large metal spoon immediately ladle into hot glasses or jars, leaving 1/2-inch space at top of glasses or jars. Let jam stand to cool. Makes 3 to 4 pints.

Jan says, "You may add raspberries or blackberries to the plums. It is delicious."

STRAWBERRY JAM

1 10-ounce package frozen strawberries, sliced
1 cup sugar
1 tablespoon pectin

Combine ingredients in large bowl. Cook 4 minutes and 3 seconds on high setting or 6 minutes on simmer. Pour in a jar and refrigerate. Makes 1 pint.

Jan says, "This is a good microwave jam."

FREEZER STRAWBERRY PRESERVES

2 cups crushed fresh strawberries
4 cups sugar
3/4 cup water
1 box (1 3/4-ounce) powdered fruit pectin

Crush berries, measure into large saucepan. Stir in sugar and mix well. Combine water and pectin in a separate saucepan, bring to a boil. Boil 1 minute stirring constantly. Stir into fruit mixture and continue stirring 2 minutes. Ladle into freezer containers or glasses and cover with lids. Let stand until set (about 24 hours).

Store in freezer up to 1 year. These preserves can be taken directly from freezer to table, as they do not completely freeze. They will not keep for a long time in the refrigerator.

Jo says, "These preserves are really delicious. Try them on ice cream, if there is any left after serving them with hot toasted English muffins or homemade biscuits." Makes 5 cups.

WINE JELLY

4 cups wine (red, white, rose)
6 cups sugar
1 (6-ounce) bottle liquid fruit pectin

Bring to a rolling boil the wine and sugar. Add at once the fruit pectin. Cook 1 minute longer. Skim off any froth, pour into glasses and seal.

Makes 2 pints.

Nine To Five • Quick Meals

This chapter is a minibook organized with the working person in mind. The recipes have been chosen to make life easier, but they still give you choices for entertaining in a manner that will have your guests wondering how you can be such a busy person and still manage to put it all together so effortlessly.

You'll love the speed and ease of the Busy Lady Stew, the Beer Muffins, and the Working-Girl Meat Loaf—three of our favorites.

Nine To Five

HOT ARTICHOKE DIP

1 can (14-ounce) artichokes, drained
1 cup grated Parmesan cheese
1 cup mayonnaise
1/2 small onion, chopped
1/2 teaspoon Worcestershire sauce
1/8 teaspoon garlic salt
Dash of lemon juice

Mash artichoke hearts slightly and mix with remaining ingredients. Place in 1-quart baking dish and bake in 350-degree oven for 25 minutes. Serve hot with Triscuits. Makes 2 cups.

BACON STIX

10 thin bread sticks, any flavor
5 slices bacon, halved lengthwise
1/2 cup grated Parmesan cheese

Dredge one side of bacon strip in cheese, roll it against bread stick diagonally. Place sticks on baking sheet, dish or paper plate lined with paper towels. Microwave on high 4 1/2 to 6 minutes. Roll again in cheese. Bacon stix may be made in advance and will stay crisp several hours after microwaving. Makes 10 stix.

BEEN AROUND FOR YEARS DIP

1 carton (8-ounce) sour cream
1 package Lipton dry onion soup mix

Combine, chill. That's it!!
Makes 1 1/2 cups.

BLUE CHEESE BITS

Cut one 8-ounce package refrigerated biscuits in quarters. Arrange in two 8-inch round pie plates. Melt together 1/4 cup butter and 3 tablespoons crumbled blue cheese. Pour mixture over biscuit pieces, coating well.

Bake at 400 degrees for 12 to 15 minutes or until golden brown. Serve hot. Makes 40 bits.

RAY DELL'S BUTTERFLY DIP

1 package (8-ounce) cream cheese
2 tablespoons fresh green onion, chopped
2 garlic cloves, chopped
1 cooked egg white, chopped
1/2 cup Hellman's mayonnaise
1/2 cup fresh parsley, chopped

Mix in blender. If desired, sprinkle finely chopped egg yolk on top. Serve with Triscuits. Makes 1 1/2 cups.

HOT CHEESE DIP

1 can Campbell's bean with bacon soup
1 stick Kraft garlic cheese
1 cup sour cream
2 teaspoons green onion (chopped)

Heat soup and cheese in double boiler until melted. Add sour cream and onion. Serve warm with chips. Makes 2 1/2 cups.

Nine To Five

❖❖

MAPLE BARBECUE RIBS

3 pounds baby-back pork ribs, cut individually
1 1/2 cups maple syrup
2 tablespoons chili sauce
2 tablespoons cider vinegar
2 tablespoons finely chopped onion
1 tablespoon Worcestershire sauce
1 teaspoon salt
1/2 teaspoon dry mustard
Pepper

Place ribs on baking sheet in single layer. Combine other ingredients. Brush sauce over ribs. Bake at 350 degrees for 1 1/2 hours or until tender, basting frequently with remaining sauce until ribs are glazed. May be made day ahead and refrigerated. Serves 4.

HOT CRAB DIP

1 package (8-ounce) cream cheese
1 tablespoon lemon juice
Dash of salt
1/3 cup milk
1 can drained and flaked crab

Combine cheese and milk in saucepan. Heat until cheese is melted. Add crab and salt, then add lemon. Bake at 350 degrees for 8 to 10 minutes or until bubbly. Keep warm while serving. Very good with Wheat Thins. Makes 1 1/2 cups.

EASY 'N' QUICK DIP FOR VEGGIES

1 pint sour cream
1 package Good Seasons Italian seasoning mix
1 tablespoon mayonnaise
2 teaspoons lemon juice

Combine all ingredients. Chill. Make the day before serving to bring out the full flavor. Makes 2 cups.

NACHOS

King-size corn chips
Monterey Jack cheese
   or
Jalapeno & green pepper cheese

Cut thin slice of cheese to cover each corn chip. Place under broiler until cheese melts. Serve warm. Jan says, "Make plenty for they disappear quickly."

NIPPY CHEESE DIP

2 Kraft Nippy Cheese sticks
1 stick butter
3 cans shrimp
Dash of Worcestershire sauce

Melt cheese, butter. Add 3 cans of shrimp and Worcestershire sauce. Serve in chafing dish. Makes 2 cups.

ZUCCHINI SLICES

Slice fresh zucchini, 1/4 inch thick. Sprinkle McCormick Lemon n' Herb spice on slices. Serve.

Nine To Five

PARTY DILL DIP

1 carton sour cream
1 carton or same amount Hellmann's mayonnaise
1/2 medium-size onion
1 teaspoon garlic salt
2 teaspoons dill weed
1 tablespoon parsley, chopped
1 teaspoon Beau Monde seasoning

Combine ingredients. Hollow out a round loaf of rye or pumpernickel bread. Fill hollow with chilled dip and serve, surrounded with fresh vegetables. Makes 2 cups.

QUICK CRAB SPREAD

1 package (8-ounce) cream cheese
1 bottle cocktail sauce
1 can crab, drained and shredded

Frost plate with the cream cheese. Spread cocktail sauce over cheese and spread crab meat on top. Serve with crackers. Makes 1 1/2 cups.

CHILLED AVOCADO SOUP

3 medium avocados, peeled and cut into chunks
1 cup sour cream
Juice of one lemon
1 cup half-and-half cream
1/4 teaspoon chili powder
2 cups chicken broth
Salt, red and black pepper to taste

Place all ingredients except chicken broth into blender or processor and blend until smooth. Do this in two batches so container will not be too full. Empty into large container. Stir in chicken broth, correct your seasonings and chill. Garnish with chopped onions and paprika. Serves 6.

QUICK BROCCOLI SOUP

2 packages (10-ounce size) frozen chopped broccoli
2 cans condensed cream of mushroom soup
2 soup cans milk
1/2 cup dry white wine or sherry
4 tablespoons margarine
1/4 teaspoon parsley
1/2 teaspoon dried tarragon, crushed
Dash pepper

In large saucepan, cook broccoli according to package directions. Drain. Add soup, milk, wine, margarine, parsley, tarragon and pepper. Heat through. **Do not boil or liquid will separate.** Serves 8.

GOURMET CHICKEN SOUP

1 can condensed cream of chicken soup
1 cup canned condensed chicken consomme
1/2 teaspoon tarragon
1/2 cup heavy cream
Paprika

Blend ingredients in blender till smooth or about 10 seconds. Heat thoroughly. Serve hot or chilled topped with spoonful of whipped cream sprinkled with paprika. Makes 4-5 servings.

Nine To Five

EASY ICED LEMON SOUP

1 can cream of chicken soup
1 cup light cream
1 cup chicken stock
3 tablespoons mint leaves, chopped
Juice of 2 lemons

Strain soup, add cream and chicken stock, chop mint leaves finely and add with lemon juice. Soup should be served well chilled. Serves 4.

QUICKIE STEAK SOUP

1 can (1 pound 3 ounces) Campbell's Chunky old-fashioned vegetable beef soup
1 can (10 1/2-ounce) cream of mushroom soup, diluted with one can milk

Mix soups and milk together. Heat and serve. Makes a creamy vegetable soup. Good on those cold winter nights. Serves 4.

TOMATO BOUILLON

2 cans (12-ounce size) tomato juice
Water
3 beef bouillon cubes
6 whole cloves
1/4 teaspoon cinnamon

Empty cans of tomato juice into saucepan. Add 2 cans of water, bouillon cubes, cloves and cinnamon. Heat, stirring occasionally, just to boiling point. Do not let boil. Lower heat and simmer at least 30 minutes. Pour through a strainer to remove cloves. Serve hot and add a dash of cinnamon. Serves 6.

SINGAPORE PEA SOUP

1 can (10 1/2-ounce) split pea with ham soup
1 can (10 1/2-ounce) chicken broth
1 1/2 cans milk
1 1/2 teaspoons curry powder
1/2 cup whipped cream

Stir pea soup and chicken broth together until smooth, blend in milk and 1 teaspoon curry powder. Chill. Serve in soup cups. Fold remaining 1/2 teaspoon curry powder into whipped cream. Serve in chilled cups. Place a tablespoon of whipped cream atop each serving. Garnish with fresh chives or minced scallions. Serves 5-6.

JAN AND JO'S SUPER SOUP

1 quart plus 1 cup milk
1 can (10 1/4-ounce) tomato soup, concentrated
1 can (10 1/4-ounce) cream of celery soup, concentrated
1 can (10 1/4-ounce) cream of mushroom soup, concentrated
1 can (10 1/4-ounce) split pea soup, concentrated
1 can (10-ounce) crab, broken into pieces
2 tablespoons onion, minced
1 teaspoon curry

Mix all ingredients. Heat. Great for "tail-gate picnics" or "after the game" crowds. Serves 12-14.

<><><><><><><><><><><><><><><><><><><><><><><><><><><><><><><><><><><><><><><><><><>

BROCCOLI-CAULIFLOWER SALAD

1 head of broccoli, break into bite-size pieces
1 head of cauliflower, break into bite-size pieces
1 cup chopped celery
1/2 cup chopped ripe olives
Viva salad dressing to taste.

Mix all ingredients together and refrigerate until ready to use. Serves 8-10.

CALIFORNIA SALAD

1 cup pineapple bits, drained
1 cup mandarin oranges, drained
1 cup seedless grapes
1 cup flaked coconut
1 cup mini-marshmallows
1 cup sour cream

Combine all ingredients. Refrigerate for at least 24 hours. This salad will keep nicely for several days. Serves 4-6.

CHINESE CABBAGE

1 head Chinese cabbage
1 red onion, chopped
Crumbled bleu cheese
3/4 cup French dressing or other creamy dressing
Salt and pepper

Cut chinese cabbage across into 1/2-inch strips. Toss together with onion, bleu cheese, and dressing. Salt and pepper to taste. Serves 4-6.

PEA SALAD

1 cup frozen peas, thawed and drained
1 cup chopped celery
1 tablespoon onion
1 cup cashew nuts
Bacon bits, at least 10-12 strips, fried and drained
1 cup sour cream or less

Mix together using sour cream according to taste. Serves 4.

SAUERKRAUT SALAD

1 No. 2 can sauerkraut (drained)
1 cup sugar
1 finely chopped large onion
1 finely chopped large green pepper
1 cup finely diced celery
1/4 cup chopped pimento
1/2 cup salad oil
1/4 cup wine vinegar

Combine drained kraut and sugar. Let stand 10 minutes. Drain off liquid. Combine chopped vegetables in medium bowl. Thoroughly mix vinegar and oil. Pour over vegetables. Add kraut. Chill several hours or overnight. Serves 4.

❖❖❖

SPINACH SALAD

2 bags fresh spinach (10-ounce size)
1 can bean sprouts or 1/2 pound fresh bean sprouts
2 (No. 402) cans water chestnuts (sliced)

DRESSING:
1/4 cup cider vinegar
1/3 cup catsup
1 medium red onion (cut up)
3/4 cup sugar
2 teaspoons salt
1 teaspoon Worcestershire sauce
1 cup Wesson oil
TOPPINGS:
4 hard-boiled eggs
1/2 pound bacon

Wash, stem spinach and break into bite-size pieces and drain. Drain, rinse bean sprouts and water chestnuts. Combine with spinach.

Blend all together in blender and slowly add 1 cup Wesson Oil. Top salad with 4 boiled eggs sliced in half and 1/2 pound fried bacon, crisp and crumbled. Serves 8.

VEGETABLE SALAD

1 can French-style green beans
1 can sweet peas
1 can Chinese vegetables
1 can sliced water chestnuts
1 1/2 cups sliced celery
Onion to taste
3/4 cup vinegar
1 cup sugar
1 teaspoon salt
1/4 teaspoon pepper

Drain all vegetables and combine first 6 ingredients. Heat together: 3/4 cup vinegar, 1 cup sugar, 1 teaspoon salt, 1/4 teaspoon pepper. Pour over vegetables. Let stand several hours or overnight. Serves 8.

QUICK CAESAR SALAD DRESSING

1/4 cup vinegar
2-ounce can anchovies with oil
1 tablespoon water
2/3 cup salad oil
1 package Good Season's cheese and garlic dressing

Combine vinegar, anchovies and water in blender, then slowly add salad oil and dressing mix. Can be made ahead. Makes 1 1/2 cups.

MOCK HOLLANDAISE

1/4 cup sour cream
1/4 cup mayonnaise
1/2 teaspoon mustard
1 teaspoon lemon juice
Few drops of yellow food coloring

Put all ingredients in saucepan and heat slowly until warm. Makes 1/2 cup.
Jan says, "This is very good on Eggs Benedict. It is easy to make and not as rich. You will like!"

AL'S BEER BREAD

3 cups self-rising flour
1 can (12-ounce) beer, room temperature. Do not use Coors.
5 tablespoons sugar

Mix all ingredients. Pour into greased loaf pan. Let set for 15 minutes before baking. Bake in 350-degree oven for 1 hour. Brush top with butter and Krazy Salt.

Nine To Five

BEER MUFFINS

4 cups Bisquick
2 teaspoons sugar
1 can (12-ounce) beer, room temperature.
   Do not use Coors.

Mix and fill 24 greased muffin tins. Bake at 375 degrees for 15-18 minutes.

BREAKFAST SWEET ROLLS

1 package frozen rolls (24)
1 cup chopped nuts
1/2 large package of butterscotch pudding mix
   (not instant)
1 cup brown sugar
1 stick margarine or butter
Cinnamon to taste (approximately 1 tablespoon)

Grease bundt pan and sprinkle in nuts and cinnamon, then the frozen rolls. Sprinkle pudding mix over the frozen rolls. Cook butter and sugar until dissolved, pour over rolls and cover with wax paper and cloth and leave at room temperature for 8 hours or overnight. Bake at 350 degrees for 25 minutes. Turn upside down, remove from pan. Serve warm. Serves 12-14.

Jan says, "I like to alternate the rolls with the nuts and cinnamon because it makes it more uniform."

COCONUT PECAN RING

2 packages (8-ounce size) butterflake rolls (24)
2/3 cup sugar
1/2 teaspoon cinnamon
1/4 cup milk
1/4 cup coconut, shredded
1/4 cup chopped pecans
1/2 cup powdered sugar
1 tablespoon milk
1/4 teaspoon vanilla
1/4 cup chopped pecans

Separate rolls, combine the 2/3 cup sugar and cinnamon, dipping each roll in 1/4 cup milk then in sugar mixture. Coat all sides. Place half of rolls slightly overlapping in bottom of ring mold. Sprinkle with coconut and 1/4 cup nuts. Add remaining rolls forming 2nd layer. Bake in 375-degree oven 25 to 30 minutes. Invert ring mold onto serving plate. Glaze powdered sugar with 1 tablespoon milk and vanilla. Drizzle over ring and sprinkle with nuts. Serves 8-10.

HOT GARLIC BREAD

1 loaf Italian bread
1/2 cup butter, softened
1 garlic clove, minced
1 teaspoon dried or freshly chopped parsley
1/4 teaspoon oregano
1/4 teaspoon dried dill or dill weed
3 tablespoons grated Parmesan cheese

Combine butter, garlic and herbs. Spread on bread which has been cut in half lengthwise. Sprinkle with Parmesan cheese. Place on oven sheet and place under broiler until lightly browned. Slice or serve in loaf length. If you do not wish to toast the bread, wrap in foil and heat for 15 minutes in a 400-degree oven.

HEATH BAR COFFEE CAKE

1 cup brown sugar
1/2 cup white sugar
1/4 pound butter or margarine
2 cups flour
1 cup buttermilk
1 egg
1 teaspoon vanilla
1 teaspoon baking soda
10 - 12 Heath candy bars
1 cup chopped nuts

Cream sugars and butter or margarine together. Add flour and mix until crumbly. Remove 1/2 cup and set aside for topping. Add buttermilk and egg to remainder of topping, then add baking soda and vanilla. Mix well and pour into 2 (8 x 8-inch or 8-inch round) greased and floured pans.

Crush Heath bars by taking from refrigerator and, while still in wrapper, hitting with a hammer until broken into 1/2-inch or smaller chunks. Unwrap over small bowl, to which you add chopped nuts and the 1/2 cup crumbly mix.

Mix and sprinkle evenly over both cake pans of batter. Bake at 350 degrees for 30 to 35 minutes or until done when tested with a toothpick.
Serves 8.

Jan says, "This is delicious served warm or with whipped cream as a dessert."

CRUSTY SPOON BREAD

1/2 cup cornmeal
1/4 cup flour
1 tablespoon sugar
3/4 teaspoon salt
1 teaspoon baking powder
1 egg
1 cup milk
2 tablespoons butter
1/2 cup milk

Combine dry ingredients and add 1 beaten egg and 1 cup milk. Blend well. Melt 2 heaping tablespoons of butter in baking dish, pour in batter. Pour 1/2 cup milk over top. Bake in 375-degree oven about 45 minutes.
Serves 5.

BROCCOLI CASSEROLE

2 packages (10-ounce size) frozen chopped broccoli
1/2 stick margarine
1 medium onion, chopped
1/2 cup celery, chopped
1 can cream of mushroom soup
1 can (4-ounce) chopped mushrooms
1 roll garlic cheese
1/2 cup cracker crumbs
1 tablespoon melted butter

Cook broccoli according to package directions and drain well. Saute the onion and celery in 1/2 stick margarine. Blend in the soup, mushrooms and garlic cheese. Heat until the cheese melts, mix with drained broccoli and cover with the cracker crumbs mixed with melted butter. Bake 30 minutes at 350 degrees or until brown and bubbly.
Serves 6-8.

QUICK 'N' EASY GREEN BEANS

2 cans whole green beans
1 can mushroom soup
2 tablespoons cooking sherry
1 teaspoon liquid onion or 2 tablespoons dry onion
2/3 of 1 package (8 ounce) sharp Cheddar cheese, grated
1 can water chestnuts, sliced

Combine all ingredients. Bake at 350 degrees until bubbly. Serves 8.
Note: Freezes well, but if you freeze, add water chestnuts at last minute.

❖◆❖

NO-FAIL CHEESE SOUFFLE

1/4 cup butter
1/4 cup flour
1 1/4 cup milk
1/4 teaspoon prepared mustard
1 jar (5-ounce) Kraft Sharp Cheddar cheese
3 egg yolks
1/4 teaspoon cream of tartar
3 egg whites

Mix in saucepan butter, flour, milk and mustard. When beginning to get thick add the cheese until melted. Stir in creamed egg yolks. Set aside. Beat egg whites and cream of tarter until stiff. Fold into first mixture and bake in an ungreased 1 1/2-quart casserole. Place casserole in a pan of water and bake at 350 degrees for 50 minutes. Shake and if wobbly bake a few minutes longer or test it with a straw. Serves 4.

Jan says, "This no-fail souffle is good served with a can of cream of mushroom soup slightly diluted with 1/3 cup white wine. When warm pour over souffle."

QUICK 'N' EASY CARROTS

Carrots, as many as you desire
1/4 cup butter
1/4 cup white sugar
1/4 cup brown sugar
1 tablespoon mint jelly

Cook carrots, cut into pieces, covered in 1/2- to 1-inch boiling water. Combine butter, sugars and mint jelly, simmer and pour over cooked, drained carrots. Allow to simmer enough to glaze the carrots. Serves 2.

GREEN BEANS PLUS

1 package (3-ounce) cream cheese, softened
1 small clove garlic, minced
1 tablespoon light cream
3/4 teaspoon dill seed
1/4 teaspoon salt
4 cups cooked, drained green beans

Blend first 5 ingredients. Toss with hot green beans just until cheese melts. Do this just before serving so beans stay hot. Serves 4.

CAROL'S SPINACH SOUFFLE

2 packages frozen spinach, cooked, drained, and chopped
1 carton sour cream
1 package dried onion soup

Combine all ingredients and place in greased casserole. Bake at 350 degrees for 30 minutes or until done. This is very good and almost impossible to overcook. Serves 4.

SPINACH CASSEROLE

1 pound creamed cottage cheese
1/4 pound American cheese
1/2 of 1 package frozen spinach
3 unbeaten eggs
1/4 cup butter
3 tablespoons flour

Put cottage cheese in mixing bowl. Add eggs. Add cheese in coarse chunks. Snip partially frozen spinach. Add with flour and butter to cheese mixture and stir well. Pour into buttered 1-1/2 quart casserole. Bake at 350 degrees for 1 hour. Serves 4.

OVEN FRENCH FRIES

2 medium-size potatoes (about 9 ounces each)
2 tablespoons butter or margarine
1/2 cup to 2/3 cup light cream
Salt and pepper to taste
1/2 cup grated Parmesan or Cheddar cheese

Wash potatoes. Peel and slice into french fries to your liking of size. Put potatoes on a 12 x 12-inch piece of heavy foil, pour cream over them, salt and pepper, put dots of butter and then sprinkle cheese over potatoes. Fold corners up around potatoes and secure with no air coming into foil. Place on baking sheet and bake at 400 degrees for 1 hour. Serves 2.

Jan says, "This makes a very good quick potato side dish."

MICROWAVE POTATOES ROMANOFF

2 cups frozen hash brown potatoes
1 cup cottage cheese
1/2 cup non-flavored yogurt
2 tablespoons chopped green onion
2 tablespoons chopped parsley
1 garlic clove, minced
1/2 teaspoon salt
2 tablespoons fine dry bread crumbs
1 tablespoon margarine or butter
Dash paprika

Place frozen hash brown potatoes in 1-quart casserole, cover. Microwave on high 3 minutes. Stir. Microwave on high 3 minutes longer. Add cottage cheese, yogurt, parsley, onions, garlic and salt. Mix well. Top with bread crumb, butter mixture. Sprinkle with paprika. Cover. Microwave on high 4 to 6 minutes. Let stand 5 minutes before serving. Serves 4.

RIZ SAUVAGE

2 1/2 cups wild rice
10 cups chicken broth

Place wild rice in saucepan with enough cold water to cover. Bring to a boil and strain.

Return rice to saucepan and add chicken broth. Bring to a boil again. Reduce heat and simmer about 40 minutes until all liquid is absorbed. Serve in a pre-heated vegetable dish. Serves 4.

LITTLE BAR-B-Q MEAT LOAVES

2 slightly beaten eggs
2 pounds ground beef
2 cups soft bread crumbs
3/4 cup minced onion
2 teaspoons salt
2 teaspoons prepared horseradish
1 teaspoon prepared mustard
1/4 cup milk
1/2 cup butter
1/2 cup catsup

Combine first 8 ingredients. Mix well. Shape into 4 miniature meat loaves about 4 1/2 inches in length and 2 1/2 inches wide. Place in baking dish. Heat 1/2 cup butter with 1/2 cup catsup just until butter melts. Brush over all sides of loaves generously. Bake in 350-degree oven 45 minutes. Use remaining sauce on top of loaves just before serving. Serves 4.

EASY BEEF SANDWICHES

1 pound ground beef, browned
1 can drained mushrooms
1/2 package onion soup mix

Stir the ingredients well. Put on buns according to how much you like. Grate cheese over top. Wrap each sandwich in foil and heat. These may be made ahead. Great for a picnic or have on hand in freezer when company comes to your house. Makes 6.

BUSY LADY STEW

3 pounds (or more) lean beef stew meat
3 large garlic buds, pressed
1 can beef consomme
1 can (28 ounces) tomatoes and juice
1 cup white wine
4 tablespoons tapioca
1 tablespoon brown sugar
1 teaspoon salt for each pound of meat
1 bay leaf
1 teaspoon MSG
1 teaspoon Beau Monde seasoning
1 1/2 teaspoons Italian herbs
1/2 cup prepared bread crumbs
5 or 6 potatoes, peeled and quartered
6 large carrots, cut in chunks
10 to 12 boiling onions
1 package (10 ounce) frozen green beans
1 package (10 ounce) frozen peas
1 package (10 ounce) frozen corn
2 cups water

Stir all ingredients together in a large stew pot. Cover with a tight lid and cook in a 250-degree oven for 7 to 8 hours. Remove bay leaf. Serves 12-14.

CHICKEN PIQUANT

3 pounds chicken pieces
3/4 cup white or rose wine
1/4 cup soy sauce
1/4 cup salad oil
1 cup chicken broth
2 tablespoons grated fresh ginger or 2 teaspoons powdered
1 tablespoon brown sugar
1/4 teaspoon oregano

Arrange pieces in casserole with tight-fitting lid. Combine in bowl rest of ingredients. Pour over chicken. Cover pan and bake 3/4 hour at 375 degrees. If cooking 2 chickens, bake 3/4 hour longer. Serve with rice. Serves 6.

CHICKEN-RICE BAKE

1 1/2 cups uncooked long-grain rice
1 chicken or desired pieces
Lemon juice
Garlic salt
1 package dry onion soup mix
1 can cream of mushroom soup
1 can chicken broth

Place chicken in casserole with tight-fitting lid. Sprinkle chicken with lemon juice and garlic salt. Pour rice over chicken and cover with onion soup mix, followed by mushroom soup and chicken broth. Cover tightly and bake in 350-degree oven for 1 1/2 hours. Serves 4-6.

HELENA'S CHICKEN ROQUEFORT

1 fryer (3-4 pounds)
4 ounces Roquefort cheese
1 garlic clove, chopped
1/2 pint sour cream

Season chicken and brown in butter. Do not use flour. Place in casserole. Mix in skillet in which you have browned chicken, the Roquefort cheese, crumbled, chopped garlic clove and sour cream. Heat this mixture and pour over the chicken. Bake in covered casserole at 350 degrees for 1 hour or until tender. Serves 4.

Jo says, "This is delicious served with wild rice."

HONEY-BAKED CHICKEN

4 chicken breasts
1/2 cup butter
1/2 cup honey
1/4 cup Dijon mustard
1/4 cup white raisins (optional)
Salt to taste
1 1/2 teaspoons curry powder

Melt butter in baking dish, stir in following ingredients. Roll chicken breasts in mixture to coat well. Arrange meaty side up in a single layer. Bake in 375-degree oven for 1 hour 15 minutes or until chicken is tender and well glazed. Baste with honey mixture every 15 minutes. Serves 4.

FISH-SPINACH BAKE

4 frozen breaded-battered fish portions
1 package (10-ounce) frozen chopped spinach, thawed and drained
1/2 pound fresh mushrooms, chopped
2 green onions, finely chopped
1/2 teaspoon salt
1/4 teaspoon white pepper
1/4 cup dry white wine
1 cup fresh bread crumbs
1 tablespoon chopped fresh parsley
1/4 cup butter, melted

Drain spinach thoroughly, pressing to remove excess liquid. Combine spinach, mushrooms, onions, salt, pepper and wine. Spoon mixture over bottom of buttered 11 x 7 x 2-inch baking dish. Mix bread crumbs with chopped parsley. Sprinkle half the crumbs over vegetables, drizzle with half the melted butter. Arrange fish over vegetables. Sprinkle with remaining bread crumbs and drizzle with remaining melted butter. Bake in 375-degree oven for 30 to 35 minutes or until very hot. Serves 4.

HAM-RICE BAKE

2 cups cubed ham
2 cups cooked rice
1/2 cup shredded sharp American cheese
1/2 cup evaporated milk or light cream
1 can asparagus soup
2 to 4 tablespoons finely chopped onion
3/4 cup corn flakes, slightly crushed
3 tablespoons margarine, melted

Combine ham, rice, cheese, evaporated milk, soup and onion. Spoon into a 1 1/2 quart casserole. Mix corn flakes and melted margarine and sprinkle over casserole. Bake uncovered at 375 degrees 20 to 25 minutes or until heated thoroughly and top is lightly browned. Serves 4.

GROUND MEAT CASSEROLE

1 pound ground beef
1 can (12 to 16-ounce) mushrooms
1 onion, minced
1 green pepper, chopped
1 stick butter
1 box wild rice, cooked
1 to 2 cans cream of mushroom soup
Salt and pepper to taste
Grated cheese

Saute onion, meat and green pepper in butter. Add drained mushrooms, cooked rice and soup. Pour in casserole and top with grated cheese. Bake at 350 degrees for 40 minutes. Serves 4-6.

Jo says, "Why not make 2 small casseroles and freeze one for a later date?"

9 to 5 ALSATIAN DINNER

2 pounds sauerkraut
1 can (16-ounce) applesauce
1/4 cup gin
6 frankfurters or knockwurst or bratwurst
1 can boiled potatoes

Drain sauerkraut and mix with applesauce in a large skillet. Add gin. Add meat and can of potatoes. Heat through and serve. Serves 6.

SEAFOOD FILLET MARSEILLE

1 pound fish fillets
2 tablespoons melted butter
1/2 cup chicken broth
1 teaspoon dry mustard
1/2 teaspoon tarragon

Defrost fillets if using frozen fish. Place in a single layer in buttered baking dish. Combine remaining ingredients and pour over fish. Bake in preheated 350-degree oven for 20 to 25 minutes until fish flakes easily with a fork. Serves 2.

TUNA CURRY CASSEROLE

2 cans (6 1/2-ounce size) tuna
1 can cream of mushroom soup
1 cup milk
1/4 cup chopped onion
1/4 cup chopped green pepper
1/2 to 1 teaspoon curry powder
1/4 teaspoon oregano
2 cups cooked elbow macaroni

Combine ingredients in 2-quart casserole. Bake in 350-degree oven for 30 to 35 minutes. Serves 4.

CURRIED SHRIMP

2 medium onions, chopped
2 cloves garlic, minced
4 tablespoons butter
2 pounds raw, cleaned shrimp
1 can mushroom soup
1 can cream of chicken soup
1/2 cup raisins
2 to 4 teaspoons curry powder
2 tablespoons lemon juice
1/2 cup sour cream

Cook onions and garlic lightly in butter. Add soups, raw shrimp, raisins and curry. Cook 15 to 20 minutes or until shrimp are tender. If mixture is too thin, thicken with cornstarch to suit. Add lemon juice and sour cream just before serving. Serve over rice.

Except for lemon juice and sour cream, the curry can be made a day in advance and refrigerated. If this is done, heat it slowly and stir to avoid scorching. Serves 6.

Nine To Five

SPICED PICKLED SHRIMP

2 1/2 pounds cooked shrimp
1 bunch green onions
2 tablespoons capers and juice
1 1/2 cups salad oil
1 teaspoon salt
3/4 cup vinegar
1 teaspoon Worcestershire sauce
1/4 teaspoon Tabasco sauce

Put layer of shrimp, then layer of chopped small green onions in glass container. Combine rest of ingredients to make sauce and pour over onions. This may be stored in refrigerator 1 week.

MARINATED SHRIMP

1 1/2 cups beer
1/2 teaspoon dry mustard
1/2 teaspoon celery seed
1/2 teaspoon freshly ground black pepper
2 pounds raw shrimp, shelled and deveined
3/4 cup chopped onion
3/4 cup olive oil

Combine and bring beer, mustard, celery seed, and pepper to boil. Add shrimp, cook over low heat 5 minutes. Cool. Saute onions in oil; mix the undrained onions into shrimp mixture. Marinate 24 hours in refrigerator. Drain before serving.
Serves 4-6.

TURKEY PICCATA

1 pound turkey breast slices
3/4 cup flour
3/4 cup margarine
2 lemons
16 medium fresh mushrooms, about 1/4 pound, sliced
1 cup dry white wine

Make 2 to 4 cuts through membrane on outer edges of turkey slices. Dredge each in flour and pound out to very thin even thickness, less than 1/6-inch. Continuing to dredge in flour, pounding, use all of flour or more if needed. Melt 1/2 of margarine in large skillet, adding juice of 1/2 lemon. Saute turkey slices quickly in a single layer until lightly browned, turning once. Remove turkey slices as they brown. Set aside and add more. Use remaining margarine and juice of 1/2 lemon as needed while slices brown.

After all turkey slices are browned, remove from skillet, add mushrooms and saute lightly. Stir in wine and bring to boil, scraping browned bits from sides and bottom of pan. Return turkey to pan. Thinly slice 2nd lemon, arranging slices over turkey. Reduce heat and boil gently, uncovered, for 5 minutes. Serve immediately, spooning sauce over turkey slices. Serves 4 or 5.

Jan says, "This is really company fare and you cannot tell it from veal piccata."

WORKING GIRL MEAT LOAF

1 1/2 pounds ground beef
1 can Campbell's Onion soup
1 cup Pepperidge Farm dressing (or more)

Put all ingredients into bowl and mix well. Put into greased casserole and bake at 350 degrees for 1 hour. Serves 4-6.

MICROWAVE QUAIL

4 quail
4 tablespoons melted butter
3 teaspoons Kitchen Bouquet
1 tablespoon honey
1 teaspoon Bon Appetit
6 tablespoons sherry wine
3-ounce can sliced mushrooms with liquid
2 tablespoons flour
10 x 16-inch cellophane cooking bag
Salt and pepper

Salt and pepper quail. Marinate for 10 hours in mixture of butter, Kitchen Bouquet, honey, Bon Appetit and wine. Combine mushrooms and their liquid with flour. Blend in marinade. Place in oven bag in 2-quart casserole. Place quail on top of mushroom mixture. Close bag and make 4 slits in top of bag. Cook 8 minutes in microwave range on high. Use sauce in oven bag for spooning over quail when served. Allow 2 quail per person. Serves 2.

Jan says, "This is a good recipe for the working gal, but you never know how young or old a quail is and I like to bake my quail low and long in the oven."

DORISBURGERS

Make 4 oblong patties of hamburgers and lay
    on aluminum foil, slightly overlapping
Add the following:
1 can tomatoes (reserve juice)
1/2 chopped green pepper
1 package dry onion soup mix
1 small can unchopped mushrooms
Dash of salt

Combine tomatoes, chopped green pepper, soup mix, mushrooms and salt. Cover patties.

SAUCE:
Tomato juice
2 tablespoons A.1. sauce
2 tablespoons Worcestershire sauce
1 tablespoon cornstarch

Combine ingredients. Cook until thickened and pour over meat. Seal and bake 2 hours at 350 degrees on cookie sheet. Serves 4.

BLACK FOREST CHERRY CAKE

1 package devil's food cake mix
1 cup chopped maraschino cherries
2 cups heavy cream
1/2 cup powdered sugar
1 carton (18-ounce) cherry yogurt
Few drops red food coloring

Prepare cake mix according to directions. Fold in chopped cherries, reserving a few for garnish. Pour into 2-well greased and floured 9-inch pans. Bake at 375 degrees for 25 to 30 minutes. Cool on rack for 10 minutes. Remove cakes from pan and cool thoroughly. Cut both layers in half to make 4 layers.

FROSTING:
Whip cream until stiff. Gradually add sugar. Fold in yogurt and food coloring. Spread 1 cup frosting on bottom layer and repeat on all layers. Garnish with reserved cherries and chocolate curls. Refrigerate. Serves 12.

❖❖❖❖❖❖❖❖❖❖❖❖❖❖❖❖❖❖❖❖❖❖❖❖❖❖❖❖❖❖❖❖❖❖❖❖❖❖❖

FRENCH CHERRY PIE

1 9-inch baked pastry shell
1 package (3-ounce) cream cheese
1/2 cup powdered sugar
1/2 teaspoon vanilla
1 cup whipping cream
1 can (1 pound, 5 ounce) prepared cherry pie filling

Cream cheese, powdered sugar and vanilla together. Whip cream. Carefully fold into cream cheese mixture. Pour into pastry shell. Spread evenly. Cover with prepared cherry pie filling. Chill thoroughly before serving. Serves 8.

CHOCOLATE-VANILLA WAFER PUDDING

2 bars German chocolate
4 eggs, separated
1 pint whipping cream
1/2 cup sugar
1 cup chopped pecans
1 teaspoon vanilla
3/4 pound (12-ounce box) vanilla wafers

Melt chocolate in top of double boiler, adding a tiny bit of hot water if too thick. Add well-beaten egg yolks to chocolate. Add sugar and set aside to cool. Beat egg whites very stiff and fold into cooled chocolate mixture. Whip cream and fold into chocolate mixture. Add vanilla and nuts. Place 1/2 vanilla wafer crumbs on bottom of 9 x 13-inch pan. Pour chocolate mixture on top of crumbs and sprinkle remaining crumbs on top. Refrigerate. Serves 10-12.

CINNAMON ICE CREAM

1/2 pint whipping cream
2 tablespoons sugar
1 heaping teaspoon cinnamon
1 quart vanilla ice cream

Whip the cream, add sugar and cinnamon. Soften ice cream, add cinnamon mixture and whip. Freeze. Serves 8.

FUDGE FLOAT

2 tablespoons melted margarine or butter
1 cup sugar
1 teaspoon vanilla
1 cup flour
8 tablespoons cocoa
1 teaspoon baking powder
3/4 teaspoon salt
1/2 cup milk
1/2 cup chopped nuts
Confectioners' sugar
Whipped cream (optional)

In bowl, combine butter, 1/2 cup sugar and vanilla. Mix flour, 3 tablespoons cocoa, baking powder and 1/2 teaspoon salt and add alternately with milk to first mixture, stirring until well blended. Add nuts. In shallow 1 1/2-quart baking dish, combine remaining sugar, cocoa, salt and 1 2/3 cups boiling water. Drop batter by tablespoons onto boiling mixture. Bake at 350 degrees about 45 minutes. Sprinkle with powdered sugar and, while still warm, spoon out portion of cake and cover with sauce that remains on the bottom. Top with whipped cream if desired. Serves 4-6.

COLD BUTTERED RUM

1 blender full butter pecan ice cream
1 cup white rum

Fill blender with ice cream. Add rum. Blend 20 to 30 seconds. Serve in glasses or mugs that have been in freezer for several hours. Serves 4-6.

GIRDLE-BUSTER PIE

1 graham cracker crust
1 quart coffee ice cream
1 can or jar of fudge sauce. Do not use
chocolate sauce, it will be too thin.
1/2 cup chopped nuts, any kind you desire

Soften and beat ice cream. Pour into graham cracker crust and freeze. When firm, spread chocolate sauce over top and sprinkle with nuts. Keep frozen until served. Serves 6-8.

INSTANT CREME FRAICHE

1 cup whipping cream, whipped with 2 tablespoons confectioners' sugar or to taste
3 to 4 tablespoons sour cream

Fold whipped cream into sour cream. Cover and chill until serving time. This will keep covered in the refrigerator for 1 or 2 days. Instant Creme Fraiche can be used only as an accompaniment; do not use it as an ingredient in cooking.
Makes 1 cup.

EASY LEMON CAKE

2 packages lemon cake mix
1 package (6-ounce) lemon-flavored gelatin
1 1/2 cups water
1 1/2 cups salad oil
8 eggs
1 can (6-ounce) lemonade, undiluted
2 cups confectioners' sugar

Combine cake mix and lemon gelatin; add water and salad oil. Beat for 2 minutes. Add 8 eggs and and beat 2 more minutes. Pour into 2 greased and floured 13 x 9-inch or 1 22 x 12 pan. Bake in 300-degree oven for 50 minutes in the 13 x 9 or 65 minutes in the 22 x 12 pan. When the cake is done, pierce holes with fork in the top and spread with the frosting of lemonade and powdered sugar. The frosting will trickle down the holes and into the cake. Serves 12.

COLD LEMON MOUSSE

1 can sweetened condensed milk
1/4 cup lemon juice
1 egg yolk
1 teaspoon grated lemon rind
1 cup whipped cream

Blend the milk and lemon juice by hand. Add beaten egg yolk and grated lemon rind. Mix well. Fold in stiffly beaten whipped cream. Spoon into ramekins and chill. Serves 4.

JUDY'S STRAWBERRY PIE

1 9-inch pie crust
1 cup sugar
3 tablespoons cornstarch
1 7-Up (7-ounce size)
Red food coloring
1 pint fresh or frozen strawberries
1 half pint heavy cream

Cook sugar, cornstarch and 7-Up until creamy. Add red food coloring and cool. Combine to cooled mixture 1 pint fresh or frozen strawberries (whole). If using frozen berries, drain. Top with whipped cream.
Jan says, "Crust won't get soggy if you keep mixture in refrigerator and add to crust shortly before serving." Serves 8.

VERN'S PEACH COBBLER

8 fresh peaches, sliced
Juice and rind of 1/2 lemon
3/4 cup sugar
2 tablespoons flour
1/2 teaspoon nutmeg
1/2 teaspoon cinnamon

CRUST:
3/4 cup flour
1/4 cup shortening
Salt and water

Combine ingredients, pour into flat pan. Cover with crust.

Combine flour and shortening, add pinch of salt and enough water to mix as if making a pie crust. Cover peach mixture and brush with cream and sugar. Bake 15 minutes at 450 degrees, then 30 minutes at 350 degrees.
Serves 4-6.

PRETTY PLUM CAKE

2 cups sugar
3 eggs
1 cup oil

2 small jars of plum baby food (with tapioca)
2 teaspoons red food coloring
2 cups flour
1/8 teaspoon salt
1/2 teaspoon soda
1 teaspoon cloves
1 teaspoon cinnamon
1 cup chopped nuts

Beat ingredients together. Add the following:

Mix well and pour into floured bundt pan or angel food pan. Bake 1 hour at 325 degrees.
Serves 10-12.

STRAWBERRY CAKE

1 box white cake mix (2-layer size)
4 eggs
1/2 cup water
2/3 cup Wesson oil
1 small package strawberry Jell-O
3/4 of 10-ounce package frozen strawberries, thawed and drained

Place all ingredients in mixer and beat well. Bake in greased and floured 13 x 9 x 2-inch pan at 350 degrees for 40 minutes, or until done.

TOPPING:
1/4 of 10-ounce package frozen strawberries, thawed and drained
1 stick margarine, softened
Powdered sugar to desired consistency

Combine all ingredients and spread on cooled cake. Serves 10-12.

CHOCOLATE ADDICTS FROZEN CREAM

2/3 cup canned chocolate syrup
2/3 cup sweetened condensed milk
2 cups heavy cream
1/2 teaspoon vanilla
1/3 cup slivered blanched almonds, toasted

Combine chocolate syrup, condensed milk, cream and vanilla; chill. Whip until fluffy and soft peaks form. Fold in nuts. Pile into refrigerator tray; freeze firm. Serve sprinkled with toasted almonds if desired. Serves 8-10.

QUICKIE STRAWBERRY DESSERT

2 packages Jiffy yellow cake mix
1 package (8-ounce) cream cheese
1/2 cup milk
3 cups milk
2 packages (4 1/2-ounce size) vanilla instant
   pudding
3 cups sliced strawberries

Mix cake according to directions on box. Bake in 13 x 9-inch pan. While cake is baking, mix cream cheese with 1/2 cup milk. Beat 3 cups milk and vanilla instant pudding well and add to the cream–cheese mixture. After cake has cooled spread the pudding mixture on top of cake. Add strawberries on top. Refrigerate. Serves 8 to 10.

Jan says, "This quick dessert is a delight to serve. You may use other kinds of fruit instead of strawberries."

HONEY NUT CRUNCH BARS

1/3 cup honey
1/3 cup margarine or butter
1 cup brown sugar (packed)
1/2 teaspoon ground cinnamon
1 teaspoon vanilla
5 cups Golden Grahams cereal
1 cup mixed nuts or peanuts

Grease a square pan (9 x 9 x 2-inch). Heat honey, margarine, brown sugar and cinnamon to boiling in a 3-quart saucepan. Boil 2 minutes. Remove from heat, add vanilla.

Gradually fold in cereal until completely coated. Fold in nuts. Press into greased pan. Let stand at least 1 hour. Cut into bars. Makes 24.

INDIVIDUAL BAKED ALASKA

4 brownies
1/2 pint vanilla ice cream, or flavor desired
3 egg whites
Dash of salt
6 tablespoons sugar
1/4 teaspoon cream of tartar

Bake brownies and let cool. Let eggs sit out overnight to arrive at room temperature. When ready to serve, place brownie on a cookie sheet, cut in squares, and place slice of ice cream on top of brownie. Place cookie sheet in freezer while you beat egg whites, sugar, salt and cream of tartar.

Frost brownies with egg whites. You may color if desired. Place in preheated 425-degree oven for about 3 to 5 minutes or until lightly browned. Serves 4.

BETTER THAN SEX CAKE

1 package yellow pudding cake mix
20-ounce can of crushed pineapple
1/2 cup sugar
1 package (3 5/8-ounce) instant vanilla pudding
1 carton (7-ounce) Cool Whip

Prepare cake mix as directed on package. Five minutes before cake is done, simmer can of crushed pineapple and sugar until cake is done. Remove cake from oven and punch holes all over cake with a toothpick or fork. Pour pineapple mixture over cake and allow to completely cool.

Prepare pudding mix according to directions. Put pudding on cake and let set for 15-20 minutes.

Spread a carton of Cool Whip on cake. Sprinkle with coconut and nuts. Serves 10-12.

MELTING MOMENTS

Melting Moments · Desserts

Though our dessert chapter is one of the largest in the book, we hope you'll try every single recipe. If you are looking for a great quick cake, try the Black Russian Cake. For a beautiful finale to your dinner party, turn to page 187 and bake the Brandy Refrigerator Cake topped with a frosted rose. Ever so many cakes, frostings, fillings, and sauces will tease your sweet buds. Among great make-ahead delights are the cheese cakes, Lili's Chocolate Torte, and the mousses. But if you want to dazzle, try any one of the soufflés.

If you are looking for a hot-weather dessert, check out the ice cream dishes. One of our very favorite easy, elegant treats is Bananas Flambé. You'll note that we don't have a few pies, we have many pies. You're sure to find your favorite, whether it be Pumpkin, Strawberry, Grape, Apple, or Grasshopper Pie.

We have placed cookies and candies in our Christmas chapter (Under the Mistletoe), where they can be found in the subsection called Visions of Sugarplums. Look through the Nine to Five chapter for quick and easy desserts if you are short of time.

Melting Moments

❖❖

Cakes

MOM'S ANGEL CAKE SUPREME

1 cup sifted cake flour
1 1/4 cups sifted confectioners' sugar
1 1/2 cups (12) egg whites
1 1/2 teaspoons cream of tartar
1/4 teaspoon salt
1 1/2 teaspoons vanilla
1/4 teaspoon almond extract
1 cup granulated sugar

Sift flour with confectioners' sugar 3 times. Beat egg whites with cream of tartar, salt, vanilla and almond extract until stiff enough to hold up in soft peaks but still moist and glossy. Beat in the granulated sugar, 2 tablespoons at a time, continuing to beat until meringue holds stiff peaks.

Sift about 1/4 cup of flour mixture over whites, fold in lightly with down, up and over motion, turning bowl. Fold in remainder of flour by fourths. Bake in an ungreased 10-inch tube pan in preheated 375-degree oven for about 30 minutes or until done. Invert pan, cool thoroughly. Serves 12-14.

CHOCOLATE ANGEL FOOD CAKE

Prepare Angel Cake Supreme as directed adding 1/4 cup cocoa to mixture with flour and confectioners' sugar. You can do the same with an angel food cake mix.

ANGEL FOOD WALDORF

Bake 1 package (15-16 ounce) white angel food cake mix or for a "quickie," use a bakery cake. Place cake upside down when cool; slice off entire top of cake about 1-inch down and set aside. Make cuts down into cake 1-inch from outer edge and 1-inch from edge of hole, leaving substantial "walls" on each side. With a curved knife or spoon, remove cake within cuts, being careful to leave a base of cake 1-inch thick. Place cake on serving plate.

FILLING:

3 cups whipping cream
1 1/2 cups powdered sugar
3/4 cup cocoa
1/4 teaspoon salt
2/3 cup toasted slivered almonds

In chilled bowl whip cream, sugar, cocoa and salt until stiff. Fold 1/3 cup almonds into half the whipped-cream mixture. Spoon into cake cavity, pressing firmly into cavity to avoid "holes" in cut slices. Replace top of cake and press gently. Frost cake with remaining whipped-cream mixture. Sprinkle with remaining 1/3 cup toasted almonds. Chill at least 4 hours or until set. 12 - 16 servings.

RAW APPLE CAKE

2 cups sugar
1 cup shortening
2 eggs
2 1/2 cups flour
2 1/2 teaspoons soda
1/2 teaspoon salt
1 teaspoon cinnamon
4 1/2 cups diced or chopped raw apples
1/2 cup walnuts, chopped

Cream sugar, shortening and eggs until smooth. Add flour, soda, salt, cinnamon, raw apples and walnuts.

Mix together and bake in greased and floured 9 x 13-inch pan for 45 minutes at 350 degrees. Top the cooled cake with whipped topping.

Serves 12.

APPLESAUCE SPICE CAKE

2 3/4 cups sifted all-purpose flour
1 teaspoon baking powder
1/2 teaspoon baking soda
1 teaspoon salt
1 teaspoon cinnamon
1 teaspoon ground cloves
1/4 teaspoon ground ginger
1/2 cup shortening
1 cup sugar
2 eggs
1 jar (16-ounce) applesauce
1 cup chopped walnuts
1 cup raisins
1 cup chopped pitted dates
1 cup confectioners' sugar
1 teaspoon grated lemon rind
1-2 tablespoons lemon juice

Sift together flour, baking powder, baking soda, salt, cinnamon, cloves and ginger. Cream shortening with sugar until fluffy; add eggs, beat until smooth.

Add flour mixture to creamed mixture, alternately with applesauce. Stir in walnuts, raisins and dates. Pour into a greased 9 x 9 x 2-inch pan. Bake in 350-degree oven for 1 hour, or until a toothpick inserted in center comes out clean.

Cool 10 minutes before removing from pan. Finish cooling right side up on wire rack. When cool, drizzle top with mixture of confectioners' sugar, lemon rind and lemon juice. Serves 6-8.

BLACK RUSSIAN CAKE

1 package Duncan Hines yellow cake mix
1 package (4 1/2 ounce) Jell-O instant chocolate pudding
1 cup oil
4 eggs
1/4 cup Vodka
1/4 cup Kahlúa
3/4 cup water

Beat all ingredients with mixer very well. Pour into a greased bundt pan and bake at 350 degrees for 50 to 60 minutes. Cool 1/2 hour in pan.

Sift powdered sugar over top or glaze with 1/2 cup sifted powdered sugar and additional Kahlúa to a glaze consistency. Serves 14.

Jan says, "Here is the recipe that I did not give out until the book was published. Such a special delicious cake."

Melting Moments

BRANDY REFRIGERATOR CAKE

1 cup soft butter
2 cups powdered sugar
5 egg yolks
1/2 cup brandy
1 cup toasted blanched almond slivers
1 angel food cake

FROSTING:
1 1/2 pints heavy cream
1/4 cup brandy
1/2 teaspoon vanilla
Powdered sugar

Blend butter with sugar. Beat until fluffy. Add egg yolks one at a time, beating after each addition. Blend in brandy and almonds. Mix well.

Line a rounded bowl or pan (use a mixing bowl) with wax paper. Slice angel food cake about 1/2-inch thick crosswise. (I do mine in thirds.) Place cake on bottom, layer of brandy mixture, cake, brandy mixture, cake and the remaining brandy mixture. Cover and chill overnight.

When ready to serve turn the cake out on a tray and frost with 1 1/2 pints heavy cream whipped, 1/4 cup brandy, 1/2 teaspoon vanilla and 2 to 3 tablespoons powdered sugar. Chill until ready to serve. Serves 14.

Jan says, "A flower that has been frosted in sugar looks like the finishing touch when placed on top of the cake."

RICH BROWNIE CUPCAKES

2 sticks margarine
4 ounce bar of semisweet chocolate
1 1/2 cups pecans, chopped
1 3/4 cups sugar
1 cup flour
4 large eggs
1 teaspoon vanilla

Melt chocolate and margarine. Add nuts and stir until well coated. Combine eggs, sugar, flour and vanilla. Add chocolate-nut mixture. Mix carefully only until well blended. (Do not beat). Bake in small cupcake liners. Bake in 325 degree oven for 35 minutes. Needs no frosting.

Makes 12 cupcakes.

ANNIE'S CHOCOLATE CAKE

2 cups sugar
1 stick margarine
2 eggs
1/2 cup cocoa

Cream first 4 ingredients very well. Mix rest of ingredients except water and add gradually to the first mixture.

2 cups flour
1 teaspoon baking powder
3/4 cup milk
1 teaspoon soda
1 teaspoon vanilla
1 cup boiling water

Stir water in mixture by hand. Bake at 350 degrees for 30 minutes. Makes a nice loaf or 2 9-inch round or square cake pans. Serves 12-14.

Melting Moments

CHOCOLATE BUTTERMILK CAKE

2 cups brown sugar
1/2 cup butter
3 eggs
3/4 cup buttermilk
2 1/2 cups flour
1/2 teaspoon salt
2 teaspoons soda
2 squares unsweetened chocolate, melted
3/4 cup water, boiling
1 teaspoon vanilla

Sift together flour, soda and salt. Cream sugar and butter; add chocolate. Add eggs, vanilla and milk. Blend in sifted ingredients; beat. Add water. Bake in preheated 350 degree oven for 30 minutes. Serves 10.

CHOCOLATE CHERRY CAKE

1 package fudge cake mix
21-ounce can cherry pie filling
1 teaspoon almond extract
2 eggs, beaten
1/3 cup vegetable oil

FROSTING:
1 cup sugar
5 tablespoons butter
1/3 cup milk
6-ounce package semi-sweet chocolate chips

Preheat oven to 350 degrees. Grease and flour 15 x 10-inch jelly roll pan or 9 x 12 x 2-inch baking pan. In a large bowl, combine ingredients. Stir by hand until well mixed. Pour into prepared pan. Bake jelly roll pan for 20-30 minutes. Bake the 9 x 13 pan for 25-30 minutes. While cake is cooling prepare frosting.

In a small saucepan combine sugar, butter and milk. Boil, stirring constantly, for 1 minute. Remove from heat, stir in chocolate chips until smooth. Poor over partially cooled cake. Serves 12.

FABULOUS CHOCOLATE CAKE

1 stick margarine or 1/2 margarine and 1/2 butter
2 cups sugar
2 eggs
3 squares melted chocolate
1 1/2 cups milk
1 teaspoon vanilla
1 teaspoon red food coloring
2 cups sifted cake flour
2 teaspoons baking powder
Salt
1 cup finely chopped pecans

FROSTING:
1/2 stick butter or margarine
1 1/2 squares chocolate, melted
1 beaten egg
1 teaspoon vanilla
1 box powdered sugar
1 cup pecans

Cream butter and sugar. Add eggs, one at a time, beating well after each addition. Add chocolate, then add combined liquid ingredients alternately with combined dry ingredients. Add nuts. Bake in greased and floured 13 x 9-inch pan for approximately 40 minutes at 350 degrees.

Note: Cake is delicious without pecans. Just use them in the frosting if you prefer.

Melt butter and chocolate. Add a small amount to beaten egg, then add back into chocolate mixture. Add vanilla. Stir in powdered sugar and nuts. Serves 18.

Melting Moments

CHOCOLATE CAKE ROLL

6 egg yolks
6 egg whites
1 cup powdered sugar
3 tablespoons cocoa
1 tablespoon flour
1/2 pint heavy cream

Beat egg yolks until thick; add sugar, then cocoa and flour gradually, beating constantly. Add egg whites beaten stiff.

Line a greased 14 x 10-inch jelly roll pan with waxed paper, then grease and flour the paper. Leave ends of paper showing so you can peel it off. Pour cake batter into the pan and bake for 20 minutes in a 350-degree oven. When cake is done turn out on a dampened cloth and fold over jelly roll style. When cool, open and put sweetened whipped cream between roll and frost top and sides.

FROSTING:
1/4 cup butter
3 cups powdered sugar
2 squares unsweetened chocolate
3 tablespoons cream
3 tablespoons hot coffee
1 teaspoon vanilla

Melt butter and chocolate in top of double boiler. Stir in sugar, coffee and cream. Leave over hot water 10 to 15 minutes. Add vanilla.
Serves 14-16.

JEANINE'S CARROT CAKE

2 cups sugar
4 eggs
1 1/2 cups vegetable oil
2 cups flour
1 teaspoon salt
2 teaspoons soda
2 1/2 teaspoons cinnamon
1/2 cup chopped nuts
2 1/2 cups grated carrots
1 teaspoon vanilla

Mix sugar, oil and eggs. Sift dry ingredients and add to mix. Add carrots, nuts and vanilla. Pour into 3 greased and floured 8-inch pans or a 9 x 13 x 2-inch baking pan. Bake in preheated 300-degree oven for 35 to 40 minutes.

Frost with Cream Cheese Frosting (see index) or Orange Glaze. Serves 12.

ORANGE GLAZE FOR CARROT CAKE

1 cup granulated sugar
1/4 cup cornstarch
1 teaspoon fresh lemon juice
1 cup fresh orange juice
1/2 teaspoon salt
2 tablespoons grated orange peel
2 tablespoons butter

Combine sugar and cornstarch in saucepan. Add juices slowly and stir, until smooth. Add remaining ingredients. Cook over low heat until thick and glossy. Cool and spread on cake, between layers and on top and sides. If a heavier glaze is desired, double recipe.

Melting Moments

CHOCOLATE SHEET CAKE

2 cups sugar
2 cups flour
2 teaspoons cinnamon
1/8 teaspoon salt
1 stick margarine
1/2 cup cooking oil
1/4 cup cocoa
1 cup water
2 eggs, beaten
1 teaspoon vanilla
1/2 cup buttermilk
1 teaspoon soda

Mix sugar, flour, cinnamon and salt together in a bowl. In a saucepan, mix margarine, oil, cocoa and water. Bring to a boil. Remove from heat and pour over flour mixture. Mix well. Dissolve soda in buttermilk and add eggs, vanilla and buttermilk to first mixture. Beat well. Pour into greased and floured 12 x 18-inch pan.

Bake at 400 degrees for 20 minutes or until toothpick stuck in center comes out clean.

Five minutes before cake is done, prepare icing: Makes 24 squares.

FROSTING:
1 stick margarine
4 tablespoons cocoa
7 tablespoons milk
1 package powdered sugar
1 teaspoon vanilla
1/2 cup chopped pecans

Mix margarine, milk and cocoa in saucepan and bring to a boil. Place sugar in bowl and pour hot liquid over sugar. Beat with mixer, adding vanilla and nuts. Pour over hot cake upon removal from oven. Icing will set up quickly. Serves 24.

COCONUT CREAM CAKE

1/2 cup shortening
1/2 cup margarine
2 cups sugar
5 eggs, separated
2 cups flour
1 teaspoon soda
1 cup buttermilk
1 2/3 cups flaked coconut

Blend shortening and margarine. Add sugar gradually and beat until fluffy. Add egg yolks, one at a time, beating well after each addition. Sift flour and soda. Add alternately with buttermilk, beginning and ending with the flour mixture. Add coconut to cake mixture. Beat egg whites until stiff peaks form. Fold into batter. Pour into 3 greased and floured 9-inch round cake pans and bake in preheated 350-degree oven for 25 to 30 minutes. Cool. Frost with Cream Cheese frosting (see index).

Serves 12.

VERN'S DATE CAKE

1 cup dates, chopped
1 cup boiling water
1 teaspoon soda
1 cup sugar
1/2 cup shortening
1 unbeaten egg
2 cups flour
1 teaspoon baking powder
1/2 cup nuts

Mix dates, boiling water and soda. Allow to cool. Combine sugar and shortening, cream well. Add egg, flour and baking powder. Stir in nuts and dates. Bake at 325 degrees for 50 minutes.

Serves 6-8.

Melting Moments

❖❖

COKE CAKE

2 cups flour
2 cups sugar
2 sticks butter
3 tablespoons cocoa
1 cup Coke
1/2 cup buttermilk
2 beaten eggs
1 teaspoon soda
1 teaspoon vanilla
1 1/2 cups miniature marshmallows

FROSTING:
1/2 cup margarine
3 tablespoons cocoa
6 tablespoons Coke
1 box powdered sugar (1-pound)
1 cup chopped pecans, toasted

Combine flour and sugar. Heat butter, Coke and cocoa to boiling. Pour over flour and sugar mixture and beat thoroughly. Mix beaten eggs, buttermilk, soda, vanilla and marshmallows. Add to other mixture and mix well. Batter will be thin with marshmallows floating on top. Bake in 9 x 13-inch pan for 30 to 35 minutes in 350-degree oven, or until toothpick inserted in center comes out clean.

While cake is baking bring margarine, cocoa and Coke to a boil; pour over box of powdered sugar and add chopped nuts. Spread on hot cake when it comes out of the oven. If icing is too thick, add a small amount of Coke. Serves 12.

FOOTBALL CAKE

2 packages white or yellow cake mix
3 squares unsweetened chocolate
1/2 cup plus 2 tablespoons margarine
5 cups powdered sugar
3/4 teaspoon salt
2 eggs
1/2 teaspoon vanilla

1 1/2 packages white or yellow cake mix. Bake according to directions and pour into 3 round 8-inch layer–cake pans that have been greased and floured well. After cake is cooled, cut two of the layers in half, cutting about 1/4-inch off-center. Cut remaining layer into three sections to give two rounded-end pieces and a center strip. From center strip cut off two end pieces about 2 1/4 inches long, leaving a square center piece which you won't need for football.

To assemble football with these eight pieces of cake, stand pieces upright on a board with largest in center, graduating down to smallest pieces on either end. With sharp knife trim top and sides and taper end to make the football shape.

Reassemble cake on serving plate, spreading frosting (about 1 cup) between the pieces. Frost and mold at the same time over cake to give a good football shape. Let this stand until set, then frost again. Keep in cool place until ready to decorate. Using cake decorator and lettering tube, make lacings and numerals with decorating frosting. When ready to serve slice the cake lengthwise.

Serves 16-20.

CHOCOLATE FROSTING

In top of double boiler over hot water, melt 3 squares bitter chocolate and 1/2 cup margarine. Turn into a bowl and add 1 1/2 cups powdered sugar, 1/2 teaspoon salt. Mix thoroughly. Add 2 unbeaten eggs, one at a time, beating well after each addition. Gradually beat in 2 additional cups powdered sugar. Beat until smooth.

FROSTING FOR DECORATING

Cream 2 tablespoons margarine with 1 1/2 cups powdered sugar, 1/4 teaspoon salt and 1/2 teaspoon vanilla. Add about 5 teaspoons milk or 5 teaspoons boiling water to make a stiff frosting. Beat until smooth.

Melting Moments

LAZY DAISY CAKE

1 large or 2 small eggs
1 cup sugar
1 cup flour
1 teaspoon baking powder
1 teaspoon vanilla
1 cup milk heated with 2 level tablespoons
   butter

TOPPING:
1/2 cup brown sugar
1/2 cup coconut
3 teaspoons cream
3 tablespoons melted butter
1/2 cup pecans (optional)

Beat eggs until light. Continue beating while adding sugar and vanilla. Fold in flour mixed with baking powder. Add hot milk and butter, mixing very quickly. Pour into greased and floured square baking dish. Bake in 350-degree oven for 20 minutes. While cake is hot, quickly cover with icing. Slip under broiler and brown slowly.

Combine ingredients.
Serves 6-8.

LEMON COCONUT CAKE

1 box lemon cake mix
1 box lemon instant pudding (small size)
4 eggs
3/4 cup salad oil
1 bottle (10-ounce) 7-Up

TOPPING:
1 cup sugar
2 tablespoons flour
1 stick margarine
1 cup undrained crushed pineapple
2 eggs
1 1/2 cups coconut
1 cup pecans

Place first 4 ingredients in large bowl and beat well. Use electric mixer on medium speed. Gradually add 7-Up. Mix until well-blended. Bake in greased and floured 13 x 9 x 2-inch pan at 350 degrees for 40 minutes.

Mix sugar and flour. Melt margarine in saucepan. Add pineapple and flour mixture. Cook until it starts to bubble. Beat eggs. Add small amount of hot liquid to eggs and add to first mixture. Cook until thick and eggs are cooked. Stir in coconut and pecans. Spread on warm cake. Serves 12.

MISSISSIPPI MUD CAKE

2 sticks margarine
2 cups sugar
4 eggs
1 1/2 cups flour
Dash of salt
1/2 cup cocoa
1 1/2 cups pecans
4 (1.2-ounce) chocolate bars

Mix all ingredients except chocolate bars. Bake in a 13 x 9-inch pan 35 minutes at 350 degrees. Spread with 4 chocolate (1.2 ounces each) bars. Break bars into pieces, place on hot cake. Let stand 1 minute, then spread softened chocolate with spatula to frost cake. Cool before serving.
Serves 12-14.

Melting Moments

GERMAN CHOCOLATE CAKE

Box of German chocolate cake mix
Small box (4-ounce) instant chocolate pudding
4 eggs
1/2 cup oil
8 ounces sour cream (commercial)
1/2 cup water
1 teaspoon vanilla
1 package (6-ounce) chocolate chips
1/2 cup chopped nuts

Mix together all ingredients except the nuts. Sprinkle the chopped nuts over the bottom of a greased and floured bundt pan and pour the batter over nuts. Bake at 325 degrees for 55 minutes. Glaze or sprinkle powdered sugar over top. Rich but so good. Serves 12-14.

HARVEY WALLBANGER SUPREME CAKE

1 package orange cake mix
3 3/4-ounce package instant vanilla pudding
1/2 cup vegetable oil
4 ounces frozen orange juice
4 ounces water
4 eggs
3 ounces Galliano
1 ounce vodka

Blend all ingredients in large bowl. Beat with electric mixer 5 minutes. Pour into greased and floured bundt pan. Bake in 350-degree oven 45 to 55 minutes until center springs back. Cool 15 minutes and turn out on cake plate. Drizzle glaze over warm cake.

GLAZE:
1 cup powdered sugar
1 tablespoon orange juice
1 1/2 tablespoons Galliano
1 tablespoon vodka

Combine ingredients and blend well.
Serves 12-14.

APRICOT BRANDY POUND CAKE

3 cups sugar
2 sticks margarine
6 eggs
1/2 teaspoon lemon flavoring
1 teaspoon orange flavoring
1 teaspoon butter flavoring
1/2 teaspoon rum flavoring
1 teaspoon vanilla
1/4 teaspoon almond flavoring
3 cups flour
1/2 teaspoon salt
1/4 teaspoon soda
1 cup sour cream
1/4 to 1/2 cup apricot brandy

Cream margarine and sugar. Add eggs, one at a time, beating well after each addition. Add flavorings, then sift dry ingredients together and add alternately with the sour cream and brandy to the sugar, egg mixture. Bake in a greased bundt pan at 325 degrees for 1 hour and 10 minutes. This comes out of the pan better if it is cooled for about 10 minutes.

Jo says, "I find if I bake this cake for only 1 hour it is more moist. Test with straws."

APRICOT GLAZE:
3/4 cup apricot preserves
1 tablespoon orange juice
1/2 pint heavy cream

Melt preserves in small saucepan over low heat. Stir in orange juice, then strain. When cake is cool place onto serving plate. Brush glaze over top and side of cake. Refrigerate.

TO SERVE: Garnish plate with grapes and, if desired, leaves. Cut cake into wedges. Pass whipped cream for guests to spoon over cake.
Serves 12-14.

Melting Moments

INSPIRATION CAKE

1 cup finely chopped pecans, walnuts or other nuts
2 ounces sweet or semi-sweet chocolate
2 1/2 cups all-purpose flour
4 teaspoons baking powder
1 teaspoon salt
1 1/2 cups sugar
2/3 cup shortening
1 1/4 cups milk
1 teaspoon vanilla
2/3 cup egg whites (4 large or 5 medium eggs, unbeaten)

Sprinkle nuts evenly over bottoms of 2 well-greased and lightly floured 9-inch round cake pans. Grate chocolate, reserve. Sift together in mixing bowl the flour, baking powder, salt and sugar. Add shortening, milk and vanilla. Beat 1 1/2 minutes at medium speed after blending on low speed. Add unbeaten egg whites and beat 1 1/2 minutes.

Spoon 1/4 of batter carefully into each nut-lined pan, using about 1/2 of the batter. Sprinkle with grated chocolate, half in each pan. Spoon remaining batter into pans, spreading carefully so chocolate is not disturbed.

Bake 35 to 40 minutes in 350-degree oven. Let cool in pans 10 to 15 minutes before turning out. Cool thoroughly and frost layers, nut side up, with chocolate frosting. Spread frosting between and on sides of layers, but frost only 1/2 inch around top edge of cake. Decorate chocolate frosting with reserved 1/3 cup white frosting, thinned with 1 to 2 teaspoons water for easy spreading.
Serves 12-14.

CHOCOLATE FROSTING:

2 squares (2 ounces) unsweetened chocolate
1/2 cup granulated sugar
1/4 cup water
4 egg yolks
1/2 cup butter
1 teaspoon vanilla
2 cups sifted confectioners sugar

Combine chocolate, sugar and water in saucepan. Cook over low heat, stirring constantly, until chocolate melts and mixture is smooth and thickened. Remove from heat. Add egg yolks and beat thoroughly. Cool.

Cream butter and vanilla. Gradually blend in confectioners' sugar, creaming well. Reserve 1/3 cup of this frosting to decorate cake.

Add cool chocolate mixture to remaining white frosting; beat until smooth.

PAULINE'S POTATO CAKE

2 cups cake flour
3 teaspoons baking powder
1/2 teaspoon cloves
1/2 teaspoon cinnamon
3/4 cup shortening
2 cups sugar
3 whole eggs
1 cup hot mashed potatoes
4 squares chocolate, melted
3/4 cup sweet milk
1 teaspoon vanilla
1 cup chopped nuts

Combine flour with other dry ingredients. Cream shortening and sugar, beat in eggs, one at a time. Blend in mashed potatoes and melted chocolate. Add the dry ingredients alternately with the milk to creamed mixture. Blend in vanilla and nuts. Bake in three layer pans at 355 degrees until toothpick inserted in center comes out clean.
Serves 12-14.

Melting Moments

CREAM CHEESE POUND CAKE

3 sticks margarine
1 package (8-ounce) cream cheese
3 cups sugar
6 eggs
3 cups flour
2 teaspoons vanilla
1/8 teaspoon salt

Cream margarine and cream cheese. Add sugar and beat until fluffy. Add eggs, one at a time, beating well after each addition. Add flour and salt, mix well and add vanilla. Bake in greased bundt pan for 90 minutes in 300-degree oven. Cool thoroughly before removing from pan.

Jo says, "You will find many ways to serve this delicious cake. Try it with fresh fruits, ice cream or just plain. I like to cut it in small pieces and serve it for dipping in dessert sauces with my fondue dinners." Serves 12-16.

PINEAPPLE COCONUT CAKE

1 box yellow cake mix
4 eggs
3/4 cup oil
1 bottle (10-ounce) 7-Up
1 box pineapple pudding

Place cake mix, pudding mix, oil and eggs in a large bowl. Beat well. Add 7-Up gradually and mix together until well blended. Pour into a prepared 13 x 9 x 2-inch pan. Bake at 350 degrees for 40 minutes.

FROSTING:
1 cup sugar
1 tablespoon flour
1 stick margarine
2 eggs
1 1/2 cups coconut
1 cup chopped pecans
1 cup undrained crushed pineapple

Mix flour with sugar, melt margarine in saucepan. Add pineapple and flour mixture to melted margarine. Cook until it starts to bubble. Beat eggs; add a small amount of hot liquid to eggs. Add to first mixture. Cook until thickened and eggs are cooked. Stir in coconut and pecans. Spread on hot cake. Serves 12.

PINEAPPLE SHEET CAKE

2 cups sugar
2 cups flour
2 cans (8-ounce size) crushed pineapple
2 eggs
2 teaspoons baking soda

Place ingredients in bowl and mix well. Pour into greased and floured jelly roll pan and bake at 350 degrees for 20 to 30 minutes.

FROSTING:
1 package (6-ounce) cream cheese
1 stick margarine
1 pound powdered sugar

Blend ingredients until smooth. If frosting gets too thick add a little milk until the right consistency. Serves 12.

PUMPKIN CAKE ROLL

3 eggs
1 cup sugar
2/3 cup pumpkin
1 teaspoon lemon juice
3/4 cup flour
1 teaspoon baking powder
1 teaspoon cinnamon
1/2 teaspoon ginger
1/4 teaspoon nutmeg
1/2 teaspoon salt
1 cup walnuts

Beat eggs on high speed for 5 minutes. Gradually beat in sugar. Stir in pumpkin and lemon juice. Stir together flour, baking powder, cinnamon, ginger, nutmeg and salt. Fold into pumpkin. Spread in greased and floured pan, 15 x 11 x 2-inch. Top with finely chopped walnuts. Bake at 375 degrees for 15 minutes. Turn out on a towel that has been sprinkled with powdered sugar.

FILLING:
1 cup powdered sugar
6-ounce package cream cheese
4 teaspoons butter or margarine
1/2 teaspoon vanilla

Combine ingredients. Beat until smooth. Spread over cake. Roll cake lengthwise and place in refrigerator. Serves 16.

PUMPKIN SHEET CAKE

1 1/2 cups flour
2 cups sugar
4 eggs
1 cup oil
1 teaspoon soda
1 teaspoon baking powder
3/4 teaspoon salt
2 teaspoons cinnamon
1 cup pumpkin

Mix all ingredients in a bowl and blend well. Pour into a greased jelly roll pan. Bake at 350 degrees for 20 minutes.

FROSTING:
1 package (8-ounce) cream cheese
2 pounds powdered sugar
1 teaspoon vanilla
5 tablespoons milk

Mix cream cheese, sugar and milk together. Add powdered sugar. Beat well. Add 1 teaspoon vanilla and mix until blended. Spread on cake.
Serves 12.

LAVERNA'S SPICE CAKE

1/3 cup butter
1 1/3 cups brown sugar
2 eggs
1/2 cup cold water
1 3/4 cups cake flour
1/8 teaspoon salt
3 teaspoons baking powder
1 teaspoon cinnamon
1/2 teaspoon nutmeg
1/4 teaspoon ground cloves
1 cup raisins

Sift dry ingredients. Cream butter and sugar, add eggs and cold water. Add to dry ingredients. Beat for 5 minutes. Bake in greased and floured tube pan at 350 degrees for 45 minutes.
Frost with Minute Penuche frosting. (See index).
Serves 12.

❖❖❖

WALDORF-ASTORIA CAKE

1 1/2 cups sugar
1/2 cup shortening
1 1/2 ounces red food coloring plus
   1/2 ounce water
2 eggs
1 teaspoon vanilla
2 cups flour
1 teaspoon salt
1 to 2 tablespoons cocoa
1 cup buttermilk
1 teaspoon soda
1 tablespoon vinegar

Cream sugar and shortening until fluffy, using fastest speed on mixer. Add coloring, eggs and vanilla; beat until smooth. Sift flour, salt and cocoa 3 times. Add to creamed mixture alternately with buttermilk; beat until smooth. Combine soda and vinegar; by hand, blend gently into batter. Place in 2 well-greased and floured 9-inch pans or 3 8-inch pans. Bake at 350 degrees for 30 to 35 minutes.

FROSTING:
1/4 cup flour
1 cup milk
1 cup sugar
1 cup shortening or 1/2 cup margarine and
   1/2 cup shortening
1 teaspoon vanilla
1 or 2 drops almond flavoring
Pinch of salt
1 cup coconut

Combine flour, salt and milk; cook until thick. Set aside to cool. Cream sugar and shortening; add flavoring. Add sugar mixture to cooled milk mixture; beat until fluffy enough to spread. Add the coconut gradually. 12 servings.

Jan says, "I like this frosting, but I use the Shortcut 7 Minute frosting. Jo uses the Cream Cheese Frosting" (See index).

BUNDT RUM CAKE

1 cup chopped pecans or walnuts
1 package (18 1/2-ounce) Betty Crocker Super-Moist yellow cake mix
1 package (3 1/2-ounce) instant vanilla pudding
4 eggs
1/2 cup cold water
1/2 cup Wesson oil
1/2 cup 80-proof Bacardi dark rum

Grease and flour bundt pan. Sprinkle nuts in bottom of pan. Mix cake ingredients as listed. Do not make cake as directed on package. Pour into pan over nuts. Bake 1 hour in preheated 325-degree oven. Cool. Invert on serving plate. Prick top liberally with a fork.

Drizzle some of glaze over top and sides. Allow cake to absorb glaze. Repeat until glaze is used up.

Jo says, "This cake freezes beautifully, and the longer it sits, the better it gets. It's not too sweet, so even those who aren't dessert freaks will take seconds."

GLAZE:
1/2 cup butter
1/4 cup water
1 cup granulated sugar
1/2 cup 80-proof dark rum

Melt butter, stir in water and sugar. Boil for 5 minutes stirring constantly. Remove from heat, stir in rum. Cool slightly. Serves 12-16.

Melting Moments

SHORTCAKE

2 cups flour
1/2 teaspoon salt
4 teaspoons baking powder
1 tablespoon sugar
1/3 cup shortening
1 well-beaten egg
2/3 cup milk
Fresh berries for filling

Sift dry ingredients together and work in shortening until like coarse meal. Combine egg and milk and add to dry ingredients, stirring just until blended. Turn out on lightly floured surface. Knead gently for 1 minute. Divide dough into half and pat out each to fit 8-inch layer pan. Place 1 round in pan, brush with melted butter and top with second round. For individual shortcakes, pat dough 1/2-inch thick and cut with biscuit cutters. Spread half the biscuits with melted butter and top with remaining biscuits. Bake in 425-degree oven about 25 minutes. Spread filling between and on top of layers. Serve hot with plain or whipped cream. Serves 6.

STRAWBERRY TUNNEL CAKE

1 angel food cake
1 package (8-ounce) cream cheese, softened
1 can (14-ounce) sweetened condensed milk
1/4 cup lemon juice
1 teaspoon almond extract
2 cups sliced fresh strawberries
4 cups frozen non-dairy whipped topping
Strawberries for garnish

Cut angel food cake in thirds. Set aside. In large mixing bowl, beat cheese until fluffy. Beat in sweetened condensed milk until smooth. Stir in lemon juice and extract. Mix well. Stir in strawberries and mix lightly. Starting with a third of cake, place on platter, put 1/2 of strawberry mixture on top, cake, strawberry mixture and cake. Chill 3 hours or until set. Frost with whipped topping and garnish with strawberries. Refrigerate until ready to use. Serves 12-16.

TUNNEL OF FUDGE CAKE

1 1/2 cups soft butter
6 eggs
1 1/2 cups sugar
2 cups flour
1 package (2 layer size) Double Dutch
   Frosting mix
2 cups chopped walnuts

Set oven at 350 degrees. Cream butter in large mixer bowl at high speed of mixer. Add eggs, one at a time, beating well after each addition. Gradually add sugar; continue creaming at high speed until light and fluffy.

By hand, stir in flour, frosting mix and walnuts until well blended. Pour batter into greased bundt or 10-inch tube pan. Bake at 350 degrees for 55 to 60 minutes. (Test for doneness after 60 minutes by observing dry, shiny, brownie-type crust.) Cool 2 hours; remove from pan. Cool completely before serving.

Jo says, "If you want to be really wicked, pour a little Kahlúa on cake slices and top with whipped cream." Serves 16-18.

Cookies—Bars

CREME DE MENTHE BROWNIES

1 cup sugar
1/2 cup butter or margarine
4 eggs
1 teaspoon vanilla
1 cup flour
1/2 teaspoon salt
1 can (16-ounce) Hershey chocolate syrup

Mix ingredients and spread in greased 9 x 13-inch jelly roll pan and bake at 350 degrees for 25 to 30 minutes. Cool and refrigerate.

FILLING:
2 cups powdered sugar
1/2 cup softened butter
2 tablespoons Creme de Menthe

Cream butter and powdered sugar well and slowly add Creme de Menthe. Spread on cool base and refrigerate until cold.

TOPPING:
1 cup chocolate chips
6 tablespoons butter

Melt butter and chocolate chips. Spread over Creme de Menthe layer and chill. Keep in refrigerator until serving time. Cut into squares.

Jan says, "Do you want another kiss for the cook? Then try this one." Serves 12-14.

CINNAMON GRAHAM CRACKERS

2 cups whole wheat flour
1 cup all-purpose flour
1 teaspoon baking powder
1/2 teaspoon baking soda
3/4 cup packed brown sugar
1/2 cup shortening
1/3 cup honey
1 teaspoon vanilla
1/2 cup milk
3 tablespoons granulated sugar
1 teaspoon cinnamon

Stir together whole wheat flour, all-purpose flour, baking powder, soda and 1/4 teaspoon salt. Cream together brown sugar and shortening until light. Beat in honey and vanilla until fluffy. Add flour mixture alternately with milk to creamed mixture, beating well after each addition. Chill dough several hours or overnight.

Divide chilled mixture into quarters. On well-floured surface roll each quarter to 15x5-inch rectangle. Cut rectangle crosswise into 6 small rectangles measuring 5 x 2 1/2-inches. Place on ungreased baking sheet. Mark a line crosswise across center of each small rectangle with tines of fork; score a pattern of holes on squares with fork tines. Combine granulated sugar and cinnamon; sprinkle over crackers. Bake at 350 degrees for 13-15 minutes. Remove from sheet at once. Makes 24.

❖❖❖

MOM'S DOUBLE FROSTED BROWNIES

1/2 cup butter or margarine
5 squares unsweetened chocolate
2 eggs
1 cup sugar
1/2 cup sifted all-purpose flour
1/4 teaspoon salt
1 teaspoon vanilla
1/2 cup chopped nuts
Frosting

Melt butter and 2 squares of chocolate together. Beat eggs, add sugar and mix well. Stir in chocolate mixture. Add sifted dry ingredients and vanilla and mix until smooth. Stir in nuts. Spread in buttered 11 x 7 x 2-inch pan. Bake in moderate oven (350 degrees) 20-25 minutes. Cool thoroughly on wire rack. Spread with frosting (recipe below). Then, melt remaining 3 squares of chocolate and spread on top. Chill until firm. When ready to serve, let stand a few minutes at room temperature, then cut into very small squares. Store remainder in refrigerator. Makes about 60 squares. Freezes well.

FROSTING:
1 1/2 cups sugar
1 1/3 cups butter
1/2 cup medium cream
1 teaspoon vanilla

Bring sugar, butter and cream to a boil. Cook without stirring until small amount forms a soft ball when dropped in very cold water, (236 degrees on a candy thermometer). Cool to lukewarm. Add vanilla and beat until creamy.

CHOCOLATE CHIPPERS

3/4 cup white sugar
3/4 cup dark brown sugar
1 cup shortening
2 teaspoons vanilla
1/2 teaspoon salt
2 eggs
1/2 cup peanut butter
1/2 cup applesauce
3 cups sifted flour
1 teaspoon soda
12-ounce package chocolate chips
1 1/2 cups toasted rice cereal

Combine sugars, shortening, vanilla, salt, eggs, peanut butter and applesauce. Blend well. Sift flour and soda together and add to first mixture. Mix well. Add chocolate chips and cereal. Drop by teaspoon about 3 inches apart on cookie sheet. Bake at 350 degrees for 15 minutes.
Makes 5 dozen.

CHOCOLATE NUT SLICES

4 squares (1-ounce size) unsweetened baking chocolate
2 cups sugar
1 1/2 cups butter or margarine
2 eggs
2 teaspoons vanilla
3 1/2 cups flour
4 teaspoons baking powder
1 teaspoon salt
1 cup chopped nuts

Melt chocolate and cool. Mix remaining ingredients. Add chocolate and nuts. Shape into rolls; chill until firm. Slice; roll in powdered sugar, if desired. Bake in 350-degree oven for 10 minutes. Makes 48.

❖❖

WICHITA COUNTRY CLUB DATE NUT BARS

Makes about 42 2 1/2 x 1-inch bars

Preheat oven to 325 degrees.
Sift:
   1 cup sugar
Beat until light:
   3 eggs
Add the sugar gradually. Blend these ingredients
   until very light.
Sift before measuring:
   7/8 cup all-purpose flour
Resift with:
   1 teaspoon double-acting baking powder
   1/8 teaspoon salt
If spices are desired, add:
   1/4 teaspoon each cloves and cinnamon or
      1/2 teaspoon allspice
Add the sifted ingredients to the egg mixture with:
   1 teaspoon vanilla
Beat until ingredients are well blended.
Add about:
   2 cups chopped dates
   1 cup broken nut meats
Pour the batter into a greased and floured 9 x 13-inch pan.
Bake for about 25 minutes.
When cool, cut into bars, roll in:
   Confectioners' sugar

DEVILS FOOD DROP COOKIES

1/2 cup butter
1 cup brown sugar
1 egg
1 teaspoon vanilla
2 squares (1-ounce size) unsweetened chocolate, melted and cooled
2 cups sifted all-purpose flour
1/2 teaspoon soda
1/4 teaspoon salt
3/4 cup sour cream
1/2 cup chopped California walnuts

Cream butter and sugar until fluffy; beat in egg and vanilla. Stir in chocolate. Sift dry ingredients together; add to chocolate mixture alternately with sour cream. Mix well. Stir in nuts.

Drop from teaspoon 2 inches apart on greased cookie sheet. Bake in 350-degree oven for 10 minutes or until done. Remove from cookie sheet and frost with Mocha frosting.

MOCHA FROSTING:
1/4 cup butter
2 tablespoons cocoa
2 teaspoons instant coffee
Dash of salt
1 cup confectioners' sugar
3 tablespoons milk
1 1/2 teaspoons vanilla

Cream butter, cocoa, instant coffee and salt. Slowly cream in confectioners' sugar, milk and vanilla. Beat until smooth. Frost cooled cookies. Makes 4 1/2 dozen.

Melting Moments

SANDIE'S LEMON FLUFF SQUARES

1 1/2 cups finely crushed vanilla wafers (33 wafers)
1/3 cup chopped pecans
6 tablespoons butter, melted
2 packages (3-ounce size) or 1 6-ounce package lemon flavor Jell-O
1 1/4 cups boiling water
1/2 cup whipping cream
1 package (3 3/4 or 3 5/8-ounce) instant lemon pudding mix
1 pint softened lemon sherbet

Combine vanilla wafer crumbs, pecans, butter. Reserve 1/4 cup for top; press remaining into 10 x 6 x 1 1/2-inch baking dish. Chill. Dissolve Jell-O in boiling water, cool to lukewarm. Whip cream until soft peaks form; set aside. Add dry pudding mix to Jell-O and mix well. Add sherbet. Beat at low speed until thickened and nearly set. Fold in whipped cream. Turn into baking dish; sprinkle reserved crumb mix atop. Chill at least 1 hour. Cut into squares. Serves 6.

MARBLE SQUARES

1 cup margarine
1/2 cup plus 4 tablespoons sugar
1/2 cup plus 4 tablespoons brown sugar, packed
1 teaspoon vanilla
2 eggs
2 cups flour
1 teaspoon soda
1 teaspoon salt
1 cup nuts
12-ounce package chocolate chips

Blend all ingredients except chocolate chips. Spread in 9 x 13-inch pan. Sprinkle chocolate chips over top of batter. Place in oven 1 minute. Remove from oven and run knife through the dough to make a marbleized effect. Return to oven and bake 12 to 14 minutes at 375 degrees. Cool and cut into 2-inch squares. Makes 4 dozen.

O'HENRY BARS

1 cup margarine
1 cup brown sugar
4 cups quick oats
1/4 cup syrup

Mix ingredients and spread in 9 x 13-inch pan. Bake at 350 degrees for 20 minutes.

1 cup chocolate chips
1/2 cup crunchy peanut butter

Melt chocolate chips over low heat; then stir in peanut butter. Spread over the crust after it is done baking. Cut into bars before it sets too long. (This takes a little practice.) Place bars on plate and refrigerate. Makes 12-14.

POTATO CHIP COOKIES

1 cup margarine
1 cup brown sugar
1 cup white sugar
2 eggs
2 1/2 cups flour
1 teaspoon soda
2 cups crushed potato chips
1 teaspoon vanilla
1 package (6-ounce) butterscotch chips

Cream together butter and sugars; add eggs and vanilla and beat well. Sift flour and soda together. Add to creamed mixture. Add butterscotch morsels and coarsely crushed potato chips. Drop by teaspoonful onto greased cookie sheet. Bake for 10 minutes at 375 degrees. Makes 36 cookies.

Melting Moments

PUMPKIN PIE BARS

1 cup flour
1/2 cup quick oats
1/2 cup brown sugar
1/2 cup butter
1/2 cup chopped pecans

Blend until crumbly, press into 9 x 13-inch pan with chopped pecans. Bake 15 minutes at 350 degrees.

FILLING:
13-ounce can evaporated milk
1-pound can pumpkin
2 eggs, slightly beaten
3/4 cup sugar
1/2 teaspoon each of salt, ginger and cloves
1 teaspoon cinnamon

Combine and put on baked crust. Bake 20 minutes at 350 degrees.

TOPPING:
1/2 cup pecans
1/2 cup brown sugar
2 tablespoons butter

Combine and spread over hot mixture (filling). Bake 20 minutes at 350 degrees.
Makes 20-24 bars.

RAISIN COOKIES

2 cups raisins
1 cup water
1 cup shortening
2 cups sugar
3 eggs
2 teaspoons vanilla
4 cups flour
1 teaspoon baking powder
1 teaspoon salt
1 teaspoon soda
1 teaspoon nutmeg
1 teaspoon cinnamon

Cook raisins in water for 5 minutes. Set aside. Cream shortening and sugar. Add eggs and beat well. Stir in remaining ingredients, raisins and water. Drop on cookie sheet and bake at 350 degrees for about 10 minutes. Makes 4 dozen.

SUGAR COOKIES

2 eggs
2 sticks margarine
1 cup powdered sugar
1 cup granulated sugar
1 cup oil
1 teaspoon cream of tartar
1 teaspoon salt
1 teaspoon vanilla
1 teaspoon almond extract
1 teaspoon soda
4 1/2 cups flour

Combine all the ingredients and mix well. Refrigerate for 4 hours or overnight. Roll into walnut size balls and press down with a sugar coated glass bottom. Bake at 350 degrees for 10-12 minutes. Yields 60-72 cookies.

Delectables

YIA YIA'S BAKLAVA

1/2 pound sweet butter
1/2 pound salted butter
1 pound filo sheets
2 pounds blanched almonds, chopped
1 pound shelled walnuts, chopped
1 tablespoon cinnamon
1 teaspoon allspice
1 1/2 teaspoons ground cloves
3 dozen whole cloves for garnish

Combine finely chopped almonds and walnuts with cinnamon, cloves and allspice. Melt butter. Brush bottom of 14 x 20-inch pan with butter and place one pastry sheet on bottom. Brush pastry sheet with butter. Repeat until 7 sheets line bottom of pan, brushing each sheet with butter.

Sprinkle with nut mixture; add another pastry sheet, brush with butter. Add one more sheet, brush with butter; sprinkle with nut mixture. Repeat 6 layers of nuts with 2 buttered filo sheets between layers, ending with 6 or 7 buttered pastry sheets on top. Brush top with butter and cut into diamond shapes before baking. Garnish each diamond with a whole clove.

Bake in 350-degree oven for 1 1/2 hours until golden brown. Pour cooled Baklava syrup over hot baklava.

BAKLAVA SYRUP:
1 1/2 cups white Karo syrup
2 cups honey
2 cups water
1 cup sugar
Peel of 1 lemon
Rind of 1 or 2 oranges
  (Yia Yia uses an orange zester)
2 sticks cinnamon

Bring ingredients to a boil and simmer about 10 minutes to form a thin syrup.

Remove lemon peel and cinnamon sticks. Can strain if desired.

This freezes beautifully. Makes 3 dozen.

SALLY'S CHEESECAKE

3 packages (8-ounce size) cream cheese
4 eggs
1 cup sugar
1 teaspoon vanilla

Beat in mixer. Poor into Graham Cracker Crust (see index) and bake for 25 minutes at 375 degrees.

GLAZE:
1 package frozen strawberries
1 cup sugar
2 tablespoons cornstarch
1 tablespoon (scant) lemon juice
1 tablespoon butter
2 pints fresh strawberries

Bring strawberries to a boil, add sugar and cornstarch. Cook until thick and clear. Add lemon juice and butter. Cool. Place 2 pints of fresh strawberries on top of the cooled cheesecake and spoon glaze over the top. Refrigerate.

Serves 10-12.

Melting Moments

JAN'S CHEESECAKE

CRUST:
1 1/2 cups graham cracker crumbs (about 20 crackers)
1/4 cup granulated sugar
1/2 cup melted butter

Lightly oil bottom of springform pan. Combine crumbs, sugar and butter until thoroughly mixed and press into bottom of pan. Bake 5 minutes in preheated 350-degree oven. Place on rack to cool.

FILLING:
4 packages (8-ounce size) cream cheese
1 cup granulated sugar
1 teaspoon vanilla
6 eggs

Cream cheese until light; add sugar and vanilla and cream again. Add eggs, one at a time, beating well after each addition. Pour over cooled crust. Bake 40 minutes at 350 degrees. Cool 15 minutes on rack.

TOPPING:
2 cups sour cream
1 1/3 cups granulated sugar
1 teaspoon vanilla
Cinnamon

Thoroughly mix sour cream, sugar and vanilla and pour carefully over baked cheesecake. Sprinkle with cinnamon. Bake 10 minutes at 350 degrees. Cool to room temperature and then chill 12 to 24 hours before serving. Remove side piece from pan and cut into wedges. Serves 16.

JEANINE'S CHEESECAKE

CRUST:
1 1/2 cups graham cracker crumbs
1/2 cup butter

Prepare crust by combining graham cracker crumbs and butter. Press into a 9-inch pie pan or single round cake pan.

FILLING:
1 package (8-ounce) cream cheese
1 package (3-ounce) cream cheese
1/2 cup sugar
2 eggs

Cream cheese, sugar and eggs in mixer. Pour into prepared graham cracker crust and bake at 350 degrees for 20 minutes. Cool.

TOPPING:
8 ounces sour cream
4 teaspoons sugar
1 teaspoon vanilla

Prepare topping of sour cream, sugar and vanilla. Mix well. Pour over cooled cheesecake. Return to oven and bake for 5 minutes at 350 degrees. Cool at room temperature and refrigerate overnight. Serves 10.

JOY'S CHEESECAKE

1 stick butter
1 cup sifted flour
1 egg yolk
2 tablespoons sugar
1/4 teaspoon salt
4 packages (8-ounce size) cream cheese
1 carton (16-ounce) sour cream
6 eggs
2 cups sugar
1 teaspoon vanilla

Combine butter and flour. Mix together with egg yolk, sugar and salt. Press in bottom of springform pan and bake at 400 degrees 10 to 15 minutes.
Combine cream cheese, sour cream, eggs, sugar and vanilla. Pour into baked crust and bake at 350 degrees for 1 hour. Serves 16.

MOCHA MARBLE CHEESECAKE

CRUST:
2 cups chocolate cookie crumbs
3/4 teaspoon ground cinnamon
2/3 cup melted butter

FILLING:
6 eggs
1 1/2 cups sugar
1/4 teaspoon salt
1/2 cup very strong coffee
1 teaspoon vanilla
2 cups heavy cream
1/2 cup flour
3 1/2 pints small curd cottage cheese
8 ounces semi-sweet chocolate, melted
Shaved chocolate curls for garnish

Preheat oven to 350 degrees. In a bowl mix together the chocolate crumbs, cinnamon and melted butter. Press the mixture onto the bottom and sides of a greased 12-inch springform pan. Chill thoroughly. Beat the eggs until lemon-colored. Slowly add the sugar and continue beating while adding the salt, coffee and vanilla. Whip the cream and fold into the egg mixture.

Press the cottage cheese through a sieve and stir in the flour. Fold the cottage cheese into the egg and cream mixture. Add the melted chocolate and make a few strokes with a fork to marbleize the chocolate and cheesecake mixture. Pour into the chilled crust. Bake for 1 hour 25 minutes. Turn off the heat and allow the cheesecake to stand in the oven for another hour with the door open. Remove rim of springform pan. Decorate around the bottom edge of plate with shaved chocolate curls. Serves 16.

MR. HERBERT'S BEER BATTER

2 cups flour
Touch of salt
Touch of sugar
1 bottle of beer
5 egg whites
Small amount of salad oil
Any kind of fresh fruit-strawberries, raspberries, etc.
Cinnamon sugar
Vanilla Sauce

Combine dry ingredients, except cinnamon sugar, into a mixing bowl. Using a wire whip, add beer slowly until it is a creamy consistency. Beat egg whites until they form stiff peaks and then fold them into batter. If batter is going to be sitting for a while before using it, sprinkle top with a small amount of salad oil to keep a skin from forming on the top. More beer can be added if needed.

Dry each piece of fruit completely on absorbent cloth to make sure it is without moisture. Dip each piece of fruit in the beer batter and deep fry until golden brown. Take the fruit out of hot oil and drain on absorbent toweling. Roll fruit in cinnamon sugar until evenly coated. Served on a bed of Vanilla Sauce. Serves 6.

VANILLA SAUCE

2 pints of half and half
Half of a vanilla bean
Sugar according to your taste
5 egg yolks

Bring all ingredients except eggs to a boil in a double boiler. Place 5 egg yolks in a mixing bowl and beat thoroughly with a wire whip. Add boiling cream mixture to egg yolks, stirring constantly. The best way to do this is by placing the mixing bowl in a hot water bath.

Jan says,"The Broadmoor was very gracious in sharing this recipe with me. It is a very delicious dessert. Your guests will enjoy every bite."

CHOCOLATE CHARLOTTE

FILLING:
1 1/2 pounds semi-sweet chocolate squares
1/2 cup strong coffee
3 eggs, separated
4 tablespoons sugar
1/2 cup Tia Maria liqueur
1/2 cup heavy cream

Melt the chocolate with the coffee in the top of a double boiler. When chocolate is completely melted, remove the pan from heat. Beat the egg yolks until pale yellow and stir into the chocolate. Gradually stir in the Tia Maria. Cool the mixture. In a separate bowl, beat the egg whites, gradually adding the sugar, until the whites are stiff. Whip the cream. Gently fold the whipped cream into the cooled chocolate mixture and then fold in the egg whites.

GLAZE:
1/2 pound semi-sweet chocolate
1/3 cup water

Melt chocolate in water and stir until smooth. Spread over top of mousse-cake and drizzle down sides. Chill again. Serve in slender slices. Cut while chilled.

CAKE:
Preheat oven to 350 degrees
1 package (23-ounce) brownie mix
2 tablespoons water
3 eggs

Beat ingredients together at medium speed on electric mixer until batter is smooth. Grease an 11 x 15-inch jelly roll pan. Line it with waxed paper. Grease and lightly flour the paper, shaking off any excess flour. Spread the batter evenly in the jelly roll pan. Bake for 10 to 12 minutes or until cake tests done. Turn the cake onto a rack and peel off the paper. Lightly oil a 2-quart charlotte mold and line with the cooled cake. Cut rounds of cake to fit both the top and bottom of the mold and a strip for the sides. Place the smaller round in the bottom of the pan. Wrap the strip around the inside of the mold. You will probably have to piece one section of the side to cover completely. Any patching will be covered.

Spoon the chilled filling mixture into the mold. Fit the larger round of cake on top of the mold. Chill for 3 to 4 hours, or until firm. Unmold and cover with glaze. Serves 12-14.

CHOCOLATE RING

3 ounces unsweetened chocolate
6 tablespoons (3/4-stick) unsalted butter
1/4 cup water
3 eggs, separated
1 teaspoon vanilla
3/4 cup sugar
1/4 cup all-purpose flour
1 cup whipping cream
2 tablespoons sugar
1/2 teaspoon vanilla

Preheat oven to 375 degrees. Generously butter a 4-cup ring mold. Combine chocolate, butter and water in top of double boiler and heat until melted. Transfer to a large bowl and beat in egg yolks one at a time, beating well after each addition. Add vanilla, then sugar and flour and beat about 3 minutes.

Beat egg whites until stiff but not dry. Fold into chocolate mixture. Pour into mold; set in larger pan and add hot water to come halfway up sides of mold. Bake about 40 minutes. Remove from water bath and let cool in pan about 5 minutes. Unmold onto serving plate and let cool completely.

Just before serving, whip cream with sugar and vanilla, or if you prefer, serve with Creme Anglaise (see index). Serve warm or at room temperature. Spoon into center of ring. Cut ring into thin
Serves 12-14.

Melting Moments

LILI'S CHOCOLATE TORTE

1 cup strong cold coffee
1 1/2 tablespoons sugar
2 tablespoons Grand Marnier
1/2 pound butter
2 large eggs
12 ounces melted semi-sweet chocolate
Large box of vanilla wafers
Whipping cream
Angelica
Candied cherries
Colored sugar crystals

Combine and set aside coffee, sugar and Grand Marnier. Cream butter and beat in eggs and chocolate.

Line a bread pan with foil, allowing enough foil to hang over the edges to cover the top. Arrange a layer of vanilla wafers on bottom of pan. Sprinkle generously with coffee liquid then spread with chocolate cream. Continue in layers until all of cream is used, ending with layer of wafers. Fold over foil to cover top. Set an identical pan on top of the case putting a heavy stone or brick on top of pan. Let ripen in refrigerator at least 12 to 16, preferably 24 hours. Serves 16.

To serve: Carefully remove foil. Turn out on serving platter. Frost top and sides with 1 cup whipped cream, lightly flavored with Grand Marnier. Garnish sparingly with candied cherries, angelica, colored sugar crystals. Slice thin.

Jan says, "This is truly rich, but a delight to serve."

CHOCOLATE POTS DE CREME

1 pound semisweet chocolate
1/4 cup butter (1/2 stick)
2 cups heavy cream
2 tablespoons instant coffee
5 egg yolks
5 egg whites, stiffly beaten

Melt chocolate in top of double boiler. Stir in butter until melted. Gradually stir in cream and instant coffee. Stir in beaten egg yolks. Cook over low heat, stirring constantly until mixture thickens. Cool.

Fold in stiffly beaten egg whites. Spoon into pot de creme cups. Top with lids and refrigerate 24 hours before serving. Serve with flavored creme.

FLAVORED WHIPPED CREAM:
1/2 cup cream, whipped until thick
2 teaspoons sugar
2 teaspoons ground toasted almonds
2 teaspoons coffee liqueur

To whipped cream add sugar, almonds, liqueur and continue whipping until cream is stiff and holds its shape. Serve in a beautiful bowl with the pots de Creme, allowing each guest to serve some on top of their portion. Serves 10-12.

CHERRIES ROMANOFF

1 can (17-ounce) or 1 package frozen dark sweet cherries
1 teaspoon grated orange peel
2 tablespoons orange-flavored liqueur
1 pint vanilla ice cream
1 cup heavy cream, whipped

Drain cherries, reserving the syrup. Simmer cherry syrup until reduced by half. Remove from heat and add orange peel and liqueur. Pour cherries and syrup mixture over ice cream and put a mound of whipped cream on top. Serves 4 to 6.

Jan says, "I use the canned cherries for the frozen do not have enough juice."

Melting Moments

CREME CARAMEL WITH STRAWBERRY SAUCE

CARAMEL:
1/2 cup sugar
1/2 cup water

CREME:
2 cups milk
1 tablespoon sugar
2 eggs
2 to 3 egg yolks

SAUCE:
1 pint strawberries
2 to 3 tablespoons sugar

1 souffle (1-quart) dish or charlotte mold

In heavy saucepan combine sugar and 1/4 cup of water for the caramel; cook over a low heat until dissolved. Boil syrup until rich brown in color; pour in remaining 1/4 cup water very carefully off the heat. Caramel mixture will sizzle vigorously. Cook stirring until caramel is dissolved. Pour into a bowl to cool.

Set oven at 375 degrees. Heat milk with 1 tablespoon sugar and stir until dissolved. Combine eggs and extra egg yolks and mix with a fork until smooth but not frothy. Stir in warm milk gradually, then add cooled caramel mixture. Strain this custard into the lightly oiled charlotte mold or souffle dish and cover with foil. Stand dish in pan of hot water, bake in heated oven 40 to 50 minutes or until knife inserted one inch from center comes out clean. Remove from oven and cool.

While custard bakes, hull and cut strawberries in slices. Sprinkle them with sugar and let stand for about 30 minutes. Work berries through a sieve or puree them in a blender. Turn creme caramel from the mold onto a dish and spoon strawberry sauce over the top. Serves 8-10.

CREAM PUFFS

1 cup water
1/2 cup butter
1/4 teaspoon salt
1 cup sifted flour
4 eggs

Heat water, butter and salt until boiling. Add flour all at once. Stir until mixture forms a smooth ball and leaves sides of pan clean. Remove from heat. Add eggs, one at a time, beating after each addition. Shape on ungreased sheet. Bake at 450 degrees for 15 minutes and 350 degrees for 20 to 25 minutes. Serves 12.

FILLING:

You may fill with your favorite custard or use instant vanilla pudding. Drizzle with Thin Chocolate Icing. Filled with ice cream is very good too.

THIN CHOCOLATE ICING

1 square unsweetened chocolate
2 tablespoons butter
1 cup powdered sugar
2 tablespoons boiling water

Melt chocolate and butter. Blend in sugar and water. Beat until smooth, not stiff. Drizzle over filled cream puffs.

❖❖

RAY DELL'S CREAMY CORNUCOPIAS

1/4 cup butter
1/2 cup dark corn syrup
1/3 cup flour
1/4 teaspoon cinnamon
1/4 teaspoon salt
1/2 cup finely chopped pecans

Grease large cookie sheet with shortening and flour. In saucepan, melt butter over low heat. Remove. Stir in corn syrup, flour, cinnamon and salt until smooth. Stir in pecans. Drop level tablespoons batter 4 inches apart onto sheet. Bake 6 to 8 minutes at 350 degrees. Let stand 15 to 30 seconds, until firm enough to remove with spatula. Remove one cookie at a time. Using hand and wooden spoon handle, form into cone shape.

Store in tightly covered tin. Cones will stay crisp for several weeks. Just before serving, spoon creamy filling into each cone. Makes 24.

CREAMY CORNUCOPIA FILLING

1/2 cup heavy cream
1/2 cup milk
1 tablespoon sugar
1 teaspoon vanilla
1 package (3 3/4-ounce) instant chocolate pudding

In small bowl, whip cream until stiff; refrigerate. In medium bowl, stir together: milk, sugar, vanilla and pudding. Beat 2 minutes. Fold in whipped cream. Refrigerate until serving time.

Filling may be refrigerated overnight or frozen 1 week.

VARIATION

Drop a rounded tablespoon onto lightly greased baking sheet and flatten with back of spoon to a 3-inch circle. Bake at 375 degrees about 8 minutes or until evenly browned. Remove from oven and let stand on baking sheet 1 1/2 to 2 minutes until edges are firm enough to lift with spatula. Place on inverted custard cup and allow to cool. Repeat procedure. Makes 6 cups. Fill cooled cups with ice cream. Top with brandy or sundae sauce. Sprinkle with nuts.

CREPES TIVOLI

Crepes (See Basic Crepe Recipe in index)
1 can sweetened condensed milk
1/2 cup chopped pecans
1/3 cup lemon juice
2 tablespoons brandy
1 tablespoons grated orange rind
1 teaspoon vanilla
1 cup heavy cream, whipped
1 package (10-ounce) frozen raspberries, thawed
1 teaspoon cornstarch
1 tablespoon water
1/4 cup brandy, warmed
1 pint fresh strawberries, sliced
OR: 1 package (10-ounce) sliced frozen strawberries

Prepare Crepes. Combine sweetened condensed milk, nuts, lemon juice, and 2 tablespoons brandy, orange rind and vanilla in a medium size bowl. Fold in whipped cream, refrigerate.

Sauce: Defrost raspberries and whirl at high speed in electric blender for 30 seconds. Strain into saucepan to remove seeds. Heat to simmering, then stir in cornstarch mixed with water. Cool, stirring 1 minute. Keep hot.

To serve: Spread 1/3 cup filling mixture on each crepe. Roll up and place seam side down on serving platter. Add the 1/4 cup brandy to sauce; ignite and stir until flames die. Stir in strawberries and pour over crepes. Serve 1 or 2 crepes to each person. Serves 6-8.

Melting Moments

✦✦

BURNT SUGAR DUMPLINGS

1 1/2 cups sugar
1/2 teaspoon salt
2 tablespoons butter
2 cups hot water

DUMPLINGS:
1 1/2 cups flour
2 1/2 teaspoons baking powder
1/4 teaspoon salt
2 tablespoons sugar
3 tablespoons butter
3/4 cup milk
1/2 cup chopped nuts

Brown 1/2 cup sugar in heavy skillet until golden brown. Remove from heat and add rest of sugar, salt and butter. Add hot water gradually until lumps melt. Set aside.

Sift dry ingredients together. Cut in butter, add nuts, milk and stir. Drop by medium spoonful in boiling syrup. Cover and let simmer for 15 minutes over a low heat. Serves 6-8.

ALMOND PRALINE BALLS

1 quart vanilla ice cream
1 cup toasted, slivered almonds or pecans
2 cups light cream
1/4 cup butter
1 1/2 cups light brown sugar
2 tablespoons corn syrup

Scoop 6 large balls of ice cream. Roll balls in toasted nuts and place in freezer to harden. To make sauce, combine cream, butter, sugar, and syrup in heavy saucepan; cook over very low heat, stirring constantly, until mixture is smooth and has thickened slightly, about 5 to 10 minutes. Cool stirring frequently. Serve over almond balls.

Jo says, "When I make Almond Roco candy, I save the pieces of chocolate and toasted almonds that fall off. I freeze them and roll the ice cream balls in these delicious morsels." Serves 6.

CHOCOLATE CUSTARD SQUARES

1/2 cup butter
1/2 cup powdered sugar
2 eggs, separated
4 squares bitter chocolate, melted and cooled

CUSTARD:
3 cups half and half cream
5 egg yolks
6 tablespoons sugar
Dash salt
1 1/2 teaspoons vanilla

Cream butter and powdered sugar together. Beat two egg yolks well and add to butter mixture. Stir in chocolate. Beat two egg whites until stiff and fold whites into chocolate mixture. Pour mixture into a well-greased 9 x 6 x 3-inch loaf pan. Chill several hours or until firm. Put half and half cream, five egg yolks, sugar and salt in double boiler. Place over simmering water and stir until thick. Stir in vanilla. Remove from heat and let stand until slightly warm.

To serve, divide chilled chocolate into eight squares. Place each square in a serving goblet and pour about 1/2 cup warm custard over each square. Serves 8.

ICE CREAM BALLS

Any of the following flavors ice cream may be used:

Neapolitan
Vanilla
Chocolate Chip
Coffee
Strawberry
Chocolate
Coconut

Using a scoop or a big spoon make the balls about the size of a tennis ball. Then roll the balls in white or colored coconut and place them immediately in the freezer. When ready to serve, remove the balls from the freezer and serve on a large platter or individually on a plate. These balls look very pretty on doilies. Also, you may use different sauces that your guests may ladle over the ice cream ball.

Jan says, ''I have made these for bridal showers, baby showers and other parties. They are very pretty as well as being delicious. Also you may make these ahead and put them in your freezer until ready to serve. I serve assorted cookies with them.''

BANANAS FLAMBE

4 firm ripe bananas
Lemon juice
1/2 cup flour
1 stick butter
1/2 cup brown sugar
1 teaspoon cinnamon
1/4 teaspoon nutmeg
1/2 cup Creme de Cacao
1/2 cup cognac
1 cup lightly whipped cream
2 tablespoons powdered sugar
1 cup toasted almonds

Peel bananas, slice lengthwise. Roll in fresh lemon juice to prevent browning and dust lightly with flour. In chafing dish or electric skillet, melt butter. Add brown sugar, cinnamon and nutmeg. Stir until brown sugar is dissolved. Place banana slices in hot bubbly mixture. Spoon mixture over bananas until they are well coated. Add Creme de Cacao and cook 1 minute. Add cognac and ignite. As soon as flames die, serve with sauce from chafing dish. Top with whipped cream sweetened with powdered sugar and toasted almonds.

Jo says, ''If you want to make this a real dazzler, and a rich one, spoon vanilla ice cream into hoch wine goblets (long-stemmed bubble glasses). On top of ice cream place bananas, (you will have to cut each slice in half for these glasses), then sauce, whipped cream and toasted nuts. In a word, scrumptious.''

Serves 4-6.

CHERRIES JUBILEE

1 large jar black cherry preserves
1 jar (16-ounce) black cherries
1 teaspoon almond flavoring
1 teaspoon lemon juice
1 ounce Kirsch
1 1/2 quarts vanilla ice cream

Blend all ingredients except Kirsch and ice cream. Adjust almond flavoring and lemon juice to suit own taste. Pour into a shallow skillet or flambeau pan and place over burner. Move about gently over flame until cherry mixture begins to bubble. Pour Kirsch over top and tip pan slightly downward toward flame. When sauce ignites, spoon over ice cream. Serves 12.

Melting Moments

CREME DE NOYAUX PIE
(Creme de Almond)

2 cups premium shredded coconut
2 tablespoons butter, melted
5 tablespoons Creme de Noyaux
1 1/2 quarts vanilla ice cream

Combine coconut and butter; pat firmly into a 9-inch pie pan. Bake at 350 degrees until toasted. Cool. Blend Creme de Noyaux and slightly softened ice cream. Pour into pie shell and freeze. Serves 6.

HOMEMADE ICE CREAM

3 cups milk
3 tablespoons cornstarch
1/2 teaspoon salt
5 eggs, beaten
1 can (13-ounce) Carnation milk
1 can Eagle Brand sweetened condensed milk
3 or 4 cups half and half
1 tablespoon vanilla

Cook first 3 ingredients until custard. Add 5 beaten eggs, barely cook. Cool thoroughly. Add Carnation, Eagle Brand, half-and-half and vanilla. Combine ingredients, pour into freezer. Follow directions on your freezer as to procedure for freezing.
Makes 5 quarts.

ICE CREAM PIE

1 egg white, beaten stiff
1/4 cup sugar
1 1/2 cups pecans
1/4 teaspoon salt
1 pint coffee ice cream
1 pint vanilla ice cream

Beat egg white and add salt. Beat in sugar and add pecans. Butter a 9-inch pie plate. Spoon mixture in plate as much like a shell as possible. Bake 12 to 15 minutes at 325 degrees. Do not overcook. Cool. Spoon coffee ice cream on crust, then spoon vanilla ice cream on top of coffee ice cream. Cover with plastic wrap and freeze.
Serve with Caramel Sauce. Serves 6.

CARAMEL SAUCE

3 tablespoons butter
1 cup brown sugar
3/4 cup heavy cream
Pinch of salt
1 teaspoon vanilla

Melt butter until it bubbles. Add sugar and stir until blended. Add cream, salt and vanilla. Cool. Grease wax paper and let paper sit on top of sauce 5 to 10 minutes before removing. Pour sauce over the pie and serve.

BETTY'S ICE CREAM

6 egg yolks
4 cups sugar
3 tablespoons flour
1 1/2 quarts milk
1 quart heavy cream
1 tablespoon vanilla
6 egg whites

Cook first 4 ingredients. Cool, and add heavy cream and vanilla. Beat egg whites until stiff and fold into mixture. Follow freezer directions as to procedure. Makes 6 quarts.

Melting Moments

IRMA COLUMBIA'S ICE CREAM

2 egg yolks
1/4 cup sugar
1/4 cup Karo light syrup
1 teaspoon vanilla
1 tall can evaporated milk
1/3 cup heavy cream
2 egg whites
1/4 cup sugar

Beat egg yolks until light. Add sugar and Karo syrup. Continue beating until light. Add vanilla, milk and heavy cream. Fold in stiffly beaten egg whites combined with 1/4 cup sugar. Freeze until firm. Cut up into chilled bowl and beat until fluffy but not melted. Refreeze. Makes 1 quart.

LEMON ICE CREAM

2 eggs
1/2 cup sugar
1/2 cup light corn syrup
1 1/4 cups milk
1 cup whipping cream
1/4 cup lemon juice
2 teaspoons grated lemon peel

Beat eggs until light and lemon-colored. Add sugar gradually, beating constantly. Add corn syrup, milk, cream, lemon juice and grated peel. Mix well. Freeze until firm, turn out into chilled bowl and beat until light but not melted. Return to freezer tray. Makes 6 servings.

OLD FASHIONED ICE CREAM

3 quarts milk (approximate)
7 eggs
4 cups sugar
1 quart cream
1 tablespoon vanilla

Combine 1 quart milk, eggs and sugar. Heat in top of double boiler, stirring until thick and custardlike. Remove from heat and flavor with 1 tablespoon vanilla. When cool, add quart of cream. Pour into container and fill to within 1 1/2-inch of top with remaining 2 quarts of milk.

If desired, when about half frozen, add 1 1/2 cups fresh fruit. When fruit is to be added, use 6 cups sugar in basic recipe. Use 6-quart freezer.

MOM'S FRESH PEACH ICE CREAM

1 quart peeled and mashed fresh peaches
3/4 cup sugar
3 cups milk
1 cup evaporated milk
2 cups sugar
8 egg yolks, well-beaten
3 tablespoons vanilla
1 pint heavy cream
1/4 teaspoon almond extract
3 cups milk

To mashed peaches, add sugar. Cover and let stand. Scald milk (fresh and evaporated), do not boil. Stir in 2 cups sugar until dissolved. Pour this over beaten egg yolks. Stir constantly over heat until thick. Do not boil. Chill. (Cool over ice cubes before placing in refrigerator.)

Add heavy cream, vanilla, almond extract and last 3 cups of milk before placing in freezer can.

Note: 1 quart half-and-half may be substituted for cream and milk.

Add peach mixture when ice cream is half frozen. Makes 1 gallon.

Melting Moments

ICE CREAM PUMPKIN PIE

1 quart butter pecan ice cream
1 quart pumpkin pie ice cream
1/2 pint whipping cream

30 minutes before preparing ice cream crust, put a deep 9-inch pie pan in freezer. To make crust, working quickly, line bottom and sides of frosty pan with butter pecan ice cream. Do not put ice cream on edge of pan. Build up crust 1/2 inch above edge of pan by overlapping tablespoonsful of ice cream. Freeze at least 2 hours. Slightly soften pumpkin pie ice cream and spread into ice cream crust. Freeze at least 3 hours. Allow to soften in refrigerator 10 minutes before serving. Top with whipped cream. Serves 6-8.

STRAWBERRY ICE CREAM PIE

1 can (3 1/2-ounce) or 1 1/4 cups flaked coconut
1 quart vanilla ice cream
1 1/2 cups sugared sliced fresh strawberries or 1 package (10-ounce) frozen, partially thawed
6 frozen cream toppers

TOPPERS:
1/2 cup heavy cream
2 tablespoons sifted confectioners' sugar

Toast coconut in 350 degree oven about 10 minutes, stirring frequently to brown evenly. Cool. Lightly press onto bottom and sides of generously buttered 9-inch pie pan. Stir ice cream only to soften slightly; spoon into shell and smooth top. Freeze firm. To serve, spoon strawberries over ice cream and trim with frozen toppers.

Whip cream, stir in sugar. Place heaping spoonfuls on chilled baking sheet. Freeze firm. Serves 6.

TOFFEE ICE CREAM PIE AND SAUCE

17 to 18 vanilla wafers
1/2 gallon vanilla ice cream
1 cup chopped Heath candy bars (toffee)
1 1/2 cups sugar
1 cup evaporated milk
1/4 cup butter
1/4 cup light corn syrup
Dash salt

Line bottom and sides of buttered 9-inch pan with wafers. Spoon ice cream into wafer shell, sprinkling 1/2 cup of the toffee between layers of ice cream. Store pie in freezer until serving time. Prepare toffee sauce by combining sugar, milk, butter, syrup and salt. Boil 1 minute. Remove from heat, stir in remaining toffee; cool, stirring occasionally. Serve sauce over pie wedges. Serves 6 to 8. Makes 2 1/2 cups sauce.

Jo says, "If you have made the Almond Roco candy, and have saved all the yummy little pieces that drop off in the candy tin (bag them up and freeze), substitute for the Heath bars."

JEANNE'S COUNTRY VANILLA ICE CREAM

4 eggs
2 1/4 cups sugar
5 cups milk
4 cups heavy cream
4 1/2 teaspoons vanilla
1/2 teaspoon salt

Add sugar gradually to beaten eggs. Continue to beat until mixture is very stiff. Add remaining ingredients and mix thoroughly. Pour into gallon freezer and follow freezer directions. Makes 1 gallon.

Melting Moments

LEMON CREAM

1 tablespoon cornstarch
1/2 cup sugar
3/4 cup water
2 large egg yolks
1 tablespoon grated lemon rind
1/4 cup lemon juice
1 cup heavy cream

Stir together the cornstarch and sugar in a 1 1/2-quart saucepan. Stir the water in gradually, keeping it smooth. Add the egg yolks and beat gently until blended. Cook over moderate heat, stirring constantly until mixture is clear, thickened and boiling. Remove pan from heat and stir in the lemon rind and then gradually stir in the lemon juice. Let stand at room temperature until cool to the touch. In a small bowl whip the cream until thick. Add to the cool lemon mixture and fold in until blended. Makes about 2 1/2 cups.

CHOCOLATE MINT MOUSSE

1 package (6 ounces) semisweet chocolate chips
4 egg whites, beaten stiff
1/2 cup whipped cream
4 Girl Scout thin mint cookies, coarsely ground
2 Girl Scout thin mints, finely ground for garnish

Melt chocolate chips in double boiler until soft. Cool slightly. Fold chocolate into beaten egg whites, combining thoroughly. Fold whipped cream into mixture; fold in coarsely ground mints and continue with folding motion until mixture is uniform in color. Put in sherbet glasses and garnish with the finely ground cookies. Chill until serving time.
Serves 6.

KAHLÚA MOUSSE

1 cup sugar
1 cup water
12-ounce package chocolate chips
4 eggs
1/3 cup Kahlúa
1/4 cup cognac
3 cups whipped cream
Dash of salt

Combine sugar and water in a pan and heat slowly. Put chocolate chips, eggs and salt into a blender on slow and blend until smooth. Add the syrup in slow steady stream, blend. Add liqueurs, put lid on and mix. Cool 10 minutes. Whip cream until not quite stiff, shows traces. Fold into chocolate mixture. Half of this recipe will serve 8.

MOCHA MOUSSE

6 eggs, separated
3/4 cup sugar
2 envelopes unflavored gelatin
1/2 cup cold water
1/4 cup coffee liqueur or Creme de Cacao
2 tablespoons instant coffee powder
Dash of salt
5 ounces unsweetened chocolate squares, melted and cooled
2 cups heavy cream
1/4 cup sugar

Separate eggs, set whites aside. Beat yolks with sugar until thick. Sprinkle gelatin over cold water to soften. Place over low heat to dissolve. Stir in coffee liqueur or Creme de Cacao, instant coffee powder and salt. Blend into egg yolks the melted chocolate. Beat egg whites stiff. Whip the heavy cream, folding in the 1/4 cup of sugar. Fold egg whites and whipped cream into egg yolk mixture. Turn into an 8-cup mold. Garnish with whipped cream and chocolate curls. Chill for several hours before serving. Serves 8.

STRAWBERRY OR RASPBERRY MOUSSE

1 quart strawberries or raspberries, washed
   and hulled
1/2 cup sugar
1/2 cup white wine
2 envelopes unflavored gelatin
1/2 cup cold water
1/2 cup boiling water
2 cups heavy cream, whipped

Reserve several berries for garnish. Press remaining berries through a fine sieve. Add sugar and white wine. Stir well. Chill. Soften gelatin in cold water. Add boiling water, stir to dissolve, cool. Combine gelatin and chilled berry mixture. Beat with rotary beater until fluffy and slightly thickened. Fold in whipped cream. Turn into an oiled 2-quart mold. Chill for 3 hours or longer. Unmold onto a chilled platter. Garnish with reserved berries. Serves 8.

PAVLOVA

2 egg whites, room temperature
1 teaspoon white vinegar
1 teaspoon vanilla
3 tablespoons boiling water
1 1/2 cups superfine sugar
2 cups whipping cream, beaten stiff
Kiwi fruit slices, or any type berry may be used

Preheat oven to 250 degrees. Generously grease and flour a 9-inch flan pan with removable bottom or draw a 9-inch circle of waxed paper and line a baking sheet.

Beat egg whites until soft peaks form, using low speed of electric mixer. Add vinegar and vanilla. Continue beating on high until stiff. Still on high, add water in slow steady stream and beat well. Turn mixer to low and gradually add sugar, beating constantly until thoroughly incorporated.

Turn meringue into prepared utensil, spreading evenly, slightly indenting center. If you would rather, make a free-form circle, indenting the center or raising the sides to form an edge.

Bake 1 hour. Remove from pan or paper and let dry on rack in draft-free area, or it may cool in the turned-off oven.

Spread whipped cream evenly over meringue. Decorate with fruit.

Note: Low baking is critical to the success of a large meringue. If your oven thermostat is not reliable, use an oven thermometer. This meringue will dry out more perfectly if it is allowed to stand in a cooling oven with the heat turned off for several hours. The meringue can be baked in advance and stored in a tightly covered container until it is used. Serves 8.

Jo says, "I discovered this fabulous dessert while traveling in Australia and New Zealand. After my first experience, I ordered it at various stops on the trip. A friend in Australia gave me the recipe, thus saving me from "Pavlova withdrawal" upon my return home. It is said to have been named in honor of the famous dancer. The Kiwi fruit makes it authentic, but I also had it served with strawberries and raspberries."

SAUTEED PINEAPPLE WITH CREAM

1/2 pineapple, cut into spears
4 tablespoons butter
2 tablespoons granulated sugar
2 jiggers light rum or imported Kirsch
3/4 cup heavy cream

Melt butter and saute pineapple slices in it until both sides are lightly browned. Sprinkle with the sugar; then slowly add the liquor and cook until it is almost absorbed. Pour the cream over the pineapple but do not stir. Serve as soon as the cream is hot. Serves 4.

PEACHES CARDINAL

6 large peaches, peeled and halved
6 cups water
2 cups sugar
3 tablespoons vanilla extract

In a heavy saucepan, bring water and sugar to a boil. Boil briskly for 3 minutes, then reduce heat as low as possible. Add peaches and vanilla and poach uncovered for 10 to 20 minutes or until barely tender. Refrigerate peaches in syrup until very cold.

SAUCE CARDINAL:
2 packages (10-ounce size) frozen raspberries, defrosted and thoroughly drained
2 tablespoons superfine sugar (or put regular sugar in food processor)
1 tablespoon Kirsch

Puree raspberries with spoon through a fine sieve. Add sugar and Kirsch. Refrigerate covered.

CREME CHANTILLY:
1 cup heavy cream
2 tablespoons superfine sugar (or put regular sugar in food processor)
1 tablespoon vanilla extract

Whip cream. When it thickens a little, add sugar and vanilla. Decorate peaches, which have been covered with sauce.

Note: This recipe is delicious substituting pears for the peaches. Serves 6-8.

PINEAPPLE A LA CREME ANGLAISE

1 fresh pineapple
1/4 cup light rum
1 1/2 cups heavy cream
2 tablespoons cornstarch
1/2 cup sugar
1/4 teaspoon salt
4 egg yolks
Toasted sliced almonds

Core and dice pineapple. (See index for instructions on fixing a pineapple.) Put in a glass casserole dish. Sprinkle with 2 tablespoons rum. Cover and refrigerate 1 to 2 hours.

Combine 1/4 cup cream and cornstarch until smooth. Gradually whisk in remaining cream. Beat in sugar and salt. Cook over medium heat until mixture thickens. Do not let this boil. Stir in a small amount on egg yolks. Pour back into sauce, stirring constantly, until mixture thickens. Remove from heat and stir in remaining rum. Cover sauce and chill. Spoon pineapple in dessert dishes or wine glasses and spoon the creme anglaise over each serving. Sprinkle with almonds. Serves 6.

POTS DE CREME

2 cups heavy cream
4 egg yolks
5 tablespoons sugar
1/4 teaspoon salt
1 tablespoon grated orange rind
2 tablespoons Grand Marnier

Place cream in a saucepan and bring it almost but not quite to a boil. In the meantime, beat yolks, sugar and salt until light and lemon-colored. Gradually add cream to yolks, stirring with a wire whisk. Place saucepan over low heat or in a double boiler and stir with a wooden spoon until custard thickens and coats the spoon.

Cool custard in a pan of cold water so it will stop cooking. Stir in grated orange rind and Grand Marnier. Pour custard into custard cups or pots de creme. Chill thoroughly. Serves 6-8.

❖❖❖

ATHOLL PUDDING

1/4 to 1/2 pint cream
3 tablespoons running honey, melted
1 tablespoon whiskey

Beat ingredients carefully. Put in sherbet glasses and chill. Sprinkle toasted almonds over top. Serves 2.

Jan says, "This recipe was given to me by an English girl in London. It is different and rich, but so good."

RUGALAS

2 sticks butter
2 cups sifted flour
3/4 cups sour cream
1 egg yolk
1/2 cup sugar
1 teaspoon cinnamon
1/2 cup chopped nuts

Soften butter. Mix with flour and add sour cream and egg yolk. Work into a ball. Then divide the ball into 4 smaller balls. Refrigerate for 4 hours or more. Then roll one ball out like a pizza, 1/8-inch thick. Sprinkle cinnamon, sugar and chopped nuts over the dough. Cut into 16 pieces like a crescent roll and roll up. Bake at 350 degrees for 25 minutes. Makes 50.

Jan says, "The Rugalas are not a sweet dough. It is a different cookie and raved about by all."

HOW TO PREPARE A SOUFFLE DISH

The average souffle dish will not be tall enough to accommodate a souffle after it has baked. It will need to have a "collar" made to extend the sides. This can be done by making two thicknesses of foil folded to a width of 6 inches and tied around the dish so it will extend 4 inches above the top of the dish. Generously butter the bottom and sides of the souffle dish and the insides of the collar; sprinkle with granulated sugar. Spoon the souffle mixture into the dish, filling it 3/4 full. As the souffle bakes it will puff and rise up the sides of the collar. Remove the collar carefully after the souffle has baked.

HOW TO BAKE A SOUFFLE

Low Temperature Method: Place the souffle dish in a pan of hot water. Bake in a preheated slow oven (325 degrees) for 1 to 1 1/2 hours or until a knife inserted in center of souffle comes out clean. Serve at once.

WAXED PAPER COLLAR FOR COLD SOUFFLE DISHES

Fold a 26-inch-long piece of waxed paper lengthwise into thirds. Lightly butter one side, and sprinkle with sugar. Wrap around souffle dish, sugared side against dish, to form a collar extending 2 inches above top; tie with string.

Melting Moments

COLD BRANDY ALEXANDER SOUFFLE

2 envelopes unflavored gelatin
2 cups cold water
1 cup sugar
4 eggs, separated
1 package (8-ounce) cream cheese
3 tablespoons Creme de Cacao
3 tablespoons brandy
1 cup heavy cream, whipped
Chocolate shavings

Soften gelatin in 1 cup of cold water. Stir over low heat until dissolved. Add remaining water. Remove from heat and blend in 3/4 cup sugar and beaten egg yolks. Return to heat and cook 2 to 3 minutes or until slightly thickened. Gradually add to softened cream cheese, mixing until blended. Stir in Creme de Cacao and brandy. Chill until slightly thickened. Beat egg whites until soft peaks form. Gradually add remaining sugar, beating to stiff peaks. Fold egg whites and whipped cream into cream cheese mixture. Wrap a 3-inch collar of aluminum foil around top of a 1 1/2-quart souffle dish. Secure with tape. Pour mixture into dish. Chill until firm. Garnish with chocolate if desired. Serves 8.

CHOCOLATE SOUFFLE

3 egg yolks
2 tablespoons butter or margarine
2 tablespoons all-purpose flour
1/4 teaspoon salt
3/4 cup milk
2 squares (1-ounce size) unsweetened chocolate, melted and cooled
1/2 cup sugar
2 tablespoons hot water
3 egg whites
1/2 teaspoon vanilla
Sweetened whipped cream

Beat egg yolks until thick and lemon-colored; set aside. In saucepan, melt butter or margarine. Stir in flour and salt. Stir mixture just until it starts to turn golden. Add the milk all at once. Cook, stirring constantly, until mixture is thickened and bubbly. Stir moderate amount of hot mixture into beaten egg yolks; mix well. Return to remaining hot mixture in saucepan; cook and stir 2 minutes more. Remove from heat. Stir together cooled chocolate, 1/4 cup sugar and hot water. Stir chocolate mixture into egg mixture.

Beat egg whites and vanilla until soft peaks form; gradually add remaining sugar, beating to stiff peaks. Fold the egg whites into the chocolate mixture. Turn into prepared 1 1/2-quart souffle dish (see page 219).

Bake at 325 degrees until a knife inserted just off-center comes out clean, 55 to 60 minutes. Serve immediately with sweetened whipped cream. Serves 6.

DOUBLE BOILER LEMON SOUFFLE

1 cup sugar
2 tablespoons flour
3 tablespoons lemon juice
1 cup milk
2 eggs, separated

Combine sugar, flour, lemon juice, milk and egg yolks in top of double boiler. Blend well. Beat egg whites until stiff. Fold into lemon mixture. Place over simmering water. Cover, cook 55 minutes. Do not uncover during cooking. Serve warm. Serves 4.

GRAND MARNIER SOUFFLE

2 tablespoons butter
2 tablespoons flour
1/2 cup light cream
1/2 cup sugar
4 large egg yolks
1 tablespoon grated orange rind
1/4 teaspoon salt
5 large egg whites
1/4 teaspoon cream of tartar
6 ladyfingers or 6 macaroons
1/4 cup Grand Marnier
Whipped cream, optional

Prepare a 1 1/2-quart souffle dish or casserole according to instructions on How to Prepare a Souffle Dish and set it aside. Melt the butter in a 1-quart saucepan. Remove from heat and blend in flour. Stir and cook for 1 minute. Add the cream. Reserve 1 tablespoon of the sugar to beat with the egg whites and add the remaining sugar. Mix well. Stir and cook until mixture is very thick. Remove from heat. Beat egg yolks, beat in a little of the hot mixture, and then stir into remaining hot mixture. Stir and cook 1 minute over low heat. Add orange rind. Transfer mixture to a large mixing bowl and set aside.

Add salt to egg whites and beat until they are foamy. Add cream of tartar and continue beating until egg whites stand in soft peaks. Beat in reserved 1 tablespoon of sugar. Continue beating until egg whites stand in sharp, stiff peaks. Stir 2 tablespoons beaten egg whites into cooked mixture. Carefully fold in remaining beaten egg whites. Spoon half the mixture into prepared souffle dish. Dip ladyfingers or macaroons in Grand Marnier and place them over the top, then spoon the remaining souffle mixture over them. Trace a circle around the top of the souffle and bake by the Low Temperature Method (directions under How to Bake a Souffle). Sprinkle top with powdered sugar. Serve immediately with whipped cream flavored to taste with Grand Marnier or serve with Grand Marnier Sauce. Serves 4-6.

GRAND MARNIER SAUCE:
2 cups milk
3 3/4-ounce pagkage instant vanilla pudding
1 cup Cool Whip
1/8 teaspoon salt
1/4 cup Grand Marnier
1 teaspoon orange rind, grated

Combine milk and pudding mix. Beat until mixture reaches consistency of thin custard. Fold in remaining ingredients and chill.

Jo says, "I do not always put the ladyfingers or macaroons in the souffle, just bake it without, and use the Grand Marnier Sauce, topped with toasted slivered almonds."

COLD LEMON SOUFFLE

1 tablespoon unflavored gelatin
1/4 cup cold water
5 eggs, separated
3/4 cup fresh lemon juice
2 teaspoons freshly grated lemon rind
1 1/2 cups sugar
1 cup whipping cream
Raspberry Sauce or Wine Sauce
   (see index)

Sprinkle gelatin over cold water to soften. Mix egg yolks with lemon juice and rind and 3/4 cup sugar. Place in top of double boiler and cook, stirring constantly, until lemon mixture is slightly thickened, about 8 minutes. Remove from heat and stir in gelatin until dissolved. Chill 30 to 40 minutes. Beat egg whites until stiff, gradually adding the remaining 3/4 cup sugar. Whip cream until stiff. Fold egg whites and whipped cream into the yolk mixture until no white streaks remain. Pour into a 2-quart souffle dish and chill at least 4 hours. Serve with Raspberry Sauce or Wine Sauce.
   Serves 6.

FROZEN STRAWBERRY SOUFFLE

6 large eggs, separated
2 cups pureed strawberries
1/2 cup Grand Marnier
2 cups sugar
1/4 cup orange juice
3 cups whipping cream
Chopped walnuts, pecans or pistachios
1/2 cup whipping cream
Whole strawberries
Raspberry Sauce (see index)

Beat egg yolks in large bowl until thick and lemon-colored. Add 1 cup sugar and beat until dissolved. Stir in 1/2 cup pureed strawberries. Place in top of double boiler and cook over hot water until thickened, about 15 to 20 minutes, stirring frequently. Allow to cool. Add Grand Marnier, a little at a time, until thoroughly blended.

Combine 1 cup sugar and orange juice in 1-quart saucepan. Cook, uncovered, over medium low heat, stirring until dissolved. Continue cooking without stirring until mixture reaches soft ball stage (245 degrees).

While orange juice and sugar are cooking, beat egg whites until soft peaks form. Very slowly pour in hot orange syrup, beating until stiff peaks form.

Whip cream and fold into yolk mixture. Fold in remaining strawberry puree. Gently but thoroughly fold in meringue. Spoon into oiled and collared 1 1/2-quart souffle dish. Freeze about 1 1/2 to 2 hours. When firm, carefully wrap in freezer paper, securing edges with masking tape.

To serve, remove collar and press nuts around sides or top of souffle. Whip cream and use to garnish top. Decorate with strawberries and serve with Raspberry Sauce. Serves 12-16.

STRAWBERRIES ROMANOFF

4 cups fresh strawberries
1/2 cup confectioners' sugar
1 1/2 ounces vodka
1 1/2 ounces Triple Sec
1 1/2 ounces light rum

Wash and hull strawberries and toss with sugar. Put in bowl and pour over the vodka, triple sec, and rum. Chill. When ready to serve, mound the marinated, chilled strawberries over ice cream.
   Serves 4-6.

Melting Moments

STRAWBERRY CHEESE FLAN

1/4 cup butter
1 cup flour
1/4 cup sugar
1 egg, beaten
1 teaspoon grated orange rind
1 teaspoon vanilla
2 cups orange juice
1 package (8 ounces) cream cheese, softened
1 can sweetened condensed milk
1 envelope unflavored gelatin
1 cup chopped fresh strawberries
Additional sliced fresh strawberries

In large saucepan, melt butter; stir in flour, sugar, egg, rind and vanilla. Mix well. Pat into bottom and about 1 1/2 inches up side of 9-inch springform pan. Bake 12 to 14 minutes or until lightly browned. Cool.

In larger mixing bowl, beat cheese until fluffy. Stir in sweetened condensed milk until smooth. In small saucepan, sprinkle gelatin over orange juice; let stand 1 minute. Over low heat, cook and stir until gelatin dissolves, about 5 minutes. Add to cream cheese mixture; mix well. Stir in strawberries. Pour into prepared pan. Chill 4 hours or until set. Garnish with sliced strawberries.

Serves 10-12.

COCONUT LEMON TARTS

1 cup flour
2 tablespoons sugar
1/4 teaspoon salt
1/3 cup butter
2 eggs, slightly beaten
1 cup firmly packed light brown sugar
1/2 cup chopped pecans
1 cup flaked coconut
1 tablespoon lemon juice
1 teaspoon grated lemon rind

Combine flour, sugar and salt in mixing bowl. Cut in butter until mixture resembles coarse meal. Press in bottom of an 8 or 9-inch square pan. Bake at 350 degrees for 15 minutes, or until lightly browned. Meanwhile, combine remaining ingredients and mix thoroughly. Spread over baked pastry and bake an additional 25 to 30 minutes. Loosen around edges while warm; top with lemon glaze. Cool in pan. Cut into squares.

Makes 15-20 cookies.

LEMON GLAZE:
1 tablespoon lemon juice
2/3 cup sifted powdered sugar
1 teaspoon grated lemon rind

Gradually add lemon juice to powdered sugar. Blend well and stir in grated lemon rind. Makes 1/4 cup.

MOCHA BROWNIE TORTE

1 package fudge brownie mix
1/4 cup water
2 eggs
1/4 cup chopped nuts

Heat oven to 350 degrees. Grease and flour 2 layer pans, 9 x 1 1/2-inch. Blend brownie mix, eggs, water and stir in nuts. Spread in pan and bake 20 minutes. Cool 5 minutes in pan. It should be completely cool.

FROSTING:
1 1/2 cups heavy cream
1/3 cup brown sugar
1 tablespoon instant coffee

In chilled bowl, beat cream until it begins to thicken. Gradually add brown sugar and instant coffee. Beat until stiff. Fill layers with 1 cup of mixture, frost with the rest.

Sprinkle top with chocolate curls. Chill at least 1 hour. Serves 10-12.

◇◇

SYLLABUB PUDDING

1 pint thick cream
Juice and peel of 3 lemons
6 ounces sugar
3 ounces sweet sherry
1 ounce brandy

Whip all ingredients together and pour into sherbet glasses. Serves 4.

ENGLISH TRIFLE

This confection is one of the world's greatest desserts and can be made in a variety of ways. In preparing Trifle you may make it as easy or hard on your part. Either way you choose, it turns out to be a delicious, beautiful dessert loved by all. The following are varieties that I have made and served.

TRIFLE

2 packages lady fingers
1/2 cup black or red raspberry jam
1 large can drained peach or apricot halves
1 large package vanilla pudding
1/2 pint whipping cream
1/2 cup sherry
Slivered almonds

Split ladyfingers and make sandwiches with generous amount of jam between slices. Line a pretty bowl or trifle bowl with the sandwiches, bottom of dish first, then the sides. Sprinkle with 1/2 cup sherry over the cake and then put the apricots or peaches, cut side down, on top, covering cake completely. Make pudding and spoon over fruit while warm. Cover completely and refrigerate. Can be made a day ahead.

One hour before serving, whip the cream stiff with 2 tablespoons sugar. Spoon this cream over the pudding. Decorate with glazed cherries or almonds or both. Refrigerate. Serves 10-12.

Jan says, ''You may use cherry pie filling in place of the apricots or peaches. When I have time I like to make my own custard sauce as follows:''

TRIFLE CUSTARD SAUCE

2 1/2 tablespoons cornstarch
3 cups light cream
6 egg yolks
1 cup sugar
1 1/2 teaspoons almond flavoring
1 cup whipped cream

Dissolve cornstarch in 1/4 cup cream. Beat egg yolks until light. Combine with cream and cornstarch mixture. Heat remaining cream with sugar. Pour 1 cup hot cream mixture over egg mixture, stirring constantly. Combine with the remaining hot cream mixture and return to low heat. Cook, stirring constantly until thickened. Remove from heat and add almond flavoring. Cool stirring occasionally. When completely cool fold in sweetened whipped cream.

❖❖❖

ENGLISH TRIFLE I

6 to 8 sponge cakes
3 tablespoons raspberry jam
1 can pears
1 box frozen raspberries
1 packet raspberry Jell-O
1/2 pint Trifle Custard Sauce (previous page)
Wine, if desired
Maraschino cherries

Split the sponge cakes horizontally and spread generously with raspberry jam. Cut into three or four pieces and place at the bottom of a glass dish. Strain the juice from the fruit and pour it over the sponge cakes. The addition of sherry or home-made wine to the fruit is an improvement, but it is not essential.

Put the raspberries on top of the sponge cakes, then pour on the hot custard. Put aside to set. Place pears on top of custard. Prepare raspberry Jell-O in the ordinary way by dissolving it in boiling water. When almost cold, and just beginning to set, whisk the Jell-O vigorously until it is light and frothy and resembling stiffly beaten whites of eggs. Arrange this in pyramids on top of the trifle and decorate with a few cherries and a little Angelica. Serves 10-12.

ENGLISH TRIFLE II

Arrange colorful layers of fruit, custard, and wine-soaked sponge cake topped with whipped cream and display magnificently in a beautiful and traditional footed crystal bowl.

ENGLISH TRIFLE III

Simply arrange this tasty confection in alternate layers of macaroons or ladyfingers with sugared fruits, covered with a custard and topped with meringue or whipped cream. Serve from a sparkling footed crystal bowl.

Jan says, "The above Trifle recipes come from London, England."

CHOCOLATE TRIFLE

1 box (9-ounce) chocolate cake mix or your favorite chocolate cake
1 box instant chocolate pudding
1 can dark sweet cherries
1/3 cup sherry
1 carton whipped topping

Make cake and pudding according to the box directions. Break up half of cake and put it in bottom of a trifle bowl or a pretty one that you can see through. Sprinkle 1/3 cup sherry over cake. In layers Add:
Half of pudding
Half of cherries
Half of whipped cream

Make another layer starting with cake and ending with the whipped cream. Reserve a few cherries to garnish along with a few shaved chocolate curls. Refrigerate at least 4 to 6 hours. Serves 10 to 12.

Jan says, "This is a very pretty dessert and an easy one. I always serve it at the table."

INDIVIDUAL TRIFLES

8 ladyfingers, cut into pieces
Cream sherry
1 can (14-ounce) condensed milk
2 cups sliced fresh strawberries or raspberries, well drained
1 container whipped cream topping

Place ladyfinger pieces in individual serving dishes or wine goblets. Sprinkle about 1/2 teaspoon sherry over each serving. Set aside. In bowl combine condensed milk with 1 tablespoon sherry and strawberries or raspberries. Fold in whipped topping. Spoon about 1/2 cup mixture into each dish. Chill several hours or until set. Serves 8.

Fillings & Frostings

FRENCH CREME FILLING

6 tablespoons flour
1 cup milk
1 cup sugar
1/2 pound butter or margarine
2 tablespoons vanilla

Combine flour and milk, cook until thick. Cool until ice cold. Add sugar, butter and vanilla; beat 15 minutes with electric mixer. May be used for cakes, cupcakes or doughnuts. May be kept 2 to 3 weeks in refrigerator.

LEMON FILLING FOR CAKES

3 egg yolks, well beaten
2 lemons
1/2 cup butter
1 cup sugar

Combine all ingredients and cook until thick and smooth. Cool.

CARAMEL FROSTING

1/2 cup butter or margarine
1 cup dark brown sugar, firmly packed
1/4 teaspoon salt
1/4 cup milk
1/2 teaspoon vanilla
2 cups confectioners' sugar

Melt butter or margarine in a heavy saucepan over low heat. Stir in brown sugar and salt. Bring to boil and stir constantly at a boil for 2 minutes. Remove from heat. Stir in milk, return pan to heat, bring to a full boil. Remove from heat, cool to lukewarm; add vanilla. Stir in confectioners' sugar and beat until smooth. If frosting is too thick, beat in a little more milk.

CHOCOLATE CREAM CHEESE FROSTING

1 package (3-ounce) cream cheese
3 tablespoons milk
1/8 teaspoon salt
1 teaspoon vanilla
2 squares chocolate, melted
2 cups sifted confectioners' sugar

Cream cheese and milk. Add rest of ingredients. Beat well. Let stand 3 minutes. Beat until creamy.

Melting Moments

CHOCOLATE FROSTING

1/4 cup butter, melted
1/4 teaspoon salt
1/2 cup cocoa
1/3 cup milk
1 1/2 teaspoons vanilla
3 1/2 cups powdered sugar

Combine butter, salt, cocoa; then add milk and vanilla. Stir in the sugar in 3 parts, mixing until smooth and creamy. Add more sugar to thicken or milk to thin frosting, as required for spreading consistency.

Frosts 2-layer cake.

SCHOOL DAYS FROSTING

1/4 to 1/3 cup strong coffee
2 tablespoons butter
1 square unsweetened chocolate, melted
1 package powdered sugar
1 teaspoon vanilla
Pinch of salt

Brown butter in a pan, add rest of ingredients and beat well. Spread on cooled cake.

Frosts 2-layer cake.

COCONUT-PECAN FROSTING

1 cup evaporated milk
1 cup sugar
3 egg yolks
1/4 pound margarine
1 teaspoon vanilla
1 1/3 cups coconut
1 cup chopped pecans

Combine first 5 ingredients in saucepan. Cook and stir over medium heat until mixture thickens, about 12 minutes.

Add coconut and pecans. Beat until frosting is cool and thick enough to spread. Makes 2 2/3 cups.

CREAM FROSTING

1 cup sugar
1 cup whipping cream
1 teaspoon vanilla
Yellow food coloring

Stir together sugar and cream and put in heavy utensil over medium heat. Cover. When it comes to a boil remove lid. Cook to a barely soft ball stage. Add 1 teaspoon vanilla and a dash of yellow food coloring. Put mixture in small mixing bowl and beat 2 to 3 minutes. Spread on cake. This recipe will frost an angel food cake.

CREAM CHEESE FROSTING

1/2 cup margarine, softened
1 package (8-ounce) cream cheese, softened
1 box (1-pound) powdered sugar
2 teaspoons vanilla
1/8 teaspoon salt
1/2 cup chopped nuts

Blend ingredients and spread between layers and on top and sides of 2-layer cake. Refrigerate.

DELISH FROSTING

1/4 pound margarine
1/2 cup Crisco
1 cup sugar
1 teaspoon vanilla
3/4 cup milk

Mix together all ingredients except milk; beat 5 minutes. Heat milk almost to boiling point; add 1 tablespoon at a time to mixture, beating well after each addition. This amount will frost a large layer cake.

FOUR MINUTE FROSTING

1 cup sugar
1/4 teaspoon salt
1/2 teaspoon cream of tartar
2 egg whites
3 tablespoons cold water
1 teaspoon vanilla

Place all in top of double boiler and beat over hot water 4 minutes or until of right consistency for icing. Frosts a 2-layer cake.

SEA FOAM FROSTING

1/2 cup brown sugar
1/2 cup granulated sugar
1 teaspoon Karo light syrup
1/3 cup water
1 egg white

Combine and cook first 4 ingredients until syrup spins thread. Pour over one egg white and beat until fluffy.
Keep frosted cake in refrigerator.
Frosts 1 small cake.

SHORTCUT 7 MINUTE FROSTING

1 cup white sugar
1/3 cup water
1/2 teaspoon cream of tartar
3 egg whites, beaten stiff
1 teaspoon vanilla

Boil sugar, water and cream of tartar until it begins to thread. Slowly pour syrup into stiffly beaten egg whites. Beat until soft peaks form. Add 1 teaspoon vanilla and beat until vanilla is dissolved. Frosts 1 large cake.

Jan says, "When making this frosting, I cover the pan with a lid until the syrup starts to boil. When you do this the syrup does not cake on the sides of the pan and will be a nice crystal-free frosting."

MINUTE FUDGE FROSTING

1 ounce unsweetened baking chocolate, cut up
1 cup sugar
1/3 cup milk
1/4 cup shortening
1/4 teaspoon salt
1 teaspoon vanilla

Place all ingredients except vanilla in saucepan. Bring slowly to a full rolling boil, stirring constantly, and boil 1 minute. Add vanilla and beat until thick enough to spread. If frosting becomes too thick, add 1 tablespoon cream.
Frosts 1 small cake.

❖❖

MINUTE PENUCHE FROSTING

1 cup brown sugar, firmly packed
1/4 cup milk
1/4 cup shortening
1/4 teaspoon salt
1/2 teaspoon vanilla

Cook, using same procedure as in Minute Fudge Frosting.
Frosts 1 small cake.

MOCHA CREAM FROSTING

2 squares unsweetened chocolate
1/2 cup water
1/2 cup sugar
1/2 teaspoon vanilla
2 teaspoons instant coffee
1 pint cream

Melt the chocolate in the water over low heat, stirring constantly. Add the sugar, vanilla and coffee and boil for 3 minutes. When cool, stir in stiffly whipped cream.
Frosts 1 large cake.

Pie Crusts

ALMOND CRUST

1/4 cup butter
1/4 teaspoon salt
2 tablespoons sugar
1 egg yolk
3/4 cup flour
1/4 cup finely chopped almonds

Cream butter, sugar and salt until light and fluffy. Add egg yolk and beat thoroughly. Stir in flour and almonds to make a firm dough. Press dough into a 9-inch pie pan. Refrigerate 30 minutes. Bake at 400 degrees for 15 minutes or until golden.

SPECIAL CHEESECAKE CRUST

1 cup sifted flour
1/4 cup sugar
1 teaspoon grated lemon peel
1/2 teaspoon vanilla
1 egg yolk
1/4 cup soft butter

Combine first 4 ingredients. Make a well in the center; add egg yolk and butter. Mix with hands until dough cleans bowl and forms into a ball. Wrap in waxed paper, refrigerate 1 hour. Preheat oven to 400 degrees. Grease bottom and sides of 9-inch springform pan. Press crust against pan and bake 8 to 10 minutes or until golden.

COCONUT CRUST

3 tablespoons softened butter or margarine
2 cans (3 1/2-ounce size) flaked coconut

Combine butter and coconut. Press evenly into buttered 9-inch pie plate, building up sides. Bake in 300-degree oven 20 to 25 minutes, or until crust is golden. Cool.

Melting Moments

GRAHAM CRACKER CRUST

16 large graham crackers
1/4 cup sugar
1 tablespoon flour
1 teaspoon cinnamon
4 tablespoons melted butter

Crush graham crackers. Add sugar, flour, cinnamon and melted butter. Mix all and pat into 2 9-inch pie plates. Chill well.

OLD-FASHIONED PIE CRUST
(Makes 2 crusts)

1 1/2 cups flour
1 teaspoon salt
1/2 cup plus 3 tablespoons shortening
3 to 4 tablespoons cold water

Measure salt and flour into a bowl. Add shortening, and with a fork mash into flour until it looks like coarse meal. Add cold water all at once and mix until all the flour is moistened and dough comes away from sides of bowl. Shape into balls. Flatten balls, sprinkle both sides with flour and on a board or cloth roll pastry dough into circles according to size of pie pan.

If you are baking a one-crust pie, fill pan with dough. Crimp edges and prick bottom of pan several times.

Note: Always brush pie-crust bottom with Crisco before baking! Prevents sogginess.

PIE CRUST
(Makes 3 crusts)

3 cups flour
1 1/2 teaspoons salt
1 cup plus 2 tablespoons Crisco
6 tablespoons cold water

Sift and measure flour. Sift again with the salt. Take out 1/3 cup flour and salt and mix with the cold water. Cut shortening into the flour and salt, then add the paste. Mix until it forms a soft ball. This may be rolled out at once on a lightly floured board, but the results are better if the dough has been wrapped in waxed paper and chilled first.

PIE CRUST

1/2 cup brown sugar
1/4 cup white sugar
1 cup white flour
1 cup graham flour
1/2 teaspoon salt
1 cup shortening
1/2 cup corn syrup

Blend sugars, flours, salt and shortening together until well blended. Blend in corn syrup and mold into 9-inch pan. Bake at 375 degrees for 15 to 20 minutes.

Use with chiffon and key lime pies, also cheesecake.

✧✧✧

CRISPY ICE CREAM SHELLS

1/2 cup shortening
1 package (7-ounce) creamy vanilla frosting mix
1 3/4 cup sifted flour
1/2 cup water

Blend shortening, frosting mix, flour and water in bowl until smooth. Lightly grease 5 1/2-inch circular areas on cookie sheet, about 1 inch apart. Mark a 5-inch area as a guide with a saucer or bowl on greased area. Spread 1 tablespoon of mixture with spatula evenly over marked area. Bake in moderate oven (375 degrees) for 6 to 8 minutes, or until golden brown. Working with one cookie at a time, loosen gently with broad spatula, carefully flip it over outside of an inverted custard cup. press into tricorn shape. Shells will cool and stiffen at once and may be removed from cups in 2 to 3 minutes. If the shells become too firm to remove from the cookie sheet, return to oven to soften. Repeat process until all batter is used. Fill with ice cream and spoon syrup over top. Shells may be stored in a covered container for several days. Makes 24.

Pies

TONIA'S APPLE CRISP — FOOD PROCESSOR STYLE

1 lemon
1 cup sugar
1 cup flour
1/2 teaspoon salt
1/2 teaspoon cinnamon
1/2 teaspoon freshly grated nutmeg
1/4 pound cold, sweet butter, cut into 6 pieces
2 pounds tart cooking apples (Granny Smiths), peeled, cored and cut in half
Water, enough to make 1/4 cup when added to the juice of the lemon

Steel Knife: Carefully cut only the yellow from the lemon rind and process it with the sugar until very fine. Add the flour, salt and spices. Combine. Add the cold butter and process, using quick on/off turns, until the mixture is the consistency of cornmeal. Remove and reserve.

Medium Serrated slices: Without washing bowl, slice all the apples. Pack them into a 2-quart casserole. Squeeze the lemon into a measuring cup and add water to make 1/4 cup liquid. Pour over apples.

Pat the reserved crumb mixture over the apples and bake at 375 degrees for 45 minutes. Top should be slightly brown. Serves 8.

SOUR CREAM APPLE PIE

Unbaked pastry for 9-inch single crust
6 apples, peeled and cut into eighths
3/4 cup sugar
1/3 cup flour
4 tablespoons butter
1 teaspoon cinnamon
1/4 teaspoon nutmeg
1/2 cup sour cream

Arrange apple slices in overlapping rows in pastry lined pie plate. Mix rest of ingredients except sour cream until crumbly and spoon over apples, then cover with 1/2 cup sour cream.

Bake in 400-degree oven for 30 minutes; reduce heat to 350 degrees and bake until apples are tender and crust is brown, about 25 minutes longer.

APPLE PIE

Pastry for 9-inch 2-crust pie
8 green, tart apples (Granny Smith), peeled, cored and cut into eighths
1 cup brown sugar or 3/4 cup white sugar
1/4 teaspoon nutmeg
1/2 teaspoon cinnamon
1/4 teaspoon salt
1 tablespoon lemon juice
Grated rind of 1/2 lemon
2 tablespoons butter
Cheddar cheese (garnish)

Line pie plate with pastry and arrange apple slices in layers. Sprinkle each layer lightly with mixture of sugar, spices, salt, lemon juice and rind. Save enough for top. When plate is full, dot with butter, cover with top crust. Seal and crimp edges. Bake in 450-degree oven for 15 to 20 minutes. Reduce heat to 350 degrees for 20 to 30 minutes until crust is brown and apples are tender. Serve warm with slices of cheese if desired.

1—CRUST APPLE PIE

Unbaked pastry for 9 or 10-inch single crust
1 cup light brown sugar, packed
1/2 cup all-purpose flour
1 teaspoon cinnamon
1/8 teaspoon allspice
1/8 teaspoon cloves
1/8 teaspoon nutmeg
1/2 teaspoon grated lemon peel, fresh
1/2 cup butter
6 medium-size apples (Jonathans are good)

Line pie plate with pastry. Mix sugar, flour, spices and butter with pastry blender until crumbly. Adjust spices to taste. Spread 1/3 of crumb mixture over bottom of unbaked pastry. Peel apples, core and slice; place over crumb mixture. Spoon remaining sugar and spice mixture over apples. Bake in 400 degree oven 50 to 55 minutes.

VARIATION STREUSEL TOPPING FOR 1 - CRUST APPLE PIE

1 cup Bisquick baking mix
1/2 cup chopped nuts
1/3 cup packed brown sugar
1 teaspoon cinnamon
3 tablespoons firm butter or margarine

Combine all ingredients and crumble on top of apple pie. Bake according to pie-recipe instructions.

Jo says, "Try this on peach pie sometime, or apricot, or pear. Be creative."

SOUR CREAM — APRICOT PIE

2 cups flour
3 teaspoons baking powder
1 teaspoon salt
1/2 cup shortening
1 egg
Milk

Sift and measure flour, resift with baking powder and salt. Cut in shortening. Beat and pour egg in measuring cup, add milk to make 2/3 cup. Combine wet and dry ingredients. Roll out 1/4-inch thick. Line a pan or baking dish, with straight sides and 2-inches deep, with dough. Bake 10 minutes in 450-degree oven. Brush crust with melted butter.

APRICOT FILLING:
1 package (3-ounce) cream cheese
1 1/2 cups sour cream
1 can (No. 2 1/2) drained apricot halves
3 teaspoons cinnamon
1/2 cup sugar

Whip cream cheese, stir in sour cream. Pour into baked shell. Insert in close rows the apricot halves and sprinkle heavily with cinnamon blended with sugar. Chill.

Melting Moments

BANANA—CREAM CHEESE PIE

CRUST:
9-inch pie pan
1/3 cup butter
1/4 cup sugar
1/2 teaspoon cinnamon
1 cup cornflake crumbs

Melt butter in saucepan over medium heat. Add sugar and cinnamon. Stir constantly until bubbles form around edges. Remove from heat and add cornflake crumbs. Stir thoroughly to mix, then form crust in pie pan and chill.

FILLING:
4 to 6 bananas
1 package (8-ounce) cream cheese
1 can (14-ounce) sweetened condensed milk
1/3 cup lemon juice
1 teaspoon vanilla

With mixer at high speed, beat cream cheese until smooth and creamy, add sweetened condensed milk and beat until mixed thoroughly. Add lemon juice and vanilla. Stir or fold with spoon until thickens. Slice 2 or 3 bananas onto crust to form layer. Slice remaining bananas into cream mixture and fold gently to distribute. Pour filling into crust and refrigerate 1 to 2 hours or until set.

BLUEBERRY CASSIS PIE

MERINGUE CRUST:
1/4 teaspoon salt
1 teaspoon vanilla
4 egg whites
1 cup sugar
1 teaspoon baking powder
1 cup graham cracker crumbs
1/2 cup shredded coconut
1/2 cup chopped filberts or hazelnuts

Preheat oven to 350 degrees. Prepare the crust by adding salt and vanilla to egg whites and beat until foamy. Add sugar in a slow stream and continue beating until egg whites form shiny peaks. Combine the baking powder, crumbs, coconut and nuts. Fold the mixture into the beaten egg whites. Spread in a well greased and floured 9-inch pie pan, making the rim slightly thicker than the center. Bake for 30 minutes. Cool.

FILLING:
3 cups fresh or frozen blueberries
1 cup sugar
3 tablespoons flour (more if the berries are very juicy)
1/4 teaspoon salt
1 tablespoon lemon juice
2 tablespoons Creme de Cassis
3 egg yolks, beaten

If you are using fresh blueberries, pick through them to remove any stems. Place berries, sugar, flour, salt, lemon juice, Creme de Cassis and beaten egg yolks in the top of a double boiler and cook over simmering water until the mixture thickens (about 10 minutes).

Pour berry mixture into the pie shell and chill. When ready to serve, whip the cream and fold in sugar to taste and 1 tablespoon Creme de Cassis. Mound the cream on top of the pie.

TOPPING:
1 cup heavy cream
1 to 3 tablespoons sifted confectioners' sugar
1 tablespoon Creme de Cassis

BRANDY ALEXANDER PIE

1 9-inch graham cracker pie shell
1 cup sugar
6 eggs, beaten
1 package unflavored gelatin
1/2 cup water
2 cups whipping cream
1 tablespoon Creme de Cacao
1 tablespoon brandy
3/4 cup semi-sweet chocolate shavings

Slowly add sugar to eggs, beating until fluffy. Dissolve gelatin in water and bring to quick boil. Slowly pour hot gelatin over egg mixture, stirring briskly. Cool and chill in refrigerator until thickened but not set. Whip cream until stiff but not dry, and gently fold into well-chilled egg mixture. Add Creme de Cacao and brandy and spoon mixture into pie shell. Sprinkle generously with chocolate shavings.

CHOCOLATE CHIFFON PIE

1 envelope (1 tablespoon) unflavored gelatin
1/4 cup cold water
1/2 cup water
1 teaspoon instant coffee
2 squares (1-ounce size) unsweetened chocolate
3 egg yolks
1/2 cup sugar
1/4 teaspoon salt
1 teaspoon vanilla
1/2 cup sugar
3 stiff-beaten egg whites
1 recipe Coconut Crust (see index)
Whipped cream

Soften gelatin in 1/4 cup cold water. In saucepan, combine 1/2 cup water, coffee and chocolate. Stir over low heat until blended. Remove from heat. Add softened gelatin and stir until dissolved. Beat egg yolks until thick and lemon-colored; gradually beat in 1/2 cup sugar; add salt and vanilla. Gradually stir in chocolate mixture.

Chill until partially set. (Mixture should mound; if it doesn't, chill a bit longer.) Stir until smooth. Beat remaining 1/2 cup sugar into egg whites. Fold into chocolate mixture. Pour into cooled coconut crust. Chill until firm. Top with whipped cream and drizzle with Syrup Trim.

SYRUP TRIM:
1 1/2 tablespoons light corn syrup
1/2 ounce square unsweetened chocolate

Combine corn syrup and melted chocolate. Stir over low heat until blended. Cool.

CHOCOLATE PECAN PIE

1/2 cup butter, melted
1 cup sugar
1 cup white corn syrup
4 eggs, slightly beaten
1 teaspoon vanilla
1 cup whole pecans
3/4 cup chocolate chips

Combine all ingredients. Pour into unbaked 9-inch pastry shell. Bake at 350 degrees for 45 to 50 minutes. Cool completely.

Melting Moments

POLLY'S CHOCOLATE PIE

2 cups milk
3/4 cup sugar
2 1/2 squares chocolate
2 tablespoons cornstarch
2 tablespoons flour
3 eggs
1/4 teaspoon salt
1 teaspoon vanilla
Small lump of butter

Add chocolate to milk and heat in top of double boiler over boiling water. When chocolate is melted beat mixture with egg beater. Mix sugar, flour, cornstarch and salt together and add gradually to mixture. Stir constantly and cook until it is thick enough for the spoon to leave an indentation. Turn down heat and continue cooking 10 to 15 minutes longer, stirring constantly in order to cook the cornstarch thoroughly.

Beat egg yolks slightly and vigorously stir a little chocolate mixture into yolks. Add this to double boiler, stirring vigorously to mix egg yolks before they can coagulate. Cook for 3 minutes longer. Remove from stove and add butter and vanilla. Cool. Turn into a 9-inch baked pie shell. Top with meringue or whipped cream.

Jan says, "This pie takes a little longer than most pies these days, but is well worth it. It is a recipe from a wonderful woman who helped my mother years ago."

DERBY DAIQUIRI PIE

1 package unflavored gelatin
1/2 cup granulated sugar
1/4 teaspoon salt
5 egg yolks
1/2 cup freshly squeezed lime juice
1/4 cup frozen orange juice concentrate, thawed
1 ounce light rum
5 egg whites
1/2 cup granulated sugar
1 pie shell (9-inch)
1 cup whipping cream
3 tablespoons confectioners' sugar, sifted fine
1 ounce light rum
1 teaspoon lime peel, grated fine

In heavy saucepan stir together gelatin, sugar and salt. Blend in egg yolks, lime and orange juices. Stirring, bring to boil over medium heat. Remove from heat, add 1 ounce of light rum and blend thoroughly. Place in refrigerator and chill, stirring occasionally until mixture mounds from a spoon.

Beat egg whites into soft peaks, gradually adding 1/2 cup granulated sugar. Continue beating until stiff peaks are formed. Gently fold gelatin mixture into beaten egg whites.

Pour into cool pie shell and chill until firm. To serve, whip cream, adding confectioners' sugar and final ounce of rum. Top pie and dust with lime peel.

HEATH BAR PIE

1 graham cracker crust
1 carton Cool Whip
6 Heath bars, crushed
1/3 cup rum
2 tablespoons instant coffee

In mixing bowl, dissolve coffee in the rum. Fold in Cool Whip. Add crushed Heath bars, but reserve some to sprinkle over the top. Fill graham cracker crust with mixture. Sprinkle with the reserved Heath bar pieces. Freezes well!

Melting Moments

GRAPE PIE

5 1/3 cups Concord grapes
1 1/3 cups sugar
1/4 cup flour
1 1/4 teaspoons lemon juice
1/4 teaspoon salt
2 tablespoons butter

Prepare pastry for 2-crust 10-inch pie. Remove and save skins from grapes. Put pulp in saucepan without water and bring to rolling boil. While hot, rub through strainer to remove seeds. Mix strained pulp with skins.

Mix sugar and flour. Combine with grapes. Sprinkle with lemon juice and salt. Pour into prepared pie shell. Dot with butter. Cover with top crust which has slits in it.

Put pie plate on cookie sheet. Place on center rack of oven and bake at 425 degrees for 35 to 45 minutes until crust is browned nicely and juice begins to bubble through slits in crust. Serve cool.

Jo says, "This is a once a year happening at our home. It is a bit of extra effort with the grapes but the smell, taste and purple teeth are all worth it."

GRASSHOPPER PIE

24 cream-filled chocolate cookies, finely crushed
1/4 cup butter, melted
1/4 cup green Creme de Menthe or you may substitute 1/4 cup milk, a few drops green food coloring and a few drops peppermint extract
1 jar marshmallow creme
2 cups heavy cream, whipped

Combine cookie crumbs and butter. Press into 9-inch spring pan. Save 1/2 cup of mixture for topping. Add Creme de Menthe or milk to marshmallow creme. Mix until well blended. Fold in whipped cream. Pour in pan. Sprinkle with remaining crumbs. Freeze.

Jo says, "For individual desserts, use paper muffin cup liners. Place in metal muffin tins to hold shape while freezing. Fun to serve at patio buffets."

KEY LIME PIE

1 teaspoon grated lime rind
1/2 cup fresh key lime juice
4 egg yolks, beaten until thick
1 can sweetened condensed milk
1 stiffly beaten egg white

MERINGUE:
3 egg whites
1/4 teaspoon cream of tartar
6 tablespoons sugar

Mix first 4 ingredients and fold into egg white. Turn into pastry shell. May use 9-inch baked pie shell or graham cracker crust. Beat 3 egg whites with 1/4 teaspoon cream of tartar until they are frothy. Slowly add 6 tablespoons of sugar. Beat until the meringue stands in peaks. Mound on top of filled pie, carefully smoothing the edge fast against the crust. Bake in a preheated 400-degree oven for 10 to 15 minutes until golden brown. Let cool to room temperature, then refrigerate at least one hour before serving.

Jo says, "Some prefer whipped-cream topping rather than the meringue. If not making meringue topping, bake pie filling as above, cool and refrigerate. Simply whip a carton of cream to which you add sugar to taste. Spread on chilled pie and garnish with thin lime slices. It's yummy!"

Melting Moments

HEAVENLY PIE

CRUST:
1 cup sugar
1/4 teaspoon cream of tartar
4 egg whites

Sift together sugar, cream of tartar. Beat egg whites until stiff, add sugar mixture slowly. Line a 9-inch glass pie plate with mixture. Bake at 250 degrees for 1 hour.

FILLING:
4 egg yolks
1/2 cup sugar
3 tablespoons lemon juice
1 teaspoon grated lemon rind
1 pint cream, whipped

Beat egg yolks with sugar, add lemon juice and rind. Cook in double boiler until thick. Cool. Combine 1/2 pint whipped cream after egg-lemon mixture has cooled. Pour into crust and spread with the other 1/2 pint of whipped cream. Chill.

VARIATION FOR FILLING

CHIFFON FILLING:
4 egg yolks, beaten
1 cup sugar
1/3 cup lemon juice
1/2 teaspoon salt
1 tablespoon gelatin
1/2 cup cold water
1 teaspoon lemon rind
4 stiff-beaten egg whites
1 cup heavy cream, whipped

Cook egg yolks, 1/2 cup sugar, lemon juice and salt in double boiler to custard consistency, stirring constantly. Add gelatin softened in cold water and grated lemon rind. Chill.

When mixture begins to thicken, fold in egg whites combined with rest of sugar. Pour into baked meringue shell and chill until firm, 2 or 3 hours. Spread with whipped cream before serving. All but adding the whipped cream can be done the day before serving.

LEMON CLOUD PIE

1 cup all-purpose flour, sifted
1/2 teaspoon salt
1/3 cup shortening
1 egg, slightly beaten
1 teaspoon grated lemon rind
1 tablespoon lemon juice

Sift flour and salt into mixing bowl. Cut in shortening until particles are fine. Combine egg, lemon rind and lemon juice. Sprinkle over mixture, stirring with fork until moist enough to hold together. Add water if necessary. Form into ball.

Roll out on floured surface to circle 1 1/2 inches larger than inverted pie pan. Fit into pan. Trim edge; place extra pieces in a baking pan. Fold edge to form rim; flute. Prick shell. Bake shell and pieces in 400-degree oven for 12 to 15 minutes. Prepare filling.

LEMON CHEESE FILLING

3/4 cup sugar
1/4 cup cornstarch
1 cup water
1 teaspoon grated lemon rind
1/3 cup lemon juice
2 egg yolks, slightly beaten
4 ounces cream cheese
2 egg whites
1/4 cup sugar

Combine sugar, cornstarch, water, lemon rind, lemon juice and egg yolks in saucepan. Cook over medium heat, stirring constantly until thick. Add cream cheese; blend well. Cool. Beat egg whites until soft mounds form. Gradually add 1/4 cup sugar; beat until stiff peaks form. Fold into lemon mixture. Spoon into pie shell. Chill. Sprinkle crumbled pastry around edge.

Melting Moments

LEMON CHIFFON PIE

CRUST:
16 graham crackers, crushed
1/2 cup butter, melted

FILLING:
4 egg yolks
1/2 cup sugar
Juice and grated rind of 1 lemon
1 teaspoon unflavored gelatin
1/3 cup water
4 egg whites
1/2 cup sugar
1 cup heavy cream, whipped

Combine cracker crumbs and melted butter. Mix and pat gently into 9-inch pie pan. Prick and bake at 350 degrees for 15 minutes.

Beat egg yolks until light, add sugar. Place in double boiler and cook to custard consistency. When almost done, add lemon juice and rind and gelatin dissolved in water. Cool.

Beat egg whites until stiff, gradually adding the sugar. Add to the cooled lemon-egg mixture, folding well. Pour into pie shell. Chill. Serve with whipped cream topping.

LEMON CHESS PIE

3 large eggs
1/4 cup lemon juice
4 teaspoons grated lemon rind
1/4 cup milk
1 3/4 cups sugar
1 tablespoon flour
1 tablespoon cornstarch
3 tablespoons melted butter

Beat eggs well. Add lemon juice, rind and milk. Add dry ingredients which have been mixed together. Add melted butter. Pour in unbaked pie shell. Bake 10 minutes at 400 degrees then 45 minutes at 325 degrees. Top will be golden brown and shiny when done.

JEANNIE'S LEMON PIE

1 prepared pie shell
2 egg yolks, beaten
Juice of 2 lemons
1 cup sugar
5 tablespoons cornstarch
1 tablespoon butter

MERINGUE:
3 egg whites
6 teaspoons sugar

Blend ingredients well. Add 2 cups boiling water to mixture. Cook until thick, stirring constantly. Remove from fire and add 1 table-spoon butter. Cool before pouring into pie shell. Be sure pie crust is also cool. Add meringue and brown, about 15 minutes in 350 degree oven.

Beat 3 egg whites with 2 teaspoons sugar to each egg white, adding the sugar very slowly to the whites. Beat until whites stand in stiff peaks, spread over pie, making sure to cover to edge of crust. Brown about 15 minutes in 350-degree oven.

PECAN PIE

4 large eggs, beaten
2/3 cup firmly packed brown sugar
1/4 teaspoon salt
1 1/3 cups light corn syrup
1/4 cup melted butter
1 teaspoon vanilla
1 1/2 cups pecan halves

Preheat oven to 400 degrees. Combine eggs and sugar in mixing bowl, beat until blended.

Add salt, corn syrup, butter, vanilla and pecans. Mix well. Pour into prepared pie shell. Bake in 400-degree oven for 15 minutes. Reduce heat to 350 degrees and bake for 25 to 35 minutes more or until set in center. Let cool before serving.

Melting Moments

JEANNE'S LIME PIE

1 prepared pie shell
1/2 cup cold water
7 level tablespoons cornstarch
1 1/2 cups hot water
1 1/4 cups sugar
2 eggs, yolks slightly beaten
3 limes or 1/3 cup lime juice
1 teaspoon grated lime rind
1 tablespoon butter
Few drops green food coloring

Mix cold water and cornstarch to thin paste. Combine hot water and sugar in top of double boiler. Add cornstarch and cold water and cook until mixture begins to thicken. Stir a small amount of mixture into slightly beaten egg yolks, pour back into heated mixture, and cook a few minutes longer. Add lime juice, rind, butter and blend. Add green coloring. Pour into prepared pie shell. Top with whipped cream.

MACADAMIA NUT CHIFFON PIE

4 ounces fresh macadamia nuts. If using salted nuts, rub with toweling to remove as much of the salt as possible.
1/2 cup sugar
1 package unflavored gelatin
2 tablespoons cornstarch
1/4 teaspoon salt
1 package (3-ounce) cream cheese, softened
1/4 cup sour cream
1 1/2 cups milk
2 eggs, separated
2 to 3 tablespoons dark rum
1 cup whipping cream
1 baked 10-inch pie crust

Preheat oven to 350 degrees. Chop nuts and place in single layer on baking sheet. Toast about 8 minutes or until golden brown. Set aside.

Combine sugar, gelatin, cornstarch and salt in blender. Add cream cheese and sour cream. Blend, adding milk gradually and continue blending until smooth. You may need to blend mixture in two batches to prevent overflowing.

Place mixture in top of double boiler and cook over gently boiling water until thick and smooth, stirring constantly, about 15 minutes.

Whisk some of the mixture into egg yolks and return to pan, stirring as it continues to cook for 2 to 3 minutes. Remove top of double boiler and set aside to cool slightly. Beat egg whites until stiff peaks form. Stir rum into cooled filling mixture. Fold in egg whites. Chill until thickened but not firm.

Whip cream until stiff and fold into filling with half the toasted nuts. Pour into prepared pie crust. Chill two hours or longer. Sprinkle top with remaining nuts just before serving.

MACADAMIA NUT PIE

4 eggs, slightly beaten
3/4 cup sugar
1 1/2 cups light corn syrup
1/4 teaspoon salt
1 1/2 cups Hawaiian macadamia nuts, chopped reserving 2 tablespoons for garnish
1 1/2 teaspoons vanilla
1 unbaked pie shell
1 cup heavy cream, whipped

Combine eggs, sugar, syrup, nuts, salt and vanilla. Pour into unbaked pie shell and bake at 350 degrees for about 10 minutes. Reduce temperature to 325 degrees and bake 30 minutes more. Cool and ring with whipped cream before serving. Garnish with reserved nuts.

Melting Moments

MILE HIGH PIE
(STRAWBERRY OR RASPBERRY)

CRUST:
1 1/4 cups sifted flour
1/2 cup brown sugar
3/4 cup melted butter
1/2 cup chopped pecans

Combine ingredients and put on a Teflon-lined jelly roll pan. Stir with fork during baking at 350 degrees until bubbly and crumbly, about 15 minutes. Cool until you are able to handle it. Pat into 10-inch pie pan.

FILLING:
2 egg whites, at room temperature
1 cup sugar
1 tablespoon lemon juice
1 package (10-ounce) frozen strawberries or raspberries, partially thawed.
If you use frozen raspberries, put fruit through a sieve to remove most of the seeds.
1 cup whipping cream, beaten stiff

Beat egg whites to fluffy, not even bubbly. Add berries, lemon juice and sugar. Beat at high speed for 15 minutes. Mixture will become a big fluff. Fold into whipped cream. Pour into pie shell and freeze 6 hours or overnight. Trim with whole berries, if in season.

VARIATION I

If making a raspberry pie, add 1/2 teaspoon almond extract to the whipped cream before folding into raspberry mixture. Instead of the above crust make the almond pastry shell (see index).

VARIATION II

This recipe can be made following the same directions but sprinkle 2/3 of the crumbs for shell into a 9 x 13 x 2-inch baking pan. Top mixture with remaining crumbs. Freeze as directed and cut into squares. Garnish with a whole berry.

PEACH CREAM CHEESE PIE

1 baked pie shell (9-inch)
1 jar baby food puree peaches
2 tablespoons cornstarch
3/4 cup sugar
1/2 cup water
2 tablespoons lemon juice
1 package (3-ounce) cream cheese
1/4 cup fine sugar
4 cups sliced peaches

Combine cornstarch and sugar, blend in peach puree, water and lemon juice. Bring to boil until thick and clear. Remove from heat, cool.
Beat together cream cheese and sugar until smooth. Spread evenly in pie shell. Spoon sliced peaches over cream cheese. Pour cooled puree mixture over the sliced peaches. Chill.

Melting Moments

JANE'S PUMPKIN CHIFFON PIE

3 eggs, separated
1 cup sugar
1 1/4 cups canned pumpkin
1/2 cup milk
1/2 teaspoon salt
1 1/4 teaspoons pumpkin-pie spice
1 package unflavored gelatin
1/4 cup cold water
Whipped cream (garnish)

Combine egg yolks, 1/2 cup sugar, pumpkin, milk, salt and spice. Cook in top of double boiler until thick. Soak gelatin in cold water for 5 minutes, add to pumpkin mixture which has been removed from heat. Mix and cool. When thickened, beat egg whites until foamy, then gradually add remaining 1/2 cup sugar. Beat until egg whites hold stiff peaks. Fold into pumpkin mixture. Pour into 9-inch pastry shell. Chill. Garnish with whipped cream.

FAVORITE PUMPKIN PIE

1 unbaked 10-inch pie shell
2 cups canned pumpkin
3/4 cup sugar
1/2 teaspoon salt
1/2 teaspoon ginger
1/2 teaspoon nutmeg
3 eggs
1/2 cup milk
1/4 cup bourbon
3/4 cup whipping cream
2 teaspoons apricot glaze:
    1 jar (11-ounce) apricot preserves,
    4 tablespoons apricot brandy. Combine in blender or food processor.
2/3 cup firmly packed brown sugar
3 tablespoons melted butter
1 tablespoon whipping cream
1/8 teaspoon salt
1/2 cup chopped pecans
1/2 cup pecan halves
1/2 pint heavy cream
Bourbon (garnish)

Preheat oven to 425 degrees. Combine pumpkin, sugar, 1/2 teaspoon salt, ginger, nutmeg, eggs, milk, 1/4 cup bourbon and 3/4 cup whipping cream in large bowl. Mix until well blended. Paint pastry shell with apricot glaze. Pour in pumpkin mixture. Bake for 15 minutes. Reduce heat to 350 degrees and bake 30 to 40 minutes longer or until filling has set. Test with knife inserted 1-inch from center. When it comes out clean, pie is done. Cool until lukewarm.

Combine brown sugar, melted butter, whipping cream, salt, and chopped pecans. Spread evenly on top of filling. Decorate with pecan halves. Broil 3 inches from low heat until surface begins to bubble. Watch carefully to avoid scorching. To serve, whip cream, fold in bourbon to taste and serve with warm pie.

SHERRY ALMOND PIE

4 tablespoons unflavored gelatin
5 tablespoons cold water
3 cups hot milk
1/8 teaspoon salt
8 tablespoons sugar
3 egg yolks
3/4 teaspoon almond extract
3 tablespoons sherry wine
3 egg whites
2 baked pie shells (8-inch)
1 cup heavy cream
6 teaspoons chopped salted almonds

Dissolve gelatin in cold water. Add hot milk then salt, 4 tablespoons sugar, 3 egg yolks beaten slightly. Cook in double boiler, stirring constantly until slightly thickened. Remove from heat. Add almond extract and wine. Cool. Beat egg whites. Add remaining sugar gradually, beating constantly. Pour into custard mixture. Pour into pie shells. Chill. Top with whipped cream. Make grooves in cream and fill with salted almonds.

HOLIDAY PUMPKIN — PECAN PIE

1 unbaked 9-inch pastry shell
2 eggs
3/4 cup brown sugar, firmly packed
1 can (1-pound) pumpkin
1/2 teaspoon salt
1 teaspoon ground cinnamon
1/2 teaspoon ground ginger
1/4 teaspoon ground cloves
1/2 teaspoon ground nutmeg
1 can (14 1/2-ounce) evaporated milk
1/2 cup coarsely chopped pecans
1/2 cup brown sugar, firmly packed
2 tablespoons softened butter or margarine

Heat oven to 425 degrees. Prepare crust according to a favorite recipe. Beat eggs slightly in large bowl. Add 3/4 cup brown sugar, pumpkin, salt, and spices, mix well. Stir in evaporated milk.

Pour mixture into pastry shell, bake 15 minutes. Reduce oven heat to 375 degrees. Bake 30 minutes longer or until blade comes out clean when inserted 1 inch from center of pie. Cool completely on wire rack.

Combine brown sugar, nuts and butter, mix well. Spread gently over cooled pie. Be careful all custard is covered. Place under broiler, 5 inches below heat, for 3 minutes or until mixture begins to bubble. If overcooked, top will burn and become syrupy. Cool.

STRAWBERRY CREAM PIE

1/2 cup sugar
1/4 cup cornstarch
1/4 teaspoon salt
1 3/4 cups milk
2 egg yolks, slightly beaten
1 teaspoon vanilla
1/2 pint heavy cream, whipped
1 baked (9-inch) pastry shell
1 pint strawberries
Strawberry Glaze

Stir together sugar, cornstarch and salt in a 2-quart saucepan. Gradually stir in milk until smooth. Stir in egg yolks. Stirring constantly, bring to boil over medium-low heat and boil 1 minute. Remove from heat; stir in vanilla. Cover pan with waxed paper. Refrigerate until cool. Fold in whipped cream until well blended. Spoon into pastry shell. Refrigerate 1 hour. Garnish with sliced strawberries and spoon Strawberry Glaze over strawberries. Serves 8.

STRAWBERRY GLAZE:
1/2 cup fresh strawberries, mashed
1 1/2 teaspoons cornstarch
2 tablespoons sugar
1/2 cup water

In small pan stir together cornstarch and sugar. Gradually stir in water until smooth. Stir in mashed strawberries, stirring constantly. Bring to a boil over medium heat and boil 1 minute. Cool. Makes 3/4 cup.

Sauces

CHANTILLY CREAM

1 cup heavy cream
2 tablespoons powdered sugar

In small bowl, mix cream and sugar. Refrigerate until well chilled. Beat until stiff. Serve with cold souffles or fresh fruit. Makes 2 cups.

Melting Moments

CREME de NOYAUX SAUCE
(CREAM OF ALMOND)

1 1/2 cups whipping cream
1/2 cup powdered sugar
2 tablespoons Creme de Noyaux or Cream of Almond liqueur

Whip cream to soft peaks in a large bowl. Blend in powdered sugar; mix liqueur into the mixture. Delicious over fruits and/or pound cake.
Makes 2 cups.

CREME ANGLAISE

1 cup heavy cream
1 cup milk
4 egg yolks, room temperature
1/3 cup sugar
2 tablespoons Cointreau, cognac or rum (optional)
1 teaspoon vanilla
1 teaspoon finely grated lemon or lime zest

Scald cream and milk in small heavy saucepan over medium heat; remove from heat. Whisk egg yolks and sugar in top of double boiler until thickened and pale yellow; gradually stir in hot cream mixture in thin steady stream. Cook custard mixture over simmering water, stirring constantly, until it reaches 170 degrees on candy thermometer, about 10 minutes. Mixture should be thickened enough to coat a spoon. Remove from heat; stir in liquor and vanilla. Blend well. Cool to room temperature, stirring occasionally. Cover and chill 4 to 6 hours before serving. Custard will thicken as it cools. Stir in lemon or lime zest to taste just before serving. Makes 2 cups.

APRICOT — WALNUT SAUCE

1 1/2 cups apricot jam
1/2 cup water
1 tablespoon sugar
1 teaspoon grated orange rind
2 tablespoons rum
1/2 cup chopped walnuts

Combine the apricot jam, water, sugar and orange rind in a heavy saucepan. Bring to a boil and simmer for 5 minutes, stirring constantly. Remove from heat and stir in the rum. If you want a smooth sauce, you can sieve it at this point. Stir in the walnuts.
Bake a box of gingerbread mix. Spoon the sauce over the warm gingerbread. Makes 2 cups.

WARM BOURBON SAUCE

1 1/2 cups dark corn syrup
3/4 cup sugar
3/4 cup firmly packed brown sugar
2/3 cup evaporated milk
3 tablespoons corn oil
Dash of salt
1/4 to 1/3 cup bourbon

Combine ingredients except bourbon in medium saucepan and mix well. Place over medium heat and stir constantly until mixture comes to a boil. Let boil, stirring occasionally, for 5 minutes. (Milk will look curdled.) Remove from heat and let cool 15 minutes. Transfer to blender, add bourbon and mix until smooth. Reheat before serving. Sauce will keep for one month in refrigerator. Makes 4 cups.
Note: This sauce is very good served over Chocolate Cake Roll or Sour Cream Pound Cake.

Melting Moments

ENGLISH CUSTARD SAUCE

1/3 cup sugar
1 tablespoon cornstarch
2 cups milk
2 tablespoons butter or margarine
6 egg yolks
1 1/2 teaspoons vanilla extract
1/2 cup heavy cream

Combine sugar and cornstarch in medium saucepan. Gradually add milk, stirring until smooth; add the butter. Cook over medium heat, stirring constantly, until mixture is thickened and comes to a boil. Boil 1 minute. Remove from heat.

In another bowl slightly beat egg yolks. Gradually add a little of the hot mixture, beating well. Stir into rest of the hot mixture; cook over medium heat, stirring constantly, just until mixture boils. Remove from heat; stir in vanilla.

Strain custard into bowl. Refrigerate, covered, until cool. Stir in heavy cream. Return to refrigerator until well chilled. Makes 2 1/2 cups.

1-2-3 FUDGE SAUCE

1 can (14 1/2-ounce) evaporated milk
2 cups sugar
3 squares unsweetened baking chocolate

Melt in top of double boiler. Cook and stir with whisk until it starts to thicken. Sauce can be served warm or stored in the refrigerator and used cold. Makes 3 cups

MINCEMEAT TOPPING FOR ICE CREAM

1 16-ounce jar mincemeat
1/2 cup sherry

Combine mincemeat and sherry. Cook mixture until it bubbles. Makes 2 1/2 cups.

PRALINE CRUNCH ICE CREAM TOPPING

1/2 cup butter
1 cup brown sugar, firmly packed
1/2 cup chopped pecans
2 1/4 cups crushed cornflakes

Place butter and sugar in saucepan and bring to a boil. Boil for just 2 minutes. Add the nuts and cornflakes and toss with a fork to coat with the syrup. Cool and serve on ice cream. Makes 2 cups.

RASPBERRY SAUCE

1 tablespoon cornstarch
1/4 cup butter or margarine
1 cup sugar
1 cup raspberries, crushed
1/2 teaspoon fresh lemon juice

Combine cornstarch with 1 tablespoon cold water; stir to make a smooth paste. Melt butter or margarine in saucepan. Stir in sugar, raspberries and cornstarch mixture; bring to a boil, stirring constantly. Boil 1 minute. Remove from heat; stir in lemon juice; cool. Makes 1 1/2 cups.

RASPBERRY SAUCE FOR COLD SOUFFLES

2 packages frozen raspberries
2 tablespoons Cointreau

Thaw raspberries and puree in blender until smooth. Strain through a sieve and add Cointreau. Chill. Makes 1 cup.

Melting Moments

SABAYON SAUCE

4 egg yolks
2 tablespoons sugar
1/4 cup Grand Marnier
1/3 cup heavy cream, whipped

In top of double boiler, beat egg yolks until thick with electric mixer at medium speed. Gradually beat in sugar, beating until mixture is light and forms soft peaks. Place double boiler top over simmering water, making sure the water in the bottom is not touching the base of the top. Slowly beat in the Grand Marnier; continue beating until mixture is fluffy and mounds, about 5 minutes. Remove top of double boiler from hot water; set in ice water. Beat until the custard mixture is cool. Gently fold in the whipped cream. Cover the sauce and refrigerate until serving time. Serve over 1 quart of fresh strawberries or fresh raspberries or 3 packages (10-ounce size) frozen berries. Makes 1/2 cup.

GLAZED STRAWBERRIES

1 package (10-ounce) frozen raspberries, thawed
1 tablespoon cornstarch
2 tablespoons brandy
2 pints strawberries, hulled

Drain raspberries, reserving liquid. Combine cornstarch and raspberry liquid until smooth in saucepan. Bring to boil, stirring constantly, and boil 1 minute. Remove from heat; stir in brandy. Pour over strawberries; toss to coat well. Cover. Refrigerate until chilled. Serves 4-6.

WINE SAUCE FOR COLD SOUFFLES

1/2 cup sugar
1 tablespoon cornstarch
1/2 cup water
2 tablespoons fresh lemon juice
1 teaspoon freshly grated lemon rind
2 tablespoons butter
1/2 cup dry white wine

Combine the sugar and cornstarch in a small saucepan. Stir in water, lemon juice and lemon rind until smooth. Add butter. Bring to a boil, lower heat and cook until thickened. Remove from heat. Add wine, stirring constantly. Chill. Makes 1 1/2 cups.

Heirlooms · Recipes from the Past

This chapter is rich with treasures from the past and family heirlooms passed from generation to generation. We hope you'll try our favorites, like Aunt Tottie's Icebox Rolls and the recipe for Kolaces. With all the gourmet candies in the marketplace today, the Innes Fudge still ranks among the best. And if you haven't had Peanut Butter Syrup on your pancakes or waffles, try our recipe.

GRANNY, WHAT WAS IT LIKE WHEN MUMMY WAS LIKE ME?

RECIPE FOR A GOOD DAY

"A huge measure of faith. An equal portion of work. A full cup of courage. One small can of patience. A constant sprinkling of prayer. A level teaspoon of meditation. A pinch each of fun, good humor, and cheerfulness. Two heaping tablespoons of compromise. A dash of quietness.

And love enough to tie all together to the consistency of firm serenity. The preparation time is 24 hours. Cooking time is daily. Set the fire low, steady, and consistent.

This recipe can be prepared with equal ease for 10 persons, or 2, or everyone you meet and invite to your house. And it may be served with a variety of side dishes to heighten its flavor and durability."

FISHHOUSE PUNCH

36 lemons, halved
4 gallons water
6 cups sugar
1 fifth dark rum
1 fifth bourbon
1 fifth peach brandy

Place halved lemons, water and sugar in large pot and bring to boil. Reduce heat and simmer until liquid is diminished by half. Remove lemons and discard. Add rum, bourbon and peach brandy. Garnish with lemon slices and chill for a day. The longer it chills, the better it gets.

DADDY'S SUMMER COOLER

Into a 16-ounce glass pour:
1 1/2 ounce vodka
1/2 lime, well squeezed, drop rind into glass
1 to 3 tablespoons orange juice concentrate, to taste
1 cup 7-Up or Sprite
Large sprig of fresh mint. Twist mint to crush leaves and stems a bit to release flavor.
Lots of crushed ice

Jo says, "It is almost a necessity to play 18 holes of golf on a hot day to fully appreciate the Cooler. This is THE traditional drink of my family in the summer months. Memories flood my mind as I picture my Daddy coming in off the course, wiping his brow as he made his Cooler on the way to the shower.

It has held the place of honor at holidays and birthdays, backyard parties and just 'you and me' times. Funny though, they never taste the same as when Daddy made them."
Note: The heavier the glass the better.

AUNT GINA'S CHEESE BALLS

4 cups shredded Cheddar cheese
2 sticks butter
2 cups flour
2 teaspoons dry mustard
1/2 teaspoon Worcestershire sauce
Few dashes Tabasco sauce
1 teaspoon chili powder

Set Cheddar cheese and butter out at room temperature until soft enough to blend on mixer. Add remaining ingredients. Chill in refrigerator for at least 1 hour. Roll into 1-inch balls and bake at 400 degrees for 12 to 15 minutes. These can be frozen.

Jo says, "These will flatten out to wafer size while baking, so don't panic, you've done them correctly."

❖◆❖

FRUIT FRENCH DRESSING

1/3 cup sugar
1 teaspoon salt
1 teaspoon paprika
Juice of 1 orange
Juice of 1 lemon
1 tablespoon vinegar
1 cup salad oil
1 teaspoon grated onion

Combine ingredients in bottle or jar; cover and shake thoroughly. Makes 1 3/4 cups.

MOTHER'S THICK OIL DRESSING

2 egg yolks
2 cups Wesson oil
Juice of 1 large lemon
3/4 teaspoon salt

Make sure the mixing bowl and beaters are ice cold. Beat the egg yolks until smooth. Add the Wesson oil very, very slowly, beating well until all blended. Add lemon juice and salt. Refrigerate.

Jan says, "Memories, memories. This dressing is delicious on a wedge of lettuce or for sandwiches." Makes 2 1/2 cups.

MOM'S TOMATO ASPIC

1 tablespoon gelatin
2 tablespoons cold water
2 tablespoons boiling water
1 can (10 1/2-ounce) tomato soup
2 cups tomato juice
1 package (3 1/2-ounce) lemon gelatin
1/8 teaspoon salt

Soak gelatin in cold water. Dissolve it in boiling water. Add tomato soup. Heat tomato juice and dissolve it in the package of lemon gelatin. Combine the 2 mixtures and add salt. Pour into greased mold and chill. Serves 8.

STEWED APPLES

2 pounds apples
2 tablespoons butter
1/2 cup sugar
1/2 cup water
1/2 cup white wine
1 small piece lemon peel
1 tablespoon lemon juice

Wash apples; peel and core. Cut into thick slices. Saute in butter 2 or 3 minutes. Sprinkle with sugar. Add water, wine, lemon peel, and lemon juice. Cover; cook slowly until apples are tender. Serves 4.

HONEY CARROTS

10 to 12 small carrots
3 tablespoons butter or margarine
1 tablespoon brown sugar
2 tablespoons honey
2 tablespoons finely chopped parsley or
  fresh mint

Cook carrots in small amount boiling, salted water 15 minutes or until tender. Melt butter; add sugar, honey, and carrots. Cook over low heat, turning until well glazed. Sprinkle with chopped parsley or mint. Makes 4-6 servings.

DADDY'S JATERNICE
(Bohemian Pork-Liver Sausage)

3 1/2 or more pounds pork shoulder
  (Boston Butt)
2 or 3 pork hearts
1 pork liver (2 pounds or more)
2 or 3 pork ears (optional)
1 loaf bread
3 tablespoons salt (more or less to taste)
1 tablespoon pepper (to taste)
6 cloves garlic
1 tablespoon allspice
1 tablespoon ginger
1 tablespoon ground cloves

Cut pork in pieces, split hearts and place in cooking vessel, with ears, using part of salt and pepper and cover with water. Bring to boil and cook over low heat about an hour, then add liver and cook until done. Add water while cooking if necessary. (Reserve broth.)

Let cool for handling. Grind meat and have bread dried and ground. Mix meat, seasonings, bread crumbs, minced garlic and broth to consistency desired. Place in loaf pans and refrigerate or freeze. To serve, cut meat in strips and heat in oven until warmed to desired heat.

If stuffing, casings can be purchased at some meat markets. The mixture must be of thinner consistency. Garlic quantity should be according to taste of maker and/or users. Likewise with salt and pepper.

Note: Bones in pork should be removed before grinding. Hearts, liver and ears to be ground as they are. All meat products to be inspected and cleaned before cooking. Makes 10 pounds.

Jo says, "I've helped my Daddy make this sausage many times never with a recipe. The last time he made it I finally stayed right by his side until completion and got these ingredients."

AUNTIE K'S SCALLOPED OYSTERS 1940's

1 quart oysters
1/2 cup melted butter
2 cups cracker crumbs
1 tablespoon lemon juice
1/2 cup cream
2 tablespoons sherry
1 tablespoon Worcestershire sauce
1/4 teaspoon Tabasco sauce
1/4 teaspoon salt
1/4 teaspoon pepper

Drain liquid from oysters, reserving 1/4 cup liquid. Set aside. Wash oysters. Butter a shallow 2-quart baking dish. Cover bottom with crumbs, put in half of oysters, pour half of melted butter and lemon juice over them. Add another layer of crumbs, then remaining oysters and butter. Sprinkle with salt and pepper. Cover top with crumbs. Then strain 1/4 cup oyster liquid and add to 1/2 cup cream, sherry, Worcestershire and Tabasco. Heat and pour over oysters. Bake for 20 minutes at 425 degrees. Serves 10.

❖❖❖

DADDY'S SPICY SAUCE FOR SEAFOOD

1/2 cup chili sauce
1/2 cup catsup
3 tablespoons lemon juice
1 tablespoon horseradish
1 tablespoon mayonnaise
1 teaspoon Worcestershire sauce
1 teaspoon grated onion
1 tablespoon finely diced celery
1/4 teaspoon salt
3 drops Tabasco sauce
Dash of pepper

Combine all ingredients and chill.
Makes 1 1/2 cups.

DENVER BISCUITS

2 cups scalded milk
1/2 cup solid vegetable shortening
1/2 teaspoon salt
2 tablespoons sugar
2 packages yeast
1/4 cup water
Flour
2 teaspoons baking powder
1/2 teaspoon salt

Dissolve yeast in water. Combine and add first 4 ingredients to yeast. Add flour to make mixture like a cake mixture. Allow to rise double its bulk. Then add 2 teaspoons baking powder, 1/2 teaspoon soda. Also enough flour to hold together. The less flour the lighter they will be.

Roll on floured board. Cut with biscuit cutter. Allow to rise again double its size. Bake in 375 to 400-degree oven, 10 to 12 minutes according to how brown one likes them. Makes 20-24.

MRS. LANDRETH'S BOSTON BROWN BREAD 1940

2 cups graham flour
1 cup white flour
2 cups sour milk
2 level teaspoons soda
1/2 cup molasses
1/4 cup white sugar
1/2 cup raisins
1/2 cup nuts
1 teaspoon salt

Mix dry ingredients, except soda, with nuts and raisins. Use enough white flour to coat raisins and nuts. Mix sour milk and molasses with soda; then stir in gradually the dry ingredients.

Put into 3 1-pound coffee cans with covers, and allow to stand for 1 hour in warm place. Leave lids on and bake 45 minutes in moderate oven.

Note: Because today's coffee cans have plastic lids, you will need to cover the cans with heavy aluminum foil before baking.

JOSA'S SPOON BREAD

1 1/2 cups cornmeal
1 pint milk
2 teaspoons baking powder
3 eggs, separated
1 teaspoon salt

Scald meal with enough boiling water to wet without becoming soft. Let cool, then add 1 teaspoon salt and the milk a little at a time. Beat yolks until creamy, the whites until stiff. First add the yolks, then the baking powder and lastly, the egg whites. Pour in a buttered baking dish. Set in pan of hot water to bake at 375 degrees for 1 hour, 10 minutes or until done. Serves 6-8.

Heirlooms

KOLACES 1930
(A Bohemian Christmas Tradition)

1 teaspoon compressed yeast
1 tablespoon sugar
2 tablespoons flour
2 tablespoons lukewarm milk
4 cups flour
1/4 cup sugar
1 teaspoon salt
1 cup lukewarm milk
1/4 cup butter, melted
1 egg
1/2 teaspoon grated lemon peel
1 teaspoon vanilla

PRUNE MIXTURE FOR KOLACE:
Cook and cool 2 pounds prunes. Seed and mash with potato masher. Add sugar, cinnamon, ground cloves and nutmeg to taste. Add enough prune juice to make a thick mixture.

Jo says, "Apricot puree is also delicious. Mom always used prunes."

GINGERBREAD:
Bake one package gingerbread mix. Cool and crumble. Do not use top or bottom crust. Sprinkle on top of prune mixture.

Place yeast in a bowl, sprinkle with sugar and stir until mixture liquefies. Add 2 tablespoons flour and 2 tablespoons milk; blend. Cover with a cloth and let rise in a warm place for 5 to 10 minutes. Add all other ingredients; mix well with a wooden spoon. Remove dough from bowl, knead on floured pastry board until smooth and does not stick. Return to bowl, sprinkle with flour, and cover with cloth. Let rise in a warm place 30 to 60 minutes or until almost doubled.

Punch down, form into small balls. Roll balls into flat rounds about 3 inches across by 1/2 to 3/4-inch thick. Let rise a short time. Bake in 350 degree oven until lightly brown. Remove from oven and brush with melted butter. Cover with prune mixture and top with crumbled gingerbread and sprinkle with melted butter. Top with whipped cream. Makes 24.

Jo says, "Kolaces are well locked in my memories of childhood on Christmas Eve. Mother would prepare the dough in advance and Christmas Eve afternoon would roll out and bake the Kolaces for our annual Christmas Eve buffet.

We are still having Christmas Eve celebrations and never without Kolaces. If we are lucky, there will be some left for Christmas morning to eat while opening packages or for nibbling while the turkey is being stuffed."

AUNT TOTTIE'S ICE BOX ROLLS

1 quart milk, lightly scalded
1 cup shortening, melted
1 cake yeast
1/2 cup lukewarm water
1 cup sugar
1 cup mashed potatoes
Salt
10-12 cups flour
2 teaspoons baking powder
1 teaspoon soda

Mix shortening with milk and cool. Dissolve 1 cake yeast in 1/2 cup lukewarm water. When milk is cool, add 1 cup sugar and 1 cup mashed potatoes and salt to taste. Add yeast to this mixture. Add 1 sifter of flour, 2 teaspoons baking powder and 1 teaspoon soda. Beat well and add flour to make dough. Stir until all flour is moistened. Cover and refrigerate.

When ready to use, pinch off desired amount, form into shapes, let rise and bake at 400 degrees for 15 minutes. Makes 8 dozen.

Ever essay ("try" is what I mean) popovers? Or do yours pop under? Always use general purpose flour, and try salad oil for shortening. Best cook in the world let me in on that last item.

AUNTIE K'S ORANGE BREAD 1930

1 egg
1 cup sugar
2 tablespoons melted butter
1 cup milk
2 1/3 cups flour
1/2 teaspoon salt
3 1/2 teaspoons baking powder
1 cup Candied Orange Peel (recipe below)

Beat egg well and add sugar. Add melted butter. Sift flour, salt, baking powder together and add alternately with milk, saving about 1/4 of the flour mixture. Add orange peel to the 1/4 flour mixture so peel is well-floured and add to other ingredients. Beat well. Bake 1 1/2 hours at 350 degrees on second oven rack. Roll in towel when first cool. Makes 1 loaf.

CANDIED ORANGE PEEL

1 1/2 cups cut-up peel
1 1/4 cups sugar
1/4 to 1/3 cup water

Soak 4 orange halves in cold water overnight or all day. Take out pulp. Place in cold water and cook until tender. Cut in tiny pieces. Cook until there is not much moisture left.

WAFFLES

2 cups flour
1 tablespoon sugar
1/2 teaspoon salt
4 level teaspoons baking powder
2 eggs, separated
1 1/4 cups milk
1/4 cup melted butter

Sift dry ingredients together. Beat egg yolks. Add 1 1/4 cups milk to egg yolks and mix. Add to flour mixture. Add 1/4 cup melted butter. Beat whites and fold in mixture. Cook immediately. Serves 8.

HOE CAKES

1 cup flour
2 tablespoons sugar
2 tablespoons baking powder
1 teaspoon salt
2 cups corn meal
2 eggs
1 cup milk
1/4 cup corn oil
1 can (16 ounces) yellow creamed corn

Sift flour, sugar, baking powder and salt. Add other ingredients. Drop by tablespoons on preheated electric griddle. Makes 20.

JOSEPHINE GAMBRILL'S BANANA CAKE 1930

2 cups flour
3 teaspoons baking powder
1/4 teaspoon salt
1/2 cup butter
1 cup sugar
2 eggs (whole)
3/4 cup milk
1 teaspoon vanilla
1 cup mashed bananas

Mix well. Bake at 375 degrees for 30 to 35 minutes in layer pans or 350 degrees for 50 minutes in loaf pan.

Heirlooms

LAVERNA'S SPICY CHOCOLATE CAKE

3/4 cup shortening
1 1/2 cups sugar
3 eggs
1 3/4 cups flour
3/4 cup sour milk or buttermilk
1/2 teaspoon salt
2 tablespoons cocoa
1 teaspoon cinnamon
1/2 teaspoon soda
1/2 teaspoon baking powder
3/4 teaspoon nutmeg
1 teaspoon vanilla
1/2 cup toasted nuts (almonds, pecans, hazelnuts)

Cream shortening and sugar. Add eggs, add sifted dry ingredients alternately with milk. Add vanilla and nuts. Pour into greased and floured 8-inch layer pans or loaf pan. Bake in 350-degree oven for 30 to 35 minutes or until toothpick inserted in center comes out clean. When cool, frost with caramel or fudge frosting. Serves 6.

AUNT MARIE'S CHOCOLATE CAKE 1920's

2 cups brown sugar
1/2 cup butter
Add:
1 beaten egg
2 1/2 cups flour
3/4 cup buttermilk
1 cake chocolate, melted
3/4 cup cold water
1 teaspoon soda
1 teaspoon vanilla

Blend well. Pour into greased and floured loaf pan. Place in cold oven and bake at 350 degrees 35 to 40 minutes. Serves 10-12.

MRS. BUTLER'S CUP CAKES 1930's

1/2 cup butter
1 cup sugar
2 egg yolks
1/2 cup sweet milk
1/4 teaspoon soda
2 egg whites
1/2 teaspoon cream of tartar
1 3/4 cup cake flour, sift before measuring
1/2 teaspoon vanilla

Cream shortening, add sugar gradually, beat until light. Add beaten egg yolks. Sift dry ingredients together, add alternately with milk. Add vanilla. Fold in stiffly beaten egg whites and bake at 325 degrees for 20 to 25 minutes.
Makes 12-15 cupcakes.

MOTHER'S CALVIN COOLIDGE SOUR CREAM CAKE

7/8 cup sugar
1 cup heavy sour cream
1 cup flour, rounded
2 eggs
1 teaspoon baking powder
1/2 teaspoon soda
1 teaspoon vanilla

Put all ingredients in bowl. Beat 2 minutes. Bake in a 9 x 9-inch pan for 20 to 25 minutes at 350 degrees.
Ruby says, "Makes lovely tea cakes. If making for gals, omit vanilla and use 1/2 teaspoon almond flavoring." Serves 8.

❖❖

MOM'S WHITE FRUIT CAKE 1930's

4 cups cake flour
1 teaspoon baking powder
1/2 teaspoon soda
1/2 teaspoon salt
1/2 pound each: crystallized orange peel,
    lemon peel, pineapple and red cherries,
    finely cut
1 pound raisins
1/2 pound citron, finely cut
1 pound blanched almonds, finely cut
1 cup butter
1 1/2 cups sugar
1 tablespoon lemon juice
10 egg whites, stiffly beaten

Sift flour once, measure, add baking powder, soda and salt and sift together three times. Sift one cup flour mixture over fruit and nuts. Mix well.

Cream shortening, add sugar gradually and cream until light and fluffy. Add remaining flour mixture to creamed mixture, a small amount at a time. Beat after each addition until smooth. Add lemon juice, fruits and nuts. Fold in egg whites.

Pour into paper lined tube pan or bread pans 2 x 2 3/4 x 4 1/2 inches. Bake in slow oven (250 degrees) for 2 1/2 hours. Then increase to 300 degrees for 15 minutes. Makes 6 pounds of fruit cake.

Jo says, "Mom made these cakes before she was married, while she was still a career girl. She took orders for them during the holidays."

LITTLE GRANDMA'S GRAHAM GEMS 1885

1 egg, beat with fork
1/4 cup cooking oil
1 cup sour milk
1 teaspoon salt
1 cup flour
1 cup graham flour
1/4 cup sugar
2 teaspoons baking powder
1/2 teaspoon soda

Combine all ingredients. Bake in greased gem pan until center is done. Toothpick inserted in center will come out clean.

Note: Really need an old-fashioned cast-iron gem pan. They are different from muffin pans.

Makes 12.

GINGERBREAD

1 cup brown sugar
2 eggs, well beaten
3/4 cup melted shortening
3/4 cup molasses
3 cups flour
1 teaspoon baking soda
1/4 teaspoon salt
1 teaspoon ginger
1/2 teaspoon cloves
1 teaspoon cinnamon
1 cup sour milk

Combine sugar, eggs, shortening, and molasses. Sift flour. Measure and sift with baking soda, salt, and spices. Add flour mixture alternately with milk. Beat until well blended. Pour into well-oiled 9 x 13-inch pan. Bake in 375-degree oven for 40 to 45 minutes. Serves 8-10.

HOLIDAY COOKIES

1 cup margarine
1/2 cup brown sugar
1/2 cup white sugar
2 3/4 cups flour
1 egg
2 tablespoons orange juice
1 tablespoon orange rind
1/4 teaspoon salt
1/4 teaspoon soda
1/2 cup pecan meats

Cream shortening, add sugar gradually. Add beaten egg, orange juice and rind. Sift flour, salt, and soda together. Add, with nuts, to creamed mixture. Form into rolls. Wrap in wax paper and store in refrigerator. Slice thin. Bake at 375 degrees for 12 to 15 minutes on a greased cookie sheet. Makes 7 dozen.

Ruby says, "You may use this recipe for cut-out cookies."

HONEY DATE STICKS

1 cup sifted flour
1 1/2 teaspoons baking powder
1/4 teaspoon salt
1/4 cup melted butter or salad oil
1 cup honey
1 cup finely cut dates
1 cup chopped walnuts
3 eggs
Powdered sugar

Sift together dry ingredients, except powdered sugar, adding dates and walnuts. Set aside. Beat eggs until lemon color. Add butter and honey to egg mixture, mixing well. Blend into the dry ingredients.

Pour into greased 8 x 8 x 1-inch pan. Bake at 350 degrees for 40 minutes. Cool slightly and cut into 1 x 3-inch strips. Remove with spatula and roll in powdered sugar. Makes 18 sticks.

GRANDMOTHER'S JELLY ROLL 1900

5 eggs
1 cup sugar
1 cup flour
2 teaspoons baking powder
Pinch salt
Lemon extract, to taste
1 cup raspberry preserves, or your choice of
    preserves or jelly
Confectioners' sugar

Combine all ingredients except preserves and confectioners' sugar. Prepare 15 1/2 x 10 1/2 x 1-inch jelly roll pan by greasing, then line bottom of pan with waxed paper.

Pour batter into pan and bake at 400 degrees for 9 minutes or just until surface springs back when gently pressed with fingertip. While cake is baking, sift confectioners' sugar on a clean tea towel, forming a 15 x 10-inch rectangle.

Invert baked cake on sugar, gently peel off waxed paper.

Starting with narrow end, roll up cake, towel and all; place seam side down on wire rack to cool, about 20 minutes.

Gently unroll cake, remove towel. Spread with preserves, roll up again. Place seam side down on serving plate; let stand, covered, at least 1 hour before serving.

To serve; sift confectioners' sugar over top, slice on diagonal. Serve with sweetened whipped cream if desired. Serves 16.

GRANDMOTHER'S DATE-NUT BREAD 1923

1 cup dates, sliced
1/2 cup nuts
1 cup sugar
1 egg
1 tablespoon butter
2 cups flour, sifted
1/2 teaspoon salt
1 teaspoon cinnamon
1 teaspoon soda
1 cup boiling water

Cream butter and sugar. Add egg and beat. Add salt, soda and cinnamon to flour. Add dates and nuts to sugar-butter-egg mixture. Combine two mixtures. Add 1 cup boiling water over all. Stir until you cannot see flour. Pour into greased, wax-paper-lined loaf pan. Bake at 350 degrees for 1 hour.

AUNTIE K'S CUP CAKES 1938

3/4 stick butter
1 cup sugar
2 eggs, separated
2 cups cake flour
1/2 cup milk
2 teaspoons baking powder
3/4 teaspoon vanilla
1/2 teaspoon lemon extract

Cream butter and sugar, add egg yolks and cream well. Add dry ingredients alternately with milk. Beat egg whites and fold into mixture, add vanilla and lemon extract.

Bake at 325 degrees for 20 to 25 minutes. Frost with choice of frosting. Makes 16 cup cakes.

LEMON FLUFF

Beat 2 egg yolks until thick. Put in top of double boiler. Add the juice of 1 lemon, 2 tablespoons hot water, 2/3 cup confectioners' sugar and the rind of 1 lemon. Cook over hot water, stirring constantly for the very few minutes it takes to thicken. Remove from heat. Fold in egg whites, beaten stiff. Pour into bowl and chill. Serve alone or on raspberries or other fresh fruit. Serves 2.

AUNT JESSIE'S LEMON PIE

1 cup sugar, scant
3/4 cup water
2 tablespoons flour
Grated peel of 1 lemon
Juice of 1 lemon
2 egg yolks, beaten

Mix sugar, water, flour and lemon peel in saucepan and place over low flame. Cook for 5 minutes or until mixture is well dissolved and soft. Remove from heat. Beat egg yolks and lemon juice well and add to saucepan mixture. Put back on stove and cook until thick. Cool and pour into pie crust topped with meringue (see index). Serves 6.

❖◆◇◆❖

AUNT JESSIE'S LIEB KUCHEN COOKIES

1/2 gallon molasses
3/4 pound lard
1 1/2 cups buttermilk
1/2 cup cinnamon
2 teaspoons cloves
2 teaspoons allspice
2 tablespoons soda
1/2 to 3/4 pound chopped pecans
16 to 20 cups flour

Mix warm molasses. Add lard. When melted, add flour (which is sifted with the spices and soda) and buttermilk. Add nuts that have been mixed with flour before the dough becomes to stiff. Roll to desired thickness. Cut with cookie cutter. Bake 12-14 minutes at 350 degrees.

*Add the spices to several cups of flour and sift to promote even distribution. Ice with boiled white icing. Sprinkle with red and green sugar. Store tight in containers. Makes 10 dozen.

Jan says, "Aunt Jessie made these cookies every Christmas, even when she was in her 90's."

ICING

3 tablespoons hot water
1 cup powdered sugar
1 egg white
1/4 teaspoon cream of tartar
1/8 teaspoon salt

Stir sugar in hot water and boil until sugar dissolves. In small mixing bowl beat 1 egg white, 1/4 teaspoon cream of tartar, 1/8 teaspoon salt. Add syrup gradually. Beat on high speed until right consistency.

Jan says, "I am sure Aunt Jessie had the syrup to a slow string when tested."

MINCEMEAT CAKE   1930

1/2 cup shortening
1 cup sugar
2 eggs
1 package of 1 1/3 cups mincemeat
1 heaping teaspoon soda dissolved in 1 cup
   coffee
1 teaspoon cloves
1 teaspoon cinnamon
1 teaspoon nutmeg
2 cups flour
1 cup English walnuts

Mix in order given. Bake 1 hour 15 minutes at 325 degrees in greased loaf pan.

THREE-MINUTE FROSTING

1 egg white
3 tablespoons water
1 cup sugar
2 tablespoons white Karo

Mix top three ingredients carefully. Place over boiling water. Cook 3 minutes, stirring constantly to keep the grains from sides of the pan. Remove from heat and add 2 tablespoons white Karo. Beat until stiff. Frosts 1 large cake.

SEVEN-MINUTE FROSTING

1 egg white
1 cup sugar
1/4 cup water
1/2 teaspoon vanilla

Put egg white, sugar and water into top of double boiler. Blend with rotary beater. Have water boiling rapidly in bottom of double boiler but water should not touch top part. Place top part over boiling water. Beat constantly with rotary beater for about 7 minutes. If an electric mixer is used, it takes about 3 minutes. Remove from water, add vanilla and continue beating until lukewarm. Frosts 3 small or 1 large cake.

ORANGE CREAM FROSTING

3 cups powdered sugar
1/4 teaspoon salt
3 tablespoons margarine
1 egg yolk
3 teaspoons grated orange rind or peel
3 tablespoons orange juice
1/2 cup whipping cream

Cream 1/2 cup sugar and salt with margarine. Add egg yolk beating well. Add grated peel. Add rest of sugar and juice alternately. Whip 1/2 cup of cream and fold in above mixture.
Ruby says, "This will frost a two layer cake. Yum! Yum!"

ETHEL'S STRAWBERRY MARLO

18 marshmallows
1/4 cup milk
2 tablespoons orange juice
1 cup heavy cream, whipped
3 cups strawberries, mashed

Melt marshmallows in milk in top of a double boiler. Cool. Add orange juice and whipped cream to cooled marshmallows. Add mashed strawberries. Pour into 9-inch pie pan or ice tray. Freeze.
Jo says, "You can substitute peaches or raspberries for the strawberries." Serves 6.

AUNT MARTHA'S RED CINNAMON APPLES

2 cups sugar
2 cups water
1 stick of cinnamon
6 apples, whole or pared
1/2 teaspoon red food coloring, if desired

In a heavy saucepan put sugar, water and cinnamon stick and bring to a boil. Add apples and boil slowly until tender. If not red enough, add food coloring. Set out on wax paper to set.
Makes 6 apples

GLAZED APRICOTS

Drain 2 cans (16 ounces each) whole unpeeled apricots. Put them in a skillet with 1/2 cup granulated sugar, 1/2 cup brown sugar, 1/2 cup of the apricot syrup and 1/4 cup butter or margarine. Cook over moderate heat, turning the apricots often with a spoon. When well glazed, drain; serve hot with chicken. Serves 6.

Heirlooms

INNES FUDGE

1 egg, beat white stiff
Add yolk and beat well.
Add 3 teaspoons of heavy cream and
3 cups powdered sugar.
Beat well.
Melt 3 squares bitter chocolate and
3 tablespoons butter together.
Add to first mixture. Then add 1 cup
   nut meats and 1 teaspoon vanilla.
Drop on oil paper. Let set.

Jan says, "I found this priceless recipe among my mother's recipes. I copied it as such for the recipe is old. A very good fudge to make these days for it is economical." Makes 12-15 pieces.

GREAT GRANDMOTHER'S MINCEMEAT

6 pounds neck meat
Seed and cut four pounds raisins
Wash and dry four pounds currants
Slice thin a pound of citron
Chop fine four quarts good tart cooking
   apples
Put into a large pan together, add:
2 ounces cinnamon (2 tablespoons = 1 ounce)
1 ounce cloves
1 ounce ginger
1 ounce nutmeg
Juice and grated rind of 2 lemons
1 tablespoon salt
1 teaspoon pepper
4 cups sugar

SAUCE:
1 quart boiled cider or
   1 quart currant or grape juice
1 quart molasses
Butter

Take 6 pounds neck meat and put to boil in enough water to cover it. Take off the scum that rises when it reaches the boiling point. Add hot water from time to time until it is tender. Then remove the lid from the pot, salt, let boil till almost dry. Take from the fire and let stand overnight. Pick bones, gristle, or stringy bits from the meat, chop very fine, mincing at the same time three pounds of neck beef suet.

Put in porcelain kettle one quart boiled cider or, better still, one quart currant or grape juice, one quart nice syrup or molasses, also a good lump of butter. Let it come to boiling point and pour over the ingredients in the pan after having first mixed them well, then mix thoroughly, do not cook.

Jo says, "Great grandmother would put this in a large crock in the dark cellar, covered with a tea towel and plate. The longer it sat the better it tasted. My mother and the other children would eat it right out of the crock." Makes 16 quarts.

PEANUT BUTTER SYRUP

1 cup white sugar
1 cup brown sugar
1 cup water
1/2 cup peanut butter, crunchy
1/2 cup heavy cream

Cook water and sugars till sugars dissolve. Add cream and peanut butter. Boil well. Very good.

Jan says, "This recipe is a very old recipe. It is delicious served on biscuits, pancakes or waffles. Do serve hot." Makes 4 cups.

A thought for the day. Hot clam-and-tomato bouillon served in cups, with a very thin slice of tomato and one of lemon floated on the top. What the milliners call "a pretty conceit."

LOIS' WATERMELON PICKLES 1935

Watermelon
4 tablespoons salt
1 quart water
Alum
4 cups sugar
1 cup vinegar
3 cups water
1 tablespoon allspice
1 tablespoon whole cloves
1 large stick cinnamon

Remove green peel and all soft pink portions from watermelon. Cut green part inside the peel into 1—1 1/2-inch pieces. Cover with a brine made by dissolving salt in 1 quart of water. If not enough to cover watermelon, make another quart of water and 4 tablespoons of salt. Let stand 3 hours. Drain. Rinse in cold water.

Rinse 3 times in alum water using 1 teaspoon powdered alum for each quart of water. Rinse thoroughly through 2 clear waters.

Prepare syrup of sugar, vinegar, water, allspice, cloves and cinnamon. Add rind to syrup and boil 10 minutes. Let stand overnight in refrigerator. Next day, boil slowly until rind is clear. You need sufficient syrup to cover rind.

WATERMELON PICKLES

Watermelon
Vinegar
Sugar

Cut rind from melon that is fresh. Soak 24 hours in strong salt water. Drain. Wash. Soak in water 12 hours. To 3 pounds fruit use 1 pint vinegar and 3 1/2 pounds sugar. Let vinegar and sugar come to a boil. Add fruit, cook 15 minutes. Take out fruit. Cook vinegar down and let cool. Pour over fruit and let stand over night. Next morning take fruit out. Boil juice until thick enough to pour over fruit in jars.

*Add: 2 sticks cinnamon
1/2 dozen cloves
2 small pieces ginger

* Add to syrup before putting in fruit the last time.

Sugar and Spice · Cooking with Children

Children love to help out in the kitchen and nothing lightens up their eyes and brightens their smiles like a piece of dough to roll and cut into fanciful shapes, like the Make-a-Word Cookies, Gingerbread Men, or the Out of This World Flying Saucer Cookies. When it is party time, serve Bozo Balls or the Flowerpot Ice Cream to little guests. If your party is in the winter with snow on the ground, try Tonia's Snow Ice Cream. Your teenagers will especially enjoy the great Halloween recipes for their goblin party. And Grandma's Meat Loaf, Shush Puppies, and the Kid-size Pizza are fun to try too. For more cookie recipes refer to the index.

Sugar & Spice

MONDAY'S child is fair of face,
TUESDAY'S child is full of grace,
WEDNESDAY'S child is full of woe,
THURSDAY'S child has far to go.
FRIDAY'S child is loving and giving,
SATURDAY'S child works hard for a living,
But the child that is born on the Sabbath day
Is blithe and bonny, good and gay.

RULES FOR LITTLE COOKS

Wash your hands.
Put on your apron.
Read your recipe and have Mother help you if you
    have a question.
Are you sure you washed your hands?
Put everything you will need on the table.
Have Mother help you heat the oven.
Measure everything carefully.
If something spills, wipe it up with paper towels,
    not the kitchen towel.
Have mother help you when you are ready to put
    your dish in the oven or under the broiler and
    to take it out. Always use pot holders, do not
    use a kitchen towel.
When you are finished, clean up your kitchen and
    wash your dishes. Mother will be so proud!

YOUR VERY OWN HAND COOKIES

1/2 cup shortening, softened (half butter or
    margarine)
1 cup sugar
1 egg
1 teaspoon vanilla
2 2/3 cups flour
1 teaspoon baking powder
1/2 teaspoon soda
1/2 teaspoon salt
1/4 teaspoon nutmeg
1/2 cup sour cream

Heat oven to 425 degrees. Mix shortening, sugar, egg and vanilla. Blend in remaining ingredients. Divide dough into 3 parts. Roll each part 1/4-inch thick on floured board. Trace around your hand and cut with pastry wheel or knife. Cut remaining dough into desired shapes. Bake 6 to 8 minutes. Cool and decorate. Makes 6 hand cookies and 1 dozen 2-inch cookies.

CHOCOLATE COOKIES:
    To 1 part dough, mix in 1-ounce unsweetened chocolate, melted and cooled.

PEANUT BUTTER COOKIES:
    To 1 part dough, mix in 1 tablespoon creamy peanut butter.

MAKE-A-NAME COOKIES

Follow directions for Sugar Cookie recipe (see index). Cut round cookies and place them on cookie sheet. Before you bake them, cut them into three pieces and move them a little bit away from each other. After the cookies are baked and cooled, frost them with your favorite cookie frosting and, with a different color frosting and using a decorator tip, make all your guests names on the cookies, one letter of the name on each section you cut. You might make a few extra letters for spares, in case one gets broken.

At party time, you can make place cards for your guests by placing the sections to form their name, or let them make their own name by finding the cookie letters.

MAKE-A-WORD COOKIES

Using the above idea, make three-letter words on each cookie, then mix them all up. You and your friends will have fun putting words together.

MAKE-A-FACE COOKIES

Using the above idea, on three cookie pieces, frost and make funny faces. Decorate with coconut for hair, beards, mustaches, gumdrops, nuts, Life Savers. Put three pieces together making happy faces, sad faces, mix them all up.

Charley Parley stole the barley
Out of the Baker's shop.
The baker came out, and gave him a clout,
Which made poor Charley hop.

NO BAKES

2 cups sugar
3 tablespoons cocoa
1/2 cup milk
1/2 stick butter
1 teaspoon vanilla
3 cups quick oats, uncooked

Add milk to sugar and cocoa, cook until sugar dissolves. Add butter and boil 1 minute. Remove from heat, add vanilla and oats. Drop by teaspoon on waxed paper.

OUT-OF-THIS-WORLD FLYING SAUCER COOKIES

1 cup margarine
1 cup peanut butter
1 cup granulated sugar
1 cup firmly packed brown sugar
2 eggs
1 1/4 cups flour
1 teaspoon soda
1/2 teaspoon salt
2 1/4 cups quick oats, uncooked
1 cup Reese's Pieces or M & M's

Beat together margarine, peanut butter and sugars until light and fluffy; blend in eggs. Add combined flour, soda and salt; mix well. Stir in oats and 1/3 cup candies. To make 2 flying saucers, place half the dough (about 2 1/4 cups) on each of 2 foil-lined and greased 12–13-inch pizza pans. Spread dough to within an inch of edge of pan; sprinkle each cookie with 1/3 cup candies. Bake at 325 degrees for 30 to 35 minutes or until cookie is lightly browned. The center may appear underdone; do not overbake. Cool 10 minutes in pan. Gently remove each cookie with foil liner to wire rack; cool thoroughly. Cut into wedges or squares to serve. Makes 2 12–13 inch cookies.

Sugar & Spice

OUT-OF-THIS-WORLD FLYING SAUCER COOKIES VARIATION

To make 4 1/2-inch round jumbo cookies, omit pizza pans. Drop dough by level 1/3 cup measures onto lightly greased cookie sheet about 3 inches apart. Bake at 350 degrees for 18 to 20 minutes or until lightly browned. Immediately press 5-6 candies onto each cookie. Cool on cookie sheet 3-4 minutes; remove to wire rack to cool thoroughly. Makes 18 4 1/2-inch jumbo cookies.

GINGERBREAD MEN

1 cup shortening
1 cup sugar
1/4 teaspoon salt
1 egg
1 cup molasses
2 tablespoons vinegar
5 cups sifted flour
1 tablespoon ginger
1 teaspoon ground cloves
1 teaspoon cinnamon
1 1/2 teaspoons soda

Cream shortening, sugar and salt. Stir in egg, molasses and vinegar. Beat well. Sift dry ingredients and stir into molasses. Chill about 3 hours. On lightly floured surface roll to 1/8-inch thickness. Cut with gingerbread man cutter. Place 1 inch apart on greased cookie sheet. Bake at 375 degrees 5 to 7 minutes. Cool and remove rack.

ICING: Add a little boiling water (very little) to confectioners' sugar to make a paste that will go through a pastry tube easily. Or make the icing thinner and drizzle icing around the outside of the gingerbread man. Use raisins or red hots for buttons and eyes. Makes 4 dozen 6-inch gingerbread men.

Run, run as fast as you can,
You can't catch me,
I'm the gingerbread man!
And I can run from you, I can!

NO BAKE FUDGIE COOKIES

2 cups sugar
1/2 cup cocoa
1 stick margarine
1/2 cup cream or milk
1 teaspoon vanilla
2 1/2 cups quick oats
1/2 cup peanut butter

Cream first 4 ingredients, bring to boil. Boil 3 minutes. Remove from heat. Add 1 teaspoon vanilla, 2 1/2 cups quick oats, 1/2 cup peanut butter. Beat until thick, spoon mixture onto waxed paper. Cool.

Note: If it sets up too quick to spoon out, add more milk and return to heat just long enough to spoon out. Makes 36 cookies.

DESSERT BURGERS

2 cups flour
1/2 cup cocoa
1 1/2 teaspoons baking soda
1/4 teaspoon salt
1/2 cup margarine
1 cup sugar
1 egg
1/2 teaspoon vanilla
1 cup milk

Sift flour, cocoa, soda and salt together. Cream margarine and sugar, add egg and vanilla. Beat in flour mixture alternately with milk. Drop by tablespoons on ungreased baking sheet to form 24 rounds. Bake 7 minutes at 425 degrees or until done. Remove from sheet and cool on wire rack.

FILLING:
1/2 cup margarine
2 egg whites
1 1/4 cups confectioners' sugar
1/2 teaspoon vanilla

Cream margarine until light. Gradually add 1 cup confectioners' sugar and vanilla. Beat egg whites until foamy and add remaining sugar. Beat until well blended. Thoroughly combine mixture. Spread on flat side of 12 rounds. Top with remaining rounds. These may be stored in refrigerator. Makes 12.

RAGGEDY ANN COOKIES

1 cup brown sugar, firmly packed
1 cup shortening
1 egg
1 teaspoon maple flavoring
2 1/4 cups sifted flour
1/2 teaspoon baking powder
1/2 teaspoon salt
1 can shredded coconut (4-ounce can)
Granulated sugar

Beat together brown sugar, shortening, egg and flavoring until fluffy. Add flour, baking powder and salt, mixing well. Stir in coconut. Drop by teaspoon 2 inches apart onto greased cookie sheet. Dip bottom of greased small glass into granulated sugar and press cookie flat. Edge will be ragged. Bake at 350 degrees 10 to 12 minutes.
Makes 3 dozen.

JELLY ROLL PAN COOKIES

25 graham crackers
2 sticks of margarine
1 cup brown sugar
1 cup chopped pecans

Foil line a jelly roll pan. Melt the 2 sticks of margarine and 1 cup brown sugar together. Boil 3 minutes. Remove from heat and add 1 cup chopped pecans. Spread on crackers. Bake 10 minutes at 325 degrees. Makes 25.

ANGEL COOKIES

1 stick margarine
1 cup sugar
1/8 teaspoon salt
8 ounces dates, chopped
1 tablespoon milk
1 egg, beaten
1 cup chopped nuts
3 cups Rice Krispies

Combine margarine, sugar, salt, dates, milk, egg in saucepan. Mix well and boil 3 minutes. Remove from heat; add nuts and Rice Krispies. Mix and roll into balls, and then roll in coconut, powdered sugar or nuts.
Jan says, "Butter hands before you roll the balls." Makes 2 dozen.

Sugar & Spice

YUMMIES

1 cup white Karo syrup
1 cup white sugar
1 1/2 cups peanut butter
5 cups Rice Krispies
1 package (6-ounce) semi-sweet chocolate chips
2 packages butterscotch chips

Combine syrup and sugar. Bring to a boil and add peanut butter and Rice Krispies. Spread in a greased pan. After mixture has set up in the pan, frost with melted chocolate and butterscotch chips. cut in squares to serve. Makes 24.

GRAHAM CRACKER PUDDING

12 or 14 graham crackers, crushed
4 tablespoons melted butter
6 tablespoons brown sugar
1 package gelatin, dissolved in 1/2 cup cold water
2 cups milk, warmed
1/2 cup sugar
2 egg yolks
1 teaspoon vanilla
2 beaten egg whites
1 cup cream, whipped

Combine graham crackers, butter and brown sugar. Press into bottom of 9 x 13-inch pan. Dissolve gelatin in cold water. Beat egg yolks and add sugar. Stir in gelatin and warm milk. Cook to a thin custard (not too long); cool. Add vanilla. Beat egg whites and whip the cream and fold into the cooled mixture. Pour over graham cracker crust and refrigerate. Cut into squares to serve.

Jo says, "This was my very favorite after-school snack and lunchtime dessert. It made walking home from school at noon for just an hour worth the effort of having to run all the way back." Serves 12.

Pease pudding hot, pease pudding cold,
Pease pudding in the pot, nine days old.
Some like it hot, some like it cold,
Some like it in the pot, nine days old.

DUMP CAKE

1 can of prepared pie filling, whatever flavor you like
2 boxes Jiffy cake mix, white or yellow
1/2 cup walnut or pecan pieces
1 stick butter or margarine

Just like the name says, dump the can of pie filling into a square cake pan. On top of that dump the cake mix, spreading it out evenly over the pie filling. Sprinkle chopped pecans or walnuts on top of the cake mixture if you like. Melt a stick of butter and dump it over the cake mix. Bake at 350 degrees for about 55 minutes. Top should be slightly brown. Serve with ice cream. Serves 8-10.

Pat - a - cake, Pat - a - cake, baker's man!
Make me a cake as fast as you can.
Pat it, and prick it, and mark it with T,
And put it in the oven for Tommy and me.

FUNNEL CAKES

2 beaten eggs
1 1/2 cups milk
2 cups sifted all-purpose flour
1 teaspoon baking powder
1/2 teaspoon salt
2 cups cooking oil

In mixing bowl, combine eggs and milk. Sift together flour, baking powder and salt. Add to egg mixture; beat smooth with rotary beater. (Test mixture to see if it flows easily through funnel. If too thick, add milk; if too thin, add flour.

In 8-inch skillet, heat cooking oil to 360 degrees. Covering bottom opening of funnel with finger, pour a generous 1/2 cup batter into funnel. Remove finger and release batter into hot oil in a spiral shape. Fry till golden, about 3 minutes. Using wide spatula and tongs, turn cake carefully. Cook 1 minute more. Drain on paper toweling; sprinkle with sifted powdered sugar. Serve hot with syrup or sprinkle powdered sugar over the cake. Makes 4 cakes.

Jo says, "This recipe is for an older child, but they are fun to make and good too. Your friends will be impressed."

TIDDLYWINK CAKE

Have mother get you a box of white Jiffy cake mix. Read the easy instructions. After the cake has baked and cooled, frost with Jam Frosting.

JAM FROSTING

4 tablespoons raspberry jam
1 teaspoon water
1 cup confectioners' sugar

Put jam in a pan and stir on the stove until jam is melted. Add the water. Remove from the stove. Sift the confectioners' sugar and add to the jam. Beat it hard and spread on Tiddlywink cake.

SNOW BALLS

1 small can crushed pineapple, undrained
3 tablespoons sugar
1 tablespoon cornstarch

Combine and cook until thickened and cool.

1 box vanilla wafers
1/2 pint heavy cream
1 teaspoon sugar
1/2 teaspoon vanilla
Angel Flake coconut

Stack 4 wafers to each snowball. Spread 1 teaspoon filling between each wafer but not on top. Place in refrigerator overnight. Next morning spread with whipped cream flavored with sugar and vanilla. Cover with Angel Flake coconut. Makes 8.

A dining-room table, with children's eager, hungry faces around it, ceases to be a mere dining-room table and becomes an altar.

Sugar & Spice

Polly put the kettle on,
Polly put the kettle on,
Polly put the kettle on,
We'll all have tea.

HAWAIIAN LEMONADE

1 can (6-ounce) frozen lemonade concentrate
1 can (12-ounce) apricot nectar
1 can (12-ounce) unsweetened pineapple juice
1 small bottle ginger ale

Combine lemonade concentrate with 1 can of water. Add chilled apricot nectar and pineapple juice. Add ice and pour in ginger ale.
Serves 6-8.

CHILDREN'S PARTY PUNCH

1 can (12-ounce) frozen orange juice
1 can (6-ounce) frozen lemonade
3 pints cranberry juice
1 quart water
2 quarts ginger ale

Combine orange juice, lemonade and water with cranberry juice. Pour into a half gallon container and chill.
Pour 1/2 mixture into a large serving pitcher. Add 1 quart of ginger ale. Fill pitcher with ice.
Repeat process when necessary. Serves 20-25.

FROSTED LEMONADE

Dip rims of glasses in water, then in sugar. Let dry and fill with cold lemonade.

GREEN DRAGONS

Place several scoops of lime sherbet into a glass and fill it with Sprite. Grandpa always fixed this for grandbabies before bedtime. You can substitute orange, raspberry, or lemon sherbet if you like, but then it won't be a green dragon will it?) Make up some fun names for your own drink.

TEA PARTY SANDWICHES I

Spread slices of bread with butter, then sprinkle with cinnamon sugar. Cover with another slice of buttered bread. Cut into small pieces just the right size for you and your friends. Serve with frosted lemonade.

TEA PARTY SANDWICHES II

Using your favorite cookie cutter, cut out from a piece of white or whole-wheat bread. Spread with your favorite filling and top with another identical cut-out.

TEA PARTY TOAST

Cut the crusts from 6 slices of bread. Cut the slices from corner to corner. Toast and butter the triangles. Spread with a mixture of 1/2 cup sugar, 1/4 cup orange juice and a tiny bit of grated orange rind. Place on a cookie sheet in 350 degree oven until the tops brown slightly. Delicious for a tea party.

TOAD IN THE HOLE

Using a biscuit cutter, cut a hole in the center of a slice of bread. Butter both sides of the bread. Place bread in a greased skillet and when it is brown on one side turn it over. Break an egg into a dish and carefully pour the egg into the hole of the bread. Turn the heat down and cover the skillet. Check in a minute or so to see if the white of the egg has set. Carefully lift out with a spatula. This is very good with a couple of slices of cheese placed around the hole before you cover the skillet. The cheese will melt as the egg cooks.

FLOWERPOT ICE CREAM

1 quart of chocolate or vanilla ice cream
6 small clay flowerpots

Line clay pots with aluminum foil. (You may use ceramic or paper cups, and if this is used you do not have to line them.) Spoon 3/4 cup ice cream into each pot, packing it down well. Cover with plastic wrap or tie in plastic bag, tying securely. Freeze at least 4 hours or do several days ahead.

Jan says, "You may decorate the ice-cream pots with marshmallows, candy mints, gumdrops, to your liking."

Wouldn't it be fun to fill the flowerpot to look like a real one? Before you put the flowerpot in the freezer, sprinkle finely crushed Oreo cookies on top of the ice cream and that will make it look like dirt. Put a small straw in the ice cream and freeze. After you take it out of the freezer, insert a pretty flower in the straw and you will have your own flower garden.

TONIA'S SNOW ICE CREAM

2 cups milk
3/4 cup sugar
1 teaspoon vanilla
4 eggs, beaten
Dash salt

Combine all ingredients. Add clean, new snow until thick. You can add instant chocolate mix or strawberry for different flavors. Serves 1 hungry kid.

A pillow shaken in the sky,
See how all the feathers fly,
Little snowflakes soft and light
Make the trees and meadows white.
A pillow shaken in the sky,
See how all the feathers fly,
Little snowflakes soft and light
Make the trees and meadows white.

FUDGESICLES

4 cups whole milk
1 package chocolate pudding mix
4 tablespoons sugar

Mix ingredients together. Pour into ice trays. Freeze until solid. Makes 2 trays.

POPSICLES

1 package Jell-O
3/4 cup sugar
1 package Kool-Aid (regular)

Flavors of Jell-O and Kool-Aid should correspond. Dissolve in 2 cups boiling water. After completely dissolved, add 2 cups cold water. Pour into molds and freeze until solid. Makes 8 popsicles.

Sugar & Spice

BOZO BALLS

Ice cream balls
Ice cream cones
Doilies
Chocolate M & M's
Red-hot candies
Whipped cream or chocolate frosting

Make balls of ice cream and put each on a small doily. Place cone on each ball for clown's pointed hat. Use chocolate M & M's on ice cream for the eyes and red-hot candies for the mouth. Using frosting or whipped cream, make a scalloped clown's collar around base of ice cream ball. These may be made ahead and frozen.

Little girls from age 7 to 9 like to have a cupcake bake. Let them make their own cupcakes using a cake mix, then bake and decorate them.

LITTLE BROWN BEAR'S HOT HONEY BUTTER

1 cup honey
1/4 cup melted butter
Cinnamon and nutmeg

Warm honey and melted butter. Add cinnamon and nutmeg as desired for spicy flavor. Spread on toast. Serves 8.

MARVELOUS MARSHMALLOWS

Melt a chocolate bar in the top of a double boiler. Stick a toothpick in a marshmallow. Dip it in the chocolate and quickly roll it in chopped nuts.

CINNAMON STICKS

Cut the crusts from day-old bread and cut the bread into thick pencil sticks. Brush these all over with plenty of melted butter. Roll the strips in cinnamon and sugar and bake at 375 degrees on a greased cookie sheet, until brown and crusty.

GRANOLA

3 1/2 cups Quaker oats
3/4 cup whole wheat flour
1 cup nuts (pecans, almonds, cashews)
5/8 cup safflower oil
1/4 cup apple juice
1/4 cup honey

Mix oats, flour and nuts, add oil, juice and honey. Mix well and make 1 layer thick in 300 degree oven for 1 hour. Store in airtight container. Fills 3-pound can.

PLAY-DOUGH MIXTURE

2 cups flour
2 tablespoons cooking oil
3 tablespoons clove oil, if desired
1 1/2 cups salt
2 tablespoons cream of tartar
2 cups water

Sift flour and salt together. Combine all ingredients. Stir over low heat until mixture pulls away from the pan's edge. Wrap in foil and refrigerate until ready to use. Keep covered when not in use.

DO NOT EAT!

❖❖

Little Tommy Tucker
Sings for his supper.
What shall we give him?
White bread and butter.

CIRCUS SALAD

Place a leaf of crisp lettuce on 2 salad plates. Peel a banana and slice it down the middle and then across the middle of those pieces. You will have four pieces of banana. Put 2 pieces on each plate. Sprinkle a handful of peanuts over the bananas and put a small spoonful of mayonnaise right in the middle. Line your plates with animal crackers and you and a friend have a circus salad. Peanuts for the elephants and bananas for the monkeys.

BUNNY SALAD

Would you like to make something special? Here is an idea you might like to use at your party, Easter dinner or to suprise your mommy.

Take a half pear, preferably canned. Put it on a bed of finely shredded lettuce. Use clove eyes, marshmallow or cottage cheese tail, and ears of radish slices to complete this "cottontail."

GRANDMA'S MEAT LOAF

2 pounds ground beef
1 pound ground pork
2 cups cornflakes
1 egg
1 small can tomatoes (pour off juice, reserve)
2 tablespoons grated Parmesan cheese
2 teaspoons Italian seasoning
1 clove garlic, crushed
1 small onion, grated
Salt and pepper
1 1/2 teaspoons Worcestershire sauce

Combine all ingredients; you can use your clean hands. Place in a loaf pan, pour tomato juice over top and bake at 350 degrees for 1 hour or until done.

KID-SIZE PIZZA

Have Mother help you split an English muffin in half and broil the outside sections to brown just a little bit. Spread the insides with pizza sauce; the kind from the grocery store will be just great. Next put on in layers all your favorite toppings, browned hamburger, onions, cheese, whatever you REALLY like. Place the pizza on a baking sheet and place under the broiler to brown and melt the cheese. Watch it closely so it doesn't brown too fast and have Mother help you take it out of the oven.

This is fun to do when you have a friend staying with you, or maybe just you and Mother or Dad are having a fun day, why don't you fix lunch?

Sugar & Spice

❖❖❖

THE PANCAKE

Mix a pancake,
Stir a pancake,
　Pop it in the pan;
Fry the pancake,
toss the pancake - - -
　Catch it if you can!!

SPECIAL SUMMER SWELL-TIME SELEBRATION

This is special because all of the recipes start with an S.
Super? Sure!!

SHUSH PUPPIES

Put hot dog bun on a square of aluminum foil. Spread with mustard and ketchup. Place a slice of cheese on the bun, then the hot dog. Then put a spoonful of relish, if you like. Wrap carefully in the foil. Make one Shush Puppy for each person. Keep cool until ready to heat and eat. Then place on a cookie sheet. Bake in 375-degree oven for 12 minutes.

SWELL TIME SOMERSAULT SALAD

Tear lettuce into little bite pieces. Chop all the veggies you like, green pepper, cucumber, little green onions, radishes, whatever you want. When ready to serve, pour salad dressing, not too much, just enough to coat the leaves, tossing them over and over with a wooden salad spoon and fork, just like the chefs do.

STUFFED SELERY

Cut celery in 2-inch pieces. Stuff cream cheese or pimento cheese spread in the hollow part, or you can use the canned cheese and squirt into the celery. Sprinkle paprika over the top.

S'NICE RICE

1 cup whipping cream, whipped stiff
1/2 cup sugar
1 cup crushed pineapple
2 cups cooked rice

Add sugar to whipped cream. Mix pineapple and rice carefully and add the whipped cream. Mix well. Serve very cold. If you like raisins you might add some to the recipe. Put a red cherry on top of each dish when you serve it. It looks very snazzy. Serves 4.

❖❖

S'MORES

Why do you think these have this special name? Because they make you want some more. On a graham cracker, put 4 squares of a Hershey's bar. Toast 2 marshmallows, and when they are gooey, put them on the chocolate, pushing gently. Put another graham cracker on the top. You'll want s'more with s'milk.

You can have this Special Selebration in the winter too. Have Daddy make a nice fire in the fireplace, put a big beach towel or quilt on the floor, but not too close to the fireplace. Tell Mother it is for a drip catcher.

SHOW TIME CIRCUS COOKIES

Spread a vanilla wafer with some frosting you and Mother can buy at the store. Put another vanilla wafer on the top, to make a sandwich. You will have to make some of these for your friends, they will think you are so smart. If you like, put a little frosting on the top wafer and stand up an animal cracker on top. Line up all the cookies, you have a circus parade.

HALLOWEEN CAT CAKE

1 package chocolate cake mix
1 package fluffy white frosting mix
Coconut
Jelly beans
Candy corn
Licorice shoelaces

Make and bake the chocolate cake mix according to package directions in 2 round 9-inch pans. Cool. With ruler and toothpicks, mark a circle 1 inch in from the edge of one layer. Cut along toothpick line with a good knife, then remove toothpicks. Carefully transfer inner circle to a tray. Place the 9-inch layer just below it. Now you have the cat's "head and body." For the tail, place 1/2 of the 1-inch circle trimming next to the body. Cut 4 triangles from remaining cake for ears and feet.

Prepare 1 package of frosting mix and glue on tail, ears and feet with some of it. Now frost the whole cake. Sprinkle well with coconut. To make the face, collar, bow and claws use jelly beans and candy corn. All cats need whiskers so cut them from licorice shoelaces.

Jan says, "Extend the ears with pieces of cake and take off the tail and you will have a bunny cake for Easter."

WITCHES' BREW

1 1/2 cups orange juice
1 quart apple cider
1 cup pineapple juice
2 tablespoons sugar
1 quart ginger ale
6 to 8 small red apples

Mix orange juice, apple cider, pineapple juice, the 2 tablespoons sugar and chill. Pour into large punch bowl and add 1 quart ginger ale and the 6 to 8 small apples. You may make faces on the apples out of cloves. Makes 2 1/2 quarts.

Peter, Peter, pumpkin eater,
Had a wife and couldn't keep her,
He put her in a pumpkin shell,
And there he kept her very well.

GOBLINS AND GHOSTS LOLLIPOP COOKIES

Prepare 1 box cookie mix by directions and add 1/2 cup peanut butter. Shape dough into 1-inch balls. Place on greased baking sheets.

Cut colored drinking straws in half and insert one in each cookie. Flatten dough into a circle and press it over straws to secure them.

Bake at 375 degrees for 10 to 12 minutes. Cool and remove with spatula to wire rack.

Mix 2 cups powdered sugar with 1/4 cup boiling water and beat until smooth. Put 1/2 of the icing in a separate bowl and color with orange food coloring. With a brush or small spatula, frost half the cookies white, the rest orange. Make faces on each with chocolate bits, licorice "shoelaces" and cinnamon drops. Use a little egg white to glue them on. Paint edge of cookies with egg white, roll in chocolate jimmies to make hair.

Makes 2—2 1/2 dozen cookies.

POPCORN BALLS

7 cups popped corn
1 cup sugar
1/3 cup sugar
1/3 cup light corn syrup
1 teaspoon salt
1/4 cup butter
1 teaspoon vanilla

Mix all ingredients except vanilla and popcorn in saucepan. Cook to 250 degrees on candy thermometer or until a few drops form hard ball when dropped into cold water. Remove from heat. Stir in vanilla.

Pour in thin stream over popped corn, stirring constantly to mix well. Shape with buttered hands into balls. Makes 12 to 15 large balls.

HALLOWEEN HAYSTACKS

1 package (6-ounce) chocolate chips
1/2 cup shredded coconut
3/4 cup cornflakes or chow mein noodles

In top of double boiler melt chocolate chips over hot but not boiling water. Remove from heat and stir in 1/2 cup shredded coconut and 3/4 cup cornflakes or chow mein noodles.

Drop by teaspoon onto greased baking sheets and chill until firm. Makes about 20 haystacks.

SPOOKY CHOCOLATE PIE

Have you ever made a "spooky chocolate pie"? When your mother has extra pie crust, ask her to make you an extra shell.

In a baked pie shell fill with a recipe on the box of Jell-O instant chocolate pudding. When the pie has set, take marshmallow cream and start forming your ghost. It will be so good you will have to have a piece for the ghost.

Sugar & Spice

JACK-O-LANTERN FROSTIES

Cut a thin slice of peel from the bottoms of 6 thick-skinned oranges. Cut a 1-inch slice from the top of each (these will become the hats).

Using a spoon, scoop out pulp and white membrane from each orange. Force pulp through a strainer for juice. (Save the juice to drink.) Make faces on the shells, gluing on gumdrops and studding with whole cloves. Fill with orange sherbet or ice cream to your liking. Toothpick a red gumdrop in the center of each hat and set it on top of the sherbet. Freeze until ready to serve. Makes 6.

Georgie Porgie pudding and pie,
Kissed the girls and made them cry;
When the girls began to play,
Georgie Porgie ran away.

CARAMEL APPLES

6 wooden skewers
6 medium-sized apples
1 cup sugar
3/4 cup white corn syrup
1 can (14-ounce) Eagle Brand sweetened condensed milk
1/8 teaspoon salt
1/4 cup butter or margarine
1 teaspoon vanilla

Wash and thoroughly dry apples and insert wooden skewer into stem end of each apple. Set aside. In a heavy saucepan, combine sugar, corn syrup, condensed milk and salt. Mix well and cook over medium heat, stirring gently but constantly to 230 degrees on candy thermometer, or until small amount dropped in cold water forms a soft ball (about 30 minutes). Remove from heat. Cool slightly, stir in butter and vanilla.

Working quickly, dip apples in caramel to coat well. Place apples stem side up to harden on a buttered piece of waxed paper.

CARNIVAL POPCORN BALLS

36 vanilla caramels
3 tablespoons water
6 cups popped corn
Shredded coconut
Multicolored sugar candies

In the top of double boiler melt, while stirring, 36 vanilla caramels with 3 tablespoons water. In a big bowl, using a fork, gently mix 6 cups popped corn with the melted caramels.

Wet your hands and shape mixture into medium-sized balls. Roll each in shredded coconut and the sugar candies. Insert wooden skewers deep into balls and tie with colored black and orange ribbons. Makes 12 popcorn balls.

Under the Mistletoe · Recipes for Christmas

In this chapter we have tried to provide an abundance of ideas to help make your holiday season a joyous time for you and memorable for your family and friends. To capture the spirit and cheer, begin at your front door by following our suggestions for holiday decor throughout your home. Be sure to review the suggested menus for our Christmas buffet and dessert cart. The recipes don't necessarily appear in this chapter but are featured elsewhere in the cookbook. Consult the index.

The section called Visions of Sugarplums is crammed full of delights—Cathedral Windows, Candy Cane Cookies, Annie's Sherry Bars, just to mention a few. In Christmas Essence from Scotland, try the tantalizing Irish Truffles and the Coffee-Whiskey Trifle. To put a gleam in Santa's eye, prepare a batch of Christmas Wassail or the Candy Cane Cocktail, from the Holiday Cheer section.

The Spirit of Giving is filled with wonderful gift ideas, each conveying a personal touch. We have been known to begin our holiday cookies and candy-making as early as October. You might want to refer also to the bread chapter (Love Those Buns) and the chapter on pickles, jellies, and preserves (Sassy and Tart) for additional gift-giving suggestions. The result in December will be a dazzling array of gifts and morsels guaranteed to bring smiles and add a twinkle to the eyes of children of all ages, and a sparkle to your table.

Under The Mistletoe

TO EVERYTHING THERE IS A SEASON,
AND A TIME TO EVERY PURPOSE UNDER
THE HEAVEN..........A TIME TO KEEP.

On Christmas Day there is a magical feeling of love that spreads throughout the house. The secret to filling a house with Christmas joy is using your imagination.

Decorate your home early enough for all to enjoy. If you wait until the last week before Christmas to begin preparations, Santa might catch you under the mistletoe amid unfinished decorations.

Christmas spirit begins at your front door. Fill a grapevine basket with pinecones. Use greenery-filled jugs or baskets, a child's sled tied with a big red bow to carry out the festive mood. You may use a traditional evergreen wreath with sprigs of heather and boxwood or create a Della Robbia Christmas wreath (see index).

Christmas music playing softly in the background will warmly embrace friends and family as they enter your front door.

The halls are decked with garlands of greenery entwined with red ribbons and red birds.

The Christmas tree is a time for family togetherness whether you cut it yourself or pick one from a tree lot. Homemade ornaments, strings of popcorn and cranberries, or whatever your choice is to decorate your tree, make it a joyous tradition to share.

It is fun and makes the children feel important to have a cookie-ornament tree in their own room. Cookies may be made weeks ahead and frozen. Don't forget, when you cut them out make a hole in the top of each ornament big enough to thread a ribbon through before baking the cookies. This is a good time to make a gingerbread house for the little ones enjoyment. Teenagers love making one for the little guys.

On your mantel above a roaring fire, place a large hurricane globe on its side. Fill with fresh pine branches, holly or boxwood entwined with your choice of ribbon through its boughs. On each side of the globe use large candles with holly candle rings. Fill a brass tub or grapevine basket with greenery, pine cones or fresh red apples and set it on the hearth to the side of the fire.

Specialties from your kitchen for the people you love make it a very busy place. Since you spend so much time preparing goodies for the season, decorate your kitchen with humble trappings that take on a festive look. Use graters with votive candles inside and watch them glitter. Even pastry molds and cookie cutters make unique candle holders. Ask to borrow your child's or grandchild's blocks and spell out Merry Christmas to be placed on your windowsill or some out of the way place. Keep your "Christmas Scent" on the stove so the aroma goes throughout the house and greets your guests with a homey atmosphere.

The Christmas spirit is bountiful so we are emphasizing on the centerpiece as a sumptuous harvest of fruits, flowers and vegetables, using fresh asparagus, green onions, sugar-coated peas, avocados, black and green grapes, pomegranates, rose-shaped mints, red apples and other beautiful green vegetables.

At the pinnacle is an outburst of red and white peppermint sticks. To add an extra flair to the beautiful harvest, tie a red ribbon around the bunches of asparagus and green onions. For the finishing touch add satin Christmas balls and velvet leaves around the fruits and vegetables.

Using a white felt tablecloth create a plaid pattern from various lengths of satin ribbon.

You can add to your Christmas spirit if you don't get caught in the last-minute rush. Start your preparations early. Bread, cookies, candies and many of the buffet foods can be made and stashed in the freezer weeks ahead of the holiday.

Under The Mistletoe

Love of entertaining is a family tradition with many of us. It may be an open house, buffet or a lavish dinner. Whatever party it may be, set up your table the day before the party. Give careful thought to traffic for placement of serving pieces, napkins, plates and flatware. Place a small piece of paper in each dish with the name of the food to be served and set an appropriate utensil next to each piece. This will make it much easier and quicker when you begin filling the table.

The way food is presented and garnished is almost as important as the flavor. So use your tea cart if you have one or a small table for your dazzling desserts. Cover top of dessert cart or table with an heirloom lace runner or overlapping lace doilies. A sprig of greenery and 6" cinnamon sticks tied with satin bow of ribbons matching the buffet table will rest in one corner. Use crystal votive candles to illuminate the desserts.

For the Christmas egg nog use a large crystal or silver bowl. Brush edge with a slightly beaten egg white and sprinkle edge with colored sugar crystals. Surround the bowl with holly and crystal birds.

Have samplings of unusual tidbits throughout your living and dining room. Also, a goodie basket filled with good cheer and glad tidings is fun for all ages to be handed out as they bid you good-night and Merry Christmas.

Don't forget to hang the stockings with care, write Santa a note, recheck camera batteries so there will be memories to share.

CHRISTMAS BUFFET

Red Caviar Mousse

Fresh Shrimp Remoulade

Sweet and Sour Chicken Wings

Beer Balls

Bowls of Krazy Krunch

Platter of Veggies with Herb Mayonnaise Dressing

Rumaki

Braunschweiger Pate

Cheese and Broccoli Dip

Smoked Turkey

Egg Rolls

Cranberry Bread

Pumpkin Bread

Fruit Cake

DESSERT CART

Fresh Strawberries in Crystal Bowl

Powdered Sugar for Dipping

Bourbon Balls

Mini Mincemeat Cupcakes

Pecan Tarts

Curried Almonds

Spiced Pecans

Glazed Apricots

Coffee and Tea

Wiedekehr Johannisberg Riesling

Bolla Valpolicella

Under The Mistletoe

SANTA'S SNACK

If you have had a Christmas Eve party at your home, make up a small plate for Santa. Some cheese and crackers, perhaps a few shrimp or meatballs and some carrot sticks from the relish tray for the reindeer. If there is some left, how about a ham or turkey sandwich for the old fellow?

Place a few of your favorite cookies on the plate and fill a mug with cold milk or if Mother served it at her party, a mug of Christmas Wassail. Santa will be delighted.

Next to the plate, place a napkin for Santa to wipe his beard and write a note telling him what a good child you have been.

CHRISTMAS SCENT

This heralds the beginning of the holiday season around our homes. When the children were small they would associate it with "Cookie Baking Time."

In a small saucepan or old teakettle, pour 1 quart of water. To this add 1 tablespoon of whole cloves, 5 or 6 small sticks of cinnamon, 1 tablespoon nutmeg and, if desired, some allspice. Bring this mixture to a boil and then just let it set on stove on low heat, and allow the aroma to fill your home with heavenly holiday scents. You can keep adding water to the spice mixture for many uses, before renewing spices.

DELLA ROBBIA WREATH

WREATH MATERIALS:
20" styrofoam ring
Natural peat moss
90 evergreen branches, 6-inch length
60 floral picks (4-inch)
15 lemons
12 oranges
8 limes
12 red apples
12 green apples
1 can oak wood stain or spray stain
26 pine cones
Sprigs of bittersweet, if available

It was four hundred years ago that a Florentine family, the Della Robbias, adapted the traditional evergreen wreath of Northern Europe by adding to it the fruits and berries of the Mediterranean.

Cover ring with moss. Wire the evergreens around the ring, allowing them to softly overhang the outside of the ring 2 to 3 inches. Insert a floral pick into the base of each piece of fruit and dip the top part of the fruit into the wood stain. Let dry for one day. When dry, place the fruit on the ring. Attach the pine cones by wrapping wire around the base and wire them to the evergreens.

To hang, take a 22-inch piece of wire and wrap it twice around the top of the wreath. Secure by twisting both ends together. Take a second piece of wire (2 to 3-inch length), fold in half, thread through the first loop and twist the ends together to secure. If you make this wreath using real fruit, it should last the holiday season if hung outdoors. It will last indefinitely if artificial fruit is used.

Jan says, "If you would like to use the spray stain, you may after the wreath is finished. I wouldn't use it on the fresh fruit, just the artificial."

HOW TO PRESERVE
YOUR CHRISTMAS TREE

Here is a simple household formula for keeping your tree upstanding and fresh throughout the holiday season.

1/4 cup horticultural iron
1 gallon hot water
2 cups light corn syrup
4 teaspoons chlorinated household bleach

You can double the indoor life of most evergreens simply by standing them in this easily prepared formula. At your florist, garden supply or hardware store, ask for Green Gard, a micronized horticultural iron. The other two ingredients, corn syrup, such as Karo, and a cleaning bleach are shelf items from your grocery store. In a bowl mix the micronized iron with hot water and stir in the corn syrup and bleach. The iron will not dissolve completely; it will produce a blue-green mixture with particles which will settle to the bottom. With a saw, remove about an inch from the tree trunk to level the base and to remove any solidified resinous material. Then crush the fibers at the cut end with hammer blows, stand the tree in a tree holder and pour in the solution. Keep the holder filled throughout the holidays with warm tap water. A tree standing in plain water alone will droop, but using this formula, your tree should remain as green and open-armed as new.

PEPPERMINT POT

Shop for your candy canes first, then get a flowerpot the height of the canes.

Wash and thoroughly dry flowerpot. Remove wrappers from candy canes. Attach a thin stripe of floral clay the length of the cane and press firmly to the outside of the pot with the curved end of cane at the bottom curving outward. Continue procedure until flowerpot is covered with canes.

If the canes are not quite the height of the pot, glue a piece of red velvet ribbon at the top of the pot.

After completing canes, fill pot with cotton or artificial boxwood and decorate with red and white candy-striped bows, peppermint candies and canes. If you can find a tall peppermint striped candle, stick it in the pot before adding the greenery or cotton.

Jo says, "This makes an adorable children's Christmas table decoration. Surround the candy cane pot with Christmas Mice characters and tiny packages, wrapped in red and green foil."

CRYSTAL CHRISTMAS BOUGH

Spray (or buy) a snowy white branch. Spread rock candy crystals in shallow pan. Sprinkle with green vegetable coloring. Mix until crystals are evenly colored. Dry for 2 to 3 hours.

Prepare 1 package fluffy white frosting as directed on package. Spread a little frosting on branch, press on sugar crystals. Continue until branch is covered. Balance branch in a square of weighted Styrofoam or on heavy lead flower frog. Hang Christmas candies on branch with nylon thread or fine wire. Cover base with strings of rock candy, crystal or colored.

Under The Mistletoe

HOMEMADE CHRISTMAS ORNAMENTS

1 cup salt
2 cups flour
1 cup water

Mix salt and flour together. Add water, a little at a time. Knead 7-10 minutes until dough is smooth.

Roll dough about 1/4-inch thick, then use cookie cutters to cut basic shapes. Roll small pieces of dough for eyes, cheeks, hair, etc., and moisten with water to attach. Poke hole at top for hanger.

Bake on cookie sheet in 325-degree oven until light brown. When cool, varnish to protect from moisture, or paint any color you like.

CHRISTMAS DECORATION

1 cup sugar
1 tablespoon water
6-8 drops food color

Mix ingredients well. Pack in plastic cookie cutter. Pat very easy onto paper. Let dry 24 hours. Do not touch.

Use Elmer's glue to attach tree hangers.

Jan says, ''These decorations make very cute favors or place cards. I like the white sugar just as well as the colored sugar ones.''

"Spirit of Giving"

Use a small container like a baby food jar, jelly jar or a pottery pot. Fill with these following items and the recipe enclosed. These make great inexpensive gifts for your child's teachers, neighbors or friends.
  a. Strawberry butter
  b. Sourdough starter
  c. Hot Buttered Rum
  d. Hot Chocolate Mix
  e. Kahlúa Mix
  f. Jellies

Choose a print piece of material to fit the lid. Pink it with pinking shears and put it on top of the lid, tying it with a ribbon or yarn.

Wrap Christmas kitchen gifts in tissue or Christmas paper with herbs tied in with the ribbons.

When giving a loaf of bread, tie it up in a bandana with a wooden spoon tucked in the knot.

Bend a piece of wire into a circle and pinch the ends together. Using dry silver king artemisia, gradually weave the plants around the wire, fastening every few inches with a string. Continue to add artemisia. Then tie on bits of nutmeg, gingerroot, bay leaf, rosemary and cinnamon sticks.

Using potpourris, fill sachets that you have made. Enclose them with a gift so they can be tucked in drawers or linen closets.

Don't forget the birds. Use the smallest Styrofoam ball. Cover it with suet and roll in bird seed until it is well coated. Tie it with a small red ribbon with tiny pinecones intertwined among the ribbons on top and bottom of ball.

ORANGE POMANDER BALLS

Sometime, long before the holidays, when you go to Grandma and Grandpa's, you can take this project with you. If you aren't going visiting, perhaps someone in your family will help you, maybe big brother or sister?

Using large navel oranges, poke small holes in the orange, one at a time, with a small nail. Insert a whole clove stem into the hole. Don't use too big a nail, or the clove will fall out. The nail is just easier to poke the hole rather than using the end of the clove. It hurts the thumb.

Poke holes and place cloves all over the orange, the more the better. When you are finished with the oranges, set them aside for several weeks. The oranges dry up but the cloves will keep them from spoiling. Wrap a pretty piece of lace or velvet ribbon around the oranges, make bows on top and attach hoops for hanging. These make nice gifts for someone you love. They will enjoy hanging them and will think of you each time they look at them.

CHILDREN'S POTPOURRI

In the summer when roses are blooming and Mother's bouquet is beginning to wilt, ask her if you may have the rose petals. Remove the petals from the stem very carefully and lay them out in a single layer on paper towels. Let them dry for several days until they are brittle. Do not cover them in a jar or container until they are completely dry or they will mold.

When you are ready to make potpourri, mix some cinnamon, ground cloves, nutmeg and allspice to the petals. Mix them well, put in a pretty jar with a lid. Decorate the lid with pretty garden pictures.

If you do not want to use spices, you can mix oils of roses, lavender or other flowers with the petals. You can buy the oil at a craft shop.

To freshen potpourri, sprinkle a few drops of brandy or perfumed oils as needed.

APPLE POMANDER BALLS

Stick whole cloves in unpeeled apples and roll the apples in ground cinnamon. Bake in an oven on warm setting for about three hours. When the apples are cool, wrap them in pretty pieces of net or lace, pull up the ends and tie with a satin or velvet ribbon and decorate with some little flowers if Mother has some to let you use.

ROSE POTPOURRI

6 cups dried rose petals
1/2 teaspoon ground cloves
1/2 teaspoon ground cinnamon
1/2 teaspoon rose oil
1/2 teaspoon ground allspice
1/2 teaspoon mint flakes
1 tablespoon orris root

Add spices to dried rose petals. Sift in ground orris root. Mix in a wide bowl and pack in a large jar. Cover tightly but open the container every few days to stir the mixture.

SPICE POTPOURRI

1 quart rose petals
1/2 pint lavender flowers
1 teaspoon anise seed
1 tablespoon cloves
1 tablespoon nutmeg
1 tablespoon cinnamon
1 tablespoon crushed benzoin
Floral oil of choice (see below)

Mix rose petals with lavender flowers. Mix anise seed, cloves, nutmeg and cinnamon and crush. Add jasmine, rose geranium, patchouli or rosemary oil to crushed benzoin. Blend all together.

Under The Mistletoe

CAFE' AU LAIT MIX

1/2 cup nondairy coffee creamer
1/2 cup sugar
1/3 cup instant coffee powder

Combine ingredients in a small mixing bowl, blending well. To serve, place 1 tablespoon mix in a cup. Add 4 ounces boiling water, and stir well. Store mix in an airtight container. Yield: 20 4-ounce servings.

CAFE' MEXICANO

1 tablespoon Cafe' au Lait Mix
1 tablespoon Kahlúa or other coffee-flavored liqueur
1 teaspoon grated semisweet chocolate
Dash of ground cinnamon

Place ingredients in a cup. Add 4 ounces boiling water. Stir well. Yield: one 4-ounce serving.

MOCHA JAVA

1 tablespoon Cafe' au Lait Mix
1 tablespoon Creme de Cacao
1 1/4 teaspoons hot cocoa mix or instant chocolate malt mix

Place ingredients in a cup. Add 4 ounces boiling water. Stir well. Yield: one 4-ounce serving.

PARSLEY BUTTER

1/2 pound butter
1 teaspoon Worcestershire sauce
1/2 teaspoon A.1. sauce
1 tablespoon parsley
1 teaspoon shallots, chopped
1/4 teaspoon salt
Dash cayenne pepper

Mix ingredients in blender or mixer. Store in refrigerator. Makes 1 cup.

STRAWBERRY BUTTER

1 stick butter
1 package (10-ounce) frozen strawberries
1 cup confectioners' sugar

Thaw and bring strawberries to room temperature. Cream butter and sugar thoroughly, adding strawberries. Blend until smooth. Makes 2 cups.
Jan says, "Please use butter, not margarine. It is better and works in the sugar and strawberries."

Under The Mistletoe

NINE BEAN SOUP MIX

1 pound barley pearls
1 pound dried black beans
1 pound dried red beans
1 pound dried pinto beans
1 pound dried navy beans
1 pound dried Great Northern beans
1 pound dried lentils
1 pound dried split peas
1 pound dried black-eyed peas

Combine all beans. Divide into ten 2-cup packages for gift giving. On the jar, tie a ribbon with a recipe card with the following Nine Bean Soup.

NINE BEAN SOUP

2 cups Nine Bean Soup Mix
2 quarts water
1 pound ham, diced
1 large onion, chopped
1 clove garlic, minced
1/2 to 3/4 teaspoon salt
1 can (16-ounce) tomatoes, undrained and chopped
1 can (10-ounce) tomatoes and green chiles, undrained

Sort and wash 2 cups bean mix; place in a Dutch oven. Cover with water 2 inches above beans, and soak overnight. Drain beans; add 2 quarts water and next 4 ingredients. Cover and bring to a boil; reduce heat and simmer 1 1/2 hours or until beans are tender. Add remaining ingredients; simmer 30 minutes, stirring occasionally. Yield: 8 cups.

HOT BUTTERED RUM BATTER

1 box (1-pound) dark brown sugar
2 sticks butter
1 teaspoon nutmeg
1 teaspoon cinnamon
1/2 teaspoon cloves

Melt butter and stir in rest of ingredients. Add 1/4 to 1/3 cup water. Mix. Put in jars and refrigerate. Will keep indefinitely.

TO SERVE:
Put 1 big tablespoon batter in mug. Add 1 ounce rum and 1 cup boiling water, stir.
Jo says, "Find a roaring fire and relax. Umm."

FRIENDSHIP TEA

1 cup Tang
1 cup instant lemon tea
1 1/2 cups sugar
1 teaspoon cinnamon
1/2 teaspoon cloves
1/2 teaspoon ginger

Mix in large container, cover and store in refrigerator. When ready for a hot drink put 3 teaspoons mix into a cup, fill with boiling water.

HOT CHOCOLATE MIX

1 box (2-pound) instant Nestle's Quik
1 box (1-pound) powdered sugar
1 box (14-quart) Carnation instant milk
1 jar (6-ounce) Coffee-Mate

Mix and store in 2 (3-pound) coffee cans. When serving fill cup 1/2 full of mixture. Add hot water.

Under The Mistletoe

GLAZED APRICOTS

2 cups sugar
1 cup water
2 packages dried apricots

Bring sugar and water to boil. Turn down heat and add 2 packages dried apricots, boiling gently for 5 minutes (Watch for boiling over). Remove apricots with a fork and spread on waxed paper (not touching) for at least 20 minutes. Save syrup for next batch. Keeps in refrigerator. Press apricots into a plate of sugar with your fingers. Place on rack and let dry overnight.

Jan says, "Be sure you make this batch and more for they are very popular."

BOURBON HARD SAUCE

1/4 cup butter
1 egg, slightly beaten
3 cups confectioners' sugar
1 tablespoon bourbon whiskey

Cream butter, then gradually beat in sugar, alternately with egg and bourbon. This sauce is good on ice cream, cookies or cake. Makes 3 1/2 cups.

ORANGE PEEL PRESERVES

Peel from 4 large oranges
Water
2 cups granulated sugar

Cut orange peel into thin slivers. Place peel in 2-quart saucepan and add water to cover. Bring to a boil over high heat and boil 5 minutes. Drain and discard water. Return peel to pan and add sugar and 2 cups water. Bring to a boil and boil 30 to 45 minutes over moderate heat until thick and syrupy. Remove from heat and chill until ready to use. Makes 2 cups.

CURRIED ALMONDS

2 cups blanched whole almonds
1 1/2 tablespoons butter
1 tablespoon curry powder
1 1/2 teaspoons salt

Mix ingredients together. Place on a greased jelly-roll pan, 15 1/2 x 10 1/2-inch. Toast almond mixture in oven 15 minutes, stirring occasionally. Cool almonds completely and store in tightly covered container to use within one week. Makes 2 cups.

GOLDEN NUTS

1 1/2 cups sugar
1/4 cup water
3 tablespoons orange juice
1/4 teaspoon cinnamon
1/2 teaspoon grated orange peel
2 1/2 cups walnuts

Stir sugar with warm water, orange juice and cover. Boil 1 minute or until sugar crystals on side of pan have melted. Uncover, cook to 240 degrees on candy thermometer or until soft ball in cold water. Add 1/4 teaspoon cinnamon, 1/2 teaspoon grated orange peel, 2 1/2 cups walnuts. Stir until creamy. Put on wax paper. Makes 4 1/2 cups.

SUGARED NUTS

2 teaspoons butter
1 cup sugar
1 pound pecans
2 egg whites
1/2 teaspoon cinnamon
1/4 teaspoon cloves
1/4 teaspoon salt
1/4 cup butter

Melt 2 teaspoons butter in pan. Add nuts; put in 325-degree oven for 25 minutes.

Beat egg whites stiff with sugar, cinnamon, cloves and salt. Fold whites into nuts; stir in 1/4 cup melted butter. Spread onto cookie sheet and bake at 325 degrees for 40 minutes.

Remove and separate nuts. Cool and store in a tight container (glass jar is good). Makes 4 cups.

CRISP FRIED WALNUTS

6 cups water
4 cups walnuts
1/2 cup sugar
Salad oil
Salt

Heat water to boiling. Add walnuts and return to boiling. Cook 1 minute. Rinse walnuts under running hot water and drain. In a large bowl, gently stir warm walnuts with sugar with rubber spatula until sugar is dissolved.

Meanwhile, heat about 1-inch salad oil to 350 degrees. With slotted spoon, add about half of walnuts to oil. Fry 5 minutes or until golden, stirring often. Drain on paper towel and sprinkle lightly with salt. Toss lightly to keep nuts from sticking together. Cool. Fry remaining walnuts. Store in tightly covered container and use within 2 weeks. Makes 4 cups.

SUGAR GLAZED NUTS

4 cups nuts*
3/4 cup sugar
1/3 cup light corn syrup
1 1/2 tablespoons corn oil
Dash of salt
1/3 cup of butter
1/2 cup sugar
* May use either pecans, walnuts, almonds, cashews, macadamia or hazelnuts

Preheat oven to 250 degrees. In a 13 x 9 x 2-inch jelly roll pan spread nuts in a single layer. Bake 5 minutes. Set nuts aside. Combine sugar, syrup, oil and salt in a heavy 2-quart saucepan. Stirring constantly over medium heat, bring to a boil; boil without stirring for 5 minutes. Remove pan from heat and stir in butter until melted. Immediately pour this syrup over the nuts, stirring constantly to coat evenly. Bake in 250-degree oven, stirring the nuts intermittently until brown. This will take 60—75 minutes. Sprinkle 1/2 cup of sugar over the nuts. Spread on cookie sheets to cool completely. Separate the nuts and store in a tightly covered container. Makes 4 cups. Don't despair! The syrup tends to ball up when poured on the nuts, but keep stirring and put them in the oven and the syrup will even out.

SPICED PECANS

1 teaspoon cold water
1 egg white
1 pound large pecan halves
1 cup sugar
1 teaspoon ground cinnamon
1 teaspoon salt

Beat water and egg white until frothy. Mix well with pecans. Combine sugar, cinnamon and salt. Mix well with pecans. Spread on a cookie sheet. Bake at 225 degrees for 1 hour, stirring occasionally. Makes 2 cups.

CANDIED GRAPEFRUIT PEEL

4 large grapefruit
Water
1/2 cup light corn syrup
Sugar
1 package (3-ounce) lemon-flavored gelatin

With a sharp knife, score peel of each grapefruit into quarters (reserve fruit for salads). Trim off white membrane. Cut peel into long, thin strips.

In 4-quart saucepan over high heat, bring peel and 8 cups water to boiling. Boil 15 minutes. Drain and rinse peel. With 8 more cups water, boil peel 15 minutes again and drain.

In same saucepan over high heat, bring corn syrup, 1 3/4 cups sugar, and 1 1/2 cups water to boiling until sugar is dissolved, stirring frequently. Gently stir in peel. Reduce heat to medium-low and cook until most of syrup has been absorbed, stirring occasionally.

Remove saucepan from heat and gently stir in gelatin until dissolved; cool 10 minutes (mixture will be sticky and thin). Place 1 cup sugar on waxed paper. Lightly roll peel, a few at a time, in sugar. Place in single layer on wire racks. Let peel dry overnight. Store in tightly covered containers. Makes 1 1/2 pounds.

Prepare orange peel like the grapefruit peel but substitute oranges for grapefruit.

Jan says, "I can remember my mother making peel candy before every holiday. I remember how clear and pretty the candy was and how I didn't like it. Amazing how taste changes."

CHRISTMAS WREATHS

Mix 1/2 cup butter and 30 large marshmallows in a double boiler. Add 1/4 teaspoon green food color, 1/2 teaspoon vanilla and 3 1/2 cups cornflakes, mint extract to taste. Blend thoroughly. While warm, drop from teaspoons onto ungreased baking sheet and shape into wreaths. Dip fingers in and out of cold water if cornflake mixture is too hot. Decorate with red hots or silver dragees.

Let cool. Makes 25-30 wreaths.

Jan says, "Let the wreaths dry well. These may be frozen and ready to use when needed. The wreaths are not only good to eat, but they are very decorative on plates, used as place cards or on a cookie tree."

KRAZY KRUNCH

4 quarts popped corn
1 1/3 cups pecans
2/3 cup almonds
1 1/3 cups sugar
1 cup margarine
1/2 cup clear Karo syrup
1 teaspoon vanilla

Combine popped corn and nuts in large container. Mix sugar, margarine, and syrup. Boil 10 to 15 minutes, stirring occasionally. Remove from heat, add vanilla, and pour over corn and nuts. Mix thoroughly, spread on cookie sheets to dry. Break apart and store in tightly covered containers. Will keep for a long time. Makes 5 quarts.

OVEN-BAKED CARAMEL CORN

20 cups popcorn (about 3 large poppers)

Place corn in large roaster pan in oven at about 250 degrees, to keep warm.

SYRUP:
2 cups brown sugar
2 sticks margarine
1/2 cup white syrup
1 teaspoon salt
2 teaspoons vanilla
1/2 teaspoon baking soda

Combine first 5 ingredients and boil for 5 minutes and add 1/2 teaspoon baking soda. Remove from heat. Pour hot syrup over hot popcorn and mix. Bake 45 to 60 minutes, stirring every 15 minutes while pan is in oven.

Remove and cool, stirring occasionally to keep corn from sticking together. Keep in air-tight container. Makes 22-25 cups.

HIDDEN VALLEY CRACKERS

2 packages (11-ounce) soup crackers
1 1/2 cups light oil
2 tablespoons dill seed
1 tablespoon lemon pepper
1 package Hidden Valley Ranch salad dressing mix (original style)
1/4 teaspoon garlic powder
1/4 teaspoon onion powder

Blend in blender well. Bake 1 hour in 250-degree oven. Stir every 15 minutes to blend.

Makes 10 cups.

BOURBON BALLS

1 package (6-ounce) semi-sweet chocolate chips
1/2 cup sugar
3 tablespoons light corn syrup
1/2 cup bourbon - can use more if desired. It won't hurt the recipe.
2 1/2 cups (5 dozen) vanilla wafers, crushed fine
1 cup walnuts or pecans, chopped fine

Melt chocolate chips in top of double boiler. Remove from heat and stir in sugar and corn syrup. Blend in bourbon. Combine crushed wafers and nuts. Add chocolate mixture. Mix well. Shape batter into 1-inch balls. Roll in granulated or powdered sugar, as taste dictates. Store in covered container to ripen.

Jo says, "I usually make the bourbon balls the week after Thanksgiving so they will have plenty of time to flavor. I also add more bourbon than the recipe calls for." Makes 3 dozen.

Under The Mistletoe

"Visions of Sugarplums"

KIDDIES CANDY CANES

1/4 cup margarine
40 large marshmallows
5 cups crisp rice cereal
1/4 cup crushed peppermint candy

Melt margarine in large saucepan over low heat. Add marshmallows; stir until smooth. Remove from heat. Add cereal and candy; stir until well coated. With greased hands, shape into candy canes, using approximately 1/2 cup mixture for each. Place on greased waxed paper; cool. Decorate with a thin red or white ribbon. Makes about 1 dozen canes.

CANDY CANE COOKIES

1/2 cup solid shortening
1/2 cup butter or margarine
1 cup sifted confectioners' sugar
1 egg
1 1/2 teaspoons almond extract
1 teaspoon vanilla
2 1/2 cups all-purpose flour
1 teaspoon salt
1/2 teaspoon red food color
1/2 cup crushed peppermint candy
1/2 cup granulated sugar

Blend shortenings, sugar, egg and flavorings. Mix flour and salt; stir into shortening mixture. Divide dough in half. Blend food coloring into one half.

Using 1 teaspoon dough, roll a 4-inch strip from each color. Make smooth, even strips by rolling them back and forth on lightly floured board, like you used to make "snakes" with clay as a child. Place strips side by side, press lightly together and twist like a rope (see sketch). Do one cookie at a time so strips do not become too dry to handle. Place on ungreased baking sheet. Curve top down to form a handle.

Bake in 375-degree oven 9 minutes or until lightly browned. While still warm, carefully remove from baking sheet with spatula and sprinkle with mixture of candy and sugar. If you do not wish to use peppermint, you can use coarse pink decorators' sugar. Makes 4 dozen.

CATHEDRAL WINDOWS

12-ounce package chocolate chips
1 stick margarine
1 cup chopped nuts
8-ounce package miniature colored marshmallows
Coconut

Melt chocolate chips and margarine together; cool. Pour over marshmallows; add nuts. Mix well. Cover sheet of aluminum foil with coconut; pour mixture over and shape into roll. Refrigerate overnight. Slice in 1/4-inch slices. Makes 3 dozen.

MOM'S CHOCOLATE CHIP COOKIES

1 1/2 cups flour
1 teaspoon salt
1 cup shortening
3/4 cup brown sugar
3/4 cup granulated sugar
2 eggs, unbeaten
1 teaspoon soda dissolved in 1 teaspoon
   hot water
1 cup chopped pecans
1 package (12-ounce) semi-sweet chocolate
   chips
2 cups Quaker oats
1 teaspoon vanilla

Cream shortening and sugars, add eggs and soda mixture, mix well. Add remaining ingredients, mixing well. Drop by 1/2 teaspoons on greased cookie sheet. Bake at 375 degrees for 10-12 minutes. Makes 48.

JEANNE'S CHOCOLATE CHIP COOKIES

3/4 cup granulated sugar
1 1/2 cups brown sugar
1 1/2 cups shortening
3 eggs
1 1/2 teaspoons vanilla
3 cups plus 6 tablespoons flour
1 1/2 teaspoons salt
2 packages (12-ounce size) Nestle's chocolate
   chips
1 cup pecans (optional)

Cream sugars, shortening and eggs. Add vanilla. Add dry ingredients, then chips and nuts. Mix well. Drop by teaspoons on greased cookie sheet. Bake for 10-12 minutes in 375-degree oven. Don't overbake. Makes lots! Makes 50.

Jo says, "A pitcher of cold milk is a must to have nearby as these come out of the oven."

CHOCOLATE MARSHMALLOW COOKIES

1 cup sugar
1/2 cup shortening
2 eggs
1 3/4 cups flour
1/2 cup cocoa
1 teaspoon soda
1/2 teaspoon salt
1 teaspoon vanilla
Pecans
Marshmallows

FROSTING:
1 package (6-ounce) chocolate bits
1/4 cup margarine
1/2 cup evaporated milk
Powdered sugar

Mix all ingredients, except pecans and marshmallows. Place a few pecans in clusters on greased cookie sheet. Roll dough in small walnut-size balls and press onto pecan clusters; press a pecan lightly on top of each cluster. Bake for 8 minutes at 350 degrees. Cut marshmallows in half; place a half cut side down on each cookie. Return to oven; bake for two minutes only.

Boil chocolate bits, milk and margarine for two minutes. Remove from heat; add powdered sugar until spreading consistency. Spread over cookies. Makes 4 dozen.

COCOA BARS

1/4 cup butter or margarine
1 cup sugar
1 teaspoon vanilla
2 eggs
1/4 cup milk
1 cup sifted flour
2 tablespoons cocoa
1/4 teaspoon salt
1/2 cup chopped walnuts

Cream butter to soften. Gradually add sugar and vanilla, creaming well. Beat in eggs, one at a time. Stir in milk. Sift dry ingredients together; stir into creamed mixture. Add nuts. Spread in a greased 9 x 9 x 2-inch pan. Bake in 375-degree oven for 20 minutes or until done. Frost immediately with Cocoa Frosting.

COCOA FROSTING:
1 1/2 teaspoons soft butter or margarine
1 1/2 tablespoons cocoa
1 tablespoon milk
1/4 teaspoon vanilla
2/3 cup sifted confectioners' sugar

Cream butter and cocoa, add milk and vanilla. Stir in confectioners' sugar and mix well. Spread on cake. Cool cake and cut into bars. Makes 2 dozen.

COCONUT JOYS

1/2 cup (1 stick) butter
2 cups powdered sugar
3 cups coconut
2 squares unsweetened chocolate, melted

Melt butter, remove from heat. Add sugar and coconut, mix well. Shape into balls and make indentation in center of each ball. Fill centers with melted chocolate. Chill until firm. Store in covered container in refrigerator. Set out to room temperature before serving to allow chocolate to soften. Makes 24 bars.

KRUNCHY COOKIES

1 cup vegetable shortening
1 cup brown sugar
1 cup white sugar
1 teaspoon vanilla
2 eggs
2 cups sifted flour
1/2 teaspoon salt
1 teaspoon soda
1/2 teaspoon baking powder
2 cups oatmeal
2 cups Rice Krispies
Coconut and nuts (optional)

Cream shortening and sugars until light and fluffy. Add vanilla and eggs. Beat well. Sift flour, salt, soda and baking powder together, stir into above mixture. Add oatmeal and Rice Krispies (and nuts or coconut if desired).

Drop by spoon on greased cookie sheet. Bake 8 to 10 minutes in 350-degree oven. Makes 7 dozen.

AUNT VIRGINIA'S COOKIES

1 cup butter
1 cup sugar
1 egg
2 1/2 cups flour (scant)
1 teaspoon vanilla

Heat oven to 350 degrees. Mix all of the ingredients and drop from spoon (about the size of a quarter) onto cookie sheet. Bake until golden, just beginning to brown on the bottom. Do not overbake. Makes 4 dozen.

EARTHQUAKE COOKIES

1/2 cup vegetable oil
4 squares (4 ounces) unsweetened chocolate, melted
2 cups granulated sugar
4 eggs
2 teaspoons vanilla
2 cups all-purpose flour, sifted then measured
2 teaspoons baking powder
1/2 teaspoon salt
1 cup powdered sugar

Mix oil, chocolate and sugar. Blend in one egg at a time until well mixed. Add vanilla. Stir flour, baking powder and salt into the oil mixture. Chill several hours or overnight.

Heat oven to 350 degrees. Drop teaspoonsful of cookie dough into powdered sugar. Roll in sugar and shape into balls. Place 2 inches apart on a greased baking sheet. Bake for 10 to 12 minutes. Be careful to not overbake. Makes 6 dozen.

GIRDLE BUSTER BARS

1 package yellow cake mix
1 stick butter
1 box powdered sugar
4 eggs
1 package (8-ounce) cream cheese

Melt butter and add, with 1 egg, to cake mix. Mix until well blended. Divide into 2 parts and spread into 2 8-inch greased and floured cake pans. Mix powdered sugar, 3 eggs, and cream cheese. Pour onto mixture in cake pans. Bake at 350 degrees for 1 hour. Cool 10 minutes. Cut each pan into 16 pieces.

LEMON SQUARES

2 cups flour
1 cup (2 sticks) butter or 1 stick butter and 1 stick margarine
1/2 cup powdered sugar
4 eggs
4 tablespoons lemon juice
2 cups sugar
4 tablespoons flour
1 teaspoon baking powder
1/2 teaspoon salt

Melt butter in 9 x 13-inch pan. Mix 2 cups flour and powdered sugar. Pour into pan and stir with butter. Press down firmly. Bake 20 minutes at 350 degrees. Beat together eggs and lemon juice. Sift together 2 cups sugar, 4 tablespoons flour, baking powder and salt. Add sifted mixture to egg and lemon juice. Pour mixture on top of baked crust while it is hot. Bake 25 minutes more at 350 degrees. Remove from oven and sift powdered sugar over top while cake is hot. Cut and serve. Makes 36 squares.

ORANGE ICEBOX COOKIES

1 cup butter (or 3/4 cup margarine)
1/2 cup granulated sugar
1/2 cup light brown sugar
1 egg
3 cups flour
1/2 teaspoon salt
1/4 teaspoon baking soda
Grated rind of 1 orange
2 tablespoons orange juice
1 teaspoon vanilla
1/2 cup chopped toasted almonds

Cream butter and sugars. Beat in egg. Sift together flour, salt and baking soda. Blend into egg mixture. Mix in orange rind and juice, vanilla and chopped nuts. Chill dough until stiff enough to shape into rolls (make them about 1 1/2 to 2 inches in diameter, 8 to 10 inches long). Wrap each in aluminum foil and freeze. To bake, slice cookies 1/8-inch thick. Place on lightly greased baking sheet and bake in 375-degree oven for 12 to 15 minutes. Makes 5 dozen.

Under The Mistletoe

MINI MINCEMEAT NUT CAKES

1/2 cup butter or margarine
1/3 cup dark brown sugar, firmly packed
3 eggs
2 1/2 cups sifted flour
1 teaspoon salt
1 teaspoon baking powder
1/2 teaspoon baking soda
1 can sweetened condensed milk
2 2/3 cups (28-ounce jar) mincemeat
2 cups California walnuts, coarsely chopped

Cream butter and sugar in bowl until fluffy. Add eggs; mix well. Sift together dry ingredients. Add to butter mixture, alternating with condensed milk. Blend. Stir in mincemeat and walnuts. Line 1 1/2-inch cupcake pans with 2-inch paper liners. Drop heaping teaspoons of batter into each liner. Bake in 350-degree oven for 20 to 25 minutes. Cool. Decorate with frostings, nuts or holiday cookie sprinkles. Makes 5 dozen.

Jo says, "If you have trouble finding the 1 1/2 inch cupcake pans and tiny liners, check your kitchen speciality shops, or during the holidays, many Christmas shops will carry the liners. If you cannot find pans, use paper liners, triple thick on cookie sheet. Fill and bake as directed."

PEANUT BUTTER COOKIES

1/2 cup shortening (half butter or margarine)
1/2 cup peanut butter
1/2 cup granulated sugar
1/2 cup packed brown sugar
1 egg
1 1/4 cups flour, sift before measuring
1/2 teaspoon baking powder
3/4 teaspoon baking soda
1/4 teaspoon salt

Mix shortening, peanut butter, sugars and egg thoroughly. Blend all dry ingredients; stir into shortening mixture. Chill dough.

Heat oven to 375 degrees. Roll dough in 1 1/4-inch balls. Place 3 inches apart on lightly greased baking sheet. Flatten crisscross style with fork dipped in flour. Bake 10 to 12 minutes. Makes 3 dozen.

PEANUT BUTTER DESSERT BARS

Prepare dough for Peanut Butter Cookies. Chill 1 hour. Heat oven to 375 degrees. Using cookie press with star plate, make 2 1/2 inch fingers. Bake 8 to 10 minutes. When cool, dip ends in melted chocolate (4 small plain chocolate bars), then in 3/4 cup salted crushed peanuts. Makes 6 dozen.

PEANUT BUTTER CUPS I

1 1/2 cup graham crackers, crushed
2 sticks butter, melted
1 box powdered sugar
1 cup peanut butter
1 package (12-ounce) chocolate chips, melted

Mix all ingredients except chocolate chips. Press into a buttered 9 x 13-inch pan. Spread melted chocolate chips over mixture. Refrigerate until firm. Warm slightly at room temperature and cut into squares. Makes 4 dozen.

Under The Mistletoe

PEANUT BUTTER CUPS II

1 cup graham crackers, crushed
1 stick butter, melted
2 cups peanut butter
2 1/2 cups powdered sugar
1/2 cup brown sugar
1/2 teaspoon vanilla
1 package (12-ounce) chocolate chips, melted

Mix all ingredients together, except the chocolate chips. Press into buttered 9 x 13-inch pan. Spread melted chocolate chips over mixture. Refrigerate until firm. Warm slightly at room temperature and cut into squares. Makes 4 dozen.

SALTED PEANUT COOKIES

1 cup melted butter
2 cups brown sugar
2 eggs, beaten well
2 cups flour
1 teaspoon baking powder
1 teaspoon soda
1 teaspoon vanilla
2 cups oatmeal
1 cup cornflakes
2 cups whole salted peanuts

Cream butter and sugar, add eggs, beating well, and add flour, baking powder and soda. Mix well and add vanilla, oatmeal, cornflakes and peanuts. Drop by spoon on greased cookie sheet. Bake at 350 degrees for 10 to 12 minutes. Makes 50.

PECAN TARTS

1 cup margarine
1/2 cup sugar
2 egg yolks
1 teaspoon almond extract
2 cups sifted flour
1/3 cup Karo dark syrup
1 cup confectioners' sugar
1 cup chopped pecans
Pecan halves for tops

Mix 1/2 cup margarine and 1/2 cup sugar. Stir in 2 egg yolks, 1 teaspoon almond extract and 2 cups sifted flour. Press evenly into tiny tart shells or muffin cups. Bake in 400-degree oven for 8 to 10 minutes.

Bring to a boil 1/2 cup margarine, 1/3 cup Karo dark syrup and 1 cup confectioners' sugar. Stir in 1 cup chopped pecans and spoon into shells. Top with pecan halves. Bake in 350-degree oven for 5 minutes. Makes 24.

SERENDIPITIES

1 cup shortening
1 cup brown sugar
1 cup white sugar
2 eggs
1 teaspoon soda
1 1/2 cups flour
1 cup oats
1 cup chocolate chips
1 cup chopped pecans

Blend shortening and sugars, add eggs, blend well. Sift soda and flour and add to shortening-sugar mixture. Add oats, chocolate chips and pecans. Pour into greased and floured 9 x 13-inch pan and bake in a preheated 350-degree oven for 30 minutes. Cool and cut into squares. Makes 24.

Under The Mistletoe

ANNIE'S SHERRY BARS

4 ounces baking chocolate
1 cup margarine
4 eggs
2 cups sugar
1 cup flour
1/4 teaspoon salt
1 teaspoon vanilla
Nuts, optional
1/2 cup butter
4 cups powdered sugar
1/4 cup half-and-half
1/4 cup sherry
1 package (12-ounce) chocolate chips
3 tablespoons half-and-half
4 tablespoons butter

Melt baking chocolate and margarine together. Add eggs, sugar, flour, salt, vanilla and nuts. Spread this mixture in a 10 x 15-inch jelly roll pan and bake at 350 degrees for 20 to 25 minutes. Refrigerate until cool.
FILLING:
Cream 1/2 cup butter and powdered sugar well and slowly add half-and-half cream and the sherry. Mixture should be light and fluffy. Spread on cool base and refrigerate until cold.
TOPPING:
Melt package of chocolate chips and add 3 tablespoons half-and-half and 4 tablespoons butter. When filling is cold, spread on top and keep in refrigerator until serving time. Cut into squares.
Jan says, "Don't back off from this recipe. It is truly one of the best. You will be declared a winner." Makes 4 dozen.

SHORTBREAD COOKIES

4 cups flour
1 pound butter
1 cup sugar
1 teaspoon vanilla

Cream butter and sugar thoroughly. Gradually add flour to mixture, then vanilla. If dough seems too soft, add a little more flour. Chill dough for several hours until stiff enough to work with. Drop by teaspoons onto ungreased cookie sheet. Bake at 300 degrees for 15 minutes or until slightly brown. (Watch bottoms so they don't get too brown.) Store in covered container. Freeze very well. Makes 50 squares.

MADELYN'S SLEEP COOKIES

2 egg whites
1/8 teaspoon salt
1/4 teaspoon cream of tartar
2/3 cup sugar
1 teaspoon vanilla
1/4 teaspoon almond extract
1 cup pecans or walnuts, chopped
3/4 cup chocolate chips

Preheat oven to 350 degrees. Beat egg whites until frothy. Add cream of tartar and salt. Gradually add sugar, vanilla and almond extract. After mixture has stiffened and formed peaks that shine, stop beating. Fold in nuts and chocolate chips.
Grease 2 cookie sheets. With teaspoon drop bite-size mounds on sheet. Place cookie sheets in oven. Turn off heat, leaving in the oven until morning. Do not peek. Put cookies in air-tight container until ready to use. Makes 60 to 70 cookies. Makes 3 dozen.

SIX LAYER COOKIES

1 stick melted butter
1 cup graham cracker crumbs
1 cup coconut
1 package (12-ounce) chocolate chips
1 cup chopped nuts
1 can Eagle Brand sweetened condensed milk

Place ingredients in 8 x 8-inch pan in the order given. Bake 35 to 45 minutes at 350 degrees.

Jo says, "You can make 7-layer cookies substituting the 12-ounce package of chocolate chips for 1 6-ounce package of chocolate chips and 1 6-ounce package of butterscotch chips. This recipe is really good and rich!" Makes 16.

SNICKERDOODLES

1/2 cup sweet butter
3/4 cup sugar
1 whole egg
1 egg yolk
1 2/3 cups flour
1/2 teaspoon baking soda
1/2 teaspoon nutmeg
1/2 cup walnut pieces
1/2 cup raisins

Cream butter and sugar. Beat in whole egg and egg yolk. Sift flour and soda with 1/2 teaspoon nutmeg. Mix into batter. Fold in nuts and raisins. Drop from a teaspoon 2 inches apart onto a buttered cookie sheet. Sprinkle with sugar and cinnamon. Bake at 375 degrees for 10 to 12 minutes. Makes 5 dozen.

SAINT NICKERDOODLES

Use Snickerdoodle recipe except sprinkle with green decorators' sugar instead of cinnamon and sugar.

ROLLED SUGAR COOKIES

1 cup butter
2 cups sugar
1 cup sour cream
3 eggs
1 1/2 teaspoons soda
4 cups flour (approximately, no more than 4)

Cream butter and sugar. Add sour cream and eggs, mixing well. Stir in flour and soda. Chill dough. Roll out dough on floured board and cut into shapes. Bake at 375 degrees for about 10 minutes.

Jo says, "Keep dough well chilled before and during the rolling out. Take just a small amount from refrigerator at a time." Makes 7 dozen.

SUGAR COOKIES

1/2 cup shortening
1/2 cup margarine
1 cup sugar
1 egg
2 1/2 cups flour
1/2 teaspoon soda
1 teaspoon vanilla
2 tablespoons milk

Cream shortening, margarine and sugar. Mix well and add 1 egg until batter is creamy. Add flour, soda and vanilla, mixing well after each addition. Blend in 2 tablespoons milk.

Drop by teaspoon on a greased baking sheet. Flatten each ball with a sugar-dipped glass bottom. Bake at 400 degrees for 8 minutes. Makes 5 1/2 dozen.

Under The Mistletoe

CHOCOLATE SUGARPLUMS

2 cups coarsely chopped pecans
2 cups coarsely chopped unblanched almonds
1 cup orange-peel preserves, chopped
3/4 cup coconut
1/4 cup undiluted orange juice concentrate
1 package (12-ounce) semisweet chocolate chips
1 large egg, beaten
Confectioners' sugar

Mix pecans, almonds, orange-peel preserves, coconut and orange juice in a large bowl. In a small saucepan over hot water melt chocolate. Cool 15 minutes. Beat in egg until mixture is smooth. Stir chocolate into nut mixture. When thoroughly mixed, let stand 20 to 30 minutes, until firm enough to handle. With buttered hands, shape into walnut-size balls. Roll in confectioners' sugar. Chill until ready to serve. Makes 60 pieces.

CHINESE TIMBALES

1 egg
1/2 cup milk
1 tablespoon sugar
1/2 teaspoon salt
1/2 teaspoon cooking oil
1/2 cup flour

Combine slightly beaten egg, milk, sugar, salt and oil. Sift flour slowly into mixture, beating constantly until smooth. Set aside until bubbles subside. Heat fat to 360 degrees. Heat Timbale iron in oil, shake off and dip into batter. Do not let batter cover top of iron. Dip into hot oil, holding a few seconds, then shake off. Turn when edges are brown.
Sprinkle with powdered sugar when cool. Makes 8-10.

TOFFEE BARS

1/2 cup butter or margarine, softened
1/2 cup sugar
1/2 teaspoon salt
1 cup all-purpose flour
1 can (14-ounce) sweetened condensed milk
2 tablespoons butter or margarine
1/4 teaspoon salt
2 teaspoons vanilla
Fudge Frosting

Cream 1/2 cup butter, sugar and 1/2 teaspoon salt; stir in flour. Pat into ungreased 13 x 9 x 2-inch baking pan. Bake at 350 degrees until lightly browned, about 15 minutes. In heavy saucepan, cook and stir sweetened condensed milk, 2 tablespoons butter, and 1/4 teaspoon salt over low heat until butter melts. Cook and stir for 5 minutes over medium heat. Mixture will thicken and become smooth. Stir in vanilla. Spread over baked layer. Bake at 350 degrees until golden, 12 to 15 minutes. Spread warm cookies with Fudge Frosting.

FUDGE FROSTING:

FROSTING:
2 tablespoons butter
1 (1-ounce) square unsweetened chocolate
1 1/2 cups powdered sugar, sifted
1 teaspoon vanilla

In saucepan, melt butter and chocolate over low heat, stirring constantly. Remove from heat; stir in powdered sugar and vanilla. Blend in about 2 tablespoons hot water until pourable consistency. Spread over top, and wait one hour until chocolate sets. Cut into squares. Makes 48.

Under The Mistletoe

LEMON WINE COOKIES

2 cups flour
Pinch of salt
1/2 cup shortening
1/3 cup sugar
Grated rind of 1 lemon
2 egg yolks
1 tablespoon sherry

TOPPING:
1 cup powdered sugar
1 to 2 tablespoons lemon juice
1 tablespoon chopped pistachio nuts

Preheat oven to 350 degrees. Sift flour and salt. Rub in shortening with fingertips until mixture is crumbly. Stir in sugar and lemon rind. Mix egg yolks with sherry, add to lemon mixture and knead dough lightly with hand until smooth. On floured board, roll out dough 1/8-inch thick and cut into 3-inch rounds. Set on greased baking sheet. Bake 8 to 10 minutes or until just beginning to brown. Transfer to wire rack to cool.

Sift powdered sugar. Stir in enough lemon juice to make a stiff paste. Set bowl over pan of hot water and warm the icing until tepid; it should coat the back of a spoon. If it is too thin, beat in more powdered sugar. Coat cookie and sprinkle a few chopped pistachios in the center of each. Makes 24 cookies.

WINDSOR COOKIES

2 cups flour
2/3 cup shortening
1/4 cup sugar
1 1/2 cups brown sugar
2 tablespoons flour
1/4 teaspoon baking powder
2 eggs
1/2 cup chopped pecans
1/2 cup coconut
1 teaspoon vanilla

FROSTING:
Juice of 1/2 lemon
Juice of 1/2 orange
2 tablespoons butter
Enough powdered sugar for spreading
    consistency

Combine flour, shortening and 1/4 cup sugar. Mix and pat in bottom of 9 x 13-inch pan. Bake 10 minutes in 375-degree oven.

Beat eggs until light. Add brown sugar gradually and beat well. Sift flour, baking powder and pinch of salt over nuts and coconut. Add to egg mixture and blend thoroughly. Add vanilla and spread over crust and bake 15 minutes at 375 degrees. Cool, and spread with frosting.

Combine juices, butter and powdered sugar and spread over top layer. Cut into squares and store in covered container. Do not freeze. Makes 3 dozen.

BUTTER LOGS

2 1/4 cups flour
1 cup powdered sugar
1/2 teaspoon salt
1/4 teaspoon cream of tartar
1/4 teaspoon soda
1 egg, slightly beaten
1 tablespoon water
1 cup soft butter

Mix flour, sugar, salt, soda and cream of tartar. Cream butter well, add egg and water, then mix in dry ingredients to form dough. Chill for easier handling. Shape by teaspoons into logs, balls or crescents. Place on ungreased cookie sheets. Bake at 350 degrees for 12 to 15 minutes, until a delicate golden brown. While warm, roll in powdered sugar. Makes 5 dozen.

Under The Mistletoe

CHRISTMAS RUM CAKE

Before you start, sample the rum and check for quality. Good, isn't it? Now, go ahead. Select a large mixing bowl, measuring cup, etc., and check the rum again for quality. It must be just right. Try it again. With an electric beater, beat one cup butter in a large fluffly bowl. Add one teaspoon sugar and beat again. Meanwhile, make certain the rum is of best quality.

Add two large eggs and two cups dried fruit and beat well -- until bery high. If fruit gets stuck in beater, pry it out with screwdriver. Sample rum again, checking for consistency. Next sift in 3 cups baking powder, add a pink of rum, 1 seaspoon toda and 1 cup of pepper -- or is it salt? Anyway, don't fret. Just test the rum again. ZOWIE........

Now, sift in half a pint of lemon juice, fold in chopped buttermilk and add strained nuts. Shample the rum again.

Now, one bablespoon srown tugar or whatever color is around. Mix well. Grease oven and turn on cake pan to 350 degrees. Now pour the whole mixture into the oven and......oops..... Now, where'd I put that mop?

On second thought, and also third and fourth, forget the oven, forget the cake, check the rest of the rum and go to bed!

PLUM PUDDING

2 cups ground suet
2 cups raisins
2 cups walnuts
2 eggs
2 cups buttermilk
2 cups sugar
3 cups flour
2 cups currants
2 teaspoons soda
2 teaspoons cloves
2 teaspoons cinnamon

Mix all ingredients together. Fill 10 to 12 1-pound coffee cans 2/3 full. Cover. Place in roaster in small amount of water. Steam 2 1/2 hours. Leave in cans or remove when cool and wrap in aluminum foil and store in refrigerator or freezer.

PLUM PUDDING SAUCE

1 cup brown sugar
1 cup white sugar
1 1/2 cups water
3 tablespoons flour
1 teaspoon vanilla
2 tablespoons butter

Mix sugars and flour; add water and cook until thick. Add vanilla and butter. At this point you may desire to add a jigger of liquor. Serve very hot over plum pudding which has been reheated in a double boiler. Makes 3 1/2 cups.

Under The Mistletoe

HOLIDAY PUDDING

1 package (14-ounce) gingerbread mix
1/4 cup sherry
3/4 cup orange juice
1/2 teaspoon grated orange peel
1/2 cup chopped walnuts
Golden Sherry Sauce - to be served in a bowl
Hard Sauce Snowballs

Preheat oven to 350 degrees. Prepare gingerbread according to package directions using sherry and orange juice for liquid called for. Add orange peel and walnuts. Turn batter into a well-greased 6-cup mold (batter should fill mold 1/2 to 2/3 full). Bake in preheated oven 50 to 55 minutes, until pudding tests done. Serve warm with Golden Sherry Sauce.

GOLDEN SHERRY SAUCE:
1/2 cup granulated sugar
1/2 cup packed brown sugar
1/4 cup heavy cream
1/8 teaspoon salt
1/4 cup sherry
1 teaspoon grated lemon peel

Combine sugars, cream and salt in saucepan. Heat slowly to boiling, stirring often. Add sherry and lemon peel. Heat slightly to blend flavors. Makes 1 1/3 cups.

HARD SAUCE SNOWBALLS:
1/2 cup soft butter or margarine
3 1/2 cups sifted powdered sugar
1 teaspoon brandy
Coconut

Beat butter, powdered sugar and brandy. Shape into small balls and roll in flaked coconut. Place around edge of pudding, decorate with a few sprigs of holly.

If you prefer to serve a "soft" hard sauce, beat in a little additional brandy or cream. Spoon onto the pudding. Recipe makes 1 1/2 cups of "soft" hard sauce or 16 balls.

WHITE CHRISTMAS FRUIT CAKE

1 pound butter or margarine
3 cups white sugar
6 egg yolks, beaten
5 cups flour
1 bottle (2-ounce) lemon extract
1 pound white raisins
4 ounce candied cherries
4 ounce candied pineapple
4 cups pecan pieces
1 teaspoon soda dissolved in 1 tablespoon warm water
3 tablespoons spiced peach juice
6 egg whites

Cream butter and sugar, add egg yolks. Combine raisins, nuts and candied fruit in part of the flour. Add rest of flour gradually to creamed mixture, then add floured raisins, nuts, candied fruit, lemon extract, spiced peach juice and soda mixture. Mix well.

Beat egg whites until they stand in peaks and fold lightly into above mixture.

Grease pans and line with brown paper. This recipe will make 2 angel food tube-pan cakes. Bake for 90 minutes in 250-degree oven. After baking, slip out of pan and paper will slip off or it may be left in paper. Wrap in foil and store in freezer where it will mellow and become even more delicious. Serves 32.

ORANGE SLICE FRUITCAKE

1 cup butter
2 cups sugar
4 eggs
1/2 cup buttermilk
1 teaspoon soda
1 pound orange slice candy
3 1/2 cups flour
4-ounce can coconut
2 1/2 cups chopped pecans
1/2 pound dates, cut thin

Cream butter and sugar. Add eggs, one at a time. Combine soda and flour and add to creamed mixture alternately with buttermilk. Add orange slice candy. Mix in pecans, coconut and dates. Pour into greased angel food pan. Bake at 250 degrees for 2 1/2 hours. Remove from pan and pour mixture of one cup orange juice and 2 cups confectioners' sugar over hot cake. Make this at least 3 weeks before Christmas. Keep in refrigerator. Makes 16-18 slices.

CHRISTMAS ESSENCE FROM SCOTLAND

Jan says, ''My sister spent two years in Scotland and brought back these tried and true recipes of Scottish friends.''

MONICA'S SCONES

8 ounces self-rising flour
Pinch of salt
1 teaspoon soda
2 ounces butter
2 ounces powdered sugar
4 ounces soured milk or 1 pot of yogurt

Put flour, salt, soda in bowl. Rub in butter. Add sugar. Mix until a soft dough with milk or yogurt. Knead lightly on floured board and roll to 1/2-inch thickness. Cut as desired and bake 10 to 12 minutes in hot oven (450 degrees). Makes 1 dozen.

DOREEN'S MELTING MOMENTS

7 ounces margarine
2 ounces icing sugar
4 ounces plain flour
2 ounces self-rising flour

2 ounces margarine
4 ounces icing sugar
Semi-sweet melted chocolate

Cream margarine and sugar. Add the 2 flours by degrees. Place small balls on greased baking trays 2 inches apart and mark with top of fork. Bake in brisk oven at 375 degrees until golden brown, about 15 minutes. Cool and ice. Sandwich together with the following butter icing.

Beat margarine and sugar well. Dip end of the cookie in semi-sweet melted chocolate. These cookies should be cut into 1 x 3-inch slices. Like fingers. Makes 1 dozen.

CHOCOLATE CARAMEL FINGERS

BASE:
Cream 4 ounces margarine with 2 ounces sugar. Add 5 ounces flour, mixing well. Spread in greased small pan (8 x 8-inch). Bake for 5 minutes and then reduce heat to 285 degrees for 20 minutes.

FILLING:
Melt 4 ounces margarine, 2 tablespoons light Karo syrup, 1 small can evaporated milk, 4 ounces fine sugar in pan slowly. When it comes to boiling, boil 5 minutes exactly, stirring all the time until fudgelike. Cool slightly and pour on base. Then spread on top of the above mixture 6 ounces melted semi-sweet chocolate and mark with the back of a fork. Cut into fingers when cold. Makes 8.

DOREEN'S PEPPERMINT SLAB

4 ounces margarine
2 ounces sugar
1 cup flour
1 cup coconut
3 teaspoons drinking chocolate
(Nestle's chocolate powder)

Combine ingredients and spread into Swiss (8 x 8-inch) pan. Press in pan well. Bake at 350 degrees 20 to 25 minutes.

FILLING:
10 ounces icing sugar (powdered)
1/2 teaspoon peppermint flavor
1/2 teaspoon green coloring

Mix ingredients well and put on the above cooled base. Top with 6-ounces semi-sweet melted chocolate. Makes 8-10.

MONICA'S SHORTBREAD

8 ounces butter
3 ounces sugar
6 ounces plain flour
4 ounces ground almonds
Few drops of vanilla essence

Gently melt the butter in a pan. Remove from heat. Combine rest of ingredients and add to butter. Mix well and press into a flat greased tin.
Bake at 325 degrees for 15 minutes or until golden brown. Makes 6-10.

IRISH TRUFFLES

5 tablespoons coconut
4 tablespoons oats
2 tablespoons cocoa
3 tablespoons sugar
2 ounces butter
2 tablespoons milk
2 ounces vermicilla (chocolate crinkles)
Raisins, walnuts or rum (optional)

Melt butter. Mix dry ingredients except coconut and vermicilla. Add milk and melted butter. Form into balls (walnut size). Roll in coconut or vermicilla. Makes 1 dozen.

COFFEE-WHISKEY TRIFLE

1 tablespoon cornstarch
2 tablespoons sugar
3 egg yolks
2 cups half-and-half

Place cornstarch, sugar and egg yolks in bowl. Mix well together. Add this mixture to well heated half and half cream and continue to mix thoroughly. Cook mixture until thick. Cool.

1/2 of basic sponge cake (see next page)
1/2 pint very strong coffee
1 1/2 pints custard
1/4 gill whiskey
4 ounces semi-sweet chocolate, grated
1/2 cup heavy cream, whipped lightly
4 ounces chopped pecans

Line a glass bowl with pieces of sponge cake. Scattering the nuts, mix coffee and whiskey together and pour over the cake. Gently poke the cake down in the bowl. Cover with custard and top with whipped cream. Sprinkle with grated chocolate and refrigerate several hours.
1/4 gill = 1/2 cup. Serves 8-10.

Under The Mistletoe

BASIC SPONGE CAKE

3 large eggs
4 ounces sugar
3 ounces flour, sifted
1 tablespoon hot water
Pinch of salt
1 tablespoon soft butter
1 teaspoon vanilla essence

Place eggs, vanilla, sugar in bowl. Beat with mixer about 5 minutes until it is really, really thick. Fold the flour and salt into the egg mixture with a metal spoon. Do not stir or beat. Fold in water, butter and pour into 2 well-greased, floured 7 to 8-inch tins. Bake 15 to 20 minutes until golden brown and springy in the center. Cool.

Jan says, "This Coffee-Whiskey Trifle is very good. The sponge cake is really a sponge cake."

ALMOND ROCO

2 cups sugar
2 cups butter
1/3 cup water
2 cups almonds, sliced and browned in the oven
2 large (8 ounces each) chocolate bars

Mix sugar, butter and water in large saucepan. Cook over high heat until color becomes tan and gets to hard-crack stage (285 degrees). Pour over sliced almonds spread out on a jelly-roll-size buttered pan. Cool slightly. Lay chocolate pieces on warm candy, let melt. Spread evenly with a knife. Let it "set up" over night and break in pieces when set. Keep in covered container. Makes 2 pounds.

MOTH BALLS

4 tablespoons powdered sugar, rounded
1 1/4 sticks butter
1 tablespoon water
1 teaspoon vanilla
2 cups sifted flour
2 cups pecan halves

Cream butter and sugar, add water, vanilla, then flour and nuts. Roll into balls and bake on cookie sheet at 300 degrees 1 hour or longer, just until bottoms are beginning to become golden. When cool, roll in powdered sugar. Freezes well. Makes 24.

Jo says, "This is a traditional Christmas cookie in my family. When I would come home from college for the holidays, Mom would have the cookie jar full. I have had many breakfasts of just moth balls and a big glass of milk.

If I couldn't make any other holiday goodie, this is the one that would have to be done. I would double the recipe, though, because this one won't last."

CHOCOLATE BON-BONS

2 pounds of powdered sugar
1/2 pound of margarine (softened)
1 can Eagle Brand milk
2 cups chopped pecans
1 large can Angel Flake coconut
1 teaspoon vanilla
1 teaspoon butter flavoring
1 large bag of chocolate chips
1 bar paraffin

Mix and combine first 3 ingredients with the next 4 ingredients. Chill. Form in balls and chill again. Melt 1 bar of paraffin in separate pan. Melt one large bag of chocolate chips. When chocolate chips are melted, gradually add paraffin. Dip balls in chocolate with toothpicks and cool on wax paper. Store in refrigerator at least 2 hours.

Makes 100 balls.

Under The Mistletoe

BOSTON CREAM CANDY

3 1/2 pounds sugar (7 cups)
1 1/2 pints thick cream (3 cups)
1 pound white syrup (2 1/4 cups)
1 teaspoon salt
1 tablespoon vanilla
1 teaspoon lemon extract
1 teaspoon butter extract
2 cups chopped candied cherries
2 cups chopped green candied cherries
2 cups chopped candied pineapple
3 cups chopped pecans
2 cups chopped English walnuts
2 cups chopped Brazil nuts

Prepare all fruits and nuts. Grease 2 loaf pans 5 x 9-inch. Line them with waxed paper and leave 2 or 3 inches over the sides. Mix cream, syrup, sugar and salt in a large deep kettle with a wooden spoon and stir over high heat until it boils. Turn to medium heat, stirring occasionally until it forms a soft ball in cold water or registers 250 on a candy thermometer. Remove from heat and set kettle in cold water in sink and stir vigorously for about 5 minutes. When it turns slightly creamy, add flavorings and set out of water onto table and continue beating. Add fruits and nuts. Mix thoroughly and pour into pans and pat down with spoon. Let cool, then remove with the edges of the waxed paper. Wrap in foil or waxed paper. Store in air-tight cans if desired. Let mellow until the holidays. Slice 1/2-inch slices like bread and cut into pieces. Makes 40 pieces.

Jo says, "You better have a man handy to assist on this one. The stirring can be difficult."

LOIS' BROWN SUGAR CANDY

2 cups brown sugar
1 cup white sugar
1 cup milk
1/8 teaspoon soda
1 tablespoon butter or margarine
1/4 teaspoon salt
1 cup Grape Nut Flakes

Boil all ingredients except Grape Nut Flakes to soft ball stage (234-238 degrees on candy thermometer). Cool to room temperature. Add Grape Nut Flakes. If desired, add 1/2 cup raisins, dates or nuts. Beat until stiff enough to knead. Turn onto board dusted with powdered sugar and knead until smooth. Shape into a roll and slice. Makes 24 slices.

AUNT MARY'S CARAMELS

2 cups sugar
1 1/2 cups white syrup
3/4 cup butter
1 can evaporated milk (13-ounce)
Enough chopped walnuts to cover a 9 x 9-inch pan
1 teaspoon vanilla

Mix all ingredients except vanilla in heavy kettle, saving out 1 cup (8 ounces) milk. Boil over medium heat for 3 minutes. Add remaining 1 cup milk and cook about 25 minutes stirring, constantly over medium heat to firm ball stage. Take off heat and add 1 teaspoon vanilla. Pour into well-greased 9 x 9-inch pan. Cover with walnuts and cool at room temperature overnight. Cut into small pieces and wrap in waxed paper. Makes 80 to 90.

Under The Mistletoe

CHOCOLATE CHIP COOKIE BRITTLE

1 cup butter
1 teaspoon vanilla
1 teaspoon salt
1 cup sugar
2 cups unsifted flour
1 package (6-ounce) chocolate chips
1 cup chopped pecans

Mix butter, vanilla and salt. Add sugar, flour and chocolate chips. Mix well. Press evenly onto a greased 15 x 10 x 1-inch cookie sheet with sides. Press pecan pieces on top. Bake for 25 minutes at 375 degrees. When done, turn cookie sheet upside down, releasing entire sheet of cookie onto paper toweling. When cool, break into pieces. Store in covered container. Freezes well. Makes 24 pieces.

HOLIDAY DELIGHT

3 cups sugar
1 cup light corn syrup
1 1/2 cups coffee
1 1/2 teaspoons vanilla

1/2 pound Brazil nuts - cut into two pieces
1/2 pound shelled pecans, coarsely broken
1/2 pound walnuts, coarsely broken
1/2 pound candied cherries, halved
1/2 pound candied pineapple, cut in pieces

Combine the first 3 ingredients and cook to soft ball stage (236 degrees) over medium heat. Remove from heat and begin beating immediately. It will begin to thicken and change color. Add 1 1/2 teaspoons vanilla and continue beating. Have ready the fruits and nuts and add slowly to cooked mixture.

When all are added, mixture will be thick and sticky. Pack in waxed-paper-lined loaf pan. Press firmly with wet spoons. Place in refrigerator. Will keep for months. Makes 5 dozen.

HOLIDAY DIPPED CREAMS

4 ounces cream cheese, softened
2 tablespoons margarine
1 1/2 tablespoons peanut butter
1/8 teaspoon vanilla
1 package (1-pound) confectioners' sugar
1/4 cup chopped pecans
1 package (12-ounce) chocolate chips
1/2 block paraffin, shaved
Red and green decorator icing

Soften cream cheese in microwave or over a pan of simmering water. Blend cream cheese and margarine. Add peanut butter, vanilla, pecans and sugar. Shape into balls. Chill. Place chips and paraffin in 3-quart bowl. Melt in pan over simmering water or on medium in microwave until paraffin is melted. Stir well. Dip each cream cheese ball into chocolate. Place on wax paper to cool. When cool, decorate with icing. Store in refrigerator. Freezes well. Makes 2 pounds.

DELUXE CHOCOLATE FUDGE

3 cups (3 6-ounce packages) semi-sweet chocolate chips
1 cup butter or margarine
2 cups marshmallow whip
2 teaspoons vanilla
2 cups coarsely chopped nuts
1 large can (14 1/2-ounce) evaporated milk
3 1/2 cups white sugar

Measure first 5 ingredients into a large bowl. Combine milk and sugar in saucepan; bring to a boil and cook 12 to 15 minutes, stirring constantly. Pour this mixture over ingredients in bowl. Stir until completely combined. Pour into greased 13 x 9 x 2-inch pan; chill for several hours before cutting. Store in covered container in refrigerator. Makes 2 pounds.

CHRISTMAS FANCIES

3 cups white sugar
1 cup white Karo syrup
1 1/2 cups light cream
1/8 teaspoon salt
1 teaspoon vanilla
4 drops lemon juice
1 cup whole Brazil nuts
1 cup whole English walnuts
1 cup whole hazelnuts
1 cup whole pecan halves
1 cup blanched almonds
1 cup candied cherries, cut in half
1 cup candied cut pineapple
1/2 cup green cut cherries or green cut
    pineapple
Note: Can use whole nuts, or halves.

In deep kettle cook 3 cups sugar, 1 1/2 cups light cream, 1 cup white syrup, 1/8 teaspoon salt on high heat, stirring constantly. When a rolling boil starts, reduce the heat to medium and begin timing. From the boiling point, cook on medium heat for 23 minutes, stirring gently every so often. Test for soft ball stage in cold water (238 degrees on a candy thermometer). When it meets this test, it is ready to take off the stove.

Beat with a wooden spoon until warm; add vanilla, lemon juice and mix well. Mix nuts and fruits together and add to candy mixture. Quickly mix all well. Pour into buttered dish, 9 x 10-inch. Candy must sit 24 hours at room temperature or in refrigerator; it might take longer in rainy weather. It will turn white when it sets up. Don't cover the dish while it is sitting 24 hours. If it gets moist, it will not set right.

Cut and store in tin boxes or jars. It will keep indefinitely. You may halve the recipe, timing the cooking 11 1/2 minutes. You may fix it to your own taste, leaving out the nuts or fruit, fixing it plain, experiment. Makes 70-80 pieces.

FABULOUS FUDGE

2 1/4 cups sugar
3/4 cup evaporated milk
1 cup marshmallow cream or 16 large
    marshmallows
1/4 cup butter or margarine
1/4 teaspoon salt
1 package (6-ounce) semi-sweet chocolate
    morsels
1 teaspoon vanilla
1 cup chopped nuts (optional)

Combine sugar, milk, marshmallow cream, butter and salt in a heavy 2-quart saucepan. Cook, stirring constantly, over medium heat until mixture comes to a boil. It will be bubbling all over the top. Boil and stir 5 minutes more. Take off heat. Stir in chocolate morsels until completely melted. Add vanilla and nuts. Spread in buttered 8-inch square pan. Cool and cut into 30 pieces. Store in covered container.

Jo says, "Experiment with this recipe. Add some instant coffee for mocha fudge. Try rum flavoring, or peppermint. Add black walnuts or hazelnuts for a different nutty flavor. So good."

SEA FOAM NUT FUDGE

6 cups white sugar
3 cups whipping cream
1 pint white Karo syrup
3 cups chopped walnuts
1 teaspoon salt
1 teaspoon vanilla

Put sugar, salt, syrup and cream in a large pan and cook over very low heat to avoid scorching, stirring occasionally. Cook until firm ball stage, 245 degrees on candy thermometer, or when a small amount forms a firm ball when dropped in a small amount of ice water. Take off heat and beat until mixture creams like fudge. Add vanilla and nuts. Do not beat this candy until it loses its shine. Makes 4-5 dozen.

MILLIONAIRES

1 package (14-ounce) caramels
2 tablespoons milk
2 cups chopped pecans
1 package (12-ounce) chocolate chips
1/3 block paraffin, shaved

Place unwrapped caramels in a 3-quart bowl. Add milk. Place over a pan of hot water or in a microwave, stirring every minute until caramels are melted. Stir until smooth. Add pecans, mixing well. Drop by teaspoon onto waxed paper. Cool and chill. In a 3-quart bowl, combine chocolate chips and paraffin. Melt over water until melted or in microwave. Stir well. Dip caramel-nut center into chocolate and return to wax paper. Chill. Store candy in refrigerator. This candy freezes well. Makes 40 pieces.

PANOCHA

2/3 cup (6-ounces) evaporated milk
1 cup white sugar
1 cup brown sugar
1/8 teaspoon salt
1 tablespoon butter
1 cup coarsely chopped pecans

In heavy saucepan, mix milk, sugars and salt. Heat slowly to boiling, stirring constantly. Cook to 236 degrees (soft ball stage) stirring often. Remove from heat, add butter. Cool undisturbed 20 minutes, then beat until it thickens and begins to lose its gloss. Quickly stir in nuts and spread in buttered 8-inch square pan. Cool and cut. Makes about 1 1/2 pounds.

VARIATIONS:
1. Mix 2 teaspoons instant coffee powder with sugars.
2. Add 2 teaspoons grated orange peel while beating candy.

SOUR CREAM PANOCHA

2 cups brown sugar
1 cup sour cream
1/2 cup chopped nuts

Combine sugar and sour cream in heavy pan. Lower heat and stir until boiling. Cook to soft ball stage (238 degrees). Remove from heat and cool to 110 degrees. Do not stir while cooling. Add nuts and beat until mixture loses shine. Spread in greased 8-inch square pan. When set, cut in squares. Makes 1 1/2 pounds.

◈◈◈

TONIA'S WHITE TAFFY

2 cups white sugar
1/2 cup light corn syrup
2/3 cup water
1/8 teaspoon salt
1 teaspoon vanilla

Mix all ingredients except vanilla. Cook to hard ball stage (268 degrees on candy thermometer). Add vanilla and pour onto greased cookie sheet. Let it cool until you can poke it with your finger and the hole stays. Then if it is cool enough, put cornstarch all over your hands, pick it up and make it into a ball and pull and pull and pull.

Keep it up until it gets light and bubbly. Then stretch it out into a long rope and cut it in small pieces. Store in a container with a tight lid.

You can add peppermint, lemon, strawberry or any flavoring you like, or food coloring, just use a tiny drop at a time to taste.

TRUFFLES

7 ounces bittersweet chocolate cut in
    1-inch pieces
1/2 cup whipping cream
2 tablespoons butter
1/4 cup powdered sugar, measured then
    sifted
2 egg yolks
1 to 2 tablespoons dark rum or to taste
Unsweetened cocoa
Coarsely chopped toasted nuts

Combine chocolate, cream and butter in top of double boiler over simmering water. Add sugar and yolks and whisk until smooth. Remove from heat and add rum to taste. Place in flat glass dish and chill until workable, about 2 hours in refrigerator or 1 hour in freezer. Shape into small balls, roll in cocoa and/or nuts. Place in paper candy cups and refrigerate until hardened. Store in covered container in refrigerator.

Note: Try substituting different flavor for the rum, amaretto, Grand Marnier, kirsch, coffee, Frangelico.

Makes 3 dozen.

MOCHA TRUFFLES

1 package (12-ounce) chocolate chips
1/4 cup sweetened condensed milk
1 tablespoon instant espresso coffee powder
2 tablespoons coffee-flavor liqueur
1/8 teaspoon salt
Cocoa

Melt chocolate chips in double boiler over moderate heat, stirring occasionally. Stir in sweetened condensed milk, espresso coffee powder, coffee-flavor liqueur and salt until well mixed. Refrigerate mixture about 30 minutes or until easy to shape.

With hands dusted with cocoa, shape a rounded teaspoon of chocolate mixture into a ball. Roll ball immediately in more cocoa. Repeat with remaining mixture. Store in covered container to use within 2 weeks. Makes 50 candies.

Under The Mistletoe

CHRISTMAS WASSAIL

6 sticks cinnamon
18 whole cloves
1 teaspoon whole allspice
3 medium oranges
6 cups apple juice
1 pint cranberry juice
1/4 cup sugar
1 teaspoon bitters
1 cup rum

Stick equal amount of cloves into the three oranges. Add all ingredients, except rum, in a large pan. Simmer for 15 minutes. Remove spices, add rum and serve hot. Makes 8 cups.

HOLIDAY CRANBERRY PUNCH

2 cups water
1 1/2 cups sugar
4 cinnamon sticks
1 quart cranberry juice
1 quart water
2 cups orange juice
2 tablespoons lemon juice

Simmer water, sugar, and cinnamon sticks for 10 minutes. Stir in cranberry juice, water, orange juice and lemon juice. Simmer 30 minutes. Do not let boil. Serves 10.

CANDY CANE COCKTAIL

Peppermint Schnapps
Club soda
Candy canes or sticks

Put a jigger of Peppermint Schnapps into a wine glass. According to taste add club soda. Place a candy cane in the glass with the hook of the cane over the rim of the glass.

Jan says, "This drink is not only fun to serve, but it is good after a meal. It really is a ladies drink; serve after luncheon."

AN OLD CHRISTMAS GREETING

Sing hey! Sing hey!
For Christmas Day
Twine mistletoe and holly,
For friendship glows
In winter snows,
And so let's all be jolly.

R.S.V.P. · Entertaining

Comments we hear over and over when we give demonstrations and classes are "I'm not creative," "I can't arrange a centerpiece," "How do you make it look so easy?" In this chapter we tell you how with orchestrated events like our Candlelight Dinner (a night to remember) and family-style picnics with suggested menus and unique ways of decorating your own backyard. The ideas presented in the Bridesmaids' Luncheon and Wedding Brunch are helpful for planning these memorable events, and there are additional ideas for brunches and parties for friends. For your holiday dinner don't miss Tonia's Thanksgiving Turkey. It is a real masterpiece and detailed instructions are given.

If entertaining is a frightening thought to you, start small. Don't plunge into planning for a large group until you are comfortable. Practice makes perfect.

FAMILY STYLE PICNIC I

Chicken and Ribs

Helena's Barbeque Sauce

Baked Beans I or II

Broccoli-Cauliflower Salad

Potato Salad (The Best)

Fresh Fruit Platter

Fresh Tomato Platter

Homemade Vanilla Ice Cream with Sauces

Carrot Cake

Lemonade

Coffee - Iced Tea

Picnic in the park or a picnic in your own backyard, the choice is yours.

On the 4th of July use the good ole' red, white and blue colors. This is a good time to use sheets for the tables. Either navy blue, white or striped. Red and blue bandanas are great for napkins. They look cute stuffed in paper cups at each place.

Ask the tree climbers to help you hang clusters of balloons with various lengths of red, white and blue ribbons.

Consider decorating your buffet table with helium balloons. They are pretty anchored in a large basket of flowers. You may even like to have one helium balloon in your Uncle Sam's hat on the individual tables. This effect is worth the extra effort.

Balloons, flags and the red, white and blue will make everyone a Yankee Doodle Dandy.

FAMILY STYLE PICNIC II

Get your cucumber peelings to keep the ants away, because we are spreading our patchwork quilts on the ground. You may stake each corner of the quilt adding 3 to 5 helium balloons to each stake. Also, if the tree climbers crew are still working, get them to put up the multicolored clusters of balloons tied with multicolored ribbons.

Baskets, baskets. Use a very large basket full of garden flowers in the center of each quilt. Different sizes and shapes of baskets may be used for serving the food. Taking the colors from your quilts, buy inexpensive material for napkins. Use your pinking shears to do the edges and tie them with different colored yarn.

Spread the beautiful array of food on a separate quilt to be used as "the buffet table." Hire a guitarist and dance on the grass.

❖❖

ELEGANT PICNIC

Tipsy Fruit

Fruit Cheese Ball

Cold Broccoli Soup

Poached Salmon with Cucumber Sauce

Curried Chicken Salad

Gazpacho Salad

Black Russian Cake

Strawberry Cake

French Bread

Chenin Blanc Wine

Coffee - Iced Tea

Let's change the pace of a regular picnic. Surprise your friends and invite them to your elegant picnic. Ask them to wear long dresses, floppy hats and the husbands to wear straw hats and bow ties. Dressing up makes it fun for everyone.

Decorate small trees and shrubbery with tiny Christmas lights throughout your back yard. Also line your driveway or walk to the backyard with luminaria sacks.

Set small tables with old lace tablecloths and silver for this gourmet evening. Baskets of garden flowers adorn the center of each table. If you can't rummage up old cloths, buy inexpensive bright material and use pinking shears to cut the cloth and napkins.

On the buffet table, use a watermelon basket for the centerpiece adorned with mint leaves and flowers. If your table is large enough, use candles with hurricane lamps.

After having your spirits, pass trays of cold broccoli soup served in crystal or silver cups and let your guests enjoy while you are adorning the buffet table.

Use small touches like butter balls or butter molded in silver or crystal small bowls topped with parsley.

With a touch of nostalgia, you'll send your guests home dreaming of the "Good ol' days."

BY CANDLELIGHT

Cocktails

Chutney Cheese Ball

Shrimp Remoulade

Beef Tenderloin

Bernaise Sauce

Mrs. Appleyard's Patrician Potatoes

Tomatoes A La Provencal

Overnight Green Tossed Salad

Vera's French Bread

Ice Cream Pie with Caramel Sauce

Coffee - Iced Tea

For this special occasion, fill your home with candlelight. Just be sure no candle poses a hazard.

At this dinner, try the bare look on your table using your silver or crystal. Arrange white candles in silver or crystal candlesticks of different heights, and set them on a 24-inch strip of mirror. The reflection will truly make it a candlelight affair.

Practice folding or tying napkins in interesting shapes or use napkin holders.

If you have a party of 8 or more, it would be advisable to use place cards which could be placed by each votive candle.

This dinner would be a good time to use party service plates. Have them sitting on your table when your guests come to the table. Use the service plates for the appetizer and main course place setting, removing them when you serve the dessert.

After returning to the living room, offer your guests an assortment of liqueurs. This will be the finishing touch to an elegant evening.

EASTER DINNER

Greek Roast Leg of Lamb

Asparagus Au Gratin

Parsley New Potatoes

24-Hour Fruit Salad

Hot Cross Buns

Strawberry Mousse

Flowerpot Ice Cream

Coffee - Iced Tea

Easter. What a lovely time to have a spring dinner after the winter months. Whether it is for family, friends or an Easter egg hunt for the children, it is a time to welcome another season!

Now it is time to get out your light, airy tablecloth. If you do not have one, try a pretty spring colored or flowered sheet. Use a light colored basket according to the size of your table. Fill it with baby's breath, daffodils and tulips. Pick up individual water tubes at a florist's so you can put your flowers in them to keep them fresh. Baby's breath or statice do not need to be put in water. If you want to save your Easter eggs for the hunt, use Easter lilies. Put the plant or plants in a silver or glass bowl according to how many lilies you have and cover the bottom with Easter grass. Don't pack the grass around the bottom. Keep it airy and scatter a few chocolate or plastic eggs among it.

Tie pastel ribbons with a dime store chicken around your napkins for holders.

Do not forget to have one golden egg in the hunt. The child who finds it gets a prize. It also would be nice to have a child's dessert. Leave the strawberry mousse served in champagne glasses for the adults. Use the flowerpot ice cream for the children (see index). Put coconut and jelly beans on top for decorations. Bless you!

BRIDESMAIDS LUNCHEON

Mimosa Cocktail

Baked Brie with Almonds

Spinach Balls

Lemon Soup

Apricot Souffle with Chicken Salad

Apple Muffins

Brandy Refrigerator Cake

Coffee - Tea

Create a warm, friendly atmosphere using your silver or crystal. Use your prettiest tablecloth, one of organdy, lace or cutwork.

Place a large lace or straw hat on its side for your centerpiece. A container inside the crown will hold either fresh or silk flowers using the bride's colors. On each side of the hat arrange three branch candelabra holding contrasting candles. In center holder of candlestick place a smaller arrangement of flowers matching the centerpiece.

Another eye-catching centerpiece is a small silver-sprayed paper parasol that lies open on its side with a bridelike bouquet of white freesia or roses and greens wired to the handle with ribbon. Favors at each place are tiny sprayed parasols, artificial lilies of the valley and silver ribbon. Use silver paper doilies for coasters on a colored cloth. Place gifts the bride has chosen for her attendants on the table as place cards.

Fill a silver or crystal punch bowl with the Mimosa cocktail and have an ice heart floating on top. Serve the cold lemon soup in small crystal cups or glasses from a crystal pitcher and let the girls help themselves.

If you can't find a small parasol or are not able to make one, look for an antique parasol with a pretty handle. Trim the upended open parasol with lace and bows. Use ivy and small roses around the umbrella.

Since this is a feminine luncheon create an intimate relaxing atmosphere.

❖❖❖

WEDDING BRUNCH

Wedding Punch

Cucumber Canapes

Hot Shrimp Balls in Pineapple Mustard Sauce

Sherried Chicken Livers

Eggs Elegante'

Baked Fruit

French Breakfast Puffs

Sour Cream Coffee Cake

Champagne

Cover your tables in raspberry linens. French nosegays of violets accented with pink sweetheart roses top tall silver candelabra. Cascading from the top, ribbon streamers in shades of violet, lavender, raspberry and avocado give a Maypole effect to the table.

Use raspberry candles.

On your entry-hall table and any other dramatic places in your home, coffee table, and/or top of mantel, place bouquets of tulips, hyacinths, forsythia and pink and white azaleas.

If your tables are small, use the large arrangement above for the buffet table and on the individual tables place pink quince baskets, using ribbons of the accenting colors around the baskets.

NEW YEAR'S BRUNCH

Bloody Marys

Cheese Ball and Crackers

Bowls of Party Snack

Coon Cheese Appetizers

Hoppin' John

Corn Bread

Marinated Veggies

Football Cake

Coffee

If you have taken down your Christmas tree and decorations, decorate your house by arranging evergreen and football mums in wooden or copper containers. If you do not have either, use baskets. Make pennants of your team and stick them in the containers along with your mums.

Set up a buffet table using a football blanket for the tablecloth and with an arrangement of football mums in the center of the table or at the end. Have a football fashioned of popcorn to hold the coon cheese appetizers. Use the popcorn ball recipe (see index). Form popcorn into football shape. Cut licorice strips into lengths to make the football lacings. Wrap flatware in colorful napkins that match the football blanket. If you have a football helmet, use it to stand the rolled-up napkins. It would be fun to have paper plates that have the name of the team you are rooting for. You can order them out of gift catalogs. Order at least 3 weeks before the party.

Have each person write his or her choice of the final score for each game and put these in separate baskets, one basket per bowl game. When the games are over, those who came closest to guessing the final scores win the kitty! Happy New Year!

❖❖

NEW ORLEANS BRUNCH

Ramos Gin Fizz

Hot Artichoke Cheese Squares

Shrimp Balls

Sausage Stuffed Eggs

Garlic Cheese Grits

Baked Pineapple

Praline Rolls

Coffee

Strains of Dixieland jazz will greet your guests as they arrive.

Decorate your tables with arrangements formed from men's plastic straw hats. These are available at novelty shops. Wrap a colored ribbon around the hat for a band, invert hat and fill with cut flowers, making a French bouquet. Place hats in the center of tables covered with crisp white linen cloths. Use colored napkins tied into a loose knot.

On the buffet, use straw hats and decorative jazz instruments. These are available at floral or novelty shops.

While guests are enjoying their Ramos Gin Fizz, have teenage daughters or friends dressed in French maid's costumes pass the cheese squares and shrimp balls.

This brunch is nice to give at the beginning of your city's Jazz festival, or before departing on a trip to New Orleans.

SOME SUNDAY MORNING BRUNCH

Brandy Milk Punch

Cocktail Cheese Balls

Sunday Eggs

Fresh Fruit Bowl with Orange Dressing

Sticky Buns

Coffee

Many of us like a brunch on Sunday morning If you are a lucky lady, the man of the house will do the cooking. Whether he uses our menu or not, why don't you help him by setting the table. Use your colored place mats according to the season. If you don't have napkin rings give your napkins a slight knot and place them between your place setting.

Look in your cupboard for a different container to hold fresh flowers, silk flowers, bittersweet; perhaps a 12-inch clay saucer with plants in it, spring blossoms, or fall bouquets (you have picked). Maybe a large bird nest in a tree branch standing in moss to conceal the bottom of the branch with a bird perched on a limb.

If you have a casual brunch, use different dishes to compliment the mood. Improvise and use your imagination. Mix and match.

❖❖❖

HOLIDAY DINNER

Pumpkin Soup

Roast Turkey

Cornbread Stuffing

Refrigerator Mashed Potatoes

Aunt Fanny's Baked Squash

Vegetable Trio

Cranberry Sauce

V-8 Aspic Salad

No Knead Butterhorn Rolls

Cranberry Bread

Pumpkin Cake Roll

Pecan Pie

Coffee

The harvest of bountiful food and nature's celebration of color makes Thanksgiving truly a blessing.

In keeping with the beauty of nature use your lovely bare wood tabletop, devoid of cloth dressing. Use the traditional cornucopia or a lovely brass, copper or wooden tray, bowl or basket. Abundantly fill with vegetables, fruits, nuts and berries. Among these use branches of bittersweet, pheasant feathers, wheat or leaves. Intertwine with gold, rust or burgundy velvet ribbon.

Stand tall brass candlesticks, 1 or 3 on each end of your arrangement. Use candles that match the velvet ribbon.

Hollow out a pumpkin, cleaning it completely and making sure you don't punch a hole in it. Serve the pumpkin soup from the shell at the table, or you might like to serve it in the living room as the first course.

If your table has not grown, but the family has and the children have their own special table, it's important they don't feel excluded. So, make an apple turkey for each child and set it at his place on the table.

Using a large red apple, cut a head for the turkey from brown construction paper, doubling the paper for extra strength and leaving the fold at the very top of the head. Glue on moveable bead eyes, and color the "gobbler" red. Insert the neck into a slit in the large end of the apple.

You can find packages of bright-colored feathers at a craft shop or you can use quail feathers for the turkey's tail. Punch several holes with a toothpick around the stem end of the apple. Insert as many feathers as you desire. Stand the turkey on three wooden toothpicks arranged in a triangle. Plastic toothpicks are not strong enough to hold the weight. If you want, you might attach a namecard for each child to his own turkey's leg.

We feel this is such a special holiday. It is more relaxed than the bustling Christmas season and what a wonderful time for all the family to be together. Before the day is over, it will go into each heart and mind as being the "Best One Yet."

❖❖

TONIA'S THANKSGIVING TURKEY

Jo says, "A friend gave this project to my daughter, Tonia, when she was 9 years old. She and her friends had a marvelous time and many giggles assembling it. I was called upon for help in cutting Styrofoam and 'pushing picks.' Children will need assistance. The finished product held a place of honor, the centerpiece of our Thanksgiving table."

Assembly of the base and ends can be done in advance, in fact we recommend it with all the other business of the day, but the greens and fruit should be fresh. Wash endive and parsley early and place in baggies. Refrigerate until ready to use. Wash and drain fruit well, polish apples and pears.

MATERIALS:

BASE: 12 x 12 x 2-inch Styrofoam sheet
  Try to get green. It will cover easier.

PLATFORM: 8 x 8 x 2-inch Styrofoam sheet

HEAD END: 15-inch long Styrofoam piece.
  Top end 2 1/2 inches wide. Keep that width down 8 inches then begin widening to a base of 5 inches.

TAIL END: 8 inches wide at base, 9 inches high and 2-inch thick piece of Styrofoam. Trim top side so it curves.

1 medium to large pineapple
1 acorn squash
2 large bunches of bananas
15 or more green apples
  (can use part apples and pears)
12 tangerines
2 bunches green grapes
2 bunches red grapes
2 bunches dark grapes
4 packages endive
2 bunches parsley
1 package dried figs
1 box dried dates (optional)
Kumquats (optional)
Maraschino cherries
Colored feathers (may be obtained at a craft shop, or perhaps someone in your family has been hunting)
Wooden toothpicks
Bamboo skewers (may be obtained at a kitchen shop

ASSEMBLING THE TURKEY

Place base on table. Insert several wooden toothpicks halfway into top of base. Place 8-inch platform in center of base. Toothpicks should hold it securely.

Stand head and tail ends upright against platform on base. Secure with toothpicks and wooden skewers into base and platform. The skewers will go in easier if lightly hammered. It is much easier on hands, but be careful you don't split Styrofoam. foam.

Cover all Styrofoam pieces with endive and parsley, securing well with toothpicks.

Cut ends off pineapple, saving top. Place pineapple lengthwise on 8-inch platform between head and tail sections. Secure end sections to pineapple using long wooden skewers.

(See next page for examples.)

Using 5 or 6 toothpicks, secure the acorn squash to the top of the head section, pointed end to the front. If you will poke holes in the squash with a small nail or metal skewer, the toothpicks will go in easier. The same can be done when you begin inserting feathers. Half of the toothpick goes in the squash, the other half in the Styrofoam.

Attach multicolored feathers to the top of head. Place a dried fig on each side of head for eyes, centered with a maraschino cherry.

On each side of pineapple "body," secure a bunch of bananas for wings, letting them rest lengthwise on base, the top of bunch toward the front of turkey.

On curved "tail" section, place the leafy top of pineapple you saved on the outside, directly in the center. Secure it with toothpicks. Around this, make a row of green apples and/or pears. The second row will be red feathers and the top row tangerines. Do similar rows on the inside of section, around end of pineapple.

Now finish the "head" end by attaching large bunches of grapes down the front of the long section below the squash head. First a bunch of white grapes, next red and last, dark grapes. The more grapes you use, the more elegant the "gobbler." If single grapes fall off, just stick a toothpick in them and put them on where needed.

Stand back and look at the finished product, then fill in spaces with more feathers and endive or parsley. You can't overdo it.

We have added dates and kumquats to the list of ingredients. You might desire to use them as filler.

Note: You might make this the night before using. Wrap it in plastic and keep in garage or cool place until next day. It must be kept cool or the endive and parsley will wilt.

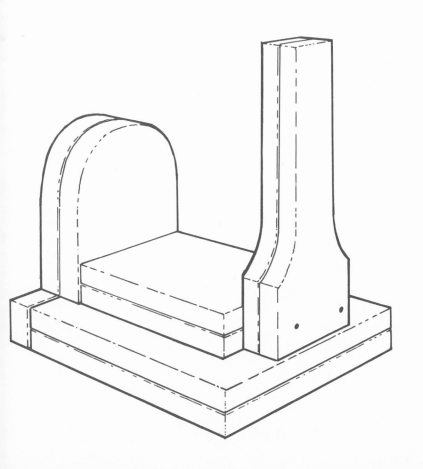

✦✦

TAXPAYER'S BAWL

Cocktails - Party Snack

Ham and Bean Soup

Steak Soup

Cornbread

Tossed Salad

Poor Boy Sandwiches
(Have guests make their own. Have trays of bread, meats, cheeses, tomatoes, onions, pickles and garnishes.)

or

Deli made in advance and wrapped to preserve freshness.

Brownies - Ice Cream
Allow guests to make their own, covering with Kahlúa, whipped cream and toasted almonds.

An April 15th party is a great tension reliever for this time of year.

Invitations: Made on brown sandwich bags, printing done in red Magic Marker pens. In one corner draw a crying face with tears. Copy will read:

Come bawl with (first names)
Saturday, April 15th
Address:
Cocktails: 7:00 p.m.
Dinner: 8:30 p.m.
Attire: Obsolete or Depreciated
R.S.V.P.: (number)
Fold sack in thirds, seal with gummed sticker.

VARIATION

Use a federal tax form page, fold in half. Take to a printer and have areas blocked out for copy. On front use man and woman cartoon characters dressed in old clothes. Put tears in their eyes.

Inside block out an area for the same copy as invitation.

Use red tablecloths and napkins. At each place use a "placemat" made of two pages of tax forms. They may need to be taped down the middle on the underside. You can do one mat and speed-print the rest.

Do not be extravagant on centerpieces. Remember, this is a "down and out" party. Consider using potted geraniums, the pot wrapped in tax forms or newspapers, tied with twine or yarn. Intersperse the plant with "burned money." At a novelty shop get a bundle of play money bills. Singe the edges with matches. Gather up one short side of the bills and wire to floral picks. You can use these anywhere else you desire in your home.

Use votive lights on the tables at each setting. Make circles of play money bills, staple or tape together and use as napkin rings.

During cocktails, serve drinks in glass jars, all sizes. They don't have to match.

Your buffet table will be the "soup line." Use newspapers or butcher paper for your "cloth." Put flowers in metal pots. Serve soup from a large metal container, using a ladle, into metal cups.

If you can find them, use large pie tins for your plates. We found them at restaurant supply houses. Aluminum foil plates will not be heavy enough to hold food well.

There are all kinds of novelty items in stores around tax day. You might want to pick up a few and award them as prizes to the best costumes, most down and out couple, etc.

Be sure to take pictures.

COME INTO OUR KITCHEN

This party is such fun and very unpredictable. When sending the invitation, it should read, "Come into Our Kitchen, featuring Chef [and your man's name]." Each invitation will request one couple to send their recipe to you for the course you specify. You will gather all the ingredients.

When guests arrive, give each gentleman a chef's hat and apron, and announce the rules of the evening.

1. Women are the bartenders. Have a couple of bells situated at strategic places so the fellows can ring for assistance.
2. The men do the cooking, but not the recipe they sent. Mix them up and designate women to assist, but not their escort. The women are not allowed to touch the food or appliances, just give verbal instructions.

This takes a little more preparation than the usual party, working out a time schedule for times in the kitchen. First couple for appetizers, second begin salad, and so on. You don't want all in the kitchen at once, so the recipes must be studied and times checked well. You and your man will prepare the meat dish, and the couples need to be told on the invitation that the recipe cannot take hours to prepare. For instance, no Jell-O salads or yeast breads.

Be sure to have a camera ready. This is one time you and your guests will not want to miss the action.

Your centerpieces will be an inverted chef's hat filled with greenery (perhaps parsley). Place a container inside to hold the shape. Stick wooden spoons, wire whisks and other kitchen utensils among the greenery.

Use metal measuring cups with votive candles at each guest's place. Set each one on a circle of cork or felt so table does not get hot.

Make place cards by cutting a strip of heavy white paper 6 inches long and 2 inches high. In center print chef and the guest's name. Form strip into a circle, staple a pouf of white tissue paper on top to form chef's hat.

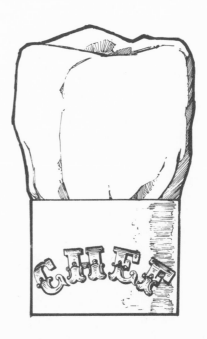

❖❖

SHHHHHH------

Don't breathe a word-------------

We're having a---------------

"POT PARTY"

WHEN:

WHERE:

R.S.V.P.

PLEASE BRING YOUR OWN POT--------------------**FONDUE, THAT IS!! ***

This invitation can be used as a card, or a clever way to present it is to type it out, wrap around a small flower pot filled with crystal rock pieces and stick a flower in the middle. They have to be hand delivered but it is so effective, people will remember you for that special effort.

There are so many ways to go on a fondue party. With the above invitation, it is fun to use "pots" for the food. Salad, bread cubes, meat, cake pieces and all the fruits can be mounded in flower pots.

When serving four at a table from one center fondue pot, there is not room for a centerpiece. Let the pot be the center. Your table will be full enough with sauces and foods. Have you ever considered a hanging basket over your table?

*On the above invitation, I have written for guests to bring their own pot. Empty, of course. You will provide the fondue. This is only if you are having several tables and do not have enough fondue pots available. You need one for every four people, at least. If you are serving cheese and a meat fondue at the same table, plan on two pots for each table.

You might wish to serve the cheese fondue during the cocktail hour from a cocktail table.

Jo says, "You don't really need to plan a party around fondue. One of my daughter's fondest childhood memories is just the family, seated on the floor around the family-room coffee table, having our own special fun-do party."

HOW TO ENJOY FONDUE

Everyone eats directly from the fondue pot, transferring food to a plate and dinner fork, as the fondue fork gets very hot. The heat of the pot must be regulated so that fondue simmers gently.

Spear cubes of bread, meat or dessert bites so that it holds firmly; if using bread, spear through the crust.

When stirring bread in cheese fondue, stir until it is entirely covered with cheese. Stirring is the first rule, it keeps the fondue smooth and creamy.

White wine or hot tea is the most suitable drink. "Coup du milieu"—"half-way drink"—is the expert's term for a small glass of Kirsch, taken during the fondue.

Legend states that if bread is lost in the fondue, a penalty is invoked. Men are fined a bottle of wine for the rest of the table and the ladies get off lightly, with a kiss for each man in the party.

Fun-Do

FUN-DO PARTY

Schloss with Cubes of Sweet Rye Bread

Fondues

Cheese - Beef

or

Chicken - Crab

Assorted Sauces

Dark Chocolate - Brandied Strawberry

Fresh Fruit and Cake Cubes

SCHLOSS

1 cup sour cream
3 egg yolks
1 tablespoon lemon juice
1/2 teaspoon dry mustard
1/2 teaspoon Worcestershire sauce
1/4 teaspoon salt

Combine and heat thoroughly, but do not boil. Serve warm in fondue pot. This is extra delicious with cubes of sweet rye bread. Makes 1 1/2 cups.

BROTH FONDUE HORS D'OEUVRES

1 1/2 pounds, prime beef, cut into chunks or thin strips
1 teaspoon salt
1/4 teaspoon pepper
2 cans (13 3/4 ounces each) chicken or beef broth
1/4 cup chopped onions or scallions
Dash ground ginger
1 tablespoon soy sauce
Sauces for dipping

Sprinkle strips of meat with salt and pepper. In fondue pot combine broth, scallions, ginger and soy sauce. Bring to boil on stove; place in fondue pot for serving. Spear meat with fondue fork and plunge into boiling broth. Cook 3-4 minutes. Dip meat into sauce of choice. Serves 4.

CHEESE FONDUE

1 clove garlic
2 cups dry white Rhine wine
1 tablespoon lemon juice
12 ounces aged Swiss cheese, grated
4 ounces natural or processed Gruyere cheese, grated
3 tablespoons flour
3 tablespoons Kirsch
1/4 teaspoon nutmeg
Dash paprika

Rub fondue pot with garlic clove. Pour wine into pot. Set over moderate heat. Heat the wine, but do not boil. Add lemon juice. Toss cheese with flour and add by handfuls, 1/3 at a time, stirring constantly with a wooden spoon or fork until cheese is melted. Bring fondue to a bubble, but do not boil. Add Kirsch, nutmeg and paprika, stirring until blended. Serves 4-6.

CHICKEN FONDUE

2 whole chicken breasts, boned and skinned
1/3 cup flour
1 egg, beaten
1 cup fine dry bread crumbs
3 cups peanut oil

Cut chicken breasts in half. Cut each half into about 14 bite-size pieces. Coat each piece in flour, dip in egg and then coat with bread crumbs. In fondue pot, heat oil to 375 degrees and place directly over flame. Spear pieces of chicken with fondue forks and dip in hot oil mixture until golden brown. Remove from fondue fork and cool slightly. Serve with Sour Cream Apricot Sauce (see next page).

Jo says, "For a variation on this recipe, I make a marinade of 1/2 cup of Wishbone Italian salad dressing and 1/2 cup orange marmalade. Marinate the pieces of chicken for several hours before cooking. Sometimes I just dip the marinated chicken in the fondue oil without the egg, bread crumb coating. Dip in sweet-sour sauce or Chinese hot mustard."

Serves 4.

CRAB FONDUE

1 pound Velveeta cheese
1/2 pound butter
1 can crab meat

Place butter and cheese in large saucepan over very low heat. Stir occasionally until melted and well-blended. Stir in crab meat and transfer to a chafing dish.

Jo says, "I improvise on this, adding sauteed onion, chopped artichoke hearts, a dash of Worcestershire sauce." Serves 4.

FONDUE BOURGUIGNON

3 pounds prime beef (sirloin or fillet)
Salt and pepper to taste
3 cups peanut oil
Assorted sauces

Let meat, cut in 1-inch cubes, stand at room temperature for at least 30 minutes. Blot excess moisture with paper towels. Lightly salt and pepper the meat. Arrange on platters and garnish with parsley or watercress. Fill the fondue pot half full of peanut oil, it may take more than 3 cups. Heat to about 375 degrees. Oil is hot enough when it browns a small cube of bread in 30 to 40 seconds. Guests place desired sauces on their plate, then spear a cube of meat with fondue fork and dip it into the hot oil; 10 to 20 seconds for rare, 50 to 60 seconds for well-done. Meat is then transferred to dinner plate and fork. Serves 4.

Fun-Do

❖❖❖

BEEF FONDUE SAUCES

HORSERADISH SAUCE:
1/2 cup mayonnaise
1/4 cup sour cream
2 tablespoons grated horseradish
Salt to taste

Mix together until smooth.
Makes 1 cup.

CURRY SAUCE:
1 cup mayonnaise
1/2 teaspoon paprika
1/2 teaspoon dried mixed herbs
1 teaspoon curry powder

Mix until smooth.
Makes 1 cup.

FONDUE SOUR CREAM APRICOT SAUCE

3/4 cup sour cream
1/2 cup apricot jam
3 tablespoons mustard

Combine all ingredients. Serve chilled.
Makes 1 1/4 cups.
Jo says, "If you prefer to use commercial sauces, there are many excellent ones on the market. I have used Sauce Robert and Sauce Diable by Escoffier. There are many sweet and sour sauces, horseradish sauce and various mustard sauces."

BRANDIED STRAWBERRY FONDUE

2 packages (10-ounce) frozen strawberries
1/4 cup cornstarch
2 tablespoons sugar
1/2 cup water
1 container (4-ounce) whipped cream cheese
1/4 cup brandy

In a saucepan, crush strawberries slightly. Blend together cornstarch, sugar and water. Add to berries. Cook and stir until thickened and bubbly. Pour into fondue pot. Place over fondue burner. Add cream cheese, stirring until it is melted. Gradually add brandy.
Spear pears, peaches, pineapple, cake cubes or marshmallows. Yummy!! Makes 2 1/2 cups.

DARK CHOCOLATE FONDUE

9 ounces Swiss milk chocolate
1 ounce unsweetened baking chocolate
1 1/2 cups light cream
2 ounces kirsch, cognac or orange Cointreau

Melt chocolate in the cream over medium heat, stirring constantly. When smooth, add liqueur. Place mixture in fondue pot and put on low setting if using electric pot or over low flame. Makes 3 cups.

"DIPPERS"
Fresh strawberries
Fresh orange sections
Fresh pineapple
Fresh bananas, cut into 1 1/2-inch pieces
Stemmed Maraschino cherries, well drained
Fresh apple cubes
Fresh pear cubes
Marshmallows
Angel food cake cubes
Cream cheese pound cake, cubed (see index)

Fun-Do

MILK CHOCOLATE FONDUE

5 3 3/4-ounce bars milk chocolate
1 cup heavy cream
2 ounces brandy

Melt chocolate in the cream over medium heat, stirring constantly. When smooth, add brandy. Makes 2 cups.

LEMON SAUCE FOR FONDUE

1 stick butter
2 cups sugar
4 tablespoons flour
2 1/2 cups boiling water
1 teaspoon lemon peel
1/8 teaspoon nutmeg
3 tablespoons lemon juice
6 cups fruit, cut into bite-size pieces

Blend butter, sugar, and flour in saucepan. Add water, stirring constantly. Mix in lemon peel and nutmeg. Bring to a boil and boil for 3 minutes, stirring constantly, until sauce is thickened. Remove from heat and blend in the lemon juice.
Makes 5 cups.

La Dolce Vita · Italian Favorites

You will find recipes for appetizers through desserts in this tribute to the good food of Italy. Some of our favorite recipes, just to mention a few, are Cannelloni (a "labor of love" dish), Pasta with Northern Italian Meat Sauce, Bellini Ice, and Crema Zabaglione Puffs. We offer an Italian Night Menu that may be prepared ahead except for the Fried Mozzarella, and toward the end of the chapter, some interesting notes on espresso and the wines of the Italian countryside.

"LA DOLCE VITA"

As we traveled throughout Italy we found the country gave us a much broader view of the Italians and their different cuisines. Anything you are excited about you want to share and that is why our Italian section is larger than the others. We so enjoyed the Italian delights that ranged from their beautiful country to their culinary arts.

Our recipes are from the top of the boot, Valle d'Aosta, Piedmonte, to the toe of the boot. Lighter, more delicate cooking is popular in northern Italy and hearty, highly seasoned cooking is done in the southern part.

The Italians love their food. They like to display it with pride. Even the vendors with their carts on the streets have their food attractively displayed. Restaurants have live fish and seafood along with meats and vegetables in cases so you can pick and choose as you come in the door.

One thing we learned in Italy was that you can never judge the quality of a restaurant by the appearance of the place.

We loved strolling the sidewalks where you'd see many cafes, patrons drinking their espresso, laughing, talking and watching people. These cafes serve breakfast in the mornings. This meal for the Italians is light, consisting of espresso and rolls. The two main meals, lunch and dinner, are lengthy and very relaxed.

We had the pleasure of eating at a particular Italian trattoria one noon. A trattoria is the homey-like atmosphere operated by a family. Italian families come in with their children and pets to have a long leisurely meal since businesses close from 12:30 to 3:30 p.m. The children behave and the cat remains sleeping on the chair until they are ready to leave.

We had a delicious meal which consisted of soup, pasta, salad and hard rolls. After we finished our meal the waiter appeared carrying a large bowl of water, a big slotted spoon and a platter of fresh fruit. It didn't take long to discover that you dip your fruit in the water (not your fingers) to wash it before eating a bite. To say the least, it was fun and unique.

Dining at the ristorante in the evening begins at 8:30 p.m. We found if you arrive early there are very few people if any. The Italians are gay and very talkative as they sip their wine leisurely while they are served each course. Dinner usually lasts between 2 to 3 hours, depending on the groups.

Our dinner began with an antipasto followed by soup or pasta. Salad was served on plates with the ingredients attractively arranged in sections on a bed of lettuce. Cruets of olive oil and wine vinegar were on the table for each person if they so desired to lace their greens. This is done in most restaurants rather than blending the greens like the Americans. The main entree consists of a variety of meats such as veal, pork, lamb, chicken, Florentine steak, seafood and varieties of pasta. Vegetables accompanying the main entree are fresh and tastefully done. Hard rolls are served throughout the dinner. It seems they have a different flavor than our yeast breads in America.

Following the main entree, the dessert consists of a variety from Cassata to fruits and cheeses. The dessert carts were lovely with their customary puddings, custards, pastries, fruit ices and homemade ice cream. House wines are superb in Italy and served throughout the meal followed by espresso and a liqueur, if so desired.

Along with the food, the atmosphere was conducive to the appetite. The tablecloths and nice big napkins were refreshing. Fresh flowers, whether at a trattoria or an elegante ristorante, always adorned the tables.

As we sat at our table devouring every morsel and detail of the evening, it was not hard to lift our glasses with a toast saying "La dolce vita," the sweet life.

ITALIAN NIGHT MENU

CAPONATA SPREAD

FRIED MOZZARELLA

ITALIAN SPRING VEGETABLE SOUP

INSALATA CAPRICCIOSA

CANNELLONI

DILLY BREAD OR FRENCH BREAD

CHIANTI OR VALPOLICELLA

ZABAGLIONE

ESPRESSO

AMARETTO OR CAPPUCCINO

ITALIAN STYLE DINNER PARTY

To set your table for an Italian dinner you may use your white linen tablecloth or runners down each side of the table, leaving the middle of the table bare. The Italians use linen tablecloths and napkins in most homes and ristorantes. Napkins may be tied with green, red or white satin or velvet ribbon. (The flag colors of Italy.)

Use a large basket lined with a large red, green and white napkin or material. Pyramid french bread, hard rolls, breadsticks, small bunches of spaghetti tied with red ribbon. Leave room for a bottle of wine (unopened), finishing the Italian touch with several bunches of grapes.

You can be more formal in your table decor. Use brass candlesticks intertwined with ivy and bunches of grapes. Tie the grapes on a stem of candlestick with green velvet ribbon. Place a votive candle on a doily at each place setting. Amber or green for the winter and a crystal or white for the summer. The Italians love using doilies and candles.

If you want to do another special touch, fix a menu card written in Italian and place it on an easel on the dining table. Or you might prefer putting the menu on a card and passing it to your guests as they have their cocktails. Believe me, your guests will love it.

Are you feeling flush? If so, give the ladies a red carnation and pin a white carnation on your male guests.

Later in the evening serve cappuccino in demitasse cups. Having this nightcap will have them thinking "La dolce vita" as they go out the door.

"Appetito-so" Appetizers

ANTIPASTO

On large platter arrange Marinated Roasted Peppers and Olive Salad, one package (8-ounce) salami, one package (8-ounce) bologna, one package (8-ounce) sliced provolone and two cans (3-ounce) sardines. Serves 6-10.

MARINATED ROASTED PEPPERS

Use 5 medium green peppers. Place on broiler rack about 6 inches from flame. Roast 30 minutes or until skins blacken and blister on all sides. Turn peppers often to prevent burning. Remove peppers from oven and cool 19 minutes. Remove skin and seeds. Cut roasted peppers into 1/2-inch strips.

In medium bowl combine peppers, 3 tablespoons red wine vinegar, 3 tablespoons Bertolli olive oil and 3/4 teaspoon salt. Cover and refrigerate. Drain before serving. Serves 4-6.

PROSCIUTTO E MELONE

Cut wedges of cantaloupe, honeydew, or watermelon. Cut the wedges into 2-inch wedges. Put 2-inch thin slices of prosciutto over each melon wedge. Add a dash of lemon juice or pepper to taste. Serves 4-6.

ITALIAN STYLE ZUCCHINI

Cut 3 medium zucchini into very thin strips. Heat 1 tablespoon butter or margarine in skillet. Add zucchini, 1/8 teaspoon salt, 1/8 teaspoon lemon pepper. Stir until tender crisp, about 3 to 4 minutes. Serves 4-6.

OLIVE SALAD

In medium bowl combine one can (6-ounce) pitted large ripe olives, drained, 1/3 cup Italian salad dressing, 1/8 teaspoon pepper. Cover and refrigerate. Drain before serving. Serves 4-6.

STUFFED MUSHROOMS PARMIGIANA

12 large fresh mushrooms
2 tablespoons butter or margarine
1 medium onion, finely chopped
2 ounces pepperoni, diced
1/4 cup finely chopped green pepper
1 small clove garlic, minced
1/2 cup finely crushed Ritz crackers
   (12 crackers)
3 tablespoons grated Parmesan cheese
1 tablespoon snipped parsley
1/2 teaspoon seasoned salt
1/4 teaspoon dried oregano, crushed
Dash pepper
1/3 cup chicken broth

Wash mushrooms, remove stems. Finely chop stems and reserve. Drain caps on paper towels. Melt butter in skillet; add onion, pepperoni, green pepper, garlic and chopped mushroom stems.

Cook until vegetables are tender but not brown. Add cracker crumbs, cheese, parsley, seasoned salt, oregano, and pepper. Mix well. Stir in chicken broth.

Spoon stuffing into mushroom caps, rounding tops. Place caps in shallow baking dish with about 1/4-inch of water covering bottom of pan. Bake uncovered at 325 degrees about 25 minutes or until heated through. Makes 12.

FRIED MOZZARELLA

Olive oil
3 eggs
Salt
12 slices Mozzarella cheese (1/2-inch thick),
   about 1 1/2 pounds
Flour, seasoned with dried Italian herbs
Bread crumbs

Heat plenty of olive oil in a deep pan. Beat eggs with salt. Coat slices of cheese with flour, dip in egg, roll in bread crumbs. Dip once again in beaten egg. Drop a few at a time into hot oil. As soon as cheese is golden brown, take it from pan with a slotted spoon and drain on paper towels. Serve immediately with or without hot tomato sauce.
Serves 4.

"Zuppa" Soup

MINESTRONE

2 tablespoons Bertolli olive oil
1 large carrot, diced
1 large celery stalk, thinly diced
1 medium zucchini, diced
1/4 pound green beans, cut,or 1 can
   green beans
1/2 small head cabbage, shredded
1 can (8-ounce) tomatoes or tomato
   sauce
1 medium onion, diced
1 small garlic clove, diced
4 cups water
2 cups tomato juice or V-8 juice
1 1/2 teaspoons salt
1/2 teaspoon oregano leaves
1/2 teaspoon tarragon
2 beef flavored bouillon cubes
1 can (10-ounce) red kidney beans or
   1 package dried pinto beans
1/2 cup spaghetti or ditali

In 4-quart saucepan over medium heat, in hot olive oil, cook carrots, celery, onion, zucchini, green beans and garlic, removing garlic after 15 minutes.

Add water and juice, salt, oregano, tarragon, cabbage, tomatoes with their liquid and bouillon over high heat. Heat to boiling, stirring. Reduce heat to low; cover and simmer 45 minutes or until vegetables are tender.

Stir in spaghetti or ditali, beans and cook until all are tender. Pinto beans usually cook longer. You may cook the beans separately and then put them through a wire sieve or whirl in blender.

Serve hot with Parmesan cheese.
Makes 12-14 cups.

ZUPPA DI PESCE

6 white-fleshed fish
2 quarts water
2 large celery stalks
1 large onion, sliced
3 sprigs parsley
2 large ripe tomatoes, diced
Salt and pepper to taste
1/2 cup ditali pasta

Place all ingredients except the pasta, salt and pepper in a 6-quart pan. Bring to boil, cover, lower the heat and simmer for 1 hour. Skim. Cool slightly and pour liquid through a fine strainer. Season. Cook the pasta in 2 quarts salted water. Do not overcook. Drain and pour cold water over pasta. Divide the pasta into 6 bowls and pour the soup over the pasta. Serves 6.

Jan says, "The pasta in soup is very popular in Italy. I got this recipe from an Italian who served it."

BRODO DI POLLO

Assortment of chicken backs, wings
    and legs (6 pounds)
Water to cover chicken pieces
2 stalks celery leaves
1 bunch parsley
3 red onions
1 clove garlic
1 shallot
Salt to taste
2 sliced carrots

Place chicken pieces in big pot and cover with water. Bring to boil and lower the heat. Simmer until scum forms, then remove scum from the surface. Continue to cook 3 hours on a very low heat. Add remaining ingredients and simmer another hour. Pour broth through strainer and refrigerate overnight. The next day remove the congealed fat from the surface of the broth. Reheat and pour the broth through cheesecloth several times. You may freeze or refrigerate the broth. Makes 2 1/2 quarts of chicken stock.

Jan says, "Making chicken stock is well worth the time. It may be heated and used as a clear soup or you may use it for gravies or adding flavor to casseroles. This chicken Brodo is delicious used like a French onion soup. We prefer it with pasta added to the cup of Brodo."

ITALIAN SPRING VEGETABLE SOUP

4 tablespoons butter
2 medium onions, chopped
4 small stalks celery and leaves, chopped
12 cups chicken broth
2 large unpeeled zucchini, thinly sliced
1 package (10-ounce) frozen green peas
1 package (10-ounce) frozen broccoli
    flowerets
1 package (10-ounce) frozen cut green
    beans
1 package (10-ounce) frozen chopped
    spinach, squeezed dry
1 cup pasta (ditali, stellina)
1 teaspoon basil
Salt and pepper to taste
1 cup Parmesan cheese, grated

Heat butter and saute onion and celery until soft. Add onions and celery to broth and bring to a boil. Add vegetables and pasta. Cook until barely tender. Add salt, pepper and basil to taste. Serve topped with grated Parmesan cheese.

Serves 24.

"Insalata"
Salad

Salads are prepared quite simply in Italy. The Italians have a variety of lettuce, fennel and others, not used by the American cook. The salads are rarely mixed with dressing. Usually cruets of oil and vinegar are on the table so each person may suit their taste. The olive oil and wine vinegars are superb. The combination of the greens and the oil and vinegar make a superb salad without the varieties that we have here in the United States.

Jan says, "The varieties that we found in Italy were as follows:"

I

1 large tomato, sliced for serving
Salt and freshly ground pepper
Crushed fresh basil or parsley to taste
Olive oil and wine vinegar in separate cruets

III

2 pounds watercress
2 tablespoons olive oil
Salt, freshly ground pepper to taste
Lemon wedges

II

Lettuce, torn
Tomatoes slices
Julienne-cut cold cooked vegetables
Olive oil
Wine vinegar

Saute the watercress in hot oil over medium heat for about 2 minutes. Serve at room temperature. Season with salt and pepper. Drizzle lightly with olive oil and serve with lemon wedges. Serves 4.

Jan says, "When serving the Italian insalata, serve the ingredients in separate sections on the salad plate. Use the cruets with the oil and vinegar or your favorite salad dressing. You may use variations of what you use on the salad plate. Mushrooms, tomatoes, onions, broccoli, peppers, eggplant, etc. I found that I really enjoyed the salad served separately instead of tossed together as we Americans do."

INSALATA CAPRICCIOSA

Hand torn lettuce
Tomato slices or chunks
Julienne-cut broccoli, cauliflower, zucchini
Olive oil
Wine vinegar
Salt and pepper

Arrange ingredients on a bed of lettuce or fresh spinach leaves. Place on a plate or in a shallow bowl. Pass the olive oil and wine vinegar in cruets.

Jan says, "This is a typical salad in Italy and guests may use the oil and vinegar to their own liking."

ANTIPASTO MISTO

4 large sliced tomatoes
1 cup tiny cooked shrimp
1 can tiny sardines
1/2 cup pickled onions
1 can anchovy fillets
1 cup black olives
1 cup green olives
1/2 cup thin strips green pepper
1/2 cup cooked broccoli flowerets
1/2 cup cooked finely minced carrots
1/2 cup cooked minced cauliflowerets
1/2 cup finely minced celery
1 cup finely chopped mushrooms
1 tablespoon capers, optional

Serve each food separately in a bowl. Arrange serving dishes on a big platter or table accompanied with Salsa Maionese. This is very good with French bread and wine. Serves 6.

SALSA MAIONESE

1 large egg
1 teaspoon Dijon mustard
3 tablespoons lemon juice
1 cup Bertolli olive oil
1 teaspoon salt

Put ingredients in blender except the olive oil. Add 1/3 cup oil, cover, and blend at high speed for about 5 seconds. Add the remaining oil in a slow steady stream. Blend until thick and smooth. Makes 1 cup plus.

CAPONATA

3/4 cup Bertolli olive oil
1 large eggplant, cut into bite-size pieces
6 medium zucchini, cut into bite-size pieces
1/2 pound thickly sliced mushrooms
1 1/2 cups chopped red onion
1 cup sliced celery
1 garlic clove, crushed
1/2 cup red wine vinegar
1/4 cup capers, drained
2 tablespoons sugar
2 teaspoons salt
1/4 teaspoon pepper
3 large tomatoes, cut into bite-size chunks
1 jar (4 1/2-ounce) pimento-stuffed olives, drained and halved crosswise

In large saucepan, heat olive oil until sizzling hot. Add eggplant, zucchini, mushrooms, onions, celery, garlic clove for 10 minutes, stirring occasionally. Stir in vinegar, capers, sugar, salt and pepper. Reduce heat to low; cover and simmer 5 to 10 minutes until vegetables are tender. Stir in tomatoes and olives. Heat to boiling. Spoon mixture into large bowl and cover and refrigerate at least 4 hours or until well chilled. Serve cold. Serves 12.

❖❖❖❖❖❖❖❖❖❖❖❖❖❖❖❖❖❖❖❖❖❖❖❖❖❖❖❖❖❖❖❖❖❖❖❖

COLD SPAGHETTI INSALATE

1 cup ripe olives, sliced
Large bunch broccoli, chopped
1 large red onion
2 cups chopped celery
1 cup mushrooms, chopped
1 package (8 ounce) spaghetti, cooked
  and drained
Wish-Bone salad dressing

Combine first 6 ingredients. After spaghetti has cooled, drizzle Wish-Bone salad dressing over mixture according to taste. Serves 10-12.

Jan says, "Coarse ground pepper is good on this salad. Use salt to taste."

Jo says, "Try this salad using the marinade for 3-bean salad. It's really delicious."

"Legumi" Vegetables

Vegetables are prepared simply in Italy. The fresh vegetables are cooked until barely tender. The Italians never overcook their vegetables. One of their favorites to serve is asparagus. It is served as a separate course. Eggplant dishes are served as appetizers, casseroles or as a separate course.

ASPARAGI MILANESE (ASPARAGUS MILAN)

Prepare asparagus according to package. You may use the canned spears. Arrange the warm asparagus on a platter and sprinkle 2 teaspoons of parsley over the top. Then drizzle Bertolli olive oil over all. Season with salt and pepper to taste.

ASPARAGI CON MAIONESE (ASPARAGUS WITH MAYONNAISE)

Prepare and drain as directed as to the kind of asparagus you use. Cool to room temperature and serve with Ruby's Homemade Mayonnaise (see index).

EGGPLANT CASSEROLE

1 1/2 pounds eggplant
Salt
Flour
1/2 cup Bertolli olive oil
2 cups tomato sauce
8 ounces thinly sliced Mozzarella cheese
1/2 cup grated Parmesan cheese

Peel and cut eggplant into 1/2-inch slices. Sprinkle both sides of eggplant with salt. Spread slices out in one layer on paper toweling for 20 to 25 minutes, then pat dry. Dip in flour and shake remaining excess flour off of eggplant.

In heavy skillet, heat 1/4 cup olive oil, brown the eggplant quickly. Add more oil as needed. Drain eggplant on paper towel. Pour 1/2 cup of the tomato sauce in a greased (lightly) baking dish. Layer eggplant, tomato sauce, Mozzarella and Parmesan cheeses. Cover and bake at 400 degrees for 20 minutes. Uncover and bake for another 10 minutes. Serves 4-6.

RISOTTO ALLA MILANESE

2 cups Italian rice or American long-grain
3/4 cup dry white wine
6-8 cups hot chicken stock, preferably home-
    made or a top-grade canned broth
1 medium yellow onion, chopped
4 tablespoons butter
1/2 cup uncooked beef marrow
1/4 teaspoon saffron, dissolved in 1 cup of stock
3/4 cup freshly grated Parmesan cheese
1/4 stick softened butter
Salt, pepper to taste

Bring the stock to a simmer in a large pot and keep it hot over a low flame.

In a heavy 3-quart saucepan, saute the chopped onion in butter until it is transparent but not brown. Stir in rice and marrow and stir-cook until meat loses color and rice is glazed. Pour in wine and cook, stirring until liquid is absorbed. Season with salt and pepper.

Add simmering stock, a cup at a time, stirring with each addition until liquid is absorbed. About halfway during the cooking time, add the 1 cup in which the saffron has been dissolved. Then add liquid in smaller amounts, about 1/2 cup at a time, and continue to stir. The risotto is ready when rice is held together in a creamy mixture—yet each grain is al dente, firm. Finish with softened butter and Parmesan cheese.   6-8 servings.

Jo says, "The amount of liquid used varies with the type of rice. Plan on one quart of liquid to one cup of rice. You may not use it all or you may need a little more. The key is adding the stock in small amounts, cooking briskly until the rice absorbs the stock, then adding additional stock until the rice is cooked and creamy. Constant watching and stirring are musts. Plan 20 to 30 minutes cooking time for risotto. There are no short cuts, nor can you make it ahead of time. Reheating will dry out the creaminess."

CARCIOFI FIORENTINA
(ARTICHOKES FLORENTINE)

1 1/2 tablespoons butter
3/4 cup mushrooms, chopped
1/2 small onion, chopped
1/2 green pepper, finely minced
8 artichoke bottoms, cooked
1 cup firm cooked cauliflowerets

SAUCE:
2 tablespoons butter
2 tablespoons sifted flour
1/2 cup light cream
1/4 cup grated Swiss cheese
1/4 teaspoon salt
White pepper and Dijon mustard to taste

Saute mushrooms, onion and green pepper in hot butter until tender. Spoon equal amounts on each artichoke bottom. Place a few cauliflowerets on each artichoke and spoon a tablespoon of sauce over each. Serve immediately.

Melt butter in a pan. Add flour, blending with whisk until smooth, then add the cream, beating continuously until the sauce is thick and smooth. Add cheese, whisking until fully mixed into the sauce. Season lightly with salt, pepper and mustard to give a zing to the sauce. Keep warm in a double-boiler until ready to serve. Makes 1 cup of sauce. Serves 8.

La Dolce Vita

ZUCCHINI AND MOZZARELLA

2 tablespoons Bertolli olive oil
1 medium red onion, diced
1 medium green pepper, diced
1 small garlic clove, minced
1 small shallot, minced
1 can (16 ounce) tomatoes
4 medium zucchini, cut into 1/4-inch slices
3/4 teaspoon salt
1/2 teaspoon sugar
1/2 teaspoon oregano
1/4 teaspoon basil
1 package (8-ounce) Mozzarella cheese, shredded

Heat olive oil until hot in 12-inch skillet over medium heat. Add onion, green pepper, garlic and shallot until tender, stirring occasionally. Add tomatoes with their liquid and next 5 ingredients. Heat to boiling. Reduce heat to low, cover and simmer until zucchini is tender-crisp, about 15 minutes, stirring occasionally to break up tomatoes. When zucchini is done, sprinkle evenly with cheese, cover and simmer about 3 minutes or until cheese is melted. Serves 8.

"Pasta"

Pasta is one of the staples in Italy. It can be served either as a main course or as a separate dish in a main meal. Now that the pasta machine is popular, more Americans are making their pasta. In the following section you will find a variety of ways to prepare the different creations.

The Italians are very proud of their pasta and the different light sauces they prepare to go with it. You do not see the sauce drenched on pasta in Italy as you do here in the United States. The Italians are geniuses with their flavorful dishes. No kitchen is without fresh or dried bunches of parsley, wild marjoram, thyme, rosemary, tarragon, bay leaves, sweet basil, sage, etc. Fennel seeds and juniper berries are the favored seasonings. Along with the spices such as cloves, coriander and saffron, the use of onions, shallots, garlic, lemon juice, vinegar and olives give the Italians a lot to choose from.

Last but not least, let us not forget the olive oil. They have the best olive oils in the world.

As you go through this Italian section you will find a variety of dishes that have been tried and true.

Jan says, "I had the pleasure to eat at my husband's relatives' home in Castel-Monte, Piedmonte, Italy. This is when I became aware of Italian food, habits and taste. The northern Italian cooking is much lighter than the southern Italian cooking which is heavy. We prefer the lighter cooking. As the true Italian says, 'After I eat dinner, I feel nothing,' meaning the dinner was a northern Italian menu. Jo and I have brought to you our recipes that we have enjoyed doing through the years. We had to choose because both of us have done a lot of Italian cooking. The more you prepare these dishes, the more you will find yourself using different herbs and such. One thing that is very important and we never deviate from is using the Bertolli olive oil or some other good oil. This makes a big difference in the taste of your dishes."

Once you have made your own pasta, you will be spoiled for life. Good luck.

P.S. Jo and I still roll our pasta out on a floured board.

PASTA I

1 1/2 cups unsifted flour
1 egg
1 egg white
1 tablespoon olive oil
1 teaspoon salt
A few drops of water

PASTA II

1 3/4 cups flour
2 large eggs
1 egg yolk
1 1/2 teaspoons oil
1/2 teaspoon salt

I put a heap of flour on my pastry board or counter, make a well in the center of the flour and put in the egg, egg white, oil and salt. Mix together with your fingers or fork. (I prefer my fingers. It is running all over, but don't despair. Keep gathering it up and form it into a rough ball.) Moisten any remaining dry bits of flour with drops of water and press into the ball. Knead the dough on the floured board working in a little more flour if it's sticky.   After 10 minutes, the dough should be shiny and elastic. Wrap it in wax paper and let the dough rest for at least 10 minutes before rolling it.

Divide the dough into 2 balls. Place 1 ball on floured board and flatten with your hand into an oblong 1-inch thick.   Dust the top lightly with flour. Use your rolling pin and start at one end of the oblong and roll it lengthwise away from yourself.   Turn the dough crosswise and roll across its width.   Repeat, turning and rolling the dough until it is paper thin. If at any time the dough begins to stick, lift if carefully and sprinkle more flour on it. Don't get discouraged. This takes time and practice. But oh, it is worth it. Makes 3/4 pound.

CANNELLONI

After rolling dough paper thin, cut it into about 35 rectangles 2 x 3 inches. I have found by experience after cutting these strips, I still roll each strip until paper thin. Seems like each strip still gets thinner, and that is what you need.   Bring the water to boiling in a large pot. Drop the pasta pieces in the boiling water and stir gently with a wooden fork or spoon for a few moments to be sure they don't stick to one another or to the pot. Bring the water back to boiling point and cook the pasta over high heat, stirring occasionally until the pasta is tender but not soft. This process takes 5 to 8 minutes.   Drain, cool slightly, then spread the pasta pieces side by side on wax paper to dry. The pasta can be refrigerated for a day or two. Wrap in wax paper or foil. Makes 20.

RAVIOLI

Divide the pasta dough into 4 pieces and roll out the first fourth of the dough as thin as possible. Cover the rolled pasta with a damp cloth to keep it from drying out and roll out the second fourth to a similar size and shape.   Using the first sheet of rolled-out pasta like a checkerboard, place a mound of filling (next page) every two inches across and down the pasta. Dip a pastry brush or your finger into a bowl of water and make vertical and horizontal lines in a checkerboard pattern on the sheet of pasta, between the mounds of filling. Carefully spread the second sheet of rolled-out pasta on top of the first one, pressing firmly around the filling and along the wet lines. With a ravioli cutter, cut the pasta into squares along the wet lines.   Separate the mounds of filling and set them aside on wax paper. Continue on to the next 2 fourths of dough. Makes 40.

La Dolce Vita

CHEESE FILLING FOR RAVIOLI

1 1/2 cups sieved ricotta cheese
3 large egg yolks
3/4 cup freshly grated Parmesan cheese
1 teaspoon salt
1 tablespoon dried parsley
Freshly ground pepper to taste

In a large bowl, mix the cheeses, 3 egg yolks, salt, parsley and the ground pepper. Stir gently together until they are well mixed. Put a well rounded teaspoon of filling on each checkerboard of the pasta.

To cook: Drop a few ravioli at a time into 6 to 8 quarts of boiling water. To keep them from sticking together gently stir with a wooden spoon. Cook about 8 to 10 minutes or until they are tender. Remove them gently with a slotted spoon and drain on wax paper or a kitchen towel. Serves 4.

MEAT FILLING FOR RAVIOLI

3 tablespoons sweet butter
3 tablespoons finely chopped onions
3/4 pound ground raw veal
1 package (10 ounce) frozen chopped spinach, defrosted
3/4 cup freshly grated Parmesan cheese
3 eggs
1 teaspoon salt
Pinch of nutmeg

Melt the 3 tablespoons sweet butter in a small pan and saute the onions until transparent and soft. Add the veal and cook slowly, stirring constantly until the veal loses its red color and no liquid remains in the pan. In another mixing bowl stir together the chopped spinach that has been squeezed thoroughly, grated Parmesan cheese and a pinch of nutmeg. Add to veal mixture. In another bowl, beat the eggs lightly and add them to the onion, veal and spinach mixture. Add salt according to taste. Put a well rounded teaspoon of filling on each checkerboard of the pasta and continue to cook as mentioned in the Cheese Filling.

To serve: Top with Tomato Sauce and fresh Parmesan cheese. Serves 6.

LASAGNE & FETTUCCINE:

Prepare pasta recipe on page 337. Dust the rolled dough lightly with flour and let it rest for 10 minutes. Then gently roll it out into a jelly-roll shape. With a long sharp knife, slice the roll crosswise into even strips. 1/4-inch wide for fettuccine and 1/2 to 2 inches wide for lasagne. Unroll the strips and let them dry on wax paper. In the same way, roll, shape and slice the second half of the dough. Makes 1 pound.

PIZZA

2 packages dry yeast
1 1/4 cups warm water
Pinch of sugar
3 1/2 cups flour
1 teaspoon salt
1/4 cup olive oil

FILLINGS:

You may use any toppings that you like. Use your imagination. Use 1/2 cup of tomato sauce on bottom, topping with ground beef or sausage, herbs, green peppers, mushrooms, capers, pepperoni slices or any other desirable combinations. Don't forget the cheeses. Use Mozzarella or Parmesan. Bake at 450 degrees for 10 to 15 minutes.

Jan says, "You do not see a lot of pizza in Italy. It is used as a snack food. Many restaurants in Rome start serving pizza after midnight. Also pizza is served individually. So you might want to make smaller pizza. The Italians like to serve large 40-inch pizza in Naples."

Makes 2 12-inch pizzas.

Sprinkle yeast and pinch of sugar into warm water. Let stand for 3 minutes, then stir mixture until it is completely dissolved.

Into a large bowl, sift flour and salt. Make a well in center of flour and pour in yeast mixture and 1/4 cup olive oil. Mix dough with your fingers or fork. Keep working dough into a rough ball. Place ball on a floured board and knead it for 15 minutes until it is smooth. Be sure it is shiny and elastic. (You may do this on your mixer.) Dust dough with flour and put it in a large clean bowl and cover. Let rise until dough has doubled in size. This depends on the warmth of your room. Do keep it warm and out of drafts.

Preheat oven to 450 degrees. Punch dough down and knead it a minute or so. Work flour into it if it is sticky. With palm of your hand flatten the ball into a circle about 1 inch thick. Keep stretching and turning the circle. You might divide this dough into 2 circles, depending on the size you want your pizza. Most pizza pans fit one of the balls of dough. After you have worked pastry to about 10 inches across and 1/8-inch thick, lightly grease pastry with oil or Crisco. This keeps filling from seeping into crust.

CANNELLONI

2 tablespoons Bertolli olive oil
1 large garlic clove, minced
1/2 cup finely minced onion
1 shallot
1 package (10-ounce) frozen chopped spinach, defrosted and squeezed dry
2 tablespoons butter
1 pound ground chuck
2 chicken livers
5 tablespoons Parmesan cheese
2 tablespoons heavy cream
2 eggs, slightly beaten
1/2 teaspoon oregano
1/2 teaspoon basil
1 teaspoon ground pepper
Salt

SAUCES:
Jan's Tomato Sauce (page 350)
Besciamella Sauce (page 349)

Heat olive oil in large skillet until moderately hot. Add onions, garlic, shallot until golden brown and soft. Stir in spinach and cook for 3 or 4 minutes, stirring constantly. When moisture is gone and spinach sticks lightly to pan, put mixture into a bowl. Melt 1 tablespoon butter in same skillet and lightly brown meat. Add meat to onion mixture and set aside. Heat 1 tablespoon butter in skillet and cook livers, turning constantly until firm. Chop them coarsely. Then add livers to mixture in bowl along with Parmesan cheese, cream, eggs, oregano and basil. Mix all ingredients together well; add salt and pepper. Prepare Sauces.

❖❖❖

ASSEMBLING THE CANNELLONI

Preheat oven to 375 degrees. Place a tablespoon of filling on the bottom third of each pasta rectangle and roll them up. Pour a cup of tomato sauce over the bottom of a 13 x 9 x 2-inch baking dish. Then lay cannelloni side by side in one layer of tomato sauce. Pour the besciamella sauce over it and spoon the rest of tomato sauce over all. Sprinkle 2 tablespoons grated Parmesan cheese over the top. Bake cannelloni uncovered in 375-degree oven for 20 minutes. Serves 8-10.

Jan says, "Let this cool for 5 minutes. Either serve it individually on the dinner plate or directly from the dish. Cannelloni freezes very well. I call this a 'labor of love' dish for it does take time, but it is well worth it. I do believe it is the Ferrari of all Italian dishes."

SHORT–CUT CANNELLONI

3 large eggs
1/4 teaspoon salt
1 1/2 cups light cream
1 1/4 cups sifted flour
2 tablespoons olive oil
Butter

Beat eggs, salt and cream together until light and foamy. Add flour and beat until smooth, then add the oil and refrigerate several hours or overnight. Pour 1 teaspoon oil in seasoned crepe pan and add 1/2 teaspoon butter to the pan and place over medium-high heat. Wait until it sizzles. Ladle just enough batter into pan so the surface is barely covered when you rotate it around. Put the pan back on the heat until the crepe appears set. Do not turn. Remove from pan. Add more butter and repeat until batter is used. Makes 20 crepes. Cool and cover with wax paper. These are good to freeze.

FILLING:
1 pound cut-up Mozzarella cheese
1/4 pound chopped ham
5 large egg yolks

Add cheese and ham to besciamella sauce, mixing thoroughly. Cool. Add egg yolks, stirring well with whisk, and cook over lowest heat for 10 minutes, stirring constantly with the whisk. Let cool. Spoon about 3 tablespoons of filling down the center of the browned side of each crepe. Roll and place in two well-greased 13 x 9 x 2-inch pans. Spoon tomato sauce over the top of cannelloni crepe. Bake in preheated oven (375 degrees) for 15 to 20 minutes. Sprinkle with Parmesan cheese just before serving. Makes 20 cannelloni, serving 6.

Jan says, "If you want to do this ahead, refrigerate the cannelloni, covered, then spoon the sauce on it just before baking."

❖•❖

FETTUCCINE

6 to 8 quarts water
1 tablespoon olive oil or salad oil
1 tablespoon salt
1/4 pound fettuccine

Bring the water, oil and salt to a bubbling boil in a large pan or kettle. Drop fettuccine noodles in it and stir gently with a wooden spoon for a few minutes to prevent the noodles from sticking to one another or the pan. Boil over high heat, stirring occasionally. The pasta should be tender in 8 to 10 minutes. (Test it by tasting, or if it breaks easily between the fingers it is done.) Immediately drain the pasta. Toss immediately with the different sauces as follows. Serves 2.

BUTTER AND CHEESE SAUCE

1/4 pound butter, softened
1/2 cup heavy cream
1/2 cup freshly ground Parmesan cheese
Black pepper, coarsely ground

Taste for flavor and serve the fettuccine immediately. Pass the extra grated cheese.
Jan says, "I do not salt my fettuccine. It takes on a different texture when salted. Let your guests salt their own." Serves 2.

CLASSIC SAUCE

1/4 cup butter
1 small garlic clove, minced
2 egg yolks, slightly beaten
1 cup light cream
1 teaspoon salt
Ground nutmeg
1 cup grated Parmesan cheese

Melt butter in a small pan. Saute garlic clove a few minutes and remove pan from heat. Beat 2 egg yolks slightly in a small bowl, adding the cup of light cream. Stir egg and cream mixture into butter-garlic pan and return to heat. Heat slowly, stirring often, but do not boil. Season with 1 teaspoon salt and a dash of ground nutmeg. Pour over pasta. Add 1 cup grated Parmesan cheese.
Serves 4.

GREEN FETTUCCINE WITH PEAS AND PROSCIUTTO

SAUCE:
1 tablespoon olive oil
1 tablespoon butter
1/2 cup chicken broth
1 small garlic clove, minced
1/4 cup freshly grated Parmesan cheese
1 package (10-ounce) frozen tiny peas
Salt and freshly ground white pepper

PASTA:
1/4 pound green fettuccine
1 tablespoon olive oil
1 tablespoon butter
1/4 cup freshly grated Parmesan cheese
Salt and freshly ground white pepper
1 ounce prosciutto, or thinly sliced ham, cut into short strips 1/4-inch wide
Freshly grated Parmesan cheese

Heat oil with butter in medium saucepan over medium heat. Add broth and garlic and bring to simmer. Add 1/4 cup Parmesan and cook, stirring constantly, until cheese is melted and sauce is slightly thickened, about 5 to 10 minutes. Add peas and continue cooking until barely tender. Season with salt and white pepper. Keep warm.
Cook pasta in large amount of rapidly boiling water until al dente (firm). Drain well. Return pasta to pot with remaining oil and butter and toss until butter is melted. Add 1/4 cup Parmesan and toss again. Season with salt and pepper. Turn into heated serving dish. Top with sauce and sprinkle with proscuitto. Serve with additional Parmesan. Serves 2.

ITALIAN GNOCCHI

3 packages (10-ounce) frozen chopped spinach, drained well
6 tablespoons butter
1 1/4 cups fresh ricotta cheese
3 large beaten eggs
1/2 cups unsifted flour, heaping
1/4 cup freshly grated Parmesan cheese
3/4 teaspoon salt
Freshly ground pepper to taste
1/4 teaspoon nutmeg
2 to 3 tablespoons butter, melted
1/3 cup grated Parmesan cheese

In 6 tablespoons hot butter in large skillet, cook spinach, stirring just enough to dry out. Add ricotta cheese; cook, stirring several minutes or until well blended.

In medium bowl, beat eggs slightly; beat in flour until smooth. Add 1/4 cup Parmesan cheese, 3/4 teaspoon salt, pepper and nutmeg; mix well. Stir in spinach-cheese mixture; mix well. Refrigerate until firm, several hours.

In large kettle bring 4 quarts water to boiling; add 1 tablespoon salt and 1 tablespoon oil.

Form dumplings: With floured hands, carefully shape chilled mixture into balls, 1 1/2 inches wide. Drop gently into boiling water, about one third at a time. Simmer 5 minutes, or until gnocchi rise to top of water. Lift out with slotted spoon; drain on paper towels.

Continue shaping and cooking until all are cooked. Arrange gnocchi in a single layer in a greased shallow heat-proof dish (about 9 x 13 inches). Sprinkle with 2 to 3 tablespoons melted butter, then with 1/3 cup grated Parmesan cheese.

Broil about 4 inches from heat, until heated through and golden brown, between 3 to 5 minutes. Makes 28 gnocchi. Serves 6.

Jan says, "You may place the gnocchi in warm shallow soup bowls and drizzle them with melted butter and sprinkle with grated Parmesan cheese."

The correct pronunciation is "nyawky." "These gnocchi are delicate, fluffy, incredibly light and habit forming!"

LASAGNE (EASY)

1 1/2 pounds ground beef
1 teaspoon oregano
2 tablespoons olive oil
1/2 cup onion, chopped
2 cloves garlic, minced
   Brown and add:
1 can (1 pound) tomatoes
1 can (8-ounce) tomato sauce
1 1/2 teaspoons salt
1/2 teaspoon pepper
1 tablespoon sugar
1 package lasagne noodles
1/2 pound Velveeta cheese
1 can (3-ounce size) Parmesan cheese

Cook top 10 ingredients for 20 minutes. Prepare lasagne noodles according to package. Cool.

Put noodles in large Pyrex dish. Slice 1/2 pound Velveeta cheese over noodles. Pour sauce over noodles and add 1 can grated Parmesan cheese. Bake at 350 degrees for 30 minutes. Serves 8-10.

La Dolce Vita

LASAGNE

PART 1:
1 pound ground beef
1 garlic clove, minced
1 tablespoon parsley flakes
1 tablespoon oregano
1 small onion, chopped
1 1/4 teaspoons salt
1 can tomatoes
2 cans (6-ounce size) tomato paste

Brown meat slowly and spoon off all fat. Add the next 7 ingredients. Stir well. Heat slowly for 45 to 60 minutes. The mixture should be thick.

Prepare lasagne noodles according to package instructions, unless you have made your own.

PART 2:
3 cups cottage cheese
2 eggs, beaten
2 tablespoons parsley
2 teaspoons salt
1/2 teaspoon ground pepper
1 package lasagne noodles
1 pound Mozzarella cheese
1/2 cup Parmesan cheese

Mix first 5 ingredients into bowl. Place half of noodles in a 13 x 9 x 2-inch baking dish. Spread half cottage cheese mixture over noodles, half Mozzarella cheese, half meat sauce and repeat layers. Sprinkle Parmesan cheese over top. Bake at 375 degrees for 30 minutes. Let lasagne cool for 10 minutes before cutting. Serves 10.

Jan says, "I have used green spinach noodles instead of lasagne noodles. Gives it a different flavor and flair."

LASAGNE ROLL-UPS

12 noodles
1 tablespoon Bertolli olive oil
1 package (10-ounce) frozen spinach, thawed and squeezed dry
2 tablespoons minced onion
1 small garlic clove, minced
1 container (16-ounce) ricotta cheese
1/3 cup Parmesan cheese
1/2 teaspoon salt
1 egg
2 1/2 cups Jan's Italian tomato sauce
1 cup shredded Mozzarella cheese

Cook lasagne noodles according to package directions. In 2-quart saucepan heat olive oil, cook onions and garlic clove. Stir about 5 minutes until tender and clear. Add spinach and stir until dry. Remove pan from heat and stir in ricotta cheese, Parmesan cheese, salt and egg.

Drain lasagne noodles and put in single layer on wax paper to drain and dry. Evenly spread cheese mixture on lasagne noodles. Roll up each noodle jelly-roll fashion. In a 9 x 13 x 2-inch baking dish, spoon about 1 cup of tomato sauce. Arrange rolled noodles seam-side down in sauce. Top with remaining sauce and sprinkle shredded Mozzarella cheese. Cover with loose foil and bake for 30 minutes in a 375-degree oven. Be sure the dish is bubbly and the cheese is melted. Serves 6.

SOUFFLE DI PASTA

1/2 pound small egg noodles or fettucine noodles
1/3 pound freshly grated Parmesan cheese
1/2 cup plus 1 tablespoon butter or margarine
1 2/3 cups hot milk
Salt and pepper to taste
1/2 pound boiled ham, finely chopped
1 package (10-ounce) frozen chopped spinach,
 thawed and squeezed dry
5 ounces Swiss cheese
6 large eggs, separated

Cut butter in chunks and add to hot milk, stirring until butter is melted. Add cheeses, ham, spinach and seasonings. Let mixture cool. Add egg yolks, slightly beaten, and mix thoroughly. Cook fettucine or noodles in boiling salted water. Drain thoroughly and fold in cheese-egg mixture. Beat egg whites until soft peaks form. Fold into noodle mixture. Butter bottom of a 2-quart souffle dish. Turn souffle mixture into dish. Bake at 350 degrees for 40 to 50 minutes. Ten minutes before removing from oven, increase temperature to 450 degrees. Allow to stand 5 minutes before serving. Serves 6-8.

MANICOTTI

1 1/2 pounds ground beef
1/2 medium onion, chopped
1 clove garlic, minced
1 tablespoon olive oil or salad oil

Put ingredients in large skillet. Brown, drain off excess fat and cool. Add:

1 cup bread crumbs
1 tablespoon chopped parsley
1/2 pound Mozzarella cheese, grated
1 teaspoon salt
1/4 teaspoon pepper
2 eggs, slightly beaten
1/2 cup milk
Manicotti shells

Use the commerical manicotti shells and cook according to box instructions. Mix ingredients thoroughly and stuff into 10 to 12 shells. Place stuffed shells in a single layer in greased 9 x 13-inch glass dish. Pour 2 cups tomato sauce (see index) over the shells and sprinkle with Parmesan cheese. Cover in 350-degree oven 25 to 35 minutes. Serves 4 to 6.

Jan says, "You may use the canned tomato sauce if you are in a hurry, but I prefer the homemade sauce."

SAUCE:
American Beauty Italian Style
 Spaghetti Sauce Mix:
1 package sauce mix
2 cans (6-ounce size) tomato paste
3 cups water
2 teaspoons oil

Bring to boil. Cover and simmer 10 minutes.

CHEESE FILLING FOR MANICOTTI:
1/2 pound Mozzarella cheese
2 pounds cottage cheese
2 eggs, slightly beaten
1/2 pound Parmesan cheese
2 tablespoons chopped parsley
1 teaspoon salt
1/4 teaspoon pepper
1 tablespoon sugar

Combine ingredients and fill cooked Manicotti shells. This recipe fills 20 shells.

Pour tomato sauce over shells. Bake in 350-degree oven 20 to 25 minutes.

JONNIE MOSETTI

2 large green peppers
2 pounds onions
1 large stalk celery
1 stick butter
3 pounds ground chuck
1 can (12-ounce) tomato paste
1 can (6-ounce) tomato paste
1 can tomato soup
4 cans mushrooms, drained
2 tablespoons Worcestershire sauce
1/2 teaspoon Tabasco sauce
1/4 cup olive juice
1 can (6-ounce) stuffed olives
1 package (16-ounce) wide egg noodles,
   cooked
2 cups sharp cheddar cheese, grated

Cut green peppers, onions and celery into chunks and saute in butter. Add ground chuck and cook until meat loses its color. Add cans of tomato paste and tomato soup, mushrooms, Worcestershire sauce, Tabasco sauce and olive juice.

Cook for 15 minutes then add stuffed olives (whole) and cooked noodles. Spoon into greased baking dish and cover with grated cheese. Bake at 350 degrees for 1 hour or until hot in the center. Serves 12-16.

PESTO DIVINO

1 recipe Basic Pesto (see index)
2 pounds spaghetti, cooked according to
   package directions
6 tablespoons butter

Cook spaghetti, drain quickly and pour into a hot serving dish. Toss with butter, add pesto sauce to taste and toss well. Serves 8.

RAVIOLI CASSEROLE

Tomato sauce recipe (see index)
1 pound ground beef
1 medium onion, chopped
1 clove garlic, finely chopped
2 tablespoons olive oil
1 teaspoon basil
1 tablespoon oregano
1 tablespoon sugar
3 tablespoons Parmesan cheese
1 tablespoon wine vinegar
1 package (10-ounce) frozen chopped spinach
1/2 teaspoon salt
1/2 teaspoon pepper
1 package (8-ounce) shell macaroni, cooked
1 cup shredded sharp American or cheddar
   cheese
1/2 cup soft bread crumbs
2 well-beaten eggs
1/4 cup Bertolli olive oil

Brown ground beef, onion and garlic in olive oil. Cook spinach per package directions. Drain and reserve the liquid. Add enough water to liquid to make one cup. Combine tomato sauce, spinach liquid, seasonings, wine vinegar, and Parmesan cheese into meat mixture. Combine spinach with macaroni, Cheddar cheese, bread crumbs, eggs and 1/4 cup olive oil. Spread the spinach mixture in a 13 x 9-inch baking dish. Top with meat mixture. Sprinkle with Parmesan cheese. Bake at 350 degrees for 30 minutes or until very hot. Let stand 5 to 10 minutes before serving. Serves 10.

La Dolce Vita

SPAGHETTI LOAF

2 1/2 cups light cream
1/2 cup plus 2 tablespoons butter
2 1/2 cups dry white bread crumbs
2/3 teaspoon thyme
1 tablespoon salt
1 1/4 cups grated Cheddar cheese
1/3 cup minced onion
5 tablespoons finely chopped green pepper
2 1/2 pimentos, slivered
2 1/2 tablespoons finely chopped parsley
7 eggs, well beaten
1 1/4 cups cooked spaghetti

Heat cream and butter until butter melts. Pour over bread crumbs mixed with thyme and salt. Let stand 10 minutes. Add remaining ingredients in order listed. Mix well. Pour into a well-buttered 9 x 5 x 2 3/4-inch loaf pan. Place in a baking pan half full of water. Bake in 350-degree oven for 1 1/2 hours or until a knife comes out clean from center of mixture. Remove and cool 2 to 3 minutes. Turn out and serve with cheese—mushroom sauce. Serves 12.

CHEESE — MUSHROOM SAUCE

1 onion, peeled and finely chopped
3 tablespoons butter
2 pounds button mushrooms, wiped clean
2 tablespoons flour
1 cup light cream
1 1/2 cups grated Cheddar cheese
1/2 teaspoon salt
1/8 teaspoon pepper

Saute onion in butter until transparent; do not brown. Add whole mushrooms. Cover and simmer until just tender. Blend in flour and add cream to make a sauce. Add cheese, salt and pepper. Cook and stir until cheese melts. Makes 5 cups.

TORTELLINI IN CREAM SAUCE

3 quarts water
1 tablespoon salt
2 pounds fresh or frozen cheese stuffed tortellini
2 cups heavy cream
1/2 teaspoon salt
1/8 teaspoon Tabasco sauce, or to taste
Freshly ground white pepper
1 cup freshly ground Parmesan cheese, or to taste

Heat water in large heavy saucepan over high heat to boiling; add 1 tablespoon salt. Stir in tortellini, cover and cook over high heat until water returns to a rolling boil. Immediately uncover; stir once, boil until tortellini are almost tender, about 5 minutes.

Drain tortellini thoroughly in large colander; spoon onto warmed, heat-proof serving platter. Cover loosely with foil, place platter in oven set at lowest setting.

Heat heavy cream in large skillet over medium heat to boiling. Boil until thickened and slightly reduced, about 5 minutes. Remove from heat. Season with 1/2 teaspoon salt and Tabasco sauce and pepper to taste. Stir in reserved tortellini; return to medium heat. Cook, stirring gently once or twice, until pasta is tender, 3 to 5 minutes. Remove from heat. Sprinkle with 1 cup Parmesan cheese; stir gently to blend. Spoon onto heated platter and serve with additional Parmesan, if desired. Serves 8.

La Dolce Vita

PASTA WITH NORTHERN ITALIAN MEAT SAUCE

6 tablespoons butter
1/2 pound smoked ham, chopped coarsely
2 medium carrots, finely chopped
1 celery stalk, finely chopped
1 small onion, finely chopped
2 tablespoons olive oil
3 cups finely chopped top round steak
1/4 pound lean pork
1/2 cup dry white wine
1 can (10 1/2-ounce) beef broth
1 can (6-ounce) tomato paste
1 1/2 teaspoons brown sugar
1 1/2 teaspoons salt
1/2 teaspoon cracked pepper
1 cup heavy cream
1/2 pound chicken livers
1 tablespoon minced parsley
1 teaspoon nutmeg
Lasagne noodles, fettuccine or spaghetti
1 tablespoon salt
1 tablespoon oil

Besciamella Sauce

Melt 4 tablespoons butter in large skillet. When butter is hot, add ham, carrots, celery and onion. Cook for 10 minutes or until lightly browned and tender, stirring frequently. Transfer this mixture to a bowl. Heat 2 tablespoons olive oil in the same skillet. Add the top round and lean pork. Stir the meat constantly to break up any lumps. Pour the wine, increasing the heat over the meat. Stir mixture until liquid in skillet has cooked away. Add meat to bowl of vegetables. Stir in tomato paste, brown sugar and beef broth. Set aside. Melt 2 tablespoons butter in same skillet and cook chicken livers 3 or 4 minutes until they are lightly browned. Chop chicken livers into small pieces, set them aside. Put the vegetable-meat mixture back into skillet and simmer 45 minutes, partially covered, stirring frequently. Then add chopped cooked livers, parsley, nutmeg, salt, pepper and heavy cream. Let it heat through.

Cook the lasagne noodles in 6 quarts water, 1 tablespoon salt, 1 tablespoon oil. Set the pot under cold running water to cool the pasta. Then lift the strips out of the pot and spread them side by side on paper towels to drain.

Spread a layer of the northern meat sauce over the bottom of a 13 x 9 x 2-inch buttered dish. Spread about 1 cup of Besciamella sauce. (See index). Lay one third of the lasagne noodles on the besciamella, overlapping the strips. Repeat the layers of meat sauce, besciamella and noodles. Sprinkle with grated Parmesan cheese. Bake 30 minutes in a 350-degree oven. Serves 8-10.

BECHAMEL SAUCE

1/4 cup butter
1 small onion, chopped and sauteed in 1/4 cup butter
3 tablespoons flour
1 teaspoon instant chicken broth, or chicken cube
1/4 teaspoon pepper
2 cups milk or light cream

Cook first 5 ingredients, stirring constantly until mixture bubbles 2 minutes. Stir in 2 cups milk or light cream and cook, stirring constantly, until sauce thickens and bubbles 3 minutes. Remove from heat and immediately serve over hot drained pasta. Makes 2 1/2 cups.

"Pollo & Carne"
Chicken & Meat

CHICKEN BOCCA

8 chicken breasts, boned
8 thin slices boiled ham
5 slices Mozzarella cheese, halved
2 medium tomatoes, seeded and chopped
1/2 teaspoon dried basil
1/2 cup dry bread crumbs
3 tablespoons grated Parmesan cheese
3 tablespoons snipped parsley
6 tablespoons butter or margarine, melted

Place a piece of clear plastic wrap over a cutting board. Place chicken, boned side up, on plastic wrap. Working from the center out, pound lightly with meat mallet to 5 x 5 inches. Remove wrap. Place a ham slice and half slice cheese on each cutlet, cutting to fit. Top with some tomato and a dash of basil. Tuck in sides. Roll up jelly-roll style, pressing to seal well. Combine bread crumbs, Parmesan and parsley. Dip chicken in butter, then roll in crumbs. Place in shallow baking pan. Bake in 350-degree oven 40 to 45 minutes. Serves 8.

OSSO BUCO

4 tablespoons butter
1/4 cup flour
2 teaspoons salt
1/4 teaspoon freshly ground pepper
6 to 7 pounds veal shank, sawed, not chopped, into 8 pieces, each 3 inches long, and tied with string to hold meat together
3 tablespoons olive oil
1 1/2 cups coarsely chopped onion
1 cup thinly sliced, pared carrot
1/2 cup diced celery
2 garlic cloves, crushed
3 cups drained canned whole tomatoes, coarsely chopped
1 cup dry white wine
1 teaspoon dried basil leaves
1 teaspoon dried thyme leaves
7 sprigs of parsley
1 bay leaf

On sheet of wax paper, combine flour, salt and pepper; rub into veal shanks, coating them well on all sides. Choose a Dutch oven that has a tight lid and is large enough to hold the pieces of veal snuggly standing up in 1 layer. Melt the butter over medium heat; add olive oil and brown veal shanks, 3 at a time, turning them to brown well on all sides. Add more oil if needed. Remove shanks as browned and set aside. To drippings in Dutch oven, add onion, carrot, diced celery, and garlic. Saute stirring until onion is tender. Add tomatoes, wine, basil, thyme, parsley sprigs and bay leaf. Bring mixture to boiling.

Reduce heat and add the browned veal shanks. Using tongs, place shanks in upright position so that round bone with marrow faces up. The liquid should come halfway up the side of the veal. Cover and bake in a regulated oven so the casserole is simmering gently. Baste occasionally. Veal will be tender between 1 hour and 30 minutes to 2 hours depending on size.

Meanwhile, prepare Gremolata in small bowl. To serve, arrange the pieces of veal on a heated platter and spoon the sauce and vegetables from the casserole around them. Sprinkle the top with Gremolata (next page). Serves 6-8.

GREMOLATA

1 tablespoon lemon peel
1 teaspoon crushed garlic
3 tablespoons finely chopped parsley

Mix in small bowl the ingredients. Add half of the Gremolata to cooked veal shanks; simmer covered, 5 minutes. Remove strings. Place on platter as described on previous page.

Jan says, "Osso Buco, in Italian, means marrow-bone, the round bone in the shin of a calf. Milan has made this cut of meat famous all over the world. Osso Buco is traditionally served with risotto or plain buttered pasta."

"Salsa"
Sauces

BESCIAMELLA SAUCE

6 tablespoons butter
6 tablespoons flour
1 cup milk
1 cup heavy cream
1 teaspoon salt
1/2 teaspoon nutmeg
1/4 teaspoon pepper

In heavy saucepan, melt butter over moderate heat. Remove pan from heat and add flour. Pour in milk and cream all at once, stirring constantly until flour is dissolved. Return pan to heat and cook slowly. When sauce begins to thicken on the spoon or whisk, remove from heat and season with salt, pepper and nutmeg. Makes 2 1/2 cups.

PESTO GENOVESE
(HERB SAUCE)

1 cup fresh basil leaves
1 clove garlic, minced
1 shallot, minced
1/4 cup Bertolli olive oil
1 1/2 tablespoons milk
2 tablespoons grated Parmesan cheese
2 tablespoons grated Romano cheese

Put the basil, garlic, shallot, oil and milk in blender. Mix at low speed for 1 minute. Add the cheeses. Mix on low speed 1/2 minute more and then 1/2 minute on high speed. Makes 3/4 cup.

Jan says, "This sauce must be eaten as soon as you make it or it tends to darken. But it is worth the last-minute task. I serve this on fettuccine or spaghetti."

JAN'S TOMATO SAUCE

2 tablespoons Bertolli olive oil
1 large onion, chopped fine
2 garlic cloves, minced
1 shallot, minced
2 tablespoons oregano leaves
2 tablespoons minced parsley
1 tablespoon basil
1/2 teaspoon rosemary
1 teaspoon coarse pepper
1 teaspoon salt
2 teaspoons sugar
2 tablespoons vinegar

Simmer ingredients slowly for about 1/2 hour. Add:

2 cans (6-ounce) tomato paste
2 cans (15-ounce) Hunt's tomato sauce with tomato bits
2 cans (15-ounce) peeled tomatoes
1 can (8-ounce) tomato sauce

Simmer all ingredients together slowly for 2 to 3 hours.

Jan says, "I prefer the tomato sauce with tomato bits. (It's a good substitute for the pear-shaped tomatoes used by the Italians.) This sauce freezes beautifully. I always keep a batch in the freezer so when I make Italian dishes it is already made. I know that a good sauce is the secret to the dishes. Since this recipe makes a large amount, you can use half the Tomato Sauce as a meat sauce."

Makes 10-12 cups.

Meat Sauce: Brown 2 pounds of ground beef or Italian sausage and mix with the Tomato Sauce.

"Desserts"

BELLINI ICE

2 pounds ripe peaches
4 to 6 tablespoons sugar
2 tablespoons water
1 1/2 cups Italian spumante (Be sure to use an Italian spumante and not a grapy-tasting wine)

Peel peaches, cut each in half, discard pits, and puree fruit in food processor or blender. There should be about 3 1/2 cups puree. If peaches are out of season, use frozen peaches, but not canned.

Stir 2 tablespoons water into 4 tablespoons sugar. Heat to boiling. Remove from heat and stir into peach puree. Stir in spumante and place in freezer until firm. Break into chunks and puree, in batches, in food processor until smooth but not liquefied. Taste and add 1 or 2 more tablespoons sugar if necessary. Refreeze immediately. Serve in champagne goblets. Makes 5 cups.

Jo says, "A fond memory of Venice were Bellinis, a mixture of fresh peaches and champagne. I was thrilled to get this recipe."

AMARETTO STRIPS

2 eggs
2 tablespoons sugar
1/2 cup melted butter
1/2 cup milk
1/3 cup Amaretto liqueur
1 teaspoon lemon rind, grated
4 cups unsifted flour
1 teaspoon baking powder
Oil for deep frying
Confectioners' sugar

In a bowl, beat eggs with sugar until fluffy. Stir in butter, milk, Amaretto and lemon rind. Stir in flour and baking powder. Knead dough on a lightly floured surface until elastic and smooth. Roll out dough to form a 24 x 15-inch oblong 1/8-inch thick. With a sharp knife, cut dough into 2 x 5-inch strips. Drop strips into deep hot oil (360 degrees) and fry 2 minutes on each side until golden brown. Drain on paper toweling. Cool and sprinkle with confectioners' sugar. Makes 36.

ITALIAN ICE CREAM CAKE

5 packages (3-ounce) ladyfingers
1/4 cup light rum
2 pints Neapolitan ice cream, slightly softened
1 pint coffee ice cream, softened
2 tablespoons chopped pecans
Maraschino cherries or shaved chocolate curls

Slice ladyfingers. Use to line sides and bottom of 9-inch springform pan. Sprinkle ladyfingers with rum. Spread Neapolitan ice cream over fingers. Spread coffee ice cream over Neapolitan. Sprinkle with nuts. Cover; freeze until firm. Remove from pan. Let stand 15 minutes before serving. Garnish with maraschino cherries or shaved chocolate curls. Serves 12-14.

ITALIAN CASSATA ICE CREAM

1 quart vanilla ice cream
3 tablespoons dark rum
3/4 cup mixed candied fruit
1/2 cup chopped walnuts
1/2 cup coarsely grated semisweet chocolate
3/4 cup heavy cream, whipped stiff

Pour rum into a small bowl and stir in the candied fruit. Soak fruit for 25 minutes. Allow ice cream to soften in refrigerator for about 20 minutes. Spoon softened ice cream into a large bowl. With a spatula fold in fruit and rum, walnuts, and grated chocolate. Then gently fold in whipped cream.

Pour mixture into a 2-quart mold that has smooth round sides, so it will be easier to unmold the cassata at serving time. Freeze overnight. Before serving, allow the cassata to soften in refrigerator for about 10 minutes. Then unmold cassata by wrapping a hot towel around the bowl for 10 seconds or more. Turn mold upside down on a platter. Decorate around the cassata with flowers, mint leaves or sugared roses. Serve cassata at the table. Serves 12.

SICILIANA CASSATA

9 x 3-inch pound cake
1 pound ricotta cheese
3 tablespoons whipping cream
1/4 cup sugar
3 tablespoons orange liqueur
3 tablespoons chopped mixed candied fruit
2 ounces semisweet chocolate, coarsely chopped

CHOCOLATE FROSTING:
1 package (12-ounce) semisweet chocolate, cut in small pieces
3/4 cup strong coffee
1 cup unsalted butter, cut into 1/2-inch pieces, chilled

Slice off ends of pound cake. Cut cake horizontally into 1/2 to 3/4-inch thick pieces. Put ricotta cheese through a coarse sieve. Beating constantly on electric beater, add cream, sugar and orange liqueur with the ricotta cheese. With rubber spatula, fold in candied fruit and chocolate.

Center a layer of pound cake on a flat platter and spread generously with ricotta mixture. Place another layer of cake on top, keeping sides and ends even, and spread with more ricotta filling. Repeat until all cake layers are assembled and filling is gone. End with cake on top. Refrigerate until ricotta is firm, about 2 hours.

Melt 12 ounces of chocolate with coffee in a heavy pan over low heat. Stir constantly until chocolate has completely dissolved. Remove from heat and beat in butter, a dab at a time. Beat until mixture is smooth. Chill until it is spreading consistency. With a metal spatula, spread frosting evenly on top, sides and ends of cake. Cover loosely with plastic and refrigerate for at least a day before serving.

Before serving, put cake on a decorative plate and either use pastry tube flowers or real flowers that have been dipped in egg white and sugar. Serve at the table. Serves 8-10.

CENCI ALTA FLORENTINA

2 cups all-purpose flour
2 whole eggs
2 egg yolks
3 tablespoons rum
Confectioners' sugar
Oil for frying
Salt

Place 1 3/4 cups of the flour in a large bowl, making a well in the center, and add eggs, egg yolks, rum, 1 tablespoon confectioners' sugar and salt. Using your hands or a fork mix until all flour is mixed and you can gather it into a rough ball. Sprinkle remaining 1/4 cup of flour on a board or pastry cloth and knead for 10 minutes, until extra flour is worked into dough and the dough is smooth. Cover with damp cloth and let rest 30 minutes. Heat 3 or 4 inches of oil to 350 degrees in a deep fryer or heavy saucepan.

On floured board or cloth, roll out 1/4 of dough at a time. When paper thin, cut dough with a pastry wheel or sharp knife into strips, 6 to 7 inches long, 1/2-inch wide. Tie strips into loose knots and deep fry 4 at a time for 1 to 2 minutes or until golden brown. With tongs transfer to paper towels to drain. Just before serving, sprinkle Cenci with confectioners' sugar. Makes 3 dozen.

La Dolce Vita

CANNOLI

2 cups ricotta cheese
1 cup heavy whipped cream
3 tablespoons confectioners' sugar
2 tablespoons candied fruit
1 1/2 teaspoons vanilla extract

PASTRY:
1 cup flour
1/4 teaspoon salt
1 tablespoon sugar
1 tablespoon soft butter
1/4 cup white wine
Vegetable oil for frying

Put ricotta in a bowl. Fold in whipped cream, adding sugar as you fold. Chop candied fruit into tiny slivers; fold in all but a teaspoonful. Add vanilla. Refrigerate until shells are cooked and ready to be filled.

PASTRY:
Place flour in a mound on pastry board or clean table. Make well in center, measure in salt, sugar and soft butter. Add wine and with fork, stir in center. Keep stirring until most of flour is absorbed. You can work paste with your hands. Knead until smooth. Roll out no thicker than a noodle, cut into 3 1/2-inch squares, using 5-inch long, 1-inch diameter forms. Place forms diagonally on squares. Wrap pastry around form, one corner over the other. Press corners together. If corners don't stick, moisten finger with water, apply to contact point and press again. Cover the bottom of the frying pan with about 3/4-inch vegetable oil; heat to 375 degrees. If you don't have a thermometer, drop in a bit of dough. If dough blisters immediately and turns toast color, the temperature is right. Cannoli cooks very fast and swells in size. Turn them carefully side by side until done. When crisp remove them from the pan. Give a gentle push with a fork to slip the fried cannoli off. Be careful you don't burn your fingers. Use pliers or tongs. Drain on paper towels. Continue procedure until all are fried. When all are done, fill cannoli from one end to the other. Press filling gently and be sure cannoli is full. Scrape ends to smooth cream. Dip ends in candied fruit. Makes 16-18.

FLORENTINES

1/2 cup sifted flour
1/4 teaspoon soda
Dash of salt
1/4 cup butter
1/3 cup firmly packed brown sugar
2 tablespoons light corn syrup
1 egg, well beaten
1/2 cup flaked coconut
1 teaspoon vanilla
2 squares semisweet chocolate
1 tablespoon butter
3 tablespoons milk

Sift flour with soda and salt. Cream butter; gradually add sugar, beating until light and fluffy. Add corn syrup and egg, blending well. Stir in flour mixture, coconut and vanilla. Drop by teaspoons onto greased baking sheets, about 2 inches apart. Bake at 350 degrees about 10 minutes. Remove baking sheets from oven. Cool 1 minute. Remove wafers quickly from baking sheets. (If wafers harden on pan, return to oven for a few minutes.) Partially melt chocolate with butter over very low heat. Remove from heat, and stir rapidly until entirely melted. Blend in milk. Drizzle in a lacy pattern over the wafers. Let stand until chocolate is firm. Makes 4 dozen.

SPUMA DI ZUCCA CON AMARETTO

8 large eggs, separated, room temperature
1 cup granulated sugar
2 tablespoons unflavored gelatin
1/3 cup Amaretto liqueur
3 1/2 cups canned pureed pumpkin
1/2 teaspoon ground cinnamon
1/2 teaspoon grated nutmeg
1/4 teaspoon ground cloves
2 cups heavy cream

TOPPING:
2 cups whipping cream
4 tablespoons Amaretto liqueur
1/2 cup slivered almonds, toasted golden brown

Beat egg yolks with sugar until very thick and light in color. Do not underbeat. Soften gelatin in liqueur over hot water and set aside. Combine softened gelatin with egg mixture. Add pumpkin and spices, mixing thoroughly. Chill mixture, stirring often, until it just begins to set.

Whip the room-temperature egg whites until stiff peaks form. Gently fold into pumpkin mixture. Whip cream to soft peaks; fold gently into the mixture. Spoon mousse into stemmed goblets. Chill for several hours or overnight. Before serving, whip 2 cups cream with Amaretto until soft peaks form. Top with a scoop of the cream and sprinkle toasted almond slivers on top. Serves 8.

ZABAGLIONE

6 egg yolks
1/4 cup sugar
1/2 cup Marsala
1 cup heavy whipping cream

In double boiler over simmering water, beat egg yolks and sugar until pale yellow and fluffy. Gradually add Marsala and continue beating until Zabaglione becomes thick enough to hold shape on a spoon. Cover and refrigerate until mixture is slightly cooled.

In small cold bowl with mixer on medium speed, beat cream until soft peaks form. Reserve 1/4 cup whipped cream for garnish. With wire whisk or rubber spatula, fold remaining whipped cream into cooled egg-yolk mixture. Spoon into six parfait glasses. Garnish with a scoop of reserved whipped cream. Cover and freeze until firm. Will take about 4 hours. When serving, let parfaits stand at room temperature 10 minutes. Makes 6.

Jan says, "This Zabaglione may be served hot or cold. I like to serve it after I have added the Marsala and it has become thick to pour into wine glasses and serve it warm."

CREMA ZABAGLIONE PUFFS

2 cups Zabaglione
1 pint heavy cream
1 tablespoon sugar
1 recipe cream puffs (see index)

Make zabaglione and let it cool. Whip cream, slowly adding sugar until very stiff. Gently fold in the cold zabaglione. Mix very carefully. Cover and freeze until firm. Fill cream puffs and place the puffs back in the freezer. When ready to serve the puffs, take out of freezer and pour chocolate sauce over them. Serves 12.

Jan says, "Your guests will love you."

SPUMONE

For a mold, chill a 1-quart bowl in freezer. Follow directions on how to form the layers. To simplify, you can layer horizontally in a 9 x 12-inch pan. The other is more dramatic if served at the table.

EGGNOG LAYER:
1 pint Eggnog ice cream
3 maraschino cherries
         or
1 pint French vanilla ice cream
Rum flavoring to taste
3 maraschino cherries

Stir ice cream just to soften; stir in rum flavoring to taste, if using French vanilla ice cream. Refreeze only enough to be workable. Spread quickly in a layer over bottom and sides of chilled bowl. Place cherries in center. Return to freezer and freeze firm.

PISTACHIO LAYER:
1 pint French vanilla ice cream
1 teaspoon pistachio extract
Few drops of green food coloring
1/4 cup finely chopped unblanched almonds
   or pistachio nuts
         or
1 pint Pistachio ice cream
1/4 cup finely chopped almonds or pistachios
Green food coloring if desired

Stir ice cream just to soften, stir in extract, food coloring and nuts. Refreeze only enough to be workable. Quickly spread over top and sides of Eggnog layer. Freeze firm.

CHOCOLATE LAYER:
1/2 cup heavy cream
1/4 cup instant cocoa

Combine cream and instant cocoa; whip until mixture holds in peaks. Quickly spread over Pistachio layer, covering completely. Freeze.

RASPBERRY LAYER:
1 package (10-ounce) frozen red raspberries or
   strawberries, thawed
1/2 cup heavy cream
1/4 cup sifted confectioners' sugar
 Salt

Drain berries, sieve. Combine cream, confectioners' sugar, and a dash of salt; whip until mixture holds in peaks. Fold in sieved berries. (Add a few drops of red food coloring if needed.) Pour into center of mold and smooth top; cover with foil. Freeze 4 hours or overnight. Serves 12.

TO SERVE:

Peel off foil. Invert on chilled serving plate. Rub outside of bowl with towel wrung out of warm water to loosen ice cream. Lift off bowl. Top spumone with cherry or a sprinkling of chopped almonds, pistachio nuts, or chocolate curls. Pour Hennessy five-star cognac over each serving.

"Espresso" Coffee

ESPRESSO

Coffee was first brought to Italy in 1615. To an Italian, coffee is espresso. It is very strong and is brewed from a special bean, prepared with a machine by forcing steam through coffee grounds. It is served in demitasse cups with sugar, but no cream. Italians drink espresso only at the very end of their meal.

Caffé Cappuccino is made by combining steaming espresso with an equal quantity of steaming milk. Pour into tall cups and serve with a dollop of whipped cream.

CAPPUCCINO

1 package sweet chocolate mix
1 ounce cognac
6 ounces strong hot coffee

Mix chocolate, cognac and coffee. Stir well and serve with whipped cream on top.

CREAMY CAPPUCCINO

1 quart vanilla ice cream
1 quart chocolate ice cream
1/2 pint cream (half-and-half)
1 cup strong hot coffee
1 jigger each, brandy, cognac, Kahlúa and rum

Melt ice cream in large container over low heat. Add rest of ingredients and serve hot.

Jan says, "If you have an espresso coffee maker, use it for the true Cappuccino coffee. If you don't have one, ask for one for Christmas. A neat and unusual gift."

VARIATIONS OF CAPPUCCINO

Add zip with 1 tablespoon almond-flavor liqueur for each 6-ounce cup.

Espresso Romano: The Romans enjoy it with a twist of fresh lemon peel.

Caffé Latte: The Italian version of Cafe au lait, a morning eye-opener blend of strong coffee poured with hot milk into large coffee cup.

Iced Cappuccino: Prepare cappuccino and allow to cool, then pour over ice cubes and top with whipped cream, ground cinnamon or nutmeg.

"Vino"
Wine

Wine to Italians is like Coca-Cola to Americans. Wine is served at a meal in Italy like we are served water at our tables. The Italians like their wine at room temperature. Remove the cork from the bottle an hour or so before serving as it enhances the flavor.

BAROLO - Greatest of the Piedmontese reds. It is smooth with a high alcoholic content. Should be at least 3 years old. Best with lamb and roast beef.

BARDOLINO - A light red with a dry, spicy flavor. Good with lean beef, chicken and veal.

VALPOLICELLA - A dark, mellow red from Verona. Nice to serve at formal meals. It is a wine that won't overpower delicate flavors of a meal.

FRASCATI - The table wine of Rome. It is not expensive, but it is a temperamental wine. It can either be good or bad.

RAVELLO ROSATO - A delicate sweet rose grown near Salerno. It has a light fruity taste that goes with rich desserts.

VERDICCHIO DEI CASTELLI DI JESI - A dry white wine with a slight bitter taste. A nice table wine that is good with fish.

CHIANTI - A fresh, fruity, dry wine that is best with roast beef and lamb.

BROLIO - A fine Chianti wine that has a rich and subtle flavor.

SOAVE - Considered one of the finest of Italian white wines. It is mild and delicate. It should be well chilled. Serve with fish courses and antipasto.

ORVIETO - A pretty gold-color wine that has a smooth taste. Serve chilled with fish. Also can be served with desserts.

SUGGESTED WINE LIST

WHITE WINE

1980 Bianco di Custoza, Martini & Rossi
1980 Bianco di Custoza, Tommasi
1980 Soave Classico Superiore, Bolla
1980 Soave Classico Superiore, Santa Sofia
1980 Soave Classico Superiore, Villa Banfi
1979 Pinot Grigio del Veneto, Torresella
1980 Chardonnay delle Venezia, Torresella
1979 Tocai del Piave, Ponte
1979 Verduzzo del Piave, Ponte

RED WINE

1978 Bardolino, Bolla
1978 Bardolino Classico Superiore, Lamberti
1978 Bardolino Classico Superiore, Lenotti
1978 Bardolino Classico Superiore, Masi
1979 Bardolino Classico Superiore, Bertani
1978 Valpolicella, Bertolli
1978 Valpolicella Classico, Bolla
1979 Valpolicella Classico Superiore, Lamberti
1978 Valpolicella Classico Superiore, Masi
1978 Valpolicella Valpantina, Secco-Bertani
1977 Valpolicella Classico Superiore, Tommasi, Vigneto Rafael
1975 Merlot del Piave, Viticoltore

CHAMPAGNE

Martini & Rossi, Asti Spumante

La Fiesta Grande · Mexican Menus

We begin this chapter with two wonderful party menus complete with decorating ideas and then move on to recipes for appetizers such as Cold Curried Avocado Soup, Quesadillas, Deep Fried Stuffed Jalapeños, and Super Nachos, and such wonders as Molded Guacamole Ring and Ensalada de Arroz. The entree selections offer choices such as Green Chile Burritos, Fiesta Chicken and Shrimp Casserole, Jeanne's Sour Cream Enchiladas, and the ever-popular Paella. Top off your fiesta with Bunuélos I or II with Cinnamon Sugar Syrup, Fiesta Chocolate Cake, or Flan de Naranja.

LA FIESTA GRANDE I

Sangria - Margaritas - Mexican Beer

Hot Chili Dip - Chips

Deep Fried Stuffed Jalapenos

Super Nacho

Refried Beans

Guacamole - Fresh Vegetable Platter

Green Chili Burritos

Chili Rellenos

Sour Cream Enchiladas

Chicken Enchiladas

Salsa

Bunuelos - Cinnamon Sugar Syrup or Honey

Mandarin Orange Cake

Coffee

PARTY I

Color, color and more color adds to the excitement of this party. It is not the time to be bashful about decorating.

Your invitations can be made by cutting paper shapes of large flowers, a Mexican sun burst or large sombrero. If they are large enough, you can fold them in half or thirds, seal with a bright-colored seal and mail without an envelope.

Upon their arrival, your guests will be greeted by twinkling clear Christmas lights in the trees and the profusion of color elsewhere.

Yellow, green, hot pink, red, blue, all of them, from the large paper flowers you have massed in every possible place to different color cloths on each table, using serapes (shawls) crisscrossed on the tables to form "place mats" or squares of fringed burlap over the colored table skirt.

Large paper flowers will form your centerpieces with votive lights at the individual places. Have your candelabra high enough so the candles are not close to the paper flowers. Place maracas and castanets among the flowers.

If you choose to not use candelabra, an inverted sombrero filled with flowers is very effective.

Cover the buffet table with a bright cloth. Stand one or several pinatas on a 6 x 12-inch raised platform. Mound flowers and greenery around it and scatter many votives on the table.

Fill brown or bright-colored paper sacks about a fourth full with a layer of sand. Place a candle or votive light in each sack and line your driveway, sidewalk and poolside. These are called luminarias and are quite effective.

To brighten your pool, place a votive candle and glass in the center of an aluminum foil pan, small pie size. Secure glass with a bit of florist's clay. Place a bright flower in each pan, light the candles with a long handled match and set afloat in the pool. The more of these, the lovelier the glow in your pool.

Arrange to have a strolling guitarist or perhaps a mariachi band to add to the festivities.

As your guests depart, they will be filled with the message you conveyed so beautifully with your warmth and hospitality: "Mi casa es su casa."

LA FIESTA GRANDE II

Sangria - Margaritas

Chili Con Queso

Gazpacho Salad

Fiesta Chicken and Shrimp Casserole

Molded Guacamole Ring with Tomatoes

Orange Flavored Cream Cheese with Fruit

Mexican Wedding Cakes

Fiesta Chocolate Cake

PARTY II

Use red tablecloths for this party, with an over-skirt of black lace, red napkins. Use black wrought-iron candelabra and red candles. Miniature Spanish dolls and fans at the base of the candelabra lend a nice effect.

The floating candles in the pool as described in the first party are also lovely here.

Cover the buffet table in red with lace over-cloths. Place a very tall black wrought-iron candelabra in the center of the table, holding many candles covered by hurricane lamps. These can be found at a rental shop. Mass the base with flowers.

The party is perfect for your strolling guitarist, or perhaps you are active in a dance group or a patron of the ballet or folk-dance organization. Ask if they would perform at your party.

HOT CHEESE DIP

1 can RoTel Tomatoes and Green Chili
Small box Velveeta cheese

Melt and serve in chafing dish.
Serves 10-12.

HOT CHEESE SAUCE

2 pound box Velveeta cheese
3 onions (use chopped frozen or put in processor)
2 or 3 jalapeno peppers (hot), chopped
1 pint mayonnaise

Melt first 3 ingredients and add 1 pint mayonnaise. Beat 4 to 5 minutes with mixer at 15-minute intervals. Do this twice. Store in refrigerator. Serves 16-20.

CHILI CON QUESO

1 tablespoon vegetable oil
1 large onion, chopped
1 garlic clove, minced
1 tablespoon all-purpose flour
1 tablespoon chili powder or to taste
1 can (10-ounce) tomatoes and green chilies, or 1 can (16-ounce) whole tomatoes mixed with 1/4 cup diced green chilies
1 pound processed American cheese, cut into 1-inch cubes
2 jalapeno peppers (or to taste), seeded and chopped

Heat oil in 3-quart saucepan over medium heat. Add onion and garlic and saute until onion is translucent, about 5 minutes. Stir in flour and chili powder and cook, stirring constantly, for 1 minute. Add tomatoes (and chilies if necessary) and continue cooking until thickened, about 5 to 6 minutes. Reduce heat to low and gradually add cheese, stirring constantly until cheese is completely melted. Stir in peppers. Taste and adjust seasoning. Serve hot. Makes 4 cups.

La Fiesta Grande

QUESADILLAS

1/2 pound Jack or brick cheese, cut in strips
1/4 cup chopped onion
1/4 cup jalapeno or green chili peppers cut in strips. Use less of jalapeno.
12 flour tortillas
Oil for deep frying

Lay several strips of cheese, some onion and chili pepper on each flour tortilla. Fold over and skewer with a toothpick. Fry until crisp, remove toothpicks. If using for appetizers cut in halves. Except for frying, can prepare early in day and refrigerate. Serves 12.

SALSA

1 large can tomatoes
1 clove garlic, crushed
1 onion, chopped
1 can (4-ounce) peeled green chilies, chopped, including seeds
1 teaspoon oregano
2 tablespoons wine vinegar
2 tablespoons oil
Salt and pepper to taste

Heat oil until quite hot. Add garlic and onion, stirring while mixture cooks. When onion and garlic are nicely browned, add tomatoes, chilies and rest of ingredients. Simmer uncovered 30 minutes or until a good sauce consistency, stirring often. If desired, add additional green chilies. Can be used for a dip with tortilla chips or on top of any dish as a condiment. Makes 2 cups.

COLD CURRIED AVOCADO SOUP

2 tablespoons butter
2 bunches green onions, finely chopped
3 teaspoons curry powder, less if desired
2 medium-sized avocados, peeled and chopped
8 to 10 cups chicken broth
1/2 cup plain yogurt
1/2 teaspoon salt
1 tablespoon chopped fresh dill, chives or parsley for garnish
Grated rind and strained juice of 1 lemon

Heat butter in a small skillet. Add green onions and saute for 4 minutes until tender. Add curry powder and stir for one minute. Puree curried onions, avocados, 1 cup of broth, yogurt, lemon rind and juice and salt in a food processor or blender.

Transfer puree into a large container and stir in remaining chicken broth until a desired pouring consistency. The soup will thicken as it stands. Cover and chill for 4 hours. Garnish with your desired herb. Serve with tortilla chips. Serves 8.

GUACAMOLE

4 large avocados, chopped
1 package (8-ounce) cream cheese, softened
1 large red onion, diced finely
1 large tomato, diced finely
1 tablespoon lemon juice
1 teaspoon garlic salt
1/2 teaspoon salt
1/2 teaspoon celery salt
1 large teaspoon Worcestershire sauce
Several dashes of Tabasco sauce
Dash of cayenne or chili powder

Mash chopped avocados and combine with softened cream cheese. Stir in chopped onion, tomato and remaining ingredients to taste. If not serving immediately, put in a bowl, place an avocado seed in the middle of the guacamole, cover and refrigerate. The seed will help keep the guacamole from turning brown before serving. Serve with corn chips or delicious with fresh vegetables.
Makes 2 cups.

La Fiesta Grande

HOT CHILI DIP

2 cans Hormel chili without beans
1 medium box Velveeta cheese
1 onion

Melt and serve hot with Fritos.
Makes 4 cups.

ORANGE FLAVORED CREAM CHEESE

3 ounces cream cheese, softened
1 teaspoon orange juice
1 teaspoon Grand Marnier
1/2 teaspoon grated orange peel
1 tablespoon powdered sugar

Mix ingredients together. Refrigerate until ready to use. Let soften before serving. Especially good served as a spread for pears, apples, and other fresh fruit. Makes 3/4 cup.

GARBANZO BEAN DIP

1 can garbanzo beans
1/2 teaspoon salt
Pepper to taste
1/4 teaspoon garlic powder
2 tablespoons salad oil
1 teaspoon lemon juice
1/8 teaspoon Accent

Drain beans and blend all ingredients. This dip is good with vegetables as well as crackers.
Makes 1 cup.

GAZPACHO

1/2 cup olive oil
1/2 cup lime juice
6 cups V-8 juice
2 cups beef broth
4 tomatoes, peeled and finely chopped
1/2 cup onion, finely minced
2 cups celery, finely minced
1 1/2 cucumbers, seeded and finely diced
1 clove garlic, pressed
1/3 cup snipped parsley
1/4 teaspoon Tabasco sauce
1 teaspoon Worcestershire sauce
1/2 teaspoon pepper, freshly ground
Optional: Sour cream
　　　　 Fresh mushrooms, sliced

GARNISHES: Served in separate bowls
2 cups croutons
2 cups green pepper, diced
2 cups scallions, chopped
2 cups cucumbers, diced

Beat oil and lime juice together. Stir in V-8 juice, beef broth, vegetables and seasonings. Adjust the seasonings and chill for at least 3 hours. Serve as prepared or add large tablespoon of sour cream and 1/4 cup sliced fresh mushrooms to each serving. Makes 14 cups.

Jo says, "If serving from a tureen, freeze a tray or two of Beefamato or Clamato juice and put into soup. The frozen juice will keep the gazpacho cold without diluting the flavor."

DEEP FRIED STUFFED JALAPENOS

This recipe will be based upon the number of stuffed jalapenos you wish to make. Wash peppers, make a slit on one side of each pepper and remove seeds. Saute enough ground beef for peppers and add enough commercial taco sauce to have the meat stick together. Grate cheddar cheese. Stuff peppers with meat, taco sauce mixture, put cheese on top and mash it into meat mixture. Prepare a thick batter out of fish and chip dip. Roll the peppers in the batter and deep fry. Serve hot.

MICRO-NACHOS

16 large tortilla chips
4 ounces shredded Monterey Jack cheese
2 tablespoons shredded cheddar cheese, optional

Place a sheet of wax paper on a 10-inch glass or paper plate. Cover with tortilla chips. Sprinkle with cheese. Microwave at "medium" for 1 1/2 to 2 1/2 minutes, until cheese melts, rotating once or twice.

You may vary the nachos by putting a small slice of jalapeno pepper or stuffed olive on each chip before sprinkling with cheese.

SUPER NACHO

1 1/2 pounds lean ground beef
1 cup chopped onion, sauteed
Salt, pepper and garlic powder to taste
1 tablespoon chili powder
1 can (4-ounce) chopped green chilies
2 cans (16-ounce each) refried beans
4 cups Monterey Jack cheese, grated
1 bottle of green taco sauce
Chopped green onions in middle
1 small can chopped black olives for second circle
Avocado dip (can be homemade or frozen for third circle)
1 carton sour cream for outside circle

Brown beef in a small amount of oil and add the next 4 ingredients. Mix well. Spray a large pizza pan with Pam, or two 9-inch pie plates if you desire to make 2 nachos. Spread with refried beans and top evenly with meat mixture. Top with 4 cups Monterey Jack cheese, grated. Sprinkle over the top 1 bottle of green taco sauce. Refrigerate or freeze at this point if serving later.

When ready to serve, bake 20 to 30 minutes at 400 degrees. Take out of oven and sprinkle on top the remaining ingredients in concentric circles.
Serves 10-12.
Serve hot with Fritos or Doritos.

TORTILLA SOUP

8 corn tortillas, sliced in thin slivers
1 quart hot water
4 heaping teaspoons chicken bouillon
1 can tomatoes
Butter, melted, for frying onions
1 onion, thinly sliced
1/2 teaspoon ground cumin
Grated cheese, Longhorn Cheddar or Jack

Fry tortilla strips until crisp; set aside. Add bouillon to hot water, mix, and add tomatoes. Fry onion in butter until brown, add cumin. Mix into soup and simmer 30 minutes. Add tortillas at the last minute. Top with grated cheese and serve. Serves 4.

La Fiesta Grande

ENSALADA DE ARROZ

1/2 cup olive oil
1/4 cup orange juice
1/4 cup vinegar
1/2 teaspoon salt
2 teaspoons grated onion
1 tablespoon minced parsley
2 tablespoons chopped pimento
1 or 2 cans artichoke hearts, as desired
4 cups cooked rice
1 tomato, cut in wedges
1 orange, cut in sections
6 small radishes
1 tablespoon capers

Combine olive oil, orange juice, vinegar, salt, onion, parsley, pimento, and artichoke hearts. Marinate 30 minutes. Add the rice. Toss and blend. Arrange on platter with tomato wedges, orange sections, and radishes as garnish. Sprinkle capers over top. This is delicious with barbecue.
Serves 6-8.

GAZPACHO SALAD

8 cucumbers, peeled and diced
16 tomatoes, seeded and finely diced
8 green peppers, seeded and finely slivered
4 onions, finely chopped
Juice of 4 lemons
24 rolled anchovies
24 halved black olives

Arrange this salad in a clear glass bowl, alternating layers of the top 4 ingredients, making at least 8 layers.
Sprinkle vegetables with lemon juice while preparing them. Sprinkle layers with salt and pepper. Intersperse vegetables with anchovies and black olives.

DRESSING:
6 to 8 garlic cloves
1/2 teaspoon salt
Ground cumin seed
1 cup vinegar
2 cups olive oil
4 tablespoons shallots, finely chopped

DRESSING:
In a wooden mixing bowl mash 6-8 cloves of garlic to a paste with 1/2 teaspoon salt and a pinch of ground cumin seed. Beat in 1 cup vinegar and 2 cups olive oil. Stir in 4 tablespoons finely chopped shallots. Pour this over salad and chill 2 to 3 hours.
Serves 12.

MOLDED GUACAMOLE RING

1 1/2 envelopes (1 1/2 tablespoons) unflavored gelatin
1/2 cup cold water
3/4 cup boiling water
2 tablespoons lemon juice
1 1/4 teaspoons salt
1 tablespoon grated onion
2 dashes Tabasco sauce
2 1/2 cups mashed avocado
1 cup sour cream
1 cup mayonnaise

Soften gelatin in cold water; dissolve in boiling water. Add lemon juice, salt, onion, and Tabasco. Cool to room temperature; stir in avocado, sour cream and mayonnaise. Turn into a 6-cup mold; chill until firm, 5 to 6 hours or overnight. Unmold on serving plate. Fill center with chilled seafood or chicken salad. Surround with cherry tomatoes.
Serves 8-10.

La Fiesta Grande

MEXICAN SALAD

1 pound ground beef
1/4 cup chopped onion
2 cups kidney beans, drained
1/2 cup French's Catalina dressing
1/2 cup water
1 tablespoon chili powder
4 cups shredded lettuce
1/2 cup sliced green onion
1 package (8-ounce) sharp Cheddar cheese, grated

Brown meat, add onion and cook until tender. Stir in beans, dressing, water and chili powder. Simmer 15 minutes. In a bowl, combine lettuce and green onion. Add meat sauce and 1/2 cheese. Toss and sprinkle with remaining cheese. To serve, have small bowls of sour cream, taco sauce and chopped avocado for guests to use as garnish. Serves 12.

MEXICAN SPOON BREAD

1 can (16-ounce) cream style yellow corn
3/4 cup milk
1/3 cup cooking oil
2 eggs, slightly beaten
1 cup yellow cornmeal
1/2 teaspoon soda
1 teaspoon salt
1 can (4-ounce) diced green chilies
1 1/2 cups shredded cheddar cheese

Mix all ingredients except chilies and cheese in order given. Pour half of batter into greased 9 x 9-inch baking dish and spread with chopped green chilies and 1/2 of cheese. Spread remainder of batter and top with remaining cheese. Bake 45 minutes in 400-degree oven. Remove from oven and allow to cool just enough to set a bit before cutting. Serves 8.

REFRIED BEANS

2 cups pinto beans, soaked overnight
1 1/2 teaspoons salt
1 1/2 cups chopped onion
3 cloves crushed garlic
1/2 cup chopped green pepper
2 teaspoons ground cumin
1/4 teaspoon pepper
3 tablespoons oil

Cook beans in water, partially covered, about 1 1/2 hours. Check periodically that beans are always covered with water. When beans are soft, drain and mash well.

Heat oil in skillet. Saute onions, garlic, cumin and 1/2 teaspoon salt. Saute until soft, add green pepper, cover and simmer 5 minutes. Add the beans to vegetables with 1 teaspoon of salt and pepper. Toss in skillet for a few minutes.

Serves 4-6.

BRAZILIAN RICE

3 cups boiled rice
1/4 cup melted butter
4 beaten eggs
1 pound grated sharp cheese
1 cup milk
1 package frozen spinach, cooked and drained
1 tablespoon chopped onion
1 teaspoon Worcestershire sauce
1 teaspoon salt
1/2 teaspoon marjoram
1/2 teaspoon thyme
1/2 teaspoon rosemary

Prepare rice. Melt butter and add remaining ingredients. Mix sauce well then stir in rice. Pour into oblong baking dish, set in pan of water. Bake at 350 degrees for 30 minutes. Cut into squares to serve. This is good reheated. Serves 8.

SPANISH RICE

1/4 pound rice, boiled with 1/2 teaspoon salt
1/2 pound ground beef, fried
1/2 of a No. 2 can tomato paste
1/2 chopped pepper
1 small onion, chopped
1/4 teaspoon chili powder
1/4 teaspoon paprika
3/4 teaspoon salt

Mix all ingredients together and bake in a greased baking dish for 1 hour in a 325-degree oven. Serves 4.

GREEN CHILE BURRITOS

2 pounds lean pork, diced
3 cans (10 1/2-ounce) chicken broth
2 cans (7-ounce) chopped mild green chiles
1 can (16-ounce) tomatoes, chopped
12 white flour tortillas
2 cans (16-ounce) refried beans
Flour
2 cups (8 ounces) grated Cheddar cheese
3 cups shredded lettuce
3 tomatoes, chopped

Simmer pork in broth until tender and thoroughly cooked. Add chiles and canned tomatoes. Simmer 15 to 20 minutes. Spread each tortilla with refried beans. Using a slotted spoon, put some pork mixture on each tortilla, reserving liquid to serve as sauce. Roll each tortilla and place in a shallow greased baking dish. Bake uncovered at 350 degrees for 15 minutes or until hot. Thicken sauce with a little flour and spoon over burritos. Serve topped with grated Cheddar, shredded lettuce and chopped tomato. Serves 12.

CHILI PIE

8 to 10 canned whole green chilies
1/2 pound (8 ounces) Monterey Jack cheese, grated
5 eggs, lightly beaten
2 1/2 tablespoons whipping cream
2 tablespoons minced onion
3/4 teaspoon salt
1/2 teaspoon minced garlic
Freshly ground pepper

Preheat oven to 325 degrees. Generously grease 10-inch pie plate or shallow casserole. Line plate with split chilies, covering completely and extending up sides as much as possible.

Combine eggs, cheese, cream, onion, salt, garlic and pepper in blender and mix on low speed about 2 minutes. Carefully pour into pie plate and bake until set, about 30 minutes. Let cool slightly before cutting into wedges. Makes 1 10-inch pie.

La Fiesta Grande

FIESTA CHICKEN AND SHRIMP CASSEROLE

1 large chicken, cut into 8 pieces,
  or if you prefer you may use 8 meaty pieces,
  thighs, legs, breasts
1/2 teaspoon salt
1/4 teaspoon cracked black pepper
1/4 cup olive oil
3/4 cup chopped onions
1 1/2 teaspoons minced garlic
3 tablespoons flour
1/2 pound cooked ham, diced
1/4 teaspoon paprika
1 cup white wine
1/2 pound medium shrimp
2 tablespoons chopped parsley

Wash, dry, salt and pepper chicken pieces. Heat oil and saute chicken in skillet until golden (about 10 minutes). Transfer to a 2 1/2 — 3-quart casserole. Cook onions and garlic in skillet until golden. Mix in flour and, stirring constantly, cook for 1-2 minutes. Stir in ham, paprika, wine and bring to a boil over high heat. Pour over chicken and bring casserole to boil. Lower heat, cover and simmer 30 minutes.

Shell shrimp, devein, wash under cold water and set aside. Pierce a chicken thigh to test for doneness. Continue cooking until meat is no longer tinged with pink. When chicken is done, arrange shrimp on top of chicken and cook 5 minutes or until shrimp are pink. Sprinkle with parsley and serve with rice. Serves 6.

CHILI RELLENOS

3 cans (4-ounce size) chopped green chiles,
  drained (use mild peppers)
1 pound sharp Cheddar cheese, grated
3 eggs
1/2 teaspoon salt
1/2 cup flour
2 cups milk

Starting with green chiles and ending with cheese, place both in layers in a 9 x 13-inch baking dish. Mix together eggs, salt, flour and beat well. Add milk and pour over layered ingredients. Bake 1 hour at 300 degrees. Serves 6.

CHEESE AND ONION ENCHILADAS

1 1/2 pounds lean ground beef
1-2 tablespoons oil
3 tablespoons fresh chili powder
1/2 teaspoon salt
1/2 teaspoon pepper
1/2 teaspoon ground cumin
1 clove crushed garlic
1 1/2 cups water
2 tablespoons masa harina
8-10 corn tortillas
1 onion, chopped
1 pound mild cheddar cheese, grated

Brown meat in oil. Add chili powder and spices. Mix masa harina with water and add to meat. Cook about 20 minutes. Soften tortillas in hot oil. Dip tortillas in meat sauce, and fill them with cheese and onion. Roll up and place in 9 x 13-inch baking dish, seam side down. Pour remaining meat sauce over top. Sprinkle some cheese over top. Bake at 325 degrees 25 to 30 minutes, until bubbly. Casserole may be prepared ahead and baked when needed. Serves 8-10.

La Fiesta Grande

CHICKEN ENCHILADAS

1 can (16-ounce) tomatoes
1 can (4-ounce) green chili peppers, drained and seeded
1/2 teaspoon ground coriander
1/2 teaspoon salt
1 cup sour cream
2 cups finely chopped cooked chicken
1 package (3-ounce) cream cheese, softened
1/4 cup finely chopped onion
3/4 teaspoon salt
12 flour tortillas
Cooking oil
1 cup shredded Monterey Jack Cheese

Place tomatoes, chili peppers, coriander and salt in blender. Cover, blend until smooth. Add sour cream; cover and blend just until smooth. Set aside. Mix chicken, cream cheese, onion and 3/4 teaspoon salt. In a skillet heat a small amount of oil. Dip tortillas, one at a time, into hot oil, fry just until limp, a few seconds per side. Drain on paper toweling. Spread chicken mixture on tortillas; roll up. Place seam side down in a 12 x 7 x 2-inch baking dish. Pour tomato mixture on top. Cover with foil; bake at 350 degrees for about 30 minutes. Remove foil; sprinkle with cheese. Return to oven until cheese melts. Serves 6.

Jo says, "If using commercial tortillas, dip each into boiling water for just a second right before filling. This will soften them and prevent them from unrolling or cracking."

ENCHILADA PIE

1 can enchilada sauce
1 can (8-ounce) tomato sauce
1 pound lean ground beef
1 medium onion, chopped
Dash of chili powder
12 corn tortillas
Melted butter
2 cups cheddar cheese, grated

Mix enchilada sauce and tomato sauce. Brown the beef and onion; add 1/2 of the tomato sauce, chili powder and heat. Butter 6 corn tortillas and lay them in the bottom of a large casserole. They will overlap. Pour meat and tomato mixture over tortillas, and sprinkle with 1 cup grated cheese. Then dip 6 more tortillas in melted butter to make a second layer; add the other half of tomato mixture without meat. Cover top with 1 cup of shredded cheddar cheese and bake 1 hour at 250 degrees. Serves 4-6.

Jo says, "I add more sauce to the meat if necessary so it will not be dry."

JEANNE'S SOUR CREAM ENCHILADAS

2 cans cream of chicken soup
2 cups sour cream
1 small can or jar of green salsa
1/2 cup chopped green onions
1 teaspoon M.S.G.
1 teaspoon salt
1/2 pound Monterey Jack cheese, grated
1/2 pound cheddar cheese, grated
12 flour tortillas
1 large or 2 small cans enchilada sauce
Chopped onions

Combine soup, sour cream, salsa, onions, M.S.G. and salt. Warm enchilada sauce. Using 1 tortilla at a time, place about a tablespoon of sauce in the middle and spread to coat. Next, put a dollop of soup mixture on one edge and a sprinkle of cheese. Roll up and place in a baking dish. Continue until pan is full. Pour remaining enchilada sauce over all; sprinkle cheese down the center and sprinkle a few chopped onions. Bake in a slow oven until warmed through and bubbly.

If you prefer to use corn tortillas, fry them first in a little hot oil and drain before rolling. The salsa is hot so you may want to use just half; experiment to taste. Serves 8.

MEXICAN-STYLE STEAK

2 pounds round steak - 1/2-inch thick
3 tablespoons all-purpose flour
   Pepper
1 1/2 teaspoons salt
2 tablespoons salad oil
1 recipe Salsa (see index)
1 can (6-ounce) broiled mushroom crowns,
   drained and halved

Cut steak into 6 serving pieces. Combine flour, salt and a dash of pepper; dredge meat in mixture. In skillet, heat oil. Brown meat on both sides in hot oil. Remove meat and arrange in a shallow baking dish. Pour half the salsa over meat. Cover; bake in 325-degree oven for 2 hours or until tender, adding mushrooms last 10 minutes. Skim off excess fat. Serve with fried rice. Heat remaining salsa. Pass with meat.

PAELLA

1/2 cup olive oil
1 onion, chopped fine
2 pounds chicken pieces
1 pound chorizos (Spanish sausage) or
   hot Italian sausage, 1-inch in diameter,
   cut in thin slices
1/2 pound diced pork loin
4 cloves garlic, minced
1/3 cup fresh parsley, minced
1 can (8-ounce) stewed tomatoes
6 cups chicken broth
1 1/2 teaspoons salt
1 teaspoon powdered saffron
2 cups rice
16 raw clams, scrubbed
16 mussels
16 raw medium shrimp, with shells
2 lobster tails, cut into 1-inch long segments
1/2 pound squid (optional), cleaned and cut
   into 1-inch pieces
1 medium green pepper, quartered
2 pimentos, quartered
1 package frozen lima beans, cooked according to
   package directions and drained
1 can artichoke hearts, drained and sliced in half
1 small can peas, drained
4 hard-boiled eggs, shelled and halved, for garnish

Heat olive oil until very hot in large, heavy skillet. Add onion, chicken, sausage and pork. Saute ingredients, turning frequently, until brown and almost done.

Push sauteed ingredients to side of pan, making a space in the center. Mix minced garlic and parsley with stewed tomatoes. Pour into center of pan and saute 3 to 5 minutes.

Add chicken broth, salt and saffron. Boil briskly for 5 minutes. Add rice. Cook, covered, about 25 minutes, being careful not to let rice on bottom of pan stick and burn.

Add clams, mussels, shrimp, lobster and squid. Cook 8 to 10 minutes until shrimp turn pink.

Check rice. If it is undercooked, add some water and cook longer.

Arrange pepper, pimento, lima beans, artichoke hearts, peas and boiled egg halves over mixture in the last minute for decoration.

Remove paella from stove, let stand, covered, for 5 minutes so flavors will blend. Serves 8.

CHICKEN TACOS

6 corn tortillas
12 ounces cooked, diced chicken
4 ounces minced onion
7 ounces jalapeno sauce
1/2 cup finely shredded lettuce
1 small fresh tomato
3 ounces grated Monterey Jack cheese

Fry tortillas individually in deep fat. While frying, place a one-inch spatula in middle of tortilla slightly above the level of fat. Be careful that the ends of tortillas do not close or you will not be able to stuff them. When tortillas are crisp and golden-brown, remove from oil and cool. Mix chicken with jalapeno sauce; spoon into pocket of tortilla. Next, sprinkle a little onion and cheese, then the lettuce, across the fold of tortillas. Place some finely diced tomato into each end of the tortilla (at the fold). When tacos are filled, they should be served at once. Beef or pork can be substituted for the chicken. Makes 6.

BUNUELOS I

12 flour tortillas
Coconut oil
Melted butter
Cinnamon
Sugar
Allspice

Deep fry tortillas one by one in coconut oil on both sides until light brown and crisp. Place on paper towels. Brush with melted butter, sprinkle with cinnamon, sugar and allspice. Serve with cinnamon, sugar syrup or honey and vanilla ice cream. Makes 12.

BUNUELOS II

4 cups sifted flour
2 tablespoons sugar
1 teaspoon baking powder
2 teaspoons salt
2 eggs, beaten
3/4 cup milk
1/4 cup melted butter

Sift dry ingredients into a bowl. Beat together eggs and milk and add to dry ingredients. Add butter and mix into a dough that can be handled. Turn dough onto very lightly floured board and knead until smooth. Divide into 25 pieces and shape into balls. Cover and let stand 25 minutes. Roll each ball onto lightly floured board into a large, round, very thin tortilla. Keep remaining pieces covered with a towel to prevent drying. Let stand 5 minutes and fry individually in deep hot (375-degree) coconut oil until golden brown on both sides, about 2 to 3 minutes. Drain on paper towels and sprinkle with sugar, cinnamon and allspice. Makes 25 balls.

Pass Cinnamon Sugar Syrup in a pitcher.

CINNAMON SUGAR SYRUP

1 1/2 cups sugar
1/2 cup water
2 tablespoons light corn syrup
1 cinnamon stick or pinch of ground cinnamon

Combine ingredients in 1-quart saucepan. Bring to boil, shaking pan gently until sugar dissolves, then boil without stirring until thick and syrupy, 8 to 10 minutes. Discard cinnamon stick.

Bunuelos will become soggy quickly when syrup is drizzled over top. Serve immediately.

Bunuelos can be stored with cinnamon-sugar sprinkling for several days in air-tight container. Makes 2 cups.

La Fiesta Grande

FIESTA CHOCOLATE CAKE

3/4 cup semisweet chocolate chips
1/2 cup walnuts
2 1/2 teaspoons cinnamon
3 eggs
1/2 cup sugar
1/2 cup light brown sugar
2 tablespoons butter
1 cup buttermilk
1 teaspoon vanilla
2 cups sifted flour
1 1/2 teaspoons baking powder
1/2 teaspoon baking soda
1/4 teaspoon salt

Grease a 10-inch tube pan. In a blender, grate the chocolate chips and walnuts. In a large bowl, beat the eggs. Add sugar, brown sugar and butter. Beat well. Fold in the chocolate mixture and add cinnamon, buttermilk and vanilla. Gently fold in flour, baking powder, soda and salt until no dry ingredients are visible. Pour into prepared pan and bake at 350 degrees for 45 to 60 minutes. Cool in pan for 5 minutes. Turn out of the pan to cool completely. Split horizontally into 3 layers. Spread with chocolate frosting. Serves 12-14.

CHOCOLATE FROSTING:
1 6-ounce package semisweet chocolate chips
1 cup sour cream (8 ounces)
1 teaspoon instant coffee granules, mixed with just enough hot water to dissolve
1/4 teaspoon ground cinnamon

Melt chocolate chips over hot water in a double boiler. Stir in instant coffee, sour cream and cinnamon. Spread on cake.

MANDARIN ORANGE CAKE

1 cup sugar
1 egg
1 teaspoon soda
1 teaspoon vanilla
1 small can mandarin oranges, drained
1 cup flour
Pinch of salt
1/2 cup chopped nuts (optional)

Combine egg, sugar, soda, vanilla, oranges and flour. Mix for three minutes. Add salt and nuts and mix well. Pour into greased and floured 8 x 8-inch pan. Bake at 350 degrees or until springs back. Cool and cover with topping. Serves 8.

TOPPING:
1/2 cup brown sugar
3 tablespoons butter or margarine
3 tablespoons milk

Combine brown sugar, butter and milk. Boil about 3 minutes and pour over cooled cake. Serve with whipped topping.

MANDARIN ORANGE CAKE II

1 package buttercake mix
1 stick butter
1 can mandarin oranges
1/4 cup oil
1 small package instant vanilla pudding

Combine all ingredients and bake at 325 degrees until done. Follow cake-mix directions for size of pan. Cool and frost.

TOPPING:
1 9-ounce tub Cool Whip
1 small can crushed pineapple, undrained
1 small package instant vanilla pudding

Combine all ingredients and frost cooled cake. Serves 10.

La Fiesta Grande

MEXICAN FRUIT CAKE

2 eggs
2 cups sugar
2 teaspoons baking soda
2 cups flour
1 can (20-ounce) crushed pineapple with juice
1 cup chopped nuts

Blend eggs and sugar. Add baking soda and flour. Mix in the pineapple, stir well. Add chopped nuts. Bake in greased and floured 9 x 13-inch pan at 350 degrees for 35 minutes. Cool.

FROSTING:
1 8-ounce package cream cheese, softened
1 stick margarine, softened
1 teaspoon vanilla
2 1/2 cups powdered sugar

Combine cream cheese and margarine. Add vanilla, beat in powdered sugar. Frost cake. Serves 12.

MEXICAN WEDDING CAKES

1/2 pound (2 sticks) butter
5 tablespoons powdered sugar
2 cups sifted cake flour
1 cup chopped nuts
1 tablespoon vanilla

Cream butter and sugar. Add flour and vanilla; blend well. Stir in nuts; shape into crescents. Bake on ungreased cookie sheet at 325 degrees for 12 to 15 minutes or until very lightly browned. Cool. Put waxed paper on tray or cookie sheet and sprinkle paper with powdered sugar. Place crescents down on powdered sugar, sift more powdered sugar on top. Layer in box or big pan. Cover. Makes 5 dozen.

Jo says, "These are very fragile, delicate cookies. Be careful handling. They are well worth the effort — a wonderful ending to your Mexican fiesta."

PUMPKIN RICE PUDDING

1 16-ounce can pumpkin
3/4 cup sugar
1 teaspoon cinnamon
1/2 teaspoon salt
1/2 teaspoon ground ginger
1/4 teaspoon ground cloves
2 slightly beaten eggs
1 13-ounce can evaporated milk
2/3 cup uncooked quick-cooking rice
1/2 cup raisins

Combine first 6 ingredients. Add eggs. Stir in milk. Stir in rice and raisins. Pour into 1 1/2-quart casserole. Place in shallow pan on oven rack; pour hot water around casserole into pan to a depth of 1 inch. Bake at 350 degrees for 15 minutes; stir until well combined. Bake until a knife inserted just off-center comes out clean, 50-60 minutes more. Serves 6-8.

FLAN De NARANJA
ORANGE CUSTARD

CARAMEL:
12 ounces sliced almonds, toasted
2 cups granulated sugar
1/4 cup water

CUSTARD:
1 pint milk
1 quart light cream
1 vanilla bean
1 ounce sugar
6 eggs
1 teaspoon granulated orange rind
4 ounces orange juice

Begin by making caramel. Dilute sugar in water, place on burner, boil until mixture is reduced and golden brown in color. Add sliced almonds. Pour into custard cups, filling to divide evenly among 8 to 10 cups. Let stand until cool. Prepare the custard by boiling half of the milk and half of the cream with the vanilla bean. Reduce mixture to about 1 cup. Remove from burner. Add the remainder of the cold milk and cream and the rest of the ingredients. Mix well. Fill custard cups. Bake in 325-degree oven for about 25 minutes. Test with toothpicks.

Jo says, "Remember to set custard cups in a small amount of water."

ESPONJOSA
(COLD CARAMEL SOUFFLE)

6 egg whites (3/4 cup)
3 1/4 cups superfine granulated sugar
English Custard Sauce (see index)

Let egg whites warm to room temperature, about an hour, in the large bowl of electric mixer. In the meantime, place 1 1/2 cups sugar in a heavy medium skillet. To carmelize, cook over medium heat, stirring, until sugar is compeltely melted and begins to boil. Syrup should be a medium brown. With a pot holder hold a 1 1/2-quart oven casserole and pour in hot syrup all at once. Tilt and rotate casserole until bottom and side are thoroughly coated. Set on wire rack and cool. Beat egg whites at high speed until very stiff, about 5 minutes. While continuing to beat, gradually pour in 1 1/4 cups sugar in a continuous stream. This takes about 3 minutes. Scrape side of bowl with scraper and beat 10 minutes. About 5 minutes before beating time is up, place 1/2 cup sugar in heavy medium skillet and carmelize as with the other 1 1/2 cups of sugar. Remove from heat and immediately place skillet in a pan of cold water for a few seconds, or until the syrup is thick, stirring constantly.

With beater at medium speed, gradually pour syrup into beaten egg-white mixture. Scrape side of bowl with scraper. Return to high speed and continue beating 3 minutes longer. Preheat oven to 250 degrees. Turn egg-white mixture into prepared casserole, spreading evenly. Set in large baking pan; pour boiling water to 1-inch depth around casserole. Bake 1 hour or until meringue seems firm when gently shaken and rises about 1/2 inch above casserole. Meanwhile, make English Custard Sauce. Remove casserole from water; place on wire rack to cool. Refrigerate 6 hours or overnight.

To unmold: Run a spatula around edge of meringue to loosen. Hold casserole in pan of very hot water for at least 1 minute. Invert onto serving dish. Pour some of the sauce over meringue, and pass the rest. 8 servings.

Girl Talk · Helpful Hints

Pssssst . . . Jo, have you heard that when making fruit salad, put the salad dressing in the bowl first—then cut the fruit into it? This keeps the fruit from darkening! And . . . adding a teaspoon of sugar to the vase will eliminate the "nose-tickling smell" of marigolds. And Jan, if you want to know about measurements and metric measures . . . just look in this section. Don't forget, Jo, there is a neat page on the uses of herbs and spices.

Prepare your own stock - beef and chicken - on a rainy day. Pour the stock into ice-cube trays and freeze it. These may be kept in plastic bags, ready for use. Measure the amount of liquid in the cubes and place enough cubes to make one cup of stock in separate plastic bags, ready to use as needed. Be sure to label your bags with the amount and type of stock.

You can prevent a souffle from falling by refrigerating the mixture for at least an hour before adding beaten egg whites.

Add 1 teaspoon unflavored dissolved gelatin to whipped cream and it will hold up longer.

You can freeze mushrooms (preferably sliced) by dropping into boiling water for 1 or 2 minutes; drain. Seal in air-tight container. Freeze until ready to use.

Peel cloves of garlic and keep in a jar filled with vegetable or olive oil in refrigerator. Will keep indefinitely and the garlic-flavored oil makes a wonderful base for salad dressing.

Food for houseplants: Mix one envelope Knox unflavored gelatin with one cup very hot water to dissolve. Then slowly add 3 cups of cold water to make a quart of liquid. Prepare only as much as you plan to use at one time. Once a month, use the mixture as part of your watering pattern.

Food for African Violets, Geraniums and other houseplants: To 1 gallon of water add 1 teaspoon baking powder, 1 teaspoon Epsom salts, 1 teaspoon saltpeter and 1/4 teaspoon ammonia. Use mixture once a month.

To cut a cake easily, use a wet knife.

Roll a lemon on a hard surface before using — you will get more juice out of it.

A pinch of salt in coffee before perking improves its flavor.

White wine for fish, red wine for meat — brings out the flavor.

Once opened, keep coffee in tightly sealed container in the refrigerator — it will stay fresh.

Never throw the water away in which vegetables have been boiled. Save in containers and use for soups and stews. Vitamins aplenty.

To sour milk, add 1 teaspoon of vinegar.

Poke holes in potatoes with an aluminum skewer —they will bake quicker.

Caps of nail polish and glue will not stick if once opened, you grease the screw threads before putting cap back on.

Inexpensive substitute for sour cream:
    1 cup cottage cheese
    2 teaspoons lemon juice
    Blend until creamy in a blender.

When making jelly, shave paraffin into bottom of jar and pour hot jelly over it; it will melt and rise to the top and seal the jelly. After this is completely cold, paraffin usually pulls away from the jar, thus another layer is recommended to pour around the edges to ensure a secure seal.

Just a dash of Worcestershire adds zip to hot mulled cider, pumpkin pie, spice cookies.

A clever wife found out how to remove cooking odors from the house—she quit cooking.

Egg-peeling tip: by adding salt to the water in which you are hard-boiling eggs, you harden the shell and it is easier to peel.

Cheese grates easily if it has been chilled first. So grate it the moment you take it from the refrigerator.

Brown sugar will never get hard if you keep it covered in the refrigerator, or leave a piece of apple in it while it sits in the cupboard.

Greasing a measuring cup before you put molasses or corn syrup in it will avoid sticking.

For something different, try chopped mint or flavoring in cream dressing for a fruit salad.

To keep fruit pies from running over in oven while baking, use macaroni as "smoke stacks" in top crust to allow steam to escape.

For baked potatoes in a hurry, boil them in salted water for about 10 minutes before putting them in a 400-degree oven. Don't forget to grease and prick them.

Overcooked potatoes can become soggy when milk is added. Sprinkle with dry powdered milk and you'll have fluffy potatoes.

Never cut salad greens with a knife — it bruises them. Tear the pieces gently.

Chop fresh parsley by snipping with scissors.

Cut raw bacon by snipping with scissors.

Slice mushrooms with an egg slicer.

Store mushrooms in a paper bag. Mushrooms are the freshest when the gills are not open.

Dust your cake before icing with a little flour or cornstarch. The icing won't run off.

Avoid soggy pie crusts by brushing the crust with the beaten white of an egg, or Crisco, then sprinkle lightly with flour.

Eliminate air bubbles in a cake by rapping pans sharply on countertop before placing in the oven.

Yeast doughs will rise properly if you set the bowl on an electric heating pad set on low. Place a piece of foil between the pad and bowl.

Add 1 tablespoon of vinegar to the fat in which you are going to fry. It keeps food from absorbing too much fat and will eliminate the greasy taste.

Eliminate fat from soup and stew by dropping ice cubes into the pot. Stir and the fat will cling to the cubes. Discard the cubes before they melt. Lettuce leaves will absorb fat also. Place a few in the pot.

Always preheat oven for at least 10 minutes unless otherwise stated in the recipe.

Lower the oven temperature by 25 degrees when using glass ovenware.

Paprika will not turn dark if kept in the refrigerator.

Brussels sprouts should be cut with an X in the stem end to ensure faster cooking.

Broccoli spears should be slit in the stem end several times so they will cook faster.

Cut cinnamon rolls with a double strand of thread rather than a knife—it won't break down your dough.

A souffle will remain light and fluffy if 1/4 teaspoon cream of tartar is added to egg whites during mixing.

A pinch of sugar will sometimes hide an excess of salt.

To ensure against curdling when making tomato soup, add tomato juice to milk, not vice versa.

Use tongs, not fork, to turn meat when cooking. Piercing will allow juices to escape.

When making white sauce, do not use an aluminum pan. Sauce will absorb gray color.

Cake, biscuit and pancake mix should never be sifted.

1 cup of chopped frozen onions equals 1 large onion chopped.

Use dried bread and leftover crackers to make your own bread and cracker crumbs. Use a blender.

Refrigerate leftover wine to use for cooking.

Crisp up crackers, cereal, taco shells, chips in a warm oven.

When covering a pie with meringue, be sure the topping touches the edge of the crust so it doesn't shrink from the sides.

If mailing cookies, pack them in popcorn.

One half-pound of cheese yields two cups when shredded.

Brown soup bones under the broiler before adding to the soup kettle. Your soup will have a wonderful brown taste and color.

White pepper is stronger than black; use only half as much.

To liquefy sugared honey, stand jar in hot water, or put in warm oven.

To blanch almonds, cover shelled nuts with boiling water, cool and slip off skins.

Grease the pot in which you are going to melt chocolate. You won't lose any from sticking to the pan.

Roll pie pastry between two sheets of waxed paper. No sticking and no mess.

Bury avocados in flour to hasten ripening.

You can soften brown sugar, coconut and hardened marshmallows by putting them in a pan and setting a cup full of water next to them in the pan. Cover the pan and place in the oven on low heat for a while.

You can make your own superfine sugar by processing granulated sugar in the blender until fine.

If your mayonnaise curdles, start over with another egg yolk and add the curdled mayonnaise drop by drop.

If Hollandaise curdles, remove from heat and beat in 1 teaspoon hot water, a few drops at a time. Do not return to heat. Serve warm or at room temperature.

Another cure for curdled Hollandaise — gradually beat 1 well-beaten egg into the hot liquid. The same applies to curdled custard.

Mashed potatoes will be fluffier if you add a pinch of baking soda to the warm milk and butter.

Hard-boiled eggs: Put eggs in salted cold water. Bring slowly to a boil, take off heat, cover and let sit 17 minutes. Douse immediately in cold water until ready to peel.

When hard-boiling eggs, pierce the broad end with a pin first to prevent cracking.

To determine whether an egg is fresh without breaking the shell, immerse the egg in a pan of cool salted water. If it sinks to the bottom, it is fresh. If it rises to the top, it is stale.

Adding 1 tablespoon of water per egg white will increase the quantity of beaten egg whites for meringue.

Beaten egg whites will be more stable if you add 1 teaspoon cream of tartar to each cup of egg whites (7 or 8 eggs).

If egg shells are stuck to the carton, just wet the carton and the eggs can be easily removed.

Egg whites can be stored in the refrigerator for several weeks if placed in a sealed jar.

Egg yolks can be kept fresh for several days if you cover them with cold water and store in the refrigerator.

Extra large eggs may cause cakes to fall. It's best to use medium to large eggs in baking.

Egg whites will yield more volume if beaten at room temperature.

To divide an egg, beat first, then measure.

When whipping cream, chill cream, bowl and beater well.

Cream whipped ahead of time will not separate if you add 1/4 teaspoon of unflavored gelatin per cup of cream.

Add a lump of butter or a few teaspoons of olive oil to the water, rubbing it around the top of the pan will keep rice, macaroni and spaghetti from boiling over or sticking together.

Remove the bitter taste from curry and chili powder by adding it to the recipe during the browning and not directly to the sauce.

Perk up soggy lettuce by adding lemon juice to a bowl of cold water and letting lettuce soak for about an hour in the refrigerator.

Use cocoa rather than flour to dust pans for chocolate cake.

Try mixing oregano with a little salad oil and rub over roast before cooking.

Poppy seeds sprinkled over cooked buttered noodles give them a different flavor.

Mix sage with the flour in which you dust chicken-very good.

Brush bread and rolls with beaten egg and sprinkle sesame seeds generously over before baking.

Thyme added to butter for baking and broiling all seafoods and chicken is delicious.

To remove fish odor from hands, rub hands with salt and wash with cold water.

Marshmallows are easier to cut if blades of scissors are buttered and dipped in hot water.

Did you ever start to make something that called for brown sugar but didn't have any? This can easily be taken care of if you have some molasses. When the recipe calls for a cup of brown sugar, just use a scant cup of white sugar and add 1 tablespoon of molasses. If the recipe calls for dark brown sugar, just add more molasses. In this way you are just putting back into the sugar what was taken out in the refining process.

Before boiling milk, rinse the pan in cold water-keeps milk from sticking to the pan.

When making fruit salad, put salad dressing into bowl first, then cut fruit into it. This keeps fruit from darkening.

A little salt sprinkled in the frying pan will keep fat or lard from splattering. Also makes stove cleaning easier.

To prevent candles from dripping, put them in refrigerator for a few hours before using.

A little vinegar added to the water in which you rinse panty hose will increase their elasticity and make them run-proof.

Kitchen tools need oiling? Use glycerine — it is harmless if any accidentally gets into food.

Keep parsley fresh by placing it in fruit jar. Close lid tight and store in refrigerator.

Know your onions — shed no tears. Next time you slice onions, spear a 1-inch chunk of bread on the point of your knife before peeling. Bread absorbs those tear-jerking fumes.

Cauliflower will come to the table much whiter if a piece of lemon is added during cooking.

A few slices of lemon added to a stew will improve the flavor.

Always open cans of whole asparagus spears from the bottom so that the tips won't break as you ease them out of the can.

Fingers stained? Remove vegetable stains from your fingers by rubbing them with a slice of raw potato.

Custard will not become watery if milk is scalded before using.

Put sweet potatoes and apples in salt water after peeling — they will not turn black.

Add a bay leaf to tomato juice for a different flavor.

Add celery seed to taste to cheese, seafood or ham mixes for crackers.

To bring out a fresh flavor, sprinkle dill weed over salads.

Keep bits of cucumber peel where you see ants and they will go away.

To kill odors of shrimp while cooking, add caraway seeds to the water.

The white of an egg will remove anything — even gum from hair.

Place a bay leaf in the box or container with flour, grits, etc. No weevils — it really works.

If you soak cabbage in ice-filled water for a while before you cook it, it will not be odorous.

If you find a dog or cat stain, right away pour club soda on it and let it stand. It really works.

For 1 cup all-purpose flour — 1 cup minus 2 tablespoons whole wheat flour.

A substitute for homemade cake flour:
  2 cups all-purpose flour, minus 2 tablespoons
  2 teaspoons baking powder
  2 tablespoons cornstarch
  Mix well.

For 1 cup heavy cream — 1/3 cup butter plus about 3/4 cup milk.

For 1 whole egg — 2 egg yolks; or 3 tablespoons plus 1 teaspoon thawed frozen egg; or 2 tablespoons and 2 teaspoons dry whole-egg powder plus an equal amount of water.

For 1 ounce chocolate — 3 tablespoons cocoa plus 1 tablespoon fat.

For 1 ounce unsweetened chocolate — 3 tablespoons baking cocoa plus 1 tablespoon oil.

For 1 clove garlic — 1/8 teaspoon garlic powder.

Change the color of cut flowers by mixing food coloring in warm water and placing the stems in the solution. In several hours the stems will absorb the colors and you will see different designs on the flowers.

The best preservative for fresh-cut flowers is 2 tablespoons white vinegar and 2 teaspoons of cane sugar to 1 quart water. Vinegar inhibits growth of organisms and sugar serves as food.

Rosebuds will open faster if a lump of sugar is added to the water.

Adding a teaspoon of sugar to the vase will eliminate the "nose-tickling smell" of marigolds.

Clean plant leaves with a few drops of glycerine on a cloth.

Water your ferns once a week with weak tea.

Use melted clean snow for watering your plants. There are a lot of minerals in it.

Stale club soda is good for watering plants.

Leftover birth control pills? Dissolve one in water for violet plants.

500 mg. of Vitamin C in 1 quart of water will keep peeled and sliced fruits and vegetables from turning.

MEASUREMENTS

3 teaspoons = 1 tablespoon
2 tablespoons = 1 fluid ounce
4 tablespoons = 1/4 cup
5 1/3 tablespoons = 1/3 cup
16 tablespoons = 1 cup
8 ounces = 1 cup
2 cups = 16 ounces
16 ounces = 1 pint
16 ounces = 1 pound
4 cups = 32 ounces
32 ounces = 1 quart
4 quarts = 1 gallon
8 quarts = 1 peck
4 pecks = 1 bushel

METRIC MEASURE

Volume
1 teaspoon = 5 milliliters
1 tablespoon = 15 milliliters
1 fluid ounce = 30 milliliters
8 fluid ounces = 240 milliliters
1 pint = 480 milliliters
1 quart = 960 milliliters

Weight
1.1 ounces = 30 grams
3.6 ounces = 100 grams
9.0 ounces = 250 grams
1 pound = 454 grams
2.2 pounds = 1 kilogram

Average Can Sizes
Picnic can = 1 1/4 cups
Number 300 can = 1 3/4 cups
Number 1 can = 1 1/3 cups
Number 1 tall = 2 cups
Number 303 can = 2 cups
Number 2 can = 2 1/2 cups
Number 2 1/2 can = 3 1/2 cups
Number 3 can = 4 cups
Number 10 can = 12 - 13 cups

Bar Measurements
1 bottle wine = 24 ounces
1 wine glass = 4 ounces
1 fifth = 16 (1 1/2 ounce) jiggers

❖❖❖

HERBS AND SPICES

ALLSPICE—Cocktail Meatballs, Hamsteak, Oyster Stew, Eggplant Dishes, Barbecue Sauce.

BASIL—Cheese Stuffed Celery, Manhattan Clam Chowder, Shrimp Creole, Spaghetti, Stewed Tomatoes, Russian Dressing, Salads.

BAY LEAF—Pickled Beets, Vegetable Soup, Lamb Stew, Simmered Chicken, Bordelaise Sauce, Boiled New Potaotes, Tomato Juice Dressing.

CINNAMON—Cranberry Juice, Pork Chops, Sweet & Sour Fish, Butter Sauce for Squash, Sweet Potato Croquettes, Stewed Fruit Salad.

CAYENNE—Deviled Eggs, Oyster Stew, Barbecued Beef, Poached Salmon, Bernaise, Cooked Greens, Tuna Fish Salad.

CELERY—Cream of Corn (Seed), Meat Loaf (Seed), Chicken Croquettes (Salt), Cauliflower (Salt), Cole Slaw (Seed), Hot German Potato Salad (Seed).

CHERVIL—Fish Dips, Cream Soup, Omelet, Chicken Saute, Vegetable Sauce, Caesar Salad.

CHILI — Seafood Cocktail Sauce, Pepper Pot Soup, Chili Con Carne, Arroz Con Pollo, Meat Gravy, Corn Mexicali, Chili French Dressing.

CLOVES—Fruit Punch, Baked Fish, Sauce Madeira, Candied Sweet Potatoes, Baked Ham.

CURRY—Curried Shrimp, Cream of Mushroom Soup, Curry of Lamb, Oriental Sauces, Creamed Vegetables, Curried Mayonnaise.

DILL—Cottage Cheese, Split Pea, Grilled Lamb Steak, Drawn Butter for Shellfish, Dill Sauce for Chicken or Fish, Peas and Carrots, Sour Cream Dressing.

FILE — Fish and Creole recipes. Use in place of Okra. Do not freeze and add after cooking.

GARLIC—Clam Dip, Vegetable Soup, Roast Lamb, Garlic Butter, Eggs and Tomato Casserole, Tomato and Cucumber Salad. Recipes calling for garlic are plentiful.

GINGER—Broiled Grapefruit, Bean Soup, Roast Chicken, Cocktail Sauce, Buttered Beets, Cream Dressing for Pears, Chutney.

MARJORAM—Fruit Punch Cup, Onion Soup, Roast Lamb, Salmon Loaf, Spaghetti Sauce, Brown Sauce, Eggplant, Mixed Green Salad.

MINT—Fruit Cup, Sprinkle over Split Pea Soup, Cold Fish, Lamb, Green Peas, Cottage Cheese Salad, Tea.

MUSTARD (DRY)—Ham Spread, Lobster Bisque, Virginia Ham, Deviled Crab, Cream Sauce for Fish, Baked Beans, Egg Salad Sandwiches, Hollandaise Sauce.

NUTMEG—Chopped Oysters, Salisbury Steak, Southern Fried Chicken, Mushroom Sauce, Glazed Carrots, Sweet Salad Dressing, Sprinkle over Ice Cream.

ONION—Avocado Spread (Powder), Consommes (Flakes), Meat Loaf (Instant Minced), Fried Shrimp (Salt), Tomato (Powder), Broiled Tomatoes (Salt), Vinaigrette Dressing (Instant Minced).

OREGANO—Sharp Cheese Spread, Beef Soup, Swiss Steak, Spaghetti, Boiled Onions, Seafood, Salads.

PARSLEY—Cheese Balls, Cream of Asparagus Soup, Irish Lamb Stew, Broiled Mackerel, French Fried Potatoes, Tossed Green Salad.

PAPRIKA—Creamed Seafood Soup, Hungarian Goulash, Oven-Fried Chicken, Paprika Cream Sauce, Baked Potatoes, Cole Slaw, Garnish.

POPPY—Rolls, Butter Sauce for Vegetables, Breads, Buttered Noodles, Fruit and Vegetable Salad.

SAGE—Cheese Spreads, Consomme, Soup, Cold Roast Beef, Poultry Stuffing, Duck, Brussels Sprouts, Chicken Salad.

SAVORY—Liver Pate, Lentil Soup, Scrambled Eggs, Chicken Loaf, Fish, Beets, Red Kidney Salad.

SESAME—Topping for Hamburger Buns, Breads, Cakes Cookies, Cream Pies, Stuffings, Sauces, Vegetables.

TARRAGON—Mushrooms a la Greque, Snap Bean Soup, Marinated Lamb or Beef, Lobster, Green Sauce, Buttered Broccoli, Chicken Salad.

THYME—Artichokes, Clam Chowder, Poultry Stuffing, Bordelaise Sauce, Tomato Aspic.

TURMERIC—Adds saffronlike coloring to Rice, Chicken, Seafood, Eggs.; also good in Pickles, Relishes.

Finesse • Finishing Touches

A finishing touch adds so much to a table, whether it be lovely Butter Balls or Butter Curls, or the Crystallized Flowers atop a cake or your favorite cookies served on a Chocolate Lace Doily. We are sure you will find ideas in this section that will become part of your personal entertaining style.

❖❖

If your affair calls for several round tables, consider covering them in full-length cloths. Form the centerpiece by using an over-scale cathedral candle on each table, encircled by a wreath of flowers and greenery. This takes the arrangement away from eye level and allows guests to see each other and visit. Group several thick candles of various heights on the buffet table using larger masses of flowers and greenery.

In the fall, make a centerpiece of a bounty of fresh vegetables. Use vegetable candles if you can find them. Use wicker baskets for breads and wooden bowls for other foods.

Balloons: Wonderful to use at picnics. Peg them into the ground at different levels, hang them in clusters from tree branches. If using them for a house party, line the walk to the house or the driveway with them. Adults love them as much as children. They are very effective using one color or mixing them up, depending on the mood of your party. Having a 40th or older birthday? Order, black balloons, tied with multicolored satin ribbons or Mylar streamers.

In spring or summer, fill a large seashell (conch) with violets and baby's breath, or use your favorite flowers. Place small murex shells at individual places.

For a spring luncheon, have individual white wicker flowerpots planted with blooming bulb plants such as crocuses or hyacinths. Or fill small bowls with tight bunches of fresh mint or parsley.

Make a pyramid of artichokes. Fill in spaces with parsley.

Hollow out a small to medium pumpkin, depending on the purpose. Place a glass liner inside and fill with fresh mums. The small pumpkins are darling for individual gifts.

Fill a glass or silver bowl with Christmas greenery and/or shiny Christmas balls.

Turn a large hurricane globe on its side; fill with fresh pine branches or holly and wind your choice of ribbon through its boughs. This is beautiful on a table or mantel. Flank by large candles.

A lovely arrangement is made of various heights of 2 3/4-inch candles grouped together. Surround the base with greenery and trailing ribbon.

Make a cloth for your fall or winter buffet from an Indian print fabric. Use all shapes and forms of baskets for your service dishes and pheasant or peacock feathers for the centerpiece. If you don't wish to use baskets, how about a lot of brass? Great for a curry dinner.

Easy and elegant! Using one of your pitchers, it can range from silver to the fabulous Italian pottery, fill with abundant foliage of the day, bittersweet in the fall, pine in winter, forsythia or quince in spring, and all the flowers of summer. This is wonderful anywhere, but why not start with a brunch.

Make a pyramid of fresh apples or oranges, held together by toothpicks. On St. Patricks Day it's fun to make a pyramid of potatoes, filling in the holes with parsley and novelty pipes, green hats and shamrocks.

A beautiful holiday centerpiece can be made by forming a pyramid of navel oranges which you have studded with whole cloves. Fill the spaces with cinnamon sticks, baby's breath and, if you can find them, small tiger lilies. You must have lilies in tiny florists vials of water to keep them fresh. This is really an effective centerpiece, lovely without the lilies, dramatic with them.

Shiny new quart-size paint cans can be obtained from a paint store. Put a strip of gingham or velvet ribbon around the can, just below the rim, and make a perky bow. Fill container with floral foam. These are wonderful for patio parties or picnics. Fill with your favorite flowers, even wild flowers look smashing.

For the buffet table, pyramid them, as many and as high as you like.

For a starting idea, how about blue tablecloths, white napkins, or reverse, blue and white gingham ribbon, and marigolds or zinnias for a summer party.

Do not forget to consider the loveliness of anthemians, protea, birds of paradise and agapanthus.

Protea (the national flower of South Africa) will dry beautifully and may be kept for lasting arrangements. Agapanthus comes in a beautiful blue shade and the always elegant white. We have seen stalks of the white put in colored water. The stems soak it up and parts of the blossoms absorb the color. Very lovely.

A lovely fall arrangement can be made of shocks of wheat tied with rust, gold or wine velvet ribbons. Use candles of matching or contrasting fall colors. Pick up a few artificial quail from a floral decorator shop to intersperse in the wheat. If you do not have wheat, use the bountiful fall harvest of leaves.

One of the loveliest fall arrangements can be made up of bittersweet and peach candles and ribbon. If you want to use this idea for a dinner party, ask to see Sonia Roses; that is the shade you want if you mix it with bittersweet. Intersperse the roses with the bittersweet, velvet ribbon cascading down from tall holders.

Group 3 or 4 flowerpots in a large saucer. Place the 5th one on top so the bottom of that pot rests on the edges of the others. These are nice with potted plants, and very effective with ivy cascading down the sides. For special effect, wrap each pot with colored ribbon around the top just below the rim.

There are endless ideas for table coverings. Do you have a patchwork quilt? They are beautiful on tables. The bed linens of today offer you a myriad of choices for colors and designs.

If you have a lace tablecloth, use a colored undercloth for different occasions. Gold or brown for fall tables, red or green for the Christmas holidays, and pastels for spring and summer. Of course, the lace by itself is elegance personified.

Do you have a bottle collection? Or small boxes? How about a favorite figurine? Use them on your table; besides looking lovely, they will be topics of conversation.

Do you have a collection of picture frames? Try using them instead of place cards, pictures of each guest at their place on the table.

Baskets, baskets! ! There is such a variety of different sizes and shapes today and a never-ending way to use them attractively.

Strawberry baskets are showing up in stores. Now, doesn't that remind you of the days of yore? Spray paint your basket a bright color and start improvising on what you are going to put inside. Fun to do a bright red with the big artificial strawberries or the silk branches of strawberries. Use the white silk filler flowers such as daisies. Also, you may spray paint a color that is suitable to your choice. You may want to do one for a bride at her kitchen shower. Line it with a yard of material that has been hemmed or pinked with pinking shears. Start filling it with spices, canned goods, utensils, dish towels, etc. Put a sprig of fresh or silk flowers among the items. If you don't want to have many items, stuff tissue paper on the bottom and go from there.

Maybe you would like to do a Mother's Day basket. Fill it with gifts Mom would enjoy and use sprigs of fresh flowers among the pretty wrapped packages.

Grapevine baskets are a popular accessory. They are used on doorsteps, porches, halls, hearths, or in any room of the house. Each to his own liking. You can even put one on your dining-room table. Fill the center with spagnum moss and perch a bird, goose, duck, or your favorite "something" on top. Put nosegays of fresh silk flowers around the basket.

Whatever the season may be, it truly makes a lovely centerpiece.

While we are talking about table settings, let us not forget the quiet elegance of linens, lace, silver, crystal, china and candlelight. Always in perfect taste and so beautiful. Add to this a few pieces of your crystal collection of animals, birds, shapes, forms. Do you have a flat mirror to set the centerpiece off and add depth. Use this look to your own taste and desired effect for the evening. It can run from white roses and baby's breath to exotic French bouquets, to cut flowers from your own garden. All quite lovely.

BUTTER BALLS

Scald a pair of wooden butter paddles in boiling water for 40 seconds; chill in ice water. Cut 1/4 pound bar of firm butter in 1-inch squares. Cut each square in half; stand each half upright on paddle. Smack butter between paddles. Holding bottom paddle still, rotate top paddle to form ball. If butter clings to paddles, dip them again into hot water, then into ice water. Drop finished balls into ice water and refrigerate. Dip paddles into ice water before making each ball. Makes 4 balls.

BUTTER CURLS

Let butter curler stand in hot water at least 10 minutes. Pull curler firmly across surface of 1/4 pound bar of firm butter (butter should not be too cold or curls will break). Drop curls into ice water and refrigerate. Curler should be dipped into hot water before making each curl.

ICE RINGS

Fill a large ring mold with boiled water and let stand till cool, stirring occasionally to remove air bubbles, which would make the ice cloudy. Then freeze. To center mold with decorations such as mint leaves, berries, etc., first freeze ring a third full of water, add garnish, then add water to fill two-thirds full. Freeze again. Then fill to top and freeze again.

Use a cake decorator and pastry bags for piping frostings, whipped cream, vegetable purees, potatoes, softened cream cheese.

FROSTED GRAPES

Dip a small cluster of grapes in egg white, beaten just until frothy, to coat with a very thin film. Roll lightly in granulated sugar, shaking off excess. Allow to dry on wire rack.

MINT CUBES

Fill ice-cube trays halfway with water. Place a fresh mint leaf or two in each cube and freeze. Fill up tray with water and return to freezer.

CHOCOLATE SHELLS

2 (6-ounce) packages semisweet chocolate pieces
1 tablespoon shortening

Combine chocolate and shortening in pan over hot water, but not boiling. Cook and stir until melted. Place 12 paper cupcake liners in cupcake pans. Coat inside of each cupcake liner with 1 tablespoon chocolate mixture. Chill thoroughly until hardened. Makes 12 shells.

Jan says, "This mixture is very good to use as a topping for ice cream or pudding. Drizzle the melted mixture over it while warm.

❖❖❖

GLAZED STRAWBERRIES

1 pint large strawberries with stems
1 cup sugar
1/4 cup water
1/2 teaspoon cream of tartar

Rinse strawberries and pat dry with paper towels. Heat sugar, water and cream of tartar to boiling until sugar is completely dissolved, stirring gently. Keep the sugar off the sides of the pan by swirling a spatula around the pan. Reduce to medium-low heat and continue cooking without stirring till the temperature reaches 300 degrees, or hard-crack stage. To check, drop a small amount of syrup into a cup of cold water. If it separates and forms a ball it is ready. Grease a cookie sheet. When the syrup is ready, remove the pan from the heat and work quickly by holding a strawberry by the stem and dipping into hot syrup. Coat completely. Scrape strawberry easily against side of pan if you have excess syrup. Place strawberry on greased cookie sheet. Let the glazed strawberries stand at least 30 minutes to 1 hour before eating. They must be eaten within 2 hours for the glaze will begin to melt. Makes about 20 strawberries.

CHOCOLATE LACE DOILY

2 1/2 (4-ounce) bars German sweet chocolate or bittersweet chocolate

Use a 1-quart pie dish. Line the dish with heavy duty foil so the foil comes up on the sides securely. Chill in freezer several hours or overnight.
In a 1 1/2-quart saucepan melt the chocolate over low heat, stirring until smooth. This process is slow. Using only half the chocolate, take a small spoon, dip spoon into sauce and start swirling over the bottom and sides of the foiled plate. Return plate to freezer until firm. If the other half of chocolate has become hard, return to heat. Repeat swirling the melted chocolate over the plate and return to freezer for 1/2 hour. To unmold the chocolate doily, lift the foil from the plate. Easy, very easy, peel the foil from the chocolate. Place doily on the serving dish you are using and chill for 24 hours.
Jan says, ''Chocolate lace originated in Russia. The intricate design was formed by the women pouring the hot syrup out on the snow.''

CHOCOLATE LEAVES

8 ounces semisweet chocolate
1 tablespoon (scant) vegetable shortening
Waxy leaves

Melt chocolate and shortening in top of double boiler. Using spoon or brush, generously coat underside of leaves. Chill or freeze until firm.
Separate chocolate from leaves, starting at stem end of leaf.

✧✧

MINTS

2 1/2 cups powdered sugar, sifted
1/4 teaspoon mint flavoring
1 package (3-ounce) cream cheese
Color to suit taste

Combine ingredients and roll in small balls, then roll in granulated sugar. Shape in mold. Gently remove to foil and let set to harden.

Jan says, "This recipe is for party or wedding mints. They may be made ahead and frozen."

CRYSTALLIZED FLOWERS

3 egg whites
1 cup superfine sugar

Select winter white or brightly colored flowers with open and simple petal arrangements, such as small orchids, Peruvian lilies, azaleas, sweet peas or narcissus. Tiny rosebuds also work well, but generally avoid flowers with thick petals and pale tints.

Makes enough coating for about 2 dozen flowers (depending on size).

Line large baking sheet or tray with parchment or waxed paper. Stir egg whites, covering all parts of petals (egg white can also be brushed onto petals). Using small brush or fingers, remove any excess egg white that might cause petals to stick together. Sift or sprinkle sugar over petals, covering all of egg white and shaking flower gently to discourage clumping of sugar and petals. Softly blow on flowers to remove excess sugar; entire flower should be evenly coated. Carefully set flowers on prepared sheet or tray. Let dry in cool air 2-3 days.

FLOATING FLOWERS AND FRUIT

If you will be serving from a punch bowl, attach a few fresh flower blossoms onto picks and spear into pieces of fresh fruit to float in the punch. Arrange some flowers and greenery around the base of your punch bowl.

PINEAPPLE

Pick a golden pineapple. Cut off the top. With the pineapple standing, cut off the rind.

Leaving the pineapple whole, take 1/8 cup of salt and rub it over the pineapple well. Then rinse well under cold water. Place pineapple in the refrigerator for at least an hour or more. Slice to serve.

Jan says, "A native woman in Hawaii demonstrated this procedure. From that day on I have fixed my pineapple like she showed us. The salt enhances the flavor of the pineapple. Just be sure you rinse the salt off well. Try it . . . you'll like it."

Allece's Coffee Cake, 48
Allspice, uses for, 380
Almond(s)
    to blanch, 377
    Camembert Amandine, 10
    and Cheddar Cheese
        Appetizers, 12
    Chocolate Sugarplums with,
        295
    in Christmas Fancies, 304
    Curried, 283
    Pie
        Crust, 229
        Sherry, 241
    Praline Balls, 211
    Roco, 301
    Sugar-glazed, 284
    -Tuna Bake, 115
Alsatian Dinner, 90
    9 to 5, 177
Amaretto
    Spuma di Zucca con, 354
    Strips, 351
Angel Cookies, 264
Angel Food Cake
    Chocolate, 185
    Supreme, Mom's, 185
    Waldorf, 185
Annie's Chocolate Cake, 187
Ann's Chicken Tetrazzini, 102
Antipasto, 329
    Misto, 333
Appetizers, 9–26. See also Dip;
        Spread
    Artichoke Bottoms with Cream
        Cheese and Caviar, 9
    Artichoke-Cheese Squares, 9
    Bacon Stix, 165
    Beer Balls, 9
    Blue Cheese Bits, 165
    Braunschweiger Pâté, 10
    Broiler Cheese, 12
    Broth Fondue Hors d'Oeuvres,
        322
    Brussels Sprouts, Marinated, 10
    Camembert, Deep-fried, 11
    Camembert Amandine, 10
    Caponata, 333
    Cheddar Cheese Appetizers, 12

Cheese and Broccoli Dip, 10
Cheese and Shrimp Canapés,
    Hot, 13
Cheese Ball, 11
Cheese Balls, Cocktail, 12
Cheese Sticks, 14
Cheese-stuffed Mushrooms, 17
Chutney Cheese Pâté, 12
Crab Mousse, 13
Crab Supreme, 14
Cream Cheese Pastry for
    Canapés, 13
Cucumber Canapés, 15
Curry Balls, 16
Fruit Cheese Ball, 12
Green Pepper
    Brick, 18
    Dip, 15
Italian-style
    Antipasto, 329
    Antipasto Misto, 333
    Fried Mozzarella, 330
    Marinated Roasted Peppers,
        329
    Olive Salad, 329
    Prosciutto e Melone, 329
    Stuffed Mushrooms
        Parmigiana, 329
    Zucchini, 329
Meatballs
    Open Sesame, 16
    Oriental, 17
Mexican-style
    Chili con Queso, 360
    Micro-Nachos, 363
    Nachos, 166
    Quesadillas, 361
    Super Nacho, 363
Mushroom(s)
    à la Grecque, 18
    Shells, 19
    Stuffed with Bacon and Chive
        Cream Cheese, 16
New Potato Appetizers, 19
Olive Cheese Puffs, Hot, 13
Olive Cheese Shells, 11
Party Snack, 20
Pecans, Toasted, 26
Pickled Eggs, Hot, 15

Pumpkin Seeds, Baked, 19
Red Caviar Mousse, 11
Reuben Roll-ups, 20
Reuben Sandwiches, 20
"Roll-ups," 27
Rumaki, 21
Salmon Ball, 21
Salmon Mousse, 21
Salomi, 22
Schloss with Cubes of Sweet
    Rye Bread, 322
Sesame Chicken Bites, 14
Shrimp
    Balls, 2
    in Beer Batter, 23
    Butter, 23
    Mousse, 13
    in Pineapple-Mustard Sauce,
        Hot, 22
    Remoulade, 24
Spinach Balls, Carol's, 24
Steak Tartare, 25
Summer Sausage, 25
Sweet and Sour Chicken Wings,
    15
Tempura Batter, 26
Tomato Aspic, 26
Zucchini Slices, 166
Apple(s)
    Bread, 41
    Cake, Raw, 186
    Caramel, 274
    Chicken in Cream with, Breast
        of, 97
    Crisp, Tonia's—Food Processor
        Style, 231
    Mincemeat with, Great
        Grandmother's, 259
    Muffins
        Bran, 57
        Fresh, 58
    Pie, 232
        1-Crust, 232
        1-Crust, Streusel Topping for,
            232
        Sour Cream, 231
    Pomander Balls, 280
    Red Cinnamon, Aunt Martha's,
        258

Salad
  Spinach and, 146
  Waldorf, 148
  for Salad, Whole Cinnamon, 138
  Stewed, 248
  Vichyssoise, 71
Apple Butter, 159
  Pumpkin Fritters, 52
Apple Jack Cider, 1
Applesauce-Cinnamon Salad,
    Molded, 138
Apricot(s)
  Brandy Pound Cake, 193
  Dip, 23
  Filling, 232
  Glaze, 193
  Glazed, 258, 283
  Nut Bread, 41
    Diabetic, 41
  Soufflé Ring with Chicken Salad,
    135
  Soup with Sour Cream, 71
  -Sour Cream Fondue Sauce,
    324
  -Sour Cream Pie, 232
  Sweet Potatoes, 129
  -Walnut Sauce, 243
Artichoke
  Bottoms
    with Cream Cheese and
      Caviar, 9
    Florentine, 335
    Spinach on, 127
  Dip, Hot, 165
  Heart(s)
    -Cheese Squares, Hot, 9
    in Chicken Garden Skillet, 99
    and Shrimp Casserole, 110
Asparagus
  Fillet of Sole Gourmet with, 113
  au Gratin, 117
  with Mayonnaise, 334
  Milan, 334
  Shrimp with, Stir-fried, 109
  Soup, 71
Aspic, Tomato, 26
  Mom's, 248
  V-8, Jeanne's, 148
Atholl Pudding, 219
Aunt Fanny's Baked Squash, 129
Aunt Gina's Cheese Balls, 247
Auntie Fay's Buttermilk Hot Cakes,
    35
Auntie K's Cup Cakes 1938, 256

Auntie K's Favorite Fruit Salad,
    141
Auntie K's Orange Bread 1930,
    252
Auntie K's Scalloped Oysters
    1940, 249
Aunt Jessie's Lemon Pie, 256
Aunt Jessie's Lieb Kuchen
    Cookies, 257
Aunt Marie's Chocolate Cake
    1920s, 253
Aunt Martha's Red Cinnamon
    Apples, 258
Aunt Mary's Caramels, 302
Aunt Tottie's Icebox Rolls, 251
Aunt Virginia's Cookies, 289
Autumn Soup, 72
Autumn Tomato Bouillon, 71
Avocado(s)
  Dressing, 145
  Guacamole, 361
    Ring, Molded, 364
  to hasten ripening, 377
  Soup
    Chilled, 167
    Cold Curried, 361

Bacon
  Appetizer "Roll-ups," 27
  Mushrooms Stuffed with Chive
    Cream Cheese and, 16
  Rumaki, 21
  Stix, 165
Bagels, Elizabeth's, 42
Bahamian Conch Chowder, 72
Baked Alaska, Individual, 183
Baklava, Yia Yia's, 204
Balloons, 381
Banana(s)
  Breakfast Bars, 42
  Cake, Josephine Gambrill's
    (1930), 252
  in Cherry Salad, 137
  -Cream Cheese Pie, 233
  Flambé, 212
  Fritters, 53
  Milk Shake, 1
  Nut Bread, 43
    Mincemeat-, 42
  Nut Muffins, 58
  Sour Cream Coffee Cake, 43
Barbecue(d)
  Brisket, Vera's, 88
  Flank Steak, Stuffed, 87

Lobster Tails, 107
  Meat Loaves, Little, 174
  Ribs, Maple, 166
  Sauce, Gina's, 151
    Helena's, 151
Bardolino, 357
Barley and Beef Vegetable Soup,
    72
Barolo, 357
Bars
  Banana Breakfast, 42
  Cocoa, 289
  Date Nut, Wichita Country Club,
    201
  Girdle-buster, 290
  Honey Date Sticks, 255
  Honey Nut Crunch, 183
  O'Henry, 202
  Peanut Butter Dessert, 291
  Pumpkin Pie, 203
  Sherry, Annie's, 293
  Toffee, 295
Basil
  Pesto
    Basic Sauce, 157
    Divino, 345
    Genovese, 349
    tips on, 157
    Tomato Soup with, 81
  uses for, 380
Baskets, 382
Batter
  Beer, Mr. Herbert's, 206
  Hot Buttered Rum, 282
Bay leaf, uses for, 378, 380
Bean(s)
  Baked
    I, 117
    II, 117
  Black-eyed Peas
    Hoppin' John, 35
    Marinated, 118
  Garbanzo, Dip, 362
  Refried, 365
    Super Nacho with, 363
  Salad, Three-, 147
  Soup
    Black, San Juan, 80
    Nine-, 282
    Nine-, Mix, 282
    White, 82
Béarnaise Sauce, 152
Beautiful Fingernails Bread, 70
Beautiful Hair Cocktail, 1

Béchamel Sauce, 151, 347
Beef
    Barbecued Brisket of, Vera's, 88
    Casserole
        Ground, 177
        Ravioli, 345
    in Cheese and Onion
        Enchiladas, 367
    Chili, Loco's, 75
    Company's Coming, 88
    Corned
        and Cabbage, 87
        Reuben Roll-ups, 20
        Salad, 139
    Dorisburgers, 179
    Enchilada Pie, 368
    Fondue
        Bourguignonne, 323
        Broth, Hors d'Oeuvres, 322
        Sauce for, 324
    Goulash, Paprika, 87
    Grape Leaves Stuffed with, 88
    Jalapeños Stuffed with, Deep-
        fried, 363
    Jonnie Mosetti, 345
    Lasagne, 343
        Easy, 342
    Manicotti, 344
    Meatballs
        Beer Balls, 9
        Curry Balls, 16
        Open Sesame, 16
        Oriental, 17
        Sweet and Sour, Jean's, 85
    Meat Loaf(-ves)
        Bar-B-Q, Little, 174
        Grandma's, 270
        Italian, 85
        Working-girl, 178
    Mexican Salad, 365
    Nacho, Super, 363
    Pot Roast
        Family Request for, 89
        in Wine, 89
    Roast
        Brown, 89
        Three-Day Marinated, 89
    Salomi, 22
    Sandwiches, Easy, 175
    Sausage, Summer, 25
    Soup
        Autumn, 72
        Barley Vegetable and, 72
        Steak, 81

    Steak, Quickie, 168
Steak
    Diane, 86
    Flank, Bar-B-Cued Stuffed, 87
    Flank, with Corn Bread, 88
    Green Peppercorn, in a
        Crêpe, 84
    Marinade, 155
    Mexican-style, 369
    au Poivre Vert en Chemise,
        84
    Savory Pepper, 86
    Soup, 81
    Soup, Quickie, 168
    Tartare, 25
Stroganoff, 90
Tenderloin, 85
Tournedos, 86
Wellington, Filet of, 83
Been Around for Years Dip, 165
Beer
    Balls, 9
    Batter
        Mr. Herbert's, 206
        Shrimp in, 23
    Bread, Al's, 170
    Muffins, 171
Beet(s)
    Borscht, 73
    Pickled Baby, 159
    Salad, Molded, 135
Beignets (French Doughnuts), 45
Bellini Ice, 350
Besciamella Sauce, 349
Better Than Sex Cake, 183
"Better Wear Bibs" Shrimp, 110
Betty's Buttermilk Pancakes, 36
Betty's Ice Cream, 213
Beverages, 1–8
    Apple Jack Cider, 1
    Beautiful Hair Cocktail, 1
    Bloody Bull, 1
    Bullshot, 3
    Champagne Cocktail, 2
    Chocolate
        French, 2
        Hot, Mix, 282
    Christmas
        Café au Lait Mix, 281
        Café Mexicano, 281
        Candy Cane Cocktail, 307
        Cranberry Punch, 307
        Friendship Tea, 282
        Hot Buttered Rum Batter, 282

        Hot Chocolate Mix, 282
        Mocha, 281
        Wassail, 307
    Coffee
        Café au Lait Mix, 281
        Café Mexicano, 281
        Cappuccino, 356
        Cappuccino, Creamy, 356
        Cappuccino, Variations of,
            356
        Espresso, 356
        to improve flavor of, 375
        Irish, Buena Vista, 3
        Mocha, 281
        Punch for Brunch, Iced, 3
        Rum Cooler, 3
        to store, 375
        -Whiskey Trifle, 300
    Daddy's Summer Cooler, 247
    Daiquiri, 3
    Eggnog, 4
    The Homemade Bomb, 6
    Irish Cream Liqueur, 4
    Kir, 4
    Lemonade
        Frosted, 267
        Hawaiian, 267
    Lemon Vodka, 8
    Lime Rickey, 4
    Margaritas, 8
    Milk Shake
        Banana, 1
        Orange, 5
    Mimosa Cocktail, 6
    Mom's Favorite Kahlùa, 4
    Peach Daiquiri, 3
        Fresh, 4
    Punch
        Brandy Milk, for 2, 2
        Brandy Milk, for 30, 2
        for Brunch, Iced, 3
        Children's Party, 267
        for Fifty, 5
        Fishhouse, 247
        Gertrude's Art Gallery, 1
        Hot Spiced, 7
        Jan's, 5
        Jo's Champagne Wedding, 2
        Lime Wine, 5
        Party, 5
        Sherbet, 6
        Witches' Brew, 272
    Remos Fizz, Special, 6
    Sangria, 6

Strawberry-Orange Cooler, 6
Sunshine Slush, 7
Taos Lightning, 7
Tea
  Friendship, 282
  Vera's Spiced, 7
Tom & Jerry Batter, 8
Tumbleweeds—a Kansas
    "Happening," 8
Velvet Hammer, 8
Wines, Italian, 357
Witches' Brew, 272
Bev's Cucumbers, 159
Bev's Lamb Shank, 94
Biscuits
  Buttermilk, Mom's, 44
  Denver, 250
  Peanut Butter Syrup for, 259
  Sourdough, 67
Black Bean Soup, San Juan, 80
Black Cherry Salad, 135
Black-eyed Peas
  Hoppin' John, 35
  Marinated, 118
Black Forest Cherry Cake, 179
Black Russian Cake, 186
Blinis, Mock, 27
Blintz Bubble Ring, Dorothy's, 44
Bloody Bull, 1
Blueberry(-ies)
  Cassis Pie, 233
  -Peach Soup, 78
Blue Cheese Bits, 165
Bohemian Coffee Cake, 45
Bohemian Kolaces, 251
Bohemian Pork-Liver Sausage,
    249
Bon-Bons, Chocolate, 301
Borscht, Beet, 73
Boston Brown Bread, Mrs.
    Landreth's (1940), 250
Boston Clam Chowder, 73
Boston Cream Candy, 302
Bouillon, Tomato, 168
  Autumn, 71
  Clam and, 259
  Hot, 80
Bourbon
  Balls, 286
  with Rum and Tom & Jerry
    Batter, 8
  Sauce
    Hard, 283
    Warm, 243

Bozo Balls, 269
Brandy(-ied)
  Alexander
    Pie, 234
    Soufflé, Cold, 220
  Frosting, 187
  Milk Punch
    for 2, 2
    for 30, 2
  Refrigerator Cake, 187
  Strawberry Fondue, 324
Bran Muffins
  Apple, 57
  Six-Week, 60
Bratwurst, in Alsatian Dinner, 9 to
    5, 177
Braunschweiger Pâté, 10
Brazilian Rice, 366
Brazil Nut(s)
  in Christmas Fancies, 304
  Holiday Delights, 303
Bread(s)
  Apple, 41
  Apricot Nut, 41
    Diabetic, 41
  Bagels, Elizabeth's, 42
  Banana Nut, 43
    Mincemeat-, 42
  Beautiful Fingernails Bread, 70
  Biscuits
    Buttermilk, Mom's, 44
    Denver, 250
    Peanut Butter Syrup for, 259
    Sourdough, 67
  Boston Brown, Mrs. Landreth's
    (1940), 250
  Buns
    Hot Cross, 54
    Onion Hamburger, 61
    Sticky, 68
  Buttermilk, Ruthie's, 45
  Cinnamon, 46
  Cocoa Zucchini, 48
  Corn
    Jalapeño, 48
    Spoon Bread, Crusty, 172
    Spoon Bread, Josa's, 250
    Spoon Bread, Mexican, 365
    Sticks, 58
    Stuffing, Casserole, 70
    Stuffing, Flank Steak with, 88
  Cranberry, 46
  Crumbs, to make, 376
  Date

Loaf, Diabetic, 43
  Nut-, Grandmother's, 256
Dill Picnic Braid, 50
Dilly, 50
French
  Jeanne's, 51
  Vera's, 52
Garlic, Hot, 171
Grapenut, Joyce's, 53
Irish Soda, 54
Khachapuri, 55
Lemon Nut, 65
Mary's, 57
Monkey, 69
Muffins
  Apple, Fresh, 58
  Apple Bran, 57
  Banana Nut, 58
  Beer, 171
  Bran, Six-Week, 60
  Corn Bread, 58
  Cranberry, 58
  Cream Cheese Spiced, 59
  English, 51
  notes on, 57
  Peach, Fresh, 59
  Pineapple, 59
  Pumpkin, 60
  Raspberry, 60
Orange, Auntie K's (1930), 252
Pita, 62
Pumpkin, 64
  Muffins, 60
Reuben, 65
Rolls
  Butterhorn, No Knead, 44
  Cinnamon, 47
  Egg, Carol's, 51
  Icebox, Aunt Tottie's, 251
  Out of This World, 62
  Pecan, Jane's, 63
  Praline, 63
  Sweet, Breakfast, 171
Rye, 56
  Old-fashioned, 55
  Swedish, 56
Sheepherder's, 66
Shredded Wheat, 65
Sourdough, 67
  Jack Bread—Extra Sour, 67
Stix, Quick, 44
Swedish, Tippy's, 56
Vienna, 69
Zucchini

Bread(s): Zucchini (*cont.*)
    Cocoa, 48
    Walnut, 61
Bread and Butter Pickles, 160, 162
Breakfast Bars, Banana, 42
Breakfast dishes. *See* Brunch
    dishes
Breakfast Puffs, French, 52
Breakfast Sweet Rolls, 171
Bridesmaids' luncheon, menu and
    ideas for, 312
Brie Cheese, Broiler, 12
Brittle, Chocolate Chip Cookie, 303
Broccoli
    Casserole, 117, 172
    and Cheese Dip, 10
    Custard Mold, 27
    Fillet of Sea Trout with, Spiced,
        114
    Rice with, 126
    Salad, 136
        Cauliflower-, 169
        Cauliflower, Red Onions, and,
            136
    Soup, 73
        Quick, 167
Brodo di Pollo, 331
Brolio, 357
Broth
    Chicken, Italian-style, 331
    Fondue Hors d'Oeuvres, 322
Brownie(s)
    Crème de Menthe, 199
    Cup Cakes, Rich, 187
    Mocha Torte, 223
    Mom's Double-frosted, 200
Brown Sugar
    Candy, Lois's, 302
    to keep from getting hard, 375
    to soften hardened, 377
    substitute for, 378
Brunch, menu and ideas for,
        313–314
Brunch dishes, 27–39
    Appetizer "Roll-ups," 27
    Blinis, Mock, 27
    Broccoli Custard Mold, 27
    Chicken Casserole, Lillian's, 39
    Columbia Specials, 28
    Conch Fritters, 33
    Crab on Toast, 27
    Cream Puff Bowl, 28
    Crêpes
        Benedict, 28

I, 29
II, 29
Eggs
    Benedict, 29
    Elegante, 29
    Omelet, Basic, 36
    Poached, Harlequin, 30
    Sausage-stuffed, 30
    Scrambled Medley, Ruthie's,
        30
    Sunday, 33
French Toast, 39
    The Best, 33
Fruit(s)
    Baked, 32
    Curried, Hot, 32
    Slush, 32
    Tart, Fresh, 31
    Tipsy, 32
Grits
    Garlic Cheese, 34
    Leonardo, Baked, 34
Ham
    and Cheese Brunch, 34
    and Egg Casserole, 34
    and Red Eye Gravy, 35
    Soufflé, Prepared Ahead, 35
Hoe Cakes, 252
Hoppin' John, 35
Pancake(s)
    Buttermilk, Betty's, 36
    Buttermilk Hot Cakes, Auntie
        Fay's, 35
    Elegant, 36
    Orange, 37
    Potato, German, 37
Pears, Hot Spiced, 37
Pineapple
    Baked, 37
    with Grapes, 37
Quiche
    Crab Meat, 39
    Lorraine, 38
Sausage
    Balls, Hot, 38
    Patties, Homemade
        Seasoned, 31
    Soufflé, Prepared Ahead, 31
    -stuffed Eggs, 30
    Sherried Chicken Livers, 28
    Strawberries, Yummy, 39
    Waffles, 252
Brussels Sprouts, Marinated, 10
Buena Vista Irish Coffee, 3

Bullshot, 3
Bundt Rum Cake, 197
Bunny Salad, 270
Buns
    Hot Cross, 54
    Onion Hamburger, 61
    Sticky, 68
Bunuelos
    I, 370
    II, 370
Burnt Sugar Dumplings, 211
Burritos, Green Chile, 366
Busy Lady Stew, 175
Butter
    Apple, 159
    Balls, 383
    and Cheese Sauce, for
        Fettuccine, 341
    Curls, 383
    Herb, 154
    Honey, Little Brown Bear's Hot,
        269
    Logs, 296
    Parsley, 281
    Shrimp, 23
    Strawberry, 281
Buttered Rum Batter, Hot, 282
Butterhorn Rolls, No Knead, 44
Buttermilk
    Biscuits, Mom's, 44
    Bread, Ruthie's, 45
    Cake, Chocolate, 188
    Hot Cakes, Auntie Fay's, 35
    Pancakes, Betty's, 36
Butter Pecan Ice Cream, Cold
        Buttered Rum with, 180

Cabbage
    Chinese, 169
        Sesame, 146
    Cole Slaw
        Deluxe, 138
        Hot, 148
    Corned Beef and, 87
    Red, 118
    Scalloped, 118
    with Sour Cream, 119
Caesar Salad
    Dressing, Quick, 170
    Mom's, 136
Café au Lait Mix, 281
Café Mexicano, 281
Caffè Latte, 356

Cake(s)
  Angel Food
    Chocolate, 185
    Supreme, Mom's, 185
    Waldorf, 185
  Apple, Raw, 186
  Applesauce Spice, 186
  Banana
    Josephine Gambrill's (1930),
      252
    -Sour Cream Coffee Cake, 43
  Better Than Sex, 183
  Black Russian, 186
  Brandy Refrigerator, 187
  Brownie, Rich, 187
  Carrot, Jeanine's, 189
  Cheese
    Crust, Special, 229
    Jan's, 205
    Jeanine's, 205
    Joy's, 205
    Mocha Marble, 206
    Sally's, 204
  Cherry
    Black Forest, 179
    Chocolate, 188
    Coffee Cake, 46
  children, recipes that can be
      made by
    Dump Cake, 265
    Funnel Cakes, 266
    Halloween Cat Cake, 272
    Tiddlywink Cake, 266
  Chocolate
    Angel Food, 185
    Annie's, 187
    Aunt Marie's, 1920s, 253
    Brownie Cup, Rich, 187
    Buttermilk, 188
    Charlotte, 207
    Cherry, 188
    Fabulous, 188
    Fiesta, 371
    German, 193
    Halloween Cat Cake, 272
    Mississippi Mud, 192
    Ring, 207
    Roll, 189
    Sheet, 190
    Spicy, Laverna's, 253
    Torte, Lili's, 208
    Tunnel of Fudge, 198
  Coconut
    Cream, 190

    Lemon, 192
    Pineapple, 195
  Coffee, 47
    Allece's, 48
    Banana Sour Cream, 43
    Bohemian, 45
    Cherry, 46
    Heath Bar, 172
    Raspberry, 64
    Sour Cream, 68
  Coke, 191
  Cup
    Auntie K's, 1938, 256
    Brownie, Rich, 187
    Mincemeat Nut, 291
    Mrs. Butler's (1930s), 253
  Dump, 265
  Filling for
    French Crème, 226
    Lemon, 226
  Football, 191
  Frosting for. See Frosting
  Fruit
    Mexican, 372
    Mom's White (1930s), 254
    Orange Slice, 299
    White Christmas, 298
  Funnel, 266
  Harvey Wallbanger Supreme,
      193
  hints on, 375–377
  Hoe, 252
  Ice Cream, Italian, 351
  Inspirational, 194
  Jelly Roll, Grandmother's
      (1900), 255
  Lazy Daisy, 192
  Lemon
    Coconut, 192
    Easy, 181
  Mandarin Orange
    I, 371
    II, 371
  Mincemeat, 257
  Mincemeat Nut, Mini, 291
  Pineapple
    Coconut, 195
    Sheet, 195
  Plum, Pretty, 182
  Potato, Pauline's, 194
  Pound
    Apricot Brandy, 193
    Cream Cheese, 195
  Pumpkin

    Roll, 196
    Sheet, 196
  Rum
    Bundt, 197
    Christmas, 297
  Siciliana Cassata, 352
  Sour Cream, Mother's Calvin
      Coolidge, 253
  Spice
    Applesauce, 186
    Laverna's, 196
  Sponge, Basic, 301
  Strawberry, 182
    Tunnel, 198
  Tiddlywink, 266
  Waldorf-Astoria, 197
  Wedding, Mexican, 372
California Salad, 169
Camembert Cheese
  Amandine, 10
  Broiler, 12
  Deep-fried, 11
Canapés
  Cucumber, 15
  Hot Cheese and Shrimp, 13
Candied Grapefruit Peel, 285
Candied Orange Peel, 252
Candlelight dinner, menu and
    ideas for, 311
Candy(-ies)
  Cane(s)
    Cocktail, 307
    Cookies, 287
    Kiddies, 287
  Christmas
    Almond Roco, 301
    Boston Cream, 302
    Bourbon Balls, 286
    Brown Sugar, Lois's, 302
    Candy Cane Cookies, 287
    Candy Canes, 287
    Caramels, Aunt Mary's, 302
    Cathedral Windows, 287
    Chocolate Bon-Bons, 301
    Chocolate Chip Cookie Brittle,
      303
    Chocolate Fudge, Deluxe, 303
    Chocolate Fudge, Fabulous,
      304
    Chocolate Sugarplums, 295
    Christmas Fancies, 304
    Coconut Joys, 289
    Holiday Dipped Creams, 303
    Irish Truffles, 300

Candy(ies): Christmas (*cont.*)
 Millionaires, 305
 Panocha, 305
 Panocha, Sour Cream, 305
 Peanut Butter Cups I, 291
 Peanut Butter Cups II, 292
 Taffy, Tonia's White, 306
 Truffles, Chocolate, 306
 Truffles, Mocha, 306
 Fudge, Innes, 259
 Yummies, 265
Cannelloni, 337, 339
 assembling, 340
 Short Cut, 340
Cannoli, 353
Cantaloupe, Prosciutto and, 329
Caponata, 333
Cappuccino, 356
 Creamy, 356
 Iced, 356
 Variations of, 356
Caramel(s)
 Apples, 274
 Aunt Mary's, 302
 Chocolate Fingers, 299
 Corn, Oven-baked, 286
 Frosting, 226
 Sauce, 213
 Soufflé, Cold, 373
Carciofi Fiorentina, 335
Carnival Popcorn Balls, 274
Carol's Egg Rolls, 51
Carol's Spinach Soufflé, 173
Carrot(s)
 Cake, Jeanine's, 189
 Copper Pennies, 121
 Honey, 249
 Hungarian, 119
 with Lemon Juice, 120
 Quick 'n' Easy, 173
Cashew Nuts
 Pea Salad with, 169
 Sugar-glazed, 284
Cassata
 Ice Cream, Italian, 351
 Siciliana, 352
Casserole
 Broccoli, 117, 172
 Celery, 119
 Chicken, 97
 Piquant, 175
 Rice-, 175
 Roquefort, Helena's, 176
 and Shrimp, Fiesta, 367

Company's Coming, 88
 Eggplant, 334
 Fish-Spinach, 176
 Green Bean, 122
 Green Pepper, 122
 Ground Meat, 177
 Ham and Egg, 34
 Ham-Rice, 176
 Pea, Company, 124
 Potato, 124
 Ravioli, 345
 Seafood, Judy's, 109
 Shrimp
 and Artichoke, 110
 and Chicken, Fiesta, 367
 Spinach, 173
 Tuna Curry, 177
Cassis Blueberry Pie, 233
Cathedral Windows, 287
Catsup, Ripe Tomato, 154
Cauliflower
 Mixture, 119
 Salad
 Broccoli-, 169
 Broccoli-Red Onion, 136
Caviar
 Artichoke Bottoms with Cream
 Cheese and, 9
 Mousse, Red, 11
Cayenne, uses for, 380
Celery
 Casserole, 119
 Stuffed, 271
 uses for, 380
Cenci Alta Florentina, 352
Centerpieces, 309–17, 381
 Tonia's Thanksgiving Turkey,
 316–317
Champagne
 Cocktail, 2
 Punch, Jo's Champagne
 Wedding, 2
Chantilly Cream, 242
Charlotte, Chocolate, 207
Chateaubriand Sauce, 152
Cheddar Cheese
 Appetizers, 12
 Balls, Aunt Gina's, 247
 Chili Rellenos, 367
 Enchilada Pie with, 368
 and Ham Brunch, 34
 Jonnie Mosetti, 345
 Mexican Salad with, 365
 Olive Puffs, Hot, 13

 and Onion Enchiladas, 367
 Soufflé, No Fail, 173
 Sticks, 14
Cheese. *See also specific names
 of cheeses*
 Appetizers
 Artichoke-Cheese Squares,
 Hot, 9
 Blue Cheese Bits, 165
 Broccoli and Cheese Dip, 10
 Broiler Cheese, 12
 Camembert, Deep-fried, 11
 Camembert Amandine, 10
 Cheddar Cheese Appetizers,
 12
 Cheese Ball, 11
 Cheese Balls, Aunt Gina's,
 247
 Cheese Balls, Cocktail, 12
 Cheese Sticks, 14
 Chili con Queso, 360
 Chutney Cheese Pâté, 12
 Cream Cheese Pastry for
 Canapés, 13
 Fried Mozzarella, 330
 Fruit Cheese Ball, 12
 Micro-Nachos, 363
 Mushrooms, Cheese-stuffed,
 17
 Nachos, 166
 Olive Cheese Puffs, Hot, 13
 Olive Cheese Shells, 11
 Quesadillas, 361
 Shrimp and Cheese Canapés,
 Hot, 13
 Super Nacho, 363
 Ball(s), 11
 Cocktail, 12
 Aunt Gina's, 247
 Brazilian Rice with, 366
 Broiler, 12
 Cake
 Crust, Special, 229
 Jan's, 205
 Jeanine's, 205
 Joy's, 205
 Mocha Marble, 206
 Sally's, 204
 Cheddar. *See* Cheddar Cheese
 Chili with, 360
 Cottage
 Cake, Mocha, 206
 Dip, 14
 Lasagne with, 343

in Spinach Casserole, 173
Dip
Broccoli and, 10
Garlic, 165
Hot, 165, 360
Enchilada(s) with
Cheese and Onion, 367
Chicken, 368
Pie, 368
Sour Cream, Jeanne's, 368
Filling
for Manicotti, 344
for Ravioli, 338
Fondue, 322
Fruit Ball, 12
Garlic
Dip, 165
Grits, 34
to grate, 375
and Ham Brunch, 34
Khachapuri, 55
Lasagne, 343
Monterey Jack
Chili Pie with, 366
Nacho, Super, 363
Nachos, Micro-, 363
Quesadillas, 361
Mozzarella
Cannelloni filled with, 340
Eggplant Casserole with, 334
Fried, 330
Lasagne with, 343
Manicotti with, 344
Zucchini and, 336
Mushrooms Stuffed with, 17
Nachos, 166
Olive Puffs, Hot, 13
and Olive Shells, 11
Pâté, Chutney, 12
Quesadillas, 361
Ricotta
Cannoli, 353
Lasagne Roll-ups with, 343
Siciliana Cassata with Filling
of, 352
Sauce, 152
Hot, 360
Mushroom-, 346
Seafood in, 112
and Shrimp Canapés, Hot, 13
Soufflé, No Fail, 173
Soup, 74
in Spinach Casserole, 173
Sticks, 14

Strawberry Flan, 223
Triangles, 120
Cherry(ies)
Cake
Black Forest, 179
Chocolate, 188
Coffee Cake, 46
Jubilee, 212
Pie, French, 180
Romanoff, 208
Salad, 137
Black, 135
Pepsi-Cola–, 137
Pineapple-, Frozen, 144
Chervil, uses for, 380
Chess Pie, Lemon, 238
Chianti, 357
Chicken
Bites, Sesame, 14
Bocca, 348
Broth, Italian-style, 331
Cacciatore, 98
Casserole, 97
Lillian's, 39
Shrimp and, Fiesta, 367
in Cream with Fresh Apples,
Breast of, 97
Deglazing Sauce for, 154
Enchilada(s), 368
Fondue, 323
Garden Skillet, 99
Gumbo, 74
Honey-baked, 176
Lemon Honey Breast of, 97
Liver(s), 99
Sherried, 28
in Macadamia Nut Cream,
Baked, 99
Marengo, for Twelve, 100
à l'Orange, 97
Parmesan, 100
Party, for Eight, 101
Pie, Impossible, 93
Piquant, 175
-Rice Bake, 175
Rococo, 101
Roll-ups, Crunchy, 98
Roquefort, Helena's, 176
in the Sack, 100
Salad, 136
Apricot Soufflé Ring with, 135
Curried, 140
Gourmet, 137
Hot, 136

Sesame, Breasts, 98
Soup
Gourmet, 167
with Rice and Mushrooms, 74
Stir Fry, 102
and Stuffing Scallop, 101
Sweet and Sour, 102
Tacos, 370
Tetrazzini, Ann's, 102
Wings, Sweet and Sour, 15
Chiffon
Filling, for Heavenly Pie, 237
Pie
Lemon, 238
Macadamia Nut, 239
Pumpkin, Jane's, 241
Children, recipes that can be made
by, 261–274
Cake(s)
Dump, 265
Funnel, 266
Halloween Cat, 272
Tiddlywink, 266
Caramel Apples, 274
Cinnamon Sticks, 269
Cookies
Angel, 264
Chocolate, 261
Dessert Burgers, 264
Gingerbread Men, 263
Goblins and Ghosts Lollipop,
273
Jelly Roll Pan, 264
Make-a-Face, 262
Make-a-Name, 262
Make-a-Word, 262
No Bake Fudgie, 263
No Bakes, 262
Out of This World Flying
Saucer, 262–263
Peanut Butter, 261
Raggedy Ann, 264
Show-Time Circus, 272
Your Very Own Hand, 261
Fudgesicles, 268
Green Dragons, 267
Halloween Haystacks, 273
Ice Cream
Bozo Balls, 269
Flowerpot, 268
Snow, Tonia's, 268
Jack-O'-Lantern Frosties, 274
Jam Frosting, 266
Lemonade

Children: Lemonade (*cont.*)
  Frosted, 267
  Hawaiian, 267
  Little Brown Bear's Hot Honey
    Butter, 269
  Marvelous Marshmallows, 269
  Meat Loaf, Grandma's, 270
  Pizza, Kid-size, 270
  Play-Dough Mixture, 269
  Popcorn Balls, 273
    Carnival, 274
  Popsicles, 268
  Punch, Children's Party, 267
  rules for, 261
  Salad
    Bunny, 270
    Circus, 270
    Swell-Time Somersault, 271
  Shush Puppies, 271
  S'Mores, 272
  S'Nice Rice, 271
  Snow Balls, 266
  Spooky Chocolate Pie, 273
  Stuffed Celery, 271
  Tea Party Sandwiches, 267
  Tea Party Toast, 267
  Toad in the Hole, 267
  Witches' Brew, 272
  Yummies, 265
Children's Potpourri, 280
Chili(-es; Chiles)
  Dip, Hot, 362
  Green
    Burritos, 366
    Pie, 366
    con Queso, 360
    Rellenos, 367
    Rice with, 122
    Salsa, 361
  Loco's, 75
  Sauce, Lois's, 152
  uses for, 380
Chinese Cabbage, 169
  Sesame, 146
Chinese Timbales, 295
Chive Cream Cheese, Mushrooms
    Stuffed with Bacon and, 16
Chocolate. *See also* Mocha
  Addicts Frozen Cream, 182
  Bon-Bons, 301
  Brownies
    Crème de Menthe, 199
    Mom's Double-frosted, 200
  Cake(s)
    Angel Food, 185

Annie's, 187
Aunt Marie's, 1920s, 253
Brownie Cup, Rich, 187
Buttermilk, 188
Charlotte, 207
Cherry, 188
Fabulous, 188
Fiesta, 371
German, 193
Halloween Cat Cake, 272
Mississippi Mud, 192
Ring, 207
Roll, 189
Sheet, 190
Spicy, Laverna's, 253
Torte, Lili's, 208
Tunnel of Fudge, 198
Candies and Confections
  Bon-Bons, 301
  Chocolate Chip Cookie Brittle,
    303
  Fudge, Deluxe, 303
  Fudge, Fabulous, 304
  Holiday Dipped Creams, 303
  Millionaires, 305
  Sugarplums, 295
  Truffles, Chocolate, 306
  Truffles, Mocha, 306
Charlotte, 207
Cookies
  Caramel Fingers, 299
  children's recipe, 261
  Chippers, 200
  Chocolate Chip, Jeanne's,
    288
  Chocolate Chip, Mom's, 288
  Chocolate Chip Cookie Brittle,
    303
  Dessert Burgers, 264
  Devil's Food, 201
  Earthquake, 290
  Grasshopper Pie with Crust
    of, 236
  Marshmallow, 288
  No Bake Fudgie, 263
  Nut-Chocolate Slices, 200
  Serendipities, 292
  Sherry Bars, Annie's, 293
  Six-Layer, 294
Custard Squares, 211
Fondue
  Dark, 324
  Milk, 325
French, 2
Frosting, 188, 189, 190, 191,

194, 227
  Cream Cheese, 226
  for Fiesta Chocolate Cake,
    371
  for Siciliana Cassata, 352
Fudge
  Cake, Tunnel of, 198
  Cookies, No Bake, 263
  Deluxe, 303
  Fabulous, 304
  Float, 180
  Frosting, Minute, 228
  Frosting, for Toffee Bars, 295
  Innes, 259
  Sauce, 1-2-3, 244
Fudgesicles, 268
Hot, Mix, 282
Icing, Thin, 209
Lace Doily, 384
Leaves, 384
Mint Mousse, 216
Pie
  Chiffon, 234
  Pecan, 234
  Polly's, 235
  Spooky, 273
Pots de Crème, 208
Pudding
  Filling for Cornucopias, 210
  Vanilla Wafer-, 180
Ring, 207
Shells, 383
S'Mores, 272
Soufflé, 220
substitute for, 379
Torte, Lili's, 208
Trifle, 225
Chowder
  Clam, 73
    Boston, 73
  Conch, Bahamian, 72
  Turkey, Jack's, 81
Christmas decorations, 275–279
  Crystal Christmas Bough, 278
  decorations, 279
  Della Robbia Wreath, 277
  ornaments, 279
Christmas kitchen gifts, 279
Christmas recipes, 275–307
  Beverages
    Café au Lait Mix, 281
    Café Mexicano, 281
    Candy Cane Cocktail, 307
    Cranberry Punch, 307
    Friendship Tea, 282

Hot Buttered Rum Batter, 282
Hot Chocolate Mix, 282
Mocha, 281
Wassail, 307
Bourbon Hard Sauce, 283
Cake(s)
Mincemeat Nut, Mini, 291
Rum, 297
Sponge, Basic, 301
Candied Grapefruit Peel, 285
Candies
Almond Roco, 301
Boston Cream, 302
Bourbon Balls, 286
Brown Sugar, Lois's, 302
Candy Cane Cookies, 287
Candy Canes, 287
Caramels, Aunt Mary's, 302
Cathedral Windows, 287
Chocolate Bon-Bons, 301
Chocolate Chip Cookie Brittle, 303
Chocolate Fudge, Deluxe, 303
Chocolate Fudge, Fabulous, 304
Chocolate Sugarplums, 295
Christmas Fancies, 304
Coconut Joys, 289
Holiday Dipped Creams, 303
Irish Truffles, 300
Millionaires, 305
Panocha, 305
Panocha, Sour Cream, 305
Peanut Butter Cups I, 291
Peanut Butter Cups II, 292
Taffy, Tonia's White, 306
Truffles, Chocolate, 306
Truffles, Mocha, 306
Coffee-Whiskey Trifle, 300
Cookies
Aunt Virginia's, 289
Butter Logs, 296
Candy Cane, 287
Chinese Timbales, 295
Chocolate Caramel Fingers, 299
Chocolate Chip, Jeanne's, 288
Chocolate Chip, Mom's, 288
Chocolate Chip Cookie Brittle, 303
Chocolate Marshmallow, 288
Cocoa Bars, 289
Doreen's Melting Moments, 299

Earthquake, 290
Girdle-buster Bars, 290
Krunchy, 289
Lemon Squares, 290
Lemon Wine, 296
Madelyn's Sleep, 293
Moth Balls, 301
Orange Icebox, 290
Peanut Butter, 291
Peanut Butter Dessert Bars, 291
Peppermint Slab, Doreen's, 300
Saint Nickerdoodles, 294
Salted Peanut, 292
Serendipities, 292
Sherry Bars, Annie's, 293
Shortbread, 293
Shortbread, Monica's, 300
Six-Layer, 294
Snickerdoodles, 294
Sugar, 294
Sugar, Rolled, 294
Toffee Bars, 295
Windsor, 296
Fruitcake
Orange Slice, 299
White Christmas, 298
Glazed Apricots, 283
Hidden Valley Crackers, 286
Holiday Pudding, 298
Nine-Bean Soup, 282
Mix, 282
Nuts
Crisp Fried Walnuts, 284
Curried, 283
Golden, 283
Spiced Pecans, 285
Sugared, 284
Sugar-glazed, 284
Orange Peel Preserves, 283
Parsley Butter, 281
Pecan Tarts, 292
Plum Pudding, 297
Sauce, 297
Pomander Balls
Apple, 280
Orange, 280
Potpourri
Children's, 280
Rose, 280
Spice, 280
Scones, Monica's, 299
Strawberry Butter, 281
Christmas Scent, 277

Christmas tree
homemade ornaments for, 279
how to preserve a, 278
Chutney
Cheese Pâté, 12
Mango, 159
Cider, Apple Jack, 1
Cinnamon
Apples
Aunt Martha's Red, 258
for Salad, Whole, 138
-Applesauce, Molded, 138
Bread, 46
Graham Crackers, 199
Ice Cream, 180
Rolls, 47
Sticks, 269
Sugar Syrup, 370
uses for, 380
Circus Salad, 270
Clam Chowder, 73
Boston, 73
Cloves, uses for, 380
Cobbler, Peach, Vern's, 182
Cocktail. See also Beverages
Beautiful Hair, 1
Candy Cane, 307
Champagne, 2
Cocktail Sauce for Seafood, 153
Cocoa
Bars, 289
Frosting, 289
Zucchini Bread, 48
Coconut
Cake
Cream, 190
Lemon, 192
Pineapple, 195
Chocolate Bon-Bons with, 301
Frosting, 197
Pineapple-, 195
Ice Cream Balls, 212
Joys, 289
Lemon Tarts, 223
-Pecan Frosting, 227
Pecan Ring, 171
Pie Crust, 229
Crème de Noyaux Pie with, 213
Raggedy Ann Cookies, 264
to soften hardened, 377
Coffee
Café au Lait Mix, 281
Café Mexicano, 281
Cappuccino, 356

Coffee: Cappuccino (*cont.*)
   Creamy, 356
   Variations of, 356
  Espresso, 356
  to improve flavor of, 375
  Irish, Buena Vista, 3
  Mocha, 281
  Rum Cooler, 3
  to store, 375
  -Whiskey Trifle, 300
Coffee Cake, 47
  Allece's, 48
  Banana Sour Cream, 43
  Bohemian, 45
  Cherry, 46
  Heath Bar, 172
  Raspberry, 64
  Sour Cream, 68
Coke Cake, 191
Cole Slaw
  Deluxe, 138
  Hot, 148
Colonial Soup, 75
Columbia Specials, 28
Conch
  Chowder, Bahamian, 72
  Fritters, 33
Cookies. *See also* Bars
  Amaretto Strips, 351
  Angel, 264
  Cenci Alta Florentina, 352
  Chocolate
    Caramel Fingers, 299
    children's recipe, 261
    Chippers, 200
    Chocolate Chip, Jeanne's, 288
    Chocolate Chip, Mom's, 288
    Chocolate Chip Cookie Brittle, 303
    Dessert Burgers, 264
    Devil's Food, 201
    Earthquake, 290
    Grasshopper Pie with Crust of, 236
    Marshmallow, 288
    No Bake Fudgie, 263
    Serendipities, 292
    Six-Layer, 294
  Christmas
    Aunt Virginia's, 289
    Butter Logs, 296
    Candy Cane, 287
    Chinese Timbales, 295

Chocolate Caramel Fingers, 299
Chocolate Chip, Jeanne's, 288
Chocolate Chip, Mom's, 288
Chocolate Chip Cookie Brittle, 303
Chocolate Marshmallow, 288
Cocoa Bars, 289
Doreen's Melting Moments, 299
Earthquake, 290
Girdle-buster Bars, 290
Krunchy, 289
Lemon Squares, 290
Lemon Wine, 296
Madelyn's Sleep, 293
Moth Balls, 301
Orange Icebox, 290
Peanut Butter, 291
Peanut Butter Dessert Bars, 291
Peppermint Slab, Doreen's, 300
Saint Nickerdoodles, 294
Salted Peanut, 292
Serendipities, 292
Sherry Bars, Annie's, 293
Shortbread, 293
Shortbread, Monica's, 300
Six-Layer, 294
Snickerdoodles, 294
Sugar, 294
Sugar, Rolled, 294
Toffee Bars, 295
Windsor, 296
Florentines, 353
Gingerbread Men, 263
Goblins and Ghosts Lollipop, 273
Holiday, 255
Honey Date Sticks, 255
Jelly Roll Pan, 264
Krunchy, 289
Lemon
  Fluff, Sandie's, 202
  Wine, 296
to mail, 376
Make-a-Face, 262
Make-a-Name, 262
Make-a-Word, 262
Marble Squares, 202
No Bakes, 262
Out of This World Flying Saucer, 262–263

Peanut, Salted, 292
Peanut Butter, 261, 291
with Pecans
  Chocolate Chip, Jeanne's, 288
  Chocolate Chip, Mom's, 288
  Madelyn's Sleep, 293
  Moth Balls, 301
  Serendipities, 292
Potato Chip, 202
Raggedy Ann, 264
Raisin, 203
Rugalas, 219
Serendipities, 292
Shortbread, 293
  Monica's, 300
Show-Time Circus, 272
Sugar, 203, 294
  Rolled, 294
Windsor, 296
Your Very Own Hand, 261
Copper Pennies, 121
Corn. *See also* Popcorn
  Balls, 121
  Caramel, Oven-Baked, 286
  Relish, Lois's, 159
  Scalloped, 121
  Soup, Cream of, 75
Corn Bread
  Jalapeño, 48
  Spoon Bread
    Crusty, 172
    Josa's, 250
    Mexican, 365
  Sticks, 58
  Stuffing
    Casserole, 70
    Flank Steak with, 88
Corned Beef
  and Cabbage, 87
  Reuben Roll-ups, 20
  Salad, 139
Cornish Hens, Glazed, 103
Cornmeal Polenta, 63
Cornucopias, Ray Dell's Creamy, 210
Cottage Cheese
  Cake, Mocha, 206
  Dip, 14
  Lasagne with, 343
  in Spinach Casserole, 173
Court Bouillon, Creole, 76
Crab(meat)
  Dip, Hot, 166

Fondue, 323
Mousse, 13
Quiche, 39
and Shrimp and Water Chestnut
    Dip, 23
Spread, Quick, 167
Supreme, 14
on Toast, 27
Cracker(s)
    Crumbs, to make, 376
    Graham
        Cinnamon, 199
        Gems, Little Grandma's
            (1885), 254
        Jelly Roll Pan Cookies made
            with, 264
        Pie Crust, 230
        Pudding, 265
        S'Mores, 272
    Hidden Valley, 286
    Lavash, 49
Cranberry
    Bread, 46
    Muffins, 58
    Salad, 139
        Frozen, 139
        Molded, 139
    Sauce, 139, 153
    Whip, 140
Cream. See also Crème Fraîche;
        Sour Cream
    Chantilly, 242
    Frosting, 227
    Puff Bowl, 28
    Puffs, 209
    Sauce, Tortellini in, 346
    substitute for, 379
    Whipped
        Coffee-flavored, 208
        to keep from separating, 375,
            377
Cream Cheese
    Artichoke Bottoms with Caviar
        and, 9
    -Banana Pie, 233
    Cake
        Jan's, 205
        Jeanine's, 205
        Joy's, 205
        Sally's, 204
    Chive, Mushrooms Stuffed with
        Bacon and, 16
    Frosting, 195, 196, 227
        Chocolate, 226

for Mexican Fruitcake, 372
and Fruit Ball, 12
Holiday Dipped Creams, 303
Lemon Filling, for Lemon Cloud
    Pie, 237
Muffins, Spiced, 59
Orange-flavored, 362
Pastry, 13
Pie, Peach, 240
Pound Cake, 195
and Radish Spread, 20
Salad, Philadelphia, 144
Strawberry Flan, 223
Crema Zabaglione Puffs, 354
Crème de Almond (Crème de
    Noyaux)
    Pie, 213
    Sauce, 243
Crème Anglaise, 243
    Pineapple à la, 218
Crème Caramel with Strawberry
    Sauce, 209
Crème Chantilly, 218
Crème Fraîche, 153
    Instant, 181
Crème de Menthe Brownies, 199
Crème de Noyaux. See Crème de
    Almond
Creole Courtbouillon, 76
Creole Gumbo, 76
Crêpe(s)
    Basic
        I, 29
        II, 29
    Benedict, 28
    Green Peppercorn Steak in a,
        84
    Tivoli, 210
    Zucchini, 134
Crisping crackers, cereal, taco
        shells, chips, 376
Croissants, 49
Croquettes, Salmon, 108
Crystal Christmas Bough, 278
Crystallized Flowers, 385
Cucumber(s)
    Canapés, 15
    -Dill Sauce, 145
    Pickles(-d)
        Bev's, 159
        Bread and Butter, 160, 162
        Lime, Old South Sweet, 163
        Oil, Mrs. Penny's, 162
        Rings, Red, 160

Sweet Pickles out of Dills, 163
    Sauce, 108, 155
    Soup, Iced, 76
Cup Cake(s)
    Auntie K's, 1938, 256
    Brownie, Rich, 187
    Mincemeat Nut, 291
    Mrs. Butler's (1930s), 253
Curry(-ied)
    Almonds, 283
    Avocado Soup, Cold, 361
    Balls, 16
    Chicken Salad, 140
    Fruit, Hot, 32
    Lamb, East Indian, 94
    Potatoes, 124
    Sauce for Beef Fondue, 324
    Shrimp, 177
    Tuna, Casserole, 177
    Turkey Breast, 103
    uses for, 380
Custard
    Broccoli Mold, 27
    Chocolate, Squares, 211
    to keep from becoming watery,
        378
    Orange, 373
    Pots de Crème
        Chocolate, 208
        Orange, 218
    Sauce
        English, 244
        Trifle, 224

Daddy's Jaternice, 249
Daddy's Spicy Sauce for Seafood,
    250
Daddy's Summer Cooler, 247
Daiquiri, 3
    Peach, 3
        Fresh, 4
    Pie, Derby, 235
Date(s)
    Bread Loaf, Diabetic, 43
    Cake, Vern's, 190
    Honey Sticks, 255
    -Nut
        Angel Cookies, 264
        Bars, Wichita Country Club,
            201
        Bread, Grandmother's, 256
Decorating. See Entertaining
Decorations, 381–382
Deglazing Sauce, 154

Delarobia Salad
  Dressing for, 140
  Jane's, 140
Delish Frosting, 228
Della Robbia Wreath, 277
Denver Biscuits, 250
Dessert Burgers, 264
Desserts, 185–245. *See also*
        Cake(s); Cookies; Ice
        Cream; Pie
  Apricots, Glazed, 258
  Atholl Pudding, 219
  Baked Alaska, Individual, 183
  Baklava, Yia Yia's, 204
  Bananas Flambé, 212
  Beer Batter (for frying fruits), Mr.
        Herbert's, 206
  Burnt Sugar Dumplings, 211
  Buttered Rum, Cold, 180
  Cherries
    Jubilee, 212
    Romanoff, 208
  Chocolate Addicts Frozen
        Cream, 182
  Chocolate Charlotte, 207
  Chocolate Custard Squares, 211
  Chocolate Pots de Crème, 208
  Chocolate Ring, 207
  Cinnamon Apples, Aunt
        Martha's Red, 258
  Cobbler, Peach, Vern's, 182
  Coconut Lemon Tarts, 223
  Cornucopias, Ray Dell's
        Creamy, 210
  Cream Puffs, 209
  Crème Caramel with Strawberry
        Sauce, 209
  Crêpes Tivoli, 210
  Fudge Float, 180
  Gingerbread, 254
  Graham Gems, Little Grandma's
        (1885), 254
  Honey Nut Crunch Bars, 183
  Italian, 350–355
    Amaretto Strips, 351
    Bellini Ice, 350
    Cannoli, 353
    Cassata Ice Cream, 351
    Cenci Alta Florentina, 352
    Florentines, 353
    Ice Cream Cake, 351
    Siciliana Cassata, 352
    Spuma di Zucca con
        Amaretto, 354

    Spumone, 355
    Zabaglione, 354
    Zabaglione Puffs, Crema, 354
  Kolaces 1930, 251
  Lemon Cream, 216
  Lemon Fluff, 256
  Mexican
    Bunuelos I, 370
    Bunuelos II, 370
    Esponjosa (Cold Caramel
        Soufflé), 373
    Fiesta Chocolate Cake, 371
    Flan de Naranja (Orange
        Custard), 373
    Fruitcake, 372
    Mandarin Orange Cake I, 371
    Mandarin Orange Cake II, 371
    Pumpkin Rice Pudding, 372
    Wedding Cakes, 372
  Mocha Brownie Torte, 223
  Mousse
    Chocolate Mint, 216
    Kahlùa, 216
    Lemon, Cold, 181
    Mocha, 216
    Raspberry, 217
    Strawberry, 217
  Pavlova, 217
  Peaches Cardinal, 218
  Pineapple à la Crème Anglaise,
        218
  Pineapple Sautéed with Cream,
        217
  Pots de Crème
    Chocolate, 208
    Orange, 218
  Pudding
    Atholl, 219
    Chocolate, filling for
        Cornucopias, 210
    Chocolate-Vanilla Wafer, 180
    Graham Cracker, 265
    Holiday, 298
    Plum, 297
    Pumpkin Rice, 372
    Syllabub, 224
  Sauces for
    Apricot-Walnut Sauce, 243
    Bourbon, Warm, 243
    Bourbon Hard Sauce, 283
    Caramel, 213
    Chantilly Cream, 242
    Crème Anglaise, 243
    Crème de Noyaux (Crème de

      Almond), 243
    English Custard, 244
    Fudge Sauce, 1-2-3, 244
    Grand Marnier, 221
    Mincemeat Topping for Ice
        Cream, 244
    Plum Pudding, 297
    Praline Crunch Ice Cream
        Topping, 244
    Raspberry, 244
    Sabayon, 245
    Strawberry, Crème Caramel
        with, 209
    Toffee Ice Cream Pie and
        Sauce, 215
    Trifle Custard, 224
    Vanilla, 41, 206
    Wine, for Cold Soufflés, 245
  Strawberries Romanoff, 222
  Strawberry, Quickie, 183
  Strawberry Cheese Flan, 223
  Strawberry Marlo, Ethel's, 258
  Tonia's Apple Crisp—Food
        Processor Style, 231
  Trifle, 224
    Chocolate, 225
    Coffee-Whiskey, 300
    Custard Sauce, 224
    English, 224–225
    Individual, 226
Devil's Food Drop Cookies, 201
Diabetic Apricot Nut Bread, 41
Diabetic Date Bread Loaf, 43
Dill(y)
  Bread, 50
    Picnic Braid, 50
  -Cucumber Sauce, 145
  Dip, Party, 167
  uses for, 378, 380
Dip
  Apricot, 23
  Artichoke, Hot, 165
  Cheese
    and Broccoli, 10
    Hot, 165, 360
  Chili, Hot, 362
  Cottage Cheese, 14
  Crab, Hot, 166
  Dill, Party, 167
  Garbanzo Bean, 362
  Green Pepper, 15
  Guacamole, 361
  Onion, Been Around for Years,
        165

Ray Dell's Butterfly, 165
Salsa, 361
Shrimp, 24
    Crab, Water Chestnut, and, 23
Spinach, 25
for Veggies, Easy 'n' Quick, 166
Doreen's Melting Moments, 299
Doreen's Peppermint Slab, 300
Dorisburgers, 179
Dorothy's Blintz Bubble Ring, 44
Dorothy's Layer Salad, 142
Doughnuts, French (Beignets), 45
Dove, Baked, 104
Dressing. See also Salad Dressing
    Herb Mayonnaise, 17
    Orange Fruit, 154
Duck Breast, 103
Dump Cake, 265
Dumplings, Burnt Sugar, 211

Earthquake Cookies, 290
Easter dinner, menu and
        decorating ideas for, 311
Easy 'n' Quick Dip for Veggies,
        166
Egg(s)
    Benedict, 29
        Crêpes, 28
    Columbia Specials, 28
    Eggnog, 4
    Elegante, Brunch, 29
    and Ham Casserole, 34
    Harlequin, Poached, 30
    hints on, 375–379
    -Lemon Soup, 77
    Omelet, Basic, 36
    Pickled, Hot, 15
    Rolls, Carol's, 51
    Sausage-stuffed, 30
    Scrambled Medley, Ruthie's, 30
    Sunday, 33
    Toad in the Hole, 267
Eggnog, 4
Eggplant
    Caponata, 333
    Casserole, 334
Elizabeth's Bagels, 42
Enchilada(s)
    Cheese and Onion, 367
    Chicken, 368
    Pie, 368
    Sour Cream, Jeanne's, 368
English Custard Sauce, 244
English Muffins, 51

English Trifle
    about, 224
    I, 225
    II, 225
    III, 225
Ensalada de Arroz, 364
Entertaining
    Bridesmaids' Luncheon, 312
    Candlelight Dinner, 311
    Come Into Our Kitchen party,
        319
    Easter Dinner, 311
    Elegant Picnic, 310
    Family-style Picnic, 309
    Fondue party, 321–322
    Italian-style dinner party, 328
    La Fiesta Grande
        I, 359
        II, 360
    New Orleans Brunch, 314
    New Year's Brunch, 313
    Some Sunday Morning Brunch,
        314
    Taxpayer's Bawl, 318
    Thanksgiving Dinner, 315
    Wedding Brunch, 313
Ermadene's Cherry Tomatoes, 137
Esponjosa, 373
Espresso, 356
    Romano, 356
Ethel's Strawberry Marlo, 258

Family Request for Pot Roast, 89
Fancies, Christmas, 304
Fat, hints on cooking with, 376
Fettuccine
    Butter and Cheese Sauce for,
        341
    Classic Sauce for, 341
    to cook, 341
    dough for, 338
    Green, with Peas and
        Prosciutto, 341
    with Northern Italian Meat
        Sauce, 347
Fiesta Chicken and Shrimp
        Casserole, 367
Fiesta Chocolate Cake, 371
Filé, uses for, 380
Fish
    Fillet
        Amandine, 105
        Coconut Grove, 105
        Florentine, 106

    Marseille, 177
    Parmesan, 106
    Sea Trout with Broccoli,
        Spiced, 114
    Sole Gourmet, 113
    Supreme, 106
    Veronique, 107
    Herb-stuffed, 107
    odor of, to remove, 378
Salmon
    Ball, 21
    Croquettes, 108
    Mousse, 21, 145
    Whole Poached Fresh, 108
Snapper Normande, 113
Soup, Italian, 330
-Spinach Bake, 176
Tuna
    -Almond Bake, 115
    Casserole, Easy Fixin', 115
    Curry Casserole, 177
Fishhouse Punch, 247
Flan
    de Naranja, 373
    Strawberry Cheese, 223
Florentines, 353
Flour, substitutions for, 378–379
Flowerpot Ice Cream, 268
Flowers
    arranging, 381, 382
    Crystallized, 385
    Floating, 385
    tips on, 379
Fluff, Lemon, 256
Fondue
    Bourguignonne, 323
    Brandied Strawberry, 324
    Broth, Hors d'Oeuvres, 322
    Cheese, 322
    Chicken, 323
    Chocolate
        Dark, 324
        Milk, 325
    Crab, 323
    Lemon Sauce for, 325
    party ideas and menu, 321–322
    Sauces for Beef, 324
    Sour Cream Apricot Sauce, 324
Football Cake, 191
Ft. Lauderdale Mustard Sauce,
        156
Four-Minute Frosting, 228
Frankfurters, in Alsatian Dinner, 9
        to 5, 177

Frascati, 357
French Bread
Jeanne's, 51
Vera's, 52
French Breakfast Puffs, 52
French Cherry Pie, 180
French Crème Filling, 226
French Doughnuts (Beignets), 45
French Dressing, Fruit, 248
French Fries, Oven, 174
French Toast, 39
The Best, 33
Friendship Tea, 282
Fritters
Apple Butter Pumpkin, 52
Banana, 53
Conch, 33
Peach, Fresh, 53
Frosted Salad, 141
Frosting. See also Icing
Brandy, 187
Caramel, 226
Chocolate, 188, 189, 190, 191, 194, 227
Cream Cheese, 226
for Fiesta Chocolate Cake, 371
for Siciliana Cassata, 352
Cocoa, 289
Coconut, 197
Pecan-, 227
Pineapple-, 195
Cream, 227
Mocha, 229
Orange, 258
Cream Cheese, 195, 196, 227
Chocolate, 226
for Mexican Fruitcake, 372
for decorating, 191
Delish, 228
Four-Minute, 228
Fudge
Minute, 228
for Toffee Bars, 295
Jam, 266
Minute Penuche, 229
Mocha, 201
Cream, 229
Orange Cream, 258
School Days, 227
Sea Foam, 228
Seven-Minute, 258
Shortcut 7-Minute, 228
Three-Minute, 257

for Windsor Cookies, 296
Fruit(s). See also specific fruits
Baked, 32
Beer Batter for frying, Mr. Herbert's, 206
Cake
Mexican, 372
Mom's White (1930s), 254
Orange-Slice, 299
White Christmas, 298
Cheese Ball, 12
Chocolate Fondue for
Dark, 324
Milk, 325
Curried, Hot, 32
Floating, 385
French Dressing, 248
Salad
Auntie K's Favorite, 141
California, 169
Delarobia, Jane's, 140
Frosted, 141
Frozen, 142
Mom's Frozen, 142
tips on, 375, 378
Twenty-four Hour, 148
Slush, 32
Tart, Fresh, 31
Tipsy, 32
"Turkey," Tonia's Thanksgiving (centerpiece), 316–317
Frying, tips on, 376, 378
Fudge, Chocolate
Cake, Tunnel of, 198
Cookies, No Bake, 263
Deluxe, 303
Fabulous, 304
Float, 180
Frosting
Minute, 228
for Toffee Bars, 295
Innes, 259
Sauce, 1-2-3, 244
Fudgesicles, 268
Fun-Do party, 322
Funnel Cakes, 266

Garbanzo Bean Dip, 362
Garlic
Bread, Hot, 171
oil flavored with, 375, 376
uses for, 380
Garlic Cheese
Dip, Hot, 165

Grits, 34
Gazpacho, 362
Salad, 364
Gems, Graham, Little Grandma's (1885), 254
German Chocolate Cake, 193
German Potato Pancakes, 37
German Potato Salad, Hot, 138
Gertrude's Art Gallery Punch, 1
Ginger, uses for, 380
Gingerbread, 254
for Kolaces, 251
Men, 263
Girdle-buster Bars, 290
Girdle-buster Pie, 181
Glaze
Apricot, 193
Harvey Wallbanger, 193
Lemon, 223
Orange, for Carrot Cake, 189
Rum, 197
Strawberry, for Strawberry Cream Pie, 242
Gnocchi, spinach, 342
Goblins and Ghosts Lollipop Cookies, 273
Golden Nuts, 283
Good Day, Recipe for a, 247
Gorgonzola Dressing, 149
Goulash, Paprika, 87
Graham Cracker(s)
Cinnamon, 199
Gems, Little Grandma's (1885), 254
Jelly Roll Pan Cookies made with, 264
Pie Crust, 230
Pudding, 265
S'Mores, 272
Grandma's Meat Loaf, 270
Grand Marnier
Sauce, 221
Soufflé, 221
Grandmother's Date-Nut Bread 1923, 256
Grandmother's Jelly Roll 1900, 255
Grape(s)
Jelly, 160
Pie, 236
Grapefruit, Candied Peel of, 285
Grape Leaves, Stuffed, 88
Grapenut Bread, Joyce's, 53
Grapes

Baked Quail or Pheasant with, 104
Frosted, 383
Pineapple with, 37
Grasshopper Pie, 236
Gravy, Red Eye, Ham and, 35
Great Grandmother's Mincemeat, 259
Greek Salata, 141
Green Bean(s)
Casserole, 122
Herb, 122
Mom's, 121
Plus, 173
Quick 'n' Easy, 172
in Three-Bean Salad, 147
in Vegetable Trio with Zippy Sauce, 133
Green Chile(s)
Burritos, 366
Pie, 366
con Queso, 360
Rellenos, 367
Rice with, 122
Salsa, 361
Greengage Dessert Salad, 142
Green Mayonnaise, 155
Green Pepper(s), Sweet
Brick, 18
Casserole, 122
Dip, 15
Jelly, 160
Marinated Roasted, 329
Sausage-stuffed, 92
Steak, Savory, 86
Green Peppercorn Steak in a Crêpe, 84
Gremolata, 349
Grits
Garlic Cheese, 34
Leonardo, Baked, 34
Guacamole, 361
Ring, Molded, 364
Gumbo
Chicken, 74
Creole, 76
Shrimp, Down South, 77

Halloween Haystacks, 273
Ham. See also Prosciutto
in Alsatian Dinner, 90
Baked, 92
Balls, 93
and Cheese Brunch, 34

Chicken Bocca with, 348
Crêpes Benedict with, 28
and Egg Casserole, 34
Eggs Benedict with, 29
Loaf, Upside-Down, 93
Nut Glaze for, 156
Pie, Impossible, 93
and Red Eye Gravy, 35
-Rice Bake, 176
White Bean soup with, 82
Hamburger(s)
Buns, Onion, 61
Dorisburgers, 179
Hard Sauce
Bourbon, 283
Snowballs, 298
Harvey Wallbanger Supreme Cake, 193
Hattie's Piccalilli, 161
Hawaiian Lemonade, 267
Haystacks, Halloween, 273
Hazelnut(s)
in Christmas Fancies, 304
Sugar-glazed, 284
Hearts of Palm Salad, 144
Heath Bar(s)
Coffee Cake, 172
Pie, 235
Toffee Ice Cream Pie and Sauce, 215
Heavenly Pie, 237
Helena's Barbecue Sauce, 151
Helena's Chicken Roquefort, 176
Herb(s,-ed). See also specific herbs
Butter, 154
Fish Stuffed with, 107
Green Beans, 122
Mayonnaise Dressing, 17
Spinach, Baked, 127
Hidden Valley Crackers, 286
Hints, 375–379
Holiday Cookies, 255
Holiday Delight, 303
Holiday Pumpkin-Pecan Pie, 242
Hollandaise Sauce, 156
Easy, 127
in Large Quantity, 155
Mock, 155
Homemade Bomb, The, 6
Honey
Butter, Little Brown Bear's Hot, 269
Carrots, 249

Chicken Baked with, 176
Date Sticks, 255
to liquefy sugared, 377
Nut Crunch Bars, 183
-Poppy Seed Dressing, 149
Honeydew, Prosciutto and, 329
Hoppin' John, 35
Horseradish Sauce for Beef Fondue, 324
Hot Cross Buns, 54
Hot Dogs, Shush Puppies, 271
Houseplants, 379
food for, 375, 376
Hubble House Dressing, 150

Ice, Bellini, 350
Icebox Rolls, Aunt Tottie's, 251
Ice Cream
Balls, 212
Almond Praline, 211
Bozo Balls, 269
Betty's 213
Butter Pecan, Cold Buttered Rum with, 180
Cake, Italian, 351
Cassata, Italian, 351
Cinnamon, 180
Coconut Cream, 190
Coffee, in Girdle-buster Pie, 181
Cookie Cups for, 210
Crispy Shells for, 231
Date, Vern's, 190
Flowerpot, 268
Fudge Sauce for, 1-2-3, 244
Jack-O'-Lantern Frosties, 274
Lemon, 214
Mincemeat Topping for, 244
Peach, Mom's Fresh, 214
Pie, 213
Crème de Noyaux (Crème de Almond), 213
Pumpkin, 215
Strawberry, 215
Toffee, and Sauce, 215
Praline Crunch Topping for, 244
Snow, Tonia's, 268
Spumone, 355
Vanilla
Almond Praline Balls, 211
Baked Alaska, Individual, 183
Betty's, 213
Cherries Jubilee, 212
Cherries Romanoff with, 208
Homemade, 213–215

Ice Cream: Vanilla (*cont.*)
    Irma Columbia's, 214
    Jeanne's Country, 215
    Old-fashioned, 214
Ice Rings, 383
Icing. *See also* Frosting
    Chocolate, Thin, 209
    Confectioners', 64
    for Gingerbread Men, 263
    White, 257
Impossible Pie, 93
Innes Fudge, 259
Insalata Capricciosa, 332
Inspirational Cake, 194
Irish Coffee, Buena Vista, 3
Irish Cream Liqueur, 4
Irish Soda Bread, 54
Irish Truffles, 300
Irma Columbia's Ice Cream, 214
Italian Meat Loaf, 85
Italian recipes, 327–357
    Appetizers
        Antipasto, 329
        Fried Mozzarella, 330
        Marinated Roasted Peppers,
            329
        Olive Salad, 329
        Prosciutto e Melone, 329
        Stuffed Mushrooms
            Parmigiana, 329
        Zucchini, 329
    Artichokes Florentine, 335
    Asparagus
        with Mayonnaise, 334
        Milan, 334
    Chicken Bocca, 348
    Coffee
        Cappuccino, 356
        Cappuccino, Creamy, 356
        Cappuccino, Variations of,
            356
        Espresso, 356
    Desserts, 350–355
        Amaretto Strips, 351
        Bellini Ice, 350
        Cannoli, 353
        Cassata Ice Cream, 351
        Cenci Alta Florentina, 352
        Florentines, 353
        Ice Cream Cake, 351
        Siciliana Cassata, 352
        Spuma di Zucca con
            Amaretto, 354
        Spumone, 355

        Zabaglione, 354
        Zabaglione Puffs, Crema, 354
    Eggplant Casserole, 334
    Gremolata, 349
    Osso Buco, 348
    Pasta
        about, 336
        Cannelloni, 337, 339
        Cannelloni, Short Cut, 340
        Fettuccine. *See* Fettucine
        Gnocchi, Spinach, 342
        Homemade I, 337
        Homemade II, 337
        Jonnie Mosetti, 345
        Lasagne. *See* Lasagne
        Manicotti, 344
        with Northern Italian Meat
            Sauce, 347
        Ravioli, 337
        Ravioli, Cheese Filling for, 338
        Ravioli, Meat Filling for, 338
        Ravioli Casserole, 345
        Souffle di, 344
        Spaghetti. *See* Spaghetti
        Tortellini in Cream Sauce, 346
    Pizza, 339
    Polenta, 63
    Risotto alla Milanese, 335
    Salads
        Antipasto Misto, 333
        Insalata Capricciosa, 332
        Lettuce and Tomato, 332
        Salsa Maionese for, 333
        Spaghetti, 334
        Tomato, 332
        Watercress, 332
    Sauces
        Béchamel, 347
        Besciamella, 349
        Cheese-Mushroom, 346
        Pesto Genovese, 349
        Tomato, Jan's, 350
    Soups
        Brodo di Pollo, 331
        Minestrone, 330
        Spring Vegetable, 331
        Zuppa di Pesce (Fish Soup),
            330
    Wines, 357

Jack's Turkey Chowder, 81
Jalapeño(s)
    Corn Bread, 48
    Deep-fried Stuffed, 363

Jam
    Frosting, 266
    Strawberry, 164
Jan and Jo's Super Soup, 168
Jane's Delarobia Salad, 140
Jane's Pecan Rolls, 63
Jane's Pumpkin Chiffon Pie, 241
Jan's Cheese Cake, 205
Jan's Punch, 5
Jan's Tomato Sauce, 350
Jaternice, Daddy's, 249
Jeanine's Carrot Cake, 189
Jeanine's Cheese Cake, 205
Jeanne's Chocolate Chip Cookies,
    288
Jeanne's Country Vanilla Ice
    Cream, 215
Jeanne's French Bread, 51
Jeanne's Lime Pie, 239
Jeanne's Sour Cream Enchiladas,
    368
Jeanne's Tiropetes, 120
Jeanne's V-8 Tomato Aspic, 148
Jeannie's Lemon Pie, 238
Jean's Sweet and Sour Meatballs,
    85
Jelly
    Grape, 160
    Green Pepper, 160
    paraffin for sealing jars of, 375
    Mystery (Tomato), 161
    Pyracantha, Letha's, 163
    Sand Plum, 164
    Wine, 164
Jelly Roll Pan Cookies, 264
Jonnie Mosetti, 345
Josa's Spoon Bread, 250
Jo's Champagne Wedding Punch,
    2
Josephine Gambrill's Banana
    Cake 1930, 252
Joyce's Grapenut Bread, 53
Joy's Cheese Cake, 205
Judy's Seafood Casserole, 109
Judy's Strawberry Pie, 181
July 4th Picnic, 309

Kahlúa
    Black Russian Cake, 186
    Mom's Favorite, 4
    Mousse, 216
Key Lime Pie, 236
Khachapuri, 55
Kiddies' Candy Canes, 287

Kidney Beans, in Three-Bean
    Salad, 147
Kid-size Pizza, 270
Kir, 4
Knockwurst, in Alsatian Dinner, 9
    to 5, 177
Kolaces 1930, 251
Krazy Krunch, 286
Krunch Cookies, 289

Lamb
    Curry, East Indian, 94
    Leg of, Lonnie's Greek Roast,
        94
    Shank, Bev's, 94
Lasagne, 343
    dough for, 338
    Easy, 342
    with Northern Italian Meat
        Sauce, 347
    Roll-ups, 343
Lavash, 49
Laverna's Spice Cake, 196
Laverna's Spicy Chocolate Cake,
    253
Lazy Daisy, 192
Lemon
    Cake
        Coconut, 192
        Easy, 181
    Cheese Filling, for Lemon Cloud
        Pie, 237
    Coconut Tarts, 223
    Cream, 216
    Filling for Cakes, 226
    Fluff, 256
        Squares, Sandie's, 202
    to get more juice out of, 375
    Glaze, 223
    -Honey Breast of Chicken, 97
    Ice Cream, 214
    Mousse, Cold, 181
    Nut Bread, 65
    Pie
        Aunt Jessie's, 256
        Chess, 238
        Chiffon, 238
        Cloud, 237
        Heavenly, 237
        Jeannie's, 238
    Sauce for Fondue, 325
    Soufflé
        Cold, 222
        Double-boiler, 220

Soup
    Egg-, 77
    Iced, 77
    Squares, 290
    Vodka, 8
    Wine Cookies, 296
Lemonade
    Frosted, 267
    Hawaiian, 267
Letha's Pyracantha Jelly, 163
Lettuce, Dressing for Wilted, 150
Lieb Kuchen Cookies, Aunt
    Jessie's, 257
Lili's Chocolate Torte, 208
Lilian's Chicken Casserole, 39
Lima Beans, in Vegetable Trio with
    Zippy Sauce, 133
Lime
    Pie
        Jeanne's, 239
        Key, 236
        Rickey, 4
        Sherbet, Green Dragons, 267
        Wine Punch, 5
Little Brown Bear's Hot Honey
    Butter, 269
Little Grandma's Graham Gems
    1885, 254
Liver(s)
    Chicken, 99
        Sherried, 28
        Pork, Sausage, Bohemian, 249
Lobster
    Mousse, 13
    Tails, Bar-B-Q, 107
Loco's Chili, 75
Lois's Brown Sugar Candy, 302
Lois's Chili Sauce, 152
Lois's Corn Relish, 159
Lois's Watermelon Pickles 1935,
    260
Lonnie's Greek Roast Leg of
    Lamb, 94

Macadamia Nut(s)
    Chiffon Pie, 239
    Cream, Baked Chicken in, 99
    Sugar-glazed, 284
Madelyn's Sleep Cookies, 293
Make-a-Face Cookies, 262
Make-a-Name Cookies, 262
Make-a-Word Cookies, 262
Mandarin Orange Cake
    I, 371

II, 371
Mango Chutney, 159
Manicotti, Cheese Filling for, 344
Maple Barbecue Ribs, 166
Marble Squares, 202
Margaritas, 8
Marinade
    for Steaks, 155
    Teriyaki, 157
Marjoram, uses for, 380
Marshmallow(s)
    Cherry Salad with, 137
    Chocolate Cookies, 288
    Marvelous, 269
    S'Mores, 272
    to soften hardened, 377
    tips on, 377, 378
Mary's Bread, 57
Mayonnaise
    Asparagus with, 334
    curdled, what to do about, 377
    Green, 155
    Herb, Dressing, 17
    Italian-style, 333
Measurements, 379
Meat. *See also* Beef; Lamb; Pork;
    Veal
    Cannelloni, 339
    Company's Coming, 88
    Filling for Ravioli, 338
    Loaf(-ves)
        Bar-B-Q, Little, 174
        Grandma's, 270
        Italian, 85
        Working Girl, 178
    Mincemeat with, Great
        Grandmother's, 259
    Sauce
        Gourmet, 153
        Northern Italian, Pasta with,
            347
    Stew, Busy Lady, 175
Meatballs
    Beer Balls, 9
    Curry Balls, 16
    Ham and Ground Pork, 93
    Open Sesame, 16
        Sauce for, 16
    Oriental, 17
Melon
    Prosciutto and, 329
Menus
    Bridesmaids' Luncheon, 312
    brunch

Menus: brunch (*cont.*)
New Orleans, 314
New Year's, 313
Some Sunday Morning, 314
Wedding, 313
Candlelight Dinner, 311
Easter Dinner, 311
Fun-Do party, 322
Italian night, 328
Mexican, 359–360
picnic
elegant, 310
family-style, 309
Taxpayer's Bawl, 318
Thanksgiving Dinner, 315
Meringue Crust, for Blueberry
Cassis Pie, 233
Metric measurements, 379
Mexican parties, 359–360
Mexican recipes, 360–373
Burritos, Green Chile, 366
Cheese and Onion Enchiladas,
367
Cheese Dip, Hot, 360
Cheese Sauce, Hot, 360
Chicken and Shrimp Casserole,
Fiesta, 367
Chicken Enchiladas, 368
Chicken Tacos, 370
Chili con Queso, 360
Chili Dip, Hot, 362
Chili Pie, 366
Chili Rellenos, 367
Desserts
Bunuelos I, 370
Bunuelos II, 370
Esponjosa (Cold Caramel
Soufflé), 373
Fiesta Chocolate Cake, 371
Flan de Naranja (Orange
Custard), 373
Fruitcake, 372
Mandarin Orange Cake I, 371
Mandarin Orange Cake II, 371
Pumpkin Rice Pudding, 372
Wedding Cakes, 372
Enchilada(s)
Cheese and Onion, 367
Chicken, 368
Pie, 368
Sour Cream, Jeanne's, 368
Garbanzo Bean Dip, 362
Guacamole, 361, 364
Nacho(s), 166

Micro-, 363
Super, 363
Orange-flavored Cream Cheese,
362
Paella, 369
Quesadillas, 361
Rice
Brazilian, 366
Ensalada de Arroz (Rice
Salad), 364
Spanish, 366
Salad
Ensalada de Arroz (Rice
Salad), 364
Gazpacho, 364
Mexican, 365
Salsa, 361
Soup
Avocado, Cold Curried, 361
Gazpacho, 362
Tortilla, 363
Spoon Bread, 365
Steak, 369
Stuffed Jalapeños, Deep-fried,
363
Micro-Nachos, 363
Mile-high Pie, 240
Milk
Beautiful Hair Cocktail, 1
Brandy Punch
for 2, 2
for 30, 2
Shake
Banana, 1
Orange, 5
to sour, 375
Millionaires, 305
Mimosa Cocktail, 7
Mincemeat
-Banana Nut Bread, 42
Cake (1930), 257
Great Grandmother's
Mincemeat, 259
Nut Cakes, Mini, 291
Topping for Ice Cream, 244
Minestrone, 330
Mint
Chocolate Mousse, 216
Cubes, 383
uses for, 375, 380
Mints, 385
Minute Fudge Frosting, 228
Minute Penuche Frosting, 229
Mississippi Mud Cake, 192

Mr. Herbert's Beer Batter, 206
Mrs. Appleyard's Patrician
Potatoes, 125
Mrs. Butler's Cup Cakes 1930s,
253
Mrs. Landreth's Boston Brown
Bread 1940, 250
Mrs. Penny's Oil Pickles, 162
Mocha, 281
Brownie Torte, 223
Cream Frosting, 229
Frosting, 201
Marble Cheesecake, 206
Mousse, 216
Truffles, 306
Mom's Angel Cake Supreme, 185
Mom's Buttermilk Biscuits, 44
Mom's Caesar Salad, 136
Mom's Chocolate Chip Cookies,
288
Mom's Double-frosted Brownies,
200
Mom's Tomato Aspic, 248
Mom's White Fruitcake 1930s,
254
Monica's Scones, 299
Monica's Shortbread, 300
Monkey Bread, 69
Monterey Jack cheese
Chili Pie with, 366
Nacho(s)
Micro-, 363
Super, 363
Quesadillas, 361
Moth Balls, 301
Mother's Calvin Coolidge Sour
Cream Cake, 253
Mother's Thick Oil Dressing, 248
Mousse
Chocolate Mint, 216
Crab and/or Shrimp, 13
Kahlùa, 216
Lemon, Cold, 181
Mocha, 216
Raspberry, 217
Red Caviar, 11
Salmon, 21, 145
Strawberry, 217
Mozzarella
Cannelloni filled with, 340
Eggplant Casserole with, 334
Fried, 330
Lasagne with, 343
Manicotti with, 344

Zucchini and, 336
Muffins
  Apple
    Bran, 57
    Fresh, 58
  Banana Nut, 58
  Beer, 171
  Bran
    Apple, 57
    Six-Week, 60
  Corn Bread, 58
  Cranberry, 58
  Cream Cheese Spiced, 59
  English, 51
  notes on, 57
  Peach, Fresh, 59
  Pineapple, 59
  Pumpkin, 60
  Raspberry, 60
Mushroom(s)
  à la Grecque, 18
  Cheese-stuffed, 17
  Chicken Soup with Rice and, 74
  hints on, 375, 376
  Sauce
    Cheese-, 346
    Pimento-, Chicken and
      Stuffing Scallop with, 101
  Shells, 19
  Soup, Old-fashioned, 78
  Stuffed
    with Bacon and Chive Cream
      Cheese, 16
    Parmigiana, 329
Mustard
  Sauce, 156
    Ft. Lauderdale, 156
    Pineapple-, Hot Shrimp Balls
      in, 22
  uses for, 380
Mystery Jelly or Relish, 161
Mystery Salad, 143

Nacho(s), 166
  Micro-, 363
  Super, 363
Nassau Peas 'n' Rice, 124
New Orleans Brunch, menu and
    ideas for, 314
New Potato Appetizers, 19
New Year's Brunch, menu and
    ideas for, 313
Nine-Bean Soup, 282
  Mix, 282

Nippy Cheese Dip, 166
No Bakes, 262
No Fail Cheese Soufflé, 173
No Knead Butterhorn Rolls, 44
Noodles
  Homemade, 54
  Jonnie Mosetti, 345
Nut(s). See also specific nuts
  Apricot Bread, 41
    Diabetic, 41
  Banana Bread, 43
    Mincemeat-, 42
  Banana Muffins, 58
  Chocolate Slices, 200
  Christmas Fancies, 304
  -Date Angel Cookies, 264
  -Date Bars, Wichita Country
    Club, 201
  -Date Bread, 256
  Fudge, Sea Foam, 304
  Golden, 283
  Holiday Delights, 303
  Lemon Bread, 65
  Mincemeat Cakes, Mini, 291
  Six-Layer Cookies with, 294
  Sugared, 284
  Sugar-glazed, 284
Nutmeg, uses for, 380

O'Henry Bars, 202
Oil Dressing, Mother's Thick, 248
Okra Pickles, 162
Olive(s)
  Cheese Puffs, Hot, 13
  Cheese Shells, 11
  Salad, 329
Omelet, Basic, 36
1-2-3 Fudge Sauce, 244
Onion(s)
  about, 376, 378
  Dip, Been Around for Years, 165
  Fruit Salad Dressing, 149
  Hamburger Buns, 61
  Red
    Broccoli and Cauliflower Salad
      with, 136
  Sausage-stuffed, 120
  uses for, 380
Orange(s)
  Bread, Auntie K's (1930), 252
  Cake, Mandarin
    I, 371
    II, 371
  Cookies, Icebox, 290

Cream Cheese Flavored with,
    362
Cream Frosting, 258
Custard, 373
Fruit Dressing, 154
Fruit Salad Dressing, 150
Glaze for Carrot Cake, 189
Milk Shake, 5
Pancakes, 37
Peel, Candied, 252
Peel Preserves, 283
Pomander Balls, 280
Potpourri, Spice, 280
Pots de Crème, 218
-Slice Fruitcake, 299
-Strawberry Cooler, 6
Toast, Tea Party, 267
Oregano, uses for, 378, 380
Oriental Meatballs, 17
Oriental Salad, 143
Orvieto, 357
Osso Buco, 348
Out of This World Flying Saucer
    Cookies, 262–263
Out of This World Rolls, 62
Oven, hints on using an, 376
Oysters, Auntie K's Scalloped,
    1940s, 249

Paella, 369
Pancake(s)
  Buttermilk
    Auntie Fay's Hot Cakes, 35
    Betty's, 36
  Elegant, 36
  Hoe Cakes, 252
  Orange, 37
  Peanut Butter Syrup for, 259
  Potato, German, 37
  Sourdough, 68
Panocha, 305
  Sour Cream, 305
Panty hose, 378
Paprika, uses for, 380
Parmesan Cheese and Butter
    Sauce, for Fettuccine, 341
Parsley
  Butter, 281
  Fried, 123
  Gremolata, 349
  tips on, 376, 378
  uses for, 380
Parties. See Entertaining
Party Punch, 5

Party Snack, 20
Pasta
about, 336
Cannelloni, 337, 339
assembling, 340
Short Cut, 340
Fettuccine
Butter and Cheese Sauce for, 341
Classic Sauce for, 341
to cook, 341
dough for, 338
Green, with Peas and Prosciutto, 341
with Northern Italian Meat Sauce, 347
Gnocchi, Spinach, 342
Homemade
I, 337
II, 337
Jonnie Mosetti, 345
to keep from sticking together, 375, 377
Lasagne, 343
dough for, 338
Easy, 342
with Northern Italian Meat Sauce, 347
Roll-ups, 343
Manicotti, 344
with Northern Italian Meat Sauce, 347
Ravioli, 337
Casserole, 345
Cheese Filling for, 338
Meat Filling for, 338
Scampi Sauce, 112
Soufflé di, 344
Spaghetti
Insalata (Salad), Cold, 334
Loaf, 346
with Northern Italian Meat Sauce, 347
with Pesto-Divino, 345
Tortellini in Cream Sauce, 346
Pastry, Cream Cheese, 13
Pâté
Braunschweiger, 10
Chutney Cheese, 12
Pauline's Potato Cake, 194
Pauline's Salad Dressing, 150
Pavlova, 217
Pea(s). *See also* Split Pea Soup
Casserole, Company, 124

Green Fettuccine with Prosciutto and, 341
and Rice, Nassau, 124
Salad, 169
in Vegetable Trio with Zippy Sauce, 133
Peach(es)
Bellini Ice, 350
Blueberry Soup, 78
Cardinal, 218
Cobbler, Vern's, 182
Daiquiri, 3, 4
Fritters, Fresh, 53
Ice Cream, Mom's Fresh, 214
Marlo, Ethel's, 258
Muffins, Fresh, 59
Pie, Cream Cheese, 240
Sun Preserves, 161
Peanut Butter
Colonial Soup, 75
Cookies, 261, 291
Cups
I, 291
II, 292
Dessert Bars, 291
Syrup, 259
Yummies, 265
Peanut Cookies, Salted, 292
Pear(s)
Sherry, and Pork Chops, 91
Spiced, Hot, 37
Pecan(s)
Bourbon Balls with, 286
Chocolate Bon-Bons with, 301
Chocolate Chip Cookie Brittle with, 303
Chocolate Pie, 234
Chocolate Sugarplums with, 295
in Christmas Fancies, 304
Coconut Frosting, 227
Coconut Ring, 171
Cookies with
Chocolate Chip, Jeanne's, 288
Chocolate Chip, Mom's, 288
Madelyn's Sleep, 293
Moth Balls, 301
Serendipities, 292
Holiday Delights, 303
Millionaires, 305
in Orange-Slice Fruitcake, 299
Panocha, 305
Pie, 238
Pumpkin-, Holiday, 242

Praline Balls, 211
Rolls, Jane's, 63
Spiced, 285
Spread, 18
Sugared, 284
Sugar-glazed, 284
Tarts, 292
Toasted, 26
Pepper (spice), about, 377
Peppermint
Pot, 278
Slab, Doreen's, 300
Peppers (vegetable). *See* Green Chili(es); Green Pepper(s)
Pepsi Cola–Cherry Salad, 137
Perigeux Sauce, 83
Pesto
-Divino, 345
Genovese, 349
Sauce, Basic, 157
tips on, 157
Tomato Soup with, 81
Pheasant, Baked, 104
with White Grapes, 104
Philadelphia Cream Cheese Salad, 144
Piccalilli, Hattie's, 161
Pickles(-ed), 159
Cucumber
Bev's, 159
Bread and Butter, 162
Bread and Butter, Mom's, 160
Lime, Old South Sweet, 163
Oil, Mrs. Penny's, 162
Rings, Red, 160
Sweet Pickles out of Dills, 163
Eggs, Hot, 15
Okra, 162
Shrimp, Spiced, 178
Watermelon, 260
Lois's (1935), 260
Picnic menus and ideas, 309–310
Pie
about, 375–377
Apple, 232
1-Crust, 232
1-Crust, Streusel Topping for, 232
Sour Cream, 231
Banana-Cream Cheese, 233
Blueberry Cassis, 233
Brandy Alexander, 234
Cherry, French, 180
Chiffon, Jane's, 241

Chili, 366
Chocolate
  Chiffon, 234
  Pecan, 234
  Polly's, 235
  Spooky, 273
Crème de Noyaux (Crème de Almond), 213
Crust, 230
  Almond, 229
  Coconut, 229
  Graham Cracker, 230
  Meringue, for Blueberry Cassis Pie, 233
Derby Daiquiri, 235
Enchilada, 368
Girdle-buster, 181
Grape, 236
Grasshopper, 236
Heath Bar, 235
Heavenly, 237
Ice Cream, 213
  Strawberry, 215
  Toffee, and Sauce, 215
Lemon
  Aunt Jessie's, 256
  Chess, 238
  Chiffon, 238
  Cloud, 237
  Heavenly, 237
  Jeannie's, 238
Lime
  Jeanne's, 239
  Key, 236
Macadamia Nut, 239
  Chiffon, 239
Mile-high, 240
Peach, Cream Cheese, 240
Pecan, 238
  Pumpkin-, Holiday, 242
Pumpkin
  Bars, 203
  Chiffon, Jane's, 241
  Favorite, 241
  Ice Cream, 215
  Pecan-, Holiday, 242
Raspberry, Mile-high, 240
Sherry Almond, 241
Sour Cream-Apricot, 232
Spinach, Greek, 128
Strawberry
  Cream, 242
  Judy's, 181
  Mile-high, 240

Pimento(s)
  Cheese Spread, 19
  -Mushroom Sauce, Chicken and Stuffing Scallop with, 101
Pineapple
  à la Crème Anglaise, 218
  Baked, 37
  in Better Than Sex Cake, 183
  Cake
    Coconut, 195
    Sheet, 195
  -Cherry Salad, Frozen, 144
  to cut, 385
  with Grapes, 37
  Muffins, 59
  -Mustard Sauce, Hot Shrimp Balls in, 22
  Sautéed with Cream, 217
Pita Bread, 62
Pizza, Kid-size, 270
Plants, 379
  food for, 375, 376
Play-Dough Mixture, 269
Plum(s)
  Cake, Pretty, 182
  Dessert Salad, Greengage, 142
  Jelly, Sand, 164
  Pudding, 297
  Sauce, 297
Polenta, 63
Polly's Chocolate Pie, 235
Pomander Balls
  Apple, 280
  Orange, 280
Popcorn
  Balls, 273
  Carnival, 274
  Caramel, Oven-baked, 286
  Krazy Krunch, 286
Popovers, about, 251
Poppy Seed(s)
  -Honey Dressing, 149
  uses for, 378, 380
Popsicles, 268
Pork. See also Ham
  Burritos, Green Chile, 366
  Chops
    Ruth's, 91
    Saucy, 91
    Sherry Pears and, 91
    Smoked, in Alsatian Dinner, 90
    Sweet and Sour, 92
  Liver, Sausage, Bohemian, 249
  Ribs, Maple Barbecue, 166

Roast
  Glazed Roll, 90
  Leftover, with Fried Rice, 91
Potage St. Germain, 79
Potato(es)
  au Gratin, 123
  Baked, Sauce for, 156
  to bake quicker, 375, 376
  Baskets, 123
  Cake, Pauline's, 194
  Casserole, 124
  Chip Cookies, 202
  Curried, 124
  Mashed
    hints on, 376, 377
    Refrigerator, 125
  Mrs. Appleyard's Patrician, 125
  New, Appetizers, 19
  Oven Creamed, 126
  Oven French Fries, 174
  Pancakes, German, 37
  Parmesan, Microwave, 125
  Puffs, 125
  Romanoff, Microwave, 174
  Salad
    The "Best," 144
    Hot German, 138
  Skins, 126
  Souffléed, for Freezer, 126
  Soup, 79
  Vichyssoise, 82
Potpourri
  Children's, 280
  Rose, 280
  Spice, 280
Pots de Crème
  Chocolate, 208
  Orange, 218
Pound Cake
  Apricot Brandy, 193
  Cream Cheese, 195
Praline
  Balls, Almond, 211
  Crunch Topping, for Ice Cream, 244
  Rolls, 63
Preserves
  Orange Peel, 283
  Peach Sun, 161
  Strawberry, Freezer, 164
Prosciutto
  e Melone, 329
  Green Fettuccine with Peas and, 341

Prune mixture for Kolaces, 251
Pudding
  Atholl, 219
  Chocolate
    Filling for Cornucopias, 210
    Vanilla Wafer-, 180
  Graham Cracker, 265
  Holiday, 298
  Plum, 297
    Sauce, 297
  Pumpkin Rice, 372
  Syllabub, 224
Puffs
  Cream, 209
  French Breakfast, 52
  Olive, Hot, 13
    Cheese, 13
  Potato, 125
  Zabaglione, Crema, 354
Pumpkin
  Apple Butter Fritters, 52
  Bread, 64
  Cake
    Roll, 196
    Sheet, 196
  Muffins, 60
  Pie
    Bars, 203
    Chiffon, Jane's, 241
    Favorite, 241
    Ice Cream, 215
    Pecan-, Holiday, 242
  -Raisin Loaves, 64
  Rice Pudding, 372
  Seeds, Baked, 19
  Soup, 79
  Spuma di Zucca con Amaretto,
    354
Punch
  Brandy Milk
    for 2, 2
    for 30, 2
  Champagne Wedding, Jo's, 2
  Children's Party, 267
  Cranberry, Holiday, 307
  for Fifty, 5
  Fishhouse, 247
  Gertrude's Art Gallery, 1
  Hot Spiced, 7
  Jan's, 5
  Lime Wine, 5
  Party, 5
  Sherbet, 6
Pyracantha Jelly, Letha's, 163

Quail
  Baked, 104
    with White Grapes, 104
  Microwave, 179
  Sherry, 105
Quiche
  Crab Meat, 39
  Lorraine, 38
Quick Bread Stix, 44

Rabbit in Pepper Sauce, 96
Radish and Cream Cheese
    Spread, 20
Raggedy Ann Cookies, 264
Raisin(s)
  Cookies, 203
  -Pumpkin Loaves, 64
Raspberry(-ies)
  Coffee Cake, 64
  Crêpes Tivoli with, 210
  Marlo, Ethel's, 258
  Mousse, 217
  Muffins, 60
  Pie, Mile-high, 240
  Salad, 145
  Sauce, 244
    for Cold Soufflés, 244
  Soup, Cold, 80
Ratatouille, 131
  with Sausage, 130
Ravello Rosato, 357
Ravioli, 337
  Casserole, 345
  Cheese Filling for, 338
  Meat Filling for, 338
Ray Dell's Butterfly Dip, 165
Ray Dell's Creamy Cornucopias,
    210
Recipe for a Good Day, 247
Red Caviar Mousse, 11
Red Wine Sangria, 6
Refried Beans, 365
  Super Nacho with, 363
Relish
  Corn, Lois's, 159
  Mystery (Tomato), 161
Remos Fizz, Special, 6
Reuben Bread, 65
Reuben Roll-ups, 20
Reuben Sandwiches, 20
Rice
  Brazilian, 366
  -Chicken Bake, 175

Chicken Soup with Mushrooms
    and, 74
Fried, Encore for Roast Pork
    with, 91
Green, 126
Green Chile, 122
-Ham Bake, 176
to keep from sticking together,
    375, 377
Peas 'n', Nassau, 124
Pudding, Pumpkin, 372
Risotto alla Milanese, 335
Salad, 364
S'Nice, 271
Spanish, 366
Zucchini, 134
Ricotta cheese
  Cannoli, 353
  Lasagne Roll-ups with, 343
  Siciliana Cassata with Filling of,
    352
Risotto alla Milanese, 335
Riz Sauvage, 174
Rolls
  Butterhorn, No Knead, 44
  Cinnamon, 47
  Egg, Carol's, 51
  Icebox, Aunt Tottie's, 251
  Pecan, Jane's, 63
  Praline, 63
  Sweet, Breakfast, 171
  Out of This World, 62
"Roll-ups," Appetizer, 27
Roquefort Cheese Chicken,
    Helena's, 176
Rose Potpourri, 280
Rugalas, 219
Rum
  with Bourbon and Tom & Jerry
    Batter, 8
  Cake
    Bundt, 197
    Christmas, 297
  Coffee Cooler, 3
  Cold Buttered, 180
  Glaze, 197
  Hot Buttered, Batter, 282
Rumaki, 21
Ruthie's Buttermilk Bread, 45
Ruthie's Fruit Salad Dressing, 149
Ruthie's Scrambled Egg Medley, 30
Ruth's Pork Chops, 91
Rye Bread, 56
  Old-fashioned, 55

Sabayon Sauce, 245
Sage, uses for, 378, 380
Saint Nickerdoodles, 294
Salad
  Apples for, Whole Cinnamon,
    138
  Beet, Molded, 135
  Broccoli, 136
    Cauliflower-, 169
  Bunny, 270
  Caesar, Mom's, 136
  California, 169
  Cherry, 137
    Black, 135
    Pepsi-Cola–, 137
  Chicken, 136
    Apricot Soufflé Ring with, 135
    Curried, 140
    Gourmet, 137
    Hot, 136
  Cinnamon-Applesauce, Molded,
    138
  Circus, 270
  Corned Beef, 139
  Cranberry, 139
    Frozen, 139
    Molded, 139
  Delarobia, Jane's, 140
  Frosted, 141
  Fruit
    Auntie K's Favorite, 141
    California, 169
    Delarobia, Jane's, 140
    Frosted, 141
    Frozen, 142
    Mom's Frozen, 142
    tips on, 375, 378
    Twenty-four-Hour, 148
  Gazpacho, 364
  Greek Salata, 141
  Greengage Dessert, 142
  Hearts of Palm, 144
  Italian-style
    Antipasto Misto, 333
    Insalata Capricciosa, 332
    Lettuce and Tomato, 332
    Salsa Maionese for, 333
    Spaghetti, 334
    Tomato, 332
    Watercress, 332
  Layer, Dorothy's, 142
  Mexican, 365
  Mystery, 143
  Olive, 329

  Oriental, 143
  Overnight Green Tossed, 143
  Pea, 169
  Pineapple-Cherry, Frozen, 144
  Potato
    The "Best," 144
    Hot German, 138
  Raspberry, 145
  Rice, 364
  Sauerkraut, 169
  Spinach, 170
    à la Grecque, 146
    Apple and, 146
    Dorothy's Layer Salad, 142
    and Dressing, 147
    Flambé, 147
    Mushroom-, 147
    Oriental, 143
    Overnight Green Tossed
      Salad, 143
  Spinach Apple, 146
  Swell-Time Somersault, 271
  Three-Bean, 147
  Tomato
    Cherry Tomatoes,
      Ermadene's, 137
    Gazpacho, 364
    Italian-style, 332
    Lettuce and, Italian-style, 332
    Mystery, 143
  Turkey, 136
  Vegetable, 170
  Waldorf, 148
  Watercress, 146
Salad Dressing
  Avocado, 145
  Caesar, Quick, 170
  Delarobia, 140
  French, Fruit, 248
  for Fruit Salad, 149
    Fresh, 149
    Honey Poppy Seed, 149
    Orange, 150
    Ruthie's, 149
  for Gazpacho Salad, 364
  Gorgonzola, 149
  Hubble House, 150
  Pauline's, 150
  Thick Oil, Mother's, 248
  for Wilted Lettuce, 150
Sally's Cheese Cake, 204
Salmon
  Ball, 21
  Croquettes, 108

  Mousse, 21, 145
  Whole Poached Fresh, 108
Salomi, 22
Salsa Maionese, 333
Salt, to hide an excess of, 376
Sandie's Lemon Fluff Squares,
  202
Sand Plum Jelly, 164
Sandwiches
  Beef, Easy, 175
  Reuben, 20
  Tea Party, 267
Sangria, 6
San Juan Black Bean Soup, 80
Santa's Snack, 277
Sauce
  Apricot
    Sour Cream-, for Fondue, 324
    Walnut-, 243
  Baked Potato, 156
  Barbecue, 151
    Helena's, 151
  Béarnaise, 152
  Béchamel, 151
  Beef Fondue
    Curry, 324
    Horseradish, 324
  Besciamella, 349
  Butter and Cheese, for
    Fettuccine, 341
  Cardinal, 218
  Chateaubriand, 152
  Cheese, 152
    Hot, 360
    -Mushroom, 346
    Seafood in, 112
  Chili, Lois's, 152
  Classic, for pasta, 341
  Cocktail, for Seafood, 153
  Cranberry, 139, 153
  Cream, Tortellini in, 346
  Cucumber, 108, 155
    Dill-, 145
  curdled, cures for, 377
  Deglazing, 154
  Dessert
    Apricot-Walnut Sauce, 243
    Bourbon, Warm, 243
    Bourbon Hard Sauce, 283
    Caramel, 213
    Chantilly Cream, 242
    Crème Anglaise, 243
    Crème de Noyaux (Crème de
      Almond), 23

❖❖

Sauce: Dessert (*cont.*)
  English Custard, 244
  Fudge Sauce, 1-2-3, 244
  Grand Marnier, 221
  Mincemeat Topping for Ice Cream, 244
  Plum Pudding, 297
  Praline Crunch Ice Cream Topping, 244
  Raspberry, 244
  Sabayon, 245
  Strawberry, Crème Caramel with, 209
  Toffee Ice Cream Pie and Sauce, 215
  Trifle Custard, 224
  Vanilla, 41, 206
  Wine, for Cold Soufflés, 245
Elegante, 29
Golden Sherry, 298
Green Peppercorn, 84
Hollandaise, 156
  curdled, cures for, 377
  Easy, 127
  in Large Quantity, 155
  Mock, 155
Lemon, for Fondue, 325
Meat
  Gourmet, 153
  Northern Italian, Pasta with, 347
Mustard, 156
  Ft. Lauderdale, 156
Noisette, 156
for Open Sesame Meatballs, 16
Perigeux, 83
Pesto, 157
  Basic, 157
  tips on, 157
Pimento-Mushroom, Chicken and Stuffing Scallop with, 101
Pineapple-Mustard, Hot Shrimp Balls in, 22
Salsa, 361
Scampi, for Pasta, 112
for Seafood, Daddy's Spicy, 250
Sour Cream Apricot, Fondue, 324
Stir-fry, 157
Teriyaki, 157
Tomato
  Jan's, 350
  for Manicotti, 344

Veloute
  I, 158
  II, 158
  White, 158
    tip for making, 376
Sauerkraut, Bohemian, 127
  in Alsatian Dinner, 90
  in Alsatian Dinner 9 to 5, 177
  Salad, 169
Sausage(s)
  in Alsatian Dinner, 90
  Balls, Hot, 38
  Eggs Stuffed with, 30
  Italian, Ratatouille with, 130
  Onions Stuffed with, 120
  Patties, Homemade Seasoned, 31
  Peppers Stuffed with, 92
  Pork-Liver, Bohemian, 249
  Soufflé, Prepared Ahead, 31
  Summer, 25
Savory, uses for, 380
Schloss, 322
School Days Frosting, 227
Scones, Monica's, 299
Sea Foam Frosting, 228
Sea Foam Nut Fudge, 304
Seafood
  Casserole, Judy's, 109
  in Cheese Sauce, 112
  Cocktail Sauce for, 153
  Fillet Marseille, 177
  Paella, 369
  Spicy Sauce for, Daddy's, 250
Sea Trout, Spiced Fillet of, with Broccoli, 114
Serendipities, 292
Sesame (Seeds)
  Chicken Bites, 14
  Chicken Breasts, 98
  Chinese Cabbage, 146
  in Sauce for Open Sesame Meatballs, 16
  uses for, 380
Seven-Minute Frosting, 258
  Shortcut, 228
Sheepherder's Bread, 66
Shellfish
  Clam, Chowder, 73
    Boston, 73
  Creole Gumbo, 76
  Lobster
    Mousse, 13
    Tails, Bar-B-Q, 107

Oyster, Auntie K's Scalloped, 1940s, 249
Shrimp. *See* Shrimp
Sherbet
  Jack-O'-Lantern Frosties, 274
  Lime, Green Dragons, 267
  Punch, 6
Sherry(-ied)
  Almond Pie, 241
  Bars, Annie's, 293
  Chicken Livers, 28
  Pears and Pork Chops, 91
  Quail, 105
  Sauce, Golden, 298
Shortbread
  Cookies, 293
  Monica's, 300
Shortcake, 198
Show-Time Circus Cookies, 272
Shredded-Wheat Bread, 65
Shrimp
  and Artichoke Casserole, 110
  with Asparagus, Stir-fried, 109
  Balls, 22
    Hot, in Pineapple-Mustard Sauce, 22
  in Beer Batter, 23
  "Better Wear Bibs," 110
  Butter, 23
  and Cheese Canapés, Hot, 13
  and Chicken Casserole, Fiesta, 367
  and Crab and Water Chestnut Dip, 23
  Curried, 177
  Deep-fried Butterfly, 111
  Dip, 24
  Elegante, 110
  Étouffé, 112
  Gumbo
    Creole, 76
    Down South, 77
  Marinated, 178
  Mousse, 13
  in Nippy Cheese Dip, 166
  Remoulade, 24
  Scampi Livornese, 111
  Spiced Pickled, 178
  Thermidor, 113
Shush Puppies, 271
Siciliana Cassata, 352
Singapore Pea Soup, 168
Six-Layer Cookies, 294
Six-Week Bran Muffins, 60

Slush, Fruit, 32
S'Mores, 272
Snapper Normande, 113
Snickerdoodles, 294
Snow Balls, 266
   Hard Sauce, 298
Snow Pea Pod Soup, 78
Soave, 357
Sole Fillet, Gourmet, 113
Soufflé
   Apricot Ring, with Chicken
       Salad, 135
   Brandy Alexander
       Cold, 220
   Caramel, Cold, 373
   Cheese, No Fail, 173
   Chocolate, 220
   di Pasta, 344
   Grand Marnier, 221
   Ham, Prepared Ahead, 35
   hints on, 376
   how to bake a, 219
   Lemon
       Cold, 222
       Double-boiler, 220
   Raspberry Sauce for Cold, 244
   Sausage, Prepared Ahead, 31
   Spinach, Carol's, 173
   Strawberry, Frozen, 222
   Wine Sauce for Cold, 245
Soufflé dish, how to prepare a, 219
   waxed-paper collar for cold
       soufflés, 219
Soup. See also Bouillon; Chowder
   Apple Vichyssoise, 71
   Apricot, with Sour Cream, 71
   Asparagus, 71
   Autumn, 72
   Avocado
       Chilled, 167
       Cold Curried, 361
   Beef
       and Barley Vegetable, 72
       Steak, Quickie, 168
   Beet Borscht, 73
   Black Bean, San Juan, 80
   bones for, 376
   Broccoli, 73
       Quick, 167
   Cheese, 74
   Chicken
       Gourmet, 167
       with Rice and Mushrooms, 74
   Colonial, 75

Cream of Corn, 75
Cream of Pea, 79
Cream of Spinach, 81
Cucumber, Iced, 76
Egg-Lemon, 77
Fish, Italian Style, 330
Gazpacho, 362
Jan and Joe's Super, 168
Lemon
   Iced, 77
   Iced, Easy, 168
Minestrone, 330
Mushroom, Old-fashioned, 78
Nine-Bean, 282
   Mix, 282
Peach-Blueberry, 78
Pea Pod, 78
Potato, 79
Pumpkin, 79
Raspberry, Cold, 80
Split Pea
   Potage St. Germain, 79
   Singapore, 168
Steak, 81
   Quickie, 168
Tomato
   to keep from curdling, 376
   with Pesto, 81
Tortilla, 363
Vegetable
   Beef and Barley, 72
   Minestrone, 330
   Spring Vegetable, Italian, 331
Vichyssoise, 82
Watercress, 82
White Bean, 82
Sour Cream
   Apple Pie, 231
   -Apricot Pie, 232
   -Apricot Sauce, Fondue, 324
   Apricot Soup with, 71
   Banana Coffee Cake, 43
   Cabbage with, 119
   Cake, Mother's Calvin Coolidge,
       253
   Coffee Cake, 68
   Enchiladas, Jeanne's, 368
   Panocha, 305
   substitute for, 375
Sourdough
   Biscuits, 67
   Bread, 67
       Jack Bread—Extra Sour, 67
   Pancakes, 68

Starter, 66
Spaghetti
   Insalata (Salad), Cold, 334
   Loaf, 346
   with Northern Italian Meat
       Sauce, 347
   with Pesto-Divino, 345
Spanakopita, Jeanne's, 128
Spanish Rice, 366
Spice(s,-d)
   Cake
       Applesauce, 186
       Laverna's, 196
   Christmas Scent, 277
   Pecans, 285
Spinach
   on Artichoke, 127
   Baked Herbed, 127
   Balls, Carol's, 24
   Casserole, 173
   Dip, 25
   -Fish Bake, 176
   Fish Fillet Florentine, 106
   Gnocchi, 342
   Intrigue, 128
   Lasagne Roll-ups with, 343
   Pie, Greek, 128
   Ring with Sautéed Tomatoes,
       129
   Salad, 170
       à la Grecque, 146
       Apple and, 146
       Dorothy's Layer Salad, 142
       and Dressing, 147
       Flambé, 147
       Mushroom-, 147
       Oriental, 143
       Overnight Green Tossed
           Salad, 143
   Scalloped, 128
   Soufflé, Carol's, 173
   Soup, Cream of, 81
Split Pea Soup
   Potage St. Germain, 79
   Singapore, 168
Sponge Cake, Basic, 301
Spooky Chocolate Pie, 273
Spoon Bread
   Crusty, 172
   Josa's, 250
   Mexican, 365
Spread
   Crab, Quick, 167
   Pecan, 18

Spread (*cont.*)
  Pimento Cheese, 19
  Radish, Cream Cheese, 20
Spuma di Zucca con Amaretto, 354
Spumone, 355
Squash, Baked, Aunt Fanny's, 129
Steak, Beef
  au Poivre Vert en Chemise, 84
  Diane, 86
  Flank
    Bar-B-Cued Stuffed, 87
    with Corn Bread, 88
  Green Peppercorn, in a Crêpe, 84
  Marinade, 155
  Mexican-style, 369
  Savory Pepper, 86
  Soup, 81
    Quickie, 168
  Tartare, 25
Stew(ed)
  Apples, 248
  Busy Lady, 175
  Goulash, Paprika, 87
Sticky Buns, 68
Stir-fry Sauce, 157
Stock, to freeze, 375
Strawberry(-ies)
  baskets, 382
  Butter, 281
  Cake, 182
    Tunnel, 198
  Cheese Flan, 223
  Crêpes Tivoli with, 210
  Dessert, Quickie, 183
  Fondue, Brandied, 324
  Glaze, for Strawberry Cream Pie, 242
  Glazed, 245, 384
  Ice Cream Pie, 215
  Jam, 164
  Marlo, Ethel's, 258
  Mousse, 217
  -Orange Cooler, 6
  Pie
    Cream, 242
    Judy's, 181
    Mile-high, 240
  Preserves, Freezer, 164
  Romanoff, 222
  Sauce, Crème Caramel with, 209
  Soufflé, Frozen, 222

Yummy, 39
Streusel Topping, for 1-Crust Apple Pie, 232
Stuffing, Corn Bread
  Casserole, 70
  Flank Steak with, 88
Sugar
  Brown
    Candy, Lois's, 302
    to keep from getting hard, 375
    to soften hardened, 377
    substitute for, 378
  Burnt, Dumplings, 211
  Cinnamon Syrup, 370
  Cookies, 203, 294
    Rolled, 294
  Glazed Nuts, 284
  superfine, to make, 377
Sugared Nuts, 284
Sugarplums, Chocolate, 295
Summer Sausage, 25
Sunday Eggs, 33
Sunday Morning Brunch, menu and ideas for, 314
Sunshine Slush, 7
Super Nacho, 363
Swedish Bread
  Rye, 56
  Tippy's, 56
Sweet Potato(es)
  Apricot, 129
  Scallop, 130
  Tropical Glazed, 130
Swell-Time Somersault Salad, 271
Swiss Cheese
  in Dorothy's Layer Salad, 142
  Fondue, 322
Syllabub Pudding, 224
Syrup
  Baklava, 204
  Cinnamon Sugar, 370
  Peanut Butter, 259

Table coverings, 382
Table settings, 381–382
Tacos, Chicken, 370
Taffy, Tonia's White, 306
Taos Lightning, 7
Tarragon, uses for, 380
Tart(s)
  Coconut Lemon, 223
  Fruit, Fresh, 31
  Pecan, 292
Taxpayer's Bawl, 318

Tea
  Friendship, 282
  Spiced, Vera's, 7
Tempura Batter, 26
Teriyaki Sauce, 157
Thanksgiving Dinner, menu and ideas for, 315–317
Three-Bean Salad, 147
Three-Day Marinated Roast, 89
Three-Minute Frosting, 257
Thyme, uses for, 378, 380
Tiddlywink Cake, 266
Timbales, Chinese, 295
Tippy's Swedish Bread, 56
Tipsy Fruit, 32
Tiropetes, Jeanne's, 26
Toad in the Hole, 267
Toast, Tea Party, 267
Toffee
  Bars, 295
  Ice Cream Pie and Sauce, 215
Tom & Jerry Batter, 8
Tomato(es)
  à la Provençal, Jeanne's, 131
  Aspic, 26
    Jeanne's V-8, 148
    Mom's, 248
  Bouillon, 168
    Autumn, 71
    Hot, 80
  Catsup, Ripe, 154
  Cherry, Ermadene's (Salad), 137
  Jelly or Relish, Mystery, 161
  Pudding, 131
  Salad
    Gazpacho, 364
    Italian-style, 332
    Lettuce and, Italian-style, 332
    Mystery, 143
  Salsa, 361
  Sauce
    Jan's, 350
    for Manicotti, 344
  Sautéed, 129
  Soup
    Gazpacho, 362
    to keep from curdling, 376
    with Pesto, 81
  Spinach Ring with Sautéed, 129
Tonia's Apple Crisp—Food-Processor–style, 231
Tonia's Snow Ice Cream, 268
Tonia's Thanksgiving Turkey, 316–317

Tonia's White Taffy, 306
Torte
  Chocolate, Lili's, 208
  Mocha Brownie, 223
Tortellini in Cream Sauce, 346
Tortilla Soup, 363
Tournedos, 86
Trifle(s), 224
  Chocolate, 225
  Coffee-Whiskey, 300
  Custard Sauce, 224
  English
    about, 224
    I, 225
    II, 225
    III, 225
  Individual, 226
Truffles
  Chocolate, 306
  Irish, 300
  Mocha, 306
Tumbleweeds—a Kansas
  "Happening," 8
Turmeric, uses for, 380
Tuna
  -Almond Bake, 115
  Casserole, Easy Fixin', 115
  Curry Casserole, 177
Tunnel of Fudge Cake, 198
Turkey
  Breast, Curried, 103
  Chowder, Jack's, 81
  Piccata, 178
  Pie, Impossible, 93
  Roast, 104
  Salad, 136
Twenty-four-Hour Fruit Salad, 148

Valpolicella, 357
Vanilla
  Ice Cream
    Almond Praline Balls, 211
    Baked Alaska, Individual, 183
    Betty's, 213
    Cherries Jubilee, 212
    Cherries Romanoff with, 208
    Irma Columbia's, 214
    Jeanne's Country, 215
    Old-fashioned, 214
  Sauce, 41, 206
  Wafer-Chocolate Pudding, 180

Veal
  Filling for Ravioli, 338
  Parmesan, 96
  Scallops, Gourmet, 95
  Shank, Osso Buco, 348
Vegetable(s)
  Dip for, Easy 'n' Quick, 166
  hints on, 375, 376, 378, 379
  Marinated, 132
  Medley, 132
  Ratatouille, 131
    with Sausage, 130
  Salad, 170
  Soup
    Beef and Barley, 72
    Minestrone, 330
    Spring Vegetable, Italian, 331
  Stir-fried, 132
  Trio with Zippy Sauce, 133
V-8 Tomato Aspic, Jeanne's, 148
Velveeta Cheese
  Dip, Hot, 360
    Chili, 362
  Lasagne with, 342
  Sauce, Hot, 360
Velvet Hammer, 8
Vera's Barbecued Brisket, 88
Vera's French Bread, 52
Verdicchio dei Castelli di Jesi, 357
Vern's Date Cake, 190
Vern's Peach Cobbler, 182
Vichyssoise, 82
Vienna Bread, 69
Vodka, Lemon, 8

Waffles, 252
  Peanut Butter Syrup for, 259
Waldorf-Astoria Cake, 197
Waldorf Salad, 148
Walnut(s)
  -Apricot Sauce, 243
  Bourbon Balls with, 286
  in Christmas Fancies, 304
  Crisp Fried, 284
  Fudge, Sea Foam, 304
  Golden, 283
  Holiday Delights, 303
  Madelyn's Sleep Cookies with,
    293
  Mincemeat Cakes, Mini, 291
  Sugar-glazed, 284
  Zucchini Bread, 61

Wassail, Christmas, 307
Water Chestnut and Shrimp and
  Crab Dip, 23
Watercress
  Salad, 146
    Italian-style, 332
  Soup, 82
Watermelon
  Pickles, 260
    Lois's (1935), 260
  Prosciutto and, 329
Wax Beans, in Three-Bean Salad,
  147
Wedding Brunch, menu and ideas
  for, 313
Wedding Cakes, Mexican, 372
White Christmas Fruitcake, 298
White Sauce, 158
White Wine
  Kir, 4
  Lime Punch, 5
Wichita Country Club Date Nut
  Bars, 201
Wild Rice, 133, 174
Windsor Cookies, 296
Wine
  about, 375, 376
  Italian, 357
  Jelly, 164
  Sauce, for Cold Soufflés, 245
Witches' Brew, 272
Worcestershire sauce, about, 375
Working-girl Meat Loaf, 178
Wreath(s)
  Christmas, 285
  Della Robbia, 277

Yia Yia's Baklava, 204
Yummies, 265

Zabaglione, 354
  Puffs, Crema, 354
Zucchini
  Boats, Stuffed, 133
  in Caponata, 333
  Cocoa Bread, 48
  Crêpes, 134
  Italian-style, 329
  and Mozzarella, 336
  Rice, 134
  Slices, 166
  Walnut Bread, 61
Zuppa di Pesce, 330